Views from the Center

The CCCC Chairs' Addresses
1977–2005

edited by

Duane Roen

ARIZONA STATE UNIVERSITY

Published in cooperation with
the National Council of Teachers
of English/Conference on College
Composition and Communication

BEDFORD / ST. MARTIN'S   Boston ● New York

In memory of Doris June Roen, 1928–2005

For Bedford/St. Martin's

Developmental Editor: Gregory S. Johnson
Senior Production Editor: Michael Weber
Production Supervisor: Matthew Hayes
Art Director: Lucy Krikorian
Text Design: Anna Palchik and Dorothy Bungert
Copy Editor: Denise Quirk
Cover Design: Donna Lee Dennison
Composition: Macmillan India Inc.
Printing and Binding: Haddon Craftsmen, an R. R. Donnelley & Sons Company

President: Joan E. Feinberg
Editorial Director: Denise B. Wydra
Editor in Chief: Nancy Perry
Director of Marketing: Karen Melton Soeltz
Director of Editing, Design, and Production: Marcia Cohen
Managing Editor: Erica T. Appel

NCTE Stock No. 56274
Published in cooperation with the National Council of Teachers of English/Conference on College Composition and Communication
1111 W. Kenyon Road
Urbana, Illinois 61801-1096
www.ncte.org

For information, write: Bedford/St. Martin's, 75 Arlington Street, Boston, MA 02116
(617-399-4000)

ISBN: 0-312-43813-3

EAN: 978-0-312-43813-5

Acknowledgments

Donald C. Stewart. "Some History Lessons for Composition Teachers" from *Rhetoric Review*, Vol. 3, No. 2, January 1985. Reprinted by permission of Lawrence Erlbaum Associates, Inc.
(Acknowledgments and copyrights are continued at the back of the book on pages 491–492, which constitute an extension of the copyright page. It is a violation of the law to reproduce these selections by any means whatsoever without the written permission of the copyright holder.)

Although the formal CCCC Chairs' addresses were not instituted until 1977, the individuals who led the organization before that year shaped CCCC in many important ways. We honor them with this photograph.

Celebrating the twenty-fifth anniversary of CCCC in Philadelphia, Pennsylvania, in March 1976.

Standing, left to right: Richard Beal, 1965 Chair; Wallace Douglas, 1969 Chair; Edward P. J. Corbett, 1971 Chair; Elisabeth McPherson, 1972 Chair; James D. Barry, 1973 Chair; Richard Larson, 1974 Chair; Lionel Sharp, 1975 Chair; Marianna Davis, 1976 Chair. *Seated, left to right:* John Gerber, 1949–1950 Chair; Harold B. Allen, 1952 Chair; Francis Shoemaker, 1957 Chair; Priscilla Tyler, 1963 Chair; Robert Gorrell, 1964 Chair.

Preface

Words from Richard Lloyd-Jones's Chair's address of 1977 and Vivian Davis's address the following year have served as the inspiration for the title of this collection, *Views from the Center: The CCCC Chairs' Addresses, 1977–2005*:

> I don't want to see the view from the center to be the view along a political line, but rather the view from the middle of the universe. We are the ones at the center who reach to all the other disciplines and to all other people. We synthesize knowledge and unite people. By our force, we draw from the wisdom of other disciplines and in making it ours, transform it by combining it in new ways. The instrument of language which we play soothes the savage breast, opens the secret places, and weds the separate selves. And it is the common property of all faithful people. That's why I want to speak of the view from the center.
>
> —RICHARD LLOYD-JONES, 27

> We are indeed in the muddle of things—on our own against the cross currents of change. What more daring time to be alive? What more treacherous time to live?
>
> To be, however, at the center of things, as Richard Lloyd-Jones explained our position metaphorically last year, means to be always in the public view, to be defined and stereotyped, reviled and praised as others judge us from their own perspectives. It may seem wise to make metaphors acceptable to ourselves and define ourselves, ignoring what anyone else has to say about who we are or what we do. But the fact is that what we do, or do not do, can have effect, sometimes direct and immediate, on the world around us.
>
> —VIVIAN DAVIS, 26

Just as Richard Lloyd-Jones and Vivian Davis inspired the title for this collection with their words, all of the CCCC Chairs from the last three decades have made significant contributions to the project. Of course, each of them wrote an address that appears in the collection. Beyond that, the living Chairs wrote reflections to shed light on their thinking at the time of the addresses — or on how their thinking has changed over the years. For chairs who were no longer living or otherwise unable to write reflections, I called on their close colleagues and friends to write about the addresses.

Editing this collection has been one of the most rewarding undertakings of my career. From the moment that Nancy Perry of Bedford/St. Martin's first discussed the concept with me, I realized how important it was to publish a collection like this one. Since then, that realization has intensified. I am very fortunate to have had the opportunity to edit the collection.

It was important to complete the project now, while most of the CCCC Chairs from 1977 to 2005 are still available to reflect on their addresses. Sadly, several of them had passed before I began working on the collection, and a few left us while I was editing their addresses. Further, because several of the addresses never appeared in *College Composition and Communication* or any other journal or book, this collection makes them available for future scholars.

The CCCC Chairs' addresses tell much about our field. First, they illustrate how well we have chosen the leaders of the organization. This volume clearly demonstrates the immense talent and dedication of the CCCC Chairs, each of them committed to enhancing the organization. Second, the addresses also chronicle many vital professional and broader social issues of the last three decades. The Chairs have reminded us that we all need to stay focused on such matters as equal access to education and economic opportunity for all.

Early in the process of developing this collection, I contacted some of the pre-1977 Chairs to see if it might be possible to include the earlier addresses. However, as I explain in the introduction, before 1977 Chairs often did not have any kind of major speaking role at the annual meeting. Nonetheless, it was exciting to talk with some of the early legends of the organization.

While reading the Chairs' reflections and drafting the introduction for this collection, I became curious about other scholars' memories of hearing the addresses. That curiosity led me to invite some colleagues in the profession to share their thoughts on what it was like listening to one or more of the addresses. I hope that those memories, which appear at the end of the Introduction, have resonance for readers.

As I worked on this collection, I communicated with the Chairs and other contributors via scores of e-mail messages, phone calls, and letters. Those exchanges often provided me with ideas for the Introduction, and they confirmed the choice of the title for the collection. I also corresponded regularly with Nancy Perry, and those conversations yielded many additional ideas. In short, it takes a village to build a collection like this one.

Near the end of this project, the profession experienced a moment of collective sadness and loss when John Lovas passed away on June 21, 2005. In the days that followed, the listservs in the field were filled with remembrances of a man who enriched the lives of family, friends, colleagues, and students. I hope that John's words in this collection will serve to remind us of all that he did to make life better for so many people. Then, on July 22, 2005, the profession lost one of its most prolific and influential scholars when Maxine Hairston died at the age of eighty-three. Even though we will miss her, we are fortunate that she has left us the gift of her published work.

Acknowledgements

I owe many thanks to the wonderfully professional and supportive team at Bedford/St. Martin's. First, this project exists because Charles Christensen, former president of Bedford/St. Martin's, developed the concept for such a collection.

I am also grateful to Joan Feinberg, current president of Bedford/St. Martin's, for her strong commitment to the collection. This project is yet another example of Bedford/St. Martin's many contributions to our field.

I thank Nancy Perry for her inspired vision and unwavering support. In our many telephone, online, and face-to-face conversations, she offered insightful suggestions that have greatly strengthened this project.

I thank Greg Johnson for all that he did to move the manuscript into production. He made the process as painless as possible by handling hundreds of details efficiently, effectively, and enthusiastically. Moreover, while working together on this project, Greg and I developed a lasting bond because both of us lost a parent in the summer of 2005—my mother, Doris June Roen, and his father, Ralph Michael Johnson.

I also enjoyed working with Michael Weber. He skillfully guided the project through production.

Just as Kathleen Blake Yancey has contributed so much to the profession during the past few decades, she has offered me much moral and intellectual support. I could not have done this project without her encouragement.

Several NCTE staff members helped with this volume. I am grateful to Zarina Hock, director of book publications and senior editor, for her enthusiastic support. Jacqui Joseph-Biddle, director of conventions; Eileen Maley, convention manager; and Margaret Chambers, division director of publications, all helped to find NCTE's archival materials, housed at the University of Illinois.

Amelia Herb deserves much praise for searching the CCCC archives at the University of Illinois. Carefully examining programs for the annual meetings, Amy found valuable information that has helped to shape this project. I greatly value her dedicated effort and contagious enthusiasm. I thank Gail Hawisher for recommending Amy to me, and I thank the University of Illinois library staff for providing access to important records.

Kelli Custer, who is writing a wonderfully insightful dissertation on the recent CCCC Chairs, has been an inspiration throughout this project. Similarly, Derek Mueller, who is studying some lexical features of the addresses, has helped me to think more carefully about the addresses.

Lisa Ede, who edited the important collection of the Braddock Essays, has been a role model as both a scholar and a person. The world needs more people like Lisa Ede.

My daughter, Hanna Roen, helped with photocopying—with a smile on her face and a song in her heart.

For nearly three decades, Maureen Roen, my partner and friend, has eagerly discussed my publishing projects, offering suggestions that have made each of them better. A writer and Web designer, she has taught me more than is readily apparent in my work.

I have had the good fortune of working with supportive mentors and colleagues. At the University of Wisconsin-River Falls, where I was a graduate student, Nicholas Karolides served as a model scholar and friend. While I was a doctoral student at the University of Minnesota, I learned much from Gene Piché, Mike Graves, Rick Beach, and Robin Brown, as well as other fine faculty there.

When I finished graduate school, I was hired for the position that Lillian Bridwell-Bowles had left at the University of Nebraska. In Lincoln, I continued to learn much from my friends and colleagues Les Whipp, John Hollowell, Paul Olson, Dudley Bailey, Alan Lempke, and Joy Ritchie.

At the University of Arizona, where I spent eleven happy years, I was fortunate to have worked closely with Charles Davis, Theresa Enos, Jan Swearingen, Tom Miller, Marvin Diogenes, Clyde Moneyhun, Stewart Brown, Roger Gilles, Vicky Stein, Tom Willard, Yvonne Merrill, Tilly Warnock, and John Warnock.

At Syracuse University, I had equally fine colleagues in Margaret Himley, Louise Whetherbee Phelps, Carol Lipson, Keith Gilyard, Ken Lindblom, Laura Gray-Rosendale, Nancy Hahn, Faith Plvan, James Comas, and Jim Zebrowski.

My good fortunes have continued at Arizona State University, where I have enjoyed much friendship and intellectual stimulation from David Schwalm, John Ramage, Maureen Daly Goggin, Frank D'Angelo, Greg Glau, Barry Maid, Glenn Irvin, Patricia Webb, Sharon Crowley, Keith Miller, Peter Goggin, Elaine Maimon, Nancy Gutierrez, Neal Lester, Dan Bivona, Barry Maid, Duku Anokye, Susan Ledlow, Laura Bush, Judy

Grace, Nancy Clemens, Janel White-Taylor, Jim Blasingame, Alleen Pace Nilsen, Ken Donelson, Bob Shafer, April Summitt, Sheryl Rinkol, Bette Bergeron, Glenn Irvin, Ian Moulton, Karen Bollermann, Lenore Brady, Jerry Jakubowski, and Lynn Nelson. Each and every one of these colleagues has enriched my professional and personal life, and I owe them much.

Graduate students, too many to name here, have rejuvenated my thinking for almost three decades. They have also made me very proud.

Finally, I wish to express my great admiration for the CCCC Chairs. They represent the very best in our field and in higher education more generally.

–Duane Roen
Arizona State University

WORKS CITED

Custer, Kelli. "Driven Identities: How Leaders in Composition/Rhetoric are Shaping the Field." Diss. Indian U of Pennsylvania, forthcoming.

Davis, Vivian I. "Our Excellence: Where Do We Grow from Here?" *College Composition and Communication* 30 (1979): 26–31.

Ede, Lisa. "Reading—and Rereading—the Braddock Essays." *On Writing Research: The Braddock Essays, 1975–1998*. Ed. Lisa Ede. New York: Bedford/St. Martin's, 1999.

Lloyd-Jones, Richard. "A View from the Center." *College Composition and Communication* 29 (1978): 24–29.

Contents

Introduction:
The CCCC Chairs'
Addresses

T HE BIRTH OF CCCC

As John Gerber ("Three-Year"), Jerome Archer, David Bartholomae, Lisa Ede, and Maureen Daly Goggin have chronicled, the Conference on College Composition and Communication can be traced to 1947, when the National Council of Teachers of English (NCTE) and the Speech Association of America collaborated to sponsor a conference in Chicago to provide a forum for "those interested in the teaching of reading, writing, and speech to college freshmen" (17). That meeting attracted approximately two hundred participants.

At its annual November convention in 1948, NCTE scheduled a session on first-year composition: Three Views of Required English. Some persons participating in that session requested that NCTE develop a greater focus on college-level writing and speech. In response to that request, the NCTE Executive Committee authorized a two-day spring conference, which was held in Chicago on April 1–2, 1949. More than five hundred scholars participated in this meeting. (See Note 1.)

In November 1949, at a luncheon meeting at the NCTE convention in Buffalo, the NCTE Executive Committee formally established the Conference on College Composition and Communication for an initial period of three years. Without a moment's delay, participants at the luncheon meeting elected the first officers of CCCC: John C. Gerber, chairman; George Wykoff, secretary; Wilbur Hatfield, treasurer; and Charles W. Roberts, editor.

In the first issue of *College Composition and Communication* in 1950, John Gerber explained the exigency for forming the organization:

> Someone has estimated that there are at least nine thousand of us teaching writing in college courses in composition and communication. Faced with many of the same problems, concerned certainly

1

CONFERENCE ON
COLLEGE FRESHMAN COURSES
IN
COMPOSITION AND COMMUNICATION

Sponsored by

The National Council of Teachers

of English

★

Friday and Saturday

April 1 and 2, 1949

★

The Stevens Hotel

CHICAGO

with the same general objectives, we have for the most part gone our separate ways, experimenting here and improving there. Occasionally we have heard that a new kind of course is working well at Upper A & M or that a new staff training program has been found successful at Lower T. C. But we rarely get the facts. We have had no systemic way of exchanging views and information quickly. Certainly we have had no means of developing a coordinated research program.

To meet such obvious needs the Conference on College Composition and Communication has been formed. ("The Conference")

Gerber ended the description with an invitation that still defines the organization today:

We believe that the activities of this new organization are aimed at practical needs in the profession, that the standards of the profession will be raised because of them. We hope that you and others from your institution will join the CCCC, not because we are after a large membership as such but because we want your information and ideas in exchange for our own.

At the 1951 annual CCCC meeting, leaders from the organization, including John Gerber and Harold Allen, met with representatives from the

National Society for the Study of Communication, an affiliate of the National Speech Association that formed in 1949, to explore the possibility of merging the two organizations. As noted in the published report on the session, the two fledgling affiliate organizations shared common interests, and their relationship was marked by "a high degree of cooperation and mutual friendliness" ("The N.S.S.C. and the C.C.C.C." 15). In the end, though, "the conclusion reached by the panel was there was too much difference between the two organizations to make a merger practical and desirable, but that a high degree of cooperation was already in evidence and should be further encouraged" (15). One can't help but wonder what CCCC would be like today if the discussion had gone in another direction. Would oral communication play a larger role in CCCC if the two organizations had merged?

ANNOUNCEMENT

The Conference on College Composition and Communication will hold its annual spring meeting at the Hotel Carter in Cleveland on March 28 and 29, 1952.

The program will include two general sessions: the first, on "What Employers Expect from the Freshman Course"; the second on "What Other Departments Expect from the Freshman Course"; three sessions devoted to some fifteen or twenty workshop topics; and two groups of panel discussions on such topics as "Audio-Visual Aides," "Sources of Information for the Study of Communication." There will also be a report at the luncheon meeting on a survey of teacher preparation for college courses in composition and communication.

The spring meeting is not restricted to members of the CCCC; all persons interested in composition and communication courses at the college level are cordially invited to attend.

(See Note 2.)

In her historical study of CCCC, Nancy Bird mentions that after granting CCCC two consecutive terms of three years each, the NCTE Executive Committee voted in 1955 to grant permanent status to the Conference on College Composition and Communication. It is interesting to note that the covers of the programs for 1951–1954 include the phrase "*An Affiliate of* the National Council of Teachers of English." In

1955, however, the cover includes a phrase that must have been a great point of pride for those who worked so diligently to establish the organization: "*A Permanent Group within* the National Council of Teachers of English."

Gordon Wilson, in reflecting on the early years of CCCC, suggests the strong feelings of those who helped build the organization: "Aggrieved by the discrepancy between our status and our function and impelled by our interest, we set out to change things: to shape programs and textbooks, to lighten loads and make the budgets heavier. For many of us the conferences gave us the first sense of being professionals" (128). Wilson's words still ring true for many in the field at the beginning of the twenty-first century.

The early chroniclers of CCCC, such as John Gerber, Jerome Archer, Gordon Wilson, and Nancy Bird, make some effort to note the membership numbers for various years, suggesting that the Herculean efforts of the early organizers helped to grow the membership. The following chart gives a sense of that growth:

Year	Membership
March 1950	297
November 1950	446
1953	339
1959	2,604
1964	4,052
1966	5,317

THE CCCC CHAIRS' ROLES

In 1949, the year I was born, John C. Gerber served as the first Chair of the Conference on College Composition and Communication, establishing a long succession of distinguished leaders for the organization. In this collection, however, the first CCCC Chair's address is that of Richard Lloyd-Jones, who in 1977 became the first CCCC Chair to deliver a formal address at the opening general session of the annual meeting. That tradition has continued to this day.

As specified in the "Constitution and By-Laws of The Conference on College Composition and Communication," the "Chairman" has nine responsibilities, including one visible role at each annual meeting: "(2) Preside at all business meetings of the CCCC and of the Executive Committee unless unavoidably absent" (22). Before 1977, each CCCC Chair had some sort of informal speaking role at the annual meeting, usually at the general session. However, none of those speeches was considered a formal Chair's address at the opening general session. As the table titled "An Overview of CCCC Chairs' Conference Roles" indicates, the Chairs' roles varied greatly at the annual meetings from 1949 to 1976. The annual secretaries' reports usually indicate what the Chairs did. For instance, as Gladys K. Brown, CCCC secretary in 1956, reports in the minutes of the Executive Committee meeting, "Chairman Irwin Griggs extended greetings and introduced all persons present. He presented the agenda of usual length with an added sheet of Recommendations to the Executive Committee made by individual Committee members, by officers and former officers, and by certain 1956 Workshops" (115).

> CCCC and New York City in the
> spring—irresistible. The dates are
> **THURSDAY, FRIDAY, and SATUR-**
> **DAY, MARCH 22, 23, and 24, 1956,**
> the headquarters the **HOTEL STATLER.**
> Send for room reservations early.
>
> *Excerpt from "CCCC Spring Meeting, 1956"*

The role of the CCCC Chair changed, though, when Vivian Davis took action in the mid 1970s: "In 1976, when I was Assistant Chair, and therefore program chair, I held court in Philadelphia to ask anyone who wanted to make suggestions for the next program to talk with me. One suggestion was that the Chairs give speeches to open the conference each year. I thought that it was a good idea, so here we are with this publication" (Personal communication). When Lloyd-Jones's address was published in *College Composition and Communication* in 1978, Edward P. J. Corbett, the editor of the journal, commemorated this event by including the following note on the first page of the article: "This article, a condensed version of the keynote address at the convention in Kansas City, Missouri, March 31, 1977, represents a 'first' in the history of CCCC. This was the first time that the current Chair of the CCCC delivered a formal address at the opening General Session—*Editor's note*" (24).

TABLE 1 An Overview of CCCC Chairs' Conference Roles Prepared by Duane Roen and Amelia Herb

Year	CCCC Chair (* deceased)	Site	Conference Theme	Session Type	Speech Title (ST = Session Title)	Published Title	CCC Article: Year, Vol. No., Pages
1949	John C. Gerber* State University of Iowa	Chicago		First session	ST: Concepts Basic to Freshman Courses in Composition and Communication		
1950	John C. Gerber* State University of Iowa	Chicago		General session	ST: Let's Face the Facts about Writing; A Look at Our Common Problems		
1951	George S. Wykoff* Purdue University	Chicago		Address	"Let's Apply Some Logic"		
1952	Harold B. Allen* University of Minnesota	Cleveland		First general session	ST: What Employees Expect from College Courses in Composition and Communication		
1953	Karl W. Dykema* Youngstown College	Chicago		First general session	ST: How to Talk with People		
1954	T. A. Barnhart* State Teachers College, St. Cloud, Minnesota	St. Louis		First general session	ST: Fields for Research in Composition and Communication, and an Illustration		

Year	Speaker	City	Session	Session Topic	Publication
1955	Jerome W. Archer, Marquette University	Chicago	First general session		
1956	Irwin Griggs*, Temple University	New York	First general session		
1957	Francis Shoemaker, Teachers College, Columbia University	Chicago	First general session	ST: The Challenge of Numbers: Some Current Solutions for Teaching Maximum Numbers with Limited Faculty	"The Challenge of Numbers" 1957, 8.3, 131–32
1958	Robert E. Tuttle, General Motors Institute	Philadelphia	First general session	ST: The Freshman Course: A Reappraisal of Aims and Content	
1959	Albert R. Kitzhaber, University of Kansas	San Francisco	First general session	ST: Emphases in the Composition/Communication Course	"The Gifted Student and the Not-So-Gifted" 1959, 10.1, 5–6
1960	Glen Leggett*, University of Washington	Cincinnati	First general session		
1961	Erwin R. Steinberg, Carnegie Institute of Technology	Washington, D.C.	First general session	ST: Writing for the Federal Government	"Writing for the Federal Government" 1961, 10.3, 130–31

(continued)

TABLE 1 (Contd.)

Year	CCCC Chair (* deceased)	Site	Conference Theme	Session Type	Speech Title (ST = Session Title)	Published Title	CCC Article: Year, Vol. No., Pages
1962	Francis E. Bowman Duke University	Chicago	Language, Grammar, Verbal Learning, Composing	General meeting	ST: Language and Culture		
1963	Priscilla Tyler Harvard University	Los Angeles	The Content of English	General session I	ST: The Content of English		
1964	Robert M. Gorrell University of Nevada	New York	Freshman English: Return to Composition	General session I	ST: The Status of Freshman English		
1965	Richard S. Beal* Boston University	St. Louis	Appraisals and Prospects	General session			
1966	Gordon Wilson* Miami University, Ohio	Denver		General session I			
1967	Richard Braddock* University of Iowa	Louisville		General session and Chair's address			
1968	Dudley Bailey University of Nebraska	Minneapolis		General session I			

Year	Chair / Institution	Location	Title	Session		Published title	Citation
1969	Wallace W. Douglas* Northwestern University	Miami Beach		General session	ST: College Composition: Tradition, Innovation, Abolition		
1970	Ronald E. Freeman* UCLA	Seattle		General session I	ST: Foreseeing the 1970s		
1971	Edward P. J. Corbett* Ohio State University	Cincinnati	Coming Together: SOS from the Darkling Plain	General session			
1972	Elisabeth McPherson* Forest Park Community College	Boston	Reconsidering Roles: What Are We About?	General session			
1973	James D. Barry* Loyola University, Chicago	New Orleans	Issues, Challenges, and Opportunities	General session I			
1974	Richard L. Larson Herbert Lehman College	Anaheim		Welcome			
1975	Lionel R. Sharp Cazenovia College	St. Louis		Welcome			
1976	Marianna W. Davis Benedict College	Philadelphia	What's REALLY Basic?	Welcome			
1977	Richard Lloyd-Jones University of Iowa	Kansas City	200 Plus One: Communicating the Third American Century	Chair's address	"A View of the Center"	"A View from the Center"	1978, 29.1, 24–29

(continued)

TABLE 1 (Contd.)

Year	CCCC Chair (* deceased)	Site	Conference Theme	Session Type	Speech Title (ST = Session Title)	Published Title	CCC Article: Year, Vol. No, Pages
1978	Vivian I. Davis Bishop College	Denver	Excellence in What We Do: Our Attitude Toward Teaching Composition	Chair's address	"Excellence: Where Do We Grow from Here?"	"Our Excellence: Where Do We Grow from Here?"	1979, 30.1, 26–31
1979	William F. Irmscher University of Washington	Minneapolis	Writing: A Cross-Disciplinary Enterprise	Chair's address	"Writing as a Way of Learning and Developing"	"Writing as a Way of Learning and Developing"	1979, 30.3, 240–44
1980	Frank D'Angelo Arizona State University	Washington, D.C.	Writing: The Person and the Process	Chair's address	"Regaining Our Composure"	"Regaining Our Composure"	1980, 31.4, 420–26
1981	Lynn Quitman Troyka Queens-borough Community College	Dallas	Our Profession: Achieving Perspectives for the 80s	Chair's address	"Perspectives on Legacies and Literacy"	"Perspectives on Legacies and Literacy in the 1980s"	1982, 33.3, 252–62
1982	James Lee Hill Albany State College	Washington, D.C.	Serving Our Students, Our Public, and Our Profession	Chair's address	"Beyond Access to Education—Literacy and Learning in Perspective"	unpublished	
1983	Donald C. Stewart* Kansas State University	Detroit	The Writer's World(s): Achieving Insight and Impact	Chair's address	"Some History Lessons for Composition Teachers"	"Some History Lessons for Composition Teachers"	Rhetoric Review, 1985, 3.2, 134–43

Year	Chair	Location	Convention Theme	Type	Address Title	Published Title	Citation
1984	Rosentene B. Purnell, California State University—Northridge	New York	Making Writing the Cornerstone of an Education for Freedom	Chair's address	"Using Language to Unlock the Limits"	unpublished	
1985	Maxine Hairston*, University of Texas, Austin	Minneapolis	Making Connections	Chair's address	"Breaking Our Bonds but Reaffirming Our Connections"	"Breaking Our Bonds and Reaffirming Our Connections"	1985, 36.3, 272–82
1986	Lee Odell, Rensselaer Polytechnic Institute	New Orleans	Using the Power of Language to Make the Impossible Possible	Chair's address	"Crisis and Renewal: A Maturing Discipline"	"Diversity and Change: Toward a Maturing Discipline"	1986, 37.4, 395–401
1987	Miriam T. Chaplin, Rutgers University	Atlanta	The Uses of Literacy: A Writer's Work in and out of the Academy	Chair's address	"Issues, Perspectives and Possibilities"	"Issues, Perspectives and Possibilities"	1988, 39.1, 52–62
1988	David Bartholomae, University of Pittsburgh	St. Louis	Language, Self, and Society	Chair's address	"The Reach of Composition"	"Freshman English, Composition, and CCCC"	1989, 40.1, 38–50
1989	Andrea A. Lunsford, Ohio State University	Seattle	Empowering Students and Ourselves in an Interdependent World	Chair's address	"Composing Ourselves: Politics, Commitment, and the Teaching of Writing"	"Composing Ourselves: Politics, Commitment, and the Teaching of Writing"	1990, 41.1, 71–82
1990	Jane E. Peterson, Richland College	Chicago	Strengthening Community through Diversity	Chair's address	"Valuing Teaching: Assumptions, Problems, and Possibilities"	"Valuing Teaching: Assumptions, Problems, and Possibilities"	1991, 42.1, 25–35

(continued)

TABLE 1 (Contd.)

Year	CCCC Chair (* deceased)	Site	Conference Theme	Session Type	Speech Title (ST = Session Title)	Published Title	CCC Article: Year, Vol. No., Pages
1991	Donald McQuade University of California, Berkeley	Boston	Times of Trial, Reorientation, and Reconsideration: A Fin de Siècle Review/Prophecy	Chair's address	"Living In—and On—the Margins"	"Living In—and On—the Margins"	1992, 43.1, 11–22
1992	William W. Cook Dartmouth College	Cincinnati	Contexts, Communities, and Constraints: Sites of Composing and Communicating	Chair's address	"Writing in the Spaces Left"	"Writing in the Spaces Left"	1993, 44.1, 9–25
1993	Anne Ruggles Gere University of Michigan	San Diego	Twentieth-Century Problems, Twenty-First Century Solutions: Issues, Answers, and Actions	Chair's address	"Kitchen Tables and Rented Rooms: The Extracurriculum of Composition"	"Kitchen Tables and Rented Rooms: The Extracurriculum of Composition"	1994, 45.1, 75–92
1994	Lillian Bridwell-Bowles University of Minnesota	Nashville	Common Concerns, Uncommon Realities: Teaching, Research, and Scholarship in a Complex World	Chair's address	"Freedom, Form, Function: Varieties of Academic Discourse"	"Freedom, Form, Function: Varieties of Academic Discourse"	1995, 46.1, 46–61

1995	Jacqueline Jones Royster, Ohio State University	Washington, D.C.	Literacies, Technologies, Responsibilities	Chair's address	"When the First Voice You Hear Is Not Your Own"	"When the First Voice You Hear Is Not Your Own"	1996, 47.1, 29–40
1996	Lester Faigley, University of Texas, Austin	Milwaukee	Transcending Boundaries	Chair's address	"Literacy after the Revolution"	"Literacy after the Revolution"	1997, 48.1, 30–43
1997	Nell Ann Pickett, Hinds Community College	Phoenix	Just Teaching, Just Writing: Reflection and Responsibility	Chair's address	"The Community College as Democracy in Action"	"The Two-Year College as Democracy in Action"	1998, 49.1, 90–98
1998	Cynthia L. Selfe, Michigan Technological University	Chicago	Ideas, Historias y Cuentos: Breaking with Precedent	Chair's address	"Literacy, Technology, and the Politics of Education in America"	"Technology and Literacy: A Story about the Perils of Not Paying Attention"	1998, 50.3, 411–36
1999	Victor Villanueva, Washington State University	Atlanta	Visible Students, Visible Teachers	Chair's address	"The Tree and the Woods: Racism and Multiculturalism"	"On the Rhetoric and Precedents of Racism"	1998, 50.4, 645–61
2000	Keith Gilyard, Penn State University	Minneapolis	Educating the Imagination: Re-imagining Education	Chair's address	"Identities and the 'Dream': Dilemmas for Composition at the Turn of the Century"	"Literacy, Identity, Imagination, Flight"	2000, 52.2, 260–72
2001	Wendy Bishop*, Florida State University	Denver	Composing Community	Chair's address	"Against All Odds: Composition and Rhetoric in Our Times"	"Against the Odds in Composition and Rhetoric"	2001, 53.2, 322–35

(continued)

TABLE 1 (Contd.)

Year	CCCC Chair (* deceased)	Site	Conference Theme	Session Type	Speech Title (ST = Session Title)	Published Title	CCC Article: Year, Vol. No., Pages
2002	John C. Lovas* DeAnza Community College	Chicago	Connecting the Text and the Street	Chair's address	"The Universal, the Common, the Collegial: The Many Voices of Our Professional Conversations"	"All Good Writing Develops at the Edge of Risk"	2002, 54.2, 264–88
2003	Shirley Wilson Logan University of Maryland	New York	Re-writing Theme for English B: Transforming Possibilities	Chair's address	"Changing Missions, Shifting Positions, and Breaking Silences"	"Changing Missions, Shifting Positions, and Breaking Silences"	2003, 55.2, 330–42
2004	Kathleen Blake Yancey Clemson University	San Antonio	Making Composition Matter: Students, Citizens, Institutions, Advocacy	Chair's address	"Made Not Only in Words: Composition in a New Key"	"Made Not Only in Words: Composition in a New Key"	2004, 56.2, 297–328
2005	Douglas Hesse Illinois State University	San Francisco	Opening the Golden Gates: Access, Affirmative Action, and Student Success	Chair's address	"Who Owns Writing"		

ANNOUNCING
THE TWENTY-EIGHTH ANNUAL CONVENTION
of
THE CONFERENCE ON COLLEGE COMPOSITION AND COMMUNICATION

being held at the

Radisson-Muehlback Hotel

Baltimore and Wyandotte at 12th

Kansas City, Missouri

March 31 through April 2, 1977

THEME: Two Hundred Plus One: Communicating the Third American Century

PROGRAM HIGHLIGHTS: *Address from the Chair:* Thursday, morning, March 31, 9:45. **Richard (Jix) Lloyd-Jones**, University of Iowa, Chair-man, CCCC, communicates with the membership.

Luncheon for Directors of Freshman Composition, Noon, Thursday, March 31. **Jack H. White**, Chair. Speakers: **Vincent Gillespie**, Kansas State University, and **William (Bill) Lutz**, Rutgers.

Addresses on the Theme: Thursday, March 31, 8:30 p.m. Speakers: **Juanita V. Williamson**, LeMoyne-Owen College, **Roger Schustereit**, Bee County College; **Norman Russell**, celebrated Native-American Poet, Central State University.

> BANQUET, Friday evening, April 1, 8 p.m. Speaker: **E. R. Ted Braithwaite**, esteemed and prolific author, professor. His best seller, *To Sir with Love*, became a movie. His current work, *Honorary White*, details the poignant experiences in apartheid South Africa.

(See Note 3.)

Editors of *College Composition and Communication*

It's important to mention the editors of *College Composition and Communication*. Because all but three of the addresses (James Lee Hill's, Rosentene B. Purnell's, and Donald C. Stewart's) were published in the organization's journal, the editors had some hand in how the addresses were made available to the profession. Interestingly, some of the editors also served as Chairs of the organization—George S. Wykoff, Francis E. Bowman, William F. Irmscher, Edward P. J. Corbett, and Richard L. Larson.

Editors of *College Composition and Communication*

Charles W. Roberts	March 1950–May 1952
George S. Wykoff	October 1952–December 1955
Francis E. Bowman	February 1956–December 1958
Cecil B. Williams	February 1959–May 1959
Francis E. Bowman	October 1959–October 1960
Cecil B. Williams	December 1960–December 1961
Ken Macrorie	February 1962–December 1965
William F. Irmscher	February 1965–December 1973
Edward P. J. Corbett	February 1974–December 1979
Richard L. Larson	February 1980–December 1986
Richard C. Gebhardt	February 1987–December 1993
Joseph Harris	February 1994–December 1998
Marilyn M. Cooper	February 1999–December 2004
Deborah H. Holdstein	February 2005–

When I asked Joseph Harris about editing the Chairs' addresses during his tenure as editor of the journal, he indicated that he used a light hand because the publication of each address was intended to serve archival purposes—to provide a written record of what listeners experience at the annual meeting.

FEATURES OF THE ADDRESSES

In the pages that follow, I note some of the salient common features that mark the CCCC Chairs' addresses. As Ellen Barton does in her study of the addresses, I comment on the Chairs' evocative gestures toward teaching, service, research, disciplinarity, and interdisciplinarity. Of course, these topics are important to the CCCC Chairs, as well as to the organization and all of us who live and work in the field. However, I also note some other features of the addresses, especially those that resonate with my experience in the field. I hope that these points also resonate with the experiences of many readers. I try to illustrate the kinds of characteristics that Andrea Lunsford attributed to our field and the organization when she spoke on the fortieth anniversary of CCCC:

> As you know, our history as a profession—certainly in the span of CCCC's life—is not easily perceived as proceeding in an ordinary and traditional academic way—a clear setting out of boundaries, a staking of territory and then a rigorous defense of those boundaries, hedging certain subjects and people in, keeping others out. Instead, our field has seemed more heterogeneous, more expansive and inclusive, gaining, in Kenneth Burke's words, "perspectives by incongruity" rather than following some linear path to academic disciplinarity. The CCCC Chair's address has provided one means of articulating such perspectives and, as expected, engendering debate. (71–72)

A Range of Scholarship

The CCCC Chairs' addresses exemplify the range of scholarly work that has defined the field and the organization. Long before Ernest Boyer offered his revolutionary taxonomy of scholarship in 1990 in *Scholarship Reconsidered,* our field was engaged in the full range of scholarly activity. Nonetheless, Boyer's views have helped to legitimize our work. In Boyer's classification system, scholarship has four distinct but interrelated functions: *discovery, application/engagement, integration,* and *teaching and learning,* and the CCCC Chairs have understood the importance of all four functions.

The scholarship of *discovery* is what academics traditionally consider to be research—inquiry without immediately recognizable application to problems in the world. Although the CCCC Chairs' addresses reflect the solid underpinnings of discovery, all of them extend, in one way or another, into the other forms of scholarship.

Moving beyond the scholarship of discovery, Boyer notes, the scholarship of *application/engagement* encourages the scholar to ask, "How can knowledge be responsibly applied to consequential problems?" (21). The

CCCC Chairs' addresses reflect a vigorous response to this question. For instance, in her 1984 address, Rosentene Purnell provided a list of social, economic, and education challenges in the United States, including inequitable educational opportunities: "School populations follow, by and large, the economic and residential patterns of the community where the schools are. Student performance, predictably, follows the quality of teaching and learning environments—even when students are bussed to other communities" (p. 117 in this volume). Of course, today Purnell's words make us think of the No Child Left Behind Act, which promised to alter these patterns but has fallen far short of its intended goals because of inadequate federal funding and faulty design.

Purnell suggests that there is an even bigger problem, though—one that has persisted far too long: "Lack of understanding across racial/ ethnic, religious, and class lines may be the greatest challenge facing the world today" (p. 117 in this volume). If anything, this problem has grown since 1984, and it has recently been especially troubling in places such as Iraq, Bosnia-Herzegovina, Rwanda, Afghanistan, Israel, and Sudan. Because we have turned our attention and resources to these trouble spots in other parts of the world since 9/11, it has been too easy to forget that the problem still persists in the United States—nearly three decades after the Ann Arbor decision, four decades after the Civil Rights Act of 1964 and the Voter Rights Act of 1965, and five decades after *Brown v. Board of Education.*

I share Rosentene Purnell's hope that education will help solve the lack of understanding that plagues the world, but there are days when I think that Candide was a sour pessimist. To solve the problem, Lillian Bridwell-Bowles, in her 1994 address in Nashville, suggests that "Academic discourse must help us and our students create community in a world that often seems torn apart by difference" (47).

In the scholarship of *integration*, Boyer asserts, the scholar is committed to "making connections across the disciplines, placing the specialties in larger context, illuminating data in a revealing way, often educating nonspecialists, too" (18). Lee Odell, in his 1986 address, clearly is interested in the scholarship of integration when he poses the question, "What does each of us need to do in order to contribute to the advancement of learning in our discipline?" (397). He responds to this question by encouraging scholars to draw on work in fields that have been popular shopping malls for us—cognitive psychology, literary theory, linguistics, rhetoric. He especially advocates for cognitive psychology and attention to research from earlier eras, cautioning us that "it is too easy to overlook elements of our history that reinforce and enrich our current work" (399).

Andrea Lunsford endorses Odell's exhortation in her 1989 address when she describes the ways in which we should "compos[e] ourselves in at least two ways: *historically* and *subjectively*" (72) (Lunsford's emphasis). If we compose ourselves effectively, Lunsford notes, we can combat those who would compose us in ways that violate our values—exploitative administrators, E. D. Hirsch, Alan Bloom, Charles Sykes. As we compose ourselves we should be mindful of our values, which can be described with adjectives such as "interdisciplinary," "non-hierarchical," "collaborative," "dialogic," "heteroglossic," "democratic" (76). As we work to compose ourselves, Lunsford urges us to use methods that are consistent with our values: "Listen. Then listen closer" (78).

In Boyer's fourth category, the scholarship of *teaching and learning*, we examine our teaching with the same rigorous standards that we apply to other forms of scholarship. That is, we invite other scholars to scrutinize our work with students just as we invite them to examine our claims in other forms of scholarship. The scholarship of teaching and learning is part of a continuum: (1) effective teaching, (2) scholarly teaching, and (3) the scholarship of teaching and learning.

Effective Teaching. The CCCC Chairs have consistently exemplified the highest levels of commitment to teaching. Of course, they demonstrate a commitment to "effective teaching," teaching that results in students' learning, and members of the organization should be very proud of that. For instance, in the first formal Chair's address, Richard Lloyd-Jones argues that our teaching must be like the roof of a well-constructed building: "Most buildings are eventually built up to the roof, so by analogy, instruction in writing should be complete as the roof is complete, long enough before one's death rattle that we'll have enough years in the completed house to pay the mortgage by writing well" (25).

William F. Irmscher, in his 1979 address, focuses strongly on learning—on writing as a way of learning, not only in writing classrooms but also in classrooms in other disciplines. The subject of his address was timely because it coincided with a rapid increase in programs in writing across the curriculum (WAC) and writing in the disciplines (WID)—a movement that David Russell has described in detail. Irmscher makes a strong case for WAC and WID programs by offering some theoretical explications of writing's effectiveness in promoting learning, including an observation that is common in WAC/WID literature: "Writing brings thought into consciousness, making it available both for us and others to see" (243).

Scholarly Teaching. In addition to considering effective teaching, though, the Chairs' addresses at the annual spring meeting demonstrate commitments to "scholarly teaching," which Lee Shulman, president of the Carnegie Foundation for the Advancement of Teaching, defines as "teaching that is well grounded in the sources and resources appropriate to the field" (49).

Among those who have advocated for scholarly teaching is Donald Stewart, who in his 1983 address argues that "a writing teacher's development can be measured by the degree to which that person has become liberated from current-traditional rhetoric. And the progress of that liberation,

I further believe, is closely linked to that person's accumulating knowledge of the history of composition as a discipline" (134). For many readers of this collection, Stewart's thesis brings to mind Daniel Fogarty's coining the term "current-traditional rhetoric" in 1959 and Richard Young's fuller explication of the term two decades later. As Stewart argues deftly for studying the history of rhetoric and teaching in our field, he offers a condensed history in which he invokes such names as Plato, John Genung, Adams Sherman Hill, Ken Donelson, Frank D'Angelo, Albert Kitzhaber, James Britton, Robert Connors, Barrett Wendell, and Fred Newton Scott.

Even though Stewart spoke at a time when digital technology was just becoming widely available to teachers and students, he offered a profound observation: "New technology gives us a means for doing our work in new and more efficient ways. But if we define the work to be done in outdated terms, we have gained nothing. We may even be doing positive harm" (143). Of course, leaders in digital pedagogies, such as those active in organizations like EDUCAUSE (www.educause.edu) are still repeating that refrain twenty years after Stewart uttered it.

The Scholarship of Teaching and Learning.   At another level of commitment to teaching, more than almost any other field in higher education, the leaders of CCCC have frequently voiced the organization's dedication to "scholarship of teaching and learning," which Lee Shulman defines as "that which occurs when our work as teachers becomes public, peer-reviewed and critiqued, and exchanged with other members of our professional communities so they, in turn, can build on our work. These are the qualities of all scholarship" (49). In working with students, the CCCC Chairs, like so many other members of the organization, have modeled the kinds of reflective practice that Donald Schön has described and advocated in *Educating the Reflective Practitioner.*

Vivian Davis, in her 1978 address, is blunt in her imperative that "we must do something to improve the quality of the teaching of composition in institutions of higher learning" (29). If we consider our attention to teaching, though, our field fares relatively well. On many campuses in this country, writing programs have long been known for their teaching support and mentoring for graduate students. Few other programs on most campuses outshine writing programs in this area. Also, as Maureen Goggin has suggested in her study of journals in rhetoric and composition, our field can take pride in the quantity and quality of journals that publish work on teaching collegiate writing—journals such as *College Composition and Communication, Teaching English in the Two-Year College, College English, Rhetoric Review, Journal of Basic Writing, WPA: Writing Program Administration, Research in the Teaching of English, Written Communication, Journal of Teaching Writing, JAC: A Journal of Composition Theory, Computers and Composition,* and *Writing Center Journal.*

When Lynn Quitman Troyka delivered her address in 1981, she drew on her own research, as well as other research such as Mina Shaughnessy's eminently influential *Errors and Expectations*. She also drew on her extensive experience working with non-traditional students at Queensborough Community College in The City University of New York. Troyka predicted that the 1980s would, among other things, be labeled "The Decade of the Non-Traditional Student" (252). Besides painting a sobering picture of the economic challenges facing non-traditional students, Troyka also examines four "legacies" that non-traditional students bring to our courses—legacies that should influence "*how* we can reach and teach, often with dramatic results" (256). The first two legacies, "Non-traditional students are highly gregarious and social" (256) and "Non-traditional students are more comfortable in an oral rather than a written mode" (258), should remind us that we should use active, learner-centered instructional practices rather than passive, teacher-centered ones. The third legacy, "Non-traditional students are holistic thinkers" (258), suggests the futility of "writing" courses that focus primarily on small, isolated sentences and paragraphs. Finally, the fourth legacy, "Non-traditional students are ambivalent about learning" (260), should resonate well with those of us who left humble homes and communities to enter the academy for life. Some of us know firsthand what Troyka means when she observes, "They want to learn, but they do not want to risk the change that such learning might bring to their lives" (260). Many of us can identify with students who worry that "mobility might subtly or dramatically separate them from friends and family" (260). Some of us have directly experienced this separation.

Like Troyka, James Lee Hill also considers issues surrounding open admissions policies that proliferated in the 1960s as we moved from "an elitist to an egalitarian higher educational system" (p. 93 in this volume). The transition has been a difficult one because our educational system "continues to define American middle-class youths as educable and college-bound, while it stereotypes poor and minority youth as unprepared and academically untalented" (p. 95 in this volume). These stereotypical views of students have led to "back-to-the-basics" composition curricula that too often ask students to focus on forms of writing while neglecting the meaningful functions and purposes of writing. These views have also helped perpetuate standardized testing for college admissions, as well as other high-stakes testing elsewhere in K-12 education. For instance, in my state, Arizona, which already suffers from one of the lowest high school graduation rates in the country, all students must pass the AIMS test (Arizona's Instrument to Measure Standards) (http://www.ade.state.az.us/standards/aims/) to earn diplomas.

Perhaps none of the other Chairs' addresses teaching as directly and thoroughly as Jane Peterson does in her 1990 address. It's an interesting coincidence that she delivered her address the same year that Ernest Boyer published his influential *Scholarship Reconsidered*. Although Peterson does not cite Boyer, she does offer similar perspectives on teaching, especially that we need to treat teaching as we treat our research—"as a mode of inquiry" (32): "The new demands of teaching simultaneously require and develop the same habits of mind that we have long associated with research and scholarship. If we expect students to be active learners, engaged in conscious theorizing and open to being transformed, we must also approach teaching as active, committed learners and knowers. . . ." (32).

EVALUATING SCHOLARSHIP

The CCCC Chairs have also displayed strong dedication to evaluating scholarly activity—whether it be discovery, application/engagement, integration, or teaching. They have modeled the evaluative rigor that Charles Glassick, Mary Huber, and Gene Maeroff have described in *Scholarship Assessed*. Glassick, Huber, and Maeroff offer six criteria for evaluating scholarship: (1) clear goals, (2) adequate preparation, (3) appropriate methods, (4) significant results, (5) effective presentation, and (6) reflective critique. That is, each category of our work must begin with clear goals. Second, once we have established those goals, we need to prepare ourselves to achieve them. Third, even though our preparation may include many methods for reaching the stated goals, we need to select the methods that will work best in any given situation—just as Aristotle's rhetor chooses the most effective means from among the available methods of persuasion. Fourth, the results of our work should be significant, meaningful, important. Fifth, if we fail to present our work effectively to others, we miss opportunities to share the fruits of our labor. Finally, we must reflect on our work if we hope to do it even more effectively in the future.

Vivian Davis, Andrea Lunsford, and Jane Peterson, for instance, argue that our research on teaching must be rigorous if we are to stave off the meddling of outsiders who purport to know what is best for our students.

Giving Voice to Marginalized Voices

It will come as no surprise to readers of this collection that each CCCC Chair's address in some way exemplifies the speaker's strong commitment to giving voice to marginalized discourses. Individually and collectively, the Chairs' addresses encourage readers to pause to respond to questions such as the following: Whom do we serve, and how well do we serve them? What are our ethical responsibilities?

For instance, Wendy Bishop reminds us that members of the profession are "appreciators of the underappreciated, individuals who challenge the odds, take on large and difficult tasks, and make much of what is generally overlooked or undervalued. It is our work and we do well to praise it" ("Against the Odds" 324).

William W. Cook draws on a line from Frederick Douglass's *The Narrative and Selected Writings* to show us the importance of bringing marginalized voices to the center of a culture's discourse because literacy can be such a powerful tool for liberation:

> I used to spend the time *in writing in the spaces left* [Cook's emphasis] in Master Thomas's copy book, copying what he had written. I continued to do this until I could write a hand similar to that of Master Thomas. Thus, after a long, tedious effort for years, I finally succeeded in learning to write (16).

Cook explains how marginalized voices can challenge a monovocal national narrative to become more polyvocal, more representative of the polyphonic culture:

> My comments will privilege those instances when the marginalized, by their very resistance to the texts of the national narrative, reconstruct such texts, instances when the very texts presented as models become refigured and transformed by the contrary voice of the formerly subjected other. Literacy and liberation are linked in such actions not because the newly literate read and internalize the values of such texts, but because they bring to the encounter with such texts a willful deconstructive point of view. Their "erased" lives become the very center of new, resistant texts, texts which displace the univocal narratives of the nation with their multi-voiced musing on nation and identity (10).

Reading Cook's address reminds us of our responsibilities as literacy educators to introduce our students—all of our students—to marginalized voices because "literacy and resistant reading are at the center of liberation and the full exercise of self as subjectivity" (10). In Bakhtinian terms, we need to provide opportunities for students to put their own perspectives—the Bakhtinian *svoj*, "one's own word, one's own world view"—in dialogue with other views—the Bakhtinian *čužoj*, "the world view of another" (Bakhtin 423). Such dialogue defines a high quality college or university education. Such dialogue defines a healthy society. To achieve such societal well being, says Jacqueline Jones Royster, "We need to get over our tendencies to be too possessive and to resist locking ourselves into the tunnels of our own visions and direct experience" (33); we need to "construct paradigms that permit us to engage in better practices in cross-boundary discourse" (37).

Anyone who has followed Anne Gere's work, especially her book *Writing Groups*, should not be surprised by her focus on composition in contexts external to institutions of high education. In her 1993 address she once again illustrates the vitality of writing in such settings as the Tenderloin District of San Francisco and the farming community of Lansing, Iowa. If we listen to voices that are often out of sight and out of mind, we can "avoid an uncritical narrative of professionalization and acknowledge the extracurriculum as a legitimate and autonomous cultural formation that undertakes its own projects" (86). If we do this, "we can learn from and contribute to composition's extracurriculum in our classes" (86).

Gere offers us advice that can make our teaching more relevant to students, who need to become lifelong learners and writers. By breaking the bonds of our preoccupation with the academic arena of life, we can work to help students see writing as relevant to the professional, civic, and personal arenas of their lives. Just as we can enrich our teaching by drawing on the extracurriculum, we can also enrich our research by focusing it on all four arenas of life. In so doing, we make our research more relevant to the general public, who, if they can see the value of our research, will be more likely to support it. Of course, this also means that we need to speak to the public more effectively and more frequently. We need to consider carefully answers to Jacqueline Jones Royster's difficult question: "How can we teach, engage in research, write about, and talk across boundaries *with* others [Royster's emphasis], instead of for, about, and around them?" (38).

Views of CCCC as an Organization

In her 2003 address, Shirley Wilson Logan analyzes CCCC's mission and position statements by drawing on such thinkers as Alice Walker, Stevie Wonder, Queen Hatshepsut, Maria Stewart, Langston Hughes, Frances Harper, Toni Morrison, Zora Neale Hurston, Ida Wells, Audre Lorde, bell hooks, Lucy Craft Laney, Sojourner Truth, Thurgood Marshall, and Anna Julia Cooper. In reviewing the eleven CCCC position statements that existed in 2003 (http://www.ncte.org/groups/cccc/positions), she responds to calls that the statements be "updated, recontextualized, or simply reaffirmed" by observing that "It may be that what we need is not so much a revising as a rereading of the statements we have already made" (333). She also uses the position statements to discuss some of our responsibilities. For instance, "we must strengthen the links between language and democracy, text and street" (335). Further, "we ought to be at the center of all policy decisions that affect the teaching and learning of communication skills" (335). Taking this last challenge seriously, CCCC and NCTE, as well as WPA, have recently taken steps to communicate more effectively with lawmakers and policy makers. It remains to be seen how effective these efforts will be.

In his 1988 address, David Bartholomae focuses primarily on CCCC as an organization. While recounting some of the interesting early history of the organization, he notes that "the history of CCCC includes the story of repeated attempts to reconstruct a unified field, to discipline this unruly discourse, to translate anxiety into security, and to replace the senior professors of literature with senior professors of composition" (44). Of course, this reconstruction has not occurred and is unlikely to occur in the foreseeable future because CCCC and its members have put students' work at the center—a point of pride. In his closing, Bartholomae offers a charge, one that the organization and its members seem to have accepted—perhaps by their nature: "The charge to this generation and the next is to keep the field open, not to close it; to provide occasions for talk, not lecture and silence; to acknowledge our roots in English, not deny them; to resist the temptations of rank and status; and to offer the invitation of others to find their work in CCCC" (49).

Building on Bartholomae's charge, Wendy Bishop admonishes us that seasoned CCCC members need to do more to welcome and nurture new members and conference-goers if we want them to remain active in the organization. This is a responsibility that we all share. She even offers advice on how to interact with audiences at the annual meeting: "Panelists are most effective when audiences feel talked with, not at" ("Against the Odds" 331).

Vexing Issues

In most of the CCCC Chairs' addresses, we find reminders of our status in departments of English, in institutions, and among the general public. In the first address in 1977, for instance, Richard Lloyd-Jones poignantly observes that "Our work in the schools is derided and under-financed at the same time that the public rages because student writing is inadequate" (28). Of course, at the time the country was abuzz with public outrage flamed by such writings as Merrill Sheils's widely read 1975 *Newsweek* article, "Why Johnny Can't Write."

Pointing to this same issue in her 1978 address, Vivian Davis admonishes us that "It may now be time that we, as a community of scholars, learn how to communicate with that other community out there who sometimes seem bent on blaming us for all that is wrong in the world and demanding that we make hay without allowing us sunshine" (26). Unfortunately, we have not made enough progress in learning how to speak to the general public. Although NCTE, CCCC, and, more recently, WPA have worked to get the message out, we as individual scholars have not done enough to communicate to the general public. If each of us would write just one essay or editorial for the general public for every ten articles or chapters that we write for peers in the profession, we could influence the public discussions about teaching and learning writing in college.

Vivian Davis also urges us to "learn the language and the methods of others who claim to measure the results of our practice and who reduce our work to standard deviations. We cannot successfully challenge their claims of reliability with philosophical oratory" (28). She also exhorts us to "bring together in one corpus the most incisive research on the teaching of composition, for research thinly spread over a wide range cannot make the impact we need to make on the whole profession" (28). A few of our colleagues have fulfilled this responsibility vigorously. For instance, George Hillocks has conducted numerous empirical studies on writing as well as rigorous meta-analysis as exemplified by *Research on Written Composition.* Edward White and Richard Haswell have published extensively on evaluation and assessment, as have Charles Cooper and Lee Odell. For the most part, though, members of our profession have preferred to pursue other kinds of scholarly activity—the many forms that Stephen North has explicated in *The Making of Knowledge in Composition.*

In his 1980 address, Frank D'Angelo recounts a political moment in which a literature colleague at Arizona State University "lost his composure" in responding to a proposal to establish a PhD concentration in rhetoric, composition, and linguistics. D'Angelo uses the occasion as an opportunity to rehearse some history, including the origins of English departments and the long scholarly tradition in rhetoric and composition. He goes on to argue that "composition can provide a unifying center for English studies as well as for the liberal arts" (423). More than twenty-five years later, our field is still struggling, but perhaps not as much as D'Angelo did, to gain respect for rhetoric and composition. Although we do have many more PhD programs now, including one that was established at Arizona State University in 1997, there are relatively few English departments in which composition enjoys an equal partnership with literature.

In Emeril style, Maxine Hairston "kicks it up a notch" by referring to colleagues in literature as "mandarins" in her CCCC address. Noting that "our experience is much like that of the women's movement" (273) and that "our worst problems originate close to home," she argues that "we will come of age and become autonomous professionals with a discipline of our own only if we can make a psychological break with the literary critics who today dominate the profession of English studies" (273). To achieve the autonomy and respect, we must, argues Hairston, "be productive researchers and scholars who contribute to the growth of our discipline" (279). And we have followed that advice, as evidenced by the proliferation of journals and presses that publish our work. In addition to the journals mentioned elsewhere in this introduction and many textbook publishers, we benefit from receptive scholarly presses such as the National Council of Teachers of English, Lawrence Erlbaum Associates, Bedford/St. Martin's, Utah State University Press, Southern Illinois University Press, Boynton/Cook-Heinemann, State University of New York Press, Parlor Press, Hampton Press, Albex, Greenwood Press, Cornell University Press, University of Pittsburgh Press, Sage Publications, Jossey-Bass, and even the Modern Language Association.

We see further evidence of that productivity in the bibliographies such as the annual *CCCC Bibliography of Composition and Rhetoric*, edited by such scholars as Erika Lindemann, and Richard Haswell's online

CompPile (http://comppile.tamucc.edu/). That productivity is further il-lustrated in Theresa Enos's substantial *Encyclopedia of Rhetoric and Com-position: Communication from Ancient Times to the Information Age*. And Lisa Ede has collected and reflected on some of the most revered research in our field—the Braddock Award winners.

Hairston also urges us to make "connections to disciplines outside our field" (279) and "with business, industry, technology, and the govern-ment" (280). Some members of our ranks are well known for making connections—for example, Linda Flower for her work with psychologist John Hayes. Of course, some among us are well known for their working in WAC and WID programs that cut across a wide range of fields—for in-stance, Chris Anson, Martha Townsend, Toby Fulwiler, Elaine Maimon, Susan McLeod, Barbara Walvoord. The same is true for work in writing centers—Lisa Ede, Muriel Harris, Christine Hult, Andrea Lunsford, Jean-nette Harris, Joyce Kinkead. Others in our ranks work in business and technical writing programs that enjoy strong connections to business and industry—for example, Kitty Locker, Barry Maid, Stephen Bernhardt.

Since Hairston's address, we have seen an explosion in graduate pro-grams in the field, as documented by Stuart Brown, Rebecca Jackson, and Theresa Enos in a special issue of *Rhetoric Review*. We have seen writing programs leave English departments in institutions such as Syra-cuse University, San Diego State University, the University of Arkansas–Little Rock, and Grand Valley State University. We have also witnessed some bloody conflicts at institutions such as the University of Texas–Austin, SUNY Albany, the University of Minnesota, and the University of Southern California.

Exploring vexing issues further, Miriam Chaplin thoughtfully ana-lyzes the social, economic, and political issues affecting the lives of stu-dents, as well as composition teachers, who struggle to succeed in a milieu of tight budgets and Procrustean approaches to accountability. When we read Chaplin's indictment of a system in which so many colleges and uni-versities pay so many teachers so little money, we must ask ourselves whether we have the will to change this immoral and pernicious system. We have endorsed various professional position statements such as the Wyoming Resolution, explicated by Linda Robertson, Sharon Crowley, and Frank Lentricchia; the one crafted by the CCCC Committee on Pro-fessional Standards for Quality Education; and the statement offered by the MLA Commission on Writing and Literature. In spite of our position statements, though, little has changed. As Eileen Schell illustrated so graphically in *Gypsy Academics and Mother-Teachers: Gender, Contingent Labor, and Writing Instruction*, employment conditions have not im-proved. If anything, employment conditions for adjunct and part-time writing instructors are worse now in 2006 than they were in 1987 at the time of Chaplin's address.

Lester Faigley uses a brief narrative of his professional career as an occasion to reflect on the field's successes and challenges, including the challenge of improving the working conditions of many postsecondary writing teachers. This narrative serves as an occasion for examining two revolutions that affect us and our work in profound ways—the digital revolution and the *"revolution of the rich"* (32). The digital revolution has meant greater access to information and exchanges of ideas for many of our students, but the digital divide is a persistent plague that exemplifies social class differences in the United States. Further, "as talk radio so vividly demonstrates, providing venues for the discussion of public issues does not necessarily lead to a more informed public, increased civic engagement, or enhanced democracy" (36). The revolution of the rich is marked by a persistent, pernicious malevolence that separates labor from wealth is such ways that the income gap between the rich and the poor continues to increase. In 2006 the dream of a global economy seems to be a nightmare for too many American workers. While investors can move their investments with relative ease within the global economy, workers are constrained by geography. Faigley observes in 1996 that "workers have not shared in the prosperity of the last 15 years" (33). That trend now has persisted for 25 years, and it seems to be headed for 35 years.

Continuing the focus on technology, Cynthia Selfe, in her 1998 address, offers a stern warning: "Allowing ourselves the luxury of ignoring technology, however, is not only misguided at the end of the 20th century, it is dangerously shortsighted" (414). It is dangerous, she argues persuasively, because "technology is now inextricably linked to literacy and literacy education in this country" (414). Also, as Faigley did in 1996, Selfe observes that the "two complex cultural formations—technology and literacy—have become linked in ways that exacerbate current educational and social inequities in the United States rather than addressing them productively" (414–15).

There is some indication CCCC and its members are paying more attention to the ways in which technology is linked to literacy and literacy education. For instance, the 1993 CCCC program (CCCC Convention, 1993) lists fourteen "Computers" sessions in the "Topic Index to Concurrent Sessions" (15). In the 2004 program (CCCC Convention, 2004) the index includes a modest twenty-two sessions under the heading "Information Technologies" (43–44). However, the 2004 program does include many other sessions in which digital technology is prominent. Also, in 2004, the CCCC Executive Committee adopted the "CCCC Position Statement on Teaching, Learning, and Assessing Writing in Digital Environments," a position statement drafted by a committee that Kathleen Blake Yancey chaired.

In her 2004 address in San Antonio, during the week that the film *The Alamo* was premiering near the convention site, Kathleen Yancey observed that "Literacy today is in the midst of a tectonic change" (298). For those who witnessed her stunning performance, which included eighty-four slides projected on two screens, the address vividly illustrated the key features of tectonic change. For those who witnessed the performance in March 2004 and then read the printed version in December of that same year, the limits of the print, especially black ink on white paper, are readily apparent.

With such compelling evidence that twenty-first-century literacy is much more than words on a page, one wonders when our writing courses will fully reflect the tectonic change that Yancey describes. There are, of course, indications that our field is trying to keep pace with literacies of our students. For instance, in the past decade we have seen a steady flow of writing textbooks that address digital technologies. More recently, we have seen a torrent of textbooks that embrace visual rhetoric. Some, such as *Picturing Texts* (Lester Faigley, Diana George, Anna Palchik, and Cynthia Selfe), *Getting the Picture* (Marcia Muth and Karla Saari Kitalong), or *Writing in a Visual Age* (Lee Odell and Susan M. Katz) offer exquisitely detailed treatments of visual literacy.

If we hope to remain relevant to our students, we must seriously respond to Yancey's sobering question, "How is it that what we teach and what we test can be so different from what our students know as writing?" (298). As we respond, we need to ponder the future of our writing programs. Will they, for example, leave English departments in increasing numbers? Will they increasingly have names such as Multimedia Writing and Technical Communication, the program that Barry Maid heads at Arizona State University East?

Victor Villanueva's 1999 address, which appeared in *College Composition and Communication* just three months after the annual meeting, is a powerful, sobering analysis of racism in the Americas since the sixteenth century. Beginning with descriptions of racism against the Incas in Peru and the Aztecs in Mexico, Villanueva vividly reminds us of the pervasiveness of racism, sexism, and other forms of prejudice, bigotry, hatred, and inequality in the United States. He also summarizes data demonstrating that higher education is no Mecca because relatively few people of color earn associate, bachelor's, master's, or doctoral degrees. For example, he notes that in 1995 Latinas and Latinos received 26 PhDs, while Americans of European descent who are not Latina/Latino earned 1,268 PhDs. Even in an inclusive organization such as CCCC, "the numbers aren't encouraging" (651). At the time of Villanueva's address, CCCC had "a 92% white membership, 5% African American, 1.4% Chicanos or Latino, 1% Asian American, and 0.5% Native American/American Indian" (651). To change these demographics, says Villanueva, we must focus on our journals, "with people of color writing frankly, sympathetically about matters concerning racism, and all of us writing about what matters to students of color. That's what will attract people of color in sufficient numbers to begin to affect racism" (652).

Keith Gilyard, who was my colleague at Syracuse University in the mid 1990s, makes thoughtful connections between social change and our teaching. In his 2000 address, he points to Martin Luther King Jr. as model for how we might craft our pedagogy: "If we agree to aim for a radical, transcultural democracy, as King did, then we need pedagogies to foster the development of the critical and astute citizenry that would pursue the task" (262). Pedagogies that support participatory democracy must, by definition, be learner-centered if they are to be effective: "For any progressive pedagogy to achieve respectable results, students, among whose ranks are some of the important outsiders we need, have to feel invested in the roles they play in the process" (269).

From my perspective as someone who directed a university-wide teaching/learning center for half a decade, writing teachers are among the most learner-centered and learning-centered teachers on any college or university campus. However, we need thoughtful reminders such as Gilyard's that our pedagogies must be built on learning goals that reflect what we value, especially social justice.

Arguing that we can do more to value the mission of community colleges, John Lovas notes that "our profession has an intellectual blind spot regarding knowledge building in and about community colleges" (274). He also questions the range of our scholarly work in the field when he aptly observes, "You cannot represent a field if you ignore half of it. You cannot generalize about composition if you don't know half of the work being done" (276).

Autobiographical Narratives

Many of the CCCC Chairs include autobiographical narratives in their addresses. As Walter Fischer has demonstrated, narratives can serve as powerful arguments. Sections of the addresses vividly exemplify Fischer's observation that "If the narrative paradigm celebrates anything, it celebrates human beings, and it does this by reaffirming their nature as storytellers" (xi). Through such narratives, as Kelli Custer reminds us in her study of recent CCCC Chairs, we can better understand how these people construct their identities in a range of professional roles—teachers, researchers, administrators.

Among the most moving narratives is Don McQuade's account of his mother's treatment in an intensive-care unit and her eventual death. He uses that story "to tell a story about writing, about writing as a matter of life and death, . . . and the importance of the work of words in the lives of our students and in our own lives" (11).

Wendy Bishop's narrative about her life in the profession and in CCCC more specifically is thought-provoking, especially in light of her recent passing. Her narrative reminds us of how much she celebrated her time with students and colleagues. Her story should motivate us to ask ourselves whether we fully appreciate the ways in which students and colleagues enrich our professional and personal lives. Her narrative also reminds us how much she enjoyed literature, especially poetry. We are also reminded that, in her writing, she was particularly fond of metaphors and mixed genres, weaving nonfiction prose with fiction and poetry. Further, as her speech and her chapter in *Living Rhetoric and Composition* vividly illustrate, she loved to read and write autobiography.

John Lovas recounts his own literacy development as part of an intricate argument that we all have a responsibility to "work to educate our fellow citizens on the moral and practical necessity of enacting professional equity, in all its forms, in all our college writing programs" (281). Lovas reminds us that we have responsibilities to value a range of literacies, including "early literacy" (271), "the literacies of feminism," "the literacies of multiculturalism," "the literacies of later life," and "the literacies not yet fully developed"(273).

Lillian Bridwell-Bowles, in her 1994 address, reflects on her literacy development and concludes with a sad commentary: "But the main insight I have about my own literacy history is that none of the important or meaningful writing I have ever produced happened as a result of a writing assignment given in a classroom" (50). My guess is that most of us who work shoulder-to-shoulder with Bridwell-Bowles in this field that values writing—if we are honest with ourselves—would come to the same conclusion.

Nell Ann Pickett uses her narrative as a community college teacher to illustrate the opportunities that two-year institutions offer to nontraditional students. However, she also tells a detailed story about the prejudice that she and colleague Ann A. Laster faced—and overcame—when, as women teaching at a community college, they tried to publish a technical writing textbook. Happily, in 1998, the eighth edition of that book was published. Pickett also used the platform in Phoenix to celebrate the successes of the Two-Year College English Association (TYCA), whose mission statement and history appear on the NCTE Web site (http://www.ncte.org/groups/tyca/about).

Perhaps the most amusing narrative is Lee Odell's account of an Amtrak ride from Albany to Boston in which he stood outside on the back of a train car to enjoy "a particularly lovely bit of country: low hills with late winter patches of winter snow; bare trees silhouetted against low lying clouds; mists swirling up around the train" (400). I won't ruin the story for you by revealing further narrative details, but I do encourage you to read it when you find yourself in need of a chuckle—the kind that one experiences while listening to Garrison Keillor's weekly news from Lake Wobegon on *A Prairie Home Companion*.

Chairs' Memories of Delivering the Addresses

Shirley Logan reminds us of the world events that shocked and sobered us during the CCCC conference in New York City. Those who attended the conference will vividly remember that the hotel elevators were equipped with television monitors that broadcast the horrible events in Iraq:

> It was March 20, 2003, the day the bombing of Iraq began. The Convention was being held at the Hilton in New York City, just a few blocks from Times Square, where anti-war demonstrators were holding forth. Our own members, in the activist tradition that characterizes CCCC, had already emailed various resolutions to the officers proposing a range of activities, including setting aside a block of time in each session to debate the issues. I recall worrying less about the reception my speech would receive than about whether anyone would be there to hear it or whether there would be a mass exodus once it became clear that the officers had decided not to turn the convention into a protest rally. With CNN airing non-stop on every hotel elevator TV, it was not an event one could ignore—even if one so desired. Well, we did pause for a moment of silence in recognition of the turmoil and I made it through the speech uneventfully and sat down.
>
> But experiences like this serve to remind us that CCCC does not exist in a socio-intellectual vacuum. We must always be prepared to be responsive to the world outside our convention hotels, or to borrow a phrase from our colleague Wendy Bishop's "My Convention Poem," responsive to "the reliable ground floors of our everyday lives." (E-mail to the author)

On a lighter note, Lillian Bridwell-Bowles, a decade after her address, remembers the humorous situation in which she found herself when she spoke to those assembled in Nashville in 1994:

> My fond memory is that the microphone failed in Nashville about five minutes into my address. Bill Cook had to hoist me up onto a stage where country singers had just performed. Thanks, Bill. I delivered my address with no lectern and worried the whole time that I would drop my papers and that they would be scattered across Music City. Meanwhile, the video camera was trained on the podium where it videotaped no one, but my voice can be heard on the tape, as if it were being piped in from a distance, which it was. It was one of my more disembodied performances. (E-mail to the author)

Some of the CCCC Chairs' memories are what one would expect of someone addressing several thousand colleagues. For instance, Anne Ruggles Gere recalls that, "It was San Diego (not Phoenix), the sun was shining, and as I looked out on that sea of familiar faces made dear through all my years in CCC, I stopped breathing. A video made that day includes a longish pause before I began speaking" (E-mail to the author).

In the opening of her 1989 address, Andrea Lunsford recounts a dream that she had the night before she spoke to those assembled in Seattle. While the dream must have been terrifying for her that night, it evoked much laughter the next morning. In the dream, every page of her script had one word on it: *linguine*. Lester Faigley fondly remembers Lunsford's linguine story in 1996 when he tells about his own anxiety-producing dream. In it, many of his friends were exiting the auditorium just as he was entering the room to speak.

Nell Ann Pickett also notes the nervousness that she experienced when she addressed the audience in Phoenix in 1997, an address that I remember vividly because I served as Local Arrangements Chair that year: "This morning, a friend and predecessor in this office—Lynn Troyka—holds a copy of the text I'm reading from. So no matter how my knees shake or my voice quivers, this address—now that it's written—will be given" (91).

Cindy Selfe has mixed memories of the situation in which she found herself on the stage in 1998 in Chicago:

> I nearly passed out during my talk! I am generally anxious when speaking before large crowds anyway, and I dreaded my Chair's talk for four long years. I really would have done anything—even plan another CCCC—if they would have let me off the hook for that talk! I simply couldn't imagine following people like Maxine, Jackie, Lilly, Nell Ann and Lester with any kind of success on that particular speaking task!
>
> Needless to say, when I finally got to the podium and looked out at that ballroom with those huge blessed chandeliers, and realized that everyone was actually waiting for me to say something, I was scared witless!
>
> I was so terribly nervous, that my body responded, and I actually *did* start to black out—my vision narrowed to a pin point, everything became black, and I could hear nothing at all but the sound of the sea in my ears.
>
> I honestly do not know what brought me back from the brink— probably a deep breath, some additional oxygen in my system, and my own sense of embarrassment about being such a wienie before my friends and colleagues—whom I admire so.
>
> When students talk to me about stage fright, they have found a sympathetic ear! (E-mail to author)

CCCC Members' Memories of Chairs' Addresses

As I read the Chairs' addresses, I was struck by their reflections on earlier Chairs' addresses, which made me eager to hear other scholars' memories of the annual event. When I asked some members of the Conference on College Composition and Communication to share some of their memories, they offered a rich array of thoughtful responses:

> I remember John Lovas's address because it was from the heart and appealed to us to be better mentors. And while listening to Cindy's, I remember thinking to myself, after reading that 4Cs wanted fewer papers read word-for-word and more lively presentations and

interaction, yet experiencing Chairs' addresses to be the exact opposite, that here was someone leading by example. Though the overhead transparencies Cindy used were simple pictures of students Cindy had met in her travels and who she talked about, it was evident to me what the 4Cs' leadership expected of us in our panels and presentations. Recalling why a speech has appeal seems as interesting as the speech's content.

–CHET PRYOR
Montgomery College

• • •

One of the addresses I will always remember is Victor Villanueva's—especially when, after presenting stunning statistics about the underrepresentation of people of color in English studies, he exclaimed, "I have so little patience with reverse discrimination." It was not just what he said but how he said it that, while reminding me of the difficulty of fighting injustice, gave me the courage to keep fighting.

–PAUL MATSUDA
University of New Hampshire

• • •

The addresses I remember best, strangely, are Cindy Selfe's and Kathi Yancey's. I say "strangely" because they both were centrally concerned with technology, but that's not something I spend loads of time thinking about myself. Anyway, that's just a small personal reflection. I have to say, too, that I think of these two together because they both had such fantastic ways of presenting. That's why they both resonate—they raised important issues, but they also led me to think about form and composition.

Cindy Selfe's Chair's address still resonates with me because of the way she attached the ideas to real, actual people. It was fantastic to see (literally, on the screen at the front of the room) people and hear/think about their interactions with technologies and literacies and the issues that came attached to both. It grounded those issues in real lives, and the presentation mode was a model of innovative writing.

It wasn't just the content of Kathi Yancey's Chair's address that caught my attention, though. I found the content very, very compelling and relevant. It was also the way she framed her case—through architecture and design, through composition and cultural theory—and it was the form of that case. The slides that she used and the ways that she built her case—visual image overlapping language overlapping e-mail blurbs—were a model of the very approach to writing, and writing majors, that she discussed, and she provided a new way to make such a case.

–LINDA ADLER-KASSNER
Eastern Michigan University

• • •

I re-entered college late in life. All during the "Re-education of Luisa," I noted that most of the theories I studied came from people who were male and white. So when I attended my first Conference on College Composition and Communication in 1993, I looked forward hearing what was a first in my life—an address by a woman. Anne Ruggles Gere's address gave me hope. The metaphors she used were very familiar to me, for many Latinas gather knowledge from the kitchen table. In 1995, Jacqueline Jones Royster's address truly spoke for me and to me. I felt thrilled, proud, and truly encouraged, for many of the points she made resonated with me. Victor Villanueva's address in 1999 made me proud, for he and I share the same ethnic roots. Most importantly, Villanueva demonstrated the writing craftsmanship I long to have. Moreover, Villanueva's address fell in line with issues that I think are important; issues I seek to work with in my classrooms and institution. Subsequent addresses have contributed to my growth as a teacher, scholar; however the three firsts: a woman, a woman of color, and a man from my Puerto Rican background, engraved themselves in my heart and mind.

—LUISA RODRIGUEZ
University of Detroit Mercy

• • •

Although it speaks to my advancing age, I remember a number of Chairs' addresses as being particularly memorable, but the one that I think of first and that I write about often (and that I write about yet again in my first "From the Editor" piece in the February 2005 issue of *CCC*, the first of my editorship) is Andrea Lunsford's "Composing Ourselves." It's the epitome of the Chair's address—scholarly, smart, inspirational, an exhortation to us all to be better. I recall that I was sitting next to Lillian Bridwell-Bowles. When Andrea was finished and as the ballroom burst into steady, loud applause, Lillian leaned over and said something like, "That was everything it was supposed to be." I've never forgotten that moment. I've felt similar inspiration with Gere, Gilyard, Bartholomae, McQuade, and, come to think of it, several others—especially McQuade's use of the personal narrative as the touchstone for his address. I'm always thrilled by the ways in which our colleagues make the most of this important (and ceremonial and scholarly) moment and meet our high expectations of them.

—DEBORAH HOLDSTEIN
Governors State University

• • •

The list of titles itself forms a powerful document, one that brings into historical relief our own interpellation into the field. A compositionist of the post-Hairston generation, I found a liberating professional space in the dynamic questioning and critical reflection of each address following the "winds of change." Yet the talk that still troubles me is Jacqueline Jones Royster's "When the First Voice You Hear Is Not Your Own"; her powerful critique showed that professional space to be fractured, and the sense of professional freedom and solidarity an illusion: "I speak, but I can not be heard. Worse, I am heard but I am not believed. Worse yet, I speak but am not deemed believable" (36). Four years later, Victor Villanueva, in an adrenaline-rushing delivery, once again called attention to the inequality of our voices. Purnell, Cook, Selfe, Gilyard, Logan, too: all antiphonal responses to the professional mainstream, punctuating the narrative of professional progress, voicing, as Royster put it, a more complex reality.

–JEANNE GUNNER
Chapman University

• • •

I've been repeating a story about Jackie Royster's address ever since she delivered it to her substantial audience in Washington, D.C. After moving each one of us to think about her provocative arguments on voice, subjectivity, knowledge construction, authority, identity politics, and the need to shift the paradigm that governs the way we listen to "others," Jackie invited us to share our responses to her talk by sending an e-mail to her address which she repeated several times. At that moment, I remember, clearly, leaning over, gasping, and whispering to a colleague sitting next to me that I couldn't believe that Jackie was issuing such a powerful call. Her speech was deeply moving, and I regret now that I was not among those who responded. Besides (I was thinking at the time), she was going to be deluged with responses from hundreds of people. She certainly asked for it. But much later, I learned from Jackie that she received only a few dozen e-mails. I was amazed that she received so few responses to a speech in a room where our engagement with her was so palpable. It certainly was a clever rhetorical use of electronic "call and response," and I continue to pass on her arguments about shifting the paradigm for rhetorical listening.

–JOYCE IRENE MIDDLETON
St. John Fisher College

• • •

I heard Donald C. Stewart's Chair's address at the 1983 CCCC in Detroit when I was in my third year (the year of my qualifying exams) in my PhD program in rhetoric, linguistics and literature at the University of Southern California. I had taken a course in rhetorical theory from Don in the mid 1970s while I was completing my MA at Kansas State University. I'd heard everything Don was saying in his Chair's address before—most of it from Don himself, the rest in graduate courses at USC—or at least it seemed so then. But Don's delivery of this paper in this setting brought home to me what a privileged position I occupied as someone able to study rhetoric and composition at the graduate level at that time. In some ways it had, for me, the quality of a commencement speech, an exhortation to go forth and do the work for which I'd been prepared.

As I reread the address more than two decades later, I'm aware again of how fortunate I've been to be simply in the right place at the right time in my academic career. In an institutional culture that identifies itself as a meritocracy, as the academy does, it's a good thing to be reminded, on occasion, that luck and love have a lot to do with how things turn out.

–SHIRLEY ROSE
Purdue University

• • •

A Mini-Jeremiad: The speech that resonates most for me is Lester Faigley's "Literacy after the Revolution." Lester focuses—and rightly so—on two revolutions: "the revolution of the rich" and "the digital revolution." Lester's speech is perhaps accidentally prophetic of the worst of times to come. At least, experiencing it now from a future anterior perspective, I can only re-read or re-hear it in relation to a personal-professional-national history.

Jim Berlin closed his letters with "Yours in the Revolution." I counter-closed with "Yours in the Involution." Lester closes his speech by referring to a passage in Jim's *Rhetoric, Poetics, and Cultures*: "It is time all reading and writing teachers situate their activities within the contexts of the larger profession as well as the contexts of economic and political concerns. We have much to gain working together and much to lose working alone" (180). I still agree with this passage even though I no longer believe in the efficacy of what it suggests. I no longer believe that our "activities" or "working together" in any context (our classrooms, conferences) will bring about a revolution that is just. I do find this disparity between my agreement and disbelief disconcerting. Allegiance to friends and a cause held in common is a difficult habit (*habitus*) to break away from. It, however, must be dis-solved and replaced by a new resolve. But how is this to take place, when it appears that there is no longer a place (topos, utopos, eutopos) from which to make a resolve?

As I see it, both of Lester's revolutions are the same inasmuch as they are both driven by a capitalist-careerist economy libidinally attached to production-consumption. (How can we continue, however, to consume what we produce when it does not feed, nourish, any body politic!) The two revolutions are co-driven by some "thing" so insidious and invidious that we have no idea precisely what we are struggling against. How we might put a stop to this "thing"! We keep focusing on mirages. Focusing on, from a pathological point of view, epiphenomena. But most dangerous is that this "thing" permeates and informs our very "activities" (teaching and scholarship) and our "working together" (co-laboring). We cross-contaminate. And so, what have we wrought? What monsters? To consume the very foundations of our raison d'être? Our activities and archives give evidence of our creating more and more of what Peter Sloterdijk calls an "enlightened false consciousness" among ourselves, students, and citizens (*Critique of Cynical Reason*). A profound cynicism. We enlighten ourselves and students, but with the side effect of cynicism. We praise the light but fail to see what lurches in the shadows, the dark side of reason.

Bonds, attachments, libidinal or otherwise, to the past, are near impossible to break. To betray. And yet, we must betray, productively, this habitual horizon of the Enlightenment. We must perform the extra-ordinary, extra-vagrant, in our search for new notions outside of traditional identities and communities. For if we do not, we will but produce only more eternal returns of the same old same. Monsters. The revolution gone bad. Mad. Sad. There is nothing worse for us and our students than a chic cynicism and incipient melancholia. . . . But have I presupposed what I should not have? For, as Marx says, in defining pure ideology: "They do this without being aware of it" (*Capital* I).

–VICTOR J. VITANZA
University of Texas, Arlington

• • •

It's no surprise, considering the circumstances, that the one speech that really stands out for me was the most political one: Maxine Hairston's rabble-rousing attack on the lit folk in the English department. She encapsulated all the buried sense of inferiority and resentment in the audience and got the crowd to cheering and applauding like nothing I've heard before or since. The echoes are still being heard, as in the recent discussion on the WPA listserv, and the issues are as alive now as they were then. But overall the issues were far more complex than her speech allowed and I still think (as I wrote in my 1989 book) that marriage counseling is a better idea than divorce for writing programs. Maybe I'm saying that the genre of the Chair's address is more political than philosophical or academic, that it's NOT the place for great or new ideas, despite the efforts of the speakers.

–EDWARD WHITE
University of Arizona

• • •

There are a number of extremely fine addresses that I will always remember. But Victor Villanueva's and Keith Gilyard's are standouts for me. They were both very passionate speeches by accomplished rhetors with broad minds and hearts. In part I recall them simply because of how much I admire these two people and their work—and the ways in which they continue to influence my own thinking and teaching. And, in part they stick with me most because both of these folks gave their talks at critical historical moments—when rhetoric and composition studies' own exclusionary histories were catching up with it, and we all most needed to examine our own practices in terms of race, class, ethnicity, and gender issues. And I know that their voices are still echoing in a lot of our heads. We know that despite the hard fight these moments are still very much with us—and that so much more work still needs to be done.

—LAURA GRAY-ROSENDALE
Northern Arizona University

• • •

When I think back on the many CCCC addresses I've heard the last eleven years, the most memorable for me was that of Cindy Selfe. Most vivid in my mind are the pictures of the individual students she flashed on the screen as she talked. Rather than a more abstract presentation, her bringing us the students she works with reinforced for me the main point of our profession: the struggling writers in our classrooms. Often they seem to get lost in the mix as we debate various means of teaching composition. The visuals she showed us as well as the words from *their* mouths, not ours, remain with me today. Also, I saw Cindy's approach as not only the synecdoche for our field, but also of her own work: always student-centered, always compassionate, always situated, and always focused on the real center of our profession.

—BARBARA HEIFFERON
Clemson University

• • •

I vividly remember Peterson, in the beginning of her 1990 address, asking audience members to stand if they had ever taught at a community college or been a community college student. Several hundred people stood and cheered—as did I. Her address on the value of teaching, and later addresses by Nell Ann Picket and John Lovas, reminds us that most writing instruction in higher education occurs in two-year colleges. If this profession wants to bring about social justice and economic equity, we need to situate more of our work in community colleges. That's where the students are.

—KATE MANGELSDORF
University of Texas-El Paso

• • •

When Shirley Logan gave this splendid address, I thought how wonderful it is that she wants to and that she can evoke the voices that have guided and nourished her. Shirley shows the active legacy of the voices we hear, remember, and express in our own ways in the light of evolving insights and experience. By melding autobiography and scholarship, Shirley quoted those voices that mean so much to her. I think that's what Bakhtin meant by the words "internally persuasive discourse." One very splendid moment occurred when Shirley mentioned and pointed to her family. That underscored the human element—the kinds of familial collaboration, sacrifice, and celebration that need to happen when a member gives the kind of selfless service that Shirley Logan does.

—JOSEPH JANANGELO
Loyola University of Chicago

• • •

Two things struck me as I looked over the list of CCCC addresses Duane sent. One, I was startled to recognize that I've now been attending CCCC for nearly twenty years and have a nearly immutable routine ingrained: the WPA breakfast at 7:00 a.m. and then the stroll over to the convention center for the Opening Address. And two, while no one address stands out, the sum of them reminds me that our profession is marked by eloquentia, that we, as represented by those we choose to lead us, are rhetors and so very capable of performing what we teach.

—STUART BROWN
New Mexico State University

• • •

I look forward with pleasure to this collection of 4Cs Chairs' addresses tracking the issues defining our field's three decades, but more importantly to me, for the decade and a half when I have belonged in and to the field.

I do not use the word *belonged* lightly, because being a writing teacher and a member of 4Cs has been an important part of my life, and my sense of belonging has been in many ways a consequence of these Chairs' addresses.

Each speaker I have listened to since 1992 has managed to overcome the problem of 4Cs—its size, threatening to swallow so many of us, making us feel as if belonging were more an act of paying dues than being. But as I have listened as an anonymous member of the huge and overwhelming audience, these speakers have spoken like friends. They have of course been eloquent, insightful, visionary, but I have cared less about that than their attitude toward their field and audience, as if they were by accident on the stage, and that maybe an hour or so later, we would be having coffee together in an obscure corner of one of those equally overwhelming hotels.

That's what I have appreciated about these Chairs. I have taken away with me their manner of address. This edition will be important, but it will be only the trace of what was said.

—IRVIN PECKHAM
Louisiana State University

• • •

The idea of living on the boundaries is at once exciting and dangerous for educators. My memories of the 4Cs and the addresses in general have focused on the issues of boundaries and their importance to us. We are border people, always finding ourselves on the edges of society, cultures, and disciplines. Rhetoric and composition are disciplines that are natural work sites for differences. Through our craft and art we encourage our students to think and to be participants in a democracy. This is more important than ever before because we are a part of a diverse society that is trying to understand how to get people together on the boundaries of their lives and interests. We are outlaws in our institutions and our communities since we are the ones who must advocate for the voices that are silenced and work for social justice by ensuring inclusion. We help people find ways to gain access to decision makers and have an influence on them. At a time when extremes have the greater share of influence, we must become, I think, an example of a tenacious middle. We can, I believe, seek to organize transformation rather than confrontation for its own sake. This is why Donald McQuade's address remains with me today. Our commitment to being on and living in the boundaries is our commitment to being facilitators of transformation.

–REX VEEDER
St. Cloud State University

• • •

In the late 1980s, I was fortunate to study with Victor Villanueva at Northern Arizona University, so I expected Victor's address at the 1999 Cs to be thoughtful and moving and wide-ranging, which it was— we'd learned in grad school that Victor was all of those things. Victor is, above all, a teacher, and I know there was no one in his CCCC audience who didn't learn from his stories, his experiences, his ideas, and especially, from his *challenge* to all of us to see and defeat racism wherever we find it.

–GREG GLAU
Arizona State University

NOTES

1. The 1949 CCCC program was republished as four pages at the front of the 1999 program book. This marked the fiftieth anniversary of the organization.
2. The announcement for the 1952 meeting appears on page 35 of the December 1951 issue of *College Composition and Communication*.
3. The announcement for the 1977 annual CCCC meeting appears on page 102 of the February 1977 issue of *College Composition and Communication*.

WORKS CITED

Archer, Jerome W. "Six-Year History of the CCCC." *College Composition and Communication* 4 (1955): 221–23.

Adler-Kassner, Linda. E-mail to author. 31 December 2004.

Bakhtin, Mikhail. *The Dialogic Imagination: Four Essays by M. M. Bakhtin*. Ed. Michael Holquist. Trans. Caryl Emerson and Michael Holquist. Austin: U of Texas P, 1981.

Bartholomae, David. "Freshman English, Composition, and CCCC." *College Composition and Communication* 40 (1989): 38–50.

Barton, Ellen L. "Evocative Gestures in CCCC Chairs' Addresses." *History, Reflection, and Narrative: The Professionalization of Composition, 1963–1983*. Ed. Mary Rosner, Beth Boehm, and Debra Journet. Stamford; Ablex, 1999. 235–54.

Berlin, James A. *Rhetorics, Poetics, and Cultures: Refiguring College English Studies*. Urbana: NCTE, 1996.

Bird, Nancy K. "The Conference on College Composition and Communication: A Historical Study of Its Continuing Education and Professionalization Activities, 1949–1975." Diss. Virginia Polytechnic Institute and State U, 1977.

Bishop, Wendy. "Against the Odds in Composition and Communication." *College Composition and Communication* 53 (2001): 322–35.

———. "Heart of Gold." *Living Rhetoric and Composition: Stories of the Discipline*. Ed. Duane H. Roen, Stuart C. Brown, and Theresa Enos. Mahwah: Erlbaum, 1999. 25–35.

Boyer, Ernest. *Scholarship Reconsidered: Priorities of the Professoriate*. Princeton, NJ: Carnegie Foundation for the Advancement of Teaching, 1990.

Bridwell-Bowles, Lillian. "Freedom, Form, Function: Varieties of Academic Discourse." *College Composition and Communication* 46 (1995): 46–61.

———. E-mail to author. 18 November 2004.

Brown, Gladys K. "Secretary's Report No. 17." *College Composition and Communication* 8 (1957): 115–16.

Brown, Stuart. E-mail to author. 6 January 2005.

Brown, Stuart, Rebecca Jackson, and Theresa Enos. "The Arrival of Rhetoric in the Twenty-First Century: The 1999 Survey of Doctoral Programs in Rhetoric." *Rhetoric Review* 18 (2000): 233–42.

CCCC 1993 Convention. Twentieth-Century Problems, Twenty-First Century Solutions: Issues, Answers, Actions. Urbana: NCTE, 1993.

CCCC 2004 Convention. Making Composition Matter: Students, Citizens, Institutions, Advocacy. Urbana: NCTE, 2004.

CCCC Committee on Professional Standards for Quality Education. "CCCC Initiatives on the Wyoming Conference Resolution: A Draft Report." *College Composition and Communication* 40 (1989): 61–72.

"CCCC Position Statement on Teaching, Learning, and Assessing Writing in Digital Environments." 22 December 2004. <http://www.ncte.org/groups/cccc/positions/115775.htm>.

"CCCC Spring Meeting, 1956." *College Composition and Communication*. 7.1 (1956): 3–5.

Chaplin, Miriam T. "Issues, Perspectives and Possibilities." *College Composition and Communication* 39 (1988): 52–62.

"Constitution and By-Laws of The Conference on College the Composition and Communication." *College Composition and Communication* 3.3 (1952): 19–24.

Cook, William W. "Writing in the Spaces Left." *College Composition and Communication* 44 (1993): 9–25.

Corbett, Edward P. J. Editor's note. *College Composition and Communication* 29 (1978): 24.

Custer, Kelli. "Driven Identities: How Leaders in Composition/Rhetoric Are Shaping the Field." Diss. Indiana U of Pennsylvania, forthcoming.

D'Angelo, Frank. "Regaining our Composure." *College Composition and Communication* 31 (1980): 420–26.

Davis, Vivian I. "Our Excellence: Where Do We Grow from Here?" *College Composition and Communication* 30 (1979): 26–31.

———. E-mail to author. 27 September 2004.

Ede, Lisa. "Reading—and Rereading—the Braddock Essays." *On Writing Research: The Braddock Essays, 1975–1998*. Ed. Lisa Ede. New York: Bedford/St. Martin's, 1999. 1–27.

Enos, Theresa, ed. *Encyclopedia of Rhetoric and Composition: Communication from Ancient Times to the Information Age*. New York: Garland, 1996.

Faigley, Lester. "Literacy after the Revolution." *College Composition and Communication* 48 (1997): 30–43.

Faigley, Lester, Diana George, Anna Palchik, and Cynthia Selfe. *Picturing Texts*. New York: Norton, 2004.

Fischer, Walter R. *Human Communication as Narration: Toward a Philosophy of Reason, Value, and Action*. Columbia: U of South Carolina P, 1989.

Fogarty, Daniel. *Roots for a New Rhetoric*. New York: Teachers College P, 1959.

Gerber, John C. "The Conference on College Composition and Communication." *College Composition and Communication* 1.1 (1950): 12.

———. "Three-Year History of the CCCC." *College Composition and Communication* 3.3 (1952): 17–18.

Gere, Anne Ruggles. "Kitchen Tables and Rented Rooms: The Extracurriculum of Composition." *College Composition and Communication* 45 (1994): 75–92.

———. E-mail to author. 16 December 2004.

———. *Writing Groups: History, Theory, Implications*. Carbondale: Southern Illinois UP, 1987.

Gilyard, Keith. "Literacy, Identity, Imagination, Flight." *College Composition and Communication* 52 (2000): 260–72.

Glassick, Charles, Mary Huber, and Gene Maeroff. *Scholarship Assessed: Evaluation of the Professoriate*. San Francisco: Jossey-Bass, 1997.

Glau, Greg. E-mail to author. 7 January 2005.

Goggin, Maureen Daly. *Authoring a Discipline: Scholarly Journals and the Post–World War II Emergence of Rhetoric and Composition*. Mahwah: Erlbaum, 2000.

Gray-Rosendale, Laura. E-mail to author. 4 January 2005.

Gunner, Jeanne. E-mail to author. 4 January 2005.

Hairston, Maxine. "Breaking Our Bonds and Reaffirming Our Connections." *College Composition and Communication* 36 (1985): 272–82.

Harris, Joseph. E-mail to author. 20 December 2004.

Heifferon, Barbara. E-mail to author. 5 February 2005.

Hesse, Douglas. "Who Owns Writing." Conference on College Composition and Communication Annual Meeting. San Francisco. 17 March 2005.

Hillocks, George, Jr. *Research on Written Composition: New Directions for Teaching*. Urbana: NCTE, 1986.

Holdstein, Deborah. E-mail to author. 31 December 2004.

Irmscher, William F. "Writing as a Way of Learning and Developing." *College Composition and Communication* 30 (1979): 240–44.

Janangelo, Joseph. E-mail to author. 6 January 2005.

Lloyd-Jones, Richard. "A View from the Center." *College Composition and Communication* 29 (1978): 24–29.

Logan, Shirley Wilson. "Changing Missions, Shifting Positions, and Breaking Silences." *College Composition and Communication* 55 (2003): 330–42.

———. E-mail to author. 16 December 2004.

Lovas, John C. "All Good Writing Develops at the Edge of Risk." *College Composition and Communication* 54 (2002): 264–87.

Lunsford, Andrea A. "Composing Ourselves: Politics, Commitment, and the Teaching of Writing." *College Composition and Communication* 41 (1990): 71–82.

Mangelsdorf, Kate. E-mail to author. 5 January 2005.

Marx, Karl. *Capital: A Critique of Political Economy*. New York: Random House, 1976.

Matsuda, Paul. E-mail to author. 30 December 2004.

McQuade, Donald. "Living in—and on—the Margins." *College Composition and Communication* 43 (1992): 11–22.

Middleton, Joyce Irene. E-mail to author. 10 January 2005.

MLA Commission on Writing and Literature. "Report of the Commission on Writing and Literature." *Profession* 88 (1988): 70–76.

Muth, Marcia F., and Karla Saari Kitalong. *Getting the Picture: A Brief Guide to Understanding and Creating Visual Texts*. Boston: Bedford/St. Martin's, 2004.

No Child Left Behind. 21 January 2004 <http://www.ed.gov/nclb/landing.jhtml>.

North, Stephen M. *The Making of Knowledge in Composition: Portrait of an Emerging Field*. Upper Montclair: Boynton/Cook, 1987.

"The N.S.S.C. and the C.C.C.C.: The Report of Group Meeting III at the Spring Meeting of the Conference on College Composition and Communication at the Morrison Hotel in Chicago, March 30–31, 1951." *College Composition and Communication* 2.2 (1951): 13–15.

Odell, Lee. "Diversity and Change: Toward a Maturing Discipline." *College Composition and Communication* 37 (1986): 395–401.

Odell, Lee, and Susan M. Katz. *Writing in a Visual Age.* Boston: Bedford/St. Martin's, 2006.

Peckham, Irvin. E-mail to author. 6 January 2005.

Peterson, Jane E. "Valuing Teaching: Assumptions, Problems, and Possibilities." *College Composition and Communication* 42 (1991): 25–35.

Pickett, Nell Ann. "The Two-Year College as Democracy in Action." *College Composition and Communication* 49 (1998): 90–98.

Pryor, Chet. E-mail to author. 5 January 2005.

Purnell, Rosentene B. "Using Language to Unlock the Limits." CCCC Chair's Address. New York, 15 March 1984.

Robertson, Linda R., Sharon Crowley, and Frank Lentricchia. "The Wyoming Conference Resolution Opposing Unfair Salaries and Working Conditions for Post-Secondary Teachers of Writing." *College English* 49 (1987): 274–80.

Rodriguez, Luisa. E-mail to author. 9 January 2005.

Rose, Shirley. E-mail to author. 15 January 2005.

Royster, Jacqueline Jones. "When the First Voice You Hear Is Not Your Own." *College Composition and Communication* 47 (1996): 29–40.

Russell, David R. *Writing in the Academic Disciplines, 1870–1990.* Carbondale and Edwardsville: Southern Illinois UP, 1991.

Schell, Eileen E. *Gypsy Academics and Mother-Teachers: Gender, Contingent Labor, and Writing Instruction.* Portsmouth: Heinemann-Boynton/Cook, 1997.

Schön, Donald A. *Educating the Reflective Practitioner.* San Francisco: Jossey-Bass, 1987.

Selfe, Cynthia L. "Technology and Literacy: A Story about the Perils of Not Paying Attention." *College Composition and Communication* 50 (1999): 411–36.

———. Personal communication. 16 December 2004.

Shaughnessy, Mina. *Errors and Expectations: A Guide for the Teacher of Basic Writing.* New York: Oxford UP, 1977.

Sheils, Merrill. "Why Johnny Can't Write." *Newsweek* 8 December 1975: 58–65.

Shulman, Lee. "From Minsk to Pinsk: Why a Scholarship of Teaching and Learning." *The Journal of Scholarship of Teaching and Learning (JoSoTL)* 1.1 (2000): 48–53. 22 August 2003 <http://www.iusb.edu/~josotl/Vol1No1/shulman.pdf>.

Sloterdijk, Peter. *Critique of Cynical Reason.* Trans. Michael Eldrid. Minneapolis: U of Minnesota P, 1988.

Stewart. Donald C. "Some History Lessons for Composition Teachers." *Rhetoric Review* 3 (1985): 134–43.

Troyka, Lynn Quitman. "Perspectives on Literacies and Literacy in the 1980s." *College Composition and Communication* 33 (1982): 252–62.

Veeder, Rex. E-mail to author. 19 January 2005.

Villanueva, Victor. "On the Rhetoric and Precedents of Racism." *College Composition and Communication* 50 (1998): 645–61.

Vitanza, Victor J. E-mail to author. 29 January 2005.

White, Edward. *Developing Successful College Writing Programs.* San Francisco: Jossey-Bass, 1989.

———. E-mail to author. 3 January 2005.

Wilson, Gordon. "CCCC in Retrospect." *College Composition and Communication* 18 (1967): 127–34.

Yancey, Kathleen Blake. "Made Not Only in Words: Composition in a New Key." *College Composition and Communication* 56 (2004): 297–328.

Young, Richard. "Paradigms and Problems: Some Needed Research in Rhetorical Invention." *Research On Composing: Points of Departure.* Ed. Charles R. Cooper and Lee Odell. Urbana: NCTE, 1978. 29–48.

1977

A View from the Center

RICHARD LLOYD-JONES

T ime . . . worships language and forgives everyone by whom it lives." So said W. H. Auden in explaining why the writing of Kipling and Claudel will live, even among people who do not share their views. Although we too may disagree on politics and social customs, even on the specifics of language, still we are among those who are fascinated, entranced, and enthralled by language in general. We all turn back to favorite poems or novels or essays which present ideas we don't really approve of, which perhaps we read with the anxiety of indulging in a secret vice, but in the end the language makes us do it. We are the victims of the love of language for its own sake. In fact, we sometimes dote on the songs of the devil.

Of all the powers and principalities of language, the most powerful and insidious and exciting and puzzling is the metaphor. In an age of quantification, allegiance to the metaphor is subversive, because it upsets the deductive electronic gadgets we have elected to be our masters. Those machines need immutable categories, precisely defined. Each little quaver of doubt, each fuzzy borderline of meaning rouses the computer to be angry with the operator. The metaphor, with its dogged insistence on outright *non*sense, simply puts the machine to sleep. Only a human can find the wisdom in absurdity, and that is how we know we are not machines.

We are also political. Even if somehow anyone escaped the larger social movements of the sixties and early seventies, we have now found our own place on the public stage as, suddenly, our fellow citizens have discovered writing. Or as the press usually puts it, "the crisis in writing skills." We are invited to make statements, and we have become the subjects of editorials. Though once we might have doubted it, by the facts of

This article is a revised version of the Chair's address Richard Lloyd-Jones delivered at the CCCC Convention in Kansas City, Missouri, on March 31, 1977. It was first published in *CCC*, volume 29, number 1, February 1978.

public notice we now know that we exist. And school boards and trustees and the Olympians of the faculty respond to the editorial pronouncements as, allegedly, the Celtic chieftains took note of the bards who reported their battles. In the end, *what* had happened was what the bard *said* had happened. When the press reports a crisis, there *is* a crisis, and *we* are *it*.

When we observed the marches of the political left and the counter-marches of the political right, we noted the discomfort of the people in the center—caught in the middle, I think. We may have remembered that St. John in Revelations passed on the advice not to be lukewarm, rather to be either hot or cold lest we be spit out altogether. The Apollonian middle way was transformed into fence-straddling or paralyzed inaction. If you weren't for us, you were against us. The center was often uncomfortable.

We hardly bothered to deny the reductive simplicity of the political metaphor which forces all kinds of belief to occupy but a single spot on a line drawn between right and left. The figure may have come from the Estates General and the geography of a political meeting hall, but the effect is to reduce all of our qualifications and amplifications and cavils and contradictions to a single point on a political line. The Center perhaps can be made of the several center parties, but even they are expected to keep their opinions to one dimension of a political line.

In our classroom grading, we are much more subtle in our simplicity; we overlay a normal curve on our political base line and pretend to a second dimension. You'll note that the extra dimension does not reveal the quality of the opinion, merely the numbers who score at the same point. The center does not represent wisdom in such a diagram, merely the more numerous party. Such standards are what make standard English, the usage of the greatest number in the least well-defined situations. Remove all contextual guidance, and the odds will favor the propriety of the form of the language which might be chosen by the greatest number and offend the least. And like the learning implied by the "C" grade, such language does the world's work. The hot and cold positions in language as in politics give us life and trouble; but the center position may just be apathy, just cause for being spit out.

As you see, I can stack metaphor on metaphor, twisting the meaning and the feeling with each new vehicle. Metaphor crafting is the ethical badge of membership in our guild. Aside from having fun, we make metaphors because we believe that a metaphor offers the possibility of our escaping the prison of categorical language. We know, as the computer does not, that if we say our love is a rose, we are not just confessing to some botanical perversion. In a metaphor, we assert the-thing-which-is-not, that is, we lie in order to get at knowledge and perhaps a larger truth. If you like fancy words, we play with heuristics. We know with C. S. Lewis that real understanding and knowledge consist of having more than one metaphor to apply to a single conception so that the tenor is best revealed when the vehicles overlap, as though ideas were being sifted through meshes made with strands from different figures. *One* metaphor lies, but several in concert *lead*. The most dangerous lies are transmitted by metaphors not really recognized as metaphors, thus masquerading as categorical, computer-firm truth. Hence I ring the changes upon notions of linear centrality in order to challenge them.

At the 1976 annual meeting of CCCC, we played on another geometric metaphor and talked about ideas which are "basic." I don't recall hearing people mention much that a "base" might refer to the footing of a geometric figure. I think I did hear a few elaborations into architecture where "base" is treated as synonymous with "foundation." Whether we said it or not, however, we took for granted that whatever was really basic was the firm foundation upon which our discipline or class is to be erected. Foundations are often hidden, they are likely to be ponderous, they require excavation, but they *are* necessary. Being basic, we are important. Clearly, that is a fine figure, or so we seem to claim.

Beyond that appeal is the somewhat less evident implication that certain parts of our subject inevitably precede certain other parts. Since buildings are built, as a rule, from the bottom up, so we too must rehearse certain elementary materials until they are perfect before we can go to the second storey or the third storey, though I am not sure why we should be able to spell before we make sense. Most buildings eventually are built up to the roof, so by analogy, instruction in writing should be complete as the roof is complete, long enough before one's death rattle that we'll have enough years in the completed house to pay the mortgage by writing well. This metaphor takes us into a world where one course or a pattern of courses ought to do the job of teaching a person to write, now and forever, with possibly minor repairs as old age sets in. We thus encourage people to think that language is a child's toy rather than a person's lifelong other self.

Still, the foundation metaphor—the basic one—has lots of political appeal. Wherever else one might skimp, prudence dictates that the foundation should get its full share of effort. Perhaps the real reason for our wanting to get back to basics is not entirely a spurious nostalgia for a past we never knew. Rather it depends upon a sense that society might be willing to pay more money for something it understood as basic.

Our real trouble with that basics metaphor is that we are not able to identify satisfactorily a tenor to go along with all the architectural vehicle. Ten of us in a room manage to find ten different ways of identifying the foundations of our discipline. By the time we bicker about definitions, we have lost whatever authority we had with the public to claim competency in dealing with basics.

Another architectural image which drifts through our comments turns out, however, to be mostly anatomical. Sometimes we talk about

skeletons, particularly in reference to composing papers. We explain outlines and amplification by discussing how flesh is attached to the skeleton. Suddenly that big building turns into the human body, but that is
simply because the animal skeleton in itself has a metaphorical equivalent in the structure of a skyscraper. "Skeleton" is a very useful vehicle for
people who want to talk about form. We also extend it to speak about the
skin of a building, at least in modern architecture. We come to understand that buildings have lives of their own. They are often given pulses
and flowing blood. The skeleton of a piece of writing is more likely to be
fleshed out, but otherwise the figures are parallel.

We have more trouble applying that particular skeletal image to our
discipline as a whole, perhaps because we are so diffident in asserting
what even an apprentice in our field should know. Even when we try to
apply the image to the language itself we run into some trouble. Grammar is surely the skeleton for language. But separating the lexicon from
the grammar really isn't easy. We are of more than one mind about what
is really the deep structure.

Anyway, one of the great virtues of English is the richness of the alternatives. Not skeletal rigidity, but fleshly mutability, attracts us. A monist
will say that any particular idea can be said only one way and that a revision automatically means that we say something else. In revision, we
have *seen* again, and we have *said* again, and we have thus created a new
reality. I sympathize with the monists, but practically I find that it is
more useful to talk about different ways of saying the same thing. Oh yes,
I know if the audience is different, if the situation is different, if the
amount of explanation is different, it is no longer *it*. *It* is other. But I will
persist in my error anyway. It allows me to say more conveniently that
the choices in the language are mostly to be determined on rhetorical
grounds rather than on linguistic ones.

Those people who believe that there is one correct form of English
simply deny this rhetorical choice and insist on ontological certainty.
They are comfortable with the metaphor of the skeleton in that it implies
rigidity. If *I* am to like that figure, it is because I can see on a skeleton the
surfaces of life. I can see dialect choices, choices to define intimacy, all
sorts of choices to deal with tone and attitude—all built upon a basic
skeleton, which is in itself one chosen from many as determined by purpose and situation. The choice of *which* skeleton is the decision of
whether we want a factory or an office skyscraper or a home.

In the end, though, I had rather discard the skeletal metaphor on the
ground that it doesn't address the core needs of our profession. I want to
return to *central*.

Some will share a memory with me—the recollection of picking up
the phone, cranking one long ring, and getting "central." You could ring
various combinations of shorts and longs and get specific subscribers

directly, but if you really wanted to know what was going on in the village you rang "central."

The folks in bigger towns, which had numbers, had to call central in order to be hooked up to anybody else on the system, but their central didn't know much except numbers, and our central had a name—Mrs. Petersen— and she knew all sorts of things. Somehow, in the village, she knew who was at the bank, who had gone down to the ice house, who hadn't been feeling well. I don't know that she listened in on all the conversations, but we supposed so. She just made herself central in the life of the community. In our more urban and perhaps urbane way, we would think of her as a communication nexus, but we'd do better to remember Mrs. Petersen as Central.

You can tell that I am about to make Mrs. Petersen an emblem of us, and you can guess I'm going to try to make it very grand and very folksy at the same time. I don't want to see the view from the center to be the view along a political line, but rather the view from the middle of the universe. We are the ones at the center who reach to all other disciplines and to all other people. We synthesize knowledge and unite people. By our force, we draw from the wisdom of other disciplines and in making it ours, transform it by combining it in new ways. The instrument of language which we play soothes the savage breast, opens the secret places, and weds the separate selves. And it is the common property of all faithful people. That's why I want to speak of the view from the center.

Mrs. Petersen, our telephone central, knew everyone in the village. Carl Klaus suggested that we should study almost all of the academic disciplines (*CCC*, December 1976). His modest proposal was that we should know rhetoric, linguistics, literary criticism, cultural history, sociology, psychology, neurology, speech therapy, politics, communication theory— all that can be gathered to store in the warehouses of the mind. He does not think we will quite master it all, but he does hold us responsible for sampling in many directions—in Kaster's cove and on Ventura Heights and out on the farms west of town. I don't think he meant for us to listen in on all of the calls, but he wanted us to know when a call was made and whether folks were home and who was visiting lately.

We do not expect to rival the comprehensive mastery of Aquinas, but with suitable tentativeness, we can make use of whatever concepts come our way. We can encourage students with diverse interests and be glad when they become our teachers in the arcane lore of an exotic intellectual land. Some will provoke us to wisdom, and we will forgive those who prove to have been merely curious. Anyway we do not expect to know everything; we want to master the spaces between everything. Modern physics long since made us learn that the world out there has more space than stuff anyway, and it is in the spaces that we find relationships.

Klaus was telling us the areas in which our students should devote some study if they want to teach writing. I want to claim that our central position in scholarship is to make a coherent whole of all this diversity. He wanted us to make better teachers; I want to tell what kind of intellectual responsibility we should assume in the House of the Intellect—and in the Palaces of Power as well.

We are, after all, making progress. Gary Tate and a few of his friends implicitly have been making my point. *Teaching Composition: Ten Bibliographical Essays* is a most convenient instrument for guiding the reading of the literary student who has become aware of the importance of teaching composition in a limited market for teachers of literature. What begins for these students as adjusting to the market ends as intellectual enthusiasm for a study that they had not known existed. Tate and his authors offer evidence that serious study of composition does exist and that it represents an astonishing variety of approaches. Richard Larson's annual bibliography in *CCC* also makes the point, and at our conventions the sessions dealing with theoretical, scholarly, and research knowledge overflow. Keeping up with new work is getting harder all of the time.

In order to know more, we will have to draw into our work the scholarship of many disciplines; we will have to recognize ourselves in the roles of inter-disciplinary scholars—with all of the attendant embarrassments that come of trying to speak in fields far from one's own base. But if we do not try to be in the center of all knowledge, to report the view from the center of how disciplines interact, we deserve our present *basic* position, that is, our traditional place in the damp cellar of the house of the intellect.

Not only do we draw upon these other fields, but we can unite them. I am always vaguely amused by the complaints of English teachers that they are always chosen to take minutes and write letters. That is, they are chosen like the bards to determine what is worth remembering and to keep people in touch. So too the person who explores constantly how language determines what one can know and feel, as well as how different people relate to each other, becomes a real power in a casual society. The more the personal contacts of our culture are fleeting and specialized, the greater the need for people who understand the language in action in situations. Here too we view from the center as negotiators, explainers, and referees.

The metaphors we choose to represent ourselves determine in part how we feel about ourselves and how we are to be judged by others. Right now, for good reasons or bad ones, the society at least gives lip service to its desire to have our appointed tasks done well. Though we have seen our language debased by political equivocation and foolish advertising, we are told that the openly expressed truth matters. Though we are baffled by bureaucratic instruction and bewildered by demogogic squeals, still we hear that the culture needs the exactness of good writing. Our work in the schools is derided and under-financed at the same time that the public rages because student writing is inadequate. We are seen as purveyors of subversive literature and abettors of dissidents, even as we hear cries for help in fixing the cultural mosaic that makes up the nation. In short, we are for the moment news, and that is our opportunity.

At the same time that our newsworthiness has increased, so has our tendency to establish a sub-group to deal with every issue. In a large organization, perhaps one has to have sub-groups so that individuals can make human contact in a group small enough to be comprehended. Perhaps only in small groups can special concerns be worked out, can ideas be given enough force to be heard by the entire polity. Perhaps, in fact, if we are truly pervasive in our interests, we can expect folks with related enthusiasms to cluster together, and very likely our convention programs have become so large that no one program chair can cope with the diversity without the help of special-interest groups.

Even as I admit the usefulness of cell division, I rise to urge the importance of concentrating our new strength to accomplish general reforms in the teaching of writing while we can muster political power. We may need to create internal structures for the CCCC in order to adjust the balances among our special interests, but I think it is important that we come together to talk together about our general visions, to listen to explanations of the special studies of parts of our group so that we know more of the whole. I note in passing that some of the most exciting lessons I've had on the teaching of writing have come from NCTE colleagues who teach in the elementary schools. We need more demanding training programs for teachers; we need research programs for scholars. We need our journals not only to deal with what to do on Monday but to demonstrate our right to a central function in the academy.

If, as an organization, we are a mosaic which reflects the cultural mosaic of the nation, and I think CCCC and NCTE have tried to be such mirrors as well as mosaics—mirrors bent slightly perhaps to reveal satirically our own pretensions—then we must remember that the tiles in a mosaic, for all their separateness, fit into a whole. Whatever we do to represent our special views, we need to return to statements of our central purpose.

So it turns out that I have given not an academic paper on tropes but a sermon about our behavior. A call to action. An admonition. My text—"Time *Worships* Language"—I've carefully kept just below the surface, and I'll trust you to work out that theological metaphor of worship to suit your fancy. It can be extended almost indefinitely, and it could allow me a grandiloquent peroration, but since this age of studied offhandedness belongs to our telephone operator, Mrs. Petersen, I will simply suggest that we avoid the wastefulness of sectarian division and urge you all, as we perform the rites of instruction, to "Keep the Faith, Babies."

In the early seventies, the press rediscovered a crisis in writing skills. One can find similar discoveries among the scribes of Sumer and regularly thereafter. One can expect the views with alarm to resurface far into the future. Writing—the use of language generally—is so central to human values that almost any facet of behavior can be reduced to a complaint on literary style.

The battle cry then was "Back to Basics." In part, it may have been a response to statements by CCCC and NCTE on the students' rights to their own language, at least in personal and classroom discourse. There had been a "minimum essentials" fad that concentrated almost entirely on cosmetic surfaces of writing. I imagine, though, that the flurry of feature articles was really an anguished response to the perceived complexity and ambiguity of modern life. Whatever the cause, it led to the theme of the 1976 CCCC convention—"What's REALLY Basic?" Clearly, the "really" was intended to suggest that popular discussions were not getting the point.

During the same time, the first graduate programs in rhet/comp were emerging, mostly in departments of English. Autodidacts had made themselves into specialists for decades, but the increasing size of colleges, the expansion of research and scholarship in the areas relating to composition, and the bureaucratizing of knowledge in colleges made formal specialization necessary. One problem was that the self-taught specialists had quite different formulas for defining their work. Another was that academic establishments had trouble imagining that people who often taught the least mature students could really deal in sophisticated ideas.

In this context, CCCC was redefining itself as well as the field. At the 1976 meeting, Janice Lauer and Janet Emig gave keynote addresses emphasizing scholarship, and seven regular sessions on research drew overflow crowds. Civil rights, the Vietnam War, and the growth of mass testing programs were part of discussions about classroom goals. Although computers were not yet moving into the sessions, papers about film were challenging the usual limits of what was composition. The organization was in ferment, and one does not have to look far to find current analogs for these debates.

I thought it was time for the Chair to issue a challenge more expansive than what was contained in the 1977 convention theme, "200 Plus One: Communicating the Third American Century." As it happened, I was teaching a course on style, and metaphor was a major topic for examination. I had already been put off by the metaphor of "basic," so I was struggling for a way to represent the importance of our work and still remain faithful to ideas of social mutability. The rural telephone lines of the thirties offered possibilities. Now, almost a third of a century later, the vehicle may be too exotic for current readers to evoke any sentimental warmth, but then one could imagine social cohesion and practical knowledge represented in the voice of one woman.

The issues have not changed much, but the details of practical life have. Higher education is clearly a commodity. The organizational confusion that was becoming evident at the time of the founding of CCCC is now just part of life. The somewhat scattered reforms of the seventies have been worn into ruts that make new changes difficult. Perhaps a look at the old metaphors in this speech will prompt a chorus of new ones.

—RICHARD LLOYD-JONES,
EMERITUS
University of Iowa

1978   *Our Excellence: Where Do We Grow from Here?*

VIVIAN I. DAVIS

I f to live in difficult times is to be blessed, we are indeed fortunate. The present tension between what is expected, what is wished for, and what we seem to be able to achieve is most frustrating, because things have not so much changed as they are in the process of change. Promises are not so much broken as they are not fulfilled. We live in what I call an age of "ad hoc-ism." Everything is constantly in flux. We seem hardly able to focus our vision before what we thought we were seeing has flipped out of view. It is as if bicentennial minutes have somehow come to life. Our greatest commitment is to be committed, but it is almost impossible to be *for* any one cause without appearing, at least, to be against some other equally deserving of our support. Every problem seems so intricately twisted into a whole net of problems that it is considered naive to talk about solving problems or to hope that anything can be made measurably better.

Old revolutions have not run their courses; rather they seem to have marched over the mountaintop, just beyond the palpable into echoes from yesteryear's fancy. We dig for our roots, summoning moments of sentimentality in the hope that some brave from the past can be today's hero, can fire our devotion and make our hearts burn alive. But we don't trust leaders or institutions or the values we used to give ourselves up to.

We are indeed in the muddle of things—on our own against the cross currents of change. What more daring time to be alive? What more treacherous time to live?

To be, however, at the center of things, as Richard Lloyd-Jones explained our position metaphorically last year, means to be always in the public view, to be defined and stereotyped, reviled and praised as others

This article is the text of the Chair's address Vivian I. Davis delivered at the CCCC Convention in Denver, Colorado, on March 30, 1978. It was first published in *CCC*, volume 30, number 1, February 1979.

judge us from their own perspectives. It may seem wise to make metaphors acceptable to ourselves and define ourselves, ignoring what anyone else has to say about who we are or what we do. But the fact is that what we do, or do not do, can have effect, sometimes direct and immediate, on the world around us. Richard Lloyd-Jones is correct: we have become news, and "that is our opportunity." It may now be time that we, as a community of scholars, learn how to communicate with that other community out there who sometimes seems bent on blaming us for all that is wrong in the world and demanding that we make hay without allowing us sunshine. Yet it is essential that we who have dedicated ourselves to the study of language and its dynamic role in human relations should take the responsibility for practicing what we believe. If we believe that language can transcend the barriers of human separation and unite us, then we ought to use it to bring ourselves and them "out there" closer together.

Presently, we are defensive, and we shy away from the opportunity, fearing that our attempts to communicate with the public may end in more conflagration than conversation. Part of that fear is a result of our own distrust of the public. We see the world divided into two camps—we "in here," and they "out there." We have a suspicion that we have been unjustly meddled with by a public that has never appreciated us enough. As in most things, there are grains of truth in our rationalizations, but we must grow beyond rationalizing to seize the moment and open ourselves to the opportunity to play new roles and experience new possibilities.

To be honest, the American people have a right to know what we do, what we do not do, and why. Not so much because they foot the bills but because the ultimate responsibility for the education of all American citizens rests squarely on the shoulders of the American people themselves. We have chosen to play significant roles in carrying out that responsibility. But we should never arrogate unto ourselves the total responsibility. For we cannot assume total authority for the education of our citizenry. Because we are essentially in partnership with the wider community attempting to share meaningfully in the working out of a community responsibility, we must be in communication with the other parts of the community.

As a profession, we know little about initiating and maintaining public dialogue; consequently, the opportunity to develop a talking relationship with the lay community is a great challenge to our growth. We appear to our critics as snobbish when we may feel unequal to the task. We need to train a new kind of practitioner—one who will know how to manipulate the modes and conventions of the popular media; one who will be at home with the speaking and writing styles that allow the public to identify with us long enough to hear what it is we want to say. At the same time, we need to develop some forums which allow the public to speak directly to us—the daily newspaper or newscast may not be the best media—if there is to be two-way exchange of ideas, clarification of issues, and correction of myths and stereotypes.

We can develop, test, and disseminate throughout the profession effective models for public dialogue. I was privileged to participate in the first of a series of seven Saturday conferences in the state of Georgia, funded by the State Commission on Humanities in response to a proposal by Jim Hill and his English Department at Albany State College. The target audience for the conferences was adults, not a student population or campus community, but civic leaders, politicians, public school teachers, business people, laypeople and parents, representative of a cross section of the population, ethnically and socially. The conferences were held in six small cities of Georgia that represent areas to which one may not usually take such programs. If the first conference was typical of the quality of participation in all of the conferences, we may already have one effective model for communicating with the public.

In its November meeting, the Executive Committee of NCTE authorized its incoming Chair to approach an investigative journalist to explore the possibility that he write an article on the issue of testing to be placed in a popular magazine. Ed Farrell suggests that we learn to piggyback— work out relationships with organizations who would be interested in helping us speak to their publics through their own publications. This week, I was happy to appear on Channel 2's "Denver Now" program to discuss our conference and our goals as composition teachers. We are making gradual steps toward open dialogue with the public, but I am not sure that we feel comfortable with the task as something that a professional organization ought to be doing. Certainly it is an ambitious move to make, but if an informed public is our best weapon against the loss of freedom and human dignity, we cannot ignore the challenge. It seems reasonable to assume that our work would have increased likelihood of support in an environment of goodwill and informed interest which I believe can come from two-way communication between ourselves and the larger public. An honest effort at communicating with the world beyond our own profession should have the sanguine effect of allowing us to learn more about ourselves and what we are doing, how we fail and why we succeed. I am indeed sensitive to the question, "What have we to say to the public?" The answer is not "those things we agree on" but another question—"What do we know about ourselves that will help the public understand what we do and what they can help us do to teach and to learn more about how to teach writing?"

Three years ago when NCTE met in San Diego, a resolution came to the floor of the business meeting intended to instruct teachers not to claim success in print for approaches or materials they used in their classrooms unless there was documented evidence that would verify their claims. I do not remember what happened to the resolution, but I do remember that there was vigorous debate about it. Essentially, two views were promulgated: (1) English teachers lack the expertise, time, or money to do controlled experiments in their classes, and should, therefore, merely describe any examples of what they believe to be good practice and not make any evaluation of it; (2) English teachers know better than anyone else what is succeeding or failing in the classroom because they are there doing what is being done, and therefore, they should say, authoritatively, what is successful practice. I said then what I believe now to be an honest appraisal of the state of our art: we don't know what we are doing.

Of course in an intuitive, philosophical way we know what we do, but generally we are suspicious of any analytical approach that attempts to quantify and measure what occurs in the classroom. Consequently, we are overwhelmed and baffled by those who tell us that they are able to test us and objectively evaluate us. Though we are doing more research and experimentation in our discipline than ever before, we are not, on the whole, sophisticated about the methods of statistical analysis. Most of us were trained before research was thought of as a way to assess our work. Consequently, we have not ourselves designed the tests and measures that would be adequate to evaluate the teaching of composition. Rather, we have become easy prey for those who have their own vested interests for claiming to be able to appraise our teaching. The truth is, if any valid test of teaching as it affects student writing is to be designed, we will have to do it ourselves. For that reason, we must learn the language and the methods of others who claim to measure the results of our practice and who reduce our work to standard deviations. We cannot successfully challenge their claims of reliability with philosophical oratory.

Perhaps we need a special conference on research in composition with the impact of Project English of a decade ago. We must pose and clarify the questions to which we need answers and thereby provide guidelines for future studies so that our research and experimentation will follow the needs of the profession rather than the special interests of circumstances of the individual researcher. We need to bring together in one corpus the most incisive research on the teaching of composition, for research thinly spread over a wide range cannot make the impact we need to make on the whole profession. Our best research needs to be interpreted, replicated, and widely published. Gaps need to be filled in and earlier works updated. Our most significant theories about the teaching of composition should be submitted to tests of verifiability. A good example is Professor Marzano's article on path analysis in the current volume of *Research in the Teaching of English*. We need to develop experimental designs and identify analytical methods especially adaptable to our own discipline. While we must borrow from other disciplines to do this important work, we cannot depend on others to have the required sensitivity to the complexities of the composition process that we have. As long as others know more about what we do than we know, we will find ourselves at their mercy for funding, for professional prestige, and for answers to fundamental questions about our own discipline.

Once I worked in a poultry house to earn money to attend college. When I first began my job there, I was sensitive to everything about the place: the stench took my breath away; the noise set off detonators in my head; the steamy humidity made me weak; and the terrible act of rationalized, routinized killing of dumb birds made me retch. At first, I cringed every time I disemboweled another fated bird, and I swore that I would never again eat chicken or eggs or chicken soup (which is not even made from chickens) as long as I lived. I admired the arrogant resistance of the hen that tried to peck, the rooster that gathered himself in one last futile attempt to spur just as the tobacco-chewing female chicken-killer's knife opened the spurting jugular stream. But after a summer in that feathery hell, Wadley's Poultry, it all became the same to me—a way to earn enough money to get to school that fall. Oh, I was still too chicken to kill a chicken, but gutting their denuded carcasses was what I was paid to do, and I learned to count success by the number of dead chickens I relieved of their guts without getting the mess squirted in my face. Sometimes it was quickening or amusing. The entrails of the conjure bird can tell fantastic tales.

Too often English teachers lose their sensitivity about the roles we have been forced to play. The joy dims and pales, but we go on teaching writing as our duty or our burden, accepting what others define as our place and our successes. The more I find out about the teaching of composition in colleges, the more I fear things have remained the same or worsened. Teachers are still overloaded. The teaching of composition is still viewed as labor and almost anybody with any kind of major in English is still considered as competent to teach writing as the best trained in our discipline. We groan and bear it, hoping the mess will not squirt in our faces. We are, albeit unwitting, accomplices to our own abuse. If we ever expect to be treated as professionals, if we ever hope to work under conditions that indicate we are valued as are all other scholars in academe, we are the ones who will have to demand that substantive changes be made in the circumstances out of which we are expected to perform the magic feat of turning every student into a polished writer in one year.

Many students do not know how to write when they come to college, and freshman composition for most of them, given the curricula of the majority of our institutions, is their last chance. It is absurd that we allow them and our schools to believe that we can essentially help them to master the writing process in a year of freshman composition. All evidence indicates that good writing is the result of processes that develop slowly. If our society wants writers, we will have to make them understand that the job cannot be done overnight and that the cost is not cheap.

Somehow, we must do something to improve the quality of the teaching of composition in institutions of higher learning. Usually, we think of teacher training, especially in-service training, as something for elementary or secondary teachers. Very little has been done about designing effective programs for retraining college English professors, yet we all know that in many classrooms students endure a quality of teaching that does more to insult them than to inspire them and, worse, that teaches them nothing about how to write. Too many college composition professors are teaching from the dictates of their own imaginings or much in the way that they were taught or after their own personal assumptions about what to do with the students they now find in their classrooms. They are unhappy because they are unsuccessful, and their students are unhappy because they cannot write. We must develop effective non-threatening models of structured programs for training the college English professor who is on the job. We must be a learning, learned society. This task is challenging, but we may be surprised to find that there is more acceptance of change in our profession than we realize. At least, we ought to bring home the opportunity to improve the quality of teaching to our own institutions. We can no longer trust voluntary study on the part of the individual practitioner if we want a prestigious community of scholars in the field of composition.

In the last decade, the 4C's, like other professional organizations, has concerned itself with increasing its minority participation and with raising its consciousness in the matter of full professional participation for women. Racism and sexism are ingrained in every facet of American life. We may even say that these twin evils define, in many measures, our way of life. No wonder then they exist within our own profession. We humanists, who know that racism and sexism are destructive of human dignity and prohibitive of the development of human potential, have become, like other segments of the population, all too accustomed to justice long denied and fearful of losing something prized if we should make real changes in the way we dispense awards and honors, in the kinds of standards we set, in the values we establish. We sense that changing things to let minorities in or to give women equal opportunity portends a fundamental difference in the way we live in America. Consequently, our steps in the direction of including everybody in are measured and slow. I recall when I made the program for Kansas City last year, I was given the mandate to increase minority participation on the program. I chose to attempt to do so by asking those who proposed sessions or workshops for the program to find minority participants for their parts of the program. Many had already included minority persons before they made their program proposals. No one refused to have a minority person in their sessions, but I was amazed that some people wrote to me saying, "I don't know any minority people in our field." One person agreed to have a minority person in the session if there were "a minority person at that level of professional growth." I think women, at least, fared better than that. But the truth is we have not, as a profession, substantially increased minority involvement or changed the role of women. I know this challenge is perhaps our most difficult one, but it must be confronted again and again, even when it may no longer be in vogue in certain circles. I wish, as I am sure you must wish, that the twin evils of sexism and racism would some night vanish while we were all asleep and that they would gather with them all the painful history with which they have cursed us. Sexism and racism, chief among the isms that divide us, are tiresome, wasteful of our energies, beneath our dignity—dangerous. But they will not magically vanish. Instead, they grow in subtle ways to plague us. You and I are, as Bob Hogan often says, "accidents." We have all been and still are the hope of some community, some family, some ethnic group. We are of the people tied to them by blood. We intimately understand their yearnings. We come from slaves, from dirt farmers, immigrants, coal miners, the ghettoes, the barrios. We are products of hard work, yes, but of some fortunate turns of events too. We, of all people, must never lose faith in our brothers and sisters who depend on us to open doors and to point them to the pathway whereby they may find their own fullest potential. If we truly believe in the power of language to unite people, then we must use it to bring people together whatever their race, their sex, or their sexual preferences, whatever their physical and mental abilities and debilities, whatever their age. This must be our continuing commitment, for all of us; if any of us are to grow to the fullness of our humanity, we must be regarded as valued, welcomed participants in the awesome experiment that is human living.

When I was a schoolgirl in Indiana (yes, I was once a girl) I think I recall our having a unique system of reporting student progress. We had report cards, but we did not have A's and B's or 1's and 2's. If my memory is accurate, we had three columns on our report cards: one labeled U for Unsatisfactory, another designated S for "Satisfactory," and the other was marked I for "Is improving." A student's progress was shown by the teacher's checkmarks in the appropriate column or columns next to each subject. I think the highest grade one could receive was a checkmark in the column labeled S and a corresponding one in the I column. Whether it was the highest possible grade or not, there was something fine and impressive to me about being marked, "Satisfactory/Is improving." It made me feel I was going someplace in the world. I wish I had titled these remarks to you today, "Satisfactory/Is Improving," because that phrase implies the kind of constant movement toward something yet to be fully accomplished, which is, I believe, the only realistic direction for our profession in these difficult times.

When I addressed the CCCC a quarter of a century ago as its Chair, I ended my remarks by explaining the grading system that we had in Indiana schools as I remembered it from childhood. Report cards then had three columns next to the title of each subject we took. The columns were labeled *U* for "Unsatisfactory," *S* for "Satisfactory" and *I* for "Is Improving." Our progress was shown by the teacher's checkmarks in the appropriate columns next to each subject. I thought the highest "grade" one could get was a checkmark in columns *S* and *I*. As I said, whether or not it was the highest possible grade, being marked "Satisfactory/Is Improving" "made me feel I was going someplace in the world." On reflection, I said I wished I had titled my remarks to the conference, "Satisfactory/Is Improving" to imply "movement toward something yet to be fully accomplished," which I believed then, and still believe to be, "the only realistic direction for our profession" in what were then, and continue to be, "difficult times."

In March 1978, my intent was to call attention to what I believed to be cutting-edge, long-term needs/concerns within our profession: to communicate more effectively with the publics we serve; to create and validate for ourselves research models capable of quantifying and objectively measuring what we do; to demand the professional status we deserve; to improve the quality of writing instruction; to move, through the power of language, beyond the violent profiles of elitism, intellectualism, classism, ageism, sexism, racism to inclusion that welcomes and values all in our quest to discover our fullest human potential.

Given the opportunity to reflect on what I said then and my feelings about it now, I thought I ought to do some research to determine what progress has been made on the issues I brought to the table. I looked for instances of progress and found that there are glimmers of change in different places where we may least expect change to occur. On the other hand, too much has remained the same. Primarily, I came to realize that our sphere of influence is not a protracted line. Our role must go beyond giving lessons, evaluating assignments, working on department and/or campus committees, publishing and presenting at learned conferences. While we may have limited authority both within the confines of our practice or outside in the sociopolitical world that defines and evaluates us, we can and do make differences—sometimes in inconspicuous ways. Often, we light only small fires. We win only skirmishes, small battles. Many times the visions we see and the dreams we dream are to come to fruition only in the lives of the next generation(s) of scholars.

Lest you think that having grown old I now counsel retreat, let me hasten to say that I believe the issues I called to mind in 1978 are not yet adequately addressed by our profession. I hope the CCCC will prioritize those concerns, and develop and disseminate methods and courses of action by which we as a profession can address them significantly throughout higher education. If we were to do so, it would give me great pleasure to evaluate our action as "Satisfactory/Is Improving," for I believe we would be going someplace in the world.

–Vivian I. Davis, Emerita
Bishop College

1979

Writing as a Way of Learning and Developing

WILLIAM F. IRMSCHER

T hose of us in composition occupy valuable territory. We are a land of jobs. We are a land of grants. We are unexplored territory. We are even represented by an organization that has surpluses—a surplus of money and a surplus of talent. But because we hold potential for development and exploitation, we are vulnerable to invaders, especially the literati, who have always been attracted by our markets; the scientific absolutists, who tend to make research a matter of figures and footnotes, seemingly unconcerned with people and purposes; and the anti-rhetoricians, who refer to writing only as a testable item, as a basic skill, or as a tool of communication that we use no more feelingly than a telephone, a tape-recorder, or a typewriter. I do not mean to strike the wrong chord at the start of Frank D'Angelo's program emphasizing trans-disciplinary concerns. We need the cross-fertilization of our discipline with others. This is not a declaration of independence or even a declaration of resistance. It is a declaration of integrity—the integrity of our own discipline as a subject worthy of research and understanding. In fact, I want to make the case that we are concerned with one of the most essential and valuable resources of anyone's education: the ability to write.

Despite our manner of regularly going about the daily business of teaching writing, we have not left our territory uncultivated. In the last ten years especially, we have acquired new expertness; we have learned new approaches. We have strong defenses. To those who do not fully appreciate the complexity of our enterprise, we can now say, "You are outdated," "You are misguided," "You are naive," "We've gone that route before, and it doesn't work." We must more and more assert the worthiness of our enterprise in terms of sound principles.

This article is a revised version of the Chair's address William F. Irmscher delivered at the CCCC Convention in Minneapolis, Minnesota, on April 5, 1979. It was first published in *CCC*, volume 30, number 3, October 1979.

During the past year, the General Education Committee of the College of Arts and Sciences at the University of Washington undertook a review of courses that would satisfy the humanities-distribution requirement for general education. The aim was to reduce the size of that list. The Committee asked the English Department, all of whose courses had previously been included, to recommend particular courses for the list that would meet criteria such as the following:

1. Does the course deal primarily with the historical and philosophical backgrounds of the field?
2. Does the content deal with the most important substantive area of the discipline for students who will in all probability take no more courses in the area?
3. Does the content attempt to distill the major concerns and essences of the discipline?

In the light of these questions, the Undergraduate Education Committee of the department recommended that all writing courses, both expository and imaginative, be dropped from the list. With reference to the expository courses, the Committee explained that these were eliminated because students ordinarily elected them for the "limited purpose of improving their writing skills."

To this proposal, those of us in the department who consider ourselves writing specialists responded, not because we were particularly optimistic about reversing the decision but because we felt obligated to point out the irony of a position that said basically that the major concern and essence of our discipline was language *to be read* but not language *to be written*. How better do we learn the complexities and subtleties of English than by attempting to compose words, literally to put together those isolated fragments of words into meaningful wholes? Writing is limited in purpose only if we see it exclusively as a skill. We must concede that at a low level of proficiency, writing may be considered only a skill, mastered by routine practice, as other skills characteristically are. We know that some adults are so completely unpracticed in writing by hand that the mechanical act of writing itself poses serious obstacles to expression. We know that those who have to be constantly concerned with fundamentals of grammatical structure and basic punctuation also view writing only as a skill that they have to learn by repetition and revision. But once we move students beyond those levels of basic proficiency, we then see new dimensions of expressiveness, inventiveness, imaginativeness, and intellectual growth that are accessible only to someone personally engaged in composing, whether that performance is acting, dancing, painting, or writing. Whatever primary motive we give to the teaching of writing, whether it is self-actualization, creative experience, discovery, or communication, writing is more than a frozen record of thinking. It is an action and a way of knowing. In Wayne Booth's article on "Kenneth Burke's Way of Knowing," Booth, in attempting to explain Burke's way of meaning, seeks a definition of knowing "that is in itself a kind of action," as opposed to knowing in the sense "of fixed concepts proved by tests of certainty."[1] Almost no one illustrates writing as a way of knowing in action better than Burke. It is writing as a generative process, as investigation, as probing, as learning in action.

Yet I would like to go further. I would like to advance the idea of writing as a way of learning about anything and everything. If you press me too hard about the breadth of that statement, I'll take refuge, as William Buckley characteristically does, by saying, "Oh well, I exaggerate a little." Or, in a Gilbert and Sullivan vein, "Well, *almost* everything." Yet I once knew a mathematics professor who required his students to verbalize every mathematical problem in all of its relationships. It was his way of teaching. It was their way of learning.

In a study of the effects of verbalization on problem-solving, Robert Gagné and Ernest Smith observed significant differences between the achievements of verbalizers and non-verbalizers. Verbalizers were clearly superior in problem-solving, particularly as tasks grew more complex. Verbalization took more time, but it forced thinking that led to fuller understanding.[2]

Writing as a form of verbalization requires even more time. Janet Emig's article entitled "Writing as a Mode of Learning" speaks of writing not just as valuable for learning or special but as unique.[3] She makes an extended comparison of talking and writing. She sees writing as unique in the learning process because it combines in one act numerous attributes that psychologists and philosophers have traditionally associated with learning strategies: it integrates the working of hand, eye, and brain. We learn by doing, we learn by seeing what we have done, and we learn by representing experience symbolically in words. Further, writing provides both immediate and long-term feedback, it makes connections, and it engages us in a personal, self-rhythmed process. In this seminal article on the subject, Janet Emig lays the groundwork for further investigation. I obviously use her thoughts as a point of departure, but I would first like to make more explicit what I think is implicit in her remarks: writing is a way of learning and, also, of developing. Peter Elbow makes a similar distinction. He defines learning as "getting new information, ideas, skills, or behavior"; developing as "moving on to a newer, more complex stage of organization in the organism's growth."[4] I am certain that the distinction is not a hard-and-fast one, nor is it linear. But it is useful to think of writing as a process of growing and maturing, in which we move from a stage of first learning the form of behavior that writing represents and, then, by exploring new connections and new combinations, developing new potentialities for knowing. When we move beyond writing as a skill, beyond writing as habit-formation, we can see writing as a way of promoting the higher intellectual development of the individual in the same sense that the human being's capacity for verbal-symbolic behavior is responsible for the superiority of our culture over that of other creatures. But if it seems that I suddenly soar high into the stratosphere of learning and development, far beyond the immediate task of teaching writing to those who are still struggling with the basic process, let me say reassuringly to those who work with basic writers that students cannot develop what they do not first possess.

In order to pursue further the idea of writing as a way of learning and developing, I would like to take a cue from Lev Vygotsky, who says that all of the higher functions in the cultural development of the individual have three things in common: awareness, abstraction, and control.[5] I would therefore like to think of writing in these three terms.

First, through writing, we learn by becoming aware of ourselves. We need not mock this function as a kind of solipsistic self-therapy. It is simply a way of becoming integrated with oneself, an intrinsic value, well said by Robert Heilman a number of years ago: "Many of us have experienced the sense of being put together by the process of putting together. We have composed, and in a sense we are composed."[6] Although we commonly think of writing as a way of connecting with the larger social order, as a form of communication, as an externalizing process, we need to see it also as a way of connecting with ourselves, an internal communication. In writing, this externalizing and internalizing occur at one and the same time. Putting out is putting in. This is learning by writing.

And further, we are all trying to make some sense out of life, especially our own: trying to become more fully aware of problems by actually defining them, trying to bridge differences by analyzing the elements of conflict, trying to clarify values by verbalizing what is good and what is not. Writing brings thought into consciousness, making it available both for us and others to see. In an elegant passage, Vygotsky writes: "The relation between thought and word is a living process: thought is born through words. A word devoid of thought is a dead thing, and a thought unembodied in words remains a shadow."[7]

And beyond these kinds of awareness, writing makes us more aware of purpose, approach, and strategy. It makes a difference what tone we adopt, what language we use, what devices we consciously employ to make our appeal. Writing makes us fully aware of ourselves as rhetorical beings.

I was once a non-writer. In junior high school, I struggled over an article on Christmas that I was supposed to write for the school paper. On the night before the deadline, when all through the house I sensed only my desperation at not knowing what to write and finding no solution in tears, my sister Esther realized the crisis and helped me sentence by sentence to the end. I know now that what I wrote on that occasion was hers, but I read the piece today as if it were mine. (That sounds like the rationale of every plagiarist.) Maybe the piece represents what I thought I could do or what I hoped I could do. In any event, it reminds me that I am still grateful for being saved in a writing situation that seemed no less threatening than disgrace itself. As an assurance to Esther—and probably to me too—I now send her copies of my books as if to say, "See, I now know how to write and to think for myself." And she is very proud of me.

I have done more than tell a story. I have *written* about the past. In the act of writing, I have distanced myself from it. I have reflected on it, intellectualized it, conceptualized it. Surely I have said things about writing in general as well as about me as a developing writer. Writing, by its very nature, encourages abstraction, and in the shuttling process from the past to the present, from the particular to the general, from the concrete to the abstract, we seek relationships and find meaning. Kenneth Pike writes, "Meaning does not occur in isolation, but only in relation to forms."[8] Writing is always different from experience, because in verbalizing the experience we transcend it by seeing it in a larger frame. Or, as James Moffett says, "The subject becomes less and less matter and more and more idea."[9] He adds, "The panic to teach exposition is partly responsible for its being taught so badly. Teachers do not feel they can take the time to let a student abstract from the ground up. But if they do not, he will never learn to write exposition" (p. 247). We can make Moffett's statement even broader: if teachers do not let students abstract from the ground up, students will never learn. I must emphasize that abstracting from the ground up is different from teaching abstractions and trying to apply them. But many teachers of writing seem not to understand that difference.

Writing is a way of engaging the world by becoming aware how our minds perceive it. Even though other modes represent ways of perceiving and structuring the world around us, writing is readily accessible to all of us because words are its vehicle. Other graphic symbol systems—those of music, mathematics, or logic—require the acquisition of a new language. Writing finds structure in words. Structure represents control. The task of knowing is not so much perceiving the complexities of simple matters as perceiving the simplicity of complex matters—like Kenneth Burke explaining the maze of lines in a photographic mural produced by the wakes of two launches proceeding side-by-side on the sea. When he perceived the pattern of interacting lines and determined the generating principle of the design, all seemed simple.[10] Learning is observing the patterns of things that otherwise seem confused and unrelated, mastering the "syntax of thought," to again use a phrase from Vygotsky.[11] Learning is seeing relationships that become the basis of discovery and development. Thus we need diversity to learn more. We need the broad emphasis of an interdisciplinary conference to provide the basis for rich analogy.

Learning through writing is also achieving a controlled synchrony of parts into wholes. Getting information is often acquiring unrelated facts. We cannot use isolated information unanchored to anything else, but if, as David Ausubel explains, we subsume material "under a relevant and more inclusive conceptual system," it becomes meaningful in terms of its new frame, and by interaction, it promotes new insights.[12] The cognitive structure of individuals determines their potential for learning and writing. To the extent that the existing cognitive structure is clear, stable, and organized, it facilitates learning. To the extent that it is ambiguous, chaotic, and fragmented, it inhibits learning.[13] Writing is a way of fashioning a network of associations and increasing our potential for learning.

Control of language ultimately translates into self-confidence and self-sufficiency. Mature writers are self-sufficient writers, resistant to outer constraints and immune to imposed controls that reduce their flexibility and independence. Finally, the control that writing represents gives us a way of saying as precisely as possible what we want to say. We often *talk* around a subject. We hint and solicit agreement by saying. "You understand, don't you? You know what I'm saying." Writing prods us to be explicit. Writing places upon us the ultimate demand for precise and accurate expression. To this end, writing is both learning and relearning. Rehearsing the thought again and again. Rephrasing it. Reconceiving it. Clarifying it. Settling finally on a configuration of meaning.

If we think of education as concerned with learning to know, finding meaning by association, organizing knowledge, and, finally, developing our capacity to use that knowledge in new situations, then certainly writing serves us all as a way of learning and developing. I would like to suggest that our integrity as teachers of writing lies not solely in being the best possible skills-technicians but in promoting composition as a way of learning and developing, basic to all disciplines.

NOTES

1. *Critical Inquiry*, 1 (Sept., 1974), 8.
2. "A Study of the Effects of Verbalization on Problem Solving" in *Readings in the Psychology of Cognition*, ed. Richard C. Anderson and David P. Ansubel (New York: Holt, Rinehart and Winston, 1965), pp. 389–390.
3. *CCC*, 28 (May, 1977), 122.
4. "Why Teach Writing?" in *The "Why's" of Teaching Composition*, ed. Philip L. Brady (Washington State Council of Teachers of English, 1978), pp. 67–68.
5. *Thought and Language*, trans. Eugenia Hanfmann and Gertrude Vakar (Cambridge, MA: MIT Press, 1962), p. 97.
6. "Except He Come to Composition," *CCC*, 21 (Oct., 1970), 232.
7. *Thought and Language*, p. 153.
8. "A Linguistic Contribution to Composition," *CCC*, 15 (May, 1964), 87.
9. "I, You, and It," *CCC*, 16 (Dec., 1965), 246.
10. *A Grammar of Motives* (New York: George Braziller, 1955), p. xi.
11. *Thought and Language*, p. 46.
12. "Cognitive Structure and the Facilitation of Meaningful Verbal Learning" in *Readings in the Psychology of Cognition*, p. 105.
13. Ibid, p. 103.

In *Teaching Expository Writing*, Irmscher affirms that "the nature of writing is the self. [. . .] Writing is a dynamic process involving choices" (11). In his 1979 Chair's address, he plainly states the idiosyncratic nature of individual writing processes and thus the necessity for teachers and writers to have the flexibility and courage to experiment with different writing methods and combinations. Additionally, Irmscher underscores that when writers muster the courage and accept the responsibility to compose, they should be perpetually afforded patience. This tenet refuses priority or privilege to published writers or unpublished writers, instructors or students, experts or novices. Irmscher underscores that neither time, place, purpose, nor perspective should exempt any writer from giving and receiving compassion.

In their 1991 "festschrift," *Balancing Acts: Essays on the Teaching of Writing in Honor of William F. Irmscher*, Virginia A. Chappell, Mary-Louise Buley-Meissner, and Chris Anderson, all past students of Irmscher, recall that "as former students," Irmscher showed them "ways of blending and merging what seemed to be conflicting points of view" (*Balancing Acts* viii). These attributes of distinction and synthesis are likewise evident in this address, as Irmscher draws a multitude of binaries, describing the multifaceted roles of writing as pedagogy, techne, episteme, and intellectual development. Such binaries as development and discovery, disgrace and pride, and thought and word generate a constellation of attributes that intricately reveal the field's vast scope.

Irmscher begins his address to the CCCC in 1979 with a similar spatial metaphor. He encapsulates the transcendent imagery of the American frontier, describing the literal and figurative field of rhetoric and composition brimming with promise, opportunity, resources, and talent in the face of the "literati," "scientific absolutists," and "anti-rhetoricians." In his time, Irmscher's speech was a treatise to those defending the field. For us now, Irmscher's speech represents the core of our disciplinary values: written language as a transformative force for self and culture. While the speech is partly a defense of Irmscher's desire to establish a doctoral program in rhetoric and composition at the University of Washington, what results is a powerful "Declaration of Integrity and Resistance" that proclaims the entire field's academic and intellectual contribution to students, universities, colleagues, and communities.

---

*Amelia Herb, who assisted in the project by researching the NCTE archives, wrote this reflection on the 1979 Chair's address.

His speech is testament that even at this early time in the field's history, there were numerous specialties represented by such diverse scholars as Emig, Elbow, Moffett, Booth, Vygotsky, Burke, and others who are the roots of the eclecticism residing in the contemporary field of rhetoric and composition today. Ultimately, Irmscher's legacy is one that unifies the field, in that he believes composition is a thorough application of rhetoric. Richard Tracey notes in his biography of Irmscher that he "embraces both rhetorical theory and applied rhetoric—that is, composition—as the two poles of a continuum, such that writing instruction is a different way of thinking about rhetoric" (179). This way of thinking about the duality of rhetoric and composition makes each half dependant on the other; thus for scholars today and those in attendance in 1979, Irmscher's principles unite what often divides loyalties or creates double binds for new and established scholars in our discipline.

–AMELIA R. HERB
University of Illinois
at Urbana–Champaign

WORKS CITED

Chappell, Virginia A., Mary-Louise Buley-Meissner, and Chris Anderson, eds. *Balancing Acts: Essays on the Teaching of Writing in Honor of William F. Irmscher*. Carbondale and Edwardsville: Southern Illinois UP, 1991.

Irmscher, William F. *Teaching Expository Writing*. New York: Holt, 1979.

Tracey, Richard. "He Takes the Teaching of Writing Seriously: A Bibliography of Works by William Irmscher." Chappell, Buley-Meissner, and Anderson 175–84.

1980

Regaining Our Composure

FRANK D'ANGELO

Several months ago, a colleague and I presented a proposal to the Ph.D. graduate committee at Arizona State University for a new concentration on the Ph.D. level in rhetoric, composition, and linguistics. Our proposal seemed reasonable enough. What we were proposing was that graduate students be given a series of options on the Ph.D. level, so that those whose primary interest was *belles lettres* could choose from among the traditional areas of English and American literature. However, those whose primary interest was language, or a broader conception of letters as exemplified by the *bonae litterae* of the Renaissance, could do half of their work in the traditional areas of literature and half of their work in rhetoric, composition, and linguistics.

We argued that students seeking degrees in order to teach and to do research face a job market very different from the one that students encountered as recently as eight or nine years ago, and drastically different from what most teachers encountered when they began. We reminded the committee of the results of the MLA Job Information List, published in the February 1978 *ADE Bulletin*, which showed a preponderance of job opportunities for people in the areas of rhetoric, composition, and linguistics. For example, of the 405 jobs advertised in '76–'77 for people with Ph.D.'s in English, 56 of those jobs were in rhetoric and composition, 53 in linguistics, and 29 in creative writing. Then in descending order, there were 18 openings in American Literature, 18 in Black Studies, 17 for generalists, 15 each in Old and Middle English Literature, 19th Century British Literature, and American Studies, 13 in Renaissance Studies, 8 in 19th Century American Literature, 7 in Colonial Literature, and so forth.

This article is a revised version of the Chair's address Frank D'Angelo delivered at the CCCC Convention in Washington, D.C., on March 13, 1980. It was first published in *CCC*, volume 31, number 4, December 1980.

We emphasized that the opportunity for serious research and scholarship in rhetoric and composition has never been better. The professional membership in the Conference on College Composition and Communication has increased dramatically over the past few years. The MLA has recognized the worth of scholarship in writing and now has a Division of the Teaching of Writing. The National Institute of Education regularly, and the Fund for the Improvement of Post-Secondary Education occasionally, provide grant money for research in composition. And the National Endowment for the Humanities supports summer (and academic year) seminars in rhetoric and composition.

But besides having their own integrity as subjects worthy of serious scholarship, courses in rhetoric, composition, and linguistics, we argued, can play a supportive role in the study of literature. Rhetorical criticism has been an important branch of literary studies in English departments for years. One influence has been that of the Chicago Critics from Elder Olson and R. S. Crane to Wayne Booth. Another influence has been that of the New Critics, who in practice, whatever may have been their aesthetic intentions, made good professional careers out of applying a few tropes such as metaphor, paradox, and irony to the study of literary texts. But rhetoric, in its relation to literature, has an even older tradition that can be traced from Aristotle and Longinus to Kenneth Burke. And some of the most interesting work in the study of literary texts is being done by critics who have been heavily influenced by various linguistic theories.

Despite what I thought of as a composed and balanced view of English studies, one of the members of the graduate committee accused me of curricular decomposition. His posture was that the English Department was guilty of fragmenting the wholeness that was the English curriculum in the late 50's and early 60's. Into the garden of English Studies, he said, we had allowed film criticism, the Bible as literature, science fiction, Black studies, feminist literature, folklore, comparative literature, the teaching of English as a second language, linguistics, and creative writing. He accused us of fostering a narrow vocationalism and of concentrating too much on "mere" literacy, as if there is anything mere about literacy. Composition, he maintained, was just so much compost, but he lost his composure when I suggested that for that very reason composition might contain the proper mixture for a fertile imagination. He lamented the sad state of English studies and grieved for *Paradise Lost*.

In response to my colleague and for the benefit of other members of the Graduate Committee, I alluded to a paper by William Riley Parker, titled "Where Do English Departments Come From?" presented to the Association of Departments of English during the November 1966 meeting of the NCTE and later published in *College English* in February 1967.[1] In that paper, Parker told his audience something that many of us in English departments would do well to heed today:

Even if history does not truly repeat itself, knowledge of it may, at least sometimes, give current problems a familiar, less formidable look. Moreover, neglect of experience, personal *or recorded*, condemns us to repeating its follies. To live intellectually only in one's own time is as provincial and misleading as to live intellectually only in one's own culture. These truisms . . . apply to the history of the teaching of English as much as they apply to the history of other matters. And they apply to the recent as well as the distant past. It can be most useful to know with certainty how raw and how new some of our problems really are.[2]

Parker went on to say that "English was born about 100 years ago."

Its mother, the eldest daughter of Rhetoric, was Oratory—or what we now prefer to call public speaking or, simply, speech. Its father was Philology or what we now call linguistics. Their marriage . . . was short-lived, and English is therefore the child of a broken home. This unhappy fact accounts, perhaps, for its early feeling of independence and its later bitterness toward both parents. I date the break with the mother, however, not from the disgraceful affair she had with Elocution, but rather from the founding of the Speech Association of America in 1914, which brought, as was hoped, the creation of many departments of speech. I date the break with the father, not from his happy marriage to Anthropology, but from the founding of the Linguistic Society of America in 1924, and the developing hostility of literary scholars to non-prescriptive grammar, new terminology, and the rigors of language study. Splinter groups form when their founders feel their interests neglected, and English teachers, absorbed in what they considered more important business, were indeed neglecting speech by 1914 and losing all vital concern with linguistics by 1924.[3]

We need to remind ourselves, Parker continued, that in most places where English was taught, it occupied a subordinate part of the curriculum. English professors originally taught courses in rhetoric, oratory, logic, moral philosophy, and philology. Later they included English literature, and also composition, which was considered to be a branch of rhetoric. Eventually, English departments were to embrace American literature, comparative literature, world literature in translation, the Bible, the humanities, American civilization, drama, theatre, journalism, creative writing, writing for engineers, and business writing.[4]

Parker's historical sketch is evidence that English has changed many times in its brief existence and that it will continue to change. Few of these changes came about as a result of conscious planning by members of English Departments. To accept rhetoric and composition, then, as legitimate parts of the graduate curriculum is not a sign of dissolution, dispersion, and decomposition. It is, rather, a sign that we are regaining our composure, taking composure to mean composition in all of its senses.

I can well understand the posture taken by some teachers of literature, worried that they might lose the few graduate students they have. I can well understand their discomfiture and discomposure. Their thinking reflects that of the profession as a whole as we enter the 80's, wondering how best we can compose ourselves and our discipline. For we are beset by a number of problems: inflation, the shrinking job market, the dwindling number of English majors, the drastic drop in college enrollments, the declining interest in literature and humanistic studies, and the crisis of literacy. These are problems that we can best solve together.

The decline of interest in literature and humanistic studies is not the fault of teachers and scholars whose primary interest is language. Universities are in financial trouble, and students are concerned about the realities of the job market. It will not help our professional situation to refuse to take responsibility for basic literacy. Nor will it help matters for teachers of composition to gloat over their new-found status or to consider a declaration of independence similar to that of the speech teachers or teachers of linguistics. Most of us are also teachers of literature. Curricular changes have been long overdue. The state of the economy has simply forced us to rethink our commitment to literacy.

We have come a long way since the first official CCCC meeting in the spring of 1950. The CCCC has provided a forum for members to talk about their needs and professional concerns: the development of writing abilities in students, the status of writing teachers, the need for strong, professional graduate training in rhetoric and composition, and the development of a body of scholarship about writing. Since that first meeting, we have achieved many of those goals. Scholars who owe a professional allegiance to the CCCC are developing an impressive body of theoretical, empirical, and pedagogical scholarship in writing. Now it is time for us to place our activities within a broader range of intellectual, social, and human thought.

My contention is that composition can provide a unifying center for English studies as well as for the liberal arts. Formerly, high schools and universities made the art of expression the field of concentration. Subjects such as history, philosophy, mathematics, and the sciences were subordinate to the mastery of the principles of reading, writing, and speaking. When literature and the classics were taught, they were taught as models of perfect expression. The educated person was one who developed habits of mind, who could select and weigh and judge the facts, and who could write and speak and think about the facts. In brief, the educated person was one who composed. Reading and writing, when taught as the art of expression, liberate the mind. Viewed in this way, English is not just another specialization, but a mode of inquiry into the ways in which all of the arts and sciences conceptualize human experience.

Scientists, for example, have recognized that language is central to the systematic understanding of nature and of human behavior. The physicist Philipp Frank, in an article titled "Contemporary Science and the Contemporary World View," has this to say about the importance of language for the scientist:

> Non-scientists often believe that science consists in making observations, in accumulating experience. But this image misses the point. At every moment of our life we perceive the data of experience, yet by recording them we do not get science. Science begins only when we invent a system of symbols which can bring order into our experience. For building up science, the creation of words and their syntax is as important as experiments. A part of our science is contained in the vocabulary and the syntax of the English, French or German that we use.[5]

What I am suggesting, of course, is that all of our symbolic actions are fundamentally rhetorical. The creative imagination of the scientist is not much different from that of the poet or of the historian. All must use language to shape the world, and all must use modes of inquiry that are ultimately rhetorical.

Philosophers of history such as W. B. Gallie have argued that history is a species of composition that depends for its intelligibility upon the mode of narration. "Every successful work of history," writes Gallie, "(of the kind that interests us all *most*) must be followable, as a unity in the way that a story is."[6] History, he goes on to say, is "basically a narrative of events in which human thought and action play a predominant part."[7] Gallie's remarks suggest that we might spend more time in the classroom focussing on the relationship between literature and other forms of discourse, such as history and scientific writing, than on trying to see literature as a thing apart. Nineteenth-century rhetoricians did not limit their discussions of the mode of narration to imaginative literature, but included discussions of history, geography, chronicle, annals, biography, autobiography, and memoir. A study of the narrative mode ought to show how narration is used as a mode of inquiry in various kinds of discourse from different disciplines.

The study of narrative modes is but one illustration of the ways in which compositional principles can inform English studies and the liberal arts. In recent years, scholars have been looking carefully at the rhetorical tropes as basic strategies for conceptualizing and understanding human experience in all the arts and sciences. Hayden White, for example, has applied Kenneth Burke's four master tropes, metaphor, metonymy, synecdoche, and irony, to the study of historical texts.[8] David Lodge has explored Jakobson's distinction between the metaphoric and metonymic poles in the modes of modern writing.[9]

Scientists have shown how analogy and metaphor enrich our understanding of the world. It matters not that scholars doing research in different fields are not self-consciously rhetorical. No matter what the name, the game's the same. Whether we call these methods of inquiry, modes, or tropes, or figures, underlying all of these inquiries we recognize the rhetorical *topoi*.

Language, then, is the bridge between the literary arts and the sciences and social sciences. As the poet Stephen Spender puts it:

> Language is the only means of communication between specialties as far apart as every individual's unique experience of his [or her] own life. Scientific specialization itself is human experience; if it is to become part of the general culture, it can only be so by communication through language. When there is a question of discussing and explaining our experiences of the other arts—music or painting— we use words. If architecture aspires to the condition of music, all human experience aspires to words.[10]

Thus far, I have barely touched upon the ways in which composition can provide a unifying center for English studies and for the liberal arts. But that position is winning support. Although some teachers might disagree about the central role that rhetoric and composition might play in unifying the curriculum, many are coming to believe that we ought to be concerned with the critical reading and writing of all kinds of texts, not just imaginative literature. History and philosophy, it can be argued, are simply different species of literary texts. There are many, however, who would not agree that we ought to be concerned with basic literacy. Student writing, they object, is not literature, and they feel that they can afford to be indifferent to it.

The reason for this attitude toward student writing is not hard to find. In an article titled "Intrinsic Criticism" that appeared in *College English* in 1974, E. D. Hirsch cited the reason, and lamented it:

> In the past few decades when we isolated the literary work of art from the continuum of discourse we were inclined to separate the teaching of literature from what is humbly called the teaching of composition. Under the dominance of intrinsic theory, composition courses, which could be called courses in the rhetoric of plain, humane prose, disappeared from the curriculum. Under the impression that literature exists in a domain separate from their own humbler efforts to write, our students were willing to discuss the subtlest stylistic nuances in poetry in uncommunicative and barbaric prose. Why not? Poetry is literature, while their stuff is just essay writing.[11]

In an article titled "Beyond Formalism, Beyond Structuralism: Jobs," Carl Woodring reinforces Hirsch's implied argument: "We ought to attend to student writing. Not their writing about works of literature. Their writing."[12] Hirsch puts the matter even more forcefully: "Bluntly, we ought to be teaching composition with as much thoughtfulness and energy as we teach great books and great works of art. Active literacy and passive literacy are not separate under the ideal of humane letters, good matter in a good manner."[13]

Reading and writing, when taught as the art of expression, should not be concerned with elite verbal artifacts, but with the verbal arts as process. The modes of discourse are merely the application of compositional means to achieving rhetorical ends. Attending to the student's writing puts emphasis on the person in the process. Although there are times when we might doubt if student writing is composed, it is never, ever compost. If students' writing lacks composure, it is because we have failed to teach them how to compose themselves.

As teachers of the art of expression, we can have no greater goal than to teach students to think effectively, to make relevant judgments, to discriminate values, and to write with as much grace and precision as possible. We should pay much more attention to the humanizing of ordinary language than we have in the past. We might take our cue from that first composition teacher, Shakespeare's Prospero, who successfully taught Caliban language. "I endow'd thy purposes with words," he tells Caliban, "that made them known." This also should be our aim—to endow student purposes with words that make them known.

NOTES

1. William Riley Parker, "Where Do English Departments Come From?" *College English*, 28 (February, 1967), 339–351.
2. Parker, p. 339.
3. Parker, p. 340.
4. Parker, pp. 346, 348.
5. Philipp G. Frank, "Contemporary Science and the Contemporary World View," *Science and Language*, ed. Alfred M. Bork (Boston: D. C. Heath and Co., 1966), pp. 8–9.
6. W. B. Gallie, *Philosophy and the Historical Understanding* (New York: Schocken Books, Inc., 1964), p. 68.
7. Gallie, p. 69.
8. Kenneth Burke, "Four Master Tropes," *A Grammar of Motives* (Berkeley: University of California Press, 1969), pp. 503–517; Hayden White, *Metahistory* (Baltimore: Johns Hopkins University Press, 1973); *Tropics of Discourse* (Baltimore: Johns Hopkins University Press, 1978).
9. Roman Jakobson, "Two Aspects of Language and Two Types of Aphasic Disturbances," *Fundamentals of Language* (The Hague: Mouton, 1956), pp. 1–48; David Lodge, *The Modes of Modern Writing* (Ithaca: Cornell University Press, 1977).
10. Stephen Spender, "Language as Communication," in *The Humanities in the Schools*, ed. Harold Taylor (New York: Citation Press, 1968), p. 83.
11. E. D. Hirsch, Jr., "Intrinsic Criticism," *College English*, 36 (December, 1974), 457.
12. Carl Woodring, "Beyond Formalism, Beyond Structuralism: Jobs." Special Joint Issue of *ADE and ADFL Bulletins* (September, 1976), p. 3.
13. Hirsch, p. 457.

In his Chair's address to the CCCC in 1980, Frank D'Angelo complained that Arizona State University had rejected a plan that he and a colleague, John Gage, offered for a full-scale PhD concentration in rhetoric, composition, and linguistics. At that time, few other universities featured a PhD track in rhetoric and composition. Over the next twenty years, however, many institutions implemented such a program. They included Arizona State, which in 1997 installed its first doctoral track in rhetoric, composition, and linguistics. Overall, the number of well-qualified, newly graduated, fully credentialed scholars in the field seems to increase every year.

In his 1980 address, D'Angelo maintained that composition can serve as "a unifying center for English studies as well as for the liberal arts." Consistent with this view, D'Angelo in the early 1990s proposed a rhetorical/cultural studies paradigm that ASU could use to organize its graduate curriculum in English. This proposal was defeated. But, after his retirement, ASU in 2003–2004 implemented a new graduate curriculum that moves roughly in that direction. He is also pleased that faculty members at ASU are now developing a proposal for an undergraduate concentration in rhetoric and composition.

An active scholar in his seventies, D'Angelo maintains a keen interest in the profession: he is now writing an essay tentatively titled "Theorizing English Studies." This piece will be consistent with the view that he articulated in the 1980 speech: "all of our symbolic actions are fundamentally rhetorical."

In his 1980 talk, D'Angelo mentioned Kenneth Burke's and Hayden White's theories of master tropes; in numerous subsequent essays, D'Angelo reflects on those conceptions and/or radically updates and reconfigures other key theories that originated in ancient Greece and Rome, including theories regarding *topoi*. Post-1980 emphases on race, class, and gender have prompted D'Angelo to encourage the study of highly cosmopolitan Hellenistic culture.

D'Angelo's commitment to the architectonic scope of rhetoric leads him to rejoice that scholars now apply rhetorical frames to visual images. Although he finds such work to be provocative and valuable, he laments the failure of certain researchers to grasp the value and adaptability of various theories from classical Greek and Roman rhetoric and from modernist and postmodernist rhetoric in

---

*Frank D'Angelo requested that his colleague and friend Keith Miller reflect on the 1980 Chair's address.

helping to analyze visual communication. Spurred by this new scholarly concern, he has, over several years, investigated images in paintings, photos, films, television commercials, maps, and computer graphics (including ones used by doctors in surgical procedures). His initial, in-progress essay on this topic is tentatively titled "Rhetoric, Poetics, and Visual Culture."

Have D'Angelo's views changed since 1980? Then he maintained that composition could be "a unifying center for English studies." Now he boisterously complains that anyone can teach anything while claiming to teach writing. He insists that, instead of providing instruction in the conventions and procedures of writing, teachers should proudly shove rhetoric into the center of their classes.

Luckily, Frank D'Angelo has helped make such a possibility far more likely now than it was when he began his career in the 1970s.

–KEITH D. MILLER
Arizona State University

1981

Perspectives on Legacies and Literacy in the 1980s

LYNN QUITMAN TROYKA

"T he Decade of the Non-Traditional Student" undoubtedly will be among the labels given to American higher education in the 1980's. More than ever before in our history, America's colleges and universities are vigorously recruiting large numbers of students who, in earlier eras, never would have thought to try to go to college. These students usually have minimal high school credentials but maximum hope that they will learn in college what they missed or what was not available in high school. This hope is fragile in the face of the demands of academe, yet as teachers of writing we have a unique chance to nurture and help fulfill these students' new expectations of themselves. To do this, we need to temper our good intentions with information and experience not usually a part of the consciousness of college faculty.

I

Some statistics and other facts about the current scene in higher education can help set into perspective the arrival on our campuses of increasing numbers of non-traditional students. In 1979, The College Board together with the American Association of Collegiate Registrars and Admissions Officers conducted a comprehensive survey of undergraduate admissions policies at a representative mix of almost 1500 colleges and universities.[1] This study revealed that only eight percent of all accredited post-secondary institutions have admissions standards that accurately can be labeled "competitive."[2] At these relatively few schools, applicants need extremely high admissions test scores and grade point averages to compete for available seats. Open admissions is the policy at thirty-four

This article is a revised version of the Chair's address Lynn Quitman Troyka delivered at the CCCC Convention in Dallas, Texas, on March 26, 1981. It was first published in *CCC*, volume 33, number 3, October 1982.

percent of the institutions; in this group, three-quarters are two-year colleges and one-quarter are four-year colleges, both public and private. The balance have selective admissions, in that all applicants who meet set standards can attend. These standards vary widely, but they are becoming more flexible so that the colleges can attract more students.

Attracting more students is of no small consequence these days. America has a shrinking pool of college students. Ten years ago, enrollments in the first grade declined significantly by over a half million, and yearly the downward trend continues. The number of eighteen year olds in this country peaked in 1979 and is conservatively predicted to decrease by twenty-five percent by the mid-1990's.[3] Thus, to protect jobs and institutions, administrators in two-year as well as four-year colleges are paying increased attention to new potential populations that comprise the group known as non-traditional.

What are the major characteristics of these non-traditional students? Generally, they are older. In the last decade, the number of college students over twenty-five years of age doubled, so that as of today one third of America's college student body is over twenty five.[4] Non-traditional students usually represent the first generation in their families to go to college. Non-traditional students are often parents, some married and some single. Most non-traditional students have jobs which often demand twenty to forty hours a week. They work on construction crews, in restaurants, as practical nurses, on the police force; some are on welfare. Many non-traditional students barely finished high school and thus were graduated without strong literacy skills. Some never finished high school and have been admitted to college on waivers.[5] Others dropped out of high school but later decided to earn an equivalency diploma, a credential more difficult to acquire than a regular diploma. Many non-traditional students are women, some of them returning to school after having started a family. Indeed, women became the new majority in the nation's college student body in 1980.[6] Not a few of the non-traditional students are foreign born: currently 300,000 foreign students attend America's colleges and universities; by the early 1990's, at least 1,000,000 such students are expected.[7]

II

For a closer look at non-traditional students, consider the urban community college where I teach. This college, one of seventeen institutions that comprise The City University of New York, has been serving non-traditional students since it opened in the mid-1960's. In recent years, however, a significantly larger percentage of students who fit the descriptors given above have been attending the college. For example, in the fall 1980 semester, in my four Developmental Writing classes, the students or their parents were from: Italy, Greece, Yugoslavia, Austria, China, India,

Pakistan, Haiti, Jamaica, Barbados, Trinidad, Puerto Rico, Ecuador, Colombia, Nicaragua, Cuba, and America. Half of my 120 students were attending college part-time, which meant that they could expect their two-year course to take four years or more. At least a dozen of my students occasionally had to bring their children to class because their baby sitters had not shown up. Thirty percent of my students were black, and twenty percent were from Hispanic roots.

The majority of students who attend this college have to take two buses or a subway and bus to reach the campus. They come at eight thirty in the morning; they come until ten thirty at night. They come in spite of being told, in most cases, that they must take what amounts to remedial writing, remedial reading, remedial mathematics, and in some cases remedial speech, all for little or no credit. Had I been told as a new college student that I had *that* much catching up to do, I am not certain that I would have had the courage to try again. But the students come. And they try. Many succeed. Often I think of William Butler Yeats' "He Wishes for the Cloths of Heaven":

> Had I the heavens' embroidered cloths,
> Enwrought with golden and silver light,
> The blue and the dim and the dark cloths
> Of night and light and the half-light,
> I would spread the cloths under your feet:
> But I, being poor, have only my dreams;
> I have spread my dreams under your feet;
> Tread softly because you tread on my dreams.

Who are these people who dream, these non-traditional students who risk time, money, and—most of all—self-esteem in the academy? Their writings reveal something of the people behind the descriptors. Here are samples from two Developmental Writing students. I offer these examples not to illustrate error, which is a currently popular way of looking at basic writing students in particular, but to identify people.

Sal is a "thirty-year man." He works for the local utility where his specialty is opening manholes that have not been touched for thirty or more years. He knows wire and cable systems old and new, and he knows how to handle the unexpected and the dangerous. Sal is twenty-six years old, the father of two. His first in-class essay was written for a departmental screening test. He chose the title "Worries Can Really Distract You."

> Worries can really distract me a lot. I worry a lot. Not on the job but about my children. How will they turn out? In the olden days you didn't have so much drugs and vandalism.

At the bottom of the page in very tiny letters Sal then printed: "Dear Dr. Troyka: Please excuse my writing. Let me know my weak points and how I can improve."

That is one side of Sal in college: tight, hesitant, worried. Here is another side, shown in his writing about a month into the semester:

> I am a psychologist of thirty-year holes. I know them and what they are hiding, often before I see them. I read maps, so I'm ready like any good doctor. I never touch at first. I size up the hole. I know that slimy, ugly insects and long fat snakes are waiting. I know that rats as big as cats will be on the sly. Sometimes the stink makes one of my men faint, or else the steps down into the hole have rotted away. My crew is always ready to start before I am. I want to get my head together. The company cares about the breakdown. I know that I can figure out what the trouble is. But I don't want to hurry. Someone might get hurt. And besides, soon there won't be many thirty-year holes left in New York. Maybe that's why I came to Queensborough.

Harriet, who prefers to be called Kee-Kee, is twenty-three, married, and works as a cashier in a local pub. She was never optimistic about holding onto her job because she had had five jobs in the two months just before she started college. Here is what Kee-Kee wrote the second week of the semester for someone in the class who was interviewing her for a report.

> I had no goal before my husband because I thought I'd marry a rich guy. I didn't marry one but there is no problem there. He has a low I.Q. (no offense). To see he got to the ninth grade with a low reading level of at least a fourth grade made me think twice. At the age of fifteen I dropped out of high school to work in a factory. The pay was awful and the labor was worst. I tried attending school again but getting high with friends seemed more important. Finally, I went for my equivalency and to my surprise my diploma arrived in the mail. Then came an unexpected but not surprising growing stomach. I was pregnant. I gave birth to a full-term stillborn baby boy. It was quite depressing.

Kee-Kee is honest and direct. As a result, her writing is memorable. Here is a paragraph she wrote about six weeks into the semester:

> I once saw a terrible automobile accident. Not long ago a band of adolescents made a name for themselves. Everyone had to pass a certain task to become an initiated member. To get up on a boardwalk with a box of pebbles and dump them on a passing car. I was jogging by the FDR Drive when the youngster dumped the stones on a beige four-door Cadillac. What a disastrous error the kid made! The driver, a middle-age lady, lost control of the wheel. She collided with a light pole which forcefully crushed her skull through the shattered windshield as her body was pressed against the dashboard now touching the car seats. There was instant death while her assassin shoved off to catch up his friends. Thus, he now belongs to the Young Daredevils.

Kee-Kee and Sal are two among many who thought they would never go to college, but they have arrived, enticed by their dreams and the hopes aroused by college recruitment campaigns and by society's newly liberal attitudes toward higher education for all.

Of course, not all who come stay. There was a vice-squad police officer who could not finish the semester because his shift rotations kept changing. There was a legal secretary who aspired to more but then was lured to move to Connecticut when her company relocated. There was Antonio, a rotund young man, who insisted on being called "Porky," and who with refreshing honesty told me after three weeks that he was leaving because "I don't want to be like you people."

On the other hand, there was Bruce, a young professional magician of amazing talent, who dazzled us with his skill but who insisted that he really was not very good because Doug Henning could do the Trunk-Switch Trick in less than half the time it took Bruce. Bruce eventually graduated and became an executive with a pickproof lock company. There was Mike, who has served a term at Attica State Prison but then went on to become a social science teacher. There was Tequila, an unmarried mother of two on welfare, who stopped out three times but finally earned her degree and went on to become a computer programmer for the welfare agency of New York State.

III

One thing is clear: As non-traditional students comprise a growing segment of the student body in America's colleges and universities, college faculty are going to become increasingly familiar with a new type of student. College faculty will soon discover that conventional teaching methods do not work well with non-traditional students.[8] These students are the ones who did not "get it" in high school; they are the ones who do not learn well from traditional lectures in the classroom; they are the ones who do not eradicate writing errors solely by doing grammar exercises in a workbook; and they are the ones who are confused or even insulted when teachers are inaccessible, detached, or unfriendly.[9]

Non-traditional students come to academe with resources not usually used or even recognized in college. They come with legacies derived from situation and from language that can enlarge the teaching repertoire that teachers of writing can use. These legacies determine not so much *what* we teach but *how* we can reach and teach, often with dramatic results. The four legacies that I discuss here apply to all writing students at all levels of fluency, but I have come to believe that they are imperative to consider when shaping instruction for non-traditional students in our basic writing and freshman English composition classes. Of course, to say that any *individual* non-traditional student brings all of these legacies to academe would be inappropriate, but my experience has convinced me that these characteristics are clearly the norm for the group.

Legacy 1.   Non-traditional students are highly gregarious and social.[10] For them, social interchange is imperative. They concretely need to feel a sense of community, of belonging to a group.[11] They literally, not figuratively, need each other. They need to be friends, and they need to have friends. Only then can they feel relaxed and safe enough to learn. Studies of conducive learning environments repeatedly show that non-traditional students attend first to social context, to getting along with other people.[12] As Kee-Kee wrote in her journal, "Friends are altogether important to me. They're my way of seeing around corners."

But the largeness of colleges militates against this need to establish social ties. The cool, detached atmospheres of our colleges simply are not environments in which non-traditional students can feel at home enough to learn, according to Patricia Cross, a leading researcher and observer of the current scene in higher education.[13] Further, Edward T. Hall, the cultural anthropologist and author of the important volumes *The Silent Language* and *The Hidden Dimension*, reports in his most recent book, *Beyond Culture*, on the mismatch between the social imperative of non-traditional students and the impersonal nature of most faculty.

> A common fault of teachers and professors is that they pay more attention to their subject matter than to their students, who frequently pay too much attention to their professors and not enough to the subject.[14]

Writing teachers have the perfect opportunity to use this legacy of imperative need for social interaction to enrich the atmospheres of their classrooms. Here is one concrete example from among many. The first day of class in my Developmental Writing classes I give out a "research questionnaire" that requires the students to find out who are the others in the classroom. To do this, the students have to move around the classroom to ask each other questions. At the end of this class session, each student has to introduce another student to the assembled group until all have been accounted for. Two things never fail to impress me about this simple activity. First, the students quickly relax and begin to smile easily, circulating from person to person and always being careful not to exclude anyone. Second when a student introduces another publicly, the introduction invariably includes words such as, "This is my friend _____" or "Meet my friend _____," yet the students were strangers only fifteen minutes earlier.

Additional interview activities of increasing complexity can build further upon the students' strong impulses toward social interaction. Such activities start with pairs of students interviewing each other while taking notes. Later these notes form the basis for written reports of the interviews. A list of questions to guide the students as they interview is crucial here. The teacher, in consultation with the class or alone, needs to sequence the questions so that they help the interviewers move from a focus on the specifics in the life of the person being interviewed to generalizations about the interviewee or about the human condition. Such a sequence helps non-traditional students with one of their typical difficulties with academic writing: moving from the concrete to the abstract. Following written reports of the interviews, written portraits of family members or of themselves prove popular with the students. Not infrequently many students have added their written portraits to the heirlooms of their families, sometimes with photographs included. One semester a particularly enterprising group of students set up a small business in their neighborhood to prepare written portraits of anyone who wanted to pay a few dollars for the service.

Legacy 2.   Non-traditional students are more comfortable in an oral rather than a written mode. They are simply more verbal orally. Non-traditional students are not solely oral people, but a large percentage are highly oral. Thomas J. Farrell, in tracing the history of the development of literacy concludes that "highly oral people relate to the world and other people in a way that is different from that of highly literate people."[15] Hall observes that oral people prefer talk not just because it is easier but because it maintains social contact. Some talk is not so much content as context.[16]

The academy tends to recoil from non-goal-oriented communication. For most college faculty, the notion that the medium is the message does not coexist easily with educated appreciation of academic discourse, written or oral. Nevertheless, teachers of writing can use this legacy of oral language to strong advantage. Simulation-games are a clear example. These activities move students from general talk to structured role playing in life-like situations that call for analysis and problem solving. Each simulation game is based on a real event in society, such as a prison uprising, the population explosion, or equal job opportunities for women.[17] Each simulation game comes with a data base that must be read, pondered, discussed with a group of peers, and finally argued with the entire class. Writing is built into the structure of each simulation game, along with provisions for oral exchanges. My research using four simulation games in one semester showed that the students who participated in the activities far excelled those who were given the same data base without any opportunity for role-playing.[18] Not only were their essays, scored holistically, significantly better, but scores on a grammar test were significantly higher.

Reading aloud to the class is another strategy teachers can use when they work from a legacy of oral language. Short pieces with accessible vocabulary and style work best, especially at first. Readings that are solely literary or very complex can be saved until later in the semester. Non-traditional students, more than most people, write with their ear as much as with their eye. But they have not been read to very much, my students say. Their mind's ear, then, has to rely too much on oral language patterns that are not always dependable for writing and editing academic prose. A side effect of reading aloud usually begins about the third week of the semester: My students start to read aloud to their children, surely a benefit for everyone involved. Conversation before or after class not infrequently drifts to discussing the children's reactions to being read to as well as the children's favorite stories and books.

Legacy 3.   Non-traditional students are holistic thinkers. They perceive the world as a whole, not as a combination of separate parts. In the language of cognitive styles, which is a field in psychology that seeks to understand the ways by which different groups of people learn most easily, non-traditional students exhibit many of the perceptual characteristics of field-dependent thinkers.[19] Life is highly context bound, filled with a complex weave of oral language, body language, awareness of and participation in a group, and information.[20]

Such students learn best with a "top-down" model of language processing.[21] They move easily from seeing the whole of a paragraph or an essay to then seeing the sentence and finally downsliding to consider the word. To start such students at the word level is clearly ill-advised.[22] My research examining the cognitive styles of students and teachers of writing shows that Developmental Writing students are open to learning when they can first see an overall context in which to place what they are studying.[23] Often referred to in the language of cognitive styles as the "global" view, such an awareness of the complete context helps non-traditional students focus and organize their learning.[24] For instance, any segment of information in a writing class, from a point in grammar to a rhetorical strategy, can be learned more successfully if its role within a complete piece of writing is made clear to the students. Non-traditional students need deliberate guidance to learn to analyze separate parts of a whole; they need coaching and reassurance when they are learning to break up long stretches of information into separate segments for the purpose of solving assigned problems.[25] In the language of logic, non-traditional students are deductive thinkers.

College faculty, on the other hand, tend to be inductive thinkers. They are comfortable with a "bottom-up" model of learning; starting with a small detail does not trouble them. They analyze and restructure information with ease, and they prefer to solve problems independently. Most important, they are usually unaware that the overall context for any separate piece of information is not self-evident.[26] When we as teachers of writing realize that there might be a mismatch between our cognitive styles and those of our non-traditional students, we can be sure to present overviews of what we are teaching and to demonstrate how parts (of a course, of an essay) work within the context of the whole—indeed how analysis of parts advances our students' understanding of the whole.

One way of giving students an overview is to show them examples of good writing by students like themselves who were enrolled during previous semesters in the same course. Such models not only demonstrate the qualities of good writing but also help students infer the goals of the course. Course goals, preferably stated explicitly in terms of both process and product, help non-traditional students place their work in a context and also help alleviate any feelings of confusion about the interrelationships among the separate aspects of their work. Especially in new situations, non-traditional students often have a low tolerance for uncertainty. If they do not know where they are headed, they are distracted by worry and wonder. Words of reassurance do not help such swirls of emotion. Concrete aids to reduce uncertainty do. For example, structured plans that guide students from generalization to support can be very reassuring to students who are most at ease when they have a clear view of what they are aiming for.

Similarly, grammar errors are more susceptible to correction when the language is explained not by abstract rules but by analysis of visible, concrete patterns. For example, a recent batch of papers written by my Developmental Writing students contained a great many comma splices. About seventy percent occurred when the second sentence started with a pronoun, as in "Thus, crime cannot be controlled, we can only try to avoid it as best we can" or "It just so happened that a young man tried to grab her chain from the outside of the bus, he did not succeed." Upon discussing this pronoun phenomenon with the students, I discovered that many assumed that a pronoun was not "as strong as a noun, so it can't start a new sentence." After we cleared up this misunderstanding, by referring to correct sentences rather than only to rules, far fewer comma splices appeared in the students' writing. Thus, a view of grammar with context at hand helped the students understand the whole picture; in fact, a common expression that comes with an insight into grammar is "now I get the picture."

Legacy 4.   Non-traditional students are ambivalent about learning. They want to learn, but they do not want to risk the change that such learning might bring to their lives. They enroll in college so that they will improve themselves, but this desire is often complicated by their usually unconscious worry that mobility might subtly or dramatically separate them from friends and family. As Irving Bieber explains in *Cognitive Psychoanalysis:*

> Dependent individuals may harbor the fear that success will evoke the wrath of those depended upon and that they will withdraw support, a threatening idea. Others may fear that success will result in isolation; that it will lose friends and the affection of loved ones, expecially family members, and especially if success is associated with upward

mobility and entry into a higher social stratum. Such fears need not be irrational. Sometimes family and friends do discourage the initiatives and success of intimates for fear of losing them. Conformity to tradition is a way of defending the family and community against the threat of disruption, but if group standards are not those of excellence, creativity, and achievement, the guilt and fear of antagonizing one's fellows by superseding them become powerful deterrents.[27]

Non-traditional students are like undecided raindrops at the Continental Divide. This learning anxiety is deeper and more pervasive than what has come to be known as writing anxiety. Those of us who teach non-traditional students have seen some of them disappear from campus immediately after a dramatic success. They never come back. Their fear wins. As teachers of writing we have to tread softly on the dreams of our students. For example, if Kee-Kee thought that she was moving too quickly away from her husband, who she felt had a low I.Q., she might have decided to leave.[28] Sal wrote "I am a psychologist of thirty-year holes" for us in his class and, he said, if we liked his writing he would show it to his wife. But he did not want to show it to his co-workers because he thought it was too well-written.

These are the legacies that our non-traditional students bring to America's colleges and universities. These "new" students are arriving in greater and greater numbers. Non-traditional students have been given access to admission; now they need access to learning. College faculty, most especially teachers of writing, can welcome these students with warm, encouraging classroom atmospheres and with informed, innovative teaching strategies that will help all students to meet the expectations they have set for themselves.

Legacies are, after all, gifts. My grandfather gave me a gift when, at the age of 93, he learned that I intended to study to become a teacher. He had me memorize this excerpt from Sayings of Our Fathers, a volume written in Hebrew during the Middle Ages:

> Much I have learned from my teachers. And more from my colleagues than from my teachers. But more still from my students than from all of them.

NOTES

1. *Undergraduate Admissions: The Realities of Institutional Policies, Practices, and Procedures* (New York: College Entrance Examination Board, 1980).
2. *Undergraduate Admissions*, p. 35.
3. Fred M. Hechinger, "Fervent Arguments in a High-Stakes Game," *New York Times*, 30 June 1980, p. C4.
4. U.S. Bureau of the Census, "Population Characteristics: Social and Economic Characteristics of Students: October 1974," *Current Population Reports* (Washington, D.C., 1974), p. 55. Also, "School Enrollment: Social and Economic Characteristics of Students: October 1978," *Current Population Reports* (Washington, D.C., 1979), p. 4.
5. *Undergraduate Admissions*, pp. 29–33.

6.   Ruth B. Cowan, "Higher Education Has Obligations to a New Majority," *Chronicle of Higher Education*, 23 June 1980, p. 48.
7.   Jane N. Danto, "Flood of Foreign Students Is Only the Beginning," *New York Times*, 3 January 1981, Education Supplement, p. 23.
8.   K. Patricia-Cross, *Accent on Learning* (San Francisco: Jossey-Bass, 1976), p. 125.
9.   Robert C. Wilson et al., *College Professors and Their Impact on Students* (New York: John Wiley and Sons, 1975).
10. Cross, p. 124.
11. John R. Everett, "Courses by TV Reaffirm Value of Classroom," *New York Times*, 30 August 1981, Education Supplement, p. 39.
12. Cross, p. 125.
13. Cross, p. 124.
14. (New York: Anchor/Doubleday, 1976), p. 77.
15. "Literacy, the Basics, and All That Jazz," *College English*, 38 (January 1977), 445.
16. Edward T. Hall, *Beyond Culture* (New York: Anchor/Doubleday, 1976), pp. 67–68.
17. Lynn Quitman Troyka and Jerrold Nudelman, *Taking Action: Writing, Reading, Speaking, and Listening through Simulation Games* (Englewood Cliffs, N.J.: Prentice-Hall, 1975).
18. Lynn Quitman Troyka, "The Effects of Simulation Games on Expository Prose Competence," Diss. New York University, 1973.
19. Cross, pp. 119–133.
20. Hall, especially Chapters 5 and 6.
21. Michael L. Kamil and P. David Pearson, "Theory and Practice in Teaching Reading," *New York University Education Quarterly*, 10 (Winter, 1979), 13.
22. In *Errors and Expectations* (New York: Oxford University Press, 1977), Mina Shaughnessy lists possible sequences for basic writing courses (pp. 285–286, 289) that imply moving from the smaller to the larger; this is, I think, a flaw in an otherwise fine book.
23. Lynn Quitman Troyka, "Cognitive or Learning Styles and Their Implications for the Composition Classroom," *Proceedings of The City University Conference on Errors and Expectations* (New York: City University of New York, 1979). A longer discussion is in preparation.
24. Herman A. Witkin et al., "Field-Dependent and Field-Independent Cognitive Styles and Their Educational Implications," *Review of Educational Research*, 47 (Winter, 1977), 21.
25. Witkin, pp. 21–25.
26. Cross, p. 125.
27. (New York: Aronson, 1980), p. 109.
28. Kee-Kee stopped out of college toward the end of the next semester.

AFTERWORD: LYNN TROYKA'S THOUGHTS UPON READING HER 1981 CCCC CHAIR'S ADDRESS

Can it be that so little has changed since 1981? The distributions I cite about types of colleges hold. The legacies I list at the end of my talk operate still. The same sorts of non-traditional, heroic students continue to work toward, and often attain, college degrees. I should have dropped "in the 1980s" from the title of my 1981 CCCC Chair's address.

Is this lack of change good or bad news? For this brief reflection, permit me to focus on my favorite topic: students, especially the so-called non-traditional ones. For these students, the news isn't good. These students, whose average age is twenty-seven, come to college after their children start school, or when they want more intellectually challenging jobs or need a degree to advance in their careers, or for myriad other reasons. Except in two-year colleges and some land-grant four-year colleges, where the ordinariness of diversity is tightly and enthusiastically woven into the fabric of the institutions, non-traditional students remain largely invisible. A huge chunk of U.S. post-secondary institutions continues to miss out on the transforming energy, richness of perspective, and keen intelligence (albeit sometimes of different sorts than many academics have become habituated to) of non-traditional students.

Too, non-traditional students now face major, dispiriting revisions in U.S. open admissions programs. In many states and other jurisdictions, the term "open admissions" has morphed into "open admissions (but only after passing a battery of tests)." The formerly hefty number of what I and many of my colleagues think of as "Second Chance Academies" is shrinking as wrong-headed politicians and college administrators aim their budget cuts at the least enfranchised.

For example, at The City University of New York (CUNY), where I taught for many years, no longer can open admissions students attend a CUNY four-year college for catch up, developmental courses. As of a few years ago, the only option is a CUNY two-year college, where overnight the new rules led to overcrowding and a drastic increase in the cadre of part-time faculty. One solution, interestingly, has become to offer developmental classes at some of the four-year college campuses where the same four-year faculty who had previously taught those courses continues to teach them, while technically the students are enrolled in community colleges.

In addition, the new CUNY rules prevent some, though not all, developmental students from simultaneously enrolling in first-year, for-credit courses. These students miss out on experiencing college-level academics, a change that ignores research. We know that chances for student success in developmental courses increase when students take one or more regular freshman courses.

Will the pendulum swing back toward the center I described in 1981? I'd wager the answer is *yes*. Higher education in the United States rests on a humanistic core. I believe that in time its underlying values will no longer be denied.

–Lynn Quitman Troyka, Emerita
The City University of New York

1982

Beyond Access to Education—Literacy and Learning in Perspective

JAMES LEE HILL

L ike our nation's economy, American higher education may be in a long-term recession, if not an actual depression. From two-year colleges to multicampus universities, American institutions of higher education find themselves in the midst of the most profound cycles of challenge and change of our generation. Many of the nation's colleges and universities, especially the least populated and endowed, are caught in the twin throes of rising costs and declining revenues; and the projected downward spiral in college enrollment may bring even tighter budgets, more personnel cutbacks, and greater reliance on federal and state governments for assistance. Additionally, since the American public is demanding immediate accountability for educational performances, the perceived inefficiencies in our institutions, whether real or imagined, are coercing colleges and universities, perhaps unwisely, to adopt the yardsticks of business and industry to measure educational success.

Indeed, the problems in higher education today are enough to disillusion the most stouthearted and dedicated among us. Despite difficult financial times in our institutions, however, many of the problems we face in higher education today, particularly in our disciplines, are only marginally related to the economic woes of our colleges and universities. Lest we go walking backward into the future, we cannot overlook the fact that many of the problems in education today—the politics of education if you will—are the direct result of a quiet, nonviolent revolution occurring in American higher education during the past several decades, one which has disrupted the status quo in our educational enterprise and has irrevocably changed how we must approach teaching and learning.

This article is a revised version of the Chair's address James Lee Hill delivered at the CCCC Convention in Washington, D.C., on March 18, 1982. It was previously unpublished.

The nonviolent revolution to which I refer is, of course, the beginning of America's grand educational experiment in moving from an elitist to an egalitarian higher educational system. In the 1960s and 1970s, America as a nation demonstrated at least the will to create full access to equality of educational opportunity; and both our federal and state governments implemented policies which moved us rapidly and effectively toward eliminating many of the financial, social, and educational barriers. In addition to the explosive growth of community colleges and the adoption of open admissions practices, institutions also implemented intensive recruitment programs to attract groups of students previously unserved; and as projected, the by-product of creating access for these students is the proliferation of remediation programs, many of which have undergone ingenious changes in terminology but have yet to achieve any significant changes in philosophies. Perhaps more than any other movement in American higher education during this century, however, our nation's effort to create access to equal educational opportunity is a historic initiative. Concomitantly, it is also one which brings waves of "new students" to our institutions, and in effect, forces us to begin to reexamine our educational pedagogies and procedures.

The dramatic increase in the democratization of education in the 1960s and 1970s created unprecedented access to education for many previously unserved students. Ill-prepared by traditional academic standards and needing a different kind of instruction, these "new students" have commanded that colleges and universities reexamine their educational priorities; and whether we like it or not, they have set a different course for the direction of American higher education, not the least of which is how we ensure that these students acquire effective communication skills. With such dramatic changes in the demography of our colleges and universities, there has also been an accompanying spirited and relentless debate about the ideologies of equal access to education and academic excellence; and at the core of this ongoing debate is a troublesome, seemingly unassailable paradox between the concepts of "equality" and "quality" in higher education. While most of us have accepted and readily embraced the concept of equal opportunity in education, the design of curricula which maximize the success potential of all students is still a very radical idea in most of our institutions.

In two of her books, *Beyond the Open Door* and *Accent on Learning*, K. Patricia Cross warned of the impending crisis that would bring waves of "new students" to our institutions. She argues that the students of the current generation come from a wide variety of backgrounds and that many are not well prepared academically, necessitating a variety of new programs to meet their needs. Sometimes variously labeled as disadvantaged, high-risk, non-traditional and underprivileged, the "new students" she describes are new, however, only in the sense that most of them would formerly not have been admitted to our colleges and universities. They are learners who were, for the most part, previously underrepresented in higher education: older adults, students from lower socioeconomic levels, ethnic minorities, laborers, night students, weekend college students, and of course, women. They differ demographically from traditional college students, and for a variety of reasons, seem to have difficulty with traditional college work. The perceived failure prevalent among many of these students who are not overly successful at what society considers their major task—getting a college education—is, in actuality, the result of the social injustices and personal tragedies which constrain many of them. "The rapid change from the call for academic excellence to the cry for equal opportunity," Cross points out, "presents an especially poignant clash of values" (Cross 1976). She reminds us, too, that contrary to the traditional university model, effective classroom instruction for these students must become the priority in higher education.

Typically, among the "new students" who now populate our classrooms are first-generation college students whose parents or other family members have never attended college. A substantial number is black, and increasingly, they represent various other ethnic minorities. One of the most vivid lessons that college offers these students is recognition of their relative standings in life. In most instances, they have come to our colleges and universities not because of their love for education but because of the continually rising educational expectations of our society. Their motivations come not from anticipated joys of learning but from their recognition that education is a socioeconomic ticket in our society. What they want from college is what they have seen others get—better jobs, more money, and higher social status.

We educators, especially language arts and composition teachers, should applaud our progress in providing access to education for these students; but at the same time, we should not be dismayed by the disruption, havoc, and disillusionment resulting from enrollment of these students in our composition classes. Again, as Cross correctly points out, we have proven that we can deliver on access to education, but we have not yet demonstrated that we can deliver an education that is attractive and useful to all of our students (Cross 1971). Outside of the academy, the overwhelming public response has been an outcry about declining academic standards in our institutions and about the advancing illiteracy Americans perceive, and the nation's outcries are admittedly worthwhile concerns. While we all want to ensure that our students demonstrate proficiency in the requisite skills of reading and writing, our nation's actions in far too many instances have translated into the widespread implementation of stopgap testing, without appropriate concerns for the detriments of the tests to these students.

Unfortunately, too, many of the present reactions are ill-conceived and are being led by uninformed boards of regents, governing boards, state legislatures, and special coalitions of educators and citizens. The supreme irony, however, is that the public outcries against the so-called declining educational standards also affect the same students to whom we have only recently provided access, students who are already victims of an educational system that has formerly omitted, patronized, or under-served them. These are also students who are victims of an educational system that continues to define American middle-class youths as educable and college-bound, while it stereotypes poor and minority youth as unprepared and academically untalented. Indeed, the stopgap tests we administer do — to no one's surprise — weed out the students whom our educational system has already labeled uneducable; and in so doing, many Americans believe, these tests will certainly ensure the academic integrity of our institutions. In condoning and administering the required tests, some of which are admittedly externally imposed, however, we continue to label and, yes, blame these students for their lack of educational exposure. What, I ask, are the reasons for which we created access to education for these students, if not to educate them? Did we reach this historic threshold in American higher education without any real assessment of the changes it would demand? Are we going to continue to blame unexposed students for their lack of preparation?

In some ways, our efforts to provide full access to higher education for these "new students" while maintaining desired standards are analogous to the phenomenon of blaming the victim, and here an old anecdote is applicable. There once was a very patriotic senator who was investigating the origins of World War II. When he learned of the bombing of Pearl Harbor and of the untold damage that occurred there (over two hundred men killed, sixteen ships sunk or damaged, and a hundred planes destroyed), he exclaimed indignantly: "What was Pearl Harbor doing in the Pacific?" I paraphrase the question from this anecdote, and I ask you: What indeed are these students doing at our institutions? More importantly, what are we doing with and for them?

The challenge of educating these "new students" has also spawned another ongoing debate in the academy and within our discipline, one which ironically parallels the access/quality paradox in American higher education. I refer here to none other than our discipline's creation of the dialectic between the "Back to Basics Movement," our national concern for correctness in language, and the New Rhetoric, our renewed interest in rhetoric. What, however, do we mean by the basics? As with the dichotomy between access and quality, our attempts to define or delineate these two topics are, to say the least, inconclusive. There is no single definition of rhetoric, as Donald C. Bryant points out in his perceptive article "Rhetoric: Its

Functions and Scope," and we regularly use the various nuances of the old rhetoric and new rhetoric. When we speak of rhetoric, do we mean the art of effective and persuasive speech and writing, or translating thought into the language of selling ideas to a particular audience? Do our concepts of rhetoric originate with the Renaissance when rhetoric became Elizabethan affectation of style, or do we accept Kenneth Burke's redefinition that rhetoric is anything one does, verbally or nonverbally, consciously or unconsciously, for the purpose of persuasion or identification? And how do we distinguish between conservative, liberal, and radical rhetoric? What then, I must ask you, is the definition of rhetoric we are using with these "new students," and is the old rhetoric disguised in new language adequate to meet their needs? For us to be effective in the teaching of composition, we must understand that the "new students" frequenting our classrooms require rhetorical experiences that are relevant, enabling, and purposeful. As Cross also reminds us, our traditional curricula may not be adequate to develop the talents and abilities of the "new students."

The term *basics* has also suffered a similar inconclusive fate. Across our nation, educators, businessmen, and others are decrying the perceived semiliteracy among high school and college students, and the overwhelming public response has given legs to the "Back to Basics Movement." Again, I must ask, what do we mean by basics? Do these basics encompass, as some suggest, only grammar, punctuation, and spelling? Do the basics include students learning to write clear simple sentences, using Standard English, or acquiring linguistics skills? Or do the basics reiterate the elitist jargon of the so-called caretakers of language, who see this recent phenomenon as the onslaught of widespread abuse of the King's English?

What, therefore, is one to make of the dialectic between the two recent movements? I would argue that the dialectic between the New Rhetoric and the basics is an artificially imposed one. If we accept the creative ideal that form follows function (and I do), this is an ideal that is equally applicable in our task of teaching writing. That is, the teaching and learning of writing should be an organic process, not one that superficially separates rhetoric and the basics. All teaching of writing implies some kind of rhetoric, how writing is produced and by what standards it should be judged. How we teach writing, how we evaluate writing, and how we describe the process of writing reflect our general assumptions about what writing is or what it should be. Whether one is discussing subject-verb agreement or the extended metaphor, there are always the larger implications about what writing is, and such assumptions, which we cannot ignore, are directly related to questions of the personal identity of the individual writer or his personal commitment.

The writing process, then, is not one which should be viewed in a piecemeal fashion. Far too often in the teaching of writing, however, we have neglected the functions of writing, concentrating primarily on the forms of writing; and we have emphasized the mechanics of writing to the detriment of purpose in writing. Since form and function in the writing process are interrelated, interdependent, and organic, it just may be possible that our overwhelming neglect of the functions of writing has resulted in some of the problems we experience in the teaching of writing and our students in learning to write. It may also be that our neglect of function has contributed to our failure to motivate the student to use acceptable language, to organize ideas in a strategic manner, or to demonstrate commitment to what they write.

Shaped by the politics of the "Back to Basics Movement," most of the remedial or compensatory programs implemented to address the educational needs of the new students have unfortunately adopted the building blocks approach, moving from word to sentence to paragraph to essay. The pedagogical rationale for this approach is that knowledge of grammar is necessary for students to write acceptable sentences and paragraphs, but does this piecemeal approach to writing obscure both the reader's and the writer's concerns with the whole structure? Perhaps it is pedagogically easier and more practical for teachers to approach the teaching of writing in this piecemeal fashion, and perhaps learning to write in this manner is easier for students, especially the underprepared student. Yet, I question whether students learning to write in this simplified manner are motivated to become interested in the effectiveness of what they write. How effective, for example, is a home decorator at designing and furnishing a house never seen?

This traditional separation of the rhetorical and the basics in the writing process is, in my opinion, an unnatural division. If the writing process is restricted solely to concerns with language propriety, then we ignore the larger political, ethical, social, and even ethnic strategies that lurk behind the compositions our students write. This is not to say, of course, that the rhetorical approach ignores the elements of writing which include what we mean by the basics—grammar, mechanics, and spelling—but these elements of writing should be considered and taught in a much broader context. Perhaps it has been our attempt to isolate the elements of the "basics" from the larger creative processes that has resulted in students not internalizing them, not making these mechanics of propriety a habitual part of their language experiences.

When one considers the rhetorical approach and the underprepared student, some may raise objections to this approach to teaching writing. The most prevalent of the arguments is that the rhetorical approach is too complex or difficult for the underprepared student. Some believe, too, that these students not only lack basic writing skills, but that they are also thoroughly unprepared to understand the psychology, logic, figurative language, diction, and advanced grammar which naturally follow in the rhetorical approach to writing. While it may be true that many of these students do not possess formal knowledge of rhetoric, it is equally true that we as composition teachers sometimes fail to realize or we ignore the fact that our students do not enter our classrooms as blank tablets. Not only do they bring their native abilities; they also bring innumerable life experiences. These students have usually had experiences which do allow us to teach such rhetorical principles as emotional, ethical, or rational appeals to an audience.

What I have attempted to suggest, here, is that there is actually not nor should there be any disparity between the concepts of the basics and rhetoric. One either approaches writing as a creative process in which form and function are interrelated or one approaches it in piecemeal fashion, preferring to emphasize parts of the writing process, not the whole. When we restrict the underprepared freshman to learning about subject-verb agreement or mechanics, however, we usually do not discover the student's potential ability or inability in other important aspects of the composing process. Teaching writing as a rhetorical process, on the other hand, allows total immersion of the student and his experiences in the creative act of writing. If I may paraphrase William E. Coles in *Teaching Composing*, we have to ensure that we create classroom environments which invite students, especially the "new students," to learn about language and themselves as language learners as they aspire to become good writers.

Using the rhetorical approach, we teachers of composition can involve students in the full range of rhetorical practices. It is a proven fact, for example, that students usually learn more rapidly and thoroughly when they develop motives for doing so. The rhetorical approach can also offer students writing experiences that are life related, productive, and real. In lieu of the often typical writing assignment on an abstract subject such as "The Meaning of Freedom," students may be directed toward writing about more concrete experiences in their daily lives and presenting their views to a predetermined, real audience, a process which certainly offers students more immediate rewards. It is this kind of writing activity, it seems to me, in which our students are more likely to develop motivations for becoming conscious of language, caring about grammatical rules, and scrutinizing choices in sentence structure. In effect, as Herzing observes in "The Rhetorical Approach to Better Writing," using the rhetorical approach in the teaching of writing involves students in effective writing experiences, not proper writing activities.

While we English teachers have worked extremely hard in the past decades to bring about educational opportunity for all of the students in our classrooms, we have by no means reached our goal. Students in our classrooms today are forcing us to acknowledge individual differences and realize that equal education is more than access; it is an affirmation of their right to a quality education. To accomplish this task, writing teachers must design and offer composition programs appropriate for all students' achievement of expected writing standards, maximizing their educational opportunity. Attainment of this goal, however, will mean nothing short of strategic reforms of our teaching/learning strategies, improvement in our instructional delivery systems and reassessment of our curricula.

It goes without saying that there is no simple or short-term solution to such a deep-seated Americanized problem, that many of the problems we confront daily in our classrooms are endemic to our traditional educational structure, and that we must begin, with purposeful reform in mind, to examine carefully the causes of the miseducation of the "new students" or their lack of preparation. Fortunately, there are signs that composition teachers, many of whom sit before me this morning, are beginning through research, redirection, and reassessment to reorder instruction to meet the needs of these "new students." It is in this endeavor that teachers of composition, more than any other of our colleagues, have an opportunity to pioneer in the instructional revolution which is already upon us.

By now we all know that there are distinct, individual differences among our students, and if we are to be successful, we must move beyond mere access to education to providing quality multicultural and multidimensional education for our students. We know, too, that the national mandate for remediation programs is not a panacea for the new instructional imperative which our students now demand. While our remedial programs may help students overcome some educational deficiencies, the real problem with many such remedial and compensatory education programs is, of course, the overwhelming tasks we assign to them. Thus, if we are to succeed in teaching all of our students, we can no longer offer curricula and methodologies aimed at conformity to mono-cultural students or imposing mono-cultural standards on our students.

Although most of us were probably educated to conform to mono-cultural standards, our students should not have to do so. In our reshaping of the teaching of composition in the future, we must implement programs that give priority (1) to student experiences in the acquisition of those basic skills on which other skills depend, (2) to experiences that develop critical thinking, (3) to instruction involving students in learning emotionally and cognitively, and (4) to instruction that enables students to raise questions and solve problems about their personal and academic development in the world around them.

If your students are anything like mine, they come to the classroom with a variety of learning styles. Some of them, for example, are incremental learners; others learn intuitively, leaping in various directions, gaining sudden insights and making generalizations; and still others may be eclectic learners who shift styles and functions according to the situation. Our success in teaching composition in the future demands, therefore, that we gear our teaching to accommodate the variety of learning styles that we encounter in our classroom.

Although we have learned much in the past few decades about how to teach composition and we continue to gain insights daily, we must in the years ahead also reexamine many of the untenable assumptions we hold about the teaching and learning. For too long, we have assumed:

1. That the specific knowledge acquired by students is related to the long-range goals that exist in our minds as teachers. (The long-term relationship between what we teach and the ways our students are eventually required to behave in society, however, it is not clear. As teachers, we can only determine the students' immediate terminal behavior and assume long-term growth.)

2. That the aptitudes, achievements, and backgrounds of students in our classrooms are equal—at least we teach that way. (This has been a primary belief or assumption underlying all college instruction. Nothing is less true. Our students differ in levels of acquisition of knowledge and skills, responses necessary in applying concepts, and motivation and learning styles.)

3. That aptitude is more important than previous achievement for attainment of knowledge. (The fact is that many of the students in our colleges and universities have earned their acceptance as freshmen based not on aptitude but on mastery of a level of knowledge prior to entrance.)

4. That all people learn in the same way and take approximately the same time to learn the same thing. (Any change in the adequacy of instruction for individual students, however, changes the relationship between their achievement and student differences.)

5. That listening to lectures and reading books are powerful means of changing students' behavior. (Though lectures and reading are important, we must not forget the changing nature of our society—technology, for example, has had a major influence on teaching and learning.)

6. That students retain knowledge without much review and/or relearning. (The fact is that we have done very little research to determine the extent to which knowledge is retained—via individuals of different lifestyles, kinds of curricula, and specific kinds of knowledge.)

7. That teaching is an art requiring no tools and no underlying technology. (Usually, our requirements of the subject matter dictate the organizational structure for teaching, but the requirements for transmitting it to students figure very little in our considerations.)

8. That the structure our disciplines impose on knowledge is the best one for transmitting knowledge or skills to students. (Students are not equal in that they learn in different ways—what is required is a commitment to individual differences and the development of learning environments adaptable to such differences.)

While literacy crises are not new, what we perceive as a current crisis of literacy provides a unique challenge for us. What began as a simple, desirable approach to equity in higher education in the 1960s and 1970s has evolved into a revolution, and although it began on the fringes of higher education, it has now evolved to the point of threatening the heart of our educational enterprise—teaching and learning. We are being forced to accept the realization that we must search out and implement new methods of teaching; for in truth, many of the old methods are no longer adequate to meet our needs as teachers or those of our students. In finding ways to move beyond mere access to quality education for all of our students, our profession can and must play a historic role, seeking the sensitive balance between our responsibilities as teachers of composition and our students' rights as learners.

The challenge for us today is even greater than the challenge of two decades ago, and the solutions to our problems will be found by those of us who still believe that learning is a right of all of our students and that the design of programs that meet their needs does not compromise our academic standards. If all of this appears to leave you with more questions than positive affirmations, then perhaps we have arrived at that moment when Gertrude Stein's final words are much in order: "If we do not know the answer, then, pray what is the question?"

I have tried here this morning to raise the questions.

WORKS CONSULTED

Baird, Craig A. *Rhetoric: A Philosophical Inquiry.* New York: Ronald, 1965.
Brazziel, William F. *Quality Education for All Americans.* Washington: Howard UP, 1974.
Bryant, Donald C. "Rhetoric: Its Functions and Scope." *Quarterly Journal of Speech* 39 (1953): 401–24.
Coles, William E. *Teaching Composing.* Rochelle Park: Hayden, 1974.
Cross, K. Patricia. *Accent on Learning.* San Francisco: Jossey-Bass, 1976.
———. *Beyond the Open Door.* San Francisco: Jossey-Bass, 1971.
Herzing, Thomas W. "The Rhetorical Approach to Better Writing." *The Idea of Composition.* Ed. Hugo Hartiz. Oshkosh: Academic, 1974.
Maxwell, Martha. *Improving Student Learning Skills.* San Francisco: Jossey-Bass, 1979.
Roueche, John, and Snow, Jerry. *Overcoming Learning Problems.* San Francisco: Jossey-Bass, 1977.

AFTERWORD: AMERICA'S GRAND HIGHER EDUCATION
EXPERIMENT: A TWENTY-TWO YEAR RETROSPECTIVE

Our nation recently celebrated, though much too quietly, one of the landmark Supreme Court decisions of the twentieth century. May 17, 2004, marked the fiftieth anniversary of *Brown v. Board of Education*, often remembered now as the judicial hammer that cracked the facade of America's racial caste system. From the 1950s to the 1980s, *Brown* transformed the demographics of public schools in America; and as intended, most public schools across America became racially mixed. Since the 1980s, however, the desegregation of public schools has reversed precipitously, nowhere more dramatically than in the American South where the 1954 decision caused the most trauma. According to a recent report of the Harvard University Civil Rights Project, southern schools have essentially resegregated, with only 30 percent of African American students attending classes at majority white public schools. In Atlanta, for example, there is not a single public high school with a majority white student population.

So, what does this profile portend for our colleges and universities? Unfortunately, the race or ethnicity of the students continues to shape attitudes and limit choices, and access to higher education is still not guaranteed. One of the most telling indices is the fact that there are more young African American males incarcerated than enrolled in college. Additionally, the College Board reports that the rising costs of college exceed the financial aid available and that inequity in access to financial aid continues; the assault on affirmative action in recent years has rendered dramatic changes in enrollment trends of minority students in many colleges and universities.

In 1982, when I gave my CCCC Chair's address, "Beyond Access to Education—Literacy and Learning in Perspective," however, I was more concerned about what changes access to higher education for waves of previously unserved students would necessitate, especially how institutions would meet these students' needs. Indeed, how would colleges and universities adjust or change their curricula, instructional approaches, pedagogies, and classroom prac- tices? While there have certainly been some important advances, including the creation of a few stellar programs across the United States, has student access changed dramatically and systemically, and how are students faring in our colleges and universities?

As we say proverbially, the jury is still out. During the last quarter of the twentieth century, remedial programs became the mantra for leveraging equal ac- cess to higher education for previously unserved students. Instead of becoming the face of higher education, however, remediation tangled with the stronger "perceptions of quality"; and like *Brown v. Board of Education*, the nation's grand experiment with equal access to higher education appears to have generated a counter trend. While the abolition of remedial programs has all but eliminated a major avenue of access to higher education for untold numbers of students, most colleges and universities, in the name of "quality," view remedial programs as stigmatization of higher education. Thus, in lieu of implementing programs to address the needs of the "new students," colleges and universities have resorted again to testing students out of access to higher education. In Georgia, for example, the university system has all but eliminated remedial education and systematically increased admissions criteria.

There appears to be ample evidence that our grand experiment with equal access to higher education has not yet rendered my concerns of twenty-two years ago null and void. Though there may have been modest improvements in access of "new students" to colleges and universities, enrollment is just the first step, and concerns about these students after access still remain. Are they well served at our colleges and universities, and are most of them receiving degrees? The *Journal of Blacks in Higher Education* reports, for example, that only two of every five black students who enter college complete degrees. I suspect, therefore, that the success of students' matriculation and continuation are integrally tied to the preparedness of colleges and universities to address their needs beyond access.

After twenty-two years, despite many indications to the contrary, I continue to believe that our nation's effort to provide equal access to higher education for all students is a historic and potentially nation-changing undertaking. I know, too, that it is in the best interest of the students we teach and the welfare of our nation. The first quarter of this new century, however, will no doubt both challenge and determine our resolve to complete the grand higher education experiment started decades ago.

–JAMES LEE HILL
Albany State University, Georgia

1983

Some History Lessons for Composition Teachers

DONALD C. STEWART

A few months ago I had a very peculiar experience. One of our older graduate students had come to my office to inquire about some courses in her program of study—I am our department's Acting Director of Graduate Studies this year—and we began a conversation which developed into a pleasant but slightly tense confrontation. *She* was trying to convince *me* that composition teaching and research were of great value and that persons with a commitment to this kind of work should receive more recognition and greater financial rewards for doing it. Since I have spent virtually all of my professional career making this argument, I was more than perplexed to be on the receiving end of it and to discover the degree of my anonymity in my own department.

Putting aside that disturbing revelation, however, I asked her if she had any idea why composition teaching and research were so lightly regarded by our profession. This was not a question she was expecting, and she seemed puzzled by it. What do you know, I asked her further, about the early development of modern English departments and the place composition instruction assumed in them? Nothing really, she said. Taking a copy of Albert Kitzhaber's doctoral dissertation, "Rhetoric in American Colleges: 1850–1900," from my desk, I handed it to her and asked her if she had ever read it. No, she had not. Have you read any histories of English or American literature, I inquired. Of course, she replied. They're basic introductions to this field for anyone planning to teach literature. Perhaps, I suggested, Kitzhaber's thesis is equally important, and in the same way, for anyone who will have to teach composition.

My lesson for this student, you see, was fundamental, and I want to use it as a point of departure for my discussion of the importance of historical

This article is the text of the Chair's address Donald C. Stewart delivered at the CCCC Convention in Detroit, Michigan, on March 17, 1983. It was first published in *Rhetoric Review*, volume 3, number 2, January 1985.

knowledge for modern composition teachers. I have become convinced that a writing teacher's development can be measured by the degree to which that person has become liberated from current-traditional rhetoric. And the progress of that liberation, I further believe, is closely linked to that person's accumulating knowledge of the history of composition as a discipline.

The term, "current-traditional rhetoric," you will recall, was coined by Daniel Fogarty in his *Roots for a New Rhetoric* (1959), but it came most forcefully to the attention of the composition teaching profession in Richard Young's "Paradigms and Problems: Some Needed Research in Rhetorical Invention" (1978). In that essay, Young summarized the salient features of current-traditional rhetoric: "emphasis on the composed product rather than the composing process; the analysis of discourse into words, sentences, and paragraphs; the classification of discourse into description, narration, exposition, and argument; the strong concern with usage (syntax, spelling, punctuation) and with style (economy, clarity, emphasis)," etc.

Now consider for a moment the most conservative of those who have inherited the current-traditional paradigm, who accept its emphases and priorities without questioning them. Because teachers at this stage of development put highest priority on superficial mechanical correctness, they drill their students in grammar, punctuation, and spelling. They are fond of formulas: five spelling, two sentence, and three subject-verb agreement errors (or whatever combination they choose) automatically earn their students' papers, regardless of their other merits, F's. Your classes, unless you are extremely fortunate, are full of students whose perceptions of what is important in writing have been shaped by such teachers. You may be wondering why I even trouble to mention them before a group which must regard them as fossils of an era which we have left far behind us. But that is the problem. These teachers are *not* exotic or extinct species. They *outnumber* us, significantly. What characterizes them most is the fact they either are never exposed to or remain untouched by the professional journals and books which would tell them what the priorities of a modern composition teacher really are. Or *were*. Ken Donelson's "Beacon Lights in the History of English Teaching," in last December's *English Education* is a remarkable record of ignored dissatisfaction with this kind of composition teaching, stretching back into the 1880's.

Teachers at this stage do not know that they have inherited the worst features of late nineteenth century composition teaching. At that time college enrollments were expanding rapidly, and an increasingly heterogeneous and unevenly prepared student body was appearing on the nation's campuses. They were part of the intense pressure that entrenched classicists were feeling to admit scientific and technical courses and English literature and the modern languages into the established curriculum. Complicating events of the time were three reports by the Committee on Composition to the Harvard Board of Overseers, in 1892, 1895, and 1897.

In essence, they were an indictment of the secondary schools for failing to teach college-bound students to spell, punctuate, and observe proprieties of usage. Their influence, coupled with that of the Harvard program, one created by A. S. Hill, who was obsessed with these mechanical matters, nullified the efforts of men like Fred Newton Scott of Michigan who sought ways of determining what was still valid in the ancient tradition of rhetoric and of adapting those findings to the teaching of writing in his era. The doctrine of correctness won the day, and it has been a force in the teaching of writing since that time.

I am aware, of course, of those today who unwillingly emphasize grammar and mechanics, even though they know better, because as one instructor in a California two-year college told me in a letter last spring, the community that pays his salary expects him to graduate students who, more than anything else, can spell, punctuate, and write grammatically correct sentences, especially those basic writers in whose papers mechanical errors are as common as nuts in a fruitcake. I appreciate the dilemma, but my question is this: where did the community get those priorities? I think that is a very important question.

I am not really optimistic about changing teachers locked in the Stone Age of our discipline. Actually, there is no need to change them. They will be replaced—they are probably being replaced right now—by micro-computers which can do the things they do more efficiently and with less resistance from students. Computers can either edit manuscripts, or by now, possibly be turning previously boring classroom drills in grammar, punctuation, and spelling into versions of Pac-Man, Frogger, or Donkey-Kong. As that happens, students may even spend their own money to do these drills.

There are, of course, many current-traditional composition teachers who have progressed well beyond this single-minded preoccupation with copy-reading skills to matters of form. Because their knowledge of the history of this discipline is very sketchy, however, I fear that they may have a false sense of being enlightened. Some are wedded intellectually to the five-paragraph essay, the "fifty-star" theme as Janet Emig calls it. The students who master this form, they say, can then write effectively on any subject and can, furthermore, move on to the more complex forms: introduction, body, and conclusion; or the patterns of narration, description, exposition, and argument and beyond that to the intricacies of the various expository modes: definition, comparison and contrast, cause and effect, analysis of process, etc. The tables of contents of many commercially successful textbooks suggest that a good number of teachers are still frozen at this stage of their development.

What can be said about the sophistication of those who live and teach at this stage? Not a lot that is very encouraging. The five-paragraph essay is a formula, not a composition. It is rule-governed, hence easy to mark, but imposing it on every subject one writes about is the equivalent of trying to put a wiggling 100-pound dog, or a barrel of apples, or several gallons of fresh maple syrup, or the unassembled parts of a ten-speed bicycle, or three different typewriters, or a wardrobe for a Florida vacation all in the same size box. Many of you know, I am sure, that I am hardly the first person to call attention to the absurdity of trying to fit several different kinds of subjects into the same verbal straitjacket: "Unless the writer takes especial care to diversify his inventive methods, there is a strong tendency after some experience to run into a certain stereotyped way of planning every subject; exemplified by the clergyman who said he always made his sermons consist of 'two points and an application.' This is evidently an unconscious surrender to the tyranny of a mental habit; and the result is that the writer does not submit implicitly to the guidance of his subject, but seeks to manipulate the thought by a preconceived scheme devised and imposed from without. Not always so undisguised as this, the same tendency may manifest itself in a craving after an equal number of subdivisions under each main heading, or after some mechanical symmetry between part and part of the plan. But however manifested, it is something against which the writer needs to be on his guard as to distrust any structure not obviously dictated, or at least made natural, by the suggestion of the subject." That observation can be found in John Genung's *Practical Elements of Rhetoric*, 1886, a textbook which, while well written and quite sensible, was hardly a radical document, even for its time.

Genung's clergyman, with his two points and an application, is clearly a first cousin to the composition teacher who promotes the five-paragraph essay or the introduction, body, and conclusion organizational pattern. There is, of course, a sense in which every composition has an introduction, body, and conclusion, but you know the kind of essay I am criticizing here: the "tell them what you are going to say, say it, then tell them that you've said it" piece. Like the five-paragraph essay, it represents a mechanical, not an organic conception of discourse. Ironically, the conception itself may have its origins in Plato's *Phaedrus* in which Socrates says that "any discourse ought to be constructed like a living creature, with its own body, as it were; it must not lack either head or feet; it must have a middle and extremities so composed as to suit each other and the whole work." The key words are *"living creature."* Socrates is comparing the structure of a piece of discourse to the organic structure of a living plant or animal. We see the separate parts of a tree, for example, but we see them as developed from one another, not as tacked together. This principle of organic unity, Fred Scott said in 1909, lay dormant for over two thousand years until it surfaced, rather surprisingly, at the end of Herbert Spencer's "The Philosophy of Style" in 1852. Scott himself championed such a conception.

The forms of discourse—narration, description, exposition, and argument—have been examined and found wanting as representations of the composing process by Kitzhaber, James Britton, and Robert Connors, our Braddock Award winner last year. Will that deter the current-traditional teacher from presenting them? No. And finally, what of the various methods of exposition—definition, comparison and contrast, cause and effect, etc.—which still dominate our best selling textbooks? They are metamorphoses of the topics of classical rhetoric, cut off from their original inventional purposes and employed in the very way Genung condemned. Frank D'Angelo has offered the only feasible theoretical defense of them: as topics in the Aristotelian sense of that term, they suggest lines of inquiry which not only generate material on a subject but also suggest patterns of development, but that is a point not well understood by most of those using them. In fact, quite the opposite is true. In the pedagogy of a current-traditional teacher without historical knowledge, they become *types* of papers for which students must find subjects. The process is psychologically inverted and barren.

What perceptions of invention do many current-traditional composition teachers have? I would say that they are pretty much limited to the occasional admonition to students to pick a subject, jot down some notes about it, limit it, and start writing. In my experience even those who have heard of the inventional procedures described by Richard Young seldom reveal a solid theoretical or practical grasp of them.

Current-traditional teachers' conceptions of style are not much more sophisticated, either. They rarely go beyond traditional textbook treatments of the word, the sentence, and the paragraph. In many instances their conception of the word is not much advanced over that of textbooks in the 1890's, their conception of the sentence is innocent of most of the findings of modern linguistics, and their conception of the paragraph is modified Alexander Bain. Even the order of their presentation of these concepts is dated; if they start with the word and end up with the whole composition, they are imitating Barrett Wendell's *English Composition*, 1891; if they reverse the pattern, they are descendants of Wendell's pupil, Henry Pearson, whose *Principles of Composition* was published in 1898. In usage, they are usually prescriptive, eager to correct infelicities, unwilling to accept the authority of modern descriptive linguists. Even in their conservatism on usage, they are not modern. In 1902, George Hempel, President of the Modern Language Association, told an Ann Arbor audience of colleagues, Michigan high school teachers, and general public that "The attitude assumed toward the mother tongue by the average teacher of English is based on antiquated and mistaken conceptions of the nature of language and the function of the teacher of English. These mistaken conceptions are not entertained by teachers only but are shared by the average educated man and woman." He attacked three misconceptions in particular: (1) that books, particularly by classic authors, not the living speech of people who use it daily, are the basis of the language;

(2) that most people use the language carelessly and badly but that somewhere educated and cultivated people speak almost perfect English; (3) that the language stands in constant danger of corruption and dilution.

To correct these misconceptions, Hempel recommended study of the life and growth of languages in general and the English language in particular, an attitude of restraint in correcting other people's speech, and intelligent listening to the language which goes on around us all the time. This descriptive approach to usage continues to be resisted by the teacher firmly rooted in the current-traditional approach to composition teaching.

Those who have outgrown the current-traditional approach, however, are our truly modern composition teachers. They have read and assimilated recent research on invention, arrangement, and style; on protocol analysis and problem-solving; on rhetorical epistemology; on the recursiveness of the composing process; on revision; on writing anxiety; on the interrelationships between rhetoric, psychology, linguistics, sociology, and other fields. They have kept abreast of modern technology and its application to our discipline, they know enough of the history of rhetoric and composition teaching to understand the place of their work in it, and they are, above all, quite sure that they are on the cutting edge of contemporary composition theory and practice.

And they very likely are. One has only to look at the titles of papers to be delivered at this convention to realize the extent to which ours has become an intellectual and professional discipline of remarkable sophistication. What even modern teachers probably do not know, however, is that many of the problems which interest them were opened for investigation by three reports of the Pedagogical Section of the Modern Language Association in 1900, 1901, and 1902. In 1900 the Section reported on responses from university English faculty in the Northern universities to these questions: (1) "Is Rhetoric . . . a proper subject for graduate work? (2) If so, what is the proper aim, what is the scope, and what are the leading problems of Rhetoric as a graduate study? (3) If Rhetoric . . . should not be admitted to the list of graduate studies, what do you regard as the strongest reasons for excluding it?" The majority responding said that rhetoric was indeed suitable for graduate study, and they specifically recommended historical studies, interdisciplinary work (particularly with psychology and linguistics), and refinements of pedagogy. In 1901 the subject was undergraduate instruction in rhetoric, and the general question being investigated was the relationship between reading and writing. Was good reading alone sufficient to develop good writers, or was additional training in composition necessary? If so, what should the nature of this training be? A majority recommended reading supplemented by good instruction in composition. The report also dealt with questions of research methodology for testing these relationships. In 1902, the Section discussed conflicting ideals in the teaching of composition: whether or not it should be principally a practical business or whether it should be authorship, the production of literature. The majority attempted to reconcile the two positions.

This burst of energy by the Pedagogical Section—and it could have laid the basis for solid theoretical and pedagogical advances in the teaching of composition for years to come—was generated, of course, by the man from Michigan, Fred Newton Scott. Suffice it to say that these ideas were not acted on, except by Scott's students, and their achievements and his have been obscured by those who determined that literary scholarship would have greatest prestige among those in the profession of English.

We return to the principal thesis of this paper: how, interesting as it may be, does historical knowledge liberate the current-traditional composition teacher from the old paradigm? I will answer that question in a moment, but first I want to make one more observation about contemporary theory and practice. Underlying much of it—and I am thinking of the most advanced kinds of work—is a tacit and very old assumption: that the production of logical and coherent discourse is an unquestioned good to which we and our students subscribe. And logic and coherence are defined in terms of particular kinds of relationships between ideas and the structures which carry them. What is coherence in a paragraph, for example? Usually, the presentation of a central idea and amplification of it which proceed with both internal and external cues which we have been conditioned to look for. In a sense, we still live in a Newtonian universe. We feel obligated to impose some kind of order on the multifarious phenomena which assail our senses daily, and we believe that we can express that order only in certain kinds of verbal structures. But a way of seeing things, we have known for some time, is also a way of *not* seeing. Four centuries ago astronomers who had accepted Ptolemy's universe were profoundly shaken by the theories of Copernicus. It is difficult for us today to fully comprehend the radical psychological adjustment which confronted them. Many, I suspect, never made it.

Loren Eiseley, in *The Immense Journey*, found a similar attitude in a friend who could not adjust to a world in which some living creatures apparently did not respect their proper domains. For example, he did not like fishes which climbed trees, caught insects flying by, and ogled him in strange ways.

But we have discovered all along that the world in which we live continually defies our categories, mocks our attempts to impose an order we desire on it. And this has happened in discourse also. Seven years ago Winston Weathers asked this question: what does one do when all of the stylistic and organizational maneuvers one has been taught are not adequate to the needs of a particular rhetorical context? Do we have alternatives which postulate new conceptions of logic and order and coherence? Do they enable us to fully respond to contexts for which our training in what he calls Grammar A has not been adequate? We do, and he cites many of them, both in the original paper which he titled "Grammars of Style: New Options in Composition" and then amplified in his book, *The Alternate Style*. This alternate grammar, not intended to replace but to supplement Grammar A, includes such strange things as crots, labyrinthine sentences, lists, double-voices, repetitions, repetends, and refrains. They have been used repeatedly by several generations of gifted writers. Are they, however, useful only to creative writers, or do they have any practical application in the world in which we teach? In some instances they are eminently more practical than the kinds of discourse we present as logical, coherent, and orderly. Suppose, Weathers says, that he discovers his oil company has billed him for $100 too much in one month. His first recourse is to write a polite and orderly Grammar A letter informing the company of the error and requesting correction of it. But no personal response to his letter and repeated dunnings tell him that he is corresponding with a computer, not a person, and an alternate strategy is called for:

To: Deep Well Oil Company

From: Credit Card # 4960-110338

For God's sake. In February—you were wrong. March—wrong. April—wrong. May—wrong. Still wrong. It's 35$. Not 135$. Have you blown a fuse? Pleaseseepreviouscorrespondence. Five service-station tickets: $7.50 + $4.25 + $10.25 + $5.00 = $35.00. You must start all over again. Recompute. You must deduct $100. I've paid. Have canceled check. $35.00. Repeat. $35.00. Repeat. $35.00. I am praying for you and your circuits, but not a penny more business with Deep Well until you correct error.

The beauty of it is that Grammar B is not all that new. Weathers quotes a wonderful letter Ambrose Bierce wrote to the editor of *The Lantern* on May 22, *1913*.

Editor "Lantern,"

Will I tell you what I think of your magazine? Sure I will.
It was thirty-six pages of reading matter.
Seventeen are given to the biography of a musician,—German, dead.
Four to the mother of a theologian,—German, peasant-wench, dead.
(The mag. is published in America, today.)
Five pages about Eugene Field's ancestors. All dead.
17 + 4 + 5 = 26.
36 − 26 = 10.
Two pages about Ella Wheeler Wilcox.
Three-fourths page about a bad poet and his indifference to—
German.

Two pages of his poetry.
$2 + \frac{3}{4} + 2 = 4\frac{3}{4}$.
$10 - 4\frac{3}{4} = 5\frac{1}{4}$. Not enough to criticise.
What your magazine needs is an editor—presumably older, preferably American, and indubitably alive. At least awake.
It is your inning.

Sincerely yours,
Ambrose Bierce

I return to the question I posed a few moments ago. How can historical knowledge liberate composition teachers from theory and practice which are dated and ineffective? The obvious answer is that the composition teacher who has it is flexible. She knows what has been tried, what has worked, and what has not. She knows the contexts in which theories have been put forth and applied; she knows those who put them forth; and she is able to detect their modern counterparts and to anticipate the appropriateness and potential effectiveness of old ideas in new garments. Even the radical Grammar B will not shake her. She has a place for it in her composition universe.

But there is a much more significant value in the kind of historical knowledge I have touched upon today. We should continually remind ourselves that ours *is* a discipline with a history and *that* history is inextricably linked, on the one hand to the history of the modern profession of English, and on the other hand to one of the oldest intellectual traditions in the Western world, the tradition of rhetoric. Acquiring such knowledge, one learns how literary study became the major preoccupation of the modern English department and composition its barely tolerated stepchild. One also learns that the most dazzling of modern machines, the computer, while radically transforming our notions of the composing process, is still part of the rhetorical tradition. Computer language is still a *language*. It must mean something, either to the machine (which is getting smarter and more personable every year), or to the person who uses the information generated by the machine. That language has a context in which it works, and it is a rhetorical as much as a technical problem to define the parameters of that context. Immediately important to us are the uses which are being made of the computer in teaching writing. Cost effective it certainly is, but who programs the machine? One director of composition at a state university wrote to me less than two months ago about the computer composition program his school has developed. He is uneasy now because 1983's technology, he is beginning to fear, is disseminating 1883's ideas about writing. It is a good thing to know this so that we will ask these important questions: who will program the composition teaching computer; how much will we insist that this programmer know about modern composition theory and practice and its historical antecedents; and what are the real limits of the computer's effectiveness?

I do not wish to conclude sounding like an adversary of progress. I am not. New technology gives us the means for doing our work in new and more efficient ways. But if we define the work to be done in outdated terms, we have gained nothing. We may even be doing positive harm. It is wise, therefore, to have the historical perspective. It gives theoretical depth and philosophical breadth to our perceptions of this most important and intriguing enterprise we call the teaching of composition. And that may be the most important history lesson that we, as composition teachers, will ever learn.

AFTERWORD: PRAGMATIC REFORM AND
VISIONARY SCHOLARSHIP*

Donald C. Stewart was in the vanguard of those scholars doing history in the late 1970s and early 1980s, groundbreaking work for an emerging field. Stewart was particularly interested in nineteenth- and twentieth-century rhetoric and writing pedagogy, and he was very vocal in championing the development of the "authentic voice" and the importance of the canon of invention. Much of his life's work was researching Fred Newton Scott (University of Michigan, 1889–1927), who, like Stewart, was a pragmatic reformer and visionary scholar who saw rhetoric as the basis of composition instruction, and who based pedagogy on experience and voice. In contrast to this philosophy was what Stewart called the "Harvardization" of American English, a concern for superficial correctness and neglect of invention strategies, which became the standard for teaching writing. In nearly all of his writings, Stewart argued that Scott was a positive counterexample to Harvard's and demonstrated how Scott's ideas on rhetoric really lay at the roots of twentieth-century theory and practice of writing instruction.

For Stewart, an historical perspective on the teaching of writing is essential. Such a perspective liberates us from current-traditional practices; progress toward liberation is linked always to a teacher's knowledge of composition's history; knowledge of our history prevents teachers from writing practices that are outdated. Our history is linked not only to traditions of rhetoric that go back 2,500 years but also to the origins of the English department.

His address to the thirty-fourth annual CCCC meeting in Detroit is the finest example of what I call Stewart's role in rhetoric and composition studies: our

---

*Theresa Enos wrote this reflection on the 1983 Chair's address.

twentieth-century Dr. Johnson of rhetoric and composition. In his address, he scolds and cajoles us not only to know our history but to use it. Stewart never shied away from telling us what we should be doing to become better scholars and teachers of writing—and knowing our history is foremost.

Even when his health began to fail in 1986—he valiantly battled multiple myeloma (a cancer of the bone marrow) for six years—Stewart was still speaking out strongly against any "sacred-cow-fad" of our profession. Along with his frequent admonitions to use our knowledge of the history of rhetoric and composition, he criticized an overreliance on collaboration and social-constructionist views of the role of invention in the writing process. In a letter to me in January 1987, he said he was getting "testier and testier, and you know what trouble I can stir up when someone writes something that raises my pedagogical hackles."

Since his passing in 1992, we really don't have a Donald C. Stewart to serve as our twenty-first-century Dr. Johnson of rhetoric and composition. For those who knew him, Don was one of a kind. And our discipline owes much to him. What he says in "Some History Lessons for Composition Teachers" is still relevant today as we begin to move beyond postmodernism and postprocess.

–THERESA ENOS
University of Arizona

1984

Using Language to Unlock the Limits

ROSENTENE B. PURNELL

Officers and Members of this, the preeminent organization in the area of college writing, the Conference on College Composition and Communication, visitors: Greetings. Thank you for the honor and privilege of serving as your Chair, 1984. Life is made up not so much of the breaths we take in a moment as of the breathtaking moments one shares with friends. In these few breathtaking moments I share with you today, I am pleased to give you an accounting of my stewardship and, secondly, to focus briefly on some of the critical challenges facing our profession, as I see them.

This year has been yet another banner year for CCCC. Among its many other stellar accomplishments, this organization now has a balanced budget and membership which shows steady growth; and it has launched the publication of a new monograph, *Studies in Writing and Rhetoric*. Composition research, especially in pedagogical theory and practice, continues at a lively pace. Increased collaborative research in such fields as ethnography, psycholinguistics, sociolinguistics, sociology, augmented by liberating pedagogy such as that of Paulo Freire, the discipline of composition studies has surely come of age. Nearly every aspect of the composing process and its product—from idea to strategy—for all student levels is being examined and analyzed by scholars in the profession. CCCC continues to lead the way.

Amid the ebb and flow of shifting social contexts, the profession can proudly point to many salutary effects of its work. Because the classroom is but a microcosm of our changing society, educational change and social progress are inextricably joined. While reports by assessment groups such as Educational Testing Service/NAEP and American College Testing

---

This article is a revised version of the Chair's address Rosentene B. Purnell delivered at the CCCC Convention in New York, New York, on March 29, 1984. It was previously unpublished.

Service indicate an appreciable increase in the performance scores of minority and lower achievers, these groups—made up principally of urban and rural Blacks, Browns, and poor Whites—still rank below the national norm, as determined by the nation's gatekeepers. Further, there is a significant decline at all levels in the use of higher-level skills such as synthesis, written analysis, and evaluation. Increasing research, along with sheer determination and limited trial-and-error classroom experimentation, has helped more than a few previously unheralded teachers to penetrate the roots of and mitigate the effects of certain intractable barriers to student learning and progress toward desired competencies.

But, as Frost would say, we have "miles to go before we sleep." Reports tell us that one out of five adults in this country (where free education is a right) is functionally illiterate. Moreover, numerous studies point to the alarming news that this is the first generation to possess fewer skills than their parents. So, our profession meets each year—and in between—to grapple with some of its most critical and perplexing issues: How to use what is known to effect meaningful change in the lives of the diverse discourse communities represented in the students served by our schools? Given the complex dimensions of the instruction and learning process, we are not yet sure of what direction to take either with those judged basic writers or with those judged more able writers to help them reach their highest potential as thinkers, definers, and shapers of their private and public worlds. Nor can we say with relative certainty—except through the dubious use of certain assessment instruments—how precise, useful, and/or valuable the test demarcations are. Certainly, today's basics are not tomorrow's basics. While psychometricians can describe relatively well what they can test, what they test is often not what is being taught. Furthermore, who really knows what the interstices designated by test scoring really mean or how other forces may intervene to impact not only a student's performance, but also the meaning of the scores? Given those facts, educators who rely upon such data need to question more scrupulously any definitive assumptions they make about student competencies. Experts recommend using multiple indicators to make decisions about students.

Certainly, as we gather here today, composition teachers recognize many urgent issues which cry out for resolution—as some of our most vocal critics (who all are our former students) continue to remind us. Time is not on our side. All signs point to 2050 as the year when minorities will become the majority in this country. Consider the implications of that reversal for the polity, voting, the tax base, the workforce. Add to that the threat of human displacement by technology and the widening gap between the haves and the have-nots. Equal educational opportunities among all segments of society—especially among many people of color—is still an unfulfilled promise. Entrenched residential patterns, racial antipathies, and indifference have all thwarted the implementation of *Brown vs. Board of Education* for over thirty years now. Today CCCC, as well as all other educational groups, are called upon to confront head on—forthrightly and sensitively—the multifaceted challenges of diversity: ethnic/racial, class, gender, ability levels, whatever among classroom populations.

School populations follow, by and large, the economic and residential patterns of the community where the schools are. Student performance, predictably, follows the quality of teaching and learning environments—even when students are bussed to other communities. The Ann Arbor case, 1979, for example, squarely placed before this nation not only the question of student success as an educational right, but also redefined the primary role and responsibility of the teacher for helping students succeed. This is not business as usual. Today, many teachers in average classrooms find themselves facing a new student population of non-traditional and underrepresented groups. Frequently, these teachers lack adequate insight into their students' psychological, social, and physical realities as these affect such students' ability to respond to the tasks presented. This lack of preparation severely limits the teacher's options for instructing this new population in composition. Moreover, there is the question of whether or not many teachers adequately understand themselves—their mettle and mentality—and how to use the available knowledge and insight equitably and humanely to help these new student writers grow and succeed.

Experts have consistently identified as the most critical issue in education today that of developing effective classroom training for urban Blacks and, concomitantly, Browns and the other disadvantaged students in this country. An educated citizenry is the heart of a democracy. Schools cannot continue to release people unprepared as writers and thinkers to flounder in college or flood the unaccommodating marketplace. For far too many students, the promise of equity and excellence is but a subterfuge for keeping them in the underclass. The quality of life in this country is jeopardized for all of its people to the extent that it fails to provide a sound education to any of its people.

Lack of understanding across racial/ethnic, religious, and class lines may be the greatest challenge facing the world today. All of us are either a part of that problem or part of its solution. Writing teachers who do not "live on [their] students' streets" may inadvertently and dangerously harbor destructive illusions and misconceptions about their students' customs, traditions, histories, and values—if they know anything at all. Somehow, gaining an authentic understanding of these realities must become an essential part of teacher training. Such cultural studies can help teachers discern the conditions under which the individual students compose themselves and their papers. How many college composition teachers, in preparing to teach, have examined—even cursorily—the historical and social backgrounds of various student populations where they teach or plan to teach? How many prior to or afterwards are provided the opportunity for either a total or limited immersion in the cultures of their prospective students?

In the multicultural society in which we now live, educators invite disaster if they omit profound cultural awareness as a part of their preparation to serve. Incidentally, but instructive in this context, two of my spiritual mentors/friends, Drs. Henry and Ella Pearson Mitchell, homiletics professors at the Interdenominational School of Theology, Atlanta, told me of an interesting capstone assignment required of all ministers in training. Since both the ministry and teaching writing involve close interaction with people, this story may be of benefit to some writing professionals. As a graduation requirement where the Mitchells teach, all ministerial interns must engage in "The Plunge." In this activity, they are sent out in groups of threes to live for a week in a remote, unknown slum or a severely depressed area. Given no money, no provisions, no lodging, not even a change of clothes—only what was on their backs, they had to survive in that setting under those conditions. Imagine what that experience taught these men and women about their level of commitment to serve people, about the harsh realities of some people into whose eyes they had, perhaps, never even looked. Certainly, these (mostly middle- to working-class) prospective ministers had never before walked in the shoes of social outcasts who had to eke out an existence, day to day. And remember, the ministers knew their sojourn was only temporary. Imagine the lessons they were taught about themselves and others. How much better must it be to preach for—or teach—someone with whom you can really empathize? Comparing this experience with our own and given our commitment to serve as writing teachers, is it probable that we can train developing writers of whom we have little or no cultural understanding?

To be sure, the composition discipline is but one component of the formal education cycle, but, arguably, it is the one on which success in all the other disciplines depends. Can we as college language teachers use our role to help students we teach find, define, and refine their own humanity—and that of those they touch? Because education is the primary key to upward mobility, the writing teacher must educate holistically— by whatever means available—the full range of our populace. To the extent that institutions fail to recruit, retain, and graduate more students from that neglected lower quartile, they help to lock that population into the meandering maze of dependency and hopelessness, limiting their benefit to both themselves and to society. As language teachers, we must orchestrate our collective skills and learning to a self-imposed score of excellence. Since excellence is a journey, not a destination, all educators must join in this work by making it their collective and individual priority to see that the genuine right to an equal educational opportunity becomes and remains a reality for every individual. Only then can the doors of the social and psychological limitations on each individual's human potential be unlocked. No barrier of any kind to a person's right to be all s/he can be is acceptable.

Some believe that if one's early education is severely compromised, that circumstance invariably predicts hopeless frustration and/or failure later on. Not necessarily. But all too often, many unsuspecting victims—the disadvantaged people of color and poor Whites among us—through no choice of their own do succumb to such a plight and are thus relegated to academic limbo and then to society's wastelands. Not surprisingly, this is the fate of many unlucky dropouts, street corner dwellers, the permanently unemployed or underemployed, welfare victims, pimps, and pushers—the perennial underclass. Think of the wasted human potential! Doubtless, many promising intellectual giants have become victim to the Sisyphean cycles of brokenness and bureaucracy in academia and the broader society. Academic institutions can and must do more to unlock the doors of opportunity and promise for the disinherited among us.

Certainly, a person—some more than others—may be crippled by such pathologies as a fractured or dysfunctional home life, inferior schooling, displacement by unforgiving technology, inadequate nutrition, abject poverty, excoriating racism, low self-esteem, and unkindled or stifled motivation and aspiration. But these obstacles can be surmounted by the determined learner being inspired through the courage and fortitude of a caring, committed teacher. Valid evidence, time and time again, proves this. For example, the success narratives generated from the work of the Historically Black Colleges and Universities (HBCUs) show that caring, committed, and competent teachers can motivate and inspire any willing learner to break through those stultifying barriers and ignite the sparks of latent genius and productive potential. They use individualized conferences, writing centers, and community involvement activities to nurture their students' growth. Look at the following record as only a brief part of the story:

> More than 80% of all Black Americans who received degrees in medicine and dentistry were trained in Howard University and Meharry Medical College. Three-fourths of all Black persons holding doctorates and four-fifths of all Black federal judges received undergraduate degrees at HBCUs, and half of the Black faculty in major research universities in the country received baccalaureate degrees at these colleges and universities. (Pinkney 84)

To be sure, not all of those talented, accomplished individuals were ill-prepared for higher study when they arrived; nor were all assailed by relatively insurmountable difficulties. I was there, but, thankfully, one of the more fortunate ones. My family, loving and supportive, was intact;

my parents were educators and landed farmers in northeast Mississippi. By precept and example, they taught my siblings and me the value of an education. I am the third generation of teachers in my family. (Two other generations follow.) A great-uncle, educated under Booker T. Washington at Tuskegee Institute, founded a school to train neglected Black youth in rural Neshoba County, Mississippi. I knew him well (longevity is another part of my heritage). Uncle Horace always challenged and encouraged us to be the best we could be. He would come to our house during summers to teach us mathematics, English, speaking, debate, personal hygiene, and sports. He taught us how to compete and offered rewards for our achievement. My family provided numerous books, magazines, puzzles, and handmade toys and clothes for my brothers, sisters, and me. I became an avid reader at the age of three, excelled in school and finished all segments of my education with honors — at least two years ahead of the average age. Nobody ever told me — either by word or action, "You don't belong here!" I never knew that some people felt that I was not supposed to score high on standardized tests because I am African American. Nor did I know that a test score could virtually determine one's destiny, or certainly limit one's upward mobility. I was just determined to always do my best, and I prevailed over every hurdle I confronted along the way, enjoying the challenge. If I were ever prejudged because of my color, I took it for ignorance and never let that deter me in any way from my goal. Not all people of color have had such grounding. Compare my story to that of some of my students at Northridge who face incomprehensible negations daily but often do not have the resourcefulness to deal with them. Of course, many of my peers were more fortunate than I. But most of the students at HBCUs were the first generation of their family to go to college and were, more or less, economically and educationally deprived — diamonds in the rough. All they needed, then and now, was someone to help them define and realize their dreams.

Not all of the HBCU alumni became or are now shining stars; but most were, and/or still are, productive citizens. This marvelous result is due primarily to the fact that some skillful, caring, and dedicated teachers took these persons as they were, nurtured, and molded them into the best they could be. Such teachers can provide not only enormous pedagogical insight, but also many effective strategies to current teachers of both non-traditional and traditional students at any level. HBCU teachers know how to apply the love, heat, pressure, power, and time to help learners succeed. Their records speak for them. Additionally, compared to the retention rates at the large state-supported and private institutions and others serving the dominant population, the HBCUs have an average retention rate of around 95 percent. Accordingly, most of their students graduate in four years. This record, it seems to me, is irrefutable evidence that neither race, color, gender, nor class hinders learning. Educators need to further explore this disparity between the progress of certain students in HBCUs and that of similar students in other academic contexts. Indubitably, teaching writing at any level is a serious, enormously demanding business. A primary requirement of this job is to believe that every student has an inalienable right and, concomitantly, a responsibility, to a sound education. One must also believe and consistently demonstrate—through word and action—that every student can and is expected to learn, given the appropriate time and means. The paramount goal of a sound education is to expand the student's range of viable options, not to limit his/her potential for a full and rewarding life. Consequently, a sound education would include requiring students to develop facility in the use of the academic discourse while exercising due respect for the students' right to their own language as affirmed in the NCTE statement on "Students' Right to Their Own Language." It goes without serious debate that what is understood to be Edited American English (EAE) is the language of academia—textbooks, tests—and of commerce; so it is an indispensable coping skill. It is the part about exercising appropriate respect for the students' home language/dialect that has generated much heated debate in our profession. This policy, adopted by CCCC, in its essence, simply urges teachers to take students where they are and help them build appropriate bridges to connect the academic world to their world. The question, primarily, is one of appropriateness for a given situation since language in and of itself is neutral. As Alice of *Wonderland* declared, one can make a word mean what one wants it to—almost.

Despite publish-or-perish mandates, workload issues, union politics, economic exigencies, status games, personal inclinations, stultifying paperwork, and inadequate budgets that many teachers face, the students must always be the teacher's major priority. They must explore innovative ways to use, for example, the writer's conference; individualize where possible. To gladly and effectively teach, those in the profession must remain in the vanguard, seeking new frontiers, ferreting out new ideas and approaches, interpreting and analyzing, discarding things that do not work and using anything that affects the success of the learning process and product. Individual members must be bold and proactive, testing unexamined assumptions, values, and biases, and above all—facing squarely our fitness for and commitment to teach all students. It may be the time for us as professionals to fortify our purpose and rethink our primary charge in at least three vital areas: how we see ourselves, how we see the students who sit in our classroom, and how we can use this awareness to liberate our pedagogy to liberate society. Only then can we can create and use the available keys to unlock the students' vast human potential for growth as writers and persons.

Doubtless, every student generation comes to the classroom with his/her own baggage, differing more in degree than kind: weak/missing background preparation, cultural miseducation, the cumulative effects of poverty, unforgiving technology, opprobrious labeling, political oppression, covert and overt racism, self-degradation, false concepts of privilege based on race or class, and a full range of other issues. Teachers often see the faces (or numbers) of these students; but because many teachers view their students through the prism of their own makeup, they never come to know the students' stories. That is a loss. In a special way, writing teachers occupy a most enviable position among teachers. The writing teacher's subject is the self: self-discovery, self-revelation. The subject is the student. In helping students shape their language and their thinking process, the teacher enables them to gain authority and to respond to and build effective relationships in the context of their expressive discourse communities. Composition teachers also have, inescapably, the concomitant responsibility. Since writing instructors teach nearly all students at some stage in their development, they can, in a major way, fix the limits of the students' future success by that English classroom experience. A teacher can build up or tear down a student's skills and/or self-image, and hence his/her will. How many times do English teachers, upon being identified as such, get: "Oh, that was my worst subject!?" Or, "I have to watch my grammar!" And we have all heard our colleagues in other departments lament: "Why can't these students write? They can't spell, use good grammar or punctuate or think. . . ." Such comments speak volumes about not only how we affect people, but also how well they understand what we do or fail to do.

I doubt not that most teachers are well-meaning, capable, hardworking, and good. But just as the Master Teacher challenged some leaders of His day—men who thought they were unquestionably the best—to be better because they had knowledge of the letter of the law but did not have true inner righteousness, I likewise must challenge the men and women in our profession to aim for even higher efficacy. By and large, English teachers are well trained, *au courant* the latest research in theories and practices in the field, committed, and assiduous, to say the least. Most teachers do not so much lack adequate knowledge as the understanding of its best use and/or the will to practice what they know. Too often other members of the profession are ruled by a textbook or current jargon—words, concepts, and previous practices. A fitting analogy to this plight is that of the rooster who lived in a barnyard next to a railroad track, along which a freight train passed every midnight. Because it was the rooster's job to announce the dawn, when he saw the train's headlight, he would crow loudly, mistaking it for dawn. Imagine the premature rumble in the barnyard!

Likewise, some researchers in our profession—under the constraints of academic and publication deadlines and such—announce prematurely their findings; and anxious pedagogues, unquestioning, follow their lead.

Consider, for example, how many in the composition field rely blindly on the presumed truth of certain labels (based on the notion of the infallibility of test scores) and substitute the label for the reality it purports to represent. What really is meant by *empty vessel; slow learner; remedial writer; reverse discrimination; part-time person*—for *faculty?* And others cling to certain code words, concepts, and practices as a subterfuge for their true intentions, e.g., tracking, extended developmental courses—overrepresented by the underrepresented. How well do these dubious labels really serve us in the complex world of helping a student develop as a writer? Les Brown, famous multimillionaire and motivational speaker, tells a story in his video *You Deserve* that is highly instructive here. As a child, Mr. Brown was labeled mentally retarded and placed in "dumbed-down classes"—until one day he came to a teacher who challenged the label and required Brown to perform. He did. From then on, Brown says, he never accepted anyone else's view of his reality. There are many such unchallenged assumptions used every day by well-meaning teachers to the detriment of students and the profession. How many, despite convincing linguistic studies, continue to teach writing as always? Rising above acquired presumption of power and privilege, exclusionist curricula, personal training, and other shortcomings, members of the profession are challenged to continue broad conversations involving all available multiethnic perspectives as they pursue realistic beliefs and authentic practices. The way to truth may lead along many divergent paths, but truth cannot only be discovered but earnestly used to guide our understanding and vivify our practices from top to bottom. Only truth is liberating. To know the truth is to be free, but to know is not, necessarily, to do.

I now turn to the winding paths that have led me to discover much about teaching writing. I also believe these experiences have made me a better teacher and person. My primary field is English Renaissance Literature: Milton and Shakespeare. I have taught in the small Open Admissions state college, the large state university, the small, private liberal arts university, and for the majority of my career, here at Northridge, a branch of the California State University, the largest state university in the world in its aggregate form. I have been department chair and professor of English, where I taught Milton and Shakespeare and other literatures. Recently, however, I have devoted myself almost exclusively to being full professor in the field of composition, as administrator, program developer, evaluator, and university coordinator. At Northridge, because I believe my first call is to serve a present need, I responded to the invitation to develop the "English" component in the interdisciplinary Department of Pan African Studies. Through all of these experiences, I have gained many valuable insights about the nature of the academic process, especially as it relates to the psychological, social, and physical contexts of writing pedagogy; and how, unnecessarily, many bureaucratic academic structures frustrate and impede learning. But the most serious impediment to learning, as I see it, is the shortage of efficacious teaching. In my administrative interactions, I have won some battles (support, fiscal, physical, ethical, and economic) and I have also lost some—not because I lacked either knowledge or probity. To say the least, I am convinced that expediency under the guise of economic constraints or personal security should never be the overriding concern of how student learning is processed. Eclectic in my approach to pedagogy, I have as my primary goal to enhance the learning of students who come from numerous, diverse backgrounds, persuasions, and levels of competencies. I believe if all students do not grow, I somehow have not taught well. My primary concern is not novelty, but efficacy.

As I explore some of the liberating truths I *have* discovered, I will use as a backdrop a relevant section from Shakespeare's *The Tempest*. This later play by the Bard of Avon, I believe, provides outstanding insight into the relationship between language transmission and learning and suggests to me a paradigm for this discussion about the use and abuse of language and how its effective transmission can serve as a key to unlock the limits on student achievement. You know the story. The shipwrecked crew of royalty and ruffians found themselves on a deserted island. They encounter the proprietor/inhabitant, Caliban, who befriends them and teaches them, as time goes on, how to survive on the island. Caliban—according to the hierarchy urged in Shakespeare's commentary on the Western imperialism of the time, and, of course, that of the interlopers—represents the "natural" man, the Other, untutored and uncultured by those imposed standards. One sees the irony of this arbitrary positioning, as Shakespeare makes him somewhat a sympathetic but rather wise figure. Caliban, who has an independence and integrity of his own, didn't need to be "discovered" by the visitors (and all that such implies). Self-actualized, he knows "where crabs grow," how to "dig . . . pig nuts," how to find "a jay's nest," and how to "get . . . Young scamels from the rock." (*The Tempest*, II.ii.160,167–75).

In return for his favors, Caliban received from the "visitors," Prospero (the presumptive ruler) and his "innocent" daughter, Miranda, the (self-serving) gift of their language. The son of the witch Sycorax, Caliban had really never before needed the gift of their tongue. But he is wise enough to know there's something "rotten in the cotton" and, under those circumstances, he needed to get with the program or be himself made unnecessary. In due course, the interlopers took over the island. They "pinned [Caliban] into a rock" and, worse, made him their "abhorred slave," when he "naturally" attempted to "people the island" with Miranda! Although the shipwrecked crew had always treated their involuntary host-benefactor with customary condescension, ironically they thought Caliban should have been grateful for the gift of their language—a gift without the giver. Nevertheless, he had a different view of both himself and their gift.

> You taught me language; and my profit on't
> Is, I know how to curse. The red plague rid you
> For learning me your language. (*The Tempest*, I.ii.363–65)

Briefly, Caliban's retort, mirroring the politics of domination, is a response to his oppressor who had enslaved him, "confined [him] into a rock," and usurped his space. He was using his only perceived weapon, hate. Hatred in one such as Caliban is understandable (but counterproductive), seeing how he had been mistreated in his own home and misled by his unworthy, unwilling allies. But, both explicitly and implicitly, Caliban's reply is quite astute in its assessment and analysis of the linguistic situation: relationships between teacher and learner, the language content, and the inseparability of these components in their use by individuals to claim and promote their power over him. This tripod suggests the framework for the possibilities of using language to unlock the limits — to remove the intractable barriers which continue to inhibit learners and frustrate teachers across all levels, or conversely.

Cultivating authentic, productive relationships between teacher and learner is the first step toward success in any transmission of knowledge. An indispensable component of any ethical language encounter — or any other human encounter — is respect. The word *respect*, at its root level, means "to look at." It is an act of recognition of one another's humanity. It is the first order of transaction between two entities. If one approaches another with preconceived notions of place and position, that view affects the relationship and the extent to which one can agree on terms of engagement. Consider, if you will, the controversy over Standard English. Much of the debate is not about language at all, but about control. Any language carries with it its value system, its histories, its mind-set, its lexicon and thinking patterns, among other things. But its transmission should also carry with it certain user options. To teach someone, one must first be perspicacious about one's motives. What does a teacher wish to do in the process — enable or cripple the student's ability to make constructive choices towards realizing his/her highest self-actualization? Or is it the teacher's role to preserve the power and position of the present structure? I believe it is the teacher's responsibility to open up available options and allow the student to choose. Otherwise it is indoctrination, not teaching.

Just as the shipwrecked crew descended on the unsuspecting Caliban, some teachers descend on their students — from the realm of presumed privilege, power, and position. They tacitly presume cardinal relationships of inferiority and superiority. Such contrived posturing tends to inhibit a teacher's respect for what students bring to the encounter and their right to it. Furthermore, some teachers may be inclined to see and use students in the way the crew saw and used Caliban, as a source of their survival, i.e., job security. As purveyors and guardians of majority privilege and power, such instructors preserve—at whatever cost—what they believe to be "universal norms." Invaders of Caliban's space, albeit accidentally, similarly the crew brought their own notions of who they were and who Caliban was or could be. Furthermore, they imposed upon Caliban their preconceived notions of irrefutable truth, good, and beauty. They applied to the situation received truth and acted upon these with "benign sovereignty." Did they know Caliban? Did they learn even a working knowledge of Caliban's language?

In the composition classroom, do you as teacher impose an immutable order on classroom/teacher exchanges? As such, are you the sole arbiter of the best and most beautiful—unassailable, unapproachable—except by your permission? Or are you secure enough to be flexible? Do you ever question the right of the text to claim the position and privilege of a (God-ordained?) power structure upheld by White, middle-class values and norms? Do you recognize other views and values as similarly legitimate? Can you look beyond superficial indications of race, class, gender, and the like to see the person in his/her individuality? It is extremely hazardous, and especially so for a teacher, to judge students by the stereotypes that permeate this society—confused and confounded by media, unenlightened homes, in myopic research, and in the Faculty Lounge. Such behaviors render a person *invisible*, in Ralph Ellison's sense. To teach, one must first get a student's attention. Invisibility renders that act impossible. Is there any wonder why many teachers fail with certain students? In the student-teacher encounter, the prism through which teachers view themselves and their relationship to the student as individual affects everything attempted by word or action.

To be efficacious, teachers must bring themselves to respect, genuinely and unapologetically, the diverse gifts students bring to every classroom, including manifestations of their authentic culture—which is often not what goes on in popular culture. Seeking a common ground across cultures, teachers must be careful to check every point of their interactions and assumptions—especially those uninterrogated assumptions of privilege and position. Attitude reflects itself, consciously or unconsciously, and renders the learning environment either fertile or sterile. The apparent ambivalence many students show about learning to write and speak so-called Standard English may be traced—logically or not—to such deep-seated teacher attitudes about themselves and to the view of the student as the Other. Teachers need to rethink and mend adverse classroom practices so that all students of diverse backgrounds can feel comfortable enough to learn. Teacher efficacy requires each of us to get beyond parroting untested views—regardless of the source—so that each person who comes to a classroom is free to discover and prize his/her own identity and voice. No one can turn back the clock, but it is never too early to begin anew as we seek to repair the damage done in this nation's classrooms (and society) and eradicate the effete practices of the past.

To open the vistas of learning wider and reprogram ourselves for success, I suggest the following poem, "The Scroll," by a third-grade class in Montgomery, Alabama. Written in 1955 and used all over this country as an inspiring, motivating mantra, it establishes a positive tone for cultivating self-esteem, self-respect, and self-knowledge. "The Scroll" has worked for over forty-five years at every level, as well as with adult learners. Affirming the students' ability to set goals, to visualize and plan their success, instead of failure, used wisely and well this poem can be just the touch needed to revitalize a classroom.

The Daily Scroll

Today, this new day, I am a successful student, overnight my mind and body have produced thousands of new cells to give me the greatest advantages possible. I am born anew, revitalized and full of energy. I am rare and valuable; unique in the entire universe. I am nature's greatest miracle in action. I have unlimited potential. I believe in my abilities, attitudes, and goals. I am worthy of greatness because I am the most important person in my world.

Today I push myself to my limits. I use the skills and knowledge from my courses every day. I begin the day with a success and end it with a success. My goals are being reached every day and I seek them eagerly.

I act positively and happily, fully accepting others and myself. I live to the fullest by experiencing life without limits. I embrace life. I approach each class, each book, and each assignment with enthusiasm, happiness, and joy. I thirst for knowledge. I look forward to reading and believing this scroll each and every day.

I am a positive and successful student. I know each step I must take to continue to be that way. I am clear on my goals and see myself reaching them. I now realize my infinite potential, thus, my burden lightens. I smile and laugh. I have become the greatest student in the world.

"The Scroll" affirms the best in each individual, evokes confidence, and locates responsibility for success where it ultimately should be, in the individual. A student who really believes the message in this poem is unleashed for success in any classroom or anywhere. That's why even "a caged bird can sing" (Paul Lawrence Dunbar's phrase).

Second, to understand how the content of English has been manipulated and possibly subverted to demean and pillage throughout the world, one should take a look at the record. History shows the explicit relationship between language dissemination and power seizure, as language and content are interdependent. One might refer to Antonio de Nebrija's observation in his introduction to the first grammar of modern European tongue, *Gramatica* (1492), in which he speaks of language as the partner of empire. Certainly, with the conquest of land went the conquest of languages and vice versa. Language and thought are inseparable; therefore, teachers must equip students to avoid the pitfalls of language abuse and safeguard their best interests by refusing to become the ally of language treason.

Finally, the content of what we teach, the tools of our trade, the instruments by which we measure the level of our success must be interrogated for their fitness in liberating the minds of our students. For example, how many ways does the English language, its dictionaries, its textbooks, its scholars, the media, and many teachers promulgate ill will and harm to nonwhite, non–middle-class people? When Caliban speaks of learning "to curse," he is evoking any use of language to demean, to condemn, to detract from, or to exploit one's humanity. That is "semantic treason," as Francis Beauvais called it—an occurrence all too prevalent in the English language, everywhere it occurs. American education, by and large, reflects an ethnocentric bias: it is rooted in the dominating Western concept of values, truth, and beauty as perceived within that ideology. The perpetuation of its myths of cultural superiority often results in the stigmatization and exploitation of those who are perceived to be different.

Language, by and large, is a primary instrument by which cultural barriers are drawn and continually reinforced. English dictionaries irresponsibly enshrine subjective, received notions and pass them on as the meanings we give to words—unassailable in their authority. Without any basis in fact, almost subconsciously—from early childhood—most people in America associate whiteness with purity and cleanliness and blackness with dirtiness and evil. Such associations become an entrenched part of the Western White psyche and mind-set. Teachers must let students know that such a negative concept of blackness is not universal; nor is that of an all positive whiteness. Teachers, further, must urge students to explore these contradictions and forms of indoctrination. There is a diversity in the way many cultures respond to color and the designated connections they make between the colors and the numerous variations in shades among so-called races. Any associations one makes are made, not born. For further profitable study, one should read Asian and African folklore, for example. As Sarah Webster Fabio, a former colleague, said: "Black is no evil thing." Nor is any other color in and of itself evil.

Haig Bosmajian, in his study of "The Language of White Racism," shows the dangerous connection between negative language and the underlying behavioral patterns of racism and power. He further offers an explanation for the continued use of biased language by Whites. He suggests that Whites hang on to this language use because it gives them a kind of "linguistic power over a victimized black American, a power most whites are unwilling or afraid to give up. A person's language is an extension of himself and to attack his use of language is to attack him" (272). Although there has been some broadening of interracial understanding since this study was released, I agree only partly with Bosmajian's observation that the problem was ever so deeply entrenched in the White psyche and for such a cause. Even so, if certain aspects of behavior are learned, they can be unlearned. Though the weapon of language is a potent one, it could never wreak the havoc it does without the aid of systemic ingrained notions of white power, position, and privilege. The ability of Whites to use language as a weapon is, I believe, overrated. Most Black Americans and others now recognizing where the real problem lies see language as just one more weapon in the arsenal of oppression by which white self-aggrandizement is ensconced and advanced. This widespread semantic treason is like a disease; it not only affects Black/White relationships, but it spreads to and negatively impacts every other identifiable group to the extent it lacks power within the existing system. The unexamined acceptance of such linguistic practices, especially in a teacher, represents a tragic failure to deal with these ingrained unexamined notions. Such teachers cannot establish the proper relationships conducive to optimal learning and unlock the human and intellectual potentiality of their students.

Simple awareness of the demeaning aspects of language use is not enough. There has to be some deliberate change in how people use language as expressed attitude to enhance positive, constructive relationships with others. Ethical, enlightened teachers cannot continue to attribute blind meaning to perceived surface realities and endow them with the status of objective fact. Such a change means more than simply doctoring the dictionaries. Lexicographers must be required to respond sensitively and adequately to the diversities of language—as they are—not as selectively seen through jaundiced eyes of white privilege. Moreover, textbooks, standardized or teacher-made tests must perceive and reflect the same standard of veracity. Items of controversy, or that reflect ill on a person, group, gender, or class should be expurgated. Such areas may be made into assignments for students to investigate, discuss, debate, and draw their own independent conclusions on. Some investigators may have to remain uncertain, but not because such a position was forced upon them. No one should accept history from its dominant perspective without scholarly objective investigation. This includes myths about Christopher Columbus, Ho Chi Minh, George Washington, Abraham Lincoln, Martin Luther King, Cesar Chavez, or Malcolm X. This pristine investigation is needed especially where language acquisition is taking place. Students must study literatures which represent the contributions of all diverse groups, with the same rigor and appreciation. Any bias in any form should be confronted, not glossed over.

Too many people of color and others are made to sit in classrooms that demean and assault their sense of self. They sit under the tutelage of those who do not truly respect them or their culture, who hug the self-serving illusion of a canon, of an exclusionary version of truth and beauty; they fiercely follow the script, not allowing fresh breezes to penetrate their space. Most teachers still teach as they were taught. The profession needs more open discussion about both the teaching of writing and the common and diverse elements among all writers. It must ask if there is a danger of valuing the research/scholarship of writing on par with the efficacy of the teaching of writing, i.e., the results it achieves with the students. The former should serve the latter. The publication impulse in composition, unlike that in the literature branch of the discipline, should never supersede the pedagogy. I don't think that the composition discipline should ever value research more than the results such research helps to achieve with the students entrusted to its care. As a vitalized profession we need to continually ask: What is the nexus between our students and our studies? There needs to be a healthy balance between research and teaching—tilted in favor of effective teaching. Most of us here today know this—which is not to say we always practice it. If we wish to move to the next level, we must make our teaching serve the highest good for all the people. Only then will we help to unlock the limits placed on the potentialities of those imprisoned by the situations of this society. We, as writing teachers, can be liberators or barriers to progress. But if we keep doing the same thing, we shall get the same results. As Duke Ellington said: "It don't mean a thing, if it ain't got that swing!"

WORKS CITED

Bosmajian, Haig. "The Language of White Racism." *College English* 31 (1969): 263–72.
"On the Students' Right to Their Own Language." Pamphlet. Urbana: NCTE, 1974.
Pinkney, Alfonso. *Black Americans*. Upper Saddle River: Prentice, 1975.
Shakespeare, William. *The Tempest. The Complete Works of Shakespeare*. Ed. Hardin Craig and David Bevington. Glenview: Scott, 1973.

AFTERWORD: RESPONDING TO CRITICAL ISSUES

In my Chair's address to the profession, I wanted to use my platform to highlight some of the critical issues facing the profession. There is a tendency to be "politically correct" in discussing certain matters, namely race and how it impacts what goes on in the classrooms of the dominant universities and colleges of this nation (elementary and secondary schools also). We look at the effects and seem afraid to confront the primary roots of the dilemma of systemic racism. At the heart of most of the educational problems the profession faces are deeply ingrained concepts of power, position, and privilege that permeate every fiber of this society. The overwhelming majority of institutions of learning serving people of color at every level are inadequate. They lack minimal resources: skilled, caring teachers and even textbooks and good libraries in many public elementary and secondary schools. These problems are confounded by unemployment, family breakdown, and other vicious pathological cycles. It is almost miraculous that students so disadvantaged can receive preparation to advance themselves and become productive members of society! Is this situation an accident or trick of the gods? Yet the media and testing agencies float negating statistics around, and people attribute this situation to the victims as though there is something inherently wrong with them. The teacher is seldom asked to examine why he or she is continually ineffective with certain students. I address this issue from the vantage point of the composition teacher and offer pertinent information to ameliorate the situation, if put into practice. We can do something about this tragic waste of human potential if we are willing.

The discipline must take a hard, honest look at its practices, its motivations, its opportunities to become agents of change in this society before the present practices and policies consume us all. In its rush toward affirmation by literature and the power structure, there is a danger that this profession—by word and action—may come to value its research more than its results with students. Are the alarming statistics on dropouts, failure, disenchantment more or less significant than the books or articles published? How many of our theories are grandfathered into our classrooms, curriculum changes, and hiring practices? To what extent is the situation a failure in teaching rather than in learning? We need to create new conversations about writers and readers. But we also need to address head on the issue of growing good teachers.

—ROSENTENE B. PURNELL
California State University,
Northridge

1985

Breaking Our Bonds and Reaffirming Our Connections

MAXINE HAIRSTON

I'm very honored to be here today. Presiding over this meeting as your chair is a moving occasion for me because CCCC is an organization that has changed my life and shaped my career. I date that career from the first CCCC meeting I attended in New Orleans twelve years ago. At the time, although I was the director of freshman English at the University of Texas, I didn't consider myself a professional writing teacher. Rather I saw myself as an assistant professor trained in literature who had asked to run the writing program and got it because no one else in the department wanted it. At the New Orleans meeting, however, I discovered that other people were also interested in teaching writing, that it was actually a discipline that had journals and a body of scholarship, and that it offered the possibility of an exciting career. That career has been more rewarding than I could have imagined twelve years ago.

When I look back on those twelve years in our profession, I find them amazing. We have achieved a kind of national recognition that didn't seem possible in 1973. We now have at least a dozen nationally recognized graduate programs granting degrees in rhetoric and composition, and more are being established every year. We are teaching courses in rhetorical history and theory that didn't exist ten years ago. Many departments are also adding positions in rhetoric and composition in their departments. In fact, the job market for rhetoric and composition faculty, both senior and junior, is excellent. We have dozens of regional writing projects for school teachers that have grown out of James Gray's Bay Area Writing Project, and writing across the curriculum has become a by-word in colleges and universities all over the country. We have at least half a dozen new journals focusing on writing and the teaching of writing, and in the past few years

This article is a revised version of the Chair's address Maxine Hairston delivered at the CCCC Convention in Minneapolis, Minnesota, on March 21, 1985. It was first published in *CCC*, volume 36, number 3, October 1985.

several scholars in the field have been awarded major grants for improving the teaching of writing. Membership in CCCC and attendance at conventions are at an all-time high, and the new people coming into the profession are energetic, enthusiastic, and bright scholars who are generating theories and doing research that is accelerating change in the discipline. We have also caught the attention of the general public, and in many ways I think the climate for doing our job is better than it has ever been.

But most encouraging to me are the major changes I have seen in the teaching of writing. The teaching assistants in my graduate classes, the apprentice teachers whom I supervise, the teachers I talk and work with at seminars and writing workshops around the country are so much better than I was when I started that there is no comparison. They like what they're doing, they are confident, enthusiastic, and committed, and they are eager to learn. I am always delighted at how many fine writing teachers I find in places like Parsons, Kansas, or McAllen, Texas, or Montgomery County, Maryland.

So I think that as a profession we have come a long way in a short time, and from a broad perspective one can say that we are doing remarkably well. But that may seem like a rose-colored view when one looks at the situation of writing teachers from the narrower perspective one gets within individual institutions. There we often find ourselves confronting the literature faculty who dominate so many departments, and we feel that we are fighting losing battles: battles to get hard money to staff the writing center, battles to establish programs for training writing teachers, or battles against staffing composition courses with underpaid, low-status part-timers. Fighting that literature faction often makes you feel like you have invaded China. You can mount an all-out assault and think you're making an impression, but when the smoke clears, nothing has changed. The mandarins are untouched.

I could cite a dozen similar examples that contradict my happy view and illustrate that we in the composition field still have major problems. And I agree. We do. But our experience is much like that of the women's movement. One can look at how far we have come and rejoice at our progress, or one can look at the barriers that still exist and become discouraged. I believe, however—and once more the situation is analogous to that of many women—that a major reason we get discouraged is that our worst problems originate close to home: in our own departments and within the discipline of English studies itself. And we are having trouble solving those problems precisely because they are so immediate and daily, and because we have complex psychological bonds to the people who so frequently are our adversaries in our efforts to make the writing programs in our departments as good as they should be and can be.

I think the time has come to break those bonds—not necessarily physically, although in some cases that may be a good idea—but emotionally and intellectually. I think that as rhetoricians and writing teachers we will come of age and become autonomous professionals with a discipline of our own only if we can make a psychological break with the literary critics who today dominate the profession of English studies. Until we move out from behind their shadows and no longer accept their definition of what our profession should be, we are not going to have full confidence in our own mission and our own professionalism. I agree that logically we should not have to choose. English studies should not be split between a commitment to teaching literature and a commitment to teaching writing. After all, what could be more central to English studies than teaching people to write? But logic has long since ceased to be a consideration in this dispute. I think that for the literary establishment, the issue is power; they do not want to relinquish their control of all of English. For us, I think the issue is survival. We must cut our psychological dependence in order to mature.

In some ways, of course, we have made the separation. We are earning our living teaching writing, and we do have our own professional meetings and journals and a developing body of scholarship. We have a sense of purpose and a camaraderie that energizes the profession. But I also see us stunted in our growth because we are not able to free ourselves from needing the approval of the literature people. We've left home in many ways, but we haven't cut the cord. We still crave love.

For example:

We keep trying to find ways to join contemporary literary theory with composition theory. Such a goal makes sense in many ways, but people who are trying to achieve it seem to be on a one-way street—they are eager to find ways by which we can use literary theory in the teaching of writing, but I hear no one talking about using what we know about writing processes to help us teach literature. Nor do I see any prospect of setting up a dialogue with the literary critics on this matter because they don't know writing theory and, as far as I know, are making no attempt to learn.

Moreover, I suspect that in many of the articles which try to link literary theory and composition theory, the authors, perhaps unconsciously, have purposes that go beyond developing new ideas about the teaching of writing. They also want to show their former mentors that even though they are now composition teachers, their hearts are still pure. They do that by demonstrating that they have read the scholarship of deconstructionism and semiotics and take it seriously. By bringing in the magic names—Cullers, Fish, Hartman, and Derrida—they signal that they have not abandoned the faith.

We have also shown our insecurity by the effusive welcomes we have given several eminent literary scholars who, distressed about the quality of their students' writing, have now and then joined forces with us to contribute their ideas about teaching writing. Their efforts were honest but had little major impact; after all, their primary interests lay elsewhere.

Still, without waiting for them to prove themselves by conference papers or committee work, we eagerly asked them to be keynote speakers and panelists, telling ourselves that if we could get them on our side, others in the literary establishment would take us more seriously and pay attention to our new discipline. The establishment, however, seems to have paid little attention. We are not being published in their journals, and they are not seeking to be published in ours.

Many of us have also revealed our nervousness about our own discipline by encouraging our graduate students to combine rhetoric and composition with literary criticism in graduate programs and their dissertations, assuming that their degrees would be more marketable in traditional English departments. That's an untested assumption, and I think it can be a damaging one. Its effect is to suggest that we fear that our own discipline may not be scholarly and substantive enough for a graduate student to specialize in it exclusively and write a dissertation in it.

Finally, in the recurring fracases with the literature people—I think of them as the Mandarin Wars—we seem always to be the ones who propose reconciliation. We are the ones who propose panels at MLA on bridging the gap between composition and literature and who edit books on the reading-writing connection. We are the ones who ask that composition people be appointed to the editorial board of *PMLA*. We are the ones who say, "But we need each other. Look how many students we teach in composition, how much money we generate for the department. If we can just focus on our common goals and talk to each other, we can work things out." We act as if we are the ones who have the most to lose in this clash of cultures we're engaged in. For that is what the Mandarin Wars are all about—they are battles against a patriarchal culture whose values we absorbed early.

But before we compromise too much, I think we need to look at that culture as it is today and decide how strongly we still believe in the values with which we were raised. And I stress "today" because I think that in many ways the culture of English studies has changed significantly in the last ten years. In my department, at least, and in many of those I hear about from my colleagues, the commitment to literature itself and to teaching students to enjoy literature that made most of us join this profession seems to have faded and to have been replaced by a commitment to criticism for its own sake. Somehow the experience of reading literature for pleasure has gotten lost. Now one can find graduate seminars in which students spend thirty minutes discussing a major novel and four hours analyzing the criticism on the book.

But in another important way English studies *hasn't* changed; in traditional departments the system still dictates that the hardest work of the department, teaching freshman writing, remains at the bottom of the social and political scale. Typically that work is done by underpaid graduate students who are given to understand that once they have served their apprenticeships and completed their Ph.D.s, they will be largely exempt from such chores. As their number has declined, an even lower class has been hired to take up the slack: anonymous, underpaid, and conveniently invisible adjunct faculty. In many schools such faculty teach the bulk of the writing courses. Tenured professors continue to do the "real" work of the department, which is understood to be teaching literature, preferably English, preferably poetry, preferably difficult. And most of the professors who specialize in these areas have not taught freshman composition in so long that they claim, with justification, that they are no longer qualified to do it.

I see no evidence that this value system is going to change in most universities. I think it reflects an elitist mindset that prefers that which is accessible only to the few and that despises the useful or the popular. The attitude is the same one that made Chinese mandarins grow long fingernails and decree that their women must bind their feet. (Notice that the women also thought the bound feet were beautiful.) And in the minds of most of today's critic-scholars, their handicaps, their inability to do useful work or communicate with non-specialists, have become advantages because they separate them from the masses. And we have to face the truth that our mandarins think we are ugly because we have short fingernails and big feet. Nothing is going to change that.

The fact that as writing teachers we are useful to them—indeed, that they probably couldn't survive without us—only makes them more contemptuous. They see us in a service role; we do the work they don't want to do, and when we accept their definition of writing courses as service courses, we ourselves denigrate what we do and buy into their value system. We take on the martyr role of faithful but underpaid and undervalued caretakers who make it possible for the elite to survive. Too often, like so many caretakers, we rationalize and romanticize our role.

Another enduring feature of traditional English departments—and, in fact, of the academic world in general—is that the faculty tends to take a Platonic view of the world, detached and slightly contemptuous of daily work and everyday concerns. Typically, academics are introverted, contemplative sorts who prefer, as Bertrand Russell says, to work in "that happy realm of exactness where pure thought can disport itself in freedom." In English studies they can come closest to finding those happy realms by focusing on writing from the past and by resolutely claiming that any practical enterprise, such as teaching technical or expository writing, is not a legitimate concern of a department of literature.

It is also clear that the scholar-critics in most departments don't believe in the teaching of writing as a discipline. They are uninterested in what we have learned about teaching writing and believe we have nothing to teach them. Some of them openly dismiss our research and scholarship as trivial. Anyone who has taught writing-across-the-curriculum work-shops will tell you that the English faculty are the least likely to attend and the most difficult to work with when they do attend.

Now I know I am generalizing and that not everyone whose primary interst is teaching and writing about literature fits the stereotype I have drawn. Almost every department has many thoughtful and open-minded scholars who enjoy teaching both literature and writing and do both rea-sonably well. They tend not to be the faculty who are politically active, how-ever; usually they just want to be left alone to pursue their scholarship. The politically active literary critics, on the other hand, are "full of passionate in-tensity" and have an effect that belies their numbers. If we are going to hold our own against them, the question we must face, the question that will not go away, is "How can we rally our forces against this intimate enemy?"

Whatever we do is going to be difficult and painful precisely because the enemy is intimate, a member of the family, and because we are going to have to take the risks that accompany assertion and separation. But I think we must begin. First, I think we need to realize that at the present time we are wasting our time trying to establish a dialogue. In addressing the mandarins, we are not in a rhetorical situation. You'll remember Lloyd Bitzer says that in order to have a rhetorical situation there has to be an *exigence* that can be modified by discourse, and there has to be an *audience* of persons who are capable of being influenced by that dis-course.[1] Chaim Perelman also reminds us that the specific requisite for argumentation is this: "the speaker can choose as his points of departure only those theses accepted by those he addresses."[2] In most of our depart-ments right now, I don't think we have either of those conditions.

We perceive an exigence—we see that much of the writing in our de-partments is being badly taught by untrained and overworked people or by disaffected literature specialists who see their students as hopeless il-literates. We see our students being short-changed, and we want to change that. We also want the literature faculty to recognize the value of what we are doing and to commit themselves to supporting writing programs and writing faculty. But those are our needs, not theirs, and they're not paying any attention. Nor will they until we force them to do so.

Nor do I think that in most institutions we are dealing with an audi-ence who is capable of being influenced by our discourse or who shares our basic premises about teaching writing. From my experience in doing faculty workshops, from talks I have heard at regional and national con-ferences, and from discussions I have had with colleagues across the country, I have to conclude that most literature faculty do not want to hear what we have to say; they already know *a priori* that the best way to teach writing is to have students read good literature and write about it. Their cry is that otherwise the courses have no content, and they refuse to concede that the content of a writing course is language and how it works. They have no interest in the new paradigm that stresses working with students during the writing process and that draws on the insights of cognitive psychology about how people learn. They prefer to teach writing by talking about literature in a teacher-centered classroom.

In many institutions, it's clear that a majority of the English department faculty do not share our conviction that English departments have an obligation to teach people to write. If students do not already know how to write when they get to college, they hold, that is somebody else's fault and we shouldn't have to deal with it. It's much easier to invoke the magic phrase "rigorous standards" and proclaim that since students should have learned to write in high school, freshman English is a remedial course that we shouldn't have to teach.

So this is the first lesson we have to learn: THEY'RE NOT LISTENING. We are wasting our energy pummeling at them and trying to get them to acknowledge our claims or our merit. As long as we do that, we are playing their game. And it's a game we can't win because they made the rules and they are the referees.

My second suggestion is that we quit wasting our time being angry. Getting angry can be useful at times, particularly if it helps one get rid of illusions and decide to take action, but staying angry consumes too much energy. When we let people keep us in an uproar, we give them too much importance and risk assuming that they are more powerful than they really are. The mandarins aren't really as monolithic and secure as we give them credit for being. Their world has changed a great deal in the past decade: fewer students are enrolling in their courses, their graduate students can't find jobs, and most of the professors themselves are no longer mobile. The openings in literature just aren't there. It's not surprising that they feel threatened by our new success. I suspect, moreover, that many of them know that they're like dinosaurs standing around waiting for the weather to change, that things are never really going to be the same again. But instead of trying to shout them down, I think we will do better to spend our energy building our own reputations and enhancing our status outside of our departments instead of over-reacting to hostility at home.

Our third important task is the same one that women and minorities have faced in the last two decades: we must pay attention to what our inner selves tell us, find our own values and listen to our own voices— values and voices that are not *against* someone else, but for ourselves. We must no longer try to be "good" by trying to live up to someone else's visions for us by saying, "Tell me what you want me to be and I'll be it. I want to please you." If we do that, when we win, we lose.

Instead, we need to listen to our voices when they tell us what is true for us even when those messages conflict with the conventional wisdom in which we have been schooled. For instance, our voices may be telling us that teaching freshmen is more rewarding than teaching graduate students; that our students are not illiterates, but intelligent, competent young people who like to write; that writing courses are not service courses, but courses in the exercise of a primary intellectual activity; that we value writing textbooks as much as we value writing scholarly books because we value teaching as much as we do scholarship. Especially we should pay attention to our own feelings when they confirm a response that some of us used to be ashamed to admit: that we genuinely enjoy teaching the writing courses that other faculty profess to despise. We must listen to our different drummer and pay attention.

For we *are* different. As writing teachers we are engaged in a dynamic and loosely-structured activity that involves intensive interaction with people. It is an activity that is tied to living language, that shifting and ambiguous medium that won't stand still to be examined and is never pure, and it is an activity that focuses on teaching a process for which there are no fixed rules and no predictably precise outcomes. We are engaged in a messy business, and *necessarily so*. And it's one that is essentially Aristotelian—pragmatic, concrete, situational, and personal.

But once we have established who we are and what we do, we face the challenge of establishing our discipline on solid ground, both in the academic community and in the community beyond the university and college. To meet that challenge, we must take a number of steps.

First, as individuals we must be productive researchers and scholars who contribute to the growth of our discipline. We cannot rely simply on being good teachers even though that may be our first priority: in the league we want to play in, that's not enough. Unless we know our past and unless we can construct theoretical frameworks that inform our practice, we will not be taken seriously. Nor should we be; being a professional means more than having a knack for one's trade.

We also have to publish: in the league we're in, that's a given. But it's useful to remember that publication does more for professionals than bring recognition and advance the state of the art. It also helps us as individuals to build the self-esteem and confidence that is especially important for beginners in an enterprise, and it gives us the rewards and reinforcement from outside our institution that most of us do not get in our own departments. Moreover, the writers and doers in a profession quickly establish a camaraderie with each other and get the important satisfaction of feeling that they are participating in a vital activity.

As scholars and writers, we also have to set high standards for our research, our conferences, our publications, and for our own writing, and we have to do first-class work in all our diverse activities. It's important, however, for us to realize that ours is a humanistic discipline, and that we cannot yield to what Lewis Thomas calls "physics envy," the temptation to seek status by doing only empirical experiments that can be objectively normed and statistically validated. If we do that we will narrow our field of inquiry to investigations that are so limited that what we find out will be worthless to us as writing teachers.

Indeed, it is precisely because our work cannot be judged by scientific standards that we have to set exacting criteria for ourselves and do rational, thorough, and informed investigation. We have to learn to formulate good questions, to examine data—especially data that come to us in language—sensitively and meticulously, to control for bias, and to be careful not to claim too much for our findings. We must demand of each other the kind of quality scholarship that will make us proud of the work being done in our field and earn us the respect of scholars outside the field. In fact, one of our major challenges now is to develop guidelines to define and govern good research.

Second, we have to extend our connections to disciplines outside our field—not only to linguistics, philosophy, cognitive psychology, and speech communication, but to less obviously connected fields such as biology, economics, and even the arts. Since rhetoric is a way of learning, every human intellectual enterprise involves writing and rhetoric, and we can learn from all disciplines and help others in all disciplines. And by establishing connections and credibility outside of English departments, we stand to improve our standing with the whole university community.

Finally, we need to reach beyond our immediate world and make connections with business, industry, technology, and the government. These institutions are running a giant educational operation, and we have an opportunity both to learn from them and to contribute to their enterprises. By working with them, we can take an active part in shaping today's information society.

If we can do all of this, we may get our literary colleagues' attention and their respect as they realize that we have gained credibility and influence outside of the department, and that we no longer look to them to validate our worth. Then they may begin to change their attitudes, decide that they need us after all, and that we should work together to resolve our differences. But that may *not* happen, too. Then what? Is separation the only answer?

Not necessarily, but at that point I think we should look at our options. Probably most composition and rhetoric faculty would prefer to keep their affiliation to English departments, and I think that that's a good solution if we can stay as equals. It is not a good solution if the patriarchal hierarchy of those departments continues to deny English departments' responsibility for teaching undergraduates to write, to demean our work, and to tilt the reward system in favor of literary criticism. We now have too many choices to accept those conditions.

As a group, one of our choices might be to work directly with a sympathetic chairman to get what we want for our writing programs; often department chairs are more practical than their faculty and want broad-based programs that serve undergraduate needs. Another option may be to enlist the help of a dean or provost who realizes how important the writing program is to the college or university. Composition faculty can also consolidate their position and expand their influence by working together to get national grants that will catch the attention of the upper administration. And in departments that have three or four rhetoric and composition faculty now and are hiring more, the answer may be "Be patient." As the new generation takes over, the power will shift.

Our most radical option, of course, would be to petition to split the composition and rhetoric program from the English department and form a department of rhetoric. If we do that, we could be helping to initiate what James Kinneavy has called the return of rhetoric from exile.[3] Rhetorical studies held the center of humanistic studies until the seventeenth century, and were a major component in American departments of English until early in the twentieth century. Then the same kind of dispute between those who wanted to focus their efforts exclusively on the study of literature and those who wanted to include the study of oral rhetoric and the craft of writing caused those committed to rhetoric to leave and form departments of speech communication. Perhaps it's time that we repeated the exodus, this time taking freshman English with us. Perhaps we should even consider joining with speech communication and journalism to form a new and vital department of language and communication, and once more make humanism and rhetoric relevant in our modern society. This option would be the most disruptive and most difficult; to me, at the present time, it would also be the best.

If you as an individual writing teacher believe that your department is hopeless, and you think you can't wait for that utopian solution, it's not too difficult to find other, more immediate, options. One is to move to another college or university. Not all departments fit the discouraging picture I have described, and many are expanding their rhetoric programs or starting new ones. You might also consider talking to the deans of some of the professional schools at your university—law or engineering, for example—about starting a writing program that would meet the special needs of their students. You could become a technical writer; you could set up a research and consulting firm; you could try to break into corporate education or become the director of writing and publicity for a bank or a computer company. Anyone who is an energetic and skillful teacher, writer, and researcher has a wide range of options open. To be sure, they all involve taking risks, and many involve giving up some of the bonuses of academia—the flexible schedules, the month-long vacations, the contact with students. But they also have their own kind of challenges and satisfactions and their own rewards, both intellectual and financial.

For anyone, these are drastic solutions, not to be undertaken lightly. There are no guarantees and not many models to look to for guidance.

But the cost in anger and frustration is also high if we do nothing, thinking that the climate is going to change if we wait long enough. If we want to cause change instead of wait for it, if we want the profession of teaching writing to become a recognized and respected intellectual discipline, we are going to have to believe in ourselves and in what we do strongly enough to be willing to take a chance and break with the power structure if necessary. We have to know that we can make it without them, for only if we are ready to leave are we going to be able to participate in the relationship as equals. When we can honestly say, "We no longer need your approval," their power over us will dissolve. But as long as we're afraid, we'll lose the struggle.

I hope that we will emerge from this dispute stronger because we have been willing to take a stand affirming that we are professional teachers of writing, and that we intend to put our primary energy into the teaching of writing and into research that informs the teaching of writing because we believe those concerns are central to English studies. By saying this we do not intend to diminish literature or the teaching of literature; we should always make that clear. But we can learn from the feminist psychologists that when we have the courage to assert ourselves, the bond of dependence can give way to a dynamic of interdependence.[4] If that happens, perhaps we can once more engage in a mutually satisfying dialogue with a group for whose traditions we once felt an affinity. By freeing ourselves, we may finally establish that dialogue. and by leaving the house in which we grew up, we may finally create the strong connection between literature and composition that most of us feel is good and natural.

NOTES

1. Lloyd Bitzer, "The Rhetorical Situation," *Philosophy and Rhetoric*, 1 (Winter, 1968), 1–15.
2. Chaim Perelman, *The Realm of Rhetoric* (Notre Dame, IN: University of Notre Dame Press, 1982), p. 21.
3. James Kinneavy, "Restoring the Humanities: The Return of Rhetoric from Exile," in *The Rhetorical Tradition and Modern Writing*, ed. James J. Murphy (New York: Modern Language Association, 1982), pp. 19–28.
4. Carol Gilligan, *In a Different Voice* (Cambridge, MA: Harvard University Press, 1982), p. 149.

AFTERWORD: REFLECTIONS ON "BREAKING OUR BONDS"

When I gave my Chair's address, "Breaking Our Bonds," to the CCCC convention in 1985, I ruffled quite a few academic feathers by being the first professional to suggest in a public forum that it was time for writing faculty to break away from English departments, psychologically and emotionally, if not physically. I urged the separation because I believed that the reward system in literature-focused English departments penalizes faculty who are committed to teaching writing. They're low men on the totem pole in both prestige and pay, and they get little encouragement to develop the solid writing courses that university students need.

I now reflect that I would have made an even stronger case for actual separation if I had fully realized then what a crucial role good writing plays in any college student's education. A well-taught composition course goes far beyond teaching students to write correctly. It engages students intellectually, challenges them to think through their assumptions, persuades them to consider their audience, leads them to discover arguments, and helps them to shape their personas to fit their writing situations. They become critical thinkers who build the confidence they need to engage in the civic and professional conversations that affect their lives, their work, and their communities. Literature teachers aren't trained for this kind of teaching, and colleges should not expect it of them. But rhetoricians, writing specialists, and communication faculty are trained to introduce students to the complex craft of writing, and they are the professionals who should design and run writing programs.

Such a program now exists at the University of Texas at Austin as the Division of Rhetoric and Composition, housed in the College of Liberal Arts and founded only eight years after I first advanced my proposal at the 1985 CCCC convention. Around that time John Ruszkiewicz, James Kinneavy, and I were urging the department, the dean of our college, and the university provost to split the writing program off from English, but with little success. Then in the late 1980s fate and politics played into our hands. A group of English department faculty who were committed to cultural studies proposed that the freshman composition course required of all entering students should become a course to raise those students' social and cultural awareness. The required text for the course, taught almost entirely by graduate assistants, would be a collection of essays on race, class, and gender. John Ruszkiewicz and I, both former directors of freshman English, vigorously opposed the proposal and voiced our objections at the departmental, college, university, and even national levels. There was also widespread opposition among faculty outside the College of Liberal Arts. The proposal was shelved, but the heated dispute made a separate writing division look more attractive to the university administration, and within two years the College of Liberal Arts created the Division of Rhetoric and Composition, giving it an independent budget and staffing it with established scholars in rhetoric and composition.

That division has been hugely successful. Its faculty and teaching assistants trained by that faculty teach all first-year required writing courses, and it offers a full array of expository writing courses and classes on the theory and practice of rhetoric and writing. It staffs and administers a writing center that offers help to all university students, it houses the Computer Writing and Research Lab, and it offers training and support to the professors in other departments who teach the substantial writing-component courses that the university requires of all students. It has a dozen full-time faculty who do research, participate in national conferences, and publish scholarly books and articles in rhetoric and writing. It also rewards graduate assistants for both teaching and research; each year it gives a prize to the TA judged best teacher for the year and another to the best graduate student research project in rhetoric. Most important, the division has a strong sense of its mission: to offer excellent writing instruction to the entire university and to support the university administration's commitment to good writing instruction as a key element of a university education.

That commitment from the top down is essential. As John Ruszkiewicz, the division's current director, points out, the program is expensive. Faculty are decently paid, and new faculty are added regularly; this past year the division hired two senior faculty, one a classical rhetorician. The division hires and trains graduate students from departments across the university to teach its freshmen; it hires no part-time faculty or lecturers. John believes, and I agree, that a program of this size and caliber can't be run cheaply. Everyone involved at all levels must believe that the whole university community benefits from a first-class writing program run by professionals and be willing to pay what it costs.

–MAXINE HAIRSTON, EMERITA
University of Texas, Austin

Note: For a comprehensive survey and discussion of writing programs at other colleges and universities, see *A Field of Dreams: Independent Writing Programs and the Future of Composition Studies*, ed. Peggy O'Neill, Angela Crow, and Larry W. Burton (Logan: Utah State UP, 2002).

1986

Diversity and Change: Toward a Maturing Discipline

LEE ODELL

Whalen we talk about history, there is always the danger of oversimplifying. In reflecting upon recent times we often focus on their uniqueness and turbulence, ignoring what they have in common with previous eras. When we consider the more distant past, we tend to think of a more serene age; the sharp edges of controversy and uncertainty become blunted by the passage of time. Yet even in acknowledging these tendencies, I think we can also acknowledge that the past two decades of our profession's history have been extraordinary.

For one thing, the past two decades have brought substantial changes in both pedagogy and scholarly procedure. In the 1960's, we rediscovered the process of invention and, recognizing that having something to say was essential for writing well, many people began teaching students to use systematic inquiry procedures: the topics of classical rhetoric, the five w's of journalism, the nine cells of tagmemic rhetoric. Furthermore, we began to attack generally shared assumptions about pedagogy and about essay structure; some people argued that outlining was not always necessary or desirable, that nobody wrote five-paragraph themes, and that lots of perfectly respectable paragraphs lacked topic sentences. We even began to criticize our knowledge about composition. Existing studies were, according to one influential text, approximately at the stage science was when alchemists were trying to turn base metals into gold. What we needed was to replace impressionistic, anecdotal studies with scientifically designed experiments.

All this change proved to be heady stuff. In fact, change was so invigorating that we kept right at it. Soon enough, talk of structured heuristic procedures was replaced by talk of cognitive processes and by instruction

This article is a revised version of the Chair's address Lee Odell delivered at the CCCC Convention in New Orleans, Louisiana, on March 13, 1986. It was first published in *CCC*, volume 37, number 4, December 1986.

in less structured discovery procedures—journals, learning logs, free writing. Furthermore, we began to criticize the critics: outlines could *too* be useful; and some paragraphs *had* to have topic sentences. And we kept changing scholarly procedure. Where once analysis of T-units had been sufficient, scholars now have to master complex schemes of discourse analysis; people who had begun to understand experimental design, analysis of variance, and standard deviation are now beginning to hear more and more talk about non-experimental methods—naturalistic observation, field notes, and triangulation.

These changes in pedagogy and scholarly procedure have been accompanied by changes in the scope of our courses. In addition to more conventional types of academic writing, students are being asked to write personal, expressive discourse as well as letters, dialogues, proposals, reports, and interviews for a wide range of audiences and rhetorical purposes. In other words, many composition courses reflect an enlarged view of what "writing" may entail.

From one perspective, all this activity is evidence of a vigorous and maturing discipline, one characterized by diverse approaches to scholarship and pedagogy, and an interest in a wide range of types of discourse. But this state of affairs can also seem overwhelming, even chaotic. Theory, research findings, pedagogical principles—almost every aspect of our professional lives is subject to continual revision; the disciplinary ground keeps shifting under our feet. Furthermore, so many diverse ideas compete for our attention that it is easy to move from one to another, without identifying and testing an idea's basic assumptions or without recognizing both the limitations and the uses of a given idea. Thus one can sympathize with a complaint once voiced by a student in a graduate course in composition, a course that placed a great deal of emphasis on primary trait evaluation. The student did not argue that primary trait evaluation was unreasonable. But she had done previous work in composition and she was concerned: "Last year the word was *holistic scoring*. The year before it was *analytic scales*. This year it's *primary traits*. What will it be next year?"

To provide a somewhat delayed answer to the student's question, it now seems as though next year's word in evaluation may not be *primary trait* or even *holistic scoring*. It may very well be *hermeneutics*. That is, some of the most promising work in evaluation seems likely to derive from work in reader-response criticism, which sees both writer and reader (or evaluator) as members of a hermeneutic circle, fellow interpreters of a text, colleagues in the effort to create meaning. Now evaluators are about to become collaborators.

That prospect is intriguing. But as one more in a long series of changes it seems incompatible with one of the few constants in our professional lives: on Monday we must meet our students and we must do something that seems likely to help them improve their writing. Given this constant, there are times when we feel frustrated or even cynical about a discipline that seems to be in a state of perpetual transition.

Although these attitudes are understandable, they are misleading. For they assume that change itself is the problem, that novelty and diversity are inherently at odds with good teaching and good scholarship. In fact, we have strong reasons for thinking that change is essential to our own intellectual lives and to the life of our discipline. One may argue that our knowledge is tentative, provisional, subject to ongoing revision. If this revision ever ends, so will our discipline. And so will our ability to survive as thinkers and as teachers. Given this point of view, I think we need to be concerned not with current trends in our discipline but rather with our relationship to those trends. In other words, the question is not, Do we approve or disapprove of the current status of our discipline? It is, rather, What does each of us need to do in order to contribute to the advancement of learning in our discipline? In the remainder of this article, I shall suggest several ways each of us might contribute to the development, the maturing of our discipline.

One contribution has to do with our assumptions about knowledge: we need to practice what we preach. In our better moments, we admit that our knowledge is limited, that we can always learn more and, on occasion, even change our mind about important issues in our profession. And we acknowledge that our understanding of a given issue is likely to be enhanced by exploring that issue from different perspectives. Thus, in order to investigate the process of composing, we draw freely upon cognitive psychology, literary theory, linguistics, rhetoric, and so on.

But we are not always at our best. Too often, we compartmentalize our knowledge about our profession and pretend to certainty in areas where we have, at most, plausible hypotheses. For example, those who use free writing or some other unstructured heuristic procedure tend to have little to say to those who value more structured, systematic procedures. People who conduct naturalistic research don't want to talk with researchers who do statistical analysis. And those who understand analysis of variance and standard deviation sometimes seem to talk only to each other. Finally, those who see themselves primarily as teachers of composition—rather than researchers or theorists—seem inclined to distrust both theory and research, relying instead on observations honed by daily experience with students. Indeed, like the blind scholars of the Indian fable, we focus, say, on the side of the elephant. And we insist that the side *is* the elephant, that others who talk of trunks and tails are, to use the very nicest term, misguided. Perhaps more than anything else, this attitude constitutes a major threat to the growth of our discipline.

One might expect members of our profession to be a little more cautious about the claims made on any given subject. After all, there is a lot of relativist talk nowadays. It is not at all unusual to hear people suggest—as I have just done—that our knowledge is tentative and subject to revision. Similarly, in much current scholarship there is at least the tacit assumption that one's understanding of a given subject is not simply a matter of recording what is "out there," objectively knowable, but is, rather, a creative process, a transaction between the knower and the known, a process that depends on interactions with others and that is enriched by contact with a wide variety of points of view.

Unfortunately, absolute certainty and compartmentalized thinking can flourish even in rather unlikely settings. At a recent conference on rhetoric and composition, the relativist point of view was put forward by one of the principal speakers at the conference. The speaker's argument was eloquent and persuasive; most of us in the audience seemed to be in wholehearted agreement that meaning is indeterminate and context-dependent. Later this speaker told me that he had come to a presentation I made, had enjoyed it, and had thought it was 85% correct. I would like to report that my first response was to remark upon the irony of such absolute certainty coming from someone who was an advocate of relativism. But my first response was "Good lord. 85%. That's only a B." In other words, my own true colors came quickly to the surface; my instinctive reaction belied the philosophical position that, earlier, I had joined in applauding. Later this speaker assured me that his initial judgment was wrong, that my presentation had been at least 87% correct. I felt a full two percent better.

As we become a bit more circumspect in our own claims to knowledge, we also need to become more aware of, to use Carl Rogers' phrase, the region of validity for competing points of view. In place of—or perhaps in addition to—asking "Is X valid?" we need to ask "Under what circumstances is X valid? From what perspectives does it make sense? What aspects of X are valid and sensible?" As we ask these questions, we become better able to make connections among apparently disparate elements of our discipline. We become able, for example, to find useful relationships between our discipline's past and its present and between what seem to be mutually exclusive views of the process of thinking that goes on while people write.

We may think it easy to dismiss as unworthy of our attention views—especially the views of previous generations—that we do not immediately find compelling. Thanks to no less an authority than I. A. Richards, it might appear that we have some justification for ignoring much of the work of the early part of this century. In his *Philosophy of Rhetoric*, Richards dismissed many composition texts of his time as containing only "the usual post-card's-worth of crude common sense." Furthermore, texts of an earlier era sometimes sound rather quaint. For example, the text *A Manual of Systematic Discourse*, written during the earlier part of this century, includes a section on oral presentations, wherein students are strongly advised to make sure that the notes for their presentations are in handwriting that is "large and clear." The rationale for this advice is that ". . . one can never foresee possibilities of bad visibility. A storm may be coming up as your time to speak arrives and the room may be dark or nearly dark. Or the electric current may have failed and the program is going forward with the aid of kerosene lamps or gas jets."

And yet this same textbook contains the following exhortation: "We must not, before beginning a sentence, decide what the end shall be; for if we do, nobody will care to hear that end. . . . We must give our thought its head, and not drive it with too tight a rein, nor grow timid when it begins to prance a bit." The author of this passage acknowledges the need to temper spontaneity and passionate self-expression with cool reason. But, he argues, "Pedantry is worse than blundering. If we care for grace and flexible beauty of language, we must learn to let our thoughts run." The extended metaphor here belongs to a much earlier generation. But the sentiments are those of Ken Macrorie attacking *Engfish* or Peter Elbow advocating that we begin our composing by writing freely, without editing or trying to predetermine the direction our thoughts will take, assuming that we can come back later to salvage and refine the most useful parts of what we have written.

My point here, then, is that it is too easy to overlook elements of our history that reinforce and enrich our current work. We are too prone to let superficial differences blind us to significant connections between past and present. Similarly, we are too willing to look for disjunctions between current schools of research or approaches to teaching and evaluation. Earlier in this essay, I referred to a graduate student who was concerned about what struck her as a relentless proliferation of strategies for evaluating writing. I do not share her apprehension about the variety of approaches. But I do think she was right to protest the tendency to emphasize the uniqueness of each of these procedures without considering possible relationships among them.

A different illustration of this tendency appears in our efforts to describe and teach the thinking processes that are essential to effective writing. Perhaps predictably, we have acted as if those efforts are unrelated or even mutually exclusive. Consider, for example, two major lines of work, one derived from rhetoric and one from cognitive psychology. Scholars in these two areas have much to teach each other; the strength of each type of work complements the strength of the other. Studies influenced by cognitive psychology have shown that while writers are in the process of writing they must engage in three major types of activity: planning, translating, and reviewing. These studies indicate that the process of planning requires writers to generate content. But these studies do not provide a comprehensive, systematic description of the intellectual strategies writers rely on when they analyze data, formulate conclusions, and, thus, generate content. By contrast, rhetoric provides potentially useful ways to categorize these strategies. But rhetoricians have not attempted to document and perhaps revise their categories by observing what writers actually do when they write.

As long as they are isolated from each other, both rhetoric and cognitive psychology are impoverished. And needlessly so. When we examine protocols of writers composing aloud, we find them performing intellectual operations described in rhetorical statements about invention. This activity may be intuitive and non-systematic, but surely it is inevitable. When we try to formulate our thoughts in language, it is difficult to avoid such activities as contrasting or classifying or speculating about causal or hypothetical sequences. As we make connections between rhetoric and cognitive psychology, both areas benefit. In exchange for providing cognitive psychology with a set of categories, rhetoricians might see those categories expanded and refined as they try to account for the complexity of the thinking that goes on while people write.

In addition to making connections among diverse scholarly works, we need, as part of our effort to help advance learning in our discipline, to identify principles that enable us to find elements that link together diverse, apparently unrelated types of communication. Without obscuring useful distinctions, we need to find ways to relate talk to writing, for example, or to relate personal letters to formal academic discourse.

This task may be less formidable than it seems, for we currently have access to research and theory that can help us understand these relationships. The problem is that we have not applied this scholarship in widely varying situations, trying to determine how it accounts for what we observe in those situations and using our observations to refine the very ideas that guide our inquiry. This seems unfortunate since our day-to-day experience is filled with opportunities to make these applications. Here is one case in point.

Several years ago, I was taking Amtrak from Albany to Boston, at a time when Amtrak had engines that would go 100 miles per hour and long stretches of track that would allow speeds of only 15 miles per hour. We were on one of those low-speed stretches when I decided to go stand on the platform at the end of the last car in the train. Over the door leading to the platform was a sign reading "Do not stand on the platform while train is in motion." But the opportunity was too good to pass up. The train was not moving fast and we were going through a particularly lovely bit of country: low hills with late winter patches of snow; bare trees silhouetted against low lying clouds; mists swirling up around the train. I was standing on the platform enjoying the romantic melancholy of the scene when an Amtrak conductor joined me. I expected a heated discussion about the reasonableness of Amtrak regulations. But no. He did nothing more than smile and nod politely. Eventually we began to talk, and I commented on the scene—the hills, the clouds, the mists. He agreed that it was, indeed lovely. Then he pointed out that just inside the door leading to the platform was the men's room. And he went on: "I don't know whether you're familiar with Amtrak policy, but when the restroom is used while the train is out on the track, the toilet is simply emptied out onto the track. So actually this mist that is swirling up around your feet . . ." He didn't have to complete the statement. And we never did get around to our discussion of Amtrak regulations.

It's probably safe to assume that this Amtrak conductor had not read much rhetorical theory, but his rhetorical strategy could easily be justified by this maxim from tagmemic theory: change takes place over a bridge of shared features. That is, if we are to accomplish any communicative purpose, we must find some common ground with our readers or listeners. We must establish or appeal to some mutual knowledge, values, or goals. Only then will we have a chance of persuading, informing, gaining sympathy, entertaining, or whatever.

From my perspective, the important thing about this principle from tagmemic theory is not just that it has parallels in the work of other theorists—in Kenneth Burke's notion of identification, for example. It appeals to me because it economically accounts for the success or failure of a wide range of communications. Further, I can use it to help students understand how to structure every level of their writing, no matter whether they are concerned with an entire essay, with a section or a paragraph within that essay, or with individual sentences. In each case students can see that they need to move from what is shared or acceptable to that which is new and perhaps troublesome.

One may easily think of other powerful theoretical concepts that link apparently diverse kinds of communication. We have, for example, only begun to understand how considerations of *ethos* or *persona* influence the reading and writing not only of literary texts but also such mundane texts as day-to-day memos and letters in the world of business and industry. No matter what theoretical concepts we may choose to apply for this purpose, we must begin to act upon those choices, testing and refining those concepts and, simultaneously, informing our teaching.

This suggestion that we begin to act upon our choices leads me to conclude by making explicit an assumption that underlies everything said thus far: the maturing of the discipline presupposes the best efforts of each member of the discipline. Each of us has the responsibility to contribute to our individual and collective understanding of how people use language to communicate.

In some ways, every aspect of our discipline seems conducive to this effort. Everywhere we look, there is both the opportunity and the means to contribute to the advancement of knowledge in our field. As a discipline, we may be unique in that the phenomena of our daily experience can be the source of basic knowledge. Moreover, some of our best current work implies that all of us should be contributing to the development of our discipline. Much of our theory, our research, and our pedagogy emphasizes the importance of each individual's engaging in the process of discovery. When our students ask us "What do you want?" in response to a particular assignment, we become cautious, even evasive. We assume that it is the responsibility of individual writers to discover for themselves the insights they will convey through their writing. We acknowledge the difficulty of this process, but we affirm that it is inherently rewarding. And certainly we feel gratified when we see our students engage successfully in that process.

For our students, then, we assume that the process of creating and revising meaning is something that is not only good for them but essential to their development as writers. The same assumption also applies to each of us. We may or may not think of ourselves as theorists or researchers. No matter. As teachers, our goal is not simply to convey knowledge but to help others learn to construct their own meaning. We accomplish this goal not simply by the exercises we use in class but by the example of our own intellectual growth. As we provide this example, we contribute to our own development as individual thinkers and teachers. And that, finally, is the best hope for the continued maturing of our profession.

AFTERWORD: ARE WE THERE YET? PROSPECTS FOR
A MATURING DISCIPLINE

It's been almost twenty years since I wrote this essay, arguing that our discipline was, if not mature, at least maturing, that we could speak of composition studies as a discipline in much the same way we could speak of literary studies as a discipline. At the time, Richard Larson, then the editor of *CCC*, suggested that I was a bit too optimistic. In his preface to the issue of *CCC* in which this essay appeared, Dick argued that our field lacked "a unifying conceptual framework, distinctive patterns of inquiry, and established standards of judgment about scholarship that many practitioners uphold" (394).

Over the years, I learned that it was a mistake to disregard what Dick Larson said, so I'll spend most of this short piece agreeing with him. As a profession, we engage in a kind of serial monogamy. We embrace one conceptual framework, then another, and then another, each time talking as though we have indeed found the love of our professional lives. Early in the relatively short life of the Conference on College Composition and Communication, we began to renounce what I. A. Richards once called the "post-card's-worth of crude common sense" found in composition textbooks of his era. Empirical work by scholars such as Francis Christensen, Richard Braddock, and Janet Emig showed us just how crude this common sense was: not all paragraphs had to have topic sentences; not all writers created careful outlines before writing. The work of these scholars marked the beginning of what some have called "the golden age of composition studies," a time when experimentation and, later, naturalistic observation promised to undergird the teaching of composition.

But by the late 1980s, this empirical work came to be labeled "positivistic" and was supplanted by work in critical theory, a form of scholarship that has held sway almost until the present time. At its best, this critical theory challenged the epistemology of some empirical work, arguing that knowledge was contingent, shaped by language and culture. At its worst, this period of scholarship replaced the "post-card's-worth of crude common sense" with the concept of "lore," a concept no more carefully articulated than the unexamined precepts Richards found in textbooks of an earlier time.

More recently still, Judith Harris has argued that some composition scholars are abandoning the "cultural studies approach" and turning to a "psychoanalytic paradigm" that sees writing as a means of psychological growth, "help[ing] students to achieve mastery over fear, prejudice, and intolerance through self-examination" (669). Will this prove to be the wave of the future? Maybe. Maybe not. But there will be a new wave. We can be certain of that.

Or almost certain. While we seem to transfer most of our professional affections almost willy-nilly (calling them paradigm shifts rather than inconstancy), we haven't entirely escaped our past. In September 2004, the *English Journal* devoted an entire issue to "Teaching Writing in the 21st Century." In that issue, three of the major articles argued about the merits of the five-paragraph theme. *The five-paragraph theme?* This is one of the major issues confronting composition specialists in the twenty-first century? What about ways students will have to communicate in the digital environment—not just e-mail but Web design? What about the role of visual information in print documents? What shall we tell students about new multimedia genres— documentaries, for example—that digital technology makes readily accessible to even very young writers? And how do we assess these new forms of communicative work?

Do I sound just the least bit cranky? OK, fair enough. But it's not because of what *English Journal* did or didn't do. Rather it's because the cartoon character Pogo had it right: "We have met the enemy and it is us." At least where conceptual frameworks are concerned, we have been too fickle in our disciplinary affections and—perhaps as a consequence—have not firmly established alternatives to five-paragraph themes and other elements of ill-founded disciplinary lore. We have become too fond of theory grounded in other theory, and too reluctant to think carefully about how well theory can help us understand what happens when people actually try to communicate in a variety of media.

So what happened to the optimism Dick Larson attributed to me? It's still here, buoyed in part by some relatively recent work by the "WPA Outcomes Statement for First-Year Composition." A steering committee from the Writing Programs Administrators was able to articulate a set of "common expectations, for students, of first-year composition programs" (323), including an awareness of purpose, an ability to "respond to the needs of different audiences" (323), and an understanding of "how genres shape reading and writing" (324). In some respects, these outcomes seem almost commonplace. But in the 1960s, at the beginning of my own career as a composition specialist, these outcomes would have seemed radical, completely unrelated to what we routinely did as teachers of writing.

So yes, we can make progress. Although our sense of desired outcomes will almost certainly continue to change, these outcomes are a dramatic improvement over the lore that guided the teaching of writing in the 1960s. As a profession we know more than we used to. Granted, that knowledge is incomplete, contingent, subject to ongoing revision. But limited as it is, our current knowledge helps us function better—as teachers, scholars, and writers. Further, the daily business of our professional lives gives us a way to grow in our own understanding, testing each new affection as it comes along, asking how well it helps us understand what is going on in our classes and in our own thinking and writing.

It is this stance with respect to knowledge that gives me the greatest hope for our profession. Change will continue to be rapid, and progress will always be slow. But at the center of the processes of change and progress we find ourselves and our students continually growing—testing, reflecting, refining our assumptions about teaching and learning. So are we there yet? Are we mature as a profession? Probably not, especially if maturity means a time of stasis, a time without change. Are we maturing as a profession? Quite possibly—at least as long as we continue to grow as professionals. And that's cause enough for optimism.

–LEE ODELL
Rensselaer Polytechnic
Institute

WORKS CITED

Harrington, Susanmarie, Rita Malencyzk, Irv Peckham, Keith Rhodes, and Kathleen Blake Yancey. "WPA Outcomes Statement for First-Year Composition." *College English* 63 (2001): 321–25.

Harris, Judith. "The Necessity of Mourning: Psychoanalytic Paradigms for Change and Transformation in the Composition Classroom." *College English* 65 (2003): 668–75.

Larson, Richard. "Editor's Note." *College Composition and Communication* 37.4 (1986): 394.

Richards, I. A. *The Philosophy of Rhetoric*. London: Oxford, 1936.

1987 *Issues, Perspectives and Possibilities*

MIRIAM T. CHAPLIN

First, a piece of personal writing.

Dear CCCC Chair:

Please share this letter with other composition teachers who may be in a predicament similar to mine.

I've tried very hard to be an effective composition teacher but I'm afraid that I am a total failure. At the end of last semester, my students in Composition 102 took the sophomore level test and 65% failed. Because the failure rate of the students was so high, I was required to take a competency test which I failed because it had math and logic in it. As a result, I lost my job and with it my insurance and pension. My house, car, Visa, American Express and Discover cards are all gone. I cannot get unemployment because I was fired.

I became mentally ill when I lost my job and used Medicaid to get into a hospital. I was only allowed to stay for 90 days and since I had nowhere to go, I became a street person. Fortunately, it is warm in Florida.

Now, Ms. CCCC Chair, that I've told you the worst, I must confess that most of this has not happened yet. But it may unless you can tell me what to do. I wrote this kind of letter because I wanted to focus your attention on my problems.

I am a non-tenured composition teacher in a large university. I teach 4 classes 4 days a week and spend two hours in the writing lab each of the four days. There is no time for me to do any kind of research and yet, I will not be tenured without it. Of course, I might not be tenured if I had publications because my institution has little respect for publications in composition.

This article is a revision of the Chair's address Miriam T. Chaplin delivered at the CCCC Convention in Atlanta, Georgia, on March 19, 1987. It was first published in *CCC*, volume 39, number 1, February 1988.

As bad as my professional life is, my performance as a teacher is worse. I seem to be unable to get even a third of my students to write an acceptable essay. I don't understand these students. They are not responsive to me at all. They will have to pass a sophomore level test and I am terribly afraid that most will indeed fail. Teachers at my institution will be held accountable for the performance of their students on this test.

I thought I was lucky to get a job after graduate school even though I earn little more than minimum wage. Now, however, I am so confused and overwhelmed, I'm not so sure. What can I do? Please help me.

Distressed composition teacher in Florida

The issues this letter raises affect all composition teachers directly or indirectly and the resolution of these issues may have a strong impact on the future of composition. Therefore, in the pages that follow I'd like to explore some of the current issues which impinge upon our discipline, discuss various perspectives and suggest possible actions that may help this composition teacher to understand and to cope with her situation.

THE ISSUES

The complex problems which interfere with the teaching-learning process as well as the professional well-being of composition teachers are not isolated. Composition is a part of higher education and the persistent problems in composition are tied to larger issues in the world, in our country, in higher education generally and in each academic institution specifically. We can never ignore the social, economic and political issues that frame education and our discipline.

The world is not the same place it was two decades ago when we began trying to explain why Johnny and Jesse could not read and write. America's image and role in today's world are insecure. Our government's responses to the questions of nuclear war, disarmament and peace, its irresponsible Iran-gate behavior, and blunders in Nicaragua and Libya all indicate that our president may be fantasizing when he says that we are better off as a nation today than we were yesterday.

Closer to home are the problems of economic upheaval which cause whole industries to dwindle or disappear carrying with them traditional jobs and institutions such as the family farm. An equally dangerous problem is the tumorous growth of the national deficit which makes America for the first time in our history a debtor nation. Present economic conditions indicate that in the future America will have to make drastic changes in its relations with other nations as well as in what it will expect from its citizens and what it will be able to offer them in exchange.

Social dislocations evident through aberrations such as drug abuse, family breakdowns, and the emergence of new incurable diseases diminish the American dream for large sectors of the population and blur the old notions that age, race, income and education are true social determinants. These national and international problems compel us to realize that the world is not only different today, but that it is not likely ever to return to what had been considered normal.

Every institution in our society and everyone involved with these institutions must confront the current issues and the complex variables they create as well as the new moralities and philosophies they spawn. We must be prepared for the possibility that the political, economic and social conditions of our society may lead to a redefinition of the meaning and role of education, particularly what we call literacy and the ways we teach people to be literate. The responses of colleges and universities to these new imperatives for change will be reflected in the kinds of students we will teach, the curriculum to which we will adhere and the way we will evaluate what was learned.

THE STUDENTS

Since the 1960s, college student populations have become extremely diverse. The increased number of Black, economically disadvantaged, bilingual and non-English speaking, veterans, women and physically handicapped students has created a new meaning of the term "college student." Admitting these students more than a decade ago led to changes in many aspects of higher education and caused latent myths and prejudices to surface. Of all the feelings aroused by the presence of these new students, none was so pervasive as the fear of eroding academic standards. Test scores gave credence to this fear and provided a means for categorically identifying the students. Colleges used admissions test scores to label many of these students remedial, developmental, marginal, below college level or high risk. These labels were believed to be true definitions of the students instead of the metaphors they really were. "Bonehead" was a colloquial term used to describe not only the writing course to which these students were assigned, but the students in the course as well.

College student populations today are somewhat different. They include fewer Black and Hispanic students, but more women, older and foreign students. Discussions about declining standards persist. But such discussions are complicated by shrinking budgets, declining enrollments and impending shortages in the traditional college-age population. The demographics show that by the year 2020, ethnic minorities will comprise a sizeable majority of the high school graduating classes in the major cities of the United States. Thus, those who predicted that the student diversity of the 1960s was but a wave that would soon ebb were inaccurate. Available student applicants will ensure diversity well into the future.

Students in the 1980s are not the idealistic revolutionaries of the 1960s. Neither are they the egocentric laissez-faire individuals of the 1970s. Students today have a future orientation that was not characteristic of earlier populations. Many of today's students have had far more experiences outside of formal education than they have had inside of it. A large percentage are independent and receive no financial support from parents. They attend college under the strain of a depressed economy and an extreme scarcity of governmental financial assistance. This kind of financial difficulty has created a sense of urgency in students and caused some of them to view their college education as a very serious affair.

Within this generation of students, there are those who have had severe educational, social and economic disadvantages. In many cases, the academic preparation of these students is limited and they are lacking the skills needed for effective communication in the academic world. In spite of this limitation, however, these students are intolerant of practice exercises and repetitive "dummy runs," to borrow Britton's term from *Language and Learning* (130). They are seeking meaningful learning experiences which allow them to relate instruction to their personal lives. Today's students adapt well to classrooms which are democratized communities of learners including the teacher. The identification of effective strategies and methodologies that will attract, stimulate, and retain this diversified group of students is a primary issue facing all institutions in higher education.

In fact, colleges today compete for the kinds of students who, two decades ago, would have been considered only for special programs, most of which did not lead to regular college degrees. In the past, the challenge to institutions of higher education was to open the door wide enough for these non-traditional students to enter, but today, colleges must reconsider the principles of democracy by making it possible for the so-called high-risk students to be educated. In other words, those days when to be a great college meant to be elitist and exclusive are gone. A great academic institution in the future will be judged by its ability to succeed in educating all of its students. You may be thinking, "There's nothing new about that." I submit to you that for higher education in America, there is much new about the matter of educating all the students.

THE CURRICULUM

The goal of most liberal arts colleges and universities as it is usually stated in their promotional materials is to acquaint students with a well-balanced program of study in fine arts, humanities, social sciences and natural sciences. Seldom do these statements commit an institution to the development of students' abilities. Thus, it is easy to conclude from the stated objectives of colleges and universities that their mission is to certify students—not to educate them. Education is a process which includes teaching, experiencing, learning, adapting, changing, creating and maturing. Education involves students in learning experiences designed to help them to develop their innate abilities to create new knowledge, to turn visions into real possibilities, to find out that they can make a difference and that making a difference matters. Certification is a process of confirming—usually it means confirming that a student has passed a certain number of prescribed courses and has achieved acceptable grades. Certification may have little to do with being educated. The issue of education as certification is the driving force behind the controversy of whether to include developmental education in college curriculums. The resolution of this controversy is of great concern to composition teachers because much of our work is developmental.

Those who believe that certification is the mission of higher education see composition courses as battlefields where competency wars are fought. The victorious students move on to higher level courses; the losers are forced out. Those, on the other hand, who believe that colleges and universities exist to educate all students perceive of composition as an integral part of higher education. They believe that skills and content are inextricably intertwined and exist mutually in a college curriculum. To this group, composition courses are not skill laboratories or battlefields; they are colloquiums where students learn to use language to form verbal transactions between their peers, the teacher and themselves.

The existence of these two perspectives on the mission of higher education and its responsibilities to students is closely related to the on-going struggle within our profession about the separation of composition and literature—a debate that is as pedagogical as it is political. Composition teachers are not the central focus of this debate because in many cases composition teachers and literature teachers are one and the same persons. It is composition as a developmental activity that is a bane to traditional English departments. Removing composition from such departments will not elevate its image in the minds of the English faculty who deplore the inclusion of developmental studies in higher education. A separation could, however, trigger a schizophrenic reaction in those literature teachers who have learned to enjoy and respect the teaching of composition.

THE NATIONAL STATUS-OF-EDUCATION REPORTS

For most of American educational history, higher education has escaped the scathing condemnations heaped upon lower levels of education by the general public. College teachers were protected from criticism because of the idea of academic freedom. Recently, this has changed; the current reform movement includes educational institutions at all levels. Spurred by an emphasis on and legislative initiatives for educational excellence, the call of national status-of-education reports on reform in colleges and universities is receiving widespread attention.

Generally, the reports start from the premise that much is wrong with higher education in America and that educational problems are partly responsible for the decline of the American image as a world leader. The reports criticize institutions for their lack of structure and depth in course content. They recommend the curtailment of specialization in undergraduate education and a return to basic liberal arts. The reports do not prescribe specific courses, but there is no doubt that they support a more traditional curriculum orientation.

Integrity in the College Curriculum, a status report on higher education prepared by the Association of American Colleges, addresses the issue of the preparation of college teachers. Stating that faculties in higher education are ill-prepared to meet the needs of students because they have had no training in methodology, the report recommends that graduate schools in all disciplines include instructional procedures in their course offerings. According to the report, service as a teaching assistant is the only preparation that most college teachers receive and the report speaks disparagingly about the use of teaching assistants. The report states: "The teaching assistantship is now a device for exploiting graduate students in order to relieve senior faculty from teaching undergraduates. The tradition in higher education is to award the degree and then turn the students loose to become teachers without training in teaching, or equally as ridiculous, to send the students off without degrees, with unfinished research and incomplete dissertations hanging over their heads while they wrestle with the responsibilities of learning how to teach. Only in higher education is it generally assumed that teachers need no preparation, no supervision, no introduction to teaching" (35).

These status reports on higher education are of great concern to the administrations and faculties of colleges and universities because they have been released at a time when student recruitment and retention are crucial to the survival of the institutions, when budgets are in retrenchment, and when other critical issues demand attention. Some of the other issues are as complex as the issues raised in the reports. For instance, most colleges and universities have a sort of three-tiered faculty. There are the senior tenured faculty who will soon retire and the junior faculty, victims of the late 1960s and early 1970s retrenchment, who became and remain academic gypsies. Increased standards and the general decline in the number of tenured positions will probably prevent many in this group from ever achieving tenure and replacing retired faculty. The third tier is composed of part-time faculty who balance the college budget, but never get into tenure-bearing or even full-time positions. The issues of instability generated from this kind of three-ring faculty circus are added to such matters as the role of athletics in higher education and the effects of the blossoming electronic and fiber optic communication systems. All of these issues interact with each other and are compounded. They lead inevitably to the issue of accountability. Accountability generates several questions about who is to be accountable and to whom accountability is due—the faculties? the students? the trustees? the government? the public? or all of the above?

EVALUATION

As accountability becomes more of an issue, there is an alarming increase in the use of standardized tests to measure what students learn as a result of instruction. In addition to statewide admissions tests in public institutions, several states are now requiring junior and senior level examinations. These assessments are designed to measure an institution's effectiveness in educating students as well as the students' abilities to perform. Testing is as much a burning issue in higher education today as it was in secondary and elementary schools a decade ago. The basic hypothesis of value-added testing, as it is called, is that objective tests can measure students' mastery of prerequisite knowledge and skills at the beginning of a course of study and are equally effective for determining how much additional knowledge was added during the course. Proponents of this method apparently assume that knowledge and skills are commodities that can be piled on top of other knowledge and skills much as one might place linens in a closet.

Many composition teachers oppose the measurement of students' progress in reading and writing with standardized testing instruments. Composition teachers view language development as a recursive process that unfolds in concert with students' cognitive, emotional and physical development. Evaluation of this process is necessary as an accompaniment to instruction, but effective evaluation involves much more than standardized tests have to offer.

First, objective tests splinter the writing process into specific measurable skills. Essay tests, scored holistically, are improved alternatives to objective tests, but an essay written as a writing sample is produced on demand in an artificial timed situation. Writing tests allow few opportunities for students to revise, edit or even reflect on what is written. Yet, writing produced under these conditions is often used to place students in composition classes and, even more disturbing, it is viewed by some teachers as a true example of students' writing abilities.

Standardized measurement of students' progress in reading is also an anathema to composition teachers. Most of the questions included in reading tests are "pre-digested." These questions call for interpretations of written material as seen through the eyes of the person who writes the questions rather than the interpretations of the students being tested. Therefore, reading tests actually measure the adaptability of students to the values and thought processes of the test developer, but the students' own abilities to interpret and question written material often remain unknown.

Language as an expression of experience is at once individual and group inspired. Students' language behaviors reveal the students' world views of reality accumulated through many different social, academic and cultural associations. Martin Buber said it best in *Between Man and Man:* "Experience comes to man as I, but it is as experience as we that he builds the common world in which he lives" (46). Even when students are reading and writing apart from other students, they are not alone. Their backgrounds of experiences are with them. George Kelly cautions, however, that students are not victims of their biographies. They are always free to alter their perceptions of realities and shift their behaviors away from former perceptions and experiences (15).

Tests which measure and document students' behaviors at a given time in a given situation under prescribed conditions provide a useful barometer of language behaviors in a particular circumstance. However, when this information is used to infer and predict language behaviors in other situations under different conditions, it may be misleading. As learning occurs, students may alter their perceptions and thus, their behaviors. A trained observer can measure language development by carefully scrutinizing students' alteration processes over a period of time. It is toward this kind of sustained evaluation of language development that testing needs to be directed.

POSSIBILITIES FOR CHANGE

Indeed, a myriad of issues impinges directly or indirectly on the teaching of composition in our colleges and universities. Some of the issues are difficult and full of inconsistencies. They will require radical changes and we may not see the result of those changes until another generation goes through college. But other issues are fairly obvious and straightforward. If we put these issues into perspective, I believe we can suggest some possibilities to our distressed colleague in Florida.

Diversity in student population, one of the issues raised in the status reports on higher education, should not be an insurmountable problem because composition teachers are no strangers to diversity. A brief glance at a CCCC convention program gives a cursory view of the diversity within our ranks. Composition includes rhetoricians, theorists, poets, historians, philosophers, reading specialists, speech therapists and computer programmers. The composition teacher's work is not confined to English Departments, and college students are not necessarily our only clients. Composition teachers can be found in several departments on college campuses; we are even called upon to teach colleagues in other disciplines how to teach and evaluate writing.

Beyond the walls of the academy are large corporations, health and legal agencies, prisons and government installations that require the services of composition teachers. Through these expanded horizons, we gain exposure to many different student populations in varied circumstances. These populations, in which there is a kaleidoscope of learning styles and cultural orientations, allow composition teachers to gain valuable experiences in educating diversified student populations.

We can use these experiences to accommodate student differences in our college classrooms by broadening the scope of materials used in instruction. Composition is not context-bound. Students cannot read reading or write writing. The content of composition is open-ended and should be chosen from many fields. Though some composition teachers, almost without exception, use literary models to teach reading and writing, literary models do not fit all content or the learning styles of all students. The same can be said for the expository essay—the only form of writing taught in some composition classes. The expository essay should be supplemented with other modes of writing which may be more compatible with the writing assignments students must complete in other disciplines.

In the same class, some students can be required to engage in original research into problems that interest them and to report their findings in writing. Other students can write position papers and give their opinions on current topics. Different textbooks and materials as well as differentiated assignments can be used within a class. Lesson planning should have the same level of diversity as the students in the class.

Composition teachers need to move away from the model of instruction based on skill proficiency or the lack of it toward a model based on students' experiential backgrounds. The skill proficiency model leads to a homogeneous identification of students. To be proficient, all students must know the same skills and be able to use them in the same way. The skill proficiency model works against diversity. The experiential background model, on the other hand, starts from the premise that each student has had experiences, but each student's experiences differ from those of other students. Experiences differ in kind, scope and intensity of effect; they can be negative and positive. Experiential differences give rise to the diversity that is inherent in students. When instruction is planned on the basis of students' positive experiences, it can capitalize on strengths instead of weaknesses. The experiential model does not portend an abdication of academic standards. Indeed, we should never abandon standards. We need, however, to make sure that the students' right to relevant instruction is not ignored as we set the standards they are expected to attain.

In his Chair's Address at the 1986 meeting of the CCCC, Lee Odell reminded us that "we are maturing as a discipline." As we grow, we must move away from the narrow perception of composition as writing. Composition includes reading, listening and speaking as well as writing. The receptive and expressive language operations are so closely related that a separation is impossible. As composition teachers make strides toward understanding the writing process, we must employ the same kind of vigorous effort to understand the processes of reading, listening and speaking and to appreciate the ways these strands of communication interact with each other. New research into the physiology of the brain and the nervous system as well as new discoveries in electronic media will provide necessary information and clearer understandings of the wholeness of communication and what that means for us in the classroom. Since words determine the ways we perceive realities, perhaps the time will soon come when we will consider the fact that the name of this organization (College Composition and Communication) suggests a separation between composition and communication. There is no such separation.

Composition teachers must close the chasm which separates us from the mainstream of education. CCCC has initiated a new committee to form links between composition teachers in secondary schools and colleges. This is an idea whose time has come, for communication with secondary schools is one of the ways we can have an effect on students' reading and writing development before they enter college.

We must be equally as concerned with the college students in teacher-preparation programs. The majority of the students who select English as a major course of study will become high school English teachers. If these English majors follow the traditional pattern of teacher preparation, they will not know how to teach writing. Yet high school English teachers must teach writing as well as literature. Many composition teachers at the college level are excellent resources for writing methodology. Beyond the freshman year, however, prospective teachers may have no contact with composition teachers. This is harmful to prospective teachers because it causes a serious gap in their preparation, but it is equally bad for composition teachers. These high school teachers will be responsible for preparing the future college students. Making sure that they are capable of doing an effective job will have the long-range effect of improving the performance of college student populations.

CONCLUSION

Preparing teachers to cope with diversity and identifying appropriate content, methodology and means of evaluating instruction and learning are the core issues in the new reform movement in higher education. These issues stand in the shadow of larger issues outside of higher education. We cannot escape the immediate issues or the more elusive ones as we search for resolutions to problems that affect the teaching of composition. Issues are resolved through positive change, and change must be made by people. Too often in American education, change is precipitated by people who operate outside educational institutions. We are currently on the brink of forced change, but the impetus can be slowed if composition teachers take the reins of their own destinies and become change agents inside and outside of their own institutions. We must structure our profession to take advantage of the potential power that is within our grasp. We must see ourselves not only as scholars but as political activists as well.

I will write to "Distressed Composition Teacher in Florida," and among other things, I will say this: "I have shared your letter with members of the Conference on College Composition and Communication. Your colleagues and I understand your problems because they are our problems as well. It is unlikely that we will be successful in solving all of the problems before us because many of them stem from the roots of issues far beyond our classrooms. However, the success of our profession and your personal success in the classroom depend on a bold confrontation of the issues that affect the teaching of composition, on the experience and knowledge that we gain as we put those issues into perspective and on our collective courage to turn possibilities into realities."

WORKS CITED

Association of American Colleges. *Integrity in the College Curriculum: A Report to the Academic Community*. 1985.

Britton, James. *Language and Learning*. Baltimore: Penguin, 1972.

Buber, Martin. *Between Man and Man*. London: Routledge & Kegan Paul, 1947.

Kelly, George. "Man's Construction of His Alternatives." *Clinical Psychology and Personality: The Selected Papers of George Kelly*. Ed. Brandon Maher. New York: John Wiley and Sons, 1969.

Odell, Lee. "A Maturing Discipline." Chair's Address. CCCC Convention. New Orleans, 13 March 1986.

AFTERWORD: FROM A DISTANCE

In 1987, I chose to begin my Chair's address with a letter from a composition teacher. The letter included references to the teacher's problematic situation. As I read the letter, I realized that the problems were not limited to that specific situation but were issues for the profession as a whole. Today, as I read and hear about CCCC, it is clear not only that the problems persist but that they are more profound.

Composition teachers continue to be second-class citizens in their institutions. Social, economic, and related issues that are paramount in American society frame the lives of today's composition teachers. While the issues are some of the same ones that I mentioned in the 1980s, composition teachers are dwarfed by America's fear of terrorist attacks, a war that directly touches the lives of many of the nation's students, and a federal deficit that practically destroys any hope of additional educational funding. In addition, they must confront widespread problems of communicable diseases, family dysfunctions, and violence on and around university campuses, as well as demand for more tolerance toward various sexual lifestyles.

Composition is central to all of these issues because language reflects students' responses to the world around them. Therefore, while NCTE and CCCC have made many attempts to bring our organizations into the mainstream of American life, I am not sure that enough teachers at the college level have realized the relationship of students' realities to their performances in composition. I am sure, however, that if there are teachers who, in Kurt Spellmeyer's words, are "squirming helplessly under the weight of tradition" (170) by holding on to the comforts that were once enjoyed, they are detached from the public world and are out of step. These methods are no longer practical or possible. Our only hope of involving students in the language arts on which composition is based is the development of new ideas that students can use to understand and relate to the situations that impinge upon their lives.

Some of the readers of this reflection will remember my constant reference to the need for sensitivity to the diversity of our students and the necessity for us to include reading, talking, and listening in our composition discussions. The diversity is still there though it may be affected by a reduction in an availability of funds for matriculation. However, composition teachers are still on the front line of contact with all students.

During the first two years of my retirement, I taught a course as an adjunct instructor at the Beaufort campus of the University of South Carolina. The students did not differ from those I had taught previously at Rutgers University in New Jersey. Then I was invited to teach English 102 at a two-year college near the Parris Island Marine Base. The students in that class were indeed diverse. In addition to the students who worked full-time jobs and were tired when they came to school, there were students who had no jobs because they did not possess the skills needed to get jobs. Primarily, the women were single mothers, and the men were marines, married and unmarried, who came from various parts of the country. The marines did not know when they would be shipped to Iraq and uncertain about their futures. There was only one student who had recently graduated from high school.

In teaching these students to express themselves in written language, I saw a real need for them to get to know one another. I did not ask them to write until I had developed trust among us that led to a comfort level on which they could write. Once they knew their classmates and me, they were eager to write about ideas and situations that they could not talk about. It was only then that I could begin to teach the skills that the college demanded. Students learned to weave the skills into their written and spoken narratives and to blend these skills into selections that they were required to read. By the end of the semester, most of the students were aware of what they needed to learn.

Some of the readers of this reflection may remember my insistence in CCCC that reading and listening be afforded a place equal to writing. Indeed, the inclusion of language arts, the diversity of students, and the involvement of the organization in the real world were the themes that I stressed as Chair and as a member of various committees.

CCCC was my first home in NCTE. I joined the organization because I needed to meet professionals with whom I could share my research interests while I became familiar with theirs. I met people who became lifelong friends— researchers and writers whom I respect. We were able to share our assessments of why we were there, how we could survive, and where we needed to go. It was indeed a worthwhile experience.

Now I write from a distance. Often a distance allows one to reflect on past actions without the passion and sense of responsibility that accompanies active participation. Retirement makes it all possible.

—MIRIAM T. CHAPLIN, EMERITA
Rutgers University

WORK CITED

Spellmeyer, Kurt. *Arts of Living: Reinventing the Humanities for the Twenty-First Century*. Albany: State U of New York, 2003.

1988

Freshman English, Composition, and CCCC

DAVID BARTHOLOMAE

P ROLOGUE

When I was invited to run for office in CCCC, like all candidates I had to put together a short statement of principle or belief for the ballot—a kind of mini-stump speech where I would set out my sense of the organization and its mission. This was a hard piece to write—"what I believe" in 200 words—and particularly hard for me since (frankly) I thought no one ever read them, that when the ballots came in the mail, people looked at the pictures, read the c.v., and pitched the rest.

And so I was taken by the number of people who have since come up to speak to me about what I wrote. I said, in brief, that I felt a great debt to CCCC, that at an early point in my career, when I felt like I was looking in as an outsider on the vast and austere corridors of adult professional life, CCCC provided a sense of community that made me believe I could get started—that there was, in fact, work for me to do, that it was good work, and that I could do it in good company. My graduate program did not give me this sense of vocation. My department could provide only a portion. No other professional organization seemed so open.

I said in that document that I felt CCCC was the organization that made work in composition possible—and in saying that, I felt its truth in the context of my personal history. I did not mean—although I could have been saying—that CCCC had or should have the authority to order or authorize work in composition, that it should determine the canon, approve methods, say Yes to some and No to others, accredit programs, unify a field that was various and disparate. I meant that CCCC (and in particular the annual meeting) seemed to me to provide the terms and context that

This article is a revised version of the Chair's address David Bartholomae delivered at the CCCC Convention in St. Louis, Missouri, on March 17, 1988. It was first published in *CCC*, volume 40, number 1, February 1989.

allowed people to get to work, and to work with energy and optimism, not cranking out just one more paper, not laddering their way up to the top, not searching for difficult texts and dull readers, not bowing and scraping before another famous book or another famous person, but doing work that one could believe in, where there was that rare combination of personal investment and social responsibility, where we felt like we could make things happen, not just in our own careers, but in the world.[1]

I can be more precise: I had just finished a dissertation on Thomas Hardy, and I could not imagine writing another paper on Hardy or the Victorians or the subjects I had presumably mastered in graduate school. I had also established a basic writing program, and the writing of my students and the problematic relationship between their work and the work of the academy; these seemed to hold all of the material I needed to make a career. I felt that in the ways people talked to each other at meetings, and that in the ways they talked about their subjects—writing and teaching—there was clearly room being made for me to get started on that career.

I was surprised at the number of people who spoke to me about those words and who said, in effect, that in saying what I did I was speaking for them. This set me to thinking about history and about generations: the people who founded CCCC; the generation of men and women, many of them now retired or on the eve of retirement, who reshaped its language and agenda in embattled times, in the 60's and 70's; and my generation, like the organization, just now reaching middle age.

I have spent much of the last year reading over the documentary record of CCCC—articles, essays, speeches, papers, secretary's reports, accounts from the "roving reporter" who, for several years, was assigned to take notes and report to the membership on the annual convention. I found it a wonderful experience. The documents are rich and various. I have been "in" composition for some time, but I had little sense of its history, particularly the history represented by the people and issues that filled the rooms of our meetings and the pages of our journal. I wanted to account for CCCC as an agent, since I had experienced it so sharply as a force in my own career. What follows is a preliminary version of that account, where CCCC stands as an organized and organizing way of speaking and thinking, with both stated and unstated projects, including the necessary project of defining and protecting its claim to a subject, what we have variously called "required English," "freshman English," and "composition."

FRESHMAN ENGLISH

CCCC was born out of the need to have a certain kind of discussion that existing venues were not making possible (not NCTE, not MLA). In fact, 4C's could be said literally to begin in a conversation that would not fit into the 1948 annual meeting of NCTE.

In 1948, NCTE featured a series of sessions on "College Undergraduate Training" at its national convention in the Stevens Hotel in Chicago. One session, on "Three Views of Required English," was chaired by John Gerber (who was to become the first chair of CCCC) and during the session one of the speakers, George Wykoff (who would become the second chair of CCCC) set aside his prepared remarks (a description of his institution's freshman course) to speak about the usefulness and value of composition. Wilbur Hatfield referred to Wykoff's impromptu remarks as "a clarion call to the profession to alert itself to improving the climate for the teaching of freshman English."[2]

The story goes that the resulting discussion was so lively and contentious that the session went well over its allotted time and threatened to keep the participants from the annual banquet, where James Michener, who had just won the Pulitzer Prize for *Tales of the South Pacific*, was scheduled to speak. The group was hesitant to let the conversation end; they complained that they were not given adequate time and wouldn't be silenced until Gerber suggested that they continue the discussion at a special conference the following spring. A committee of seven petitioned the Executive Committee of NCTE to sponsor a special 2-day conference on freshman English.[3] The proposal was approved, and the next spring—in Chicago, in 1949—500 people met to talk and read papers at a conference on "College Freshman Courses in Composition and Communication."

This was the first meeting of CCCC, even though the organization had not yet been given a name or official status. At this meeting participants unanimously passed a resolution supporting the formation of a permanent organization devoted to freshman English. Gerber presented this request to NCTE—this time requesting a separate annual meeting, a separate governing body, and a journal. After much discussion, this request was approved by NCTE at its November meeting in Buffalo in 1949.

And so CCCC became part of the council, but also a semi-independent entity. Here is John Gerber commenting on the moment in "CCCC Facts—1956":

> In true progressive fashion [CCCC] was told to do the things that would make it happy and well adjusted and not to do the things that would make it unhappy. Also, it was told that at the end of three years it might be annihilated if it had not been good. (117)

It turned out to be good enough, and at the end of its three-year trial period it was given a second three-year term; following that trial period, NCTE changed its constitution to make the conference a permanent entity. At this point CCCC established a procedure for elections and appointed a representative executive committee, drawing equally from universities, liberal arts colleges, teachers colleges, technical schools, and junior colleges. By 1950 it had a membership of 550, representing 48 states, Hawaii, and the District of Columbia.

This is the history, in brief. But it doesn't provide a satisfactory answer to the question "Why?" Why was it necessary to imagine freshman English as separate—as different enough from the other English, or the other Englishes represented in the curriculum, to require a separate professional organization?

For one thing, those responsible for freshman English felt the need to respond to two pressures, both of which threatened their interests. The first was, in John Gerber's terms, "the common enemy . . . the senior professor of literature" (*Loomings* 7). This figure is almost too familiar—this senior professor of literature. The terms we now commonly use to define college English would give prominence to the word "literature" in Gerber's statement. Against literature, that is, freshman English asserted itself as composition.

I think we need to read this differently, however. While it is true that the organization, with its need to name itself and its subject, displaced freshman "English" with freshman "composition and communication," there was much debate in the early meetings over whether composition or communication or something else altogether was the proper subject for CCCC. And the motive here was largely to make a place for a new set of interests, not merely to erase the old ones.

I think that the key word in Gerber's sentence is "senior"—the "*senior* professor of literature." The "common enemy," that is, was a version of English represented by an attenuated humanistic tradition that placed literature (a Norton-anthology-like unified body of texts) as an unquestionable center of value, and that placed the professor, who could demonstrate acceptable ways of using and responding to those texts, as the primary representative of English.

The other pressure was the pressure of numbers—the numbers of students, many of them GI's, swelling colleges and universities after the war, placing dramatic and unprecedented demands on introductory courses (courses they were said to be "unprepared to take") and requiring the creation of a new faculty to do a teaching for which their English PhD's had not prepared them. There were also, then, economic and culture forces poised to redefine English in post-secondary education.

Given these threats to the freshman course, and given the desire to do something with English and do something for students for whom the old English was an inadequate or inappropriate form of instruction, there was good cause to band together, pool information and resources, and (1) develop an agenda to give status and recognition to those teaching freshman English, (2) revise the graduate training of prospective teachers of English, and, most importantly, (3) work on developing this course, freshman English, a course without a proper subject or history—one whose name, freshman English, was an open term, indeterminate and, therefore, both inspiring and frightening.

In the documents that mark the first 15 years of CCCC, you hear this refrain over and over again: no one knows, on any given day on any given campus, what goes on in freshman English; it's there as a force on every campus, it carries a common name, but it refers to everything, anything—no one knows what it is. There was no way of speaking about reading and writing at the introductory level, where it was not yet shaped into English, no way to fix the discourse, to give the institution the feeling that it had this course in control. Everyone knew what went on in "The American Novel" or "18th Century British Literature," but this other English course was a black hole. And this was simultaneously CCCC's greatest problem—to give standards, unity, and definition to this course—and its greatest attraction, since it put its members in a position to make up English as they went along.

COMPOSITION

Having emptied English, the organization had to try to fill it again. In this gesture what came to be called "composition" participated in a project that has come to characterize modern English studies. The CCCC project paralleled developments in criticism—and in particular the New Criticism, whose beginning moment was similarly a rejection of the senior professors of literature. Criticism, as a new way of imagining how to do English, was similarly going to revive pedagogy and relocate English in the immediate experience students had with texts (that is, in the practice of reading).

This is the history I imagine, that since the 1940's there has been a continuing struggle to displace the old humanism—with its entrenched theories of knowledge, culture and pedagogy—and to replace the English of the senior professors with a new English. The opposing term for composition, then, is not literature but a version of literary study threatened not only by composition but by other critical movements in the discipline: women's studies, black studies, film studies, gay studies, critical theory, culture study, studies of working-class language and literature, pedagogy. CCCC provided a site where English was open for negotiation (or renegotiation).

Let's look briefly at the two opening talks of the first CCCC convention. I don't mean to suggest that these two talks fully represent the issues occupying the organization. Nor do I want to suggest that these two figures shaped the organization and its concerns. I want to take this moment, one that was shaped and enabled by CCCC, and use it as an example of the possibilities for representing "English" in this new place, under the aegis of this new professional organization. I'm interested in the speakers as speakers, not figures in an intellectual history.

The speakers were Richard Weaver and James McCrimmon. McCrimmon, the first to speak, cast this session as a debate (it is hard to tell whether Weaver was aware of this in advance and whether he was a willing participant), and in doing so he identified Weaver as a representative of that "English" that the new organization was poised to question or replace.[4] His point of reference was Weaver's recent *College English* article, "To Write the Truth" (10 [Oct. 1948]: 25–30). Weaver anticipated an argument in his talk, but it was not the argument he got from McCrimmon.

Weaver's talk, "Composition as a Liberal Art," was grounded in the commonplaces of the humanistic tradition. (It has a familiar ring; the language is current in today's debate on the academy and the humanities.) Weaver argued that a proper education in language can lead to a unified culture, a refined, moral sensibility, and a perception of eternal truths beyond language. Against this he posed a composition course interested only in mechanical matters, skills. He said, "And as there is a big difference between filling in blanks in a workbook and forging out of one's own chaotic thought a coherent piece of discourse, it is easier to teach the limited skill than the larger art of composition." The failure to teach the larger art was a failure of will and vision—teachers were not willing to comment on the substance of students' papers; they were not willing to take responsibility for showing students "the direction in which truth lies"; they were willing to be concerned with form and technique alone.

Surely, he said,

> it is a sign of the depth of the intellectual crisis that many have not made up their minds as to whether our colleges and universities should be centers of knowledge or centers of skepticism. I do not mean here skepticism in the sense of departing from a dogma or differing with a popular canon; I mean that skepticism which is the despair of knowledge—a feeling that one cannot know even the proximity of truth, but must, if he is a teacher, find his work in the mere churning of opinion.

And it is the study of language, he said, that can

> keep us from succumbing completely to that absurdity called "educating for a changing world." The very fact that languages carry a burden of tradition and reflect an aspiration toward logical order makes them a means of coherence and an instrument of stabilization. The work of scholars is the safeguard of continuity.

McCrimmon, on the other hand, was trying to speak for an English that took as its subject, and as its source of value, the instability of language, particularly as exemplified by the varieties of English present in the work of students.

> I think it is both absurd and detrimental to our purpose to demand that all college writing should be done at a formal level. If we judge usage by the standard of appropriateness to the occasion rather than

by an absolute standard, I think we will find that what we have lost in pedantic certainty we have gained in pedagogical effectiveness.

McCrimmon cast his argument against the notion of a single, unifying English. Can Weaver, he said, mean anything more than that "we should teach students to speak and write what has been asserted to be the truth by Plato, or Aristotle, or Thomas Aquinas, or perhaps some less remote authority?"

> If this assumption—that Truth is what the Elect say it is—is sound, the answer to what ails Freshman Composition is simple. That answer is that the course has got out of the control of the Elect and can only be saved by returning it to their control. If you believe that, you should reject the whole corpus of linguistic research, since that science is chiefly responsible for the linguistic relativism which Mr. Weaver so much deplores. If you agree with Mr. Weaver, you should denounce Bloomfield and Curme and Fries and Perrin and all other scientific grammarians, for their leadership has led us all astray. You should even withdraw from the National Council of Teachers of English, or at least purge the present membership, because the NCTE must be a most subversive organization.

On the one hand you have an argument for an idealized English with the power to unify and stabilize the culture; on the other hand, you have an argument for preserving and valuing linguistic difference.[5]

Weaver, in the *CE* article, had argued that

> Adam helped to order the universe when he dealt out these names, and let us not overlook what is implied in the assertion that the names stuck. There is an intimation of divine approval, which would frown upon capricious change.

The early work of Hayakawa and Korzybski enabled McCrimmon to imagine that the notion of a proper meaning, like the notion of a proper utterance, was available to systematic critique. If there was no necessary relationship between words and things, then there were no absolute meanings, meanings must somehow be negotiated—and that, the ways meanings and languages are negotiated individually and collectively, was what CCCC was prepared to take as its subject.

Language as an abstraction, language as practice; an idealized English, common English: these were the fundamental oppositions at play in these two speeches. This opposition is played out in any number of talks and papers in the opening years of CCCC. I could, for example, have organized a similar discussion by turning to the keynote speeches for the 2nd meeting of CCCC: Kenneth Burke's "Rhetoric—Old and New" and Rudolf Flesch's "Let's Face the Facts About Writing." CCCC enabled the expression of a fundamental anxiety about "required English," a useful anxiety that produced new ways of speaking about language, writing, and pedagogy.

The history of CCCC includes the story of repeated attempts to reconstruct a unified field, to discipline this unruly discourse, to translate anxiety into security, and to replace the senior professors of literature with senior professors of composition. There has been too much pain and disappointment for me to say this lightly, but I think it is fortunate that these attempts have largely failed.

CONFERENCE ON COLLEGE COMPOSITION AND COMMUNICATION

Chairs' addresses, like this one, customarily end by taking the long view—making proposals for future action or future direction. And since I have been exploring where we began, it seems only proper that I should offer my hopes about the future. I don't have time today to offer my reading of other key moments in CCCC history. I can't, that is, move from the 40's to the 80's except by a leap. I would, however, like to offer my sense of where we are now and where we are going.

What I would like to do is to reflect on how we talk about who we are and what we do, and how we have come to talk about these things as we do; I am interested in the terms we use to constitute our subject, the terms we take for granted and the degree to which we take them for granted. Today I'll stick to the three terms of our name—*composition, communication, conference*. These terms are our legacy; we must not betray those who have given them to us. They are also our problem, our burden, since they resist reflection and change.

Communication

This term has an interesting history. The official union of speech and writing (represented by the words *composition* and *communication* in our title) can be attributed to several factors—the existence of model freshman English courses that combined public speaking and media studies with composition and literature; the Navy V-12 program, which forced colleges and universities during the war to combine instruction in speech and written communication in freshman courses in officer training programs; and the "communications" movement, one of whose key figures was Harold Allen, the 3rd chair of 4C's and a member of the original committee of seven who founded the organization.

Many articles in the early journals were devoted to explaining the communications course—what it was and how it worked—and there was some debate over its appropriateness. In 1948 (as in 1988), there was reason to wonder what the word meant and why it was in our title. With slightly different timing, we could have been the Conference on Composition and Linguistics or the Conference on Composition and Semantics. And if these had been our names, we would be a very different organization today.

My sense is that the best way to think of the term *communication,* and the best way to think of its function in our title, is to think of it as a fortunate device, a term that keeps us from ever completely knowing our subject. Because of it, we can never simply study composition; there is always also this something else that we know is there but that we can't define. The undefinable term is evidence of our anxiety about composition as a subjectless activity, to be sure. At one time communication was the thing to be added to composition to make it respectable—to make freshman English a subject and not just the place where students worked on papers. But it was, and remains, a guarantee that there will always be a missing term, a structural presence to call into question any attempts to unify the field.[6]

Recently we have seen *communication* removed from the construction "composition and ———" and replaced with the word *rhetoric.* Characteristically, we call upon rhetoric when we want to identify our interests with some form of language study that is removed from the immediate scene of freshman English. We become rhetoricians, not just composition teachers. Rhetoric gives composition a literature, a body of theory, even a critical and scholarly project. It makes the field easier to imagine. *Rhetoric* not only displaces the term *communication;* it offers the possibility of a coherent pair.

I am continually amazed, however, by the degree to which we speak and write as though we had control of the rhetorical tradition—as though it were ours and we could name its key figures and projects. At the moment, rhetoric is very much out of our control. It seems, in fact, to defy every discipline's desire to keep order. All across the humanities and the human sciences, those undertaking critical or philosophical projects have become rhetoricians studying the discourse of their disciplines, or they are looking at the role of language in the way people negotiate power relationships, in the ways they establish knowledge and community.

I can only regret the degree to which the organization has tried to draw the line and keep this literature out of view. (I think it has much to do with the ways we are trying to preserve and honor the work of the second generation of composition scholars, those who opened the field to the classical and so-called "modern" rhetorical tradition.) Three years ago Maxine Hairston argued in "Breaking Our Bonds and Reaffirming Our Connections" that if we do not struggle to maintain our own disciplinary boundaries, we would lose our identity and disappear (*CCC* 36 [Oct. 1985]: 272–82). I am nervous about our sudden obsession with disciplinary boundaries. I regret graduate courses or graduate programs with reading lists designed to define composition and rhetoric as a set or self-contained field. I believe that to tell our graduate students to read Blair, Campbell, and Whately but not Foucault, Pratt, and Jameson is to assert the worst and most paranoid kind of disciplinary influence. It means that we will jeopardize their role in the general project that is reforming

English. And it closes the field to those with interests beyond a limited version of the rhetorical tradition.

Composition

As CCCC organized its interests, it changed the name of its subject from "required English" or "freshman English" to "composition and communication." The problem of English, by this progression, is displaced from an institutional site (a curriculum designed to produce unwilling readers and writers) or students (freshmen whose English was not yet mature) to a generalized academic subject (something located beyond either the institution and its practices, or students and theirs).

This change of terms was meant to will an academic respectability, but also to signal a conventional scholarly project for CCCC. This project never materialized, however, and largely because the membership was unwilling to turn attention away from the institution and from students. At one point, in the late 50's, there was even a proposed amendment to the CCCC constitution intended to focus the organization's efforts "upon a discipline rather than a course or a particular group of teachers." The amendment was defeated.[7]

Composition stands, then, for both an abstract subject and something materially present, a course and its students. The early work of CCCC was based on a recognition of this as a productive doubleness, a recognition that the most pressing general issues in the study of language could be represented in the work of students—that, in fact, one could study English by studying the work of students—and that students, by reflecting upon their own practice, could be brought into contact with the proper subject of English.

This was not an easy move to make, to be sure, since it also marked most dramatically the difference between freshman English and the other English. To put students' work at the center was to put Milton or Shakespeare on the margins. Now that the canon is generally under siege, and the study of culture is achieving a position of status in the academy, it is easier (not so dangerous) to imagine that composition could be the center of a professional life.

If "communication" signifies our doubt, then "composition" stands for our certainty. It is what we know, the subject we command, often so well that it is difficult to imagine it again as a subject open for question or negotiation.

It is also, in a familiar construction, half of the equation "literature and composition." There is literature and there is composition and we can either bridge the gap or show the bastards the door.

This is not, I have tried to argue, a useful construction. It is not as though there were now two solid, monolithic Englishes in a battle for power. To be sure, there are departments where composition and composition faculty are under siege. There are departments where black studies, film studies, women's studies and critical theory are under siege, to name a few similarly situated areas of scholarship. And there are success stories. There are departments where faculties of various backgrounds are teaching a variety of introductory courses—courses where student writing is central, courses where the subjects are open to negotiation and revision, courses that are neither literature courses nor composition courses but courses in something else, something that can't be named in just those terms.

CCCC's contribution to this work is derived from its historical concern for pedagogy and the classroom, for composition, for both the material and the psychological conditions affecting the production of text, and from its history as a community committed to valuing (rather than mocking) the common (and unconventional) things people do with language.

Conference

Finally, I come to the word *conference*—the word that stands for us, the 2,500 assembled in St. Louis, but also the 6,500 who are at home. Conference is a strange label for a professional organization, but in some ways apt for us, since we take such strength and pleasure from the act of meeting and talking. This is not, need I add, generally true of professional organizations.

We are at the point now where it has become possible and fashionable to speak of composition as a mature discipline. In 1956, in retrospect, Gerber said that the conference had reached a bumptious, ebullient adolescence. Thirty-three years later, when we are 39 years old, we have passed into a solid, if not completely respectable middle age.

We are financially stable, having experienced an unprecedented period of growth for a professional organization in the humanities. And we are big. From a first-year total of 297 members, we now have around 9,000. From a convention of 500 in Chicago, we now bring 2,500 people to St. Louis. In fact, we seem in disturbing ways to be getting too big to provide the sense of good-natured, knowable community that had been our hallmark in the past. While it was once possible to have a sense of everything going on at a meeting, the program has now become huge and diffuse, in some ways impossible for any single individual to comprehend. And we can point to scholarly achievements to announce our maturity: faculty holding distinguished chairs, publication series at major presses, several journals publishing an incredible range of research. We have even reached that pinnacle of disciplinary status, we now produce more words than any single person can possibly read. We cannot be kept up with.

I love, for example, to pick up the *Longman Bibliography* and page through it. To an outsider it must look like the strangest and most idiosyncratic collection of books and articles ever assembled. There is an order, to be sure, an order I admire, but it is not the kind of order we usually associate with academic life. We may be a discipline, but we are surely not disciplined in any usual sense of the term.

One way of defining maturity, then, is in terms of the literal growth of the profession. We are so many, we offer such a rich variety of voices and projects, we have established our niche in academe.

Much of the recent talk about our maturity laments this richness, seeing in it a failure to establish a philosophical or methodological center. In *The Making of Knowledge in Composition*, Stephen North asks, "Can composition really muster enough coherence to justify an autonomous academic existence, or is that just wishful thinking?" (Boynton/Cook, 1987, 374) What we need, some would say, is order: a canon, a set of texts to define the best that has been thought and said.

I have watched several of my contemporaries work on bibliographies or anthologies designed to provide necessary background to prospective students in composition. I know where these reading lists come from and I understand their order. At the same time, I know that I have read few books on these lists, or if I have read them I read them only recently. And I know that these collections of books and articles had little to do with what I take to be the essential parts of my preparation for the field, since much of that preparation came while I was doing work that was not "in" the field at all.

People of my generation have begun to call for a disciplined, ordered field, something that was not there for us when we got started, when we were in a position to believe that we were making it up as we went along, striking unusual connections, poking in strange places for sources and methods, finding subjects where no one else had bothered to look.

Here, then, is the point I want to argue. I am suspicious of calls for coherence. I suspect that most of the problems in academic life—problems of teaching, problems of thinking—come from disciplinary boundaries and disciplinary habits.

Our meetings have been devoted to possibility, with no great respect for tradition or precedent, and we are the recipients of that legacy—fractious, prone to argument, not likely, as Robert Gorrell once said, to "lapse into the lethargy of agreement." We form ourselves into small collectives—caucuses and special interest groups: these collectives fix our commitment to CCCC by establishing a place that is and is not the whole.

In our organizational history as in our research there has been a concerted effort to preserve diversity in academic life—to bring attention to those who would otherwise be ignored. And yet now, as we enter our 40's, we seem to be desperately trying to become respectable, to make the mistakes of middle age.

In 1963, a group charged with observing and evaluating the annual meeting reported with chagrin, "We still speak with many voices. We need to know what relationship these voices have to our central purpose."[8] As I see it, our central purpose has been to make room for these many voices, to imagine a multivocal, dialogical discipline that reflects in its actions its theoretical opposition to a unifying, dominant discourse. To propose a unifying tradition, a canon, disciplinary boundaries—to do this is to turn our backs on our most precious legacy, which is a willed and courageous resistance to the luxury of order and tradition. The charge to this generation and the next is to keep the field open, not to close it; to provide occasions for talk, not lecture and silence; to acknowledge our roots in English, not deny them; to resist the temptations of rank and status; and to offer the invitation to others to find their work in CCCC.[9]

NOTES

1. I am not, as I'll argue later, trying to set up an opposition between literature and composition as areas of professional activity. I am making a claim for the kind of context CCCC, at its best, creates for teachers and scholars. Paula Johnson wrote: "Literary scholarship does not strive to affect anything, except maybe an advancement in academic rank for the scholar. Composition research, on the other hand, tries to do something to what it studies. The social analogue is plain: the leisured elite and rude mechanicals." ("Writing Programs and the English Department," *Profession '80*, New York: MLA, 1980, 15.) This is a formulation whose terms I do not accept. Composition has become, certainly always was, also a way for some to do little more than advance a career (with CCCC providing place and time). And literary studies has (perhaps always) provided the occasion for individuals to do something with a subject, with the materials and conditions of its production, with the scene of instruction. I don't accept the easy terms of Johnson's formulation. I remain committed, however, to the formulation: there are forms of professional life that are deadening; there are forms that make useful work possible.

2. For much of this early history, I have relied on the secretary's report, CCCC (October 1950); the following *CCC* articles by John Gerber: "The Conference on College Composition and Communication" (March 1950), "Three-Year History of the CCCC" (October 1952), "CCCC Facts—1956" (October 1956); Gerber's *Loomings* (ED 103 893); my own correspondence with Harold Allen (1/27/88; 2/24/88); and a fine dissertation by Nancy K. Bird, "The Conference on College Composition and Communication: A Historical Study of Its Continuing Education and Professionalization Activities, 1949–1975" (Virginia Polytechnic University, 1977). Wykoff's statement is taken from "The Chicago Convention," *College English* (February 1949): 283. The 1948 meeting was preceded by a meeting in 1947 sponsored by NCTE and the Speech Communications Association devoted to the new communications skills courses designed for returning veterans. This meeting was not a success, although some of the participants were involved in the 1948 meeting.

3. The seven were: John Gerber, Carlton Wells (Michigan), Harold Allen (Minnesota), T.A. Barnhart (St. Cloud State), Mentor Williams (Illinois Institute of Technology), George Wykoff (Purdue), and Frank Bowman (Duke). The NCTE executive committee named a separate committee and authorized it to sponsor two conferences (in 1949 and 1950) on Freshman English. This committee consisted of John Gerber, George Wykoff, Harold Allen, Mentor Williams, John Cowley (Iowa State Teachers College), Clyde Dow (Michigan State Normal), Karl Dykema (Youngstown), Ada Roberts (Culver-Stockton), Ernest Samuels (Northwestern), and Samuel Weingartner (Wright Junior College).

4. Both talks can be found in the "Report of the Conference on College Freshman Courses in Composition and Communication, April 1 and 2, 1949," in the NCTE archives.

5. Let me make it clear that McCrimmon was offering a doctrine of linguistic relativism appropriate to the post-war economy. He was not looking to destabilize the class system but to make room for new candidates for the rising middle class: "If my student should later use his acquired skill to win for himself and his family a comfortable standard of living,

I am not at all embarrassed. But then I am less afraid of materialism than is Mr. Weaver—an admission which may be charged either against my philosophy or my nationality."

6. Among my list of key moments in CCCC history are the attempts to remove "communication" from our title.

7. See "Report of the Committee on Future Directions," *CCC* (February 1960): 3–7.

8. "Report of the Evaluation Committee," *CCC* (December 1963): 202. The authors include Robert Hogan, then Executive Director of NCTE; Priscilla Tyler, Chair of CCCC; and Louise Rosenblatt.

9. I'm grateful to Chris Ross for her help with the research on this project. Mike Rose and Steve Carr read an earlier draft and suggested a number of important changes. The project owes an obvious debt to Gerald Graff's *Professing Literature: An Institutional History* (Chicago: University of Chicago Press, 1987).

AFTERWORD: REFLECTION ON "COMPOSITION, FRESHMAN ENGLISH, AND CCCC"

My 1988 CCCC Chair's address was written as a reply to Maxine Hairston's 1985 Chair's address. Hairston called for composition to break free from English departments:

> I think the time has come to break those bonds—not necessarily physically, although in some cases that may be a good idea—but emotionally and intellectually. I think that as rhetoricians and writing teachers we will come of age and become autonomous professionals with a discipline of our own only if we can make a psychological break with the literary critics who today dominate the profession of English studies. (273)

It is worth noting that Hairston was less sure about the necessity of a "physical" break—that is, creating independent writing programs (like the current program at her former institution, the University of Texas). The issue at the time had to do with the traditions of scholarship that would prepare not only writing teachers but those PhDs in rapidly growing numbers who would choose to identify themselves professionally with "Composition."

I argued that English *was* an appropriate home for composition. After recalling her Chair's address, I said:

> I am nervous about our sudden obsession with disciplinary boundaries. I regret graduate courses or graduate programs with reading lists designed to define composition and rhetoric as a set or self-contained field. I believe that to tell our graduate students to read Blair, Campbell, and Whately but not Foucault, Pratt, and Jameson is to assert the worst and most paranoid kind of disciplinary influence. It means that we will jeopardize their role in the general project that is reforming English. And it closes the field to

those with interests beyond a limited version of the rhetorical tradition. (See page 177 in this volume.)

I was not thinking at the time about the administrative difficulties faced by directors of composition, many of them untenured (as I was when I first became the WPA at the University of Pittsburgh) and facing a variety of obstacles in English departments, nor was I thinking about the working conditions of most of those who were teaching composition courses—graduate teaching assistants and part-time or adjunct faculty. Or, more accurately, although I was most certainly *thinking* about these things, since they were on the minds of all those who were administering programs, I did not think to bring these issues into professional discussion. That was a blindness, of mine and the times, quite brilliantly addressed by the framers and signers of the Wyoming Resolution, who forced these issues onto conference agendas and made us realize that intellectual issues are related to material conditions, particularly in a field whose subject includes a course and a curriculum.

At the time I wrote the Chair's address, I was concerned with research and scholarship and their relationship to teaching, and I was concerned with how research and scholarship in composition could best be sponsored, valued, and rewarded. I was arguing against the turn to rhetoric and the turn to cognitive psychology as the necessary foundations or models for scholarly work in composition, and I was arguing against the contempt for literature (as an institution) and literary scholarship that was the legacy of the CCCC generation before mine, for whom "lit-er-a-ture" (pronounced as if at a tea party) was used as a negative epithet. I felt then, as I feel now, that literary training can be an appropriate training for a teacher of composition. This just seems obvious to me. Literary training prepares one to read closely, to assign value to acts of writing, to think about writing in relation to history and culture. And I was arguing that traditions of literary scholarship could be extended to work on pedagogy and student writing.

In some ways, history has shown that English Studies *has* provided a useful reference point for composition. Any review of the current literature would show that literary theory has become an important point of reference, and more and more scholars are pursuing a form of literacy studies that takes them to a history of writing and teaching in the United States as well to the history of American literature and literary culture.

At the same time, the present situation in composition is not what I had hoped for, with so many undergraduate writing programs breaking off from

English departments to become "independent" or "free-standing." Without appropriate faculty status and the research support it brings, those writing the future of composition and its scholarship will be working from a disadvantage. And without a record of substantial research, it will be hard to make the case for appropriate faculty status for professionals in the field. The proper employment of teachers, the valuing of student writing, and the future of scholarship in composition—I think these are related concerns. I think everyone will lose if composition fails to make its case within the established structures of value in the university. And I continue to believe that English departments are in the best position to support this work.

—DAVID BARTHOLOMAE
University of Pittsburgh

1989

Composing Ourselves: Politics, Commitment, and the Teaching of Writing

ANDREA A. LUNSFORD

T he tradition that has grown into the CCCC Chair's address now casts a fairly long shadow, one that has certainly shadowed me in the long months separating David Bartholomae's brilliant 1988 address and this 1989 Opening General Session. The opportunity to talk openly on a public occasion about what is uppermost in one's mind is a rare occasion indeed, and it has provided me with the luxury of long reflection. What *is* most on my mind, I idly wondered on the way home from our 1988 St. Louis meeting. And I was suddenly terrified by a kind of eerie silence between my ears—and forcefully reminded of my Granny's scorn for a fellow (the local sheriff, actually) she said had nothing much at all on his mind. "Honey, once that fellow's told you howdy," my Granny said, "he's told you all he knows." So it was a relief to me, as the months skittered past, to find that I wouldn't have to come to this session, say "howdy," and sit down. That relief has made me no less nervous, however. Just last night, in fact, I dreamed that I got up to give this address, delivered the first page, turned to page two and found only one word on it: *linguine.* I shuffled wildly through all the other pages, each of which held the same text: *linguine.* Now, I know of the strong connection in the history of rhetoric between rhetoric and cooking (see Plato; Vitanza; Crowley, "A Plea for the Revival of Sophistry"; Leonardi; and the Nutrostylistics panel of the 1985 CCCC [Brown, Faigley, Halloran, "Eating," Herrington, Lunsford, Ruszkiewicz, Secor, Selzer]), but that connection did little to calm me when I woke in a panic. So I've had to spend the morning reminding myself that I do have something to say to you other than "linguine" or "howdy."

This article is a revised version of the Chair's address Andrea A. Lunsford delivered at the CCCC Convention in Seattle, Washington, on March 16, 1989. It was first published in *CCC*, volume 41, number 1, February 1990.

Indeed, I do have some things on my mind, things I want to say about Composing Ourselves, things that relate to the fortieth birthday of the Conference on College Composition and Communication and to our coming of middle age.[1] As you know, our history as a profession—certainly in the span of CCCC's life—is not easily perceived as proceeding in an ordinary and traditional academic way—a clear setting out of boundaries, a staking of territory, and then a rigorous defense of those boundaries, hedging certain subjects and people in, keeping others out. Instead, our field has seemed more heterogeneous, more expansive and inclusive, gaining, in Kenneth Burke's words, "perspectives by incongruity" rather than following some linear path to academic disciplinarity. The CCCC Chair's address has provided one means of articulating such perspectives and, as expected, of engendering debate. Maxine Hairston presented one such perspective in her powerful "Breaking Our Bonds" address of 1985, and David Bartholomae last year placed *that* perspective into incongruity, suggesting that breaking bonds might not be as advantageous or as richly rewarding as interrogating and stretching those ties that bind us in various interdisciplinary ways.

Looked at in one way, as Bartholomae noted in his 1988 address, we have been obsessed over the last decade with defining ourselves—are we a science, or an art? Are we part of literary studies, or do we stand against the literary "mandarins"? Are we theorists or practitioners? Classicists, cognitivists, or epistemic rhetoricians? Such self-scrutiny and debate is of course not unique to composition studies; Clifford Geertz identifies such self-conscious reflection as a hallmark of the postmodern academy. But insofar as we have been intent on *defining*, I see these efforts as too often limiting and constricting. Rather than *defining* ourselves, therefore, I propose that we attend closely to *composing ourselves*, remembering always that composing entails terminologies—writings—and that, as Burke says, "any given terminology is a *reflection* of reality; but by its very nature as a terminology it must be a selection . . . and hence a *deflection of reality*" ("Terministic" 45).

Given that we may resist the seductive lure of crisp definitions, how and why should we go about composing ourselves? Let me address the "how" first and suggest that we might well concentrate on composing ourselves in at least two ways: *historically* and *subjectively*.

My appeal to history may seem surprising given the amount of work carried out in the last fifteen years on the history of rhetoric and composition: from revisionist views of the Sophists (Enos; Jarrett) and of classical (Halloran; Knoblauch and Brannon) and Enlightenment (Covino) rhetoricians; to debunkings of the same; to studies of the history of rhetoric in Canada (Hubert; Johnson) and of rhetoric and composition in the United States (Berlin; Connors; Crowley). This scholarly work provides an extremely valuable series of lenses through which to view the history of our discipline. But as a field, I have been surprised to realize, we know very, very little about the history of our subject—*writing*. "Standard" histories of writing—like those by Gelb and Gaur—focus primarily on the text itself—on the *inscribed* nature of writing. Others—anthropologists Scribner and Cole, and Goody and Watt in particular—focus only on how writing is used. Still others in classics (like Ong or Havelock) and in psychology (like Olson, and Kerckhove and Lumsden) focus primarily on how writing affects cognition. Not one of these histories take a compositional perspective—*none* focuses primarily on how writing is taught and *learned*.

In composing ourselves, we need first of all to be aware of the work of the historians, the anthropologists, the classicists, the psychologists on our subject, writing. We need, that is, to view writing from a variety of perspectives and throughout history. We need to know, for instance, that in the West, the very earliest traces of writing are inextricably tied up with commerce, with trade, with business—while in the East the earliest writing is linked to ritual and religion. We need to realize the extent to which writing—and in particular the Greek alphabet with its elegant addition of vowels—has written the "story" that is all of Western history. In particular, we need to realize the extent to which writing was necessary for the invention of the self, usually dated during the 12th century, the reification of that self in the Romantic "author," and its crossing to America as rugged individualism, self-reliance, and intellectual property, constructs which, as we know, have vested power in some groups while withholding power from others. As we trace the threads in the dense tapestry of the history of writing, we need also to realize the ways in which writing is itself a technology, a material technology. And again, we teachers of writing tend to know little about the evolution of that technology. The battle over directionality in writing, for instance—shall it go left to right, right to left, top to bottom, bottom to top, in circles, or in "boustrophedon"—like the furrows of a plow? All of these systems of directionality have had their days—and the systems are important in many ways to our history. A recent collection of essays on *The Alphabet and the Brain*, in fact, sets out a series of questions regarding directionality in writing and calls for "models which account for the mechanisms that appear to bind rightward reading to the structure of the western alphabet" (Kerckhove and Lumsden 11). What we think of today as technology—machines mostly—are often simply extensions of the technology which is writing, though the new technologies are certainly affecting that writing—blurring writing and reading and speech and hence changing the relationship between the spoken and written word.

As a technology with a very long and complex history, then, *writing*, as Derrida continuously reminds us, is implicated in all our epistemological, political, and social systems. In the face of this history—which we as teachers of writing are only beginning to explore—to say that writing is not innocent, never neutral, sounds almost quaintly understated. We need to keep this value-laden nature of the technology of writing uppermost in mind as we probe its history, as we compose ourselves into and around and within that history, so that *our* writing writes our history even as it writes us.

Beyond composing ourselves historically, however, I want to propose that we compose ourselves *subjectively* — in terms of those who have been the teachers of writing. Of such teachers, again, we know remarkably little. Of Plato, paradoxically a great teacher of the art of writing he condemned, we know a little. But of others — of Aspasia, our Mother Rhetorician, teacher of Socrates — almost nothing. Of Quintilian, a bit, though even the date of his death has been contested. But of those who taught him, almost nothing. Who taught Heloise? Who Milton? Who Martin Luther King? Who, for that matter, taught us? We know much about writers, but very, very little about the teachers of writers. It is time we began to learn, and to compose stories/narratives that allow teachers as well as writers to inhabit their spaces.

I realize that my invocation of subjectivity puts me in a very dangerous zone, for the concept of the subject is a particularly problematic one. In the 20 years since Roland Barthes announced "The Death of the Author," the constructed nature of the subject has been vigorously explored and debated. (Indeed, that debate has been of great help to Lisa Ede and me in our work on collaborative writing, and in our forthcoming book on that subject.) In spite of these problematics, however, writing teachers of all people can scarcely abandon all talk of subjects, of subjectivity, for as Jackie Jones Royster demonstrates in composing the intellectual tradition of black women, and as Mary Ellen Washington notes in her study of *Invented Lives*, many marginalized voices have written themselves into being, as subjects of their own histories.

Such writing has always been fearful — and feared. It is at the heart of Plato's distrust of writing, of the Christian Fathers' "ownership" of writing, of all efforts to keep others from writing themselves into being, of composing themselves. As James Moffett argues, teaching people to compose themselves in this way, allows for, indeed it demands, difference and diversity and thus threatens sameness and original identity by broadening through vicarious experiences. Fortunately, we have models of those who have persevered in claiming writing, who have, through writing, composed themselves. We have, most notably, the experience of black Americans, who claimed writing against almost insuperable odds, including laws which actually forbade anyone to teach a slave how to read or write (see Holt). In works such as Thomas Webber's *Deep Like the Rivers*, we hear chronicled the stories of black mothers who taught songs, stories, letters and a love of letters, who thus transmitted values and attitudes and passions, and who in so doing crafted a narrative or story very different from the "official" one society created for black people. In Herbert Gutman's *Power and Culture*, we catch a glimpse of one such teacher of writing, Mrs. Milla Grandison, a Mississippi slave woman who taught slaves in her house in the wee hours of the morning:

> Every window and door was carefully closed to prevent their discovery. In that little school hundreds of slaves learned to read and write. . . . After toiling all day for their masters they crept stealthily into this back alley, each with a bundle of pitch-pine splinters for light. . . . Her number of scholars was 12 at a time, and when she had taught these to read and write she dismissed them, and again took her apostolic number and brought them up to the extent of her ability, until she had graduated hundreds. (261)

Some of Mrs. Grandison's students wrote their own passes to Canada—they literally composed themselves as *free*.

If writing is, as I have suggested, never innocent or neutral, and if the American concept of self-identity and individual, powerful status has been restricted to certain groups, we badly need to know more about teachers like Mrs. Grandison, those whose commitment allowed them to stare down political realities and say I *will* teach writing, and I will teach a way to write a new story, a new political reality.

In this regard, we also have the example of women. As Carolyn Heilbrun says in her *Writing a Woman's Life*, "in the last third of the twentieth century," women of all colors have "broken through to a realization of the narratives that have been controlling their lives," and have begun to fashion other, more expansive narratives they can and do inhabit (60). And scholars in this room today have begun to re-examine the narrative, the story, of women in our history, the history of writing and rhetoric and the teaching of writing and rhetoric. They are studying the ways in which such women composed *themselves* and they are trying out narratives of their own. We need to listen to these stories, to these composed lives. And we need to tell the stories of other teachers of writing, of many, many others.

Why is it important that we do so, that we compose ourselves subjectively as well as historically? Because if we do not, we will be composed in the discourses, the discursive practices, the writings, of others. As Mikhail Bakhtin puts it, writing or "the word . . . is half someone else's. It becomes one's own only when the speaker [writer] populates it with his [her] own intentions [or] accent, when he [she] appropriates the word, adapting it to his [her] own semantic and expressive intention. Prior to this moment of appropriation, the word . . . exists in other people's mouths, in other people's contexts, serving other people's intentions: it is from these that one must take the word, and make it one's own" (293–94).

How do the discourses—the mouths, the words—of others compose us? Let me suggest several such compositions—to which I know you can add others. In my travels around the country this year, I have been listening to how others "compose" us, to how they describe teachers of writing. Here are two phrases I have heard used on several occasions, and always, incidently, by administrators: teachers of writing are the "floating bottom" and the "soft underbelly" of the academy. Such phrases go a long way, in my mind, toward explaining how administrators justify the exploitation of teachers of writing, and especially part-time teachers of writing. A "floating bottom" cannot be central to the mission of the academy or accorded its highest priorities and rewards. *I don't want such administrators composing us.*

As you know, we are composed in quite a different way by E. D. Hirsch—as technocrats, captains of skills and drills, who have abandoned knowledge and content and thus robbed students of an education. (For a particularly thorough critique of Hirsch, see Barbara Herrnstein Smith's essay, "Cult-Lit.") *I don't want E. D. Hirsch composing us.*

We have been composed by Alan Bloom as soft-headed know-nothings, betrayers of tradition and prepares of dimwitted, semiliterate youths. *I don't want Alan Bloom composing us.*

Ironically enough, we have been composed by Charles Sykes in his book *Profscam*, accused like our other academic colleagues of paying little or no attention to students, of scorning teaching, and of the pursuit of tenure and academic rank above all else. I'd be willing to bet that Mr. Sykes hasn't been in any of our classrooms. *And I certainly don't want Charles Sykes composing us.*

I think it is dramatically obvious why others wish—and need—to compose us. As teachers of writing have always been, we are dangerous precisely because we threaten the equilibrium, the status quo. We tip over the melting pot and allow for the play of *difference* by enabling others, our student colleagues, to compose themselves, to write themselves into being and hence to write a new and different narrative, one populated by many different and differing voices.

At its best, our field of composition studies—and CCCC, our forty-year-old professional organization and home—have managed to resist the temptation to make ourselves over in the image of traditional humanistic disciplines, defined by what we exclude, and instead have allowed for a different way to compose ourselves. We are composing ourselves, I believe, at our best according to the following characteristics:

- We are strongly interdisciplinary: we blur disciplinary boxes; we blur genres. As examples of our interdisciplinarity, I could point to many of you here in the audience today, and certainly to today's award winners, Christina Haas and Linda Flower, and Fred Standley.

- We are non-hierarchical and exploratory, intensely collaborative. Again, I could point to the large number of us who insist on sharing authorship, on formulating in our scholarship as well as in our teaching alternatives to rigid hierarchies.

- We are dialogic, multi-voiced, heteroglossic. Our classroom practices *enact* what others only talk about; they are sites for dialogues and polyphonic choruses.

- We are radically democratic and quick to use new technology to further democratize reading and writing for ourselves and our students.

- We are committed to maintaining the dynamic tension between *praxis* and *theoria*, between the political and the epistemological. Our students, of course, help us in this endeavor, for they keep us firmly situated in the experience of the classroom community, no matter how far into the thickets of theory we may explore.

In these characteristics especially, I suggest, composing ourselves makes us into a postmodern discipline, one that, to borrow from Catherine Stimpson, would set up not consensus but coalitions, that would search for "affinities," not "common identity." "Equally chary of a dominant discourse," Stimpson continues, "such a group would trust oppositional viewpoints . . . a multiplicity of oppositional voices. . . . Such a group would . . . develop an ethics that . . . delights not in the imposition of 'right' but in charity of response, clarity of speech, and self-consciousness about principles and practices" (194). I would suggest that insofar as we threaten boundaries, hegemonies of all kinds, insofar as we demonstrate charity of response, clarity of speech, and self-consciousness about principles, we are composing ourselves into a post-modern discipline, a postmodern profession.

I have presumed for too long on the charity of your response here, so let me attempt some sort of summing up. If we follow the invitation to compose ourselves in the ways I have been suggesting, what—in practical, concrete terms—will we do?

First, we will situate ourselves in the complex, problematic history of writing, trying to find ways to tell and retell that story around and through us—as Emily Dickinson says, to "tell it slant" (506–07). This task will be difficult, and to name only one obvious challenge, it will call on us to better prepare our graduate students to pursue such investigations by theorizing and historicizing writing in ways not now common to our programs and by assuring our graduate students the space and time to compose themselves into such a history.

Second, we will continue our often unspoken commitment to resist the temptations of binary oppositions—between research and teaching, theory and practice, composition and literature, teacher and student, between playfulness and seriousness. In our own discursive practices we will instead open out such oppositions to multiple interrogation and multiple understanding.

Third, we will focus our practical and theoretical gazes on the contested site of authorship and authoring, questioning, probing, excavating this site with our students and asking how and when authoring and writing differ. This goal will mean finding ways to allow for multi-voiced, polyphonic, collaborative texts, for writing that writes in the plural rather than the singular. Given the academy's valorization of the notion of original authorship and its denigration of collaborative acts, this task will demand all our composing talents.

Fourth, we will tell our stories, stories of students like those Shirley Brice Heath tells in *Ways With Words* or like those Janet Emig tells in *The Composing Processes of Twelfth Graders* and of teachers of writing such as the oral histories CCCC hopes to compose of a number of those here today, including many of our past chairs.

Fifth, we will insist, as we compose our stories, on combining the private and the public, the personal and the professional, the political and the social, in the ways Mina Shaughnessy did in the opening to her *Errors and Expectations*, as Lynn Troyka did in her own Chair's address in 1981, as Mike Rose has brilliantly and courageously done in his new book *Lives on the Boundary*.

Most of all, we will refuse to be or become composed or static. We will listen again to Burke, who says in *A Rhetoric of Motives*, "Let us try again. A direct hit is not likely [indeed possible] here. The best one can do is to try different approaches toward the same center whenever the opportunity offers" (137). So we will keep composing, keep opening out to potential ways of composing ourselves. Like Carolyn Heilbrun, we will "not believe that death should be allowed to find us seated comfortably in our tenured positions. Virginia Woolf describes this condition in *Mrs. Dalloway*—'Time flaps on the mast. There we stop; there we stand. Rigid, the skeleton of habit alone upholds the human frame. Where nothing is'" (131). Woolf describes here a life that has been rigidly and statically and passively composed. We aim rather for the active, the continuing, the gerundive and participial—*composing*.

Finally, we will value *talk* as part of the way toward composing ourselves, the kind of rich talk Shirley Heath's work both explores and celebrates, the kind of talk we are enjoying here at our 1989 convention, the kind of talk that favors many, many voices, the kind of talk that is full of listening. For teachers, this is a tall order, but one I think we can fill because we want to and because we know doing so will bring its own rewards. In a remarkably evocative poem, May Swenson focuses the shifting lens of her language on a poinsettia, turning it and shifting it through the seasons, presenting one view and then beckoning the reader to "look closer" and see with that view of the poinsettia—yet another poinsettia. Composing ourselves will call on us to look closer, in just the way Swenson demonstrates. It will also call on us to "listen closer," to listen to the voices of the other in each of us and in each other, to listen closer to the rich and complex diversity our students and classrooms bring to us.

When Jacqueline Jones Royster spoke at Ohio State University in February, 1989, she told us (among many other compelling things) that the motto of the National Association of Colored Women was "Lifting as We Climb." I've thought many times these last weeks of that motto and of an invocation given by a young woman at an Hispanic Leadership banquet I was privileged to attend last year. I wish I could repeat that invocation to you in her beautiful Spanish, but it was very much like "Lifting as We Climb." She called on all those present to "reach out a hand to all those behind even as you move forward." Lifting as we climb.

Lifting as we climb means we must reach out, stretch ourselves around new stories, around new narratives of what it means to be a teacher of writing and a writer in the twenty-first century. Look at all those of us here today, those who have been here throughout the forty years of CCCC's life and those who have more recently arrived. I hope and trust we will see a lot of lifting, a lot of climbing, a lot of reaching out. Look around. Then look closer. Listen. Then listen closer. We are here, in Seattle. We *are* composing ourselves. Thank you very, very much for letting me join in that process.

NOTE

1. CCCC first met in 1949. Our first chair was John Gerber, of the University of Iowa, and principal speakers included Richard Weaver and James McCrimmon.

WORKS CITED

Bakhtin, M[ikhail] M. "Discourse in the Novel." *The Dialogic Imagination: Four Essays*. Ed. Michael Holquist. Austin: U of Texas P, 1981. 259–422.
Barthes, Roland. "The Death of the Author." *Image—Music—Text*. New York: Hill and Wang, 1977.
Bartholomae, David. "The Reach of Composition." CCCC Convention. St. Louis, March 1988. Rpt. as "Freshman English, Composition and CCCC." *College Composition and Communication* 40 (February 1989): 38–50.
Berlin, James A. *Rhetoric and Reality: Writing Instruction in American Colleges, 1900–1985*. Carbondale: Southern Illinois UP, 1987.
———. *Writing Instruction in Nineteenth Century American Colleges*. Carbondale: Southern Illinois UP, 1984.
Bloom, Allan David. *The Closing of the American Mind*. New York: Simon, 1987.
Brooks, Charlotte K., ed. *Tapping Potential: English and Language Arts for the Black Learner*. Urbana: National Council of Teachers of English, 1985.
Brown, Betsy E. "Comestible Communication: The Rhetoric of the Power Lunch." CCCC Convention. Minneapolis, March 1985.
Burke, Kenneth. *A Rhetoric of Motives*. Berkeley: U of California P, 1962.
———. "Terministic Screens." *Language as Symbolic Action: Essays on Life, Literature and Method*. Berkeley: U of California P, 1966. 44–62.
Clark, Suzanne. "Julia Kristeva." CCCC Convention. Seattle, March 1989.
Connors, Robert J. "Angelina Grimke." CCCC Convention. Seattle, March 1989.
———. "Grammar in American College Composition: A Historical Overview." *The Territory of Language: Linguistics, Stylistics, and the Teaching of Composition*. Ed. Donald A. McQuade. Carbondale: Southern Illinois UP, 1986. 3–22.

———. "Mechanical Correctness as a Focus in Composition Instruction." *College Composition and Communication* 36 (February 1985): 61–72.

———. "The Rhetoric of Explanation: Explanatory Rhetoric from Aristotle to 1850." *Written Communication* 1 (April 1984): 189–210.

———. "The Rhetoric of Explanation: Explanatory Rhetoric from 1850 to the Present." *Written Communication* 2 (January 1985): 49–73.

———. "The Rise and Fall of the Modes of Discourse." *College Composition and Communication* 32 (December 1981): 444–55.

———. "The Rise of Technical Writing Instruction in America." *Journal of Technical Writing and Communication* 12 (1982): 329–52.

———. "Textbooks and the Evolution of the Discipline." *College Composition and Communication* 37 (May 1986): 178–94.

Covino, William A. *The Art of Wondering: A Revisionist Return to the History of Rhetoric*. Portsmouth: Boynton/Cook, 1988.

Crowley, Sharon. "The Current-Traditional Theory of Style: An Informal History." *Rhetoric Society Quarterly* 16 (Fall 1986): 233–50.

———. "The Evaluation of Invention in Current-Traditional Rhetoric: 1850–1970." *Rhetoric Review* 3 (January 1985): 146–62.

———. "Neo-Romanticism and the History of Rhetoric." *Pre/Text* 5 (Spring 1984): 19–37.

———. "A Plea for the Revival of Sophistry." *Rhetoric Review* 7 (Spring 1989): 318–34.

———. "On Poststructuralism and Compositionists." *Pre/Text* 5 (Fall-Winter 1984): 185–95.

———. "Response to Robert J. Connors, 'The Rise and Fall of the Modes of Discourse.'" *College Composition and Communication* 35 (February 1984): 88–90.

Derrida, Jacques. *Limited Inc*. Evanston: Northwestern UP, 1988.

———. *Of Grammatology*. Baltimore: Johns Hopkins UP, 1976.

Dickinson, Emily. *The Complete Poems of Emily Dickinson*. Ed. Thomas H. Johnson. Boston: Little, 1957.

Ede, Lisa. "Lucia Olbrechts-Tyteca." CCCC Convention. Seattle, March 1989.

———. "Collaborative Learning: Lessons from the World of Work." *Writing Program Administration* 9 (Spring 1986): 17–27.

Ede, Lisa, and Andrea Lunsford. "Let Them Write—Together." *English Quarterly* 18.3 (Winter 1985): 119–27.

———. *Singular Texts/Plural Authors: Perspectives on Collaborative Writing*. Carbondale: Southern Illinois UP, forthcoming.

Emig, Janet. *The Composing Processes of Twelfth Graders*. Urbana: National Council of Teachers of English, 1971.

Enos, Richard. "The Effects of Imperial Patronage on the Rhetorical Tradition of Athenia Second Sophistic." *Communication Quarterly* 25 (Spring 1977): 3–10.

———. "Emerging Notions of Heuristic, Eristic, and Protreptic Rhetoric in Homeric Discourse: Proto-Literate Conniving, Wrangling, and Reasoning." Texas Writing Research Conference. Austin, 1981.

———. "The Epistemology of Gorgias's Rhetoric: A Re-examination." *Southern Speech Communication Journal* 42 (Fall 1976): 35–51.

———. "The Features of Sophistic Composition." New Directions in Composition Scholarship Conference. U of New Hampshire, Durham, 1986.

———. "The Formulae of Sophistic Composition." CCCC Convention. Atlanta, March 1987.

———. "Rhetorical Theory and Sophistic Composition: A Reconstruction." The Report of the 1985 National Endowment for the Humanities Summer Stipend. 1986.

Faigley, Lester. "Peristalsis as Paradigm: From Process to Product." CCCC Convention. Minneapolis, March 1985.

Gaur, Albertine. *A History of Writing*. London: The British Library, 1984.

Gelb, I. J. *A Study of Writing*. 1952. Rev. ed. Chicago: U of Chicago P, 1963.

Geertz, Clifford. *Local Knowledge: Further Essays in Interpretive Anthropology*. New York: Basic Books, 1983.

Glenn, Cheryl. "Aspasia." CCCC Convention. Seattle, March 1989.

Goody, Jack. *The Domestication of the Savage Mind*. Cambridge: Cambridge UP, 1977.

———. *The Interface between the Written and the Oral*. Cambridge: Cambridge UP, 1987.

———. *The Logic of Writing and the Organization of Society*. Cambridge: Cambridge UP, 1986.

Goody, Jack, and Ian Watt. "The Consequences of Literacy." *Literacy in Traditional Societies*. Ed. Jack Goody. Cambridge: Cambridge UP, 1968. 27–68.

Gutman, Herbert G. *Power and Culture*. New York: Pantheon, 1987.

Haas, Christina, and Linda Flower. "Rhetorical Reading Strategies and the Construction of Meaning." *College Composition and Communication* 39 (May 1988): 167–83.

Hairston, Maxine. "Breaking Our Bonds and Reaffirming Our Connections." CCCC Convention. Minneapolis, May 1985. Rpt. in *College Composition and Communication* 36 (October 1985): 272–82. Rpt. in *ADE Bulletin* 81 (Fall 1985): 1–5.

Halloran, S. Michael. "Aristotle's Concept of Ethos, or If Not His, Somebody Else's." *Rhetoric Review* 1 (September 1982): 58–63.

———. "Eating Aristotle: Semiotics as Salivation in *The Name of the Rose*." CCCC Convention. Minneapolis, March 1985.

———. "On the End of Rhetoric, Classical and Modern." *College English* 36 (February 1975): 621–31.

———. "Rhetoric in the American College Curriculum: The Decline of Public Discourse." *Pre/Text* 3 (Fall 1982): 245–69.

———. "Tradition and Theory in Rhetoric." *Quarterly Journal of Speech* 62 (October 1976): 234–41.

Halloran, S. Michael, and Merrill O. Whitburn. "Ciceronian Rhetoric and the Rise of Science: The Plain Style Reconsidered." *The Rhetorical Tradition and Modern Writing*. Ed. James J. Murphy. New York: MLA, 1982. 58–72.

Havelock, Eric A. *The Muse Learns to Write: Reflections on Orality and Literacy from Antiquity to the Present*. New Haven: Yale UP, 1986.

Heath, Shirley Brice. *Ways with Words: Language, Life, and Work in Communities and Classrooms*. Cambridge: Cambridge UP, 1983.

Heilbrun, Carolyn. *Writing a Woman's Life*. New York: Norton, 1988.

Herrington, Anne J. "Wining and Dining across the Curriculum: The Smorgasbord of Discourse." CCCC Convention. Minneapolis, March 1985.

Hirsch, E.D., Jr. *Cultural Literacy*. Boston: Houghton, 1987.

Holt, Thomas. "'Knowledge Is Power': The Black Struggle for Literacy." The Right to Literacy Conference. Columbus, Ohio, September 1988.

Hubert, Henry Allan. "The Development of English Studies in Nineteenth-Century Anglo-Canadian Colleges." Diss. U of British Columbia, 1988.

Jarrett, Susan. "Toward a Sophistic Historiography." *Pre/Text* 8 (Spring 1987): 9–28.

———. "The First Sophists and the Political Implications of *Techne*." CCCC Convention. Seattle, March 1989.

———. "The First Sophists as Precursors of Humanism: Expanding the Limits of Literacy." CCCC Convention. Atlanta, March 1987.

Johnson, Nan. *Nineteenth-Century Rhetoric: Theory and Practice in North America*. Carbondale: Southern Illinois UP, forthcoming.

———. "English Composition, Rhetoric, and English Studies at Nineteenth-Century Canadian Colleges and Universities." *English Quarterly* 20.4 (Winter 1987): 296–304.

———. "Rhetoric and Belles Lettres in the Canadian Academy: An Historical Analysis." *College English* 50 (December 1988): 861–73.

Kerckhove, Derrick de, and Charles J. Lumsden, eds. *The Alphabet and the Brain*. Berlin: Springer-Verlag, 1988.

Knoblauch, C.L., and Lil Brannon. *Rhetorical Traditions and the Teaching of Writing*. Upper Montclair: Boynton/Cook, 1984.

Leonardi, Susan J. "Recipes for Reading: Summer Pasta, Lobster a la Riseholme, and Key Lime Pie." *PMLA* 104 (May 1989): 340–47.

Lipscomb-Burnett, Drema. "Sojourner Truth: A Practical Public Discourse." CCCC Convention. Seattle, March 1989.

Lunsford, Andrea. "Masticatio: A New Trope from Classical Rhetoric." CCCC Convention. Minneapolis, March 1985.

Lunsford, Andrea, and Lisa Ede. "Classical Rhetoric, Modern Rhetoric, and Contemporary Discourse Studies." *Written Communication* 1 (1984): 78–100.

————. "Why Write . . . Together: A Research Update." *Rhetoric Review* 5 (Fall 1986): 71–77.

————. "Collaboration and Compromise: The Fine Art of Writing with a Friend." *Writers on Writing*. Vol. 2. Ed. Tom Waldrep. New York: Random House, 1987. 121–28.

Lyon, Arabella. "Susanne Langer." CCCC Convention. Seattle, March 1989.

Moffett, James. "Censorship and Spiritual Education." The Right to Literacy Conference. Columbus, Ohio, September 1988.

————. *Storm in the Mountains*. Carbondale and Edwardsville: Southern Illinois UP, 1988.

Olson, David. "From Utterance to Text: The Bias of Language in Speech and Writing." *Harvard Educational Review* 47 (August 1977): 257–81.

————. "The Languages of Instruction: The Literate Bias of Schooling." *Schooling and the Acquisition of Knowledge*. Ed. R. Spiro. Hillsdale: Lawrence Erlbaum, 1977. 65–89.

————. "Mind, Media, and Memory: The Archival and Epistemological Functions of Written Text." *The Alphabet and the Brain: The Lateralization of Writing*. Ed. Derrick de Kerckhove and Charles J. Lumsden. Berlin: Springer-Verlag, 1988. 422–41.

Olson, David R., Nancy Torrance, and Angela Hillyard, eds. *Literacy, Language, and Learning: The Nature and Consequences of Reading and Writing*. Cambridge: Cambridge UP, 1985.

Ong, Walter. *Orality and Literacy: The Technologizing of the Word*. London: Methuen, 1982.

Plato. *Gorgias*. Trans. W.C. Helmbold. Indianapolis: Liberal Arts Press, 1952.

Redfern, Jenny R. "Christine de Pisan and Her Medieval Rhetoric." CCCC Convention. Seattle, March 1989.

Rose, Mike. *Lives on the Boundary*. New York: The Free Press, 1989.

Royster, Jacqueline Jones. "Muted Voices: Perspectives on Black Women as Writers of Non-Fiction Prose." The Right to Literacy Conference. Columbus, Ohio, September 1988.

————. "Contending Forces: The Struggles of Black Women for Intellectual Affirmation." Ohio State U, Columbus, Ohio, 1 March 1989.

Ruszkiewicz, John J. "A Theory of Dis-Course and Dat-Course." CCCC Convention. Minneapolis, March 1985.

Scribner, Sylvia, and Michael Cole. *The Psychology of Literacy*. Cambridge: Harvard UP, 1981.

Secor, Marie. "La Technique: An Alimentary Approach to Stylistic Analysis." CCCC Convention. Minneapolis, March 1985.

Selzer, Jack. "Upchuck Retaught: A Bulimic Finds an Authentic Voice (A Case Study)." CCCC Convention. Minneapolis, March 1985.

Shaughnessy, Mina. *Errors and Expectations: A Guide for the Teacher of Basic Writing*. New York: Oxford UP, 1977.

Smith, Barbara Herrnstein. "Cult-Lit: Hirsch, Literacy, and 'The National Culture.'" *South Atlantic Quarterly*, forthcoming.

Standley, Fred. "William Bennett, Alan Bloom, E.D. Hirsch, Jr.: 'Great Nature has another thing to do to you and me. . . .'" *Teaching English in the Two-Year College* 15 (December 1988): 266–77.

Stimpson, Catherine R. *Where the Meanings Are*. New York: Methuen, 1988.

Swearingen, C. Jan. "Inez de la Cruz." CCCC Convention. Seattle, March 1989.

Swenson, May. "Look Closer." *New Yorker* 12 December 1988: 48.

Sykes, Charles, *Profscam: Professors and the Demise of Higher Education*. Washington: Regnery Gateway. 1988.

Troyka, Lynn Quitman. "Perspectives on Legacies and Literacy in the 1980's." *College Composition and Communication* 33 (1982): 252–62.

Vitanza, Victor. "Editorial Preface 2: 'Rhetoric, Cookery, and Recipes.'" *Pre/Text* 1. 1–2 (1980): 205–14.

Washington, Mary Ellen, ed. *Invented Lives*. New York: Doubleday, 1987.

Webber, Thomas. *Deep Like the Rivers*. New York: Norton, 1978.

As I began composing this response to my 1989 Chair's
address, I had just endured the opening day of the 2004 Republican National
Convention. I felt close to tears of frustration and near-despair as speaker after
speaker evoked events of 9/11 as justification for the reelection of George W. Bush
and went on, at best, to misrepresent events and, at worst, to engage in a series of
deliberate untruths. Never had the power of ideology seemed so raw and present;
never had Orwellian doublethink and newspeak been more on display; never had I
felt more frightened for the future of the United States, for our children and
grandchildren, for our students.

By the time these remarks are published, we will know something more of
our fate, and I am very fearful that "four more years" will set back the U.S. clock—
environmentally, educationally, socially, and even militarily—for dozens if not
hundreds of years. So, it is particularly interesting and instructive to look back
fifteen years, to 1988, my year as Chair of our organization. That year, of course,
saw the election of the first President Bush, following eight years of Reaganomics.
Also in 1988, terrorism struck in Lockerbie, Scotland, as a Pan Am flight
exploded, killing 270 people; a U. S. Navy plane "accidentally" shot down an
Iranian plane, killing 290 in the Persian Gulf; and scientist James Hansen of
NASA delivered a strong warning to Congress on the effects of global warming
and the "greenhouse effect." So much for déjà vu, all over again.

In 1988, I was also at a low personal ebb, one year after a devastating divorce
and a hectic move across the country. Yet in spite of my disillusionment with the
American electorate, with the government, and with the state of my so-called life,
I came to our convention in a hopeful frame of mind, knowing that the work of
writing teachers is good and true work, that we do make differences in the lives of
millions of students, and that our subject—written and oral communication—
would be of greater and greater importance as we moved toward the twenty-first
century. I quoted Kate Stimpson, who called for a postmodern discipline that
would value not consensus but coalitions, not common identity but affinities.

Certainly I was concerned in 1988–1989, as I am today, about the state of our
discipline. I was acutely aware that, despite the exponential growth of the field,
large classes and very heavy teaching loads meant most college students were not
getting the instruction in writing that they needed or deserved, and that working
conditions for writing teachers—especially the legions of adjunct or part-time

instructors and graduate students—were difficult at best and deplorable at worst. I was also concerned about our graduate programs, which were too often failing to provide the grounding in history, theory, and practice of rhetoric and writing that I saw as crucial to the long-term success of our field. As a result of such concerns, I made a strong call for scholars and teachers of writing and rhetoric to reject the constructions of others (such as the muckraking Charles Sykes, author of *ProfScam*, or the cultural doomsayers like Alan Bloom) in favor of *composing ourselves*. Fifteen years later, I still find this a powerful metaphor for the work that lies before us.

Today, in another time of deep pessimism about so many things in our society, it is bracing and inspiring to me to see how much good work our field has accomplished in the last decade-and-a-half. We now have major studies of writing practices across the centuries, many of which draw on the wisdom of women and people of color (Logan, Hobbs, Ratcliffe, Royster, Wertheimer, Sutherland, Moss, Johnson, Mountford, Miller) as well as important studies of writing and rhetoric teachers (Kates, Adams, Brereton, Campbell, Maher, Stewart and Stewart). In 2003, a conference of the Alliance of Rhetoric Societies (ARS) explicitly joined theory and practice, declaring that rhetoric is, above all, a teaching tradition and linking that unifying goal across centuries and continents to performance. In fact, the two terms of pedagogy and performance animated the entire conference: "every keynote address touched not only on pedagogy but also on performance: the performance of teaching; the performance of civic duty and discourse; the performance of student speaking and writing; the performance of disciplinarity" (55). (Reports on and responses to this conference are in the Summer 2004 issue of the *Rhetoric Society Quarterly*.)

Readers will perhaps have noted my insistence on pairing "rhetoric and writing" throughout these remarks, and this is a point I did not feel I had to make in 1988–1989. I am more convinced than ever, however, that the field of writing studies will be impoverished if it ignores its rhetorical history and traditions. I also did not feel a need in 1988–1989 to respond to the debate on location of writing (and rhetoric) programs, since one year before, David Bartholomae had joined the argument with Maxine Hairston. We can see today, however, that our field is increasingly moving out of English departments and in some cases out of the humanities. In the 2004 Chair's address, Kathi Yancey called for new writing (and rhetoric) majors across the United States, and such majors will bring with them, I believe, new departments. So today, as we strive to stem the national tide of anti-intellectualism, unilateralism, dogmatism, and self-righteous bellicosity, we must also strive to guide the shape of our still-emerging discipline. What we call this discipline is important, as are our decisions about undergraduate and graduate curricula, our research agenda, and our goals. At the ARS conference, Jackie Royster spoke of the ideology of rhetoric (and writing) instruction, insisting that we remember that actions "always have consequences" (*Reflections* 66). This focus on consequences took Jackie to Anna Julia Cooper, who "believed in human potential, in the possibility of education for African Americans, for women, for African American women, for people who live in poverty, for all human beings." Lessons from Cooper and other leading African American women suggest that the consequences of what we do will inevitably take root in our students and that we must therefore be judged by our and our students' performances. In short, Jackie argued, our pedagogy "should be in the interest of creating people with the vision, values, and skills that will help them to make a better world" (*Reflections* 66).

This is a tall order, but it is one our field can and must take on. In my response to the ARS conference, I took this challenge to heart, arguing that we must sustain rhetoric (and writing) "as a teaching tradition that is open to all, that refuses the exclusions and exclusivities of the past, and that accepts the challenge of what Hauser calls rhetoric's 'birthright' of civic education and that Leff describes as bringing students 'to perform appropriately in the public world'" (Lunsford and Leff, 67). In my view, rhetoric (and writing) are arts that are "strategically agentive, deeply performative, devoted to ethical action and to developing all students' abilities to make a difference in the world provide a strong ground on which to build" a discipline and departments of the future, ones that will make a difference in the world and will, as Royster cautions, "only have eloquence if it has consequence" (*Reflections* 67).

–ANDREA A. LUNSFORD
Stanford University

WORKS CITED

Adams, Katherine. *Progressive Politics and the Training of America's Persuaders*. Mahwah: Erlbaum, 1999.

Brereton, John. *The Origins of Composition Studies in the American College, 1875–1925: A Documentary History*. Pittsburgh: U of Pittsburgh P, 1994.

Campbell, JoAnn. *Toward a Feminist Rhetoric: The Writing of Gertrude Buck*. Pittsburgh: U of Pittsburgh P, 1996.

Gere, Anne. *Intimate Practices: Literacy and Cultural Work in U.S. Women's Clubs, 1880–1920*. Urbana: U of Illinois P, 1997.

Glenn, Cheryl. *Unspoken: A Rhetoric of Silence*. Carbondale: Southern Illinois UP, 2004.

Hauser, Gerard A. "Teaching Rhetoric: Or Why Rhetoric Isn't Just Another Kind of Philosophy or Literary Criticism." *Rhetoric Society Quarterly* 34 (Summer 2004): 39–54. 29 July 2005. <http://www.findarticles.com/p/articles/mi_qa4142/is_200407/ai_n94124167>.

Hobbs, Catherine, ed. *Nineteenth-Century Women Learn to Write*. Charlottesville: U of Virginia P, 1995.

Horner, Bruce. *Terms of Work for Composition: A Materialist Critique*. State U of New York P, 2000.

Johnson, Nan. *Gender and Rhetorical Space in American Life 1866–1910*. Carbondale: Southern Illinois UP, 2002.

Kates, Susan. *Activist Rhetorics and American Higher Education: 1885–1937*. Carbondale: Southern Illinois UP, 2000.

Logan, Shirley Wilson, ed. *With Pen and Voice: A Critical Anthology of Nineteenth-Century African-American Women*. Carbondale: Southern Illinois UP, 1995.

———. *"We Are Coming": The Persuasive Discourse of Nineteenth-Century Black Women*. Carbondale: Southern Illinois UP, 1999.

Lunsford, Andrea A. "Composing Ourselves: Politics, Commitment, and the Teaching of Writing." *College Composition and Communication* 41 (Feb. 1990): 71–82.

Lunsford, Andrea, and Michael Leff. "Afterwords: A Dialogue." *Rhetoric Society Quarterly* 34 (Summer 2004): 55–68.

Maher, Jane. *Mina P. Shaughnessy: Her Life and Work*. Urbana: NCTE, 1997.

Miller, Susan. *Assuming the Positions*. Pittsburgh: U of Pittsburgh P, 1997.

Moss, Beverly. *A Community Text Arises: A Literate Text and a Literacy Tradition in African-American Churches*. Cresskill: Hampton, 2003.

Mountford, Roxanne. *The Gendered Pulpit: Preaching in American Protestant Spaces*. Carbondale: Southern Illinois UP, 2003.

Popken, Randall. "Edwin Hopkins and the Costly Labor of Composition Teaching." *College Composition and Communication* 55 (2004): 618–41.

Ratcliffe, Krista. *Anglo-American Feminist Challenges to the Rhetorical Traditions: Virginia Woolf, Mary Daly, Adrienne Rich*. Carbondale: Southern Illinois UP, 1995.

Rhetoric Society Quarterly. Special Issue: The Alliance of Rhetoric Societies Conference, 2003. 34 (Summer 2004).

Royster, Jacqueline Jones. "Reflections on Pedagogy in Three Frames." ARS Conference, Evanston, IL. 11–14 September 2003. 8 Aug. 2004. <http://www.rhetoricalliance .org.pdf>.

———. *Southern Horrors and Other Writings: The Anti-Lynching Campaign of Ida B. Wells, 1892–1900*. New York: Bedford/St. Martins, 1997.

———. *Traces of a Stream: Literacy and Social Change among African American Women*. Pittsburgh: U of Pittsburgh P, 2000.

Stewart, Donald, and Patricia Stewart. *The Life and Legacy of Fred Newton Scott*. Pittsburgh: U of Pittsburgh P, 1997.

Stimpson, Catherine R. *Where the Meanings Are*. New York: Methuen, 1988.

Sutherland, Christine Mason, and Rebecca Sutcliffe, eds. *The Changing Tradition: Women in the History of Rhetoric*. Lansing: Michigan State UP, 1999.

Wertheimer, Molly Meijer, ed. *Listening to Their Voices: The Rhetorical Activities of Historical Women*. Columbia: U of South Carolina P, 1997.

———. *Leading Ladies of the White House*. Lanham: Rowan, 2004.

1990 Valuing Teaching: Assumptions, Problems, and Possibilities

JANE E. PETERSON

I feel both honored and delighted to be part of this occasion when we come together not only to celebrate our diversity but also to explore the ways diversity can strengthen us. Among the recent indicators of our diversity have been the concerns presented in the Chairs' addresses at this Opening General Session. For example, in her 1987 Chair's address, Miriam Chaplin focused our attention on public education in this country and the National Education Reform Movement, calling us to "close the chasm which separates us from the mainstream of education" (60). In 1988, David Bartholomae reminded us of the origins of this organization and urged us to remain open rather than to close the boundaries by defining ourselves too narrowly as a discipline. And last year, Andrea Lunsford addressed us, compellingly inviting us to write our own history: to compose ourselves rather than be composed by others.

I too wish to put before you a matter of some importance, one I see as critical to our future. Let me begin by reviewing briefly where our organization and profession have been and are. In his 1988 Chair's address, David Bartholomae described the founding of CCCC by people who had attended the 1948 Annual Convention of the National Council of Teachers of English and felt that meeting did not provide enough time to discuss the teaching of Freshman Composition, a course that presented a new challenge to composition teachers as they dealt with the influx of students in the post World War II years. This organization, then, grew out of an immediate, concrete problem, a teaching-related problem: what to do with the required English course, Freshman Composition. And it grew out of a special need for discussion and dialogue (Bartholomae 39).

This article is a revised version of the Chair's address Jane E. Peterson delivered at the CCCC Convention in Chicago, Illinois, on March 22, 1990. It was first published in *CCC*, volume 42, number 1, February 1991.

As the dialogue continued, new needs emerged. 1963 is the year most often cited as the beginning of our modern discipline, what we are today. Edward P. J. Corbett, for instance, points to 1963 as marking the resurgence of scholarship in our field because of the frequency with which the term *rhetoric* appeared in the 1963 CCCC convention program (445). Stephen North, in *The Making of Knowledge in Composition*, uses 1963 to "date the birth of modern Composition, capital C" (15) largely because of the publication of *Research in Written Composition* by Richard Braddock, Richard Lloyd-Jones, and Lowell Schoer (17). That work reviewed existing empirical research in composition—largely applied research—and ended with a call for basic research.

Since 1963, we as a profession have been engaged in making composition a viable discipline. As signs of our success, we now point to doctoral programs in composition and rhetoric, endowed chairs, the emergence of many new journals in our field (especially in the last 15 years), the growth of this organization, the size of meetings such as this convention, and bibliographies such as Erika Lindemann's *CCCC Bibliography of Composition and Rhetoric* for 1987, a selective bibliography which has 1,813 entries.

We have become a healthy and dynamic profession through devoting the last 27 years to establishing our identity as an emerging discipline, to becoming respectable through scholarship and research.[1] These have been important and necessary years. We have *needed* the dialogues with the past and with other disciplines that scholarship provides. We have *needed* the exploration into reading, writing, and learning processes that basic research has made possible. And we have *needed* the development of new methodologies for creating knowledge in our field. Today, we probably feel better about ourselves as scholars and researchers—as composition specialists—than we ever have. But how do we feel about ourselves as composition *teachers*?

What has happened to teaching in these past 27 years? How do we view ourselves in 1990 as writing teachers? The answer to this question, I believe, is more problematic. I think most of us would agree that teaching in general is undervalued in American society. Public school teachers now talk about needing three Rs for themselves: Remuneration, Respect, and Recognition (Dichter 3). In higher education, too, teaching yields little recognition, respect, or remuneration for faculty. The rank and tenure systems of most colleges and universities have institutionalized a hierarchy that places teaching far below research and scholarship.

The dollars spent within higher education also reflect the undervalued state of teaching. Research universities not only receive more money per student, as June Jordan noted in her 1989 CCCC/College Section Luncheon speech portraying the elitism of post-secondary education in this country, but those institutions also spend less of what they receive on instruction. In 1988, the Commission on the Future of Community Colleges within the American Association of Community and Junior Colleges reported that research universities allocate 38% of their budgets to instructional-related matters such as instruction, library services, and academic-support services; four-year schools allocate 42% of their budgets to instruction and community colleges 61% (45). These spending patterns reveal the priorities within higher education—the hierarchy that operates within the larger academic community.

What about within our own profession? Do we, as members of this profession, as composition teachers ourselves, value teaching in general or the teaching of composition in particular? Sometimes we answer "yes" and sometimes "no." Let us deal with the "yes" first.

The Constitution of this organization, the organization most associated with composition teaching in colleges, asserts,

> The broad objective of CCCC is to unite teachers of college composition and communication in an organization which can consider all matters relevant to their teaching. The specific objectives are (1) to provide an opportunity for discussion of problems relating to the organization and teaching of college composition and communications courses, (2) to encourage studies and research in the field, and (3) to publish a professional journal and other materials of interest to teachers of composition and communication. (Article I, Section 2)

Teaching clearly plays a central role in our stated organizational mission and objectives, and it has in fact been valued in much of our recent work. The importance of teaching composition, for instance, is a key premise in CCCC's argument for improved conditions for part-time and temporary faculty (*Statement*). And in the *Guidelines on Scholarship* endorsed by CCCC in 1987, we advocated including writing composition textbooks and conducting workshops and seminars for faculty in other institutions as important contributions to the field, worthy of consideration in tenure and promotion reviews. In other words, we have worked to expand the range of activities considered valuable by our own institutions, and that work includes teaching-related activities. Responses to the Spring 1989 survey about our journal offer yet another form of evidence. Asked whether the Staffroom Interchange section should continue, just over 75% of the respondents answered yes (Bridwell-Bowles and Dickel). So, what we are doing and saying provides some evidence that this organization does consider teaching important.

But there's also evidence that we don't—evidence that a hierarchy exists within the profession, evidence that we consider teaching far less important than research or scholarship, evidence that our understanding of the value of teaching remains limited. Let me offer a few examples by adapting a technique from women's studies work in consciousness raising, the technique of reversals.[2]

- In discussions about who might be invited to submit an article on teaching basic writing for a festschrift, the question most likely to arise is "What has this person published?" Other questions seldom, if ever, arise: "What teaching awards has he won? How many classes of basic writing has she taught? How does she teach basic writing?" In other words, the comments we make to "qualify" people in our profession often relate to scholarship and publication, seldom to teaching, even when the topic itself is teaching.

- The question "What do I do on Monday morning?" has become symbolic of a limited hands-on interest that is often characterized as anti-intellectual while the practical questions researchers ask, such as "How can I code this protocol?" are considered important questions with many implications.

- The phrase "classroom mentality" is common and pejorative. Phrases like "library mentality," "manuscript mentality," or "research mentality" don't exist.

Other evidence: Promising graduate students are usually encouraged to seek jobs that require little teaching. And those who express a strong desire to teach—who *want* positions in two- or four-year colleges—may well hear what a friend of mine heard last fall: "Why would you want to do that? You're bright; you can do much better than that."

This undervaluing of teaching is *not* limited to those whose primary work centers on research and scholarship. Those of us who are practitioners, whose primary responsibility is teaching in a two- or four-year college, frequently undervalue teaching. We may say, "I just teach" or "I'm only a teacher." Have you ever heard someone say, "I'm just a scholar" or "I'm only a researcher"? Comments such as these suggest that many of us do not yet fully understand or value teaching as a mode of inquiry, a way of learning and knowing.

Our current attitudes toward teaching, though not desirable in my opinion, are nonetheless understandable. They are understandable from a social perspective when we consider such factors as the low pay, low prestige, and other messages we receive from our institutions and society at large. Our attitudes are also understandable from an historical perspective. I have already suggested one aspect of the historical: that to establish ourselves as a discipline we needed to focus on research and scholarship these past 27 years. Another historical factor centers on the medium of teaching, which is talk, not written discourse, the form we value most. The whole relationship of writing and speech has been a problematic one, both to us as a profession and to CCCC as a professional organization, leading us to consider dropping the word *communication* from our name because of its association with speech.[3] Historically, too, the word *teaching* has been so strongly associated with transmission models of learning, which we now find inadequate, that today the very word *teaching* seems to be suffering from a form of guilt by association with those models.

The hierarchy within the profession is also understandable from another perspective—that of our propositions. We mean something quite different when we talk about the value of teaching than when we talk about the value of research and scholarship. Our proposition that teaching has value means "value for students and through students for the larger society." It places teachers in servant roles. In contrast, the idea that research and scholarship have value means "value for the profession and for us individually, as researchers and scholars."

Although the current undervalued state of teaching may be understandable, it remains a concern. For instance, how do we argue effectively for improved conditions for part-time and temporary faculty when we ourselves have ambivalent feelings about the importance of teaching? How do we recruit new people to the profession when we ourselves consider a portion of our work comparatively unimportant? How do we convince ourselves to remain in the profession?

The time has come, I believe, for us to re-evaluate teaching, not only for the reasons I have been suggesting, which are *re*active reasons—what we can lose by not understanding the value of teaching—but for *pro*active reasons as well—what we can gain by developing a deeper understanding of the nature of teaching today.

Much had changed in recent years, and it's time to look at teaching in the light of our current theories, to recognize a new proposition. After 27 years of work, we have new, complementary, constructivist theories about writing, reading, and learning. We see writing now not as a matter of mechanically encoding a known message but as active and interactive processes of creating meaning. We see reading not as a matter of mechanically decoding a known message, but as active and interactive processes of meaning-making, of negotiating meaning between reader, writer, and text. And we see learning not as a logical, linear, predictable process but as a dynamic, active and interactive, recursive process.

The goal of education has changed too. In a "Point of View" essay in the *Chronicle of Higher Education,* Howard Gardner wrote:

> Our concept of knowledge has changed since classical times but Socrates has provided us with a timeless educational goal—ever deeper understanding. With information accumulating at an incredible rate, our students will never be able to master all of the facts of history, science, mathematics, or the humanities. Nor is it necessary that they all study everything. What does seem worthwhile is that all students acquire some basic understandings of those disciplines that constitute our major ways of making sense of our lives and our world.

To the extent that the recommendations of the 1987 English Coalition Conference, summarized in a book subtitled *Democracy through Language* (Lloyd-Jones and Lunsford), represent our beliefs about language and learning, we as a profession have adopted the same goal of basic understanding that Gardner advocates.

To achieve this goal of understanding, our practices have changed so dramatically that we may have difficulty convincing others we are teaching. Many of you have probably had an experience similar to mine. About six years ago, a new division chairperson came to observe one of my basic-writing classes as part of our formal evaluation procedure. Students were working in small groups on first drafts, and after about 10 minutes, she came over to me and whispered, "This is all very interesting, Jane, but I'm going to leave now. Please come by the office to reschedule this visit for a day when you're teaching." It's true, and I have heard similar stories from many others and even read a few (see, for instance, Emig, "Non-Magical" 135).

Such stories illustrate how acting on our emerging theories has altered the shape of our work, i.e., changed our classroom practices. As a profession we have focused on this changing shape, on exploring the implications of our theories primarily in terms of what we expect of students. This focus has been both important and appropriate, but now we need to look at the implications for ourselves. We need to explore the ways in which the nature of our work has changed and consider the proposition that teaching today—the teaching that seeks to transform classes of students into communities of readers, writers, and learners—is itself a way of learning and knowing that has value for us as well as for students.

In terms of teaching, we seem to be in a position today analogous to the position we occupied in 1963 in terms of writing, for we have not yet explored the nature of the teaching that our current theories demand—we have not yet considered basic questions about our teaching, questions like the last four proposed as "Unexplored Territory" in the 1963 *Research in Written Composition:*

> What is involved in the act of writing?
> How does a person go about starting a paper? What questions must he answer for himself?
> How does a writer generate sentences?
> Of what does skill in writing really consist? (Braddock et al. 53)

Given our new theories about reading, writing, and learning, we might profitably pose parallel questions for teaching:

- What is involved in the act of teaching?

- How does a teacher go about planning a course; what questions must he or she answer?

- How does a teacher generate dialogue?

- Of what does skill in teaching really consist?

By exploring questions like these, we can deepen our understanding of teaching and, I contend, discover in the process that the teaching our current theories call us to is itself a mode of inquiry, a way of learning and knowing for us as teachers.

We have many options for exploring the idea that teaching writing has become a way of learning and knowing. We could, for instance, take that as a proposition, as Janet Emig took the proposition that writing is a mode of learning in her article of 1977. We could compare the characteristics of the act of teaching to those of learning as Emig considered correspondences between writing and learning. We could go point by point through the same clusters Emig did, beginning with learning being multirepresentational: enactive, iconic, symbolic, involving hand, eye, and brain (124). Teaching is also multirepresentational—extraordinarily multirepresentational. We could take Emig's second area, that learning benefits from feedback, both immediate and long-term (125). Teaching certainly provides immediate and long-term feedback. We could continue, not only considering the correspondences that Emig selected but examining other aspects of learning as well to discover the ways in which teaching itself has become a mode of inquiry, a way of learning and knowing.

We could also explore teaching by comparing it to what we know about reading processes. We could consider, for instance, how teachers read the emerging text of a classroom. What texts do they bring from other classes at other times? From other meetings of this class? How do teachers read the current texts—nonverbal, written, oral—of an individual student? When, for instance, do teachers read the current text of a student against earlier texts of the same student and when against the texts of the whole class or of previous classes? How do these readings interact? How are they like or unlike reading an individual short story against the corpus of a writer's work or that of her contemporaries? What questions about language, interpretation, and learning do such readings and rereadings of multiple texts stimulate in teachers? What questions arise about connections among reading, writing, speaking, listening, and critical thinking? And if we generate and use reading-related questions such as these to explore teaching, we can also generate and use writing-related questions such as what prompts a teacher to revise.

These examples suggest only a few of the many avenues already open to us for exploring teaching as a way of learning and knowing once we posit that idea as a possibility. In addition to perusing these lines of inquiry into the nature of teaching, I hope we will begin reflecting on what our theories demand of us and what they grant us in terms of our roles.

Our current theories demand that we be more than doctors diagnosing problems and prescribing corrective measures, more than entertainers pleasing an audience, more than high priests initiating the chosen into our rituals, more than managers assigning tasks and schedules, more even than coaches who alternately model, critique, cajole, and encourage. Our theories demand that we enter classrooms as knowledgeable, committed learners, willing to join students in the process of learning. This is not a return to the rather thoughtless, atheoretical student-directed practices of 20 years ago, but a tougher stance.[4] It requires respecting students in the deepest sense and recognizing both their integrity and our own as learners.

Creating communities of learners requires something similar to Martin Buber's I-Thou relationship, a stance or relationship to students and our task that makes dialogue and genuine inquiry possible.[5] And the two are integrally related, as Paulo Freire asserts in *Pedagogy of the Oppressed:* "Only dialogue, which requires critical thinking, is also capable of generating critical thinking. Without dialogue there is no communication, and without communication there can be no true education" (81). To make dialogue possible, to create what Parker Palmer calls spaces for learning that are open, bounded, and hospitable (71), demands a great deal.

Freire describes several conditions as essential for dialogue: "a profound love for the world and for men" (77), which he explains as commitment to others; "an intense faith in man, faith in his power to make and remake, to create and recreate" (79); and hope, for "[i]f the dialogues expect nothing to come of their efforts, their encounter will be empty and sterile, bureaucratic and tedious" (80). Freire also considers humility a prerequisite to dialogue:

> Dialogue, as the encounter of men addressed to the common task of learning and acting, is broken if the parties (or one of them) lack humility. How can I dialogue if I always project ignorance onto others and never perceive my own? . . . At the point of encounter, there are neither utter ignoramuses nor perfect sages; there are only men who are attempting, together, to learn more than they now know. (78–79)

If Freire is right, our theories call us to be learners with students and require from us a new level of commitment—the passion that Michael Polanyi finds essential to knowledge as understanding:

> I have tried to demonstrate that into every act of knowing there enters a tacit and passionate contribution of the person knowing what is being known, and that this coefficient is no mere imperfection, but a necessary component of all knowledge. (312)

Much has changed in these past 27 years, and it is time to explore the implications of those changes for us as teachers—as learners and knowers. The new demands of teaching simultaneously require and develop the same habits of mind that we have long associated with research and scholarship. If we expect students to be active learners, engaged in conscious theorizing and open to being transformed, we must also approach teaching as active, committed learners and knowers: reading and rereading the multiple texts of our students and classrooms, reflecting on and consciously theorizing about what does and does not unfold, generating new questions about language and learning, remaining open to new interpretations, developing in ourselves an ever deeper understanding of our discipline—of what constitutes acts of creation and interpretation, of self-discovery, expression, and communication. Because these habits of mind, required when we act upon our theories, parallel those of the scholar who works with more traditional texts or the researcher with data, I believe that teaching writing today is not only another way of learning and knowing, another mode of inquiry, but one that offers the same intellectual stimulation and personal satisfaction that research and scholarship bestow.

In inviting us to explore the idea of teaching as a mode of inquiry, I am not suggesting that it will be—or should be—the preferred mode of learning and knowing for all of us. Too much has been discovered about multiple ways of learning and knowing for that to be even a desirable goal (Belenky et al.; Gardner, *Frames;* Myers). I am suggesting, however, that teaching be considered a third, equally valid mode.

Let me close by indicating what we have to gain by exploring the nature of teaching today and acknowledging what it has become. At the level of this organization, we can gain the possibility of a stronger community, one based on genuine mutual respect. As individuals and a profession, developing a deeper understanding of the nature of teaching can lead not only to greater self-respect and confidence but also to new knowledge. The immense gains we have made from a deeper understanding of reading, writing, and learning will be fully matched, I believe, by a deeper understanding of teaching and its transformation into a genuine way of learning and knowing.[6]

NOTES

1. Bartholomae, Hairston, and North are among those who have discussed work in our field in terms of identity and respectability, but their conclusions about the implications for us differ. Disagreement also exists about whether we have succeeded in establishing composition as a discipline. North, who contends we have not (364), reviews this debate (318–21).

   Here and elsewhere, my use of *research* and *scholarship* follows North's basic distinction, in which research includes "all modes of inquiry grounded in empirical phenomena, however conceived, as opposed to the textual phenomena/dialectical grounding of the Scholars" (136). Although I have also been influenced by North's portrayal of the devaluation of teaching within the profession since 1963 and am indebted to his discussion of the factors contributing to what he calls "a general erosion in Practitioner authority" (50), my view of teaching as a mode of inquiry, which is predicated on the dialogic implications of our current constructivist theories of reading, writing, and learning, differs from his. I do not, for instance, see today's "practice as inquiry" as being necessarily reactive (North 33) although I believe that in the past, when transmission models dominated, teaching seldom, if ever, moved into the realm of inquiry without the stimulus of an immediate problem.

2. Resources for women's studies courses in the late 1960s and early 1970s included readings and exercises that reversed gender in statements and situations to raise consciousness—to make explicit, even palpable, our tacit knowledge of the pervasiveness

of sexism in our language and culture and its negative effects on both men and women. These passages employed strategies such as substituting feminine pronouns for masculine ones and using *woman* as a generic term for *humanity;* applying statements commonly made about one gender to the other, especially traditional psychological explanations of behavior; and creating parallel situations or statements for the other gender to highlight what was not typically said or done. Although I used passages such as Theodora Wells's "A Reversal Reading" for consciousness raising in workshops and women's studies classes, I don't remember ever reading a description or analysis of the reversal technique *per se.* The strategies constituting these reversals, however, have remained with me, informing my own readings and rereadings of situations and texts, including the few examples that follow.

3. North, for example, identifies the oral medium of teaching as a significant factor in the devaluation of teaching within the profession (54). Bartholomae, in reviewing the history of CCCC and discussing each term in our name, acknowledges our current uneasiness with the term *communication* and suggests we "think of it as a fortunate device, a term that keeps us from ever completely knowing our subject" (45).

4. The pedagogy of the late 1960s and early 1970s (sometimes called the inquiry or experiential-relevance movement) was not only atheoretical but also reactive (often growing out of what was, at best, a desire to placate students, at worst disdain for students). Unlike traditional transmission models which were, in Freire's terms, all *verbalism,* that earlier inquiry movement elevated experience for its own sake—what Freire would consider *activism* instead of *praxis,* the marriage of word and work (75–76), the interplay of action and reflection that our current constructivist theories require from both students and teachers.

5. Although Buber and Freire use somewhat different terms and examples to establish the nature of dialogue, Buber focusing on relationship or stance and Freire on conditions, they cover the same territory and create similar portraits of dialogic encounters, portraits that depict all parties as engaged, committed participants who are open to being transformed. The primary difference relates to what Buber, in a 1957 Afterword to *I and Thou,* considers the "limits of mutality" in contexts such as education and therapy (177–79). There, Buber contends, dialogue can occur without the pupil (or patient) being expected to enter fully into the perspective of the other (the teacher or therapist).

6. I am especially grateful to Marion Cutler, Janet Emig, and Lynn Troyka, who each discussed ideas with me early in the process and later offered valuable suggestions on a draft. And for engaging in conversations with me about the changing nature of teaching (conversations that began in 1984 or 1985 and have shaped my thinking about teaching in untold ways), I thank Jennifer Black and Judy Lambert. I am also grateful to Jacqueline Jones Royster for encouraging me, at a critical time, to stick with this topic and "speak from the heart."

WORKS CITED

Bartholomae, David. "Freshman English, Composition, and CCCC." *College Composition and Communication* 40 (Feb. 1989): 38–50.

Belenky, Mary Field, Blythe McVicker Clinchy, Nancy Rule Goldberger, and Jill Mattuck Tarule. *Women's Ways of Knowing: The Development of Self, Voice, and Mind.* New York: Basic, 1986.

Braddock, Richard, Richard Lloyd-Jones, and Lowell Schoer. *Research in Written Composition.* Champaign: NCTE, 1963.

Bridwell-Bowles, Lillian, and Michael Dickel. "Summary Report: Statistical Information, *CCC* Review." Unpublished report prepared for CCCC Executive Committee, 1989.

Buber, Martin. *I and Thou.* 1923. Trans. with Prologue and Notes by Walter Kaufmann. New York: Scribner's, 1970.

Chaplin, Miriam T. "Issues, Perspectives and Possibilities." *College Composition and Communication* 39 (Feb. 1988): 52–62.

Commission on the Future of Community Colleges. *Building Communities: A Vision for a New Century.* Washington: AACJC, 1988.

Conference on College Composition and Communication. *Guidelines on Scholarship.* Urbana: NCTE, 1987.

———. *Statement of Principles and Standards for the Postsecondary Teaching of Writing.* Urbana: NCTE, 1989.

Corbett, Edward P. J. "Teaching Composition: Where We've Been and Where We're Going." *College Composition and Communication* 38 (Dec. 1987): 444–52.

Dichter, Susan. *Teachers: Straight Talk from the Trenches.* Los Angeles: Lowell, 1989.

Emig, Janet. "Non-Magical Thinking: Presenting Writing Developmentally in Schools." *Writing: The Nature, Development and Teaching of Written Communication.* Ed. Joseph Dominic, Carl Fredericksen, and Marcia Whiteman. Vol. 2. Hillsdale: Erlbaum, 1982. Rpt. in *The Web of Meaning: Essays on Writing, Teaching, Learning and Thinking.* Ed. Dixie Goswami, and Maureen Butler. Upper Montclair: Boynton, 1983.

———. "Writing as a Mode of Learning." *College Composition and Communication* 28 (May 1977): 122–28.

Freire, Paulo. *Pedagogy of the Oppressed.* Trans. Myra Bergman Ramos. 1968. New York: Continuum, 1984.

Gardner, Howard. *Frames of Mind: The Theory of Multiple Intelligences.* New York: Basic Books, 1983.

———. "Point of View: The Academic Community Must Not Shun the Debate over How to Set National Educational Goals." *Chronicle of Higher Education* 8 Nov. 1989: A52.

Hairston, Maxine. "Breaking Our Bonds and Reaffirming Our Connections." *College Composition and Communication* 36 (Oct. 1985): 272–82.

Jordan, June. Address. CCCC/College Section Luncheon. NCTE Convention. Baltimore, 18 Nov. 1989.

Lindemann, Erika, ed. *CCCC Bibliography of Composition and Rhetoric, 1987.* Carbondale: Southern Illinois UP, 1990.

Lloyd-Jones, Richard, and Andrea Lunsford, eds. *The English Coalition Conference: Democracy through Language.* Urbana: NCTE and MLA, 1989.

Lunsford, Andrea A. "Composing Ourselves: Politics, Commitment, and the Teaching of Writing." *College Composition and Communication* 41 (Feb. 1990): 71–82.

Myers, Isabel Briggs, with Peter S. Myers. *Gifts Differing.* 1980. Palo Alto: Consulting Psychologists Press, 1985.

North, Stephen M. *The Making of Knowledge in Composition: Portrait of an Emerging Field.* Portsmouth: Boynton, 1987.

Palmer, Parker J. *To Know as We Are Known: A Spirituality of Education.* San Francisco: Harper, 1983.

Polanyi, Michael. *Personal Knowledge: Towards a Post-Critical Philosophy.* 1958. Corrected ed. 1962. Chicago: U of Chicago P, 1962.

Wells, Theodora. "A Reversal Reading." *Association for Humanistic Psychology Newsletter.* Dec. 1970: n.pag. Rpt. in *PsychoSources: A Psychology Resources Catalogue.* Ed. Evelyn Shapiro et al. Toronto: Bantam, 1973.

AFTERWORD: OPTIMISM GAINED AND LOST

After readily agreeing to participate in this project, I found myself reluctant to reread my address for the first time since its publication. That reluctance stemmed from memories of the struggle with writing it nearly fifteen years ago. I remember wanting to follow the CCCC tradition of using the Chair's address to present an issue the Chair considers important. For me that meant suggesting that, as composition specialists, we needed to view teaching differently — as an activity to be valued, an opportunity to construct new knowledge in our field through exploration and reflection. I also remember being acutely aware of the fact that CCCC had not had a "two-year person" as Chair since Lynn Troyka in 1981. I worried that a teaching-centered topic would be expected and so listened to but not heard. How could I frame my argument to increase the odds of its being heard, discussed, and seriously debated?

Having associated the address more with anxiety than excitement, I was surprised by the optimism underlying it. In retrospect, the optimism that fueled my writing seems naïve, but 1990 appeared to be a time for hope. We were celebrating a new decade as a prelude to a new millennium. On the international scene, we had recently witnessed the fall of the Berlin Wall as concrete evidence of the dissolution of the Iron Curtain. Most of us did not see the Gulf War on the horizon, and the prospect of continued peace seemed assured. At the national level, signs that diversity was being increasingly valued appeared in multiple forms: more cities and states were recognizing Martin Luther King Day as an official holiday; openly gay men and women were running for public offices (and occasionally winning in areas other than San Francisco Bay); and textbooks in history, literature, and humanities as well as composition were including the contributions of people of color. Despite the conservatism of the National Endowment for the Humanities under Lynn Cheney and the Department of Education under William Bennett, the wave of Anglo ethnocentrism embodied in E. D. Hirsch's "cultural literacy" and Bennett's promotion of a "great works" canon had *not* taken over the American education scene in the late 1980s and seemed to be receding.

CCCC was growing and graduate programs in comp/rhetoric becoming independent of literature-centered English programs in many institutions and gaining recognition and financial support in others. We seemed to have established ourselves as a healthy discipline with multiple research methodologies, new journals, ever-growing bibliographies, and competing models of key concepts such as voice and audience. The time seemed right to argue for viewing teaching as a mode of learning and for valuing it for what it can contribute to our field—a value parallel to the value we associate with research and scholarship.

The optimism I felt then has faded, and if I were writing that speech today, it would be quite different. Although I still view teaching as a powerful but largely unexplored venue for constructing knowledge, I see the problems in higher education today as more significant than those in our discipline. In 1990 I discussed assumptions and problems that made our limited view of teaching an understandable though unfortunate one, and I don't believe much has changed.

Although good work has come out of the teacher-researcher movement, it has not been able to change attitudes about the nature of teaching. And in the intervening years, a different view of higher education has gained ground—one that poses more pressing problems.

Today's problems certainly parallel some past problems, but the implications for teaching and learning seem more serious to me. We used to be concerned about students seeing college as job training instead of education. Now we need to be concerned not only about how students view higher education but about how our own institutions view our roles and our work. Many colleges and universities have shifted to business models using "total quality improvement" (TQI or one of its relatives—CQI, TQM). Whatever the acronym, students are consumers, our customers, and we need to please them. The public, area businesses, other departments, and so forth are all "stakeholders" whose perceived views seem to have more weight than that of others in our own field. With reduced budgets, administrators fear loss of income through lower enrollment, and they urge increased retention as they lower entrance requirements, reduce support for developmental programs and writing centers, and replace retirees with adjunct and temporary faculty. Added to that is the new admonition to make learning "fun," which for many students means easy, not challenging.

So if I were speaking today, I would probably focus on the value of education, the value of teaching for students, and what we can do as a profession to promote a view that centers on critical thinking, understanding, and the production of knowledge. The value of teaching for teachers, though still an issue close to my heart, would become subordinate—again.

–JANE PETERSON
Richland College

1991

Living In—and On—the Margins

DONALD McQUADE

I would like to invoke a brief—but I think memorable—assertion from Isak Dinesen. It reads: "All sorrows can be borne if you put them into a story or tell a story about them."[1] I come to this podium this morning fully conscious of the rather daunting responsibility attached to this occasion—a responsibility heightened by what my distinguished predecessors have said in their Chair's addresses. Mindful of that tradition, I do not intend this morning to speak *for* our profession, nor to try to prepare a different focus for our individual or collective work. Nor do I intend to argue for the need to establish either greater coherence for or a different map of the shifting demarcations within the field of composition studies. Rather, I've come here prepared simply to tell a story about writing, about writing as a matter of life and death, a story about how I now know much better what I thought I had known before—about the dignity and the importance of what we try to do each day in our public and private conversations about the importance of the work of words in the lives of our students and in our own lives.

• • •

I pause nervously at the door to room 216, trying with one last deep breath to compose myself for what I have been told I'm about to see. It's late in the afternoon on January 16th, a day already shrouded by low-hung dark rain clouds and the specter of the first salvos in what will soon be a deadly and destructive war in the Gulf. I adjust my eyes to the darkness in the room, and I enter its silence. I follow the invitation of the only light that's on—a small and soft green light on the monitor next to the shapeless from on the bed. The light casts a pale glow over the motionless

This article is a revised version of the Chair's address Donald McQuade delivered at the CCCC Convention in Boston, Massachusetts, on March 21, 1991. It was first published in *CCC*, volume 43, number 1, February 1992.

figure. I stand at the foot of the bed, and I suddenly recall the smell of a decomposing body from my summers working at the beach. I decide that this odor is slightly different—that it might be a leak in the catheter that hangs nearly filled on the far side of the bed. I taste the bitterness churning in the pit of my stomach and swallow uneasily. I stare at what is in front of me, trying to figure out if it's the person I traveled across the country to see and to talk with—perhaps for the last time.

I linger there for a moment or two, and then I decide to pick up her chart—to confirm her identity and to peer at the medical staff's judgment of her illness. Standing at the foot of the bed, her past and her future in my hands, I suddenly remember that she never had a birth certificate. I recall that she told us once that there was apparently no official record of her birth—anywhere. There was only a baptismal certificate. I saw it once; it said: Adelina Pisano, Blessed Sacrament Church, January 21, 1907. She had no reason not to trust her parents when they told her she was born on Christmas Day. She always seemed pleased that I had been born on December 26th. We celebrated our birthdays together late on Christmas night, and she always had a kind word to offset the disappointment I invariably felt when our relatives wished me a Merry Christmas *and* a Happy Birthday with a single present.

But there is no voice to hear this afternoon. Her lips are motionless; the rings around her eyes underscore the darkness of her sleep. Her body seems shorter, her head smaller than the image I carry around with me. Several wisps of thin grey hair evade the snarls of the net she no doubt struggled to put on—so that she wouldn't bother the nurses with having to comb her hair before her children's arrival each day during visiting hours. Smiling at the sight of the black hair net, I remember how self-effacing she is, how she never wants to bother anyone, how she doesn't expect anything from anyone, and how—when someone does try to help her—she responds with embarrassment and with the conviction that she hasn't done anything to deserve the attention, how someone else needs it more.

She never claims any authority for herself—for her perceptions, for her experiences, for her distinctive sense of self. She habitually disqualifies her point of view—before she speaks it. I recall from my childhood her most often repeated phrase: "Go ask your father. He'll know about that." I remember her telling us that she didn't get upset when the nuns in grammar school "officially" changed her name from Adelina to Edna—to make it easier to pronounce her name. "What was I going to do? Those nuns were tough then—not like today. They all wore stiff habits, even in the summer—not like today. Then, they didn't take any guff from anybody. . . ." I can hear her constantly interrupt herself to say, "I know I shouldn't say this." The soft stillness of the body lying in that bed reminds me that she sees herself at the receiving end of experience rather than at its origins. She doesn't seem to determine the history of her own life. After she was robbed by the young man she had asked to help her cross an icy and busy street on her way to daily Mass, she told her children, "Look, you gotta take what comes your way . . . the bad with the good. But don't worry. I asked Josie the tailor to sew pockets on the inside of my overcoat. When that bum tries to steal my pocketbook again, he'll be surprised. There won't be nothing in it next time." It seemed almost as if she were eager to see him again and to stare at him with contempt. But she allows herself few instances of such sweet revenge.

As I look intently down at her, I remind myself that she never likes to call attention to herself. She talks a great deal, but always about others—and especially about her sons, about her daughters-in-law, and, whenever *anyone* would listen, about her grandchildren and how blessed—and lucky—she is. As hard as I try, I can recall no time when she allows herself to be at the center of anything public. She somehow manages to make herself inconspicuous, even the time when she was invited to City Hall to receive a certificate—suitable of course for framing—from then-Mayor Ed Koch for her volunteer work among the elderly. She was proud of her award, but modesty, if not embarrassment, seemed almost to compel her to cover at least partially her mouth whenever she spoke about the occasion. Her family seemed much more excited than she allowed herself to be, and none of us was surprised that we had a difficult time trying to find her in the official photograph: she had tucked herself into a tiny space between two beaming—and large—women at what, as fortune would have it, turned out to be the edge of photograph. As I move my eyes slowly across her deeply-lined face, I see there reminders that in virtually every significant sense, she probably still views herself as unimportant, as someone who doesn't matter, as someone who finally sees herself as fundamentally expendable.

I notice that her chest moves slowly—to the rhythm of the monitor. Her skin takes on a slightly yellow hue in the soft green light, and it drapes loosely—and even elegantly—over the small, brittle bones that somehow still keep her body together. Her wrists are attached with thin rubber tubing to the metal bed rails—to protect her, they say, from hurting herself if she suffers another stroke. I sit down at her bedside and reach for the short, stubby fingers that are open to view, fingers that I imagine still bear traces from the years she devoted to raising her children, years when, as she hesitantly told us, she "helped make ends meet" by typing address labels at the kitchen table against a never-ending cycle of pressured deadlines from an insurance company that wanted its renewal notices out on time.

Her hands are ice cold, and I slide my nervous fingers up to her wrist—in search of what I expect will be her faint pulse. I'm no longer surprised by what I see and touch. She looks as if she's dying quietly, if not peacefully.

Her arm moves slightly, and I am quickly drawn to her face, and then to her flickering eyes. She opens them and turns her head toward me—but slowly. I lean closer to her, but she doesn't speak. I sense her surprise and wait for her to say something. She looks at me with more focused attention, smiles, and tries to force words out of her body. I feel the attention in her quickening pulse and sense the emotion that pushes the words through her stiffened jaw and parched lips. Her voice finally relaxes, taking comfort in recognizing its own distinctive sound. She whispers: "Da Professor!"

She seems too weak for conversation, so I launch into a hurried—and scattered—report on her grandchildren in California. The news seems to course through her fragile veins, and I try to make her stronger with funny stories about the children, about life on the west coast, and about the trips she took with us after her husband died. I ask her if she remembers the trip on TWA to the old country—when one of my former students bumped all of us up into first class. "Somebody should fly first class," he said, "Why not you and your family?" When I remind her that I found that logic compelling, her smile broadens and deepens. She says softly: "I was a nervous wreck for the first half-hour. I had my rosary beads out. What if they found out that we didn't belong?!"

I lean back into the chair and ask: "Do you remember what happened when we landed in Rome?"

"Yeah. I wouldn't speak Italian. I didn't want to embarrass you and Susanne by speaking with such a terrible accent. They'd know I was from Brooklyn in a second. . . ." I remind myself that she won't speak for either herself or for others, and I conclude, mistakenly, that she remains not simply—but profoundly—inarticulate.

As we relax into each other's company and settle into a quiet conversation, a hospital orderly announces himself and reminds her that it's five o'clock. Positioning her dinner tray over her now raised-bed, he proudly announces, "I've got something special for you tonight. I know you gonna like this." He releases the restraints on her wrists and sweeps the metal cover from over the plate, like a magician heightening the anticipation before revealing a surprise. He backs away from the bed with the metal lid still in his hand, and as he turns to leave, he takes special pleasure in trumpeting the word "Lasagne!"

Almost immediately, her head drops, as if it has been suddenly disconnected from the rest of her body. She moves it back and forth, trying to muster a sigh of despair at the same time. She tries to arch her head back up to see if the orderly has left. "They're very nice people here," she says in a hushed voice. "They bring you your tray right to your bed. I don't want them to be insulted, but I can't eat this stuff. Look at it. They serve carrots with lasagne! I tasted the sauce yesterday." Her eyes dart toward the doorway. She tries to lean forward, but she resorts to another whisper: "They don't know how to make sauce—not like we do."

I try to reassure her that I understand. "I know," I say softly, "but try to eat it anyway. If you wanna get outta here, you have to eat. You know you need to get strong."

"I know. . . . I know. . . ." Her hand moves slowly, reluctantly toward the fork. She lifts a small lump of the lasagne from the right side of the plate, and as she moves it haltingly—and almost horizontally—across the plate toward her, the fork touches the carrots. She doesn't seem either willing or able to hold the fork any longer. Her eyes move away from the food, and she stares intently at me. Her tongue reaches the edge of her lips, but she doesn't speak.

I fill the silence with a nervous refrain: "You have to eat it if you want to get strong, if you want to get out of this place."

She forces herself to lift her right hand with her left and to move it once again toward the fork. She picks it up and tilts it slightly toward herself, perhaps hoping that some of the lasagna will slide off and onto her pale green nightgown, putting an end to the awkwardness we both feel.

But the sauce glues the pasta to the fork. "I'll try," she murmurs, "but I can't promise that I'll eat all of it. This sauce is so lousy."

"Try. . . . Do the best you can."

The second bite is even more reluctant than the first. "I can't eat it. It'll kill me."

"You gotta eat," I say, and somewhat impatiently. "All right. Leave the lasagne. Try the carrots. . . ."

She responds more quickly, and with a slightly sharper edge in her voice. "The carrots?! I just tried the lasagna. I can't eat the carrots now, not with lasagna."

"You gotta get stronger if you wanna get out of here."

"I know. But I can't eat this stuff. The lasagna and the carrots are cold. Nobody can eat cold lasagna. It'll kill me."

Her eyes reach for the cup of lime Jello. "Let me try the Jello. It's got fruit cocktail in it. What the hell can they do to Jello?!" Her fork disturbs the sheen of the Jello. The surface wobbles like she knows it should. She forces a slight smile, and as she eats it she says "Everybody knows how to make Jello."

• • •

At 7:15 that night, I'm sitting at a linen-lined table in my younger brother's dining room, eating a steaming plate of ravioli. Our eyes are glued to the television set nervously propped atop the credenza so that we could eat and watch the news before returning to the hospital. At precisely the same moment that news reports from Baghdad announce that the war has begun, raining steel on that city, the phone rings. Annoyed by the distraction, I pick it up and before I can say anything the voice on the other end urges "Come to the hospital—fast."

As soon as my brother, sister-in-law, and I arrive at room 216, we're redirected to the intensive care unit, where my older brother paces the hallway. "She's had another episode," he reports anxiously. "I don't know if she's gonna make it this time." I spend what seems like the next hour or two sitting on a vinyl-covered couch, thinking—nervously—about the word "episode." Finally, the doctor emerges and asks us to step outside the waiting room to find a corner or a wall that will provide some semblance of privacy.

"She's had another stroke, but this one is far more serious. She's also suffered respiratory arrest, but because the nurses and the doctor were working on her in less than a minute, I'm confident that there's no brain damage. We can always do a CAT-scan later. She didn't seem able to keep her food down, and it came back up into her lungs. I'm afraid she's also suffering from double pneumonia—a combination of bacterial and gastric infections in her lungs. Look, I hate to bring this up, but the hospital staff needs to know whether you'd like us to try to resuscitate her should she experience another episode like the one tonight. She's stabilized now. There isn't anything you can do for her at this point. Don't let me push you into a decision. Why don't you go home and try to get some sleep."

Even in the face of her own death, she doesn't have the opportunity to speak for herself.

• • •

The next morning brings the startling news that she's made remarkable progress during the night. We take turns going in to see her. When my brother and I reach her bedside, we're stunned by the sight of the number of tubes running into, and through, her body. While technology rained death on Baghdad and Allied forces used "smart" bombs equipped with cameras to film their own success in living color, one tiny, frail Italian woman was kept alive by six humming consoles and by what apparently was an indomitable will to live.

She looks up at us from the center of the other side of that terrifying sight. The tubes prevent her from speaking, but her eyes plead for an explanation. We tell her, as best we can, what has happened to her. We don't tell her that the doctor has asked us to decide whether *we* want the hospital to resuscitate her should she have another stroke. Neither of us is ready to say that, at least not yet. We try to keep talking, to reach beyond the veil of silence that seems to have descended over her.

The more we try to offer her encouragement, the more her eyes seem to dart around the room. She fixes her attention on the table to the right of where I'm standing. She motions toward the table with her eyes. The only items on it are a stack of the bookmark-sized prayers she carries around with her, a half-filled cup of water, a pencil, and some sheets of paper with "Mercy Hospital" written across the top and "PROGRESS NOTES" printed in large boldface beneath it. Instinctively, I gather up the prayers and ask her if she'd like me to read them to her. Her eyes dart left and right. Once again, she uses her eyes to motion toward the table. After what seemed like the longest—and most awkward—moments in my life, I finally realize that she wants me to hand her the paper and pencil. I rush to the nurse's station and ask for a clipboard. Within seconds of my return, a torrent of prose rushes across that piece of paper.

It seemed as though nothing—not her eighth-grade education, her shaky handwriting, her weak grammar, not her spotty punctuation—could encumber what she wanted, almost desperately, to tell us about what had happened to her. Here's a sampling of what she wrote:

> Last night after you left they started working on me from 8:00 to through the night. The doctors and nurses never left me. No sleep until 5:00 o'clock a.m. in the morning. They were good to me. I will not ever forget them in my prayers. They all very very nice to me and I hope you all feel the same way about them. Sorry. Bad handwriting. Love and Prayers.

She wrote virtually continuously for twenty minutes that morning, pausing only to allow us to figure out what the appropriate next question was and to press her for greater detail. She wrote until she slid into exhaustion and a deep sleep. That afternoon, as soon as we arrived, she was back at it. And the next day, when her grown grandchildren arrived, she told them slightly different versions of the same story in writing. She was proud that she had survived, but she couldn't fully release herself into saying that directly.

It seems as if she is writing to keep herself alive, almost as if her self would be lost if she stopped—lost, or suffocated, in the maze of tubes and wires and contraptions that not only were keeping her alive but also allowing her to speak from the other side of her silence. Each time we visit she pours out one "Progress Note" after another. Each becomes more detailed, more compelling. She writes, for example, about the CAT-scan they put her through on the night she suffered her last stroke. She describes feeling trapped inside that silver machine, feeling as though she had died and had been placed inside a silver casket. She writes that she felt so alone and that she is glad she can tell us about that experience, and how she hopes she won't have to go through it again. "Next time," she writes, "just bury me."

Over the course of several visits, we ease her—or she eases us—into taking up different subjects, but she invariably returns to the events surrounding her last stroke and to their aftermath. She seems to shy away from describing the central event, the "episode," in any detail, but she doesn't hesitate in the least to take us inside the world of the machines she's still hooked up to. She explains, for example, that she sometimes feels as though she no longer has a body, that she is little more than an extension of the equipment. "I don't know how I'll ever get out of this place," she writes. Yet, slowly her tone grows slightly more confident. She seems able for the first time in her notes to distance herself from the trauma by characterizing it in a phrase we heard applied for years to anything she judges unpleasant. "You have no idea. I went through the tortures of hell." Everyone smiles, knowingly. It's also time to leave. She motions me to stay, and as soon as she is sure that everyone else has left the room, she starts to write again. After about a minute, she hands me the clipboard, and smiles wistfully and coyly: "It was the bad lasagne I had. . . ."

Driving home from that evening, I take pleasure in the fact that perhaps for the first time in her life, Adelina Pisano has chosen to reserve for herself the authority to make—as well as to articulate—a decision. Needing to tell her stories, but trapped in silence, she turns to the only medium available to her: writing. Writing for her took on a life of its own; it became not only a self-affirming but also a life-affirming activity.

Another day—her final day in intensive care. The doctor reports that she's "out of the woods now" and that they plan to move her in the morning to a bed in intermediate care. We thank him for his help, and he turns toward me: "When are you going home?"

"I guess I can go back tomorrow night."

The ride to JFK is unusual; that is, it is uneventful. There is no traffic, no accidents, and I remark to my brother that the road looks "really clean," that I haven't seen a single abandoned—or stripped—car along the side of the highway. He acknowledges my point with a quick "uh huh" but never takes his eyes off the car in front of him.

The flight to San Francisco proves more intriguing. With threats of global terrorism, it's not surprising that the plane is far less than half full. Yet I can't understand why I don't sleep on the long flight home.

My body is in neutral, if not reverse, but my mind jump starts the takeoff. Before we reach cruising altitude, I realize I need to make some sense of what we all have just gone through. I order some wine—to celebrate Adelina Pisano's will to live and to toast her for caring enough about her family and finally about herself to tell them each day through her "Progress Notes" that she is alive and that she hopes—with the help of God and some good luck—to stay alive. I take pleasure and pride in the dignity of her struggle and in her resourcefulness with language and the power she now exercises over it. But I quickly caution myself to resist sentimentalizing her and what she is accomplishing as a newly-practiced, although still self-effacing writer. I remind myself of my rekindled anger about the resources of language denied to her as well as about the skills she denied to herself. I know that her resourcefulness with language is culturally as well as personally determined, but I can't decide which prevails in Adelina Pisano's life — then and now. I can't figure out where she is in relation to her own experience — whether she is at the center or at the margins of her own articulateness.

I sit in a silver cylinder at 35,000 feet, alone with my thoughts and plenty of time, so I decide to pursue some better understanding of what it means to be "marginal" or "marginalized" and to live "in" and "on" the margins. It doesn't take long for the negative associations to surface. Those who are "marginal" or "marginalized" lead lives determined — in fundamental ways — by others. Characteristically, they are reported by others to regard themselves as closed out, if not shut down, from experience. Characteristically, they are reported to be viewed — and treated — by others as though they were inert, ignored, forgotten, left out too long — like a faded shirt hanging on a clothesline at the back of an abandoned tenement.

The prevailing view of living "on the margins" doesn't differ markedly. To be "on the margins" is to be in a condition which closely approximates the limit below or beyond which something ceases to be possible or desirable. Viewed from another angle — from on the other side of a boundary — to be on the margins is to be superfluous. After all, a margin (of profit, of space, of time, of material goods) is an amount that is available — or allowed — in addition to what is estimated to be strictly necessary for or essential to a predefined purpose.

I gaze out the window and reflect on the significance the term bears when viewed from the perspective of spatial relations. To be "on" the margin means to locate oneself — or to be located — at the edge of a boundary. This place — this state of mind, this socio-economic condition, this linguistic or political or sexual identity — is in some way marked off or distinguished from the rest of what is perceived. In this sense, to be "in" or "on" the margin is to be identified as different — but negatively so — to be seen as unlike the rest. But the demarcations between the center and the margins are always in flux. And complex identities result from these shifting grounds — what Gloria Anzaldua calls "Borderlands." In a compelling blend of poetry and prose, Anzaldua describes the shadowy spaces of her own childhood along the Texas/Mexico border, caught between two cultures, and an alien in both. Anzaldua charts the intersections of ethnic, linguistic, and sexual identity with both searing insight and a powerful and cohesive vision of a dignified future for those who live in what she calls "this place of contradiction," a place where the self struggles "amidst adversity and violation; with the confluence of primordial images; with the unique positionings consciousness takes at these confluent streams; and with [an] almost instinctive urge to communicate, to speak, to write about life on the borders, life in the shadows."[2]

I realize that the terms of Adelina Pisano's life—and especially its shifting grounds—offer another confirmation of the contradictions of living "on the borders" and "in the shadows." I begin to challenge the applicability of the traditional definitions of the word "margins," each of which focuses on some limitation of the place or the person described with this term. The inaccuracies and the inadequacies of these definitions become clearer—when applied to individual acts of self-identification, to individual acts of self-articulation, when applied to speaking, thinking, and writing.

For Gloria Anzaldua—and for Adelina Pisano—to live "in" and "on" the margins might well bear more positive implications. For these two women, in very different places and in very different ways, to live "in" and "on" the margins is, in many respects, to be free: to try to reach out, to speak out from behind the veil of silence, to take risks, to take chances, to open themselves to experience in what are possibly, although not assuredly, informative and enduring ways. To live productively "in" and "on" the margins is to be "on edge," to recognize and explore both the terms for experience as well as the relations between and among the terms, those seemingly silent gaps, those seemingly still spaces between one experience and another. The voice of William James resonates as I pause to take a deep breath. "Experience itself, taken at large, can grow by its edges," James reminds me. "Life is in the transitions as much as in the terms connected: often indeed, [life] seems to be there more emphatically, as if our spurts and sallies forward were the real firing line of flame advancing across the dry autumnal field which the farmer proceeds to burn. In this line, we live prospectively as well as retrospectively."[3] I ponder those lines in James, and I *think* I understand the connection: the margin is not only a place, it is a locus for relations. It may even be an activity. It's *more*—not less—than a noun. It's a noun in process—like the word "education," or "knowledge," or "experience."

I spend the rest of the flight conjuring up images that might sharpen the distinctions between and among such terms as "margins," "borders," "edges," "boundaries," and "fringes." I think first of the students I teach. I realize that the margins are where most teachers—especially teachers of writing—live in relation to our students. It's a location (a place) as well as an opportunity for us to demonstrate (an activity) the generosity that distinguishes our work as teachers—the reciprocity we express in response to what they have written. I suddenly find it curious that teachers and students call such writing "marginal notes," and I remind myself that I need to think more often—and more seriously—about the nature and the implications of the writing I so routinely do in the classes I teach. Being "in" and "on" the margins of our students' lives is where they ordinarily expect us to be—and rightfully so. Versions of the dialectic surface in all corners of the academy. I begin to understand that the margins may well be where many students *and* faculty spend their time thinking and writing—even though every one of us is expected to do something quite different: to speak and think and write and perform at the center of the intellectual communities and the cultures in which each of us seeks to posit his or her voice.

My thoughts drift to the difficulties, to the strains, to the pain some—and perhaps many—students and teachers experience as they struggle with the pressures and expectations imposed on them: to toe the line rather than, as James says, to live *in* the line, that is to "live prospectively as well as retrospectively." Remembering my mother's eagerness—and struggle—to write prompts me to think of my student Emily Hampton, who loved to write sentences. Emily Hampton wrote many brilliant and elegant sentences. She worked relentlessly on them, shaping and reshaping them to satisfy her own extraordinary standards. But Emily Hampton had trouble seeing the relations between her sentences. Transitions—from one sentence to the next, from one paragraph to another—remained impossibly difficult for her. A perfectionist in every sense, Emily Hampton was stuck *on* the line. She had trouble living and writing either prospectively or retrospectively. Because Emily Hampton was convinced—by herself or by others—that she couldn't ever produce paragraphs and essays that would satisfy the expectations she imagined others set for her, she did violence to her sentences and finally to herself. She killed herself the day after she participated in the commencement ceremony at Berkeley. With my chin leaning on my hand, I sit staring at the seat in front of me—thinking only of my failures, for a long time.

The silence is broken by the sounds of the voices of Emily and Adelina, by the painful edges of these women's stories, and I recall another. Francine du Plessix Gray's account of a recurring—and harrowing—nightmare from her youth. "Facing a friend, I struggle for words and emit no sound," she says. "I have an urgent message to share but am struck dumb. My jaw is clamped shut as in a metal vise. I gasp for breath and cannot set my tongue free. And at the dream's end, my friend has fled, and I am locked into the solitude of silence." du Plessix Gray attributes the nightmare, at least in part, to her father's impatience with her youthful writing, to his swift and sardonic tongue, and to his having constantly interrupted her when she tried to speak. Later as a student in a workshop at Black Mountain, du Plessix Gray submitted revisions of several prize-winning stories. Her mentor, no less an imposing figure than the 6 foot 8 inch poet Charles Olson, told her, "You're writing pure junk. . . . If you want to be a writer keep it to a journal. . . . And above all don't try to publish anything for ten years."

Francine du Plessix Gray's first piece of fiction was published in *The New Yorker* one year *past* the distant deadline Olson had set for her. In struggling to come to terms with why she persisted at writing, she says: "I write out of a desire for revenge against reality, to destroy forever the stuttering powerless child I once was, to gain the love and attention that silenced child never had, to allay the dissatisfaction I still have with myself, to be something other than what I am. . . . I remain sustained," she says, "by a definition of faith once offered me by Ivan Illich: 'faith is a readiness for the surprise.' I write because I have faith in the possibility that I can eventually surprise myself."[4]

· · ·

That image of a jaw clamped shut, that sense of revenge against reality, that definition of faith, that readiness for the surprise propel me back to the place I left nearly eight hours before.

I am standing at Adelina Pisano's bedside. She finally frees herself from the machines that regulated her recovery. She can talk now, but I know that she won't — not unless she has her teeth in. We're both nervous. We hold each other's hand tightly, but stiffly. Neither of us dares to be the first to talk. I feel the quiet tension between us. I finally say: "I'm leaving tonight. I have to go. Susanne has been alone with the kids for a long time, and I start a new semester in two days."

"I understand."

I tell her how happy I am to have spent time with her, even in such difficult circumstances. I tell her how sorry I am to leave, and I try to deflect attention from my sadness by reminding her of the funny stories we traded on the first day I visited her. She looks at me and fixes my attention on her eyes for what seems like a very long minute. Finally, she speaks. "I understand. I've caused you boys too much trouble already. Don't worry about me. I'll be all right." Her voice rushes forward. "Listen, say hello to Susanne and the kids, and send me a new picture of Christine and Marc. The ones I have are getting old. I bet he's grown a lot."

She pauses, but only for a few seconds, perhaps to summon a word, to change the subject. "Oh, they say I can have a phone in my new room. Call me once in a while." She drops her hand slightly, but her eyes hold mine. "You take care of yourself, do you hear . . . and write when you get a chance."[5]

NOTES

1. This quotation from Isak Dinesen appears as an epigraph to chapter five of Hannah Arendt's *The Human Condition* (175).
2. See the "Preface" to Gloria Anzaldua's *Borderlands/La Frontera: The New Mestiza.*
3. William James makes this point in an essay, "A World of Pure Experience," in *Essays in Radical Empiricism* (42).
4. Francine du Plessix Gray's statement appeared in a *New York Times Book Review* article, "I Write for Revenge Against Reality" (3).
5. Adelina Pisano died on August 6, 1991.

For their generous encouragement and assistance in preparing several drafts of this essay, I would like to thank Patrick W. Hoy III, June Jordan, Anne Middleton, Kathleen Moran, and Nancy Sommers. I would also like to express my gratitude to the students in English 180J at the University of California, Berkeley, who read an earlier draft of this essay and offered invaluable suggestions for improving it.

WORKS CITED

Anzaldua, Gloria. *Borderlands/La Frontera: The New Mestiza.* San Francisco: Spinsters/Aunte Lute, 1987.
Arendt, Hannah. *The Human Condition.* Chicago: U of Chicago P, 1958.
Gray, Francine du Plessix. "I Write for Revenge Against Reality," *The New York Times Book Review.* September 12, 1982: 3.
James, William. "A World of Pure Experience," *Essays in Radical Empiricism.* Cambridge: Harvard UP, 1976.

AFTERWORD: "WRITE WHEN YOU GET A CHANCE"

An unlikely set of circumstances shaped the Chair's address I delivered at the 1991 CCCC in Boston: a class of 150 students, my dying mother, and a long plane ride to Boston. The experience proved to be the most instructive writing exercise of my life.

The previous year, I had the privilege and the pleasure, along with Alix Schwartz, then a PhD student at the University of California, Berkeley, of serving as architect and carpenter for the 1990 CCCC at the Palmer House in Chicago. Serving as the Program Chair is the most privileged of positions in the field of composition and rhetoric: for at least that one-year period, the CCCC Program Chair knows as much about the current state of the field as anyone. Yet with that knowledge comes the daunting responsibility the next year as CCCC Chair to speak to and for the field — to one's colleagues. Given my philosophical reluctance to speak on behalf of a large group, my academic training in literature, as well as my close reading of the distinguished tradition of CCCC Chair's addresses, I found it difficult to summon the courage to speak to and for the profession.

During the spring 1991 semester, I was teaching English 166, The Essay as Literature: Traditions and the Individual Talent, at U. C. Berkeley. At the initial class meeting, I announced to the 150 students in attendance that I would invite them to critique the draft of an essay that I would present at the CCCC meeting in Boston in late March.

During this same period, my mother, Adelina Pisano, was in a nursing home in New York City slowly dying from a series of small strokes. I decided to use the occasion of my Chair's address to write an essay about my mother and our exchanges of letters across the continent. It was the first time she and I had talked about writing, and I wanted to convey what I had learned from her soft-spoken views about its importance.

The draft of the essay I presented for the students' response had a two-part structure: a narrative focused on my mother, whose eighth-grade schooling belied her wisdom, followed by a series of inferences about the significance of writing in everyday life. At first, the students were reluctant to critique the draft — until one student said pointedly, "Why don't you do what you tell us to do: why don't you let the narrative make the point?" Another student quickly added, "Why don't you let your mother make the point?"

A third student wondered, "What was the last thing your mother said to you?" Without hesitating, I responded, "Write when you get a chance." I then said to them, "Excuse me. Give me two minutes." I wrote the last paragraph of my CCCC Chair's address standing in front of those 150 students. I then rewrote the rest of the essay on a notepad during the long, delayed flight from San Francisco to Boston. I had found an opportunity to practice what I preach and to heed my mother's sage advice.

I sent the "final" version of the essay ("Living In — and On — the Margins") to the class via fax, along with my gratitude, but they had shifted their focus to other work and to the spring break. Adelina Pisano died four months later.

> – DONALD MCQUADE
> University of California,
> Berkeley

1992

Writing in the Spaces Left

WILLIAM W. COOK

T he modern nation and its national narratives, those texts which authenticate cultural location, have become increasingly the source of contention. Evidence of such contention may be read in the persistent resistance of historically suppressed groups and individuals to accept subscription by such texts, to translate the absence and exclusion of such texts into metaphors for universality. Art, as a powerful source of national narratives (and this should surprise no one), has become the ground on which many of the battles for control have been fought. Ishmael Reed in the early 1970s spoke to the necessity for resistance, likening the struggle over control of the national narrative to sexual competition. "In the beginning was The Word and The Word is the domain of the white patriarchy. Beware. Women and natives are not to tamper with The Word" (n.pag.). This is the situation he describes in the introduction to *19 Necromancers from Now*. His artistic project, described in "When State Magicians Fail," is to "appreciably curtail Judeo-Christian culture's domination of our senses," to stage a "bloodless coup" by "a cooperative of autonomous groups who are going to come up with new ways of making America work" (qtd. in Gerald and Blecher 163). I would like to argue that our contemporary struggles with the primacy of "official histories" provides us with a useful tool for reading back through cultural history and, by doing so, reconsidering the relationship of the voice of the suppressed to the canonical texts of the dominant.

In 1882 Ernest Renan attempted a definition of nation and the manner in which national narratives served to inscribe that nation. Such national narratives are, according to Renan, tales of "a heroic past, great men, glory. . . . [They are] the capital upon which one bases a national

This article is a revised version of the Chair's address William W. Cook delivered at the CCCC Convention in Cincinnati, Ohio, on March 19, 1992. It was first published in *CCC*, volume 44, number 1, February 1993.

ideal." Such narratives privilege "common glories in the past . . . and a common will in the present" (qtd. in Bhabha 19). They assume, if not "a universal subjectivity and will, at least a national 'heimlich'" (Bhabha 2). Homi K. Bhabha in the Introduction to *Nation and Narration* observes that the narratives described by Renan are neither eternal or unshakable; rather, they are transitional, indeterminate; their vocabularies waver, terrified by "the space or race of the other" (2) — those excluded from participation in such inscription and consequently silent and marginalized. Bhabha is interested in those sites at which such narratives encounter the newly insistent voice of the once subjected. He cites Edward Said's observation that national narratives are as much the agency or force for subordination, fracturing, diffusing, and reproducing, as for producing, creating, forcing, and guiding (Bhabha 4–5). The irrefragable dream of pains suffered and the dedication to future suffering for the common glory become, in Bhabha's modernist construction, a contested site. Such narratives fracture at just those points where silenced and marginalized others claim spaces for their own counter-inscription.

In 1991 I proposed as a theme for the CCCC convention "A Time of Trial, Reorientation, and Reconsideration." This year, we turned our attention to "Contexts, Communities, and Constraints: Sites for Composing and Composition." 1993 promises us an opportunity to consider "Issues, Answers, and Actions." The comments which follow are my attempt to suggest the interconnectedness of these three themes, to reconsider some of the contexts and constraints particular to specific ideological sites for composing and communicating, to recreate the ideological contexts in which texts are inserted, and to suggest, in this reconsideration, issues and actions: spaces not completely obscured by earlier inscriptions. My comments will privilege those instances when the marginalized, by their very resistance to the texts of the national narrative, reconstruct such texts, instances when the very texts presented as models become refigured and transformed by the contrary voice of the formerly subjected other. Literacy and liberation are linked in such actions not because the newly literate read and internalize the values of such texts, but because they bring to the encounter with such texts a willful deconstructive point of view. Their "erased" lives become the very center of new, resistant texts, texts which displace the univocal narratives of the nation with their multi-voiced musings on nation and identity.

To read the multi-voiced record left by African American writers is to encounter texts which recreate again and again the same message: literacy and resistant reading are at the center of liberation and the full exercise of self as subjectivity. The multiple speaking texts to which I refer do not approach that literacy from an uncomplicated point of vantage, however. The very texts which substantiate in narrative and argument the power that is to be gained by mastery of written composition and reading undermine such an emphasis in what may be called a subversive second text, one which affirms the primacy of orality, and especially oratory, over all other language constructions. They affirm and deny (to paraphrase Ralph Ellison); they accept and reject the power of the national narrative as written. As James Olney argues in *I Was Born: Slave Narratives and Their Status as Autobiography*, writing is, in such texts, an "assertion of identity and in identity is freedom—freedom from slavery, freedom from ignorance, freedom from non-being, freedom even from time" (qtd. in Cornelius 2). Access to writing made possible, in his configuration, not only the construction of a self; it also rendered such a construction fixed and immune to the shifts and deteriorations of time.

I will privilege the nineteenth century in this discussion, for it is that period in the cultural history of the United States which is marked by a very interesting shift in discourse, a shift from oratory to poetic discourse. Individualism and romantic modes of creativity replace the collaboration and consequent epideictic rhetoric of oratory. Eighteenth-century science, for example, was belletristic, morally tinged, and the property of the educated individual. In the nineteenth century, that science became specialized and morally neutral, moving from sensory language to the marshaling of evidence. William S. McFeeley sums up the privileged position of oratory quite nicely in his 1991 biography of Frederick Douglass.

> In the public mind, oratory was not just a demonstration of great learning, though it was sometimes that, nor was it simply entertainment, though it was decidedly that as well, and people listened for hours; oratory was power. (34)

Let me begin by examining two moments in the record to which I refer, moments which converse on the topic of literacy and orality and on literacy and liberation. Olaudah Equiano (or Gustavas Vasa, the African) published his narrative in 1789. One moment in that text constitutes for me an initiating location for my theme:

> I had often seen my master and Dick employed in reading and I had a great curiosity to talk to the books, as I thought they did; and so to learn how all things had a beginning. For that purpose I have often taken up a book, and talked to it, and then put my ears to it, when alone, in hopes it would answer me; and I have been much concerned when I found it remaining silent. (43–44)

Equiano provides us here with our earliest reference to the "talking book," that text which will speak when spoken to, a text which will willingly surrender its secrets to a non-lettered conversant. At this early stage in consciousness, the naive young man seeks dialogue with, hopes to hear the voice he desires in, the texts of others. Only later does he come to the mastery which empowers his realization of the text and voice which he seeks: the record of self to which he can speak because he shares with it a life and a language. The text he seeks is the "history of neither a saint, a hero, nor a tyrant" (11). Such a record must be the product of his own inscription. Significantly, in a world which rejects full selfhood for the African American, he inscribes himself as a representative rather than an exceptional voice. He is not interested in those exceptional constructs of human desire which dominate the narratives of the world which he has unwillingly encountered—its saints, heroes and tyrants—he is interested in representation. He rejects what Edward Said has called nationalism's "heroic narratives" (qtd. in Bhabha 44).

John Sella Martin, editor of the *New Era* with Frederick Douglass from 1870–1871, restates the view of the "talking book" initiated by Equiano:

> I learned, too, from seeing them reading and writing, that they could make paper and the little black marks on it talk. It is difficult for children who see this from their earliest years to realize the incredulity with which a slave-boy ten years of age regards the achievement of reading when he notices it for the first time. For a long time I could not get it out of my head that the readers were talking to the paper, rather than the paper talking to them. When, however, it became a reality to me, I made up my mind that I would accomplish the feat myself. . . . [By] their bantering one another at spelling, and betting each on his proficiency over the other, I learned to spell by sound before I knew by sight a single letter in the alphabet. (Blassingame 709)

Frederick Douglass picks up the image of the "talking book" in his 1845 narrative, exemplifying in his echoing of Equiano, the process of imitation and repetition which Henry Louis Gates, Jr. describes as the source of that special genre called the slave narrative. In chapter four, Douglass describes himself at the nadir of his hopes. He is acutely aware that he is now a slave for life. His earlier dreams of freedom are never to be realized. At this point, he encounters that "talking book" which responds to his questions about the possibility and reality of liberation, and, in the process of responding, it instructs him in his struggle to gain an authentic voice. Douglass writes:

> the thought of being a slave for life began to bear heavily upon my heart. Just about this time I got hold of a book entitled *The Columbian Orator*. Every opportunity I got, I used to read this book. (*Narrative* 52)

What was the effect of his reading the passages which he cites as his favorites in Caleb Bingham's *The Columbian Orator* (first published in 1797), a text designed to provide, according to the title page, "a variety of original and selected pieces; together with rules . . . to improve youth and others in the ornamental and useful art of eloquence"? Was such a text silent, or was it for Douglass truly a "talking book"?

I read them over and over again with unabated interest. They gave tongue to interesting thoughts of my own soul, which frequently flashed through my mind, and died away for want of utterance. The reading of these documents enabled me to utter my thoughts. (*Narrative* 52–53).

The selections which Douglass singles out for special mention are a dialogue between a slave and his master, which ends in the master's bowing to the power of the slave's argument and granting him freedom, and a second excerpt taken from a ringing speech of Sheridan on Catholic emancipation. Douglass wants not the substance of these selections, but something else: a model of the power and possibility of language, a model for arranging words in such an effective way that they become both action and the initiator of action. More than that, Douglass was looking for the freedom that comes with literacy. He receives the gifts he seeks:

Freedom now appeared, to disappear no more forever. It was heard in every sound and seen in every thing. It was ever present to torment me with a sense of my wretched condition. I saw nothing without seeing it, and felt nothing without feeling it. It looked from every star, it smiled in every calm, breathed in every wind, and moved in every storm. (*Narrative* 53–54)

This is the new and special revelation Douglass receives: that learning to read was the "pathway from slavery to freedom" (*Narrative* 47). The result of this experience of the "talking book" is clearly provided by Douglass's using that figure *chiasmus* which he has discovered in Bingham as a marker, a metanarrative transition: "you have seen how a man was made a slave; you shall see how a slave was made a man" (*Narrative* 75). His earlier description of the freedom resulting from his reading just as clearly demonstrates his control of anaphora (patterned repetition) and *antithesis* (the yoking of opposing images and ideas in the same statement). It is, however, when he comes to describe the death of his grandmother that he demonstrates how masterful has been his appropriation of the classical rhetorical figures which he has heard in *The Columbian Orator:*

If any one thing in my experience, more than another, served to deepen my conviction of the infernal character of slavery, and to fill me with unutterable loathing of slaveholders, it was their base ingratitude to my poor old grandmother. She had served my old master faithfully from youth to old age. She had been the source of all his wealth; she had peopled his plantation with slaves; she had become a great grandmother in his service. She had rocked him in infancy, attended him in childhood, served him through life, and at his death wiped from his icy brow the cold death-sweat, and closed his eyes forever. She was nevertheless left a slave—a slave for life—a slave in the hands of strangers; and in their hands she saw her children, her grandchildren, and her great-grandchildren, divided, like so many sheep, without being gratified with the small privilege of a single word, as to their or her own destiny. And, to cap the climax of their base ingratitude and fiendish barbarity, my grandmother who was now very old, having outlived my old master and all his children, having seen the beginning and end of all of them, and her present owners finding she was of but little value, her frame already racked with the pains of old age, and complete helplessness fast stealing over her once active limbs, they took her to the woods, built her a little hut, put up a little mud chimney, and then made her welcome to the privilege of supporting herself there in perfect loneliness; thus virtually turning her out to die! If my poor old grandmother now lives, she lives to suffer in utter loneliness; she lives to remember and mourn over the loss of children, the loss of grandchildren, and the loss of great-grandchildren. . . . The hearth is desolate. The children, the unconscious children, who once sang and danced in her presence, are gone. She gropes her way, in the darkness of age, for a drink of water. Instead of the voices of her children, she hears by day the moans of the dove, and by night the screams of the hideous owl. All is gloom. The grave is at the door. And now, when weighted down by the pains and aches of old age, when the head inclines to the feet, when the beginning and ending of human existence meet, and helpless infancy and painful old age combine together—at this time, this most needful time, the time for the exercise of that tenderness and affection which children only can exercise towards a declining parent—my poor old grandmother, the devoted mother of twelve children, is left all alone, in yonder hut, before a few dim embers. She stands—she sits—she staggers—she falls—she groans—she dies—and there are none of her children or grandchildren present, to wipe from her wrinkled brow the cold sweat of death, or to place beneath the sod her fallen remains. Will not a righteous God visit for these things? (*Narrative* 59–61)

In the passage cited above, Douglass has created a great period; he has become master of the very modeling aimed at in Bingham's text. He has troped on a text not intended for his ears; has revised and reconstructed the master discourse of his day. The force of his demonstration lies in his careful construction of a great oratorical period built on the figure *epanalepsis* (he opens and closes with the same phrase, "wipe from his icy brow the cold death-sweat" and "wipe from her wrinkled brow the cold sweat of death"). Within this frame he marshals *synonymia, episeuxsis, membrum, antithesis,* and *anaphora* contrasting these elaborations with the brutal simplicity of short unadorned statements ("she stands," etc.). The result is a powerful expression of rage and righteous indignation, one shaped by the stylistic benefits of *deutero* or secondary learning. He sought information in the Bingham text (a primary learning goal) but in that seeking, derived another benefit: he found a form, a style, a mode of expression.

Douglass learned such techniques from his study of Caleb Bingham, whose criteria for inclusion of samples in his text had been their conformity to rules for classical oratory. The period, one of which I have just cited, is central to Cicero's ideal oration. It is, he argues in "On Oratory," the Greek name for a "turning point in speech": a "series of words in prose is much neater and more pleasing if it is divided up by joints and limbs than if it carried right on without a break; the limbs in question will need management" (qtd. in Matsen, Rollinson, and Sousa 198). Douglass has learned control of the period, a stylistic device which in its relationship to the text of an oration functions somewhat like the aria in an opera. Cicero in the same work identifies three levels of diction: (1) "the full and yet rounded style of oratory," (2) the "plain style that is not devoid of vigour and force," and (3) the "style which combines elements of either class and whose merit is to steer a middle course" (qtd. in Matsen, Rollinson, and Sousa 199).

The Columbian Orator belongs to a class of preliminary exercise texts called *progymnasmata*. Because the sequencing in Douglass's narrative echoes such texts, I want to clarify their content and to do so by drawing on the descriptions of such texts by Theon and Nicolaus of Constantinople. Although both ancient writers appeared in English for the first time in the 1990 *Readings from Classical Rhetoric*, their texts make clear that they are summaries of common practice in the classical world. Theon: "I shall attempt to transmit those things that it is necessary to know and to be reasonably trained in before one makes a speech" (qtd. in Matsen, Rollinson, and Sousa 254). The order of education described by both Theon and Nicolaus encompasses three stages: (1) Under a grammarian, the student learns to read and write; at this stage the student studies literature and the fundamentals of exposition. (2) Studying under a rhetorican, the student learns the techniques of persuasion. (3) The major activity at the third stage is the giving of declamations on judicial themes. First reading, then writing, and then oratory. Such a system of study conforms to the five-part scheme found in the *Rhetorica ad Herrenium* — invention, arrangement, style, memory, and delivery.

Oratory and its traditions are the silent second text of Douglass's *Narrative*. Such a conclusion can be supported by the clear sequence of language production in that text. Douglass has learned to read, and this achievement has resulted in freedom. His progress is not limited to this one stage, for reading the text of another and moving toward construction of his own text lead to the need for full development of yet another skill: "I would learn to write" (*Narrative* 55). He first wants to say "some smart as well as impressive things" (*Narrative* 52), as does the slave to his master, but he wants to do more than that. He wants to write in order to give those impressive utterances the permanence and distribution which chirographic and typographic systems make possible. He must write the self denied by the national narrative of his day. Mastery of the written text follows upon conversation with the speaking text, the "talking book." He closes his narrative with the words, "I subscribe myself, Frederick Douglass," and in so doing, he affirms his own powers of authentication and self-assertion; he subverts the custom of his day, the use of testimonies from those who hold positions of power in the community to authenticate and certify the African American voice.

The narrative is titled "A Narrative of the Life of Frederick Douglass American Slave, one *Written by Himself*" (italics mine), just as was that of Equiano. One further word on closing words and title pages in that earlier narrative is needed here. Equiano had refused to relinquish control over the life which he had inscribed and, in inscribing, created. To a reader who may find incidents in that life trifling or uninteresting, Equiano states that such is not the case with him.

> Almost every event of my life made an impression on my mind and influenced my conduct. . . . [E]very circumstance I have related was, to me, of importance. (178)

By such an assertion, Equiano resists external control of the shape and incidents of his composition. He alone is the true judge of what should be included in that work. Equiano's title page itself operates in a similar fashion when it rejects the power and right of others to name and thereby subscribe his self. Olaudah Equiano is printed in bold Gothic letters and is followed by his slave name in plain text reduced in size relative to his Igbo name. He takes back both self and control. He asserts the truth of his identity rather than accepting the constructed self of that world which has renamed him. He will be called by his rightful name. In the engraving that appears as frontispiece, he is depicted holding in his hands a Bible open to Acts 4.11: "this is the stone which was set at nought of you builders, which is become the head of the corner."

Although Douglass, after his escape from bondage, permitted a Mr. Johnson to choose a patronymic for him, he insisted on adding that name, one selected from Scott's "Lady of the Lake," to the name which he retained. He may share with Scott's Lord Douglass betrayal, exile, and restoration, but he is also different and unique. Of his name "Frederick" he says: "I must hold on to that to preserve a sense of my identity. . . . I shall continue to use it as my own" (*Narrative* 115). He will use it as his own fully aware that it is not yet his own. What he does own, if not a name, is the power of naming, and he chooses to exercise this power and become Frederick Douglass, the product of his own nomination and subscription.

Such is the case of the "talking book" of Equiano and Douglass. Both attempt to transform the silent and silencing texts which they encounter into orality and oratory, to restore the speaking power of the page, and to appropriate such power to their project of self-inscription. That such negotiations privilege orality can be situated clearly in the positioning of language activity in those texts. Douglass reads and receives a voice. Only then does he feel a determination we write.

> I used to spend the time in *writing in the spaces left* [italics mine] in Master Thomas' copy book, copying what he had written. I continued to do this until I could write a hand similar to that of Master Thomas. Thus, after a long, tedious effort for years, I finally succeeded in learning to write. (*Narrative* 56)

The free man can become the writing subject. In the spaces left he finds those uninscribed topoi necessary to his own creation. He writes a hand similar to, but not identical with, that of his model preparatory to taking full control of the text itself. Imitation and repetition lead here to creativity and liberation. Yet, it must be emphasized here that learning to read and to write do not close the record of Douglass's quest for literacy. This ultimate position is reserved for oratory. He closes his *Narrative* with still another incident focused on the liberating influence of his reading (in this instance reading the abolitionist paper *The Liberator*):

> The paper became my meat and drink. My soul was set all on fire. . . . [It] sent a thrill of joy through my soul, such as I had never felt before. (*Narrative* 119)

How is that thrill and that fire made manifest by the man who would create a rival to *The Liberator* in his own *North Star?* "On the 11th day of August, 1841, I felt strongly moved to speak" (*Narrative* 119). Here, Douglass reflects yet another echo of the second oral tradition out of which he speaks. Like those testifiers in the black church and in the conversion narratives which can be read as the generic source for the slave narrative, he can give us the day and hour when full freedom came to him; the day when my dungeon shook and my chains fell off. "I spoke but a few moments, when I felt a degree of freedom, and said what I desired with considerable ease" (*Narrative* 120). These are his closing remarks.

To situate Douglass's *Narrative* in the tradition of the black church is not to contradict the placement of that text in traditions of classical oratory, for the work under consideration here is part of a dual heritage, of two interdependent and compatible systems of oral discourse. Douglass's narrative, Robert O'Meally argues,

> does more than touch upon questions pondered by black preachers. Its very form and substance are directly influenced by the Afro-American preacher and his vehicle for ritual expression, the sermon. In this sense, Douglass' narrative of 1845 is a sermon, and, specifically, it is a black sermon. This is a text meant to be read and pondered: it is also a clarion call to spiritual affirmation and action; this is a text meant to be preached. (192–93)

And Douglass, as if to remind a reader that his is a "talking book," adds an Appendix which makes crystal clear the sermonic qualities, the *ars praedicandi*, noted in the above passage. He selects as his sermon text, one on which he will expatiate at great length, Matthew 23 and its condemnation of hypocrites and oppressors—those whited sepulchres. Both sacred and secular oratory become the instruments of Douglass's project in self-expression and self-determination: his weapons of war.

In 1945, Richard Wright published *Black Boy,* the record of his transformation from objectified other to self-defining subjectivity. The final pages of the text present us with the silent second voice of his talking book, the subverting voice of his hyperglossic text. Prior to the reading of H. L. Mencken, Wright saw "only two responses as Negro, rebellion and docility, and both were self-destructive" (Scruggs 168). Mencken showed him that words could be used as weapons and that one need not be destroyed in the process. On the contrary, language is not just a way of getting even; it is a way of saving oneself, of shaping that which threatens to destroy (Scruggs 168). How does Wright describe the debt?

> It had been my accidental reading of literary criticism that had evoked in me vague glimpses of life's possibilities. (283)

Out of the emotional impact of imaginative constructions he experiences a conversion:

> I felt touching my face a tinge of warmth from an unseen light. . . . I was groping toward that invisible light, always trying to keep my face so set and turned that I would not lose the hope of its faint promise, using it as my justification for action. (283)

Here, too, we encounter the rhetoric and imagery of that conversion, particularly the climactic moment in the sermon when the black preacher recalls his coming into the light, his realization that the truth is the light, and his calling to become a bringer of that light to others.

At the end of his narrative, Wright borrows a card and goes to the library to seek out that writer who, because he is so reviled by the white South, must be a writer worth knowing. (The exiled speak to our condition.) It is useful to recall here parallels to Douglass's situation. It was the resistance of his master to black literacy that spurred Douglass to seek that same power and freedom for which Wright yearns in his twentieth-century quest. Wright checks out two Mencken works—*A Book of Prejudices* and *Prejudices: Second Series.* The vicious satire of the essay "The Sahara of Bozart" in *Prejudices* so startles and pleases Wright that he reads it and takes notes all night on this deconstruction of the narrative of white southern cultural supremacy. Note his description of his reaction:

> Why did he write like that? And how did one write like that? Yes, this man was fighting, fighting with words. He was using words as a weapon. . . . Could words be weapons? Well, yes, for here they were. Then, maybe, perhaps, I could use them as a weapon. (272)

Wright sees and feels not only light and warmth, but, like Douglass, hears a clarion call. The possibility of power and action discovered in the Mencken texts leads him to the assurance that he can become fully human, the shaper of a self and a destiny, and not the black boy, the product of the construction of others. Again, like Douglass, he detects in those texts spaces left for his own inscription. His notes constitute the act of appropriation by which he will turn the potential of Mencken's rhetoric to his own active project; his will be the second silent text heard within his seeming imitation of Mencken. As a result of his encounter with Mencken, Wright begins the *progymnasmata* which will lead to his great sermon on the agonies and joys of self-inscription, *Native Son*. He receives his calling and his mission. He is freed from slavery and has become master of his own destiny. Note the quick succession of possessive pronouns in his declaration of that condition: "I held my life in my mind, and in my consciousness every day" (277). These are the closing words of his narrative.

If Wright, like Douglass, can move toward a great sermon by exploiting the disclosure of the uninscribed spaces in the texts of the dominant discourse of his day, Ralph Ellison's nameless protagonist in *Invisible Man* fails at this task. He is nameless because he refuses to wrest the act of naming away from others. The slips of paper he so obediently collects contain, according to Ellison, his name and the social role he is to play as defined for him by others (*Shadow* 177). In burning this collection at the end of the narrative, he provides himself with a possible self, a beginning— a beginning because he has experienced little development as a result of his experiences. Rather, he has been engaged in a continual refusal to move beyond repetition and imitation; he has rejected his own voice and chosen to let others determine what is to be said and done. He is a true victim of affirmation.

If incidents in Homer's *Odyssey* can be mated to significant moments in his life, such parallels are not completed. His is neither the completed *telemachy* or *nostoi* of the Greek text; he fails the *peria* (test of worth). Unlike Odysseus, he is an accidental rather than a willful manipulator of words. If the earlier writers experience a great conversion about which they wish to testify, Ellison's record includes many conversions and as many instances of backsliding or boomeranging (to use Ellison's own term). He is the model believer, always handy when there is a need to swell the number of the saved at the revival:

> I always tried to go in every one's way but my own. I have been called one thing and then another while no one wished to hear what I called myself. (*Invisible* 560)

He is not a self-naming Douglass or Equiano. One might argue that he had never insisted on his exclusive right to be anyone other than that nameless construction, that invisible and voiceless writer that he becomes.

If Douglass at the end of his narrative rose to speak and experienced freedom, the end of Ellison's twentieth-century slave narrative is marked or marred by the abandonment of speech. Ellison's narrator is compelled to "put invisibility down in black and white" (*Invisible* 13–14). He has put down—denigrated—the very nature and value of the struggle. He has put down his own naiveté in believing that he could triumph over the forces which are set upon controlling his life. He has put down or inscribed *their* narrative. He has put down or committed to paper the very experience of his life, a life which he has refused to speak or live. His final words—"who knows but that, on the lower frequencies I speak for you" (*Invisible* 568)—are a timid assertion as opposed to the bold assertions found in the other texts, texts that, as a result of their insistence on claiming a unique voice, become a voice for the entire congregation. His goal in life has been to speak for others. Not to but *for* them. The current may flow between his small voice and the ear of a larger congregation, but the flow is at a lower frequency. There is no true call-response communication here. Near approaches to oratorical excellence are willful imitations (see his Booker T. Washington imitation at the Battle Royal), or unconscious and unwilled tappings of cultural memory, the aesthetic traditions of the oratory of the community out of which he has come. Neither succeeds for or to others. He is misunderstood, resented, or silenced. More frequently, his attempts at oratory yield results diametrically opposed to his borrowed objectives. He writes and speaks on the line, on the white line, and seems to have no conception in his early life that there are spaces left above and below that line, spaces which are available for his own appropriation. He is shocked by the electrified rug at the Battle Royal and by the electric surge of energy coming from the crowd at the eviction and Brotherhood rally speeches. Unable to control the results of his language and exhausted by repeated attempts to do so, he settles for that modeling system which Walter Ong calls secondary orality. He turns from oratory to writing. He chooses this lower frequency in order to escape the higher voltage primary orality and eloquence which have so frequently implicated him in guilt and exposed him to vengeful attack. Eloquence and oratory with their assumption of clear and powerfully held values are exchanged for inscribed irony, that writing which says yes and no, which both affirms and denies.

Given the above argument, it is no accident that Ellison places Douglass's image in the text of his narrative in *Invisible Man*, for Douglass is the very figure, the silent other voice of the text, which undermines the assertions of the protagonist:

> Sometimes I sat watching the watery play of light upon Douglass' portrait, thinking how magical it was that he had talked his way from slavery to a government ministry, and so swiftly. Perhaps, I thought, something of the kind is happening to me. Douglass came north to escape, and find work in the shipyards: a big fellow in a sailor's suit who, like me, had taken another name. What had his true name been? Whatever it was, it was as Douglass that he became himself, defined himself. And not as a boatwright as he had expected, but as an orator. Perhaps the sense of magic lay in the unexpected transformations. (372)

Douglass is everything the young naif refuses to claim as his own. The union between reading, writing, and speech-oratory-action presented by Douglass is nowhere apparent in the Ellison narrative. For in that narrative we are presented with a man who asserts, "I am an orator, a rabble rouser" (14) and then rejects this very calling and its logical consequences in action. He refuses leadership of the "rabble" which he has aroused and finally the very function of orator. "I am? I was" (14). He has abdicated that title, for he does not see in it the great man envisioned by Ellison's namesake Ralph Waldo Emerson who argued that "there is no true orator who is not a hero. . . . [H]is speech is not to be distinguished from action" (*Letter* 113). He sees only the rabble rouser. As the Vet states, "he registers with his senses and short circuits his brain" (14). Voice spins toward silence and symbolic castration.

Douglass, unlike Ellison's protagonist, wrote in an age when oratory and eloquence were the mark of greatness. Ralph Waldo Emerson, who also haunts the narrative of Ralph Waldo Ellison, is named as yet another voice in the text in Ellison's essay "Hidden Name and Complex Fate." Emerson clarifies the role of the orator:

> The orator must always stand with forward foot in the very attitude of advancing. His speech must be just ahead of the whole human race or it is prattle. His speech is not to be distinguished from action. It is the salt and electricity of action. (Journals 425)

Ellison's protagonist lacks not only electricity but also a clear plan of action: he lacks an ideology within which to frame action. He speaks but is repeatedly ignorant of the relationship between speech and action which Emerson privileges:

> Go and hear a great orator to see how presentable truth and right are, and presentable as common facts. . . . [A] true orator will instantly show that states and kingdoms of the world, all senators,

lawyers, and rich men, are caterpillars; webs and caterpillars when seen in the light. (Journals 112)

Emerson again,

> The great orator cannot be too caught up in admiration of the rich and the powerful. He is their leader and not their follower. He speaks not to what they know: but rather, he speaks that which he knows, those truths to which they are blissfully blind. . . . [I]f the orator addressing the public assembly should attempt to make people wise in that which they already know, he would fail; but by making them wise in that which he knows, he has the advantage of the whole assembly. (Journals 122)

Can a speaker who accepts his name and the social role which he is to play from others aspire to the condition of orator described by Emerson?

> The eloquent man is he who is . . . inwardly and desperately drunk with his matter (a certain belief). . . . [T]he possession by the subject of his mind is so entire, that it ensures an order of expression which is the order of nature itself, and so the order of greatest force. . . . [T]his mind is contemplating a whole, and inflamed with the contemplation of the whole. (Journals 122)

How different from the Douglass orator, one closer to the Emerson model, is Ellison's speaker-protagonist, this man who lives in a world dominated by chirographic and typographic systems, this man who lives in a world in which speech, action, writing, and ideology are often not only disjunct but often working at cross purposes . . . blind (to use Ellison's central image) to their essential union and mutual dependence.

Further testimony to such a difference can be found in Douglass's sole attempt at an extended work of fiction, his novella *The Heroic Slave*. Madison Washington, Douglass's subject in this work, is the leader of the slave revolt on board *The Creole*, and he is by no means blinded or marginalized. He is heir in name and in eloquence to the privileged traditions of the nation. We first hear him in his own words and then through the mediating narration of the programmatically named Mr. Listwell and Mr. Grant. It is important to Douglass's argument that Listwell hears Washington before he sees him. Because Mr. Listwell does not know that the manipulator of the eloquence he hears is a black man, he judges him solely on the power of his oratory. How does he respond to such verbal powers? "The speech of Madison rang through the chambers of his entire frame," and he resolves after recovering from the shocked revelation that the owner of such eloquence is a slave to join the forces fighting for freedom. "From that hour I am an abolitionist," a man working for "the speedy emancipation of every slave in the land" (304–5).

If Ellison's protagonist can remember clearly the day he was condemned to be kept running after impossible goals, Belle Meyers Carothers, former slave, in her recollection as recorded in the Federal Writers Project on Slave Narratives can remember liberation:

> I found a hymn book one day and spelled out "When I can Read my Title Clear." I was so happy when I saw that I could read, that I ran around telling all the other slaves—
> When I can read my title clear
> To mansions in the skies,
> I'll bid farewell to every tear
> And wipe my weeping eyes. (qtd. in Cornelius epigraph)

In her experience of the hymn, Carothers reads an entitlement, one which had been denied her by those who had the power to interpret texts for those who lacked the power to do so for themselves. She sees in the text a self heretofore absent, an uninscribed space on which she writes her name. Her recreation of that text is the occasion for her action, her preaching of her liberation to the other slaves. Carothers discovers then, not Isaac Watts, composer of the hymn, but Belle Meyers Carothers, free, liberated, and self-subscribed. She does her own lining out: that technique in which the literate leads, reads, and speaks for the illiterate.

Ann Petry published *The Street* one year after Wright's *Black Boy*, but Lutie Johnson, Petry's protagonist, is neither Belle Carothers nor Wright's boy-become-man. In the final silencing of her narrative, she resembles Ellison's writer more than she does the liberated preachers found in Equiano, Douglass, and Wright. If Mencken is the enabling voice in Wright's text, a function served by Equiano's and Bingham's models in Douglass's, the voice behind Petry's text, the silent other voice, is that of Ben Franklin. That voice is oppressive and silencing while Mencken's releases power for Wright. That voice reinscribes the destructive myths of the American national narrative while Mencken's clarifies the foolishness of those myths and their vulnerability to deconstruction. Note the contrast between the closing passages of Petry's text and those already noted in Wright:

> As the train started to move, she began to trace a design on the window. It was a series of circles that flowed into each other. She remembered that when she was in grammar school, the children were taught to get the proper slant to their writing, to get the feel of the pen in their hands, by making these same circles. (Petry 435)

Lutie, the central tragic figure of Petry's text, recalls this early experience as she is abandoning everything she had hoped to build. If Wright's black boy heads for Chicago armed for action and self-assertion, she is traveling away from possibility, headed toward a certain tragic future:

> Once again she could hear the flat, exasperated voice of the teacher as
> she looked at the circles Lutie had produced. "Really," she said, "I don't
> know why they have us bother to teach you people to write." (435)

And Lutie agrees with this assessment: "What possible good has it done to
teach people like me to write?" (436). The twists and turns which she
traces on the window, those swirls and slants of the Palmer Method, are
emblematic of the twists and turns of her life, but she is incapable of understanding them or of making them over as objects of her desire. "And
as the train roared into the darkness, Lutie tried to figure out by what
twists and turns of fate she had landed on this train. Her mind balked at
the task" (436).

Petry's Lutie Johnson is silent. If literacy provides Wright with verbal
weapons which are to be more effective than those of physical violence,
the role subscribed for him in the national narrative, if his *progymnasmata* results in a powerful voice, Lutie's experience of literacy dictates another route. Like Ellison's protagonist she is an obedient reader; hers is
hardly an act of willful misreading or an act of appropriation. She ignores
the spaces in the text and concentrates on the single domineering and
dominating narrative line of Franklin. She is unable to speak, read, or
write a self, and in this silencing, she turns to "the ever darkening scar"
(426). In an attempt to reduce her adversary Boots "to a speechless mass"
(428), she strikes him repeatedly with an iron candlestick. No candle is
mentioned here, nor is light or warmth. The candlestick becomes in her
hands a weapon of destruction rather than a holder of light. "Blurred vision," "not thinking," "a walled enclosure"—these are the terms which
mark her final action in a room in which there is "no sound except her
own hoarse breathing," a room to which she had no key (430–31). She
can no more bring voice and eloquence to bear on her situation at this
final moment than she could in her earlier encounters with the super or
the lawyer. Lutie's voice is not an active part of her reading or of her final
attempt at inscription.

If Ellison's protagonist began his descent by repeating the words of
Washington's "Atlanta Exposition Address" and was haunted by the great
oratorical example of Douglass, Lutie styles herself another Benjamin
Franklin as she is pulled "down down into the basement" (Petry 63).

> She thought immediately of Ben Franklin and his loaf of bread. And
> grinned thinking, you and Ben Franklin. (63)

That most sinister figure who orchestrates her doom is named none other
than Junto, the name Franklin gave to his circle of intimates. On the train
darkened and as much a type of hell as is the cellar of Ellison's text, she is
haunted at the end by the memory of an exercise that promised, but

never led to, fluid and independent writing. Lutie preaches no great sermon. The text in which she is enclosed admits no rhetorical flourishes. She seems unaware that the myth of the white self-made man embedded in Franklin's text is not a liberating myth for a black woman in the twentieth century. Nor is it a text upon which such a woman can preach the desired sermon. Her blind adherence to that text, her silent assent to its inscription, admits of no space for her own composition. Hers is, as Toni Morrison asserts in *Beloved*, "not a story to be passed on" (275). What Lutie fails to understand is the very nature of the ideological constructs which determine the received discourse which she so uncritically accepts.

The subversion and triumph of Maya Angelou's graduation, as described in *I Know Why the Caged Bird Sings*, are, by contrast to Lutie's failure, predicated on a clear understanding of those very institutional controls and on the power of voice to resist and reconstruct. The silenced young woman of that narrative recovers voice. Mrs. Flowers, in contrast to the villainous Mrs. Hedges of Petry's *The Street*, acts as a redeemer. She teaches young Margaret that she must use the spaces left, that she must add her own voice to that of the dominant narratives, for only the sound of her own voice can convert these texts into enabling vehicles; can resist their silencing potential:

> Now no one is going to make you talk—possibly no one can. But bear in mind, language is man's way of communicating with his fellow man and it is language alone which separates him from the lower animals.
>
>   Words mean more than what is set down on paper. It takes the human voice to infuse them with the shapes of deeper meaning. (Angelou 82)

This view is "a totally new idea" to the young woman but, as the text asserts, "it seemed so valid and poetic" (82). Mrs. Flowers gives her books and she understands that "I not only must read them, I must read them aloud. She suggested that I try to make a sentence sound in as many different ways as possible" (82). Here, too, wisdom and power are to be found in oral literacy which once again is assigned a privileged position:

> She encouraged me to listen carefully to what country people called mother wit. That in those homely sayings, was couched the collective wisdom of generations. (83)

She must be "intolerant of ignorance but understanding of illiteracy."

These tales of literacy and liberation, for all their differences, agree on one very important theme: to preach the word demands possession of that word, and such possession is predicated on seizing for the creating and speaking self spaces not yet claimed by the texts of the dominant discourse. The primary or privileged texts of that discourse must not be permitted to foreclose the generation of voice by the formerly subjected, the coming to voice of the once silenced. How do we read, write, and speak the texts of our culture? Do we approach them as closed systems, that is, as spaces already covered with the inscriptions of others? Do we engage in mere exercises in composing, drawing circles and lines, or do we move beyond exercises to oration? Do we offer our narratives, our sermons on salvation, as incomplete and thus enabling texts for others? Do we become the surrogate mothers who end Shay Youngblood's narrative of emergence, *Big Mama Stories*?

This final text demonstrates in its closing paragraph the movement from margin to center which is representative of the great sermon texts which I have dealt with here:

> Each woman called me by my names as they gave my gift, hugging me, their tears mingling with mine. . . . Miss Tom gave me a book of poems by Langston Hughes. . . . I felt a cool breeze. . . . These women were my mamas. They had always been there to give me whatever I thought I needed. Standing in that circle of light behind the 8th Street Baptist Church on a clear September night I was given my name and invited into the circle of women, no longer a girl. I was a woman now. All the stories that they had told me were gifts, all the love more precious than gold. They tell me . . . now I know. (105–106)

Youngblood goes on to create her "talking book," one appropriately titled "Shakin' the Mess Outta Misery." Ours is not a foreclosed narrative or a narrative of foreclosure. There are still spaces left.

WORKS CITED

Angelou, Maya. *I Know Why the Caged Bird Sings.* New York: Bantam, 1970.

Bhabha, Homi K. *Nation and Narration.* London and New York: Routledge, 1990.

Bingham, Caleb. *The Columbian Orator.* Troy: William S. Parker, 1821.

Blassingame, John. *Slave Testimony.* Baton Rouge: Lousiana State UP, 1977.

Cornelius, Janet D. *When I Can Read My Title Clear.* Columbia: U of South Carolina P, 1991.

Douglass, Frederick. *The Heroic Slave.* Rpt. in *Three Classic Afro-American Novels.* Ed. William L. Andrews. New York: Penguin, 1990. 22–69.

———. *The Narrative and Selected Writings.* New York: Modern Library, 1984.

Ellison, Ralph. *Invisible Man.* New York: Vintage, 1972.

———. *Shadow and Act.* New York: Vintage, 1966.

Emerson, Ralph Waldo. *Journals and Miscellaneous Notebooks of Ralph Waldo Emerson.* Volume 9. Ed. William H. Gilman. Cambridge: Belknap P, 1971.

———. *Letters and Social Aims.* Boston: Houghton, 1884.

Equiano, Olaudah. *The Life of Olaudah Equiano.* Gates 1–182.

Gates, Henry Louis, Jr., ed. *Classic Slave Narratives.* New York: New American Library, 1987.

Gerald, John Bart, and George Blecher, eds. *Survival Prose.* Indianapolis and New York: Bobbs Merrill, 1971.

McFeeley, William S. *Frederick Douglass.* New York: Norton, 1990.

Martin, John Sella. "Sella Martin." Blassingame 702–35.

Matsen, Patricia, Philip Rollinson, and Marion Sousa, eds. *Readings from Classical Rhetoric.* Carbondale: Southern Illinois UP, 1990.

Morrison, Toni. *Beloved.* New York: New American Library, 1988.

O'Meally, Robert G. "Frederick Douglass' 1845 Narrative." *Afro-American Literature: The Reconstruction of Instruction.* Ed. Dexter Fisher and Robert Stepto. New York: MLA, 1979. 192–211.

Petry, Ann. *The Street.* Boston: Beacon P, 1946.

Reed, Ishmael, ed. *19 Necromancers from Now.* Garden City: Doubleday, 1970.

———. "When State Magicians Fail." Gerald and Blecher 151–63.

Renan, Ernest. "What Is a Nation?" Bhabha 8–22.

Scruggs, Charles. *The Sage in Harlem: H.L. Mencken and the Black Writers of the 1920s.* Baltimore: Johns Hopkins UP, 1984.

Wright, Richard. *Black Boy: A Record of Childhood and Youth.* New York: Harper, 1966.

Youngblood, Shay. *Big Mama Stories.* Ithaca: Firebrand, 1989.

———. "Shakin' the Mess Outta Misery." Unpublished manuscript.

AFTERWORD: THE STRUGGLE CONTINUES

I occupy at present a chair dedicated to Oratory and Belles Lettres, an assignment very appropriate to a major academic interest and avocation. The purpose of my Chair's address was to recover the oral in the word *communication* in our name. I wanted to call attention to the way in which classical rhetoric was something more than a historical curiosity. It was something more than a language structure that had to be severely reimagined if it was to be useful in our own day. I wanted to begin a kind of mini-revolution in our approaches to language and to writing. In composition classes, I do teach the major rhetorical figures, and students imitate them, filling the empty abstract bag of an oratorical figure with the concrete stuff of their own experience. This is one of the ways in which we play with language. Too many first-year students are taught to fear language, to feel not at home in it. That is why we play a great deal. Language play rounds off the ugliness of "language deprivation" and the sense of traveling on roads that belong to somebody else. I own every language and dialect of language to which I can give tongue, teeth, lips, and sweet imagination.

My interest in oratory was linked to how much such discourse remains in the traditional Black sermon that was a vital part of my own religious experience. It was also linked to the despair I feel every time political candidates stage what they call debates or present the limping language in which almost all political discourse is shrouded. Kenneth Cmiel in *Democratic Eloquence* recorded the shift from oratory to the lower-level language of the marketplace, but he could not predict how far we would go as we attempted to rid our public discourse of every vestige of grace and beauty.

I am still at the grindstone. I am bringing to completeness a new book, *African American Literature and the Classical Tradition.* This work, written in collaboration with classicist James H. Tatum, will survey in a much more detailed manner than heretofore the role of classical rhetoric and oratory in African American writing in the eighteenth, nineteenth, and twentieth centuries. It is the result of a dozen years of collaboration in the classroom and in the study. The silence of the present literature on this subject would seem to say that it is neither our tradition nor a worthwhile scholarly project. I answer in words inappropriate to my present elevated level of discourse. The struggle continues.

–WILLIAM W. COOK
Dartmouth College

WORK CITED

Cmiel, Kenneth. *Democratic Eloquence: The Fight over Popular Speech in Nineteenth-Century America.* New York: Morrow, 1990.

1993

Kitchen Tables and Rented Rooms: The Extracurriculum of Composition

ANNE RUGGLES GERE

> Two prisoners in contingent cells communicate by blows struck on the wall. The wall separates them, but it also permits them to communicate.
>
> —SIMONE WEIL

In a rented room on Leavenworth Street in the Tenderloin District of San Francisco a group of women gathers on Friday afternoons from two to five to provide one another advice and feedback on their writing. The Tenderloin District, identified by many as a home for drug dealers, welfare recipients, criminals, and mental health patients, also provides a home for several writing groups including the Tenderloin Women's Writing Workshop. Carol Heller, who has studied this group, notes that although these women have little formal education, they take their writing seriously; they offer one another encouragement as well as criticism and suggest revisions. As Carolyn, a member of the group, put it, "We can disagree with each other's views, but the point of this workshop is to do the work" (Heller, *Multiple Functions* 225).[1]

In Lansing, Iowa, a small farming community, a dozen writers gather around Richard and Dorothy Sandry's kitchen table. They meet on Monday evenings during the lull between fall harvest and spring planting and spend two hours reading and responding to one another's writing. In their prose they look at the experience of farming, old equipment, the process of milking cows, and country schools. Frequently writers talk

This article is a revised version of the Chair's address Anne Ruggles Gere delivered at the CCC Convention in San Diego, California, on April 1, 1993. It was first published in *CCC*, volume 45, number 1, February 1994.

about their plans before they begin writing, gathering suggestions and ideas for shaping their material. These writing workshops are part of what Robert Wolf, the workshop facilitator, calls the Rural Renovation Proposal, which aims to revitalize both the economy and democracy of small towns by building community and consensus among individuals who can then address local problems.

Participants in groups like the Tenderloin Women's Writing Workshop and the Lansing, Iowa, Writers Workshop represent a tiny portion of the enormous number of individuals who meet in living rooms, nursing homes, community centers, churches, shelters for the homeless, around kitchen tables, and in rented rooms to write down their worlds. These writers bear testimony to the fact that writing development occurs outside formal education. As Simone Weil reminds us, walls can be a means of communication as well as a barrier, and I propose that we listen to the signals that come through the walls of our classrooms from the world outside.

Hobbled by poverty, histories of alcoholism and drug addiction, along with the indignities of aging, the women in the Tenderloin Women's Writing Workshop take strength from finding that their experience is worth expressing. As one member of the Women's Writing Workshop says, "You write down your world and then you read it to other people and they affirm you for it" (Heller, *Writers* 6). Anita Ardell, a recovering cancer patient, expresses a similar view: "I had never before written. They've encouraged me incredibly. . . . You are given the freedom to try. You feel brave here. You feel brave at the women writers group" (Heller, *Multiple Functions* 174). Participants in the Lansing, Iowa Writers' Workshop also find that writing enhances their self esteem. Bob Leppert, a farmer with little formal education, says, "I never felt like I had anything that anyone was interested in hearing" (Wagner). Eighty-three-year-old Clara Leppert, the oldest member of the Lansing Workshop, echoes this feeling, "We didn't think we could write . . ." (*Washington Post*). Despite their inexperience, workshop participants gain confidence and begin to think of themselves as writers.

In addition to increasing positive feelings, workshops outside classroom walls discipline participants to hone their craft as writers. Mary Tall-Mountain, a member of the Tenderloin Women's Writing Workshop and a published author, explains, "They're my readers. I write down everything they say and at some point in time, when it's quiet and spiritually proper, when my mind and whole system are attuned to the writing, I go through it" (Heller, *Multiple Functions* 83). Maria Rand, another member of the workshop, affirms this: "Some of the women are hesitant because nobody ever asked them their opinions about anything. But unless you read your work and get reactions from different groups of people, you're not a writer. You're just dilettanting around. You gotta get rejected and get applause. You gotta get both sides. I'll always be in writing groups. That's where I get my energy from" (Heller, *Multiple Functions* 91–92). The Lansing,

Iowa, group also helps members develop their writing skills. A local reporter explains, "They offer positive criticism of one another's work. They read books and essays by established writers and pick the work apart, talking about the elements that make it effective" (Wagner).

Opportunities for performance provide a major incentive for writers to develop their skills. The Tenderloin Reflection and Education Center, which sponsors the Women's Writing Workshop, holds regular public readings where workshoppers present their work to a live audience. Despite the anxieties they feel at reading their writing aloud to strangers, individual members and the group as a whole enjoy the opportunity to display their work. As Heller notes, these readings strengthen the relationship between the story teller and those who hear the story, along with the larger community as a whole (Heller, *Multiple Functions* 130). The Center also helps maintain a local newsletter, *Tender Leaves*, to which workshop participants contribute regularly, and the Tenderloin's Exit Theater has produced plays written by Workshop participants. When he began working with the Lansing group, Robert Wolf explained that "public readings with discussions afterwards" would be the heart of the project (*Voices* 2). Publication also features prominently in this group's work. Several members of the workshop contributed to *Voices from the Land*, a book that has attracted national attention. Bill Welsh, one of these contributors, observes, "I never dreamed of this. I don't feel like any kind of a big shot. I still wear my overalls" (*Washington Post*).

Reaching out into the community with prose performances develops in participants the perception that writing can effect changes in their lives. The stated purpose of the Lansing, Iowa Writers' Workshop—to build community in order to solve local problems—is enacted by individual members (Wolf, *Newsletter*). Greg Welsh, a member of the Workshop, employed writing to deal with the time when his family's cattle herd was accidentally poisoned by a contaminated bale of hay. Greg explains, "Writing about it was one way for me to understand how I felt. It was a way for me to reconcile some differences I had with members of my family" (Wagner). In addition to changing the quality of personal relationships, workshop participants often use writing to alter the material conditions of their lives. A piece by one of the Tenderloin women writers led to a fundraising event for a publication called *Homeless Link* along with increased activism on behalf of homeless people, and a Black History study group developed because of another participant's play, "Ain't I Right Too?" (Heller, *Multiple Functions* 216). The public readings of the Lansing group have led individuals to consider organic alternatives to chemical farming (Wagner).

Positive feelings about oneself and one's writing, motivation to revise and improve composition skills, opportunities for publication of various sorts, the belief that writing can make a difference in individual and community life—these accomplishments of workshops outside classroom walls mirror the goals most of us composition teachers espouse for our students.

Workshops outside classroom walls frequently, however, succeed with those individuals deemed unsuccessful by their composition instructors. Few of the participants in the Tenderloin Women's Writing Workshop or the Lansing, Iowa Writers' Workshop had much formal education, and many had negative experiences with schooling. They did not think of themselves as writers because teachers had taught them they could not write. Yet these individuals wrote effectively in workshops, published their writing, and gained personal and community recognition for their work. Although it remains largely invisible and inaudible to us, writing development occurs regularly and successfully outside classroom walls.

One explanation for our relative unfamiliarity with groups such as those in Lansing and the Tenderloin lies in the way we tell our history. Like representatives of most emerging fields, we in composition studies have sought to establish our right to a place in the academy by recounting our past, and this historiography has focused inside classroom walls. One version of composition's history has concentrated on American instructional practices of the nineteenth and twentieth centuries. Albert Kitzhaber's study of rhetoric in nineteenth century American colleges helped establish this tradition. Drawing upon nineteenth-century textbooks, Kitzhaber describes the theory and practice of composition in higher education during the latter part of the nineteenth century. Historians such as Donald Stewart, Robert Connors, and James Berlin, even though they adopt differing stances toward their materials, emulate Kitzhaber's model in looking to composition texts, course descriptions, statements of instructions, and other institutional artifacts as sources for information about composition theory and practice. A related historical narrative constructs for composition a genealogy that extends back to Classical Rhetoric. Scholars such as James Murphy, Edward P. J. Corbett, and Winifred Bryan Homer have aided this construction by delineating the composition-rhetoric connections. Robert Connors, Lisa Ede, and Andrea Lunsford extol the benefits of this union, asserting that until recently "rhetorical scholars in speech communication emphasized theoretical and historical studies, while those in composition focused on pedagogy," but the wedding of rhetoric and composition had provided the former with an "outlet for application" and relieved the latter of its "historical and theoretical vacuum" (12–13). In addition, they claim, this merger has helped "to make composition and its necessary theoretical background in rhetoric acceptable to departments of English" (13).

While we might debate how acceptable composition has become in English departments, the terms in which composition's history has been represented arouse little dissent: In concentrating upon establishing our position within the academy, we have neglected to recount the history of composition in other contexts; we have neglected composition's extracurriculum. I borrow this term "extracurriculum" from Frederick Rudolph, who uses it to describe the literary clubs, the fraternity system, and the organized athletics instigated by undergraduates during the nineteenth century. Rudolph argues that this extracurriculum served to make undergraduates "a remarkably important element in the power structure of the American college" (136). Arthur Applebee also uses the term "extracurricular," but for him it describes one of three traditions—the ethical, the classical, and the extracurriculum—from which English studies emerged. Applebee defines the extracurriculum as the nonacademic tradition that contributed to the development of English studies. Like Rudolph, he employs the term extracurriculum to describe eighteenth and nineteenth century college literary clubs and recounts how these groups discussed vernacular literature not judged worthy of academic study. As Applebee explains, college literary clubs also sponsored libraries, speakers, and magazines, providing a context where students could "polish their skills in English composition" (12). Applebee's extracurriculum does not include fraternities or athletic groups but it confirms Rudolph's point that the extracurriculum lent undergraduates power in American colleges because the curriculum was adapted to their interests. Gerald Graff emulates Applebee's description of extracurricular literary clubs, noting their contribution to the development of English studies.

Significantly, Rudolph, Applebee, and Graff all describe the extracurriculum as a white male enterprise. Literary societies at women's colleges and women's literary groups on co-ed campuses receive no more attention than do those of African Americans. In addition, each of these narratives positions the extracurriculum as a way-station on the route toward a fully professionalized academic department, thereby implying that the extracurriculum withered away after helping to institutionalize English studies. There is no suggestion that the extracurriculum continues to exist or perform cultural work. This erasure of the extra-professional takes on particular irony in Graff's work as his discourse advances the very professionalism he decries. As Jonathan Freedman puts it, "The effacement or replacement of the non-academic perspective by a thoroughly academicized one that professionalism accomplished is recapitulated in the narrative form in which the story of professionalism is told."

In contrast, my version of the extracurriculum includes the present as well as the past; it extends beyond the academy to encompass the multiple contexts in which persons seek to improve their own writing; it includes more diversity in gender, race, and class among writers; and it avoids, as much as possible, a reenactment of professionalization in its narrative. In looking at the relationship between composition studies and the "outside/other" represented by the extracurriculum, my project shares much with Susan Miller's *Textual Carnivals,* a text which also discusses the extracurriculum. This excellent book has informed my thinking, and I share Miller's interest in considering the relationship between nonacademic writing and composition instruction, although Miller gives more attention to the political forces surrounding composition's institutional location, and I am more interested in the cultural work undertaken by various groups of writers, our projects converge.

My methodology for looking at composition's extracurriculum owes much to recent accounts of literacy practices outside formal education. Investigations of community literacy practices by Shirley Brice Heath, of workplace literacy by Glynda Hull, of multiple discourse communities by Patricia Bizzell, and of "unofficial literacy" by Ruth Hubbard all provide angles of vision for looking at composition's extracurriculum. They suggest the need to uncouple composition and schooling, to consider the situatedness of composition practices, to focus on the experiences of wirters not always visible to us inside the walls of the academy. Drawing on this tradition, my account focuses explicitly on self-sponsored pedagogically oriented writing activities outside the academy. In defining the extracurriculum this way, I deliberately exclude from my story the writing instruction carried out in workplaces, extension courses, and workshops for which participants pay large fees. The extracurriculum I examine is constructed by desire, by the aspirations and imaginations of its participants. It posits writing as an action undertaken by motivated individuals who frequently see it as having social and economic consequences, including transformations in personal relationships and farming practices.

Just as accounts of literacy practices outside the walls of the academy uncouple literacy and schooling, so my account of the extracurriculum of composition separates pedagogy from the traditional pedagogue. Composition's extracurriculum acknowledges a wide range of teachers, including texts published for aspiring writers. From the Colonial Period to the present, publications designed for persons who seek to improve their writing have contributed to composition's extracurriculum. One of the most popular, George Fisher's *The American Instructor: Or, Young Man's Best Companion* was first published in Philadelphia in 1748, and issued in 17 editions between 1748 and 1833. Aimed at the emerging entrepreneurs of the period, Fisher's book emphasized the importance of composition for business and asserted: "To write a good fair, free and commendable hand, is equally necessary in most if not all the affairs of life and occurrences of business" (A2). Fisher goes on to offer sentences to copy, models of letters for various occasions as well as instructions for making a quill pen, holding the pen in the hand, positioning the light, and making red and black ink. He also includes directions for keeping ink from freezing or molding: "In hard frosty Weather, Ink will be apt to freeze; which if once it doth, it will be good for nothing; for it takes away all its Blackness and Beauty. To prevent which (if you have not the Convenience of keeping it warm, or from the Cold) put a few Drops of Brandy, or other Spirits, into it, and it will not freeze. And to hinder its Moulding, put a little

Salt therein" (43). This form of composition's extracurriculum continued after the Revolutionary War with publications such as *The Complete Letter Writer* (1793), *The Farmer and Mechanic's Pocket Assistant* (1818), and *The Art of Epistolary Composition* (1826).[2]

Not only did publications like these offer an alternative to the academy's instruction in composition, they frequently criticized the way composition was taught in schools. *A Help to Young Writers,* a self-help guide published in 1836, found fault with the "vapid subjects" assigned by teachers and with the tendency of schools to teach composition as though it bore no relationship to good conversation. This self-help guide went on to assert that "composition is nothing more than conversation put on paper" and demonstrated this by advising writers in question and answer form (Heath 34).

As magazines developed during the nineteenth century, composition's extracurriculum flourished in their pages as well. As Nicole Tonkovich Hoffman has shown, Sarah Hale, editor of *Godey's Ladies Magazine* from 1828–1878, offered considerable advice to writers. Like the authors of self-help books, Hale includes material on the technology of writing. Instructions for cutting a pen-point and models of handwriting appear in the pages of *Godey's.* Hale also gives attention to the processes of writing. An 1838 column, for example, recommends what Hale calls "mental composition" for developing more active reading. According to Hale, mental composition "can be pursued at any time and place without the requisite paraphernalia of written composition. . . . it greatly conduces to the development of the judgment, to make frequent pauses, and trace out the inference, and the particular bearing and tendency of detached portions of it; and upon its completion to consider the general scope, its moral tone, the correctness of the sentiments advanced and the character of the style" (191). Hale goes on to recommend writing in response to reading, not note taking but "the keeping of a common-place book, to sketch down one's views, opinions, and sentiments, upon every subject or topic, which may have interested the mind in the perusal of a work" (191).

Godey's was not the only magazine to include advice for individuals interested in developing their composition skills, but it was the most influential women's magazine until the last two decades of the nineteenth century when it was supplanted by the more consumer-oriented *The Ladies Home Journal.* Although less didactic than *Godey's, The Ladies Home Journal* continued composition's extracurriculum. Editor Edward Bok's column in an 1890 issue of the *Ladies Home Journal,* for example, included admonitions to aspiring authors such as, "Whenever possible use the typewriter. If you have not a machine yourself, send your manuscript to some typewriting establishment and let it be copied. The expense is trifling, but the value to a manuscript can hardly be overestimated. . . . Avoid corrections, erasures and interlineations. Don't do on paper what you ought to do mentally. Again—and on this point I cannot be too emphatic—do not roll your manuscript. If there is one thing more than any other which irritates a busy, practical editor, it is a rolled manuscript" (12). An 1894 column by J. MacDonald Oxley includes directives for a "Mutual Research Club" whose "essential feature is the preparation of papers on given subjects and the rule is that each member should have a paper ready for every meeting." Oxley continues, "The modus operandi is as follows: A subject having been selected, and a night of meeting decided upon, the members proceed to prepare their papers. These, at least ten days before the meeting, are sent in to the secretary who binds them together, adding several blank pages at the back. They are then circulated among the members, who pass them on from one to the other, having first entered any note or comment that may suggest itself on the blank pages provided for the purpose. Then at the night of the meeting each member reads his or her paper, and the reading concluded, a general discussion takes place" (16).

Although we can never know precisely how these publications of composition's extracurriculum were used, their number, multiple editions, and wide circulation document that they WERE used. We can speculate that at least some of them played a role in the many self-help groups that also constituted composition's extracurriculum. The egalitarian view of knowledge that characterized European settlers who arrived on this continent led them to organize for self improvement. Cotton Mather started a self-help group in Boston during the colonial period and in 1728, Ben Franklin joined with several friends to form a mutual improvement group that required each member to "once in three months produce and read an essay of his own writing on any subject he pleased" (Goodman 98). As the new republic took shape, many young men formed self-improvement groups. In Boston in 1833, for example, more than 1500 young men belonged to groups that gave composition a central place in their activities. Individuals wrote reports on local issues and these reports were read and discussed at meetings. The Lyceum, founded in 1826, had 3000 clubs in 15 states by 1836, and fostered self-improvement through writing, as did the Chautauqua Literary and Scientific Circle (CLSC), founded in 1878. This 1904 letter from a CLSC member in Syracuse, NY, demonstrates the extracurriculum of composition in action:

> The members are expected to write two papers upon subjects assigned to them by the president who selects carefully such as pertain strictly upon the year's study. This part of the program is thoroughly enjoyed as a special effort is put forth by each member to put only such thoughts upon paper which may prove helpful. An able critic from whose valuable assistance much benefit has been derived is usually in attendance unless professional duties demand her absence. (CLSC, 1904 Record Book)

Many self-help groups included a critic among the officers. Usually elected on the basis of skill in identifying errors, this critic assumed special responsibility for noting faults of syntax and diction in papers read before the group. The critic's commentary, combined with the general club discussion, provided members significant guidance for improving their prose. The Bay View Circles, an offshoot of Chautauqua, also followed an annual course of study which included writing papers on topics under discussion. In 1897, the *Bay View Magazine,* which published the curriculum for the Circles, included this reminder: "Work has a two-fold purpose: The first is to share with the circle the results of research; the other is the benefit the member receives in knowledge and in discipline of writing." It also offered this advice: "In preparing papers, never be content to give dry and detailed facts, but invest the subject with your own individuality" (7).

Spurned by many of these groups, middle-class African Americans formed self-help associations of their own early in the nineteenth century. Typical of these, the New York Garrison Society, founded in 1834, concentrated its discussions on education and liberty and devoted its meetings to "singing, praying and the reading of original compositions" (Porter 568). Other African American expressions of composition's extracurriculum included the Philadelphia Association for Moral and Mental Improvement of the People of Color, The Young Men's Literary and Moral Reform Society of Pittsburgh and Vicinity, the New York African Clarkson Society, the Washington Convention Society, the Young Men's Lyceum and Debating Society of Detroit, and the Boston Philomathean Society. Many of these groups included both men and women, but African American women led the way in organizing single-sex forms of composition's extracurriculum by establishing ladies literary societies in Philadelphia, Washington, D.C., New York, Boston, Buffalo, and Rochester before 1836. William Lloyd Garrison, editor of the *Liberator,* addressed the Female and Literary Society of Philadelphia in 1832. When members of this society entered the meeting room, they placed their anonymous weekly compositions in a box from which they were later retrieved and criticized. Garrison was so impressed with the writing produced by The Female and Literary Society that he subsequently published several selections in *The Liberator,* thus instituting a tradition of African American clubwomen publishing their work.

Faced with the double challenge posed by their race and gender, African American clubwomen embraced writing's capacity to effect social and economic change, to enact their motto, "lifting as we climb." The Women's Era Club, founded in Boston by Josephine St. Pierre Ruffin in the latter part of the nineteenth century, issued a newspaper *The Woman's Era* in which clubwomen published their writing, and African American women appeared frequently in the pages of *The Liberator* as well as *The*

Guardian, The Conservator and *Voice of the Negro*. Prior to the Civil War, African Americans living in the south created another kind of extracurriculum in the form of secret schools. These schools—comprised of one person who could read and write and a group of individuals who wanted to learn—would meet during the night or on Sundays when slaves had a bit of free time. The mandate for graduates of these secret schools was to teach others. Kept secret because the punishment for trying to learn to read and write was severe beating or even death, these schools enabled a number of graduates to write their own passes to freedom. As Thomas Holt puts it, "Just as blacks maintained an invisible church, separate from the one that whites provided for them, they also maintained secret schools. These schools could be found in every major southern city and in countless rural communities and plantations. Their teachers were often barely literate themselves, but they passed on what little they knew to others in what one may call a chain letter of instruction" (94).

White women also contributed to composition's extracurriculum. Between 1839 and 1844, Margaret Fuller offered well-educated women subscription memberships to conversations designed to provide women an opportunity to reproduce their learning as men did, and although talk was the dominant mode, Fuller required participants to write. She explained: "At the next meeting I read these [writings] aloud and canvassed their adequacy without mentioning the names of the writers" (Hoffman 299). Clearly Fuller saw writing as a means of fostering thinking and she encouraged women to write as part of their self-education. For example, she advised one woman this way:

> I should think writing would be very good for you. A journal of your thoughts and analyses of your thoughts would teach you how to generalize and give firmness to your conclusions. Do not write down merely your impressions that things are beautiful or the reverse, but what they are and why they are. (Hoffman 302)

White women's clubs wielded considerable cultural force during the period between 1880 and 1920, and most clubs required members to write papers. The Saturday Morning Club of Boston, for example, stipulated in its bylaws: "Papers shall be read to the president (or to someone designated by her) at least a week before the discussion date" (SMC Yearbook). Since newer members wrote a higher percentage of the papers, this system of supervision guaranteed that less experienced writers received more direct instruction in this form of the extracurriculum. Elizabeth Moore et al.'s *English Composition for College Women* (1914) demonstrates the ubiquitous nature of club papers during this period by including a chapter on the club paper. In addition to sample papers and suggestions for topics, the chapter includes this description: "A club paper may be considered a popular exposition of some subject of general utility or interest" (67).

The extracurriculum of composition reached across class lines. One account of a working class women's club appears in Lucy Larcom's *A New England Girlhood*. Larcom, who worked in the textile mills of Lowell, Massachusetts, describes "The Improvement Circle" in which she and her co-workers met "for writing and discussion" (174). Papers read in the Improvement Circle were often published in "The Lowell Offering," a journal edited by a young woman who worked in the mills. Other forms of composition's extracurriculum appeared in the clubs organized in Settlements — such as Jane Addams' Hull House in Chicago, the Philadelphia Guild of Working Women, founded in 1893, and the Women's Educational and Industrial Union, founded in 1877. In these and other such associations, working class women wrote their worlds and helped one another become better writers.

This brief account documents some of the publications and groups that sustained the extracurriculum of composition in the past. Current publications such as William Zinsser's *Writing Well: An Informal Guide to Writing* and magazines such as *The Writer's Market* have taken the place of *The Young Man's Companion* and columns in *Godey's Ladies Magazine*, but today's writers continue to separate pedagogy from the classroom pedagogue and seek advice from texts in the extracurriculum. The Garrison Society's "singing, praying, and reading of original compositions" and Margaret Fuller's conversational advice to women writers may be silenced, but groups such as the Tenderloin Women Writer's Workshop and the Lansing, Iowa, Writer's Workshop have taken up their task of bringing together individuals of varying classes, genders, and races who meet to read and respond to one another's writing. These ongoing and vital manifestations of the extracurriculum challenge us to take a wider view of composition. In suggesting a more inclusive perspective, I am not advocating that composition studies work to appropriate the extracurriculum or tear down classroom walls. Rather, I propose that we avoid an uncritical narrative of professionalization and acknowledge the extracurriculum as a legitimate and autonomous cultural formation that undertakes its own projects. Such an inclusive perspective can lead us to tap and listen to messages through the walls, to consider how we can learn from and contribute to composition's extracurriculum in our classes.

That word *class* suggests possibilities, since it designates at once a political/economic social group and the site where we in composition studies enact much of our working lives. Normal usage separates social class from academic class, but a look at the origins of the word suggests a close relationship between the two. The Latin word *Classis* referred to the most prosperous Roman citizens, the ones who paid the highest taxes. In the second century Aulus Gellius used the name of these wealthy citizens to designate the best writers. As Richard Terdiman says, "This subterranean valorization of *economic power masquerading as quality* has stuck to 'class' ever since" (226). If we look at the relationships between economic power and attributions of quality in our writing classes, we cannot avoid noting that those with least economic power, often people of color, are most likely to be designated as "basic writers." Significantly, writing centers, which lie outside classes yet remain intimately related to them, offer rich opportunities for communicating with worlds outside the academy. Students often bring extracurricular texts such as self-sponsored poems, resumes, and personal letters to these liminal sites. By stepping outside our classes in both economic and academic terms, we can contribute to and learn from the extracurriculum as we reconsider relationships between economic power and attributions of quality in the writing of our student bodies.

The term *student body* suggests potential for creating another bond through the walls separating the classroom and the extracurriculum. Schooling implies a disciplining of the student's body. Nineteenth century images of classrooms with the instructor standing on a raised dais over students seated in desks bolted to the floor, of teachers caning students' bodies, and of students standing to recite have given way to the more familiar images of instructors seated near students, of moveable desks arranged in a semi-circle, and of students' fingers poised over a keyboard. But schooling in general and composition in particular still inscribes itself on students' bodies. The relaxed physical environment of the extracurriculum suggests that we rethink the relationship between physical and mental discipline. Why, for example, has the move toward whole-language pedagogies among our colleagues in elementary schools been accompanied by the introduction of cushions, beanbag chairs, and carpets in classrooms? How do we see the correlation between whole language—a pedagogy that unites reading and writing while affirming students' inherent language abilities—and a blurring of domestic and academic scenes? This blurring suggests new ways of looking at the relation of public and private life, even of eliding distinctions between the two. It also recalls the material conditions of writing. While few of us are concerned with providing our students recipes for making red ink or instructing them in ways to prevent it from molding or freezing, we do confront such complex material questions as how to provide equality of access to computers for word processing. Reconsidering the relations between domestic and classroom economies may help us develop creative responses to the material constraints of writing. Thinking along these lines we would do well to recall Kenneth Burke's image of intellectual history as a parlor where participants enter and leave the ongoing conversation. This domestic/academic image resonates with feminist explorations of the trajectories of public and private.

In urging that we look again at the relationship between domestic and academic scenes, I am emphatically not suggesting that we move away from professionalism in our field. We know too well the history of the Harvard Reports issued at the turn of the century. These reports, which had an enormously negative impact on composition studies, demonstrate what can happen when questions about composition are answered by non-professionals: The most superficial aspects of writing receive the greatest attention, and the more complicated and important questions remain unasked and unanswered. We who teach composition, and particularly we who claim membership in CCCC, have, in recent years, given considerable energy to professionalism. We have asserted that writing instructors have or require specialized training and that they deserve the respectability born of educated knowledge. I applaud these efforts, particularly where they have served to improve the working conditions of writing teachers. But I'd like to suggest that we scrutinize the culture of professionalism. For instance, professionalism incorporates both material and ideological functions. Its economic function creates a link between education and the market place by insisting, for example, that composition teachers ought to be paid adequately because they possess special training. Embracing this economic function implicates us in an ideology that justifies inequality of status and closure of access. Composition's extracurriculum can remind us of the need for increased access in writing instruction. In response we can strengthen our vigilance against reductive forms of assessment and against instructional practices and curricular plans that make writing a barrier to be overcome rather than an activity to be engaged in. We can also learn to value the amateur. The culture of professionalism, with its emphasis on specialization, abhors amateurism, but composition's extracurriculum shows the importance of learning from amateurs. After all, as the Latin root *amatus* reminds us, members of the Tenderloin Women's Writing Workshop or the Lansing, Iowa, Writers Workshop write for *love.*

An unswerving concentration on professionalism can also blind us to the power relations in our classrooms. One of the clearest messages of the extracurriculum concerns *power.* As Frederick Rudolph noted, the extracurriculum of the nineteenth century vested students with power in curriculum decisions. We see that power acknowledged (and usurped) today as student film societies become departments of and courses in film studies. In a related way composition studies can draw upon and contribute to circulations of power in its extracurriculum. Our incorporation of the workshop practices that originated in student literary societies exemplifies one way. Another is suggested by a sketch Mary TallMountain read at the Tenderloin Women Writers Workshop. This sketch portrays a fellow Indian who loses his identity and ultimately his life in San Francisco:

> I watched that man for six months in the line at St. Anthony's shelter. I watched him and watched him and watched him. I could see

beyond the dirt and all the things holding him back. He was a brave man to me. I felt he had come to the end of his way. The next thing he knew he was riding through the prairies on his horse. And the filthy street changed into the long grass in a strangely familiar valley and Bilijohn was riding. Riding. He didn't hear the high keening screech of brakes, didn't see the lithe swerve of the shining town car. He heard only a distant call: Bily! Bily John! and his own answering holler. Yeah, I'm coming as fast as I can! He didn't feel the massy jolt as the sharp hood scooped him skyward, his eyes still measuring the weeping clouds. The half-empty, gray-green bottle arced into the gutter and tumbled down the torrent of flotsam, the Thunderbird belching out of it. Indian Bilijohn galloped on through the long amber grass, heels pummeling the bright flanks. (Heller, "Writers" 77–78)

Mary TallMountain demonstrates the power of representing one's own community. In insisting on Bilijohn's dignity and humanity against mainstream accounts of poverty and alcoholism among Native Americans, she exemplifies the point made by a good deal of fashionable critical discourse: the importance of considering who will represent whom in what terms and in what language. Like medical doctors who learn from nutritionists, shamans, and artists without compromising their professional status, we can benefit from examining how the extracurriculum confers authority for representation and how we might extend that authority in our classes. Our students would benefit if we learned to see them as individuals who seek to write, not be written about, who seek to publish, not be published about, who seek to theorize, not be theorized about. Ultimately, however, we in composition studies would benefit from this shift because, as Susan Miller reminds us, "placing those who teach composition in the role of hired mother/maid has a great deal to do with the presexual, preeconomic, prepolitical subjectivity imposed on composition *students*" (192). By helping to change the subjectivities of our students, we open the possibility of enhancing our own (professional) positions.

The fact that sketches like Mary TallMountain are read regularly at the Tenderloin Women's Writing Workshop speaks to the issue of *performance* in the extracurriculum. Here, as Maria Rand says, "You gotta get rejected and get applause." Clubs that mandated oral readings of papers, the office of the critic who commented on syntax and diction in self-help groups, the presumption of the editor of *The Ladies Home Journal* that writers would be sending their manuscripts, rolled or not, to busy editors— all of these items from the history of composition's extracurriculum show the direct relationship between writing and performance. Like the British working class balladeer of the mid-nineteenth century who exchanged original compositions for a pint of ale, writers in the extracurriculum demonstrate how writing effects changes, both tangible and intangible. Thinking of writing as performance reminds us that it occupies an uncertain space between the concrete and the symbolic. This might prompt us to reconsider performance in our own teaching and research. As Porter Perrin shows, college composition before 1750 in this country centered on the declamation, a pedagogical practice which required students to read aloud to an audience compositions they had previously written. Pedagogies of performance like these reinforce writing's liminal status between materiality and idea and demonstrate it as "a centered space from which we do not exit in the same form" (Benston 435).

The transformative quality of writing's performance speaks to the cultural work it accomplishes. Within classroom walls, composition frequently serves a gatekeeping function by providing an initiation rite that determines whether newcomers can master the practices and perspectives of academic discourse. Those who do not succeed in composition classes rarely last long in higher education. For a significant number of those who survive this initiation, alienation results. These are students who succeed in composition by distancing themselves from persons and experiences important in their everyday lives. Composition thus accomplishes the cultural work of producing autonomous individuals willing to adopt the language and perspectives of others. Composition's extracurriculum frequently serves the opposite function by strengthening ties with the community. In his study of the development of schooled literacy among the British working class of the 19th century, David Vincent observes that, "Composition was eventually admitted to the official curriculum in 1871, but as a means of exploiting the Penny Post, not of imitating penny dreadfuls" (218). Penny dreadfuls, episodic narratives that rely strongly on the songs and melodramatic tales common among working class people, were held in low regard by school instructors who saw composition as a means of copying the sentences of others. Yet, as Vincent shows, working class children educated in these schools were as likely to use their skills to write penny dreadfuls as letters for the penny post. Similarly, when our own students enter the extracurriculum, they frequently write their own versions of penny dreadfuls. That is, the form and content of what they write reflects their connections with their own communities. For women of the nineteenth century the genre of club paper represented one such connection, and the extracurricular selections that students bring to our writing centers manifest another. When persons in groups such as the Tenderloin Women's Writing Workshop and the Lansing, Iowa, Writers' Workshop write about people they know, about homelessness, about farming, composition's extracurriculum accomplishes the cultural work of affirming and strengthening their connections with their own communities.

These communities outside our classroom walls have, if books on the best-seller list in recent years provide any indication, demonstrated considerable dissatisfaction with much of what transpires in higher education.

While one reasonable response is to counter with books telling the story from our side of the classroom wall, we run the risk of talking past those on the other side, of constructing walls as divisions rather than means of communicating. A more productive alternative involves considering our own roles as agents within the culture that encompasses the communities on both sides of the classroom wall.

This consideration implies rethinking the narratives we construct about composition studies. Instead of a historiography based exclusively on textbooks used in schools and colleges, on the careers and works of prominent teachers and scholars, on the curricular decisions made by universities and on texts produced by students, we can consider the various sites in which the extracurriculum has been enacted, the local circumstances that supported its development, the material artifacts employed by its practitioners, and the cultural work it accomplished. This expanded historical account will attend to the New York Garrison Club along with Porter Perrin's discussion of the teaching of rhetoric in the American college before 1750. It will recognize that a group of unschooled young men who met on Friday evenings to share and respond to one another's writing contributes to the story of composition as surely as does an examination of textbooks written by Fred Newton Scott. It will look to *Godey's Magazine* as well as Hugh Blair's *Lectures on Rhetoric and Belle Lettres* for information on how writers of another age learned their craft.

While history offers a source of inspiration for the future, its vision cannot be realized without cultural work in the present. As we consider our own roles of social agency we can insist more firmly on the democracy of writing and the need to enact pedagogies that permit connections and communication with the communities outside classroom walls. This does not mean appropriating the extracurriculum but merely assigning it a more prominent status in our discourses. Whether or not we rise to this challenge, composition's extracurriculum will persist and our students can join it as soon as they step outside our classroom walls and enter what Tillie Olson calls "all the life that happens outside of us, beyond us." We may discipline their bodies with school desks and hand positions for keyboarding, but they write outside and beyond us in an extracurriculum of their own making. They may gather in rented rooms in the Tenderloin, around kitchen tables in Lansing, Iowa, or in a myriad of other places to write their worlds. The question remains whether we will use classroom walls as instruments of separation or communication.

ACKNOWLEDGMENTS

An earlier version of this article was presented at the 1992 Penn State Rhetoric Conference, and many conference participants helped me think toward revisions. In particular, Stephen Mailloux, Deborah Minter, Jack Selzer, and Nancy Shapiro offered very useful comments. Members of my writing group—Arnetha Ball, Deborah Keller-Cohen, Rosina Lippi-Green, Pamela Moss, and Annemarie Palincsar—urged me through multiple revisions, and Karen Burke-Lefevre provided a very timely and generous reading when I needed it most. I thank them all.

NOTES

1. I am grateful to Carol Heller for sharing with me her extensive work with and ideas about the Tenderloin Women's Writing Workshop.
2. I wish to thank Deborah Keller-Cohen for introducing me to these early American texts.

WORKS CITED

Applebee, Arthur. *Tradition and Reform in the Teaching of English*. Urbana: NCTE, 1974.

Bentson, Kimberly W. "Being There: Performance as Mise-en-Scène, Abscene, Obscene and Other Scene." *PMLA* 107 (1992): 434–449.

Bok, Edward. "Editor's Column." *Ladies Home Journal* 7 (1890): 12.

Chautauqua Literary and Scientific Circle Record Book, CLSC Clubhouse, Chautauqua, New York, 1904 (unpaged).

"Column." *Bay View Magazine* 5.2 (1897): 6.

Connors, Robert, Lisa Ede, and Andrea Lunsford. *Essays on Classical Rhetoric and Modern Discourse*. Carbondale: Southern Illinois UP, 1984.

Fisher, George. *The American Instructor: Or, Young Man's Best Companion*. Philadelphia: Franklin and Hall, 1748.

Freedman, Jonathan. "Beyond the Usual Suspects: Theorizing the Middlebrow." Unpublished paper, U of Michigan, 1993.

Goodman, Nathan, Ed. *A Benjamin Franklin Reader*. New York: Crowell, 1945.

Graff, Gerald. *Professing Literature: An Institutional History*. Chicago: U of Chicago P, 1987.

Hale, Sarah Josepha. "Editor's Column." *Godey's Ladies Magazine* 16 (1838):191.

Heath, Shirley Brice. "Toward an Ethnohistory of Writing in American Education." *Writing: The Nature, Development and Teaching of Written Communication*. Ed. Marcia Farr Whiteman. Hillsdale, NJ: Lawrence Erlbaum, 1981.

Heller, Carol Elizabeth. "Writers of the Tenderloin." Unpublished essay. U of California, Berkeley, 1987.

———. "The Multiple Functions of the Tenderloin Women's Writing Workshop: Community in the Making." Diss. U of California, Berkeley, 1992.

———. *The Tenderloin Women's Writing Workshop: Until We Are All Strong Together*. New York: Teachers College Press, forthcoming.

Hoffman, Nicole Tonkovich. "Scribbling, Writing, Author(iz)ing Nineteenth Century Women Writers." Diss. U of Utah, 1990.

Holt, Thomas. "'Knowledge Is Power': The Black Struggle for Literacy." *The Right to Literacy*. Eds. Andrea A. Lunsford, Helene Moglen, and James Slevin. New York, MLA, 1990. 91–102.

Hubbard, Ruth. "Notes from the Underground: Unofficial Literacy in One Sixth Grade." *Anthropology and Education Quarterly* 20 (1989): 291–307.

Kitzhaber, Albert Raymond. "Rhetoric in American Colleges, 1850–1900." Diss. U of Washington, 1953.

Larcom, Lucy. *A New England Girlhood*. Boston: Houghton, 1889.

Miller, Susan. *Textual Carnivals: The Politics of Composition*. Carbondale: Southern Illinois UP, 1991.

Moore, Elizabeth, Dora Gilbert Tompkins, and Mildred MacLean. *English Composition for College Women*. New York: Macmillan, 1914.

Oxley, J. MacDonald. "Column." *Ladies Home Journal* 9 (1894):16.

Perrin, Porter Gale. "The Teaching of Rhetoric in the American Colleges before 1750." Diss. U of Chicago, 1936.

Porter, Dorothy B. "The Organized Educational Activities of Negro Literary Societies, 1828–1846." *The Journal of Negro Education* 5 (1936):555–576.

Rudolph, Frederick. *American College and University: A History*. New York: Vintage, 1962.

———. Saturday Morning Club Yearbook, 1898, Schlesinger Library, Cambridge, MA.

Terdiman, Richard. "Is there Class in this Class?" *The New Historicism.* Ed. H. Aram Veeser. New York: Routledge, 1989.

Vincent, David. *Literacy and Popular Culture: England 1750–1914.* Cambridge: Cambridge UP, 1989.

Wagner, Jay P. "Alamakee Farmers Cultivate Writing Habits." *Des Moines Register* 12 March 1991.

———. "Writers in Overalls." *The Washington Post.* 2 January 1993.

Wolf, Robert. *Free River Press Newsletter* 1 (January, 1993): 1.

———, ed. *Voices from the Land.* Lansing, Iowa: Free River Press, 1992.

AFTERWORD: THE THRIVING EXTRACURRICULUM

Eleven years, three computer crashes, and one move later, I no longer have a copy of my Chair's address, and I rarely read my own work in print because I don't want to face having written *that* awkward sentence, because I'm more interested in what others say, and because I'm usually thinking about new questions by the time my writing is published. But, at Duane Roen's request, I turned to the February 1994 issue of *CCC* to read the revised version of what I said. Although I don't have the original text, I have a very clear memory of April 1, 1993, when I stood before an audience of my peers in San Diego. The faces of dear friends and colleagues looking up expectantly brought me to the edge of tears, as I thought about the privilege and responsibility of the moment. My recollections also include the dreams — nightmares really — that haunted me in the days before I gave the address. I would stand to speak and discover that my text had turned to ashes, pages would be missing, I'd be unable to speak — every time I awoke in a cold sweat.

I felt anxious because I was taking a risk with my speech. I worried, as Shirley Brice Heath so astutely observed in her response, that my emphasis on the literacy practices of (mostly) women's groups could be taken as "a recitation of curiosities about the writing practices and conditions of those who have not mattered much throughout history" (98). But I had to, really had to, use the occasion of the Chair's address to talk about literacy practices enacted outside classrooms. At that point, I had done much of the archival research for my book *Intimate Practices: Literacy and Cultural Work in Women's Clubs 1880–1920* (University of Illinois Press, 1997), and all those months and years of sifting through papers, notebooks, and letters had convinced me that our field needed to shift away from, as Susan Miller put it, separating students from their culture and begin thinking of teaching as "a way to facilitate [literacy] practices already under way" (106). The extracurriculum, as I called it, needed to be much more prominent in our thinking and doing.

Looking back from the perspective of more than a decade, I am even more convinced that it was worth taking the risk. It's gratifying to know that a number of academic studies have built upon the concepts I laid out in my Chair's address and in the book that followed, but I'm even more struck by what is happening in the larger culture. As I write, a recently issued report sits on my desk. It begins, "*Reading at Risk* is not a report that the National Endowment for the Arts is happy to issue" (vii). It continues with a gloomy report on the rapid decline in literary reading in America, especially among those under thirty-five. What has received little notice is this sentence: "Contrary to the overall decline in literary reading, the number of people doing creative writing—of any genre, not exclusively literary works—increased substantially between 1982 and 2002" (22). "Substantial" means 30 percent; adults are writing 30 percent more than they did two decades ago. The extracurriculum of composition thrives.

–ANNE RUGGLES GERE
University of Michigan

WORKS CITED

Heath, Shirley Brice. "Finding in History the Right to Estimate." *College Composition and Communication* 45 (Feb. 1994).

Miller, Susan. "Things Inanimate May Move: A Different History of Writing and Class." *CCC* 45 (Feb. 1994).

National Endowment for the Arts. *Reading at Risk: A Survey of Literary Reading in America.* Research Division Report #46 (June 2004).

1994

Freedom, Form, Function: Varieties of Academic Discourse

LILLIAN BRIDWELL-BOWLES

Let me begin my address by invoking three voices other than my own: First, Langston Hughes, whom I discovered in desperation during my first year of teaching:

> Hold fast to dreams
> For if dreams die,
> Life is a broken-winged bird that cannot fly.

And then Adrienne Rich, whom I discovered in more recent years: "We might hypothetically possess ourselves of every recognized technological resource on the North American continent, but as long as our language is inadequate, our vision remains formless, our thinking and feeling are still running in the old cycles, our process may be 'revolutionary,' but [it will not be] transformative" (247–48).

And finally, Hélène Cixous: "I do not want to tell a story to someone's memory" (qtd. in Conley 1).

In my opinion, the most significant issue facing our profession as we move into the twenty-first century is embodied in these quotations: That our language and our writing should be adequate enough to make our dreams, our visions, our stories, our thinking, and our actions not just revolutionary but transformative. When Rich chooses transformative processes over revolutionary ones, she strikes a chord with me and with many others of my generation. Like Langston Hughes, we were youthful dreamers, but our visions of revolution have given way to practical questions about how we can change our two institutions, our own departments, and our own classrooms. And finally, I have invoked Hélène Cixous, who challenges me to try to think in new ways even when

---

This article is a revised version of the Chair's address Lillian Bridwell-Bowles delivered at the CCCC Convention in Nashville, Tennessee, on March 17, 1994. It was first published in *CCC*, volume 46, number 1, February 1995.

I cannot. I want to bring the passions and the dreams of transformation to our classrooms.

In the 1990s, it is not always easy to invite our students to participate in transformation, to write with passion about subjects that are complex, politically charged, politically correct, or even politically incorrect. To do so invites labels such as "tenured radical" and accusations that politics is corrupting higher education, to paraphrase Roger Kimball. To do so invites media attention to our textbooks, as was the case just last week on the Rush Limbaugh Show.[1] To do so invites departmental discord and strife, as past events at the University of Texas have taught us.

And yet, we must continue to make our classrooms vital places where students learn not only the various conventions of academic writing, but also the power of communication to change things, to transform. Academic discourse must help us and our students create community in a world that often seems torn apart by difference. As my title suggests, I want to know how the various forms and functions of academic writing have anything to do with educating ourselves for our whole lives, and by this I mean all of our multiple identities and our multiple dreams for ourselves. To be successful, we need to teach students conventional forms and better analytical skills, but also we need to encourage them to dream, to think in new cycles and to have visions for the future that are hopeful.

Some details from my personal history explain why I care about these issues. One of the things I have learned about rhetoric from feminist theory, especially bell hooks, is how very important it is to position oneself clearly with one's listeners or readers, especially when the subject is complicated.[2] My experience in this profession will resonate with some of you, particularly those who were in school during the late sixties or early seventies. Others will have had entirely different experiences, and you will agree or disagree with me for your own reasons, but I also hope that we have common professional ground.

I was born in 1947, and promptly nicknamed "Lilly," which was extremely appropriate, given the nature of my middle class, lily-white surroundings in central Florida. Our neighborhood was typical of many built by those seeking to forget what they had experienced during the Great Depression and World War II. Our home was my father's "castle" and my mother was the superwoman who ran it and orchestrated the lives of the children she considered "gifted." Our world was fairly homogenized, as many were in the 1950s. I recall hearing murmurs in the neighborhood when a Cuban doctor bought a house during the first wave of Cuban immigration before Castro's revolution. He was very "light-skinned," they said, and welcome, of course, but no one invited him or his family to dinner. I had to travel to North Carolina to my grandparents' homes to actually meet any people of color whose names and histories were accessible to me. There, as a small child, I saw my father's hand remain at his side when a friend from his childhood extended his hand in friendship, a hand that happened to be black. This act, which is indelibly recorded in my memory, made no sense to me, coming as I did from that lily-white world where white hands clasped in greeting all the time.

Perhaps, then, you can imagine my surprise when I read Zora Neale Hurston's *Their Eyes Were Watching God* and learned of another world I had never seen even though it was only a few miles down the road. I am still educating myself about that world down the road. Melissa Fay Greene's *Praying for Sheetrock*, which describes the lives of black and white families in a county intersected by Highway 17, is literally about the road we took every summer on our way back to North Carolina. My world in Florida is gone now, bulldozed and rebuilt as a fantasy world where athletes go when they win medals and diamond rings. It is no longer lily-white, but the people there still attempt to hold on to other kinds of fantasies.

I am a dreamer from that world, but until I went away to college, my dreams were, for the most part, ordinary. As Adrienne Rich suggests, my vision was formless and my thinking ran in the old cycles. The only hint of something else was that my high school counselor complained that I had an exaggerated sense of my personal rights when I refused to take the home economics course required for graduation from a Florida high school. I didn't even know the word "sexist" then; I just knew that I couldn't allow my dreams to be limited to cutting out dress patterns and going on tours of mobile home parks where we were supposed to learn how to finance a home with a kitchen like Betty Crocker's.

The writing that I did in high school was mainly summarization. The only essays that I recall at all were a halting attempt to describe the architecture of Frank Lloyd Wright, largely plagiarized by stringing together quotes from several books, and a term paper on becoming a psychologist, complete with notecards and an outline written at the last minute. Writing at that time was not a source of discovery or a way of knowing for me. I learned patterns of paragraph development and parts of speech, but I did not learn to write. I did not feel the power of the written word to change anything.

In 1965, I went off to college in yet another lily-white world, though it is now, I am told, a more colorful place. That institution began a radical transformation during the years I was there, as others did across the country, but my courses still reflected old patterns. Nearly all of the important writing that I produced was extracurricular, not a part of my "formal" education, which is one of the reasons why Anne Gere's address last year was so meaningful to me. My final exams were interrupted by the deaths of Bobby Kennedy and Martin Luther King. My real literacy education was about what was happening in the streets. Here, for example, is a poem that I found outside the classroom, a poem that I have carried in my heart for 26 years:

> I have wrapped my dreams in a silken cloth,
> And laid them away in a box of gold;
> Where long will cling the lips of the moth,
> I have wrapped my dreams in a silken cloth;
> I hide no hate; I am not even wroth
> Who found earth's breath so keen and cold;
> I have wrapped my dreams in a silken cloth,
> And laid them away in a box of gold.

That is Countee Cullen's "Epitaph For A Poet." It might have been the first piece of writing by an African American that I had ever read, for the anthologies of literature in my high school and even in the "southern literature" class that I took at Florida State University in 1970 were still lily-white. I could hardly believe that it could have been written by an African American. I could also not imagine that this African-American man was more educated than my father. Nothing in my childhood world nor in my segregated education had prepared me for this poem. It came to me from an alternative source, from the person who was the most influential teacher I had throughout late adolescence and early adulthood. This was Joan Baez, whose album, *Baptism: A Journey Through Our Time*, introduced me to poetry that mattered and politics that I was supposed to participate in. These things inspired me to write on my own, outside of school.

On the *Baptism* album, Baez read and sang other poems, anti-war poems like Wilfred Owne's parable about Abram and Isaac:

> Offer the ram of pride instead of him.
> But the old man would not so,
> but slew his son, and half the seed
> of Europe, one by one.

This was the first time that my old Sunday school lessons had any connection with the world in which I lived. And Norman Rosten's "Guernica," about the little children slain in Guernica, little children just like those in Sarajevo, Palestine, Somalia, or Haiti today:

And Walt Whitman's "I Saw The Vision Of Armies":

> I saw battle-corpses, myriads of them,
> And the white skeletons of young men—I saw them;
> I saw the debris and debris of all dead soldiers;
> But I saw they were not as was thought;
> They themselves were fully at rest—they suffer'd not;
> The living remain'd and suffer'd—the mother suffer'd,
> And the wife and the child, and the musing comrade suffer'd,
> And the armies that remained suffer'd.

These, my most important literacy lessons, were poems I found on a folksinger's record, outside the classroom, away from the places where literature was supposed to be affecting my life. So I left my lily-white world and began to learn about gaps, especially the gaps in my supposedly privileged education. I joined in marches and went off to teach high school English in a predominantly African American community where the average income per family in the county was $3,000. I began to try to figure out how I would teach these students to read and write, why and how they might or might not want to learn to talk like me. I learned a lot from them about the literatures and cultures of people who did not talk like me. Then and since, writing has also helped me to understand many issues in my personal and professional worlds. It has helped me feel a sense of personal power in my work for social change, and it has helped me with my own personal transformations.

But the main insight I have about my own literacy history is that none of the important or meaningful writing I have ever produced happened as a result of a writing assignment given in a classroom. None of it. And I had some good teachers. And, unlike many of our students, I was one of the ones for whom education supposedly worked, considering that I have a plaque with the word "Valedictorian" on it. In the ninth grade, Warrene H. Fugitt gave me A's for my book reports, all of which I have forgotten, but she also wrote on the board one day a line from Robert Browning that I wrote down in a private journal she never saw: "Ah, but a man's reach should exceed his grasp, Or what's a heaven for?" In college, I produced more "A" papers in a class taught by James McCrimmon, whose textbook in its multiple editions is legendary, but they were exercises in form, practice-writing that would prepare me for something else, later. So much of my education seemed to be about "later."

Foss, Foss, and Trapp, writing about Foucault, observe that he "saw his experience in the French educational system as a continual postponement of the promised secret knowledge. In primary school, he was told that the most important things would be revealed in the lycée. At the lycée he was told he would have to wait until his final year, only to be told at that point that the knowledge he wanted was to be found in the study of philosophy, which would be revealed at the university level" (210). The rest of his life was a search for knowledge, an archeological dig to find the secrets and structures of the knowledge he so desperately sought.

Though I hardly compare the range of my intellect to Foucault's, I can identify with parts of his quest. Like Foucault, I and many others of my generation needed alternative sources, alternative visions to learn to think in new ways, to find visions and dreams that didn't run in the same patterns. What I dream about today is that we might *more often* make our classrooms places that connect with the world outside, the here and now; places that show students the power of writing to transform—writing that is not always about later, about jobs and careers, but writing that is about themselves as people, as individuals and as citizens of various communities.

I feel a strong sense of community with colleagues in CCCC who have tried to make education and the teaching of writing "relevant" as we used to say in the 60s and 70s, but finding that sense of solidarity is more complicated than it used to be. Relevant for what? From whose perspective? Our old revolutionary rhetorics are not working. The influence of identity politics has made us cautious, fearful that we would or would not be perceived as "politically correct," depending upon our politics. Within our own profession, we now have significant differences that make it difficult for us to communicate with each other, let alone decide on curriculum, textbooks, or pedagogies. I know first-hand from the politics of my own institution that many people have a vision for education very different from mine.

In fact, it may be because we as a profession have already been transformed in so many ways so quickly that we have a whole new set of problems. As a profession, we are conflicted about the roles we and other faculty members should play in literacy development. If we read Bizzell and Herzberg's *Rhetorical Tradition* from cover to cover, as I just did this quarter in a rhetorical history seminar, we read about rhetoric's fall from grace in western curricula. At the turn of this century, as English departments in higher education established the study of literature and literary criticism as their primary interests, rhetoric and composition became merely a "service" that these departments provided. The conflicted goals of English and composition were summarized in Maxine Hairston's CCCC Chair's address in 1985 when she urged us to separate ourselves from departments that put us "at the bottom of the social and political scale" (275). During the 1970s, and especially after Hairston's rallying cry, we sent the message that we were an emerging (now middle-aged) field with a body of professional research and theory that could account for literacy development and generate methods for turning a generation of students into more literate readers and writers. We claimed we had found ways to restore rhetoric to its central and rightful place in the curriculum. Our institutions have, in many cases, believed us and have set up expensive programs, writing centers, and computer labs where our students are supposedly being remediated, educated, and trained for professional writing once they leave us.

More recently, despite Hairston's suspicion about the motive for doing so, we have centered our profession by aligning it with some of the most exciting, formerly "marginal," theoretical developments within the academy: feminist theory, multicultural and postcolonial theory, poststructuralism, and the new rhetorics with their connections to contemporary critical theory. We have learned from the black feminist theorist bell hooks about the interplay between margins and centers. In our roles as rhetoricians, we have found new alliances with those on our campuses who would see writing as a crucial site for intellectual, political, and social debate. We have even found some ways to reunite with those who had seen us as mere technicians as we talk about composition in the broader context of literacy, where reading is not separated from writing. As Hairston put it, prophetically then, "by freeing ourselves . . . and by leaving the house in which we grew up, we may finally create the strong connection between literature and composition that most of us feel is good and natural" (282).

We have accomplished a great deal, but there are problems with our success in professionalizing and theorizing our way back into the academy. Our professional solidarity may mask fundamental disagreements about pedagogical practices. In some places, our rhetorical power to convince administrators has outstripped our ability to deliver students with writing skills acceptable to institutional monitors or to employers beyond the groves of academe. We have not always reconciled our theoretical interests in the philosophical issues of language with the goals that our students and our institutions have for us. Critical theory may be helping us as academics, but is it helping our students? Has all of our transformation been more for us than for our students? Despite the efforts of many CCCC committees, including the leaders of various assessment committees and the drafters of the Wyoming Resolution, we have no universally accepted professional standards or standards for writing upon which we all agree. We have not reconciled the issues of politics and power that complicate our ability to have students write about topics such as racism, cultural misogyny, class differences, abortion, nationalistic chauvinism, and homophobia.

There are, of course, broader social and historical reasons why we have not made more progress in these areas. Our profession is more complicated now than it was earlier in the country's history, or even in the 1940s when CCCC was founded. There was a time when rhetorical education was simpler, and principles and standards were easier to write. This education was predicated on a limited number of professions, a limited number of students, a limited range of types of students, and relative uniformity about the materials and goals of institutions of higher learning. It was simpler because the notion that all people should be allowed access to literacy and to academic literacy in particular did not exist. As Henry Louis Gates, Jr., reminds us in his recent book *Loose Canons*, it was illegal in eighteenth century South Carolina for African Americans to be taught to read and write.

> Be it enacted that all and every person and persons whatsoever,
> Who shall hereafter teach,
> Or cause any slave or slaves to be taught to write,
> Or shall use or employ any slave as a scribe in any manner of

> Writing whatsoever, hereafter taught to write;
> Every such person or persons shall, for every offense, forfeit the sum of
>   one hundred pounds current money (59).

Today my university at least proclaims that we do not discriminate on the basis of race, ethnicity, religion, creed, gender, sexual orientation, physical ability, or nationality. We have made tremendous progress in naming discriminatory practices, but we have not yet eliminated them in our classroom practices.

Rhetorical education was also simpler because, among those hired to teach in higher educational institutions, you could assume that there was a fairly homogenous world view. The complexities of language theory were largely limited to two conditions: "Truth" was obvious, waiting to be conveyed by good writing or speaking, or it was probable, waiting to be discovered by the patterns of thinking embodied in rhetorical training. Before the printing press, before the "information explosion" in the twentieth century, "gathering the available means of persuasion," as Aristotle taught us, was intellectually demanding, but not without boundaries. But now, the old familiar canons have given way to Gates' loose canons; we have lost our parameters in this postmodern world. Finally, "we" were all supposedly more alike than we are today. When I first walked into the faculty club on my campus 13 years ago, I recall not seeing another woman or a person of color in a very large room that held over 150 people. Today, as we celebrate the diversity within our profession, we discover that we cannot always talk about a common "we."

However "we" define ourselves as we move into the twenty-first century, we no longer have, and most of us do not want, these limitations. We are preparing students for professions and lifestyles we can hardly imagine in our wildest dreams. We are teaching more of them than ever before. Our students come from many cultures, and they range in age from early teens to retirement age. We teach them in community colleges, in four-year liberal arts colleges, in research universities, and in alternative programs. No wonder, then, that at the annual meeting of CCCC, we should have to consider our goals for the teaching of writing and communication. For a long time, we have looked for and found common ground, common theories, common pedagogies. As we move toward a new millennium, we, along with our society and the planet, also have to come to grips with difference—among ourselves, among our students, among our institutions, among our nations as we see ourselves as global citizens.

A recent essay in *The Atlantic* entitled "Jihad vs. McWorld" suggests just one kind of tension we live with. Benjamin Barber repeats a common contemporary theme: the dialectical tension between identity politics and the struggle to build a world where we all see things through the same lens, eat the same hamburgers, wear the same brands of athletic shoes, and watch the same movies. As practitioners in the world of composition studies, some of us are confused by the rhetorical problems presented by difference vs. homogenization. This tension affects not only our view of the world, but also our language and our written texts.

If we are blessed, or cursed, with the ability to accommodate what feminist linguist Dale Spender has called a "multidimensional reality," we find ourselves changing perspectives often, really trying to see what "difference" means. Sometimes we see ourselves with a clear identity in a well-defined world. Sometimes we see ourselves as a complex of identities in a complex society. My list of identities includes, but is not limited to: baby-boomer, "white" (but with several Native American ancestors), middle-class, woman, academic with access to international conversations, middle-aged tennis player who might have been great had she started young, life partner to Rick Bowles, mother, stepmother, expatriate southerner, Presbyterian, out-of-fashion liberal, and teacher. Multiple identities, multiple languages, multiple rhetorics.

With regard to the way language works in my multiple worlds, sometimes I think truth is clear and that rhetoric and language should be transparent media for discovering and transmitting it. I remember thinking, for instance, when I sat on a jury: Did this suspect abuse this child? Yes or No? At such times, I require familiar expository forms, clear and lucid speaking and writing. At other times, the very concept of truth is so cloudy that I can hardly get my bearings or believe in a single truth. For example, what is the "real" situation in El Salvador? Whose perspective, whose version of reality, whose documents, whose language can we believe? How could we possibly write about a place like El Salvador? As Joan Didion did? With her own experience of terror? But then, if we include too much of ourselves in our writing, we might find ourselves being discounted, as Didion was in a review that described *Salvador* as "The Perils of Joan." Or like some reporters with the lens of "objectivity" and investigative journalism?[3] Or how do we write about Bosnia-Herzogovina? Or Haiti? From what vantage point should a U.S. citizen try to describe clearly the multiple perspectives that lead to violence in eastern Europe? Or in the Israeli-occupied Palestinian territories? Or, closer to home, in Los Angeles, or New York, or in my own St. Paul? How can we possibly say all we need to say about the AIDS epidemic in simple expository essays? What else might count as evidence? Journals, fiction, film, photographs, graffiti, posters? Is it better to accept the words of Randy Shilts, author of *And the Band Played On*, before he acknowledged that he had AIDS, or do we believe more of what he wrote and said afterward? How are his words altered by his death? Does his reputation in the Gay community matter as we weigh his words? What could possibly be written in a 5,000 word essay on abortion that would change anyone's mind? On complex matters such as these, we need a wide variety of forms of writing, produced from multiple perspectives, alongside a variety of other media. If form follows function, and the functions of most written language are multiple, then we need to investigate new forms.

So what does it mean to write or to learn to write from multiple perspectives? From a personal perspective, my life has been directly touched by racism, by war, by AIDS, and by the feminist movement. As I have been touched, I have changed and my language and my rhetoric have changed. Because we are in the profession we are in, many of us self-consciously reflect on these changes. This may be the one great contribution we have to make to our students, to model for them our self-reflexive analysis of our own discourse practices. Our students sometimes have difficulty imagining how radically their own language might need to change until they see how the English language has already had to change in the twentieth-century. They wonder why we still talk about sexist language, but they don't wonder any more when they read textbooks written 25 years ago. They wonder why we stress the importance of naming particular groups in careful ways, but they don't wonder any more when they read about racial strife in newspapers written in the 1930s. They also wonder whether they should trust us when we invite them to write in a variety of forms, some of them even labeled "experimental." They also wonder, sometimes, why we don't just give them the formulas and the rules and be done with it. Although some teachers and textbooks do offer students cookbooks, most of us know that the characteristics of writing in particular fields are cloudier and harder to pin down than the recipes acknowledge. The best I can do is to model for students my own process of trying to connect myself with academic writing. They have learned, just as I did, that "self" and "first person" do not belong in academic writing, so we have much in common.

If we accept multiple perspectives, an ever-changing relationship to the concepts of "truth," rapidly changing language, and complex discourse communities as inevitable characteristics of living and writing in a postmodern world, I believe we have to encourage many different kinds of writing, and not just a variety of styles of academic discourse, but experimental writing as well. In the fall of 1992, I published an essay in *CCC* on "discourse and diversity." I included a number of samples of students' writings produced in response to my invitation to attempt something "experimental." Like many of you, I often encourage students to write in ways that are unfamiliar: problem-solution essays with more than one "right" answer, parodies of academic writing, experiments with textual space, position papers from personas different from their own, and so on. Even though all of the samples came from upper division students and from graduate student seminars, some people who read the essay thought that I was writing a radical manifesto for first-year composition, that I wanted to throw out convention and encourage students to ignore standard forms.

One such respondent told me that there was no time for "alternate discourse" in the undergraduate curriculum and that I should focus on rational thought and clear exposition, rather than feminist theories of language and subjectivity. Such responses represented my worst fear: that people would see "rational" discourse as separate from the kinds of experiments I encourage, rational writing as opposed to feminist writing. A growing number of award-winning books from members of our own profession are mixing or blending different types of discourse. One of my favorites is Keith Gilyard's *Voices of the Self: A Study of Sociolinguistic Competence,* in which he juxtaposes his own personal experience of language difference with the most conventional of linguistic analyses. Many of us don't think we should separate our thinking into categories and enforce strict dichotomies, but there are many who do.

But finding our common pedagogical ground is far more complicated than simple either-or thinking about types of discourse. To assume that we can have a common language of expository rationality in opposition to what I advocated is to deny a long catalogue of differences that exist within modern (or "postmodern") postsecondary institutions. Likewise, to assume that we agree that writing in our classrooms should always be about cultural transformation is to ignore a range of differences among us. For example, there are the professional differences. Some of us are tenured, some are employed full-time but have no tenure, some are part-time, and some are students. The obvious differences in our status make us more or less willing to talk about difference. The part-time, untenured lecturer may be less likely to challenge a current-traditional paradigm than someone whose job and future are secure. But security doesn't always lead to experimentation either; often it is a ticket to complacency. Then, there are the academic aims of our institutions. Those in the most prestigious liberal arts colleges, for example, can sometimes avoid the immediate pressure to train students for jobs. While this might enable them to avoid or at least to defer the instrumental argument for conventional skills, some of the strongest proponents of "liberal arts" curricula argue loudest for conformity. The liberal arts provide, in Allan Bloom's cynical analysis, the space between an "intellectual wasteland," and the "dreary professional training" that awaits students after a baccalaureate degree (336). According to Bloom and others who share his views, the liberal arts work best when they promote a "unified view of nature and man's place in it" (347) by focusing on canonical books and rational, belletristic essays. Those who teach at public universities or in two-year colleges with a strong career orientation, with terminal degrees in majors such as law enforcement and dental hygiene, have little of this kind of luxury. Their job is to get students from point *a* to point *b* as quickly and as economically as possible. Nonprofessional reading and experimental writing are likely to be less attractive, even though their students, many of them from working-class backgrounds, may be the ones who would benefit most from interrogating the discourse practices of those in powerful positions.

A former member of the faculty at my university, Wlad Godzich, goes even further when he says that "it would not be an exaggeration to state that the effect of the new writing programs [by these he means those that have courses in writing for various fields such as business, technology, and law], given their orientation, is not to solve a 'crisis of literacy' but to promote a new culture of illiteracy, in which the student is trained to use language for the reception and conveyance of information in only one sphere of human activity: that of his or her future field of employment" (29). Godzich argues that programs in advanced, specialized composition, in league with the market forces that drive vocationalism, promote linguistic practices that fragment culture, rather than build common understanding. While he would not endorse my experimental program, he does imply that students should have instruction in "the general problematic of codes and codification in language" (29).

Within writing programs across the U.S., however, there is more diversity than Godzich suggests. In many writing-across-the-curriculum programs, for example, there are disagreements between practitioners in various fields and writing specialists from our field. For example, some of our colleagues might favor the styles in works such as *The Double Helix* or Lewis Thomas's *Lives of a Cell* over technical reports and design specifications. They might see "good" scientific writing as philosophical speculation by major scientists, often expressed in genres and on topics fairly far removed from the work that earned them their reputations. We are also familiar with the well-intentioned attempts of our colleagues who try to help students produce "good" social scientific writing, in active voice, with strong verbs and excised prepositional phrases. Such instruction is often criticized when professors in their home departments produce an entirely different style, often what is called "bad" writing in our classes, and wonder why their students' thinking was so subjective and loose. As many members of our profession have noted, discourse communities are not nearly so uniform as our textbooks sometimes suggest. As Joseph Harris has put it, "I think we dangerously abstract and idealize the workings of 'academic' discourse by taking the kinds of rarified talk and writing that go on at conferences and in journals as the norm, and viewing many of the other sorts of talk and writing that occur at the university as deviations from or approximations of that standard" (20).

Nevertheless, there are still some among us who believe that all we really need are uniformity, order, clarity, rules and principles. Allan Bloom argues, for example, that this democracy is really an anarchy, because there are "no recognized rules for citizenship and no legitimate titles to rule" (337). E. D. Hirsch and many others plead for a standard curriculum, standard ways of thinking, shared reading—common ground, in other words. On the other side, there are those who believe that difference is everything, that we should celebrate it in all forms and reject homogenization. Within our own profession, we can name those who represent these political and philosophical poles. In this address, I have argued for diversity because I believe that calls for standardization often mask white, middle-class, male-dominated traditions. Nevertheless, I want to be clear that I do not believe that diversity is an end in itself. As we try to move from "one" right way of thinking and being, let's not get stuck at the stage of "many" right ways of thinking and being, or what we criticize as "hopeless relativism." In some ways, the history of rhetoric is the conflict between those who would spell out rules for rhetorical forms vs. those who would invent new forms to construct new meanings. Surely there are times and places for difference and disagreement and times and places for commonality and community.

Richard Lloyd-Jones, in an eloquent vision of our profession, will help me to return to terra firma: "We *can* help students in a democracy understand how language both isolates and builds individuals—all at the same time—and how if we are to live together peaceably we have to learn how we are shaped by discourse as much as we shape discourse" (496). And then he offers some very practical advice: "We need to decide what teaching things we do that are too important to lose, what we can give up with no more than a token fight" (496).

What can we give up with no more than a token fight? I have a long personal list of things I can give up: silly arguments about posture and position, quibbles over the fine points of pedagogical practice, technicalities of writing assessment, narrow conceptions of modes and genres, the need to control my students' writing, and on and on. What things are too important to lose? I put one thing on my list, and after that many other things seem less important: the opportunity to see students grow, not only on the pages of their papers, but also as individuals and as citizens of larger communities. The kind of growth that I'm talking about is the ability to imagine something different, to see things in a new way, to think outside the boundaries of the familiar. That we have to do this is inescapable. Tradition and reform, permanence and change, anarchy and civilization. These pairings are familiar to us because change is inevitable. But my words have been about the freedom to imagine for ourselves what the changes ought to be. I have chosen to speak on the connections between discourse and transformation in the academy because the pressures to conform and to reproduce are so very powerful. I find myself turning again and again to Freire's *Pedagogy of the Oppressed*, especially to this passage:

> The central problem is this: how can the oppressed, as divided, unauthentic beings, participate in developing the pedagogy of their

liberation? . . . As long as they live in the duality in which *to be* is to *be like*, and to *be like* is to *be like the oppressor*, this contribution is impossible. (33)

If the one way we know to *be* is to *be like*, our visions will continue to run in the old cycles. If we don't understand history, as the saying goes, we are doomed to repeat it. If we can, as Cixous implied, only write our stories to someone else's memory, we will invent courses, syllabi, writing assignments, genres, organizations, institutions, journals, conventions, panel papers, special interest groups, and occasionally even Chair's addresses that are entirely familiar. We will not transform. My dream for all of us is that we cherish what is valuable from tradition and that we continue to find new ways of thinking, writing, and acting in the world. This is our common ground in the groves of academe.

Jim Berlin, whom we will remember throughout this convention, helped us to see different pedagogical practices built around our understanding of how language works, either as a transparent vehicle for transmitting reality, as a way of constructing reality, as a way of getting at cultural knowledge, or as a way of exploring individual voice. It was important for our profession to see how our own theoretical positions with regard to language, society, and truth influence the pedagogical practices we choose. I have attempted to place these practices within the dialectic of identity politics and society's aims for education.

Let me conclude now with the rest of Langston Hughes' poem from the book I used the first year I taught:

Hold fast to dreams
For when dreams go
Life is a barren field
Frozen with snow.

I no longer believe that I can change the world, as I did when I sang along with Joan Baez, but I do believe that I can change my own discourse practices, and in so doing, I may inspire some students in my classrooms. Kenneth Burke taught us a long time ago that rhetoric is the use of language to form attitudes and to influence action. I invite you to use writing to dream about transformations for all of us.

ACKNOWLEDGMENTS

Students in my "Feminist Writing Seminar" in the spring of 1994 read my paper and offered many suggestions for additions and notes; they helped me enormously as I tried to turn the spoken words into a written text. Jane Harred was working on the dissertation cited in the notes while I was writing my speech, and traces of our many conversations about authorship appear in my work. That I continue to learn from my students is one of the many reasons why I love our profession. My colleague Lisa Albrecht saw me through this process from the vaguest prewriting to the final draft. Like Cixous, she never fails to push me beyond my comfort level, and I am always glad when I take her advice and take more risks.

NOTES

1. The recent textbook co-authored by Andrea Lunsford and John Ruszkiewicz, *The Presence of Others*, was the focus of Limbaugh's comments about the politics of instruction on Limbaugh's show in March of 1994.
2. My essay entitled "Discourse and Diversity," published in *CCC* in 1992, contains a fuller discussion of the connections I try to make between feminist theory and writing.
3. I am indebted to Jane Harred's brilliant work on literary journalism, *Never a Copy: The Conflicting Claims of Narrative Discourse and Its Referent in the Literary Journalism of Truman Capote, Hunter S. Thompson, and Joan Didion*. I recommend her discussion of narrative theory to all who are interested in the question of perspective in nonfiction writing.

WORKS CITED

Baez, Joan. *Baptism: A Journey through Our Time.* Vanguard, VSD-79275, 1968.

Barber, Benjamin R. "Jihad vs. McWorld." *Atlantic,* March 1992: 53–62.

Bizzell, Patricia, and Bruce Herzberg. *The Rhetorical Tradition: Readings from Classical Times to the Present.* Boston: Bedford, 1990.

Bloom, Allan. *The Closing of the American Mind.* New York: Simon, 1987.

Bridwell-Bowles, Lillian. "Discourse and Diversity: Experimental Writing within the Academy," *CCC* 43 (1992): 349–68.

Conley, Verena Andermatt. *Hélène Cixous: Writing the Feminine.* 2nd Ed. Lincoln: U of Nebraska P, 1991.

Didion. Joan, *Salvador.* New York: Simon, 1983.

Foss, Sonja K., Karen A. Foss, and Robert Trapp. *Contemporary Perspectives on Rhetoric.* 2nd Ed. Prospect Heights, IL: Waveland, 1991.

Freire, Paulo. *Pedagogy of the Oppressed:.* Tr. Myra Bergman Ramos. New York: Seabury, 1970.

Gates, Henry Louis, Jr. *Loose Canons: Notes on the Culture Wars.* New York: Oxford UP, 1992.

Gere, Anne Ruggles. "Kitchen Tables and Rented Rooms: The Extracurriculum of Composition." *CCC* 45 (1994): 75–92.

Gilyard, Keith. *Voices of the Self: A Study of Language Competence.* Detroit: Wayne State UP, 1991.

Godzich, Wlad. "The Culture of Illiteracy." *Enclitic* 8.1–2 (1984): 27–35.

Greene, Melissa Fay. *Praying for Sheetrock.* New York: Fawcett, 1991.

Hairston, Maxine. "Breaking Our Bonds and Reaffirming Our Connections." *CCC* 36 (1985): 272–282.

Harred, Jane. *Never a Copy: The Conflicting Claims of Narrative Discourse and Its Referent in the Literary Journalism of Truman Capote, Hunter S. Thompson, and Joan Didion.* Diss. U of Minnesota, 1994.

Harris, Joseph. "The Idea of Community in the Study of Writing." *CCC* 40 (1989): 11–22.

Hughes, Langston. "Dreams." *Reflections on a Gift of Watermelon Pickle.* Ed. Stephen Dunning, Edward Lueders, and Hugh Smith. Glenview, IL: Scott, 1966. 129.

Hurston, Zora Neale. *Their Eyes Were Watching God.* Urbana: U of Illinois P, 1978.

Kimball, Roger. *Tenured Radicals: How Politics Has Corrupted Higher Education.* New York: Harper, 1990.

Lloyd-Jones, Richard. "Who We Were, Who We Should Become." *CCC* 43 (1992): 486–96.

Lunsford, Andrea A., and John J. Ruszkiewicz. *The Presence of Others: Readings for Critical Thinking and Writing.* New York: St. Martin's, 1994.

Pilger, John. "Having Fun with Fear." Rev. of *Salvador* by Joan Didion. *New Statesman* 6 (1983): 21.

Rich, Adrienne. *On Lies, Secrets and Silences: Selected Prose 1966–78.* New York, Norton, 1979.

Spender, Dale. *Man Made Language.* 2nd Ed. London: Routledge, 1985.

Thomas, Lewis, *The Lives of a Cell: Notes of a Biology Watcher.* New York: Viking, 1974.

Watson, James D. *The Double Helix: A Personal Account of the Discovery of the Structure of DNA.* New York: Atheneum, 1968.

Despite the realities of the world in 2004, I am still the dreamer I was when I wrote my CCCC Chair's address over a decade ago. Writing and new ways of constructing what we know through language can be transformative. Never has it been more important to dream this dream.

My address was written as I watched tracer bombs light the skies over Baghdad during the Gulf War. I am writing my response as we are engaged in yet another war without a democratic mandate, on the eve of the election of either George Bush or John Kerry. We are still seeing, with Whitman, "visions of armies." We have not offered "the ram of pride" instead of our young people. Wealth is even more unevenly distributed within our nation, and we still consume that lion's share of the world's resources without contributing to the empowerment of the oppressed that Freire described. We value production of goods over the environment.

We have not made much progress over the decade as teachers of ethical rhetoric if we measure our success by the nature of public discourse in the "information age." Granted, we have information available to us on a scale unprecedented in human history, but we and our students have been ineffective in using this sea of data to realize dreams of global peace or social justice. As academics and administrators of colleges and universities, we must still be "running in the old cycles," as Rich put it. We must still be conveying or encouraging a monolithic view of culture and language to our students. We must still be assuming that there is a common "we" and that we in the United States are the producers and receivers of the only important rhetoric. The evidence of these failures is everywhere in public media. Where is sophisticated argument on the major television networks or their cable counterparts? What do radio talk shows reveal about civility, empathy, or ethics? What is the status of factual evidence in marketing U.S. political positions? Where is debate encouraged and supported on our campuses? Who is arguing for conciliation, rather than conquest or domination? For all of my hope in alternative visions, particularly the promise of feminist rhetoric(s), I have seen little in 2004 to encourage me to believe that we teachers of ethical rhetoric have been effective.

A theme in the autobiographical part of my address is that important writing and reading was encouraged for me outside formal classrooms, in the popular culture that I consumed as an adolescent and young adult. No doubt it is a sign of my age and alienation from contemporary popular culture, but I do not now see an emphasis on these dreams. I'm not sure young people today have role models who inspire them to dream about much more than consumerism, sex, drugs, and violence. There are glimmers here and there—witness the enthusiasm among students for Howard Dean—but the big picture is disturbing to me. I hope that I am wrong, that somewhere out there—on Web sites, in chatrooms, in blogs, in music I cannot understand—there are inspiring leaders. I hear myself sounding like the people over thirty that we distrusted, and I hope that my perspective is just typical of what happens when one ages. Whether I am right or wrong about the hopes and dreams of this generation of students, we must redouble our efforts as rhetoricians to help students think and act critically in the world my generation is leaving them.

Holding fast to the dream of social transformation is still what gives my work meaning. In my lifetime, I don't remember a more critical need for ethical, responsible rhetoric.

-LILLIAN BRIDWELL-BOWLES
Louisiana State University

1995

When the First Voice You Hear Is Not Your Own

JACQUELINE JONES ROYSTER

T his essay emerged from my desire to examine closely moments of personal challenge that seem to have import for cross-boundary discourse. These types of moments have constituted an ongoing source of curiosity for me in terms of my own need to understand human difference as a complex reality, a reality that I have found most intriguing within the context of the academic world. From a collectivity of such moments over the years, I have concluded that the most salient point to acknowledge is that "subject" position really is everything.

Using subject position as a terministic screen in cross-boundary discourse permits analysis to operate kaleidoscopically, thereby permitting interpretation to be richly informed by the converging of dialectical perspectives. Subjectivity as a defining value pays attention dynamically to context, ways of knowing, language abilities, and experience, and by doing so it has a consequent potential to deepen, broaden, and enrich our interpretive views in dynamic ways as well. Analytical lenses include the process, results, and impact of negotiating identity, establishing authority, developing strategies for action, carrying forth intent with a particular type of agency, and being compelled by external factors and internal sensibilities to adjust belief and action (or not). In a fundamental way, this enterprise supports the sense of rhetoric, composition, and literacy studies as a field of study that embraces the imperative to understand truths and consequences of language use more fully. This enterprise supports also the imperative to reconsider the beliefs and values which inevitably permit our attitudes and actions in discourse communities (including colleges, universities, and classrooms) to be systematic, even systemic.

This article is a revised version of the Chair's address Jacqueline Jones Royster delivered at the CCCC Convention in Washington, D.C., on March 23, 1995. It was first published in *CCC*, volume 47, number 1, February 1996.

Adopting subjectivity as a defining value, therefore, is instructive. However, the multidimensionality of the instruction also reveals the need for a shift in paradigms, a need that I find especially evident with regard to the notion of "voice," as a central manifestation of subjectivity. My task in this essay, therefore, is threefold. First, I present three scenes which serve as my personal testimony as "subject." These scenes are singular in terms of their being my own stories, but I believe that they are also plural, constituting experiential data that I share with many. My sense of things is that individual stories placed one against another against another build credibility and offer, as in this case, a litany of evidence from which a call for transformation in theory and practice might rightfully begin. My intent is to suggest that my stories in the company of others demand thoughtful response.

Second, I draw from these scenes a specific direction for transformation, suggesting dimensions of the nature of voicing that remain problematic. My intent is to demonstrate that our critical approaches to voice, again as a central manifestation of subjectivity, are currently skewed toward voice as a spoken or written phenomenon. This intent merges the second task with the third in that I proceed to suggest that theories and practices should be transformed. The call for action in cross-boundary exchange is to refine theory and practice so that they include voicing as a phenomenon that is constructed and expressed visually and orally, *and* as a phenomenon that has import also in being a *thing* heard, perceived, and reconstructed.

SCENE ONE

I have been compelled on too many occasions to count to sit as a well-mannered Other, silently, in a state of tolerance that requires me to be as expressionless as I can manage, while colleagues who occupy a place of entitlement different from my own talk about the history and achievements of people from my ethnic group, or even about their perceptions of our struggles. I have been compelled to listen as they have comfortably claimed the authority to engage in the construction of knowledge and meaning about me and mine, without paying even a passing nod to the fact that sometimes a substantive version of that knowledge might already exist, or to how it might have already been constructed, or to the meanings that might have already been assigned that might make me quite impatient with gaps in their understanding of my community, or to the fact that I, or somebody within my ethnic group, might have an opinion about what they are doing. I have been compelled to listen to speakers, well-meaning though they may think they are, who signal to me rather clearly that subject position is everything. I have come to recognize, however, that when the subject matter is me and the voice is not mine, my sense of order and rightness is disrupted. In metaphoric fashion, these "authorities" let me know, once again, that Columbus has discovered America and claims it now, claims it still for a European crown.

Such scenes bring me to the very edge of a principle that I value deeply as a teacher and a scholar, the principle of the right to inquiry and discovery. When the discovering hits so close to home, however, my response is visceral, not just intellectual, and I am made to look over a precipice. I have found it extremely difficult to allow the voices and experiences of people that I care about deeply to be taken and handled so carelessly and without accountability by strangers.

At the extreme, the African American community, as my personal example, has seen and continues to see its contributions and achievements called into question in grossly negative ways, as in the case of *The Bell Curve.* Such interpretations of who we are as a people open to general interrogation, once again, the innate capacities of "the race" as a whole. As has been the case throughout our history in this country, we are put in jeopardy and on trial in a way that should not exist but does. We are compelled to respond to a rendering of our potential that demands, not that we account for attitudes, actions, and conditions, but that we defend ourselves as human beings. Such interpretations of human potential create a type of discourse that serves as a distraction, as noise that drains off energy and sabotages the work of identifying substantive problems within and across cultural boundaries and the work also of finding solutions that have import, not simply for "a race," but for human beings whose living conditions, values, and preferences vary.

All such close encounters, the extraordinarily insidious ones and the ordinary ones, are definable through the lens of subjectivity, particularly in terms of the power and authority to speak and to make meaning. An analysis of subject position reveals that these interpretations by those outside of the community are not random acts of unkindness. Instead, they embody ways of seeing, knowing, being, and acting that probably suggest as much about the speaker and the context as they do about the targeted subject matter. The advantage with this type of analysis, of course, is that we see the obvious need to contextualize the stranger's perspective among other interpretations and to recognize that an interpretive view is just that—interpretive. A second advantage is that we also see that in our nation's practices these types of interpretations, regardless of how superficial or libelous they may actually be within the context of a more comprehensive view, tend to have considerable consequence in the lives of the targeted group, people in this case whose own voices and perspectives remain still largely under considered and uncredited.

Essentially, though, having a mechanism to see the under considered helps us see the extent to which we add continually to the pile of evidence in this country of cross-cultural misconduct. These types of close encounters that disregard dialectical views are a type of free touching of the powerless by the power-full. This analytical perspective encourages us to acknowledge that marginalized communities are not in a good position to ward off the intrusion of those authorized in mainstream communities to engage in willful action. Historically, such actions have included everything from the displacement of native people from their homelands, to the use of unknowing human subjects in dangerous experiments, to the appropriation and misappropriation of cultural artifacts—art, literature, music, and so on. An insight using the lens of subjectivity, however, is a recognition of the ways in which these moments are indeed moments of violation, perhaps even ultimate violation.

This record of misconduct means that for people like me, on an instinctive level, all outsiders are rightly perceived as suspect. I suspect the genuineness of their interest, the altruism of their actions, and the probability that whatever is being said or done is not to the ultimate benefit and understanding of the people who are subject matter but not subjects. People in the neighborhood where I grew up would say, "Where is their home training?" Imbedded in the question is the idea that when you visit other people's "home places," especially when you have not been invited, you simply can not go tramping around the house like you own the place, no matter how smart you are, or how much imagination you can muster, or how much authority and entitlement outside that home you may be privileged to hold. And you certainly can not go around name calling, saying things like, "You people are intellectually inferior and have a limited capacity to achieve," without taking into account who the family is, what its living has been like, and what its history and achievement have been about.

The concept of "home training" underscores the reality that point of view matters and that we must be trained to respect points of view other than our own. It acknowledges that when we are away from home, we need to know that what we think we see in places that we do not really know very well may not actually be what is there at all. So often, it really is a matter of time, place, resources, and our ability to perceive. Coming to judgment too quickly, drawing on information too narrowly, and saying hurtful, discrediting, dehumanizing things without undisputed proof are not appropriate. Such behavior is not good manners. What comes to mind for me is another saying that I heard constantly when I was growing up: "Do unto others as you would have them do unto you." In this case, we would be implored to draw conclusions about others with care and, when we do draw conclusions, to use the same type of sense and sensibility that we would ideally like for others to use in drawing conclusions about us.

This scene convinces me that what we need in a pressing way in this country and in our very own field is to articulate codes of behavior that can sustain more concretely notions of honor, respect, and good manners across boundaries, with cultural boundaries embodying the need most vividly. Turning the light back onto myself, though, at the same time that my sense of violation may indeed be real, there is the compelling reality that many communities in our nation need to be taken seriously. We all deserve to be taken seriously, which means that critical inquiry and discovery are absolutely necessary. Those of us who love our own communities, we think, most deeply, most uncompromisingly, without reservation for what they are and also are not, must set aside our misgivings about strangers in the interest of the possibility of deeper understanding (and for the more idealistic among us, the possibility of global peace). Those of us who hold these communities close to our hearts, protect them, and embrace them; those who want to preserve the goodness of the minds and souls in them; those who want to preserve consciously, critically, and also lovingly the record of good work within them must take high risk and give over the exclusivity of our rights to know.

It seems to me that the agreement for inquiry and discovery needs to be deliberately reciprocal. All of us, strangers and community members, need to find ways to sustain productivity in what Pratt calls contact zones (199), areas of engagement that in all likelihood will remain contentious. We need to get over our tendencies to be too possessive and to resist locking ourselves into the tunnels of our own visions and direct experience. As community members, we must learn to have new faith in the advantage of sharing. As strangers, we must learn to treat the loved people and places of Others with care and to understand that, when we do not act respectfully and responsibly, we leave ourselves rightly open to wrath. The challenge is not to work with a fear of abuse or a fear of retaliation, however. The challenge is to teach, to engage in research, to write, and to speak with Others with the determination to operate not only with professional and personal integrity, but also with the specific knowledge that communities and their ancestors are watching. If we can set aside our rights to exclusivity in our own home cultures, if we can set aside the tendencies that we all have to think too narrowly, we actually leave open an important possibility. In our nation, we have little idea of the potential that a variety of subjectivities—operating with honor, respect, and reasonable codes of conduct—can bring to critical inquiry or critical problems. What might happen if we treated differences in subject position as critical pieces of the whole, vital to thorough understanding, and central to both problem-finding and problem-solving? This society has not, as yet, really allowed that privilege in a substantial way.

SCENE TWO

As indicated in Scene One, I tend to be enraged at what Tillie Olsen has called the "trespass vision," a vision that comes from intellect and imagination (62), but typically not from lived experience, and sometimes not from the serious study of the subject matter. However, like W. E. B. Du Bois, I've chosen not to be distracted or consumed by my rage at voyeurs, tourists, and trespassers, but to look at what I can do. I see the critical importance of the role of negotiator, someone who can cross boundaries and serve as guide and translator for Others.

In 1903, Du Bois demonstrated this role in *The Souls of Black Folk.* In the "Forethought" of that book, he says: "Leaving, then, the world of the white man, I have stepped within the Veil, raising it that you may view faintly its deeper recesses—the meaning of its religion, the passion of its human sorrow, and the struggle of its greater souls" (1). He sets his rhetorical purpose to be to cross, or at least to straddle boundaries with the intent of shedding light, a light that has the potential of being useful to people on both sides of the veil. Like Du Bois, I've accepted the idea that what I call my "home place" is a cultural community that exists still quite significantly beyond the confines of a well-insulated community that we call the "mainstream," and that between this world and the one that I call home, systems of insulation impede the vision and narrow the ability to recognize human potential and to understand human history both microscopically and telescopically.

Like Du Bois, I've dedicated myself to raising this veil, to overriding these systems of insulation by raising another voice, my voice in the interest of clarity and accuracy. What I have found too often, however, is that, unlike those who have been entitled to talk about me and mine, when I talk about my own, I face what I call the power and function of deep disbelief, and what Du Bois described as, "the sense of always looking at one's self through the eyes of others, of measuring one's soul by the tape of a world that looks on in amused contempt and pity" (5).

An example comes to mind. When I talk about African-American women, especially those who were writing non-fiction prose in the nineteenth century, I can expect, even today after so much contemporary scholarship on such writers, to see people who are quite flabbergasted by anything that I share. Reflected on their faces and in their questions and comments, if anyone can manage to speak back to me, is a depth of surprise that is always discomforting. I sense that the surprise, or the silence, if there is little response, does not come from the simple ignorance of unfortunate souls who just happen not to know what I have spent years coming to know. What I suspect is that this type of surprise rather "naturally" emerges in a society that so obviously has the habit of expecting nothing of value, nothing of consequence, nothing of importance, nothing at all positive from its Others, so that anything is a surprise; everything is an exception; and nothing of substance can really be claimed as a result.

In identifying this phenomenon, Chandra Talpade Mohanty speaks powerfully about the ways in which this culture coopts, dissipates, and displaces voices. As demonstrated by my example, one method of absorption that has worked quite well has been essentially rhetorical. In discussing nineteenth century African American women's work, I bring tales of difference and adventure. I bring cultural proofs and instructive examples, all of which invariably must serve as rites of passage to credibility. I also bring the power of storytelling. These tales of adventure in odd places are the transitions by which to historicize and theorize anew with these writers re-inscribed in a rightful place. Such a process respects long-standing practices in African-based cultures of theorizing in narrative form. As Barbara Christian says, we theorize "in the stories we create, in riddles and proverbs, in the play with language, since dynamic rather than fixed ideas seem more to our liking" (336).

The problem is that in order to construct new histories and theories such stories must be perceived not just as "simple stories" to delight and entertain, but as vital layers of a transformative process. A reference point is Langston Hughes and his Simple stories, stories that are a model example of how apparent simplicity has the capacity to unmask truths in ways that are remarkably accessible—through metaphor, analogy, parable, and symbol. However, the problem of articulating new paradigms through stories becomes intractable, if those who are empowered to define impact and consequence decide that the stories are simply stories and that the record of achievement is perceived, as Audre Lorde has said, as "the random droppings of birds" (Foreword xi).

If I take my cue from the life of Ida Wells, and I am bold enough and defiant enough to go beyond the presentation of my stories as juicy tidbits for the delectation of audiences, to actually shift or even subvert a paradigm, I'm much more likely to receive a wide-eyed stare and to have the value and validity of my conceptual position held at a distance, in doubt, and wonderfully absorbed in the silence of appreciation. Through the systems of deep disbelief I become a storyteller, a performer. With such absorptive ability in the systems of interpretation, I have greater difficulty being perceived as a person who theorizes without the mediating voices of those from the inner sanctum, or as a person who might name myself a philosopher, a theorist, a historian who creates paradigms that allow the experiences and the insights of people like me to belong.

What I am compelled to ask when veils seem more like walls is who has the privilege of speaking first? How do we negotiate the privilege of interpretation? When I have tried to fulfill my role as negotiator, I have often walked away knowing that I have spoken, but also knowing, as Anna Julia Cooper knew in 1892, that my voice, like her voice, is still a muted one. I speak, but I can not be heard. Worse, I am heard but I am not believed. Worse yet, I speak but I am not deemed believable. These moments of deep disbelief have helped me to understand much more clearly the wisdom of Audre Lorde when she said: "I have come to believe over and over again that what is most important to me must be spoken, made verbal and shared, even at the risk of having it bruised or misunderstood" (*Sister* 40). Lorde teaches me that, despite whatever frustration and vulnerability I might feel, despite my fear that no one is listening to me or is curious enough to try to understand my voice, it is still better to speak (*Black* 31). I set aside the distractions and permeating noise outside of myself, and I listen, as Howard Thurman recommended, to the sound of the genuine within. I go to a place inside myself and, as Opal Palmer Adisa explains, I listen and learn to "speak without clenching my teeth" (56).

SCENE THREE

There have been occasions when I have indeed been heard and positively received. Even at these times, however, I sometimes can not escape responses that make me most weary. One case in point occurred after a presentation in which I had glossed a scene in a novel that required cultural understanding. When the characters spoke in the scene, I rendered their voices, speaking and explaining, speaking and explaining, trying to translate the experience, to share the sounds of my historical place and to connect those sounds with systems of belief so that deeper understanding of the scene might emerge, and so that those outside of the immediacy of my home culture, the one represented in the novel, might see and understand more and be able to make more useful connections to their own worlds and experiences.

One, very well-intentioned response to what I did that day was, "How wonderful it was that you were willing to share with us your 'authentic' voice!" I said, "My 'authentic' voice?" She said, "Oh yes! I've never heard you talk like that, you know, so relaxed. I mean, you're usually great, but this was really great! You weren't so formal. You didn't have to speak in an appropriated academic language. You sounded 'natural.' It was nice to hear you be yourself." I said, "Oh, I see. Yes, I do have a range of voices, and I take quite a bit of pleasure actually in being able to use any of them at will." Not understanding the point that I was trying to make gently, she said, "But this time, it was really you. Thank you."

The conversation continued, but I stopped paying attention. What I didn't feel like saying in a more direct way, a response that my friend surely would have perceived as angry, was that all my voices are authentic, and like bell hooks, I find it "a necessary aspect of self-affirmation not to feel compelled to choose one voice over another, not to claim one as more authentic, but rather to construct social realities that celebrate, acknowledge, and affirm differences, variety" (12). Like hooks, I claim all my voices as my own very much authentic voices, even when it's difficult for others to imagine a person like me having the capacity to do that.

From moments of challenge like this one, I realize that we do not have a paradigm that really allows for what scholars in cultural and postcolonial

studies (Anzaldua, Spivak, Mohanty, Bhaba) have called hybrid people—
people who either have the capacity by right of history and development,
or who might have created the capacity by right of history and development, to move with dexterity across cultural boundaries, to make themselves comfortable, and to make sense amid the chaos of difference.

As Cornel West points out, most African Americans, for example,
dream in English, not in Yoruba, or Hausa, or Wolof. Hybrid people, as
demonstrated by the history of Africans in the Western hemisphere, manage a fusion process that allows for survival, certainly. However, it also
allows for the development of a peculiar expertise that extends one's
range of abilities well beyond ordinary limits, and it supports the opportunity for the development of new and remarkable creative expression,
like spirituals, jazz, blues, and what I suspect is happening also with the
essay as genre in the hands of African American women. West notes that
somebody gave Charlie Parker a saxophone, Miles Davis a trumpet, Hubert Laws a flute, and Les McCann a piano. I suggest that somebody also
gave Maria Stewart, Gertrude Mossell, Frances Harper, Alice Walker,
Audre Lorde, Toni Morrison, Patricia Williams, June Jordan, bell hooks,
Angela Davis and a cadre of other African American women a pencil, a
pen, a computer keyboard. In both instances, genius emerges from hybridity, from Africans who, over the course of time and circumstance,
have come to dream in English, and I venture to say that all of their
voices are authentic.

In sharing these three scenes, I emphasize that there is a pressing
need to construct paradigms that permit us to engage in better practices
in cross-boundary discourse, whether we are teaching, researching, writing, or talking with Others, whoever those Others happen to be. I would
like to emphasize, again, that we look again at "voice" and situate it
within a world of symbols, sound, and sense, recognizing that this world
operates symphonically. Although the systems of voice production are indeed highly integrated and appear to have singularity in the ways that we
come to sound, voicing actually sets in motion multiple systems, prominent among them are systems for speaking but present also are the systems for hearing. We speak within systems that we know significantly
through our abilities to negotiate noise and to construct within that noise
sense and sensibility.

Several questions come to mind. How can we teach, engage in research, write about, and talk across boundaries *with* others, instead of
for, about, and around them? My experiences tell me that we need to do
more than just talk and talk back. I believe that in this model we miss a
critical moment. We need to talk, yes, and to talk back, yes, but when do
we listen? How do we listen? How do we demonstrate that we honor and
respect the person talking and what that person is saying, or what the
person might say if we valued someone other than ourselves having

a turn to speak? How do we translate listening into language and action, into the creation of an appropriate response? How do we really "talk back" rather than talk also? The goal is not, "You talk, I talk." The goal is better practices so that we can exchange perspectives, negotiate meaning, and create understanding with the intent of being in a good position to cooperate, when, like now, cooperation is absolutely necessary.

When I think about this goal, what stands out most is that these questions apply in so much of academic life right now. They certainly apply as we go into classrooms and insist that our students trust us and what we contend is in their best interest. In light of a record in classrooms that seriously questions the range of our abilities to recognize potential, or to appreciate students as non-generic human beings, or to appreciate that they bring with them, always, knowledge, we ask a lot when we ask them to trust. Too often, still, institutionalized equations for placement, positive matriculation, progress, and achievement name, categorize, rank, and file, while our true-to-life students fall between the cracks. I look again to Opal Palmer Adisa for an instructive example. She says:

> Presently, many academics advocate theories which, rather than illuminating the works under scrutiny, obfuscate and problematize these works so that students are rendered speechless. Consequently, the students constantly question what they know, and often, unfortunately, they conclude that they know nothing. (54)

Students may find what we do to be alienating and disheartening. Even when our intentions are quite honorable, silence can descend. Their experiences are not seen, and their voices are not heard. We can find ourselves participating, sometimes consciously, sometimes not, in what Patricia Williams calls "spirit murder" (55). I am reminded in a disconcerting way of a troubling scene from Alex Haley's *Roots*. We engage in practices that say quite insistently to a variety of students in a variety of ways, "Your name is Toby." Why wouldn't students wonder: Who can I trust here? Under what kinds of conditions? When? Why?

In addition to better practices in our classrooms, however, we can also question our ability to talk convincingly with deans, presidents, legislators, and the general public about what we do, how we do it, and why. We have not been conscientious about keeping lines of communication open, and we are now experiencing the consequences of talking primarily to ourselves as we watch funds being cut, programs being eliminated, and national agencies that are vital to our interests being bandied about as if they are post-it notes, randomly stuck on by some ill-informed spendthrift. We must learn to raise a politically active voice with a socially responsible mandate to make a rightful place for education in a country that seems always ready to place the needs of quality education on a sideboard instead of on the table. Seemingly, we have been forever content to let voices other than our own speak authoritatively about our areas of expertise and about us. It is time to speak for ourselves, in our own interests, in the interest of our work, and in the interest of our students.

Better practices are not limited, though, even to these concerns. Of more immediate concern to me this year, given my role as Chair of CCCC, is how to talk across boundaries within our own organization as teachers of English among other teachers of English and Language Arts from kindergarten through university with interests as varied as those implied by the sections, conferences, and committees of our parent organization, the National Council of Teachers of English (NCTE). Each of the groups within NCTE has its own set of needs, expectations, and concerns, multiplied across the amazing variety of institutional sites across which we work. In times of limited resources and a full slate of critical problems, we must find reasonable ways to negotiate so that we can all thrive reasonably well in the same place.

In our own case, for years now, CCCC has recognized changes in our relationships with NCTE. Since the mid-1980s we have grown exponentially. The field of rhetoric and composition has blossomed and diversified. The climate for higher education has increasingly degenerated, and we have struggled in the midst of change to forge a more satisfying identity and a more positive and productive working relationship with others in NCTE who are facing crises of their own. After 50 years in NCTE, we have grown up, and we have to figure out a new way of being and doing in making sure that we can face our challenges well. We are now in the second year of a concerted effort to engage in a multi-leveled conversation that we hope will leave CCCC well-positioned to face a new century and ongoing challenges. Much, however, depends on the ways in which we talk and listen and talk again in crossing boundaries and creating, or not, the common ground of engagement.

As I look at the lay of this land, I endorse Henry David Thoreau's statement when he said, "Only that day dawns to which we are awake" (267). So my appeal is to urge us all to be awake, awake and listening, awake and operating deliberately on codes of better conduct in the interest of keeping our boundaries fluid, our discourse invigorated with multiple perspectives, and our policies and practices well-tuned toward a clearer respect for human potential and achievement from whatever their source and a clearer understanding that voicing at its best is not just well-spoken but also well-heard.

WORKS CITED

Adisa, Opal Palmer. "I Must Write What I Know So I'll Know That I've Known It All Along." *Sage: A Scholarly Journal on Black Women* 9.2 (1995): 54–57.
Anzaldua, Gloria. *Borderlands/La Frontera*. San Francisco: Aunt Lute, 1987.
Bhabha, Homi K. *The Location of Culture*. London: Routledge, 1994.
Christian, Barbara. "The Race for Theory." *Cultural Critique* 6 (1987): 335–45.

Cooper, Anna Julia. *A Voice from the South.* New York: Oxford UP, 1988.
Du Bois, W. E. B. *The Souls of Black Folk.* New York: Grammercy, 1994.
Haley, Alex. *Roots.* Garden City: Doubleday, 1976.
Hernstein, Richard J., and Charles Murray. *The Bell Curve: Intelligence and Class Structure in American Life.* New York: Free, 1994.
hooks, bell. *Talking Back: Thinking Feminist, Thinking Black.* Boston: South End, 1989.
Lorde, Audre. *The Black Unicorn.* New York: Norton, 1978.
———. Foreword. *Wild Women in the Whirl-wind.* Ed. Joanne M. Braxton and Andree Nicola McLaughlin. New Brunswick: Rutgers UP, 1990. xi–xiii.
———. *Sister/Outsider.* Freedom: The Crossing Press, 1984.
Mohanty, Chandra Talpade. "On Race and Voice: Challenges for Liberal Education in the 1990s." *Cultural Critique* 14 (Winter 1989–90): 179–208.
———. "Decolonizing Education: Feminisms and the Politics of Multiculturalism in the 'New' World Order." Ohio State U, Columbus, OH, April 1994.
Olsen, Tillie. *Silences.* New York: Delta, 1978.
Pratt, Mary Louise. "Arts of the Contact Zone." *Profession* 91 (1991): 33–40.
Spivak, Gayatri Chakravorty. *In Other Worlds: Essays in Cultural Politics.* New York: Routledge, 1988.
Thoreau. Henry David. *Walden.* New York: Vintage, 1991.
Thurman, Howard. "The Sound of the Genuine." Spelman College, Atlanta, April 1981.
West, Cornel. "Race Matters." Ohio State U, Columbus, OH, February 1995.
Williams, Patricia. *The Alchemy of Race and Rights.* Cambridge: Harvard UP, 1991.

AFTERWORD: THE REMAINS OF THE DAY

In the field of rhetoric and composition, we embrace both reflection and revision as core values, understanding the empowering effects of these commingled processes, so the opportunity to re-examine and respond publicly, rather than privately, to an artifact of my own professional work and scholarship (my 1995 CCCC Chair's address, "When the First Voice You Hear Is Not Your Own") is quite a special occasion. Because such occasions are not always comfortable or comforting, I asked myself just one critical question: Do the ideas and the viewpoint of this essay remain as perspectives that I can still stand by almost ten years later?

Quite unequivocally, I still believe that subjectivity, as amplified by concepts such as voice, vision, agency, ethos, and identity, is an instructive lens through which to analyze discourse. This belief has constituted a major focal point in all of my scholarship since the CCCC address, as illustrated by two examples. First, in *Southern Horrors* (1997) and *Traces of a Stream* (2000), I focused on the ways in which African American women writers have persistently made places in public discourses for their experiences and points of view. Second, in essays on the social construction of knowledge in rhetorical studies, as exemplified, for instance, by my coedited collection *Calling Cards: Theory and Practice in the Study of Race, Gender, and Culture* (2005), I have focused in a twofold way on (1) broadening the perspectives of what constitutes rhetorical history, theory, and practice by various shifts, given my interests in geography, gender, race, and also in the circle of what constitutes practice; and (2) the inclusion of more and different voices and experiences in re-rendering history, re-making what constitutes knowledge, and developing pedagogical practices and processes that are more meaningful for a broader range of students. What has remained crystal clear for me throughout this work is the need for transformation, for a shifting of paradigms both in the formation of usable theories in rhetorical, composition, and literacy studies and in the use of this knowledge with more generative consequence in what we do in academe and beyond.

Similarly, I continue to believe that it is important to view voice, whether written or spoken, as a thing produced and a thing heard. I remain concerned that, in the field of rhetoric and composition, we do not give enough critical attention to what it means to listen and to respond, that is, to listen to voices with critical understanding and to talk back rather than just talk also. I applaud Krista Ratcliffe for underscoring for us the concept of "rhetorical listening" (1999), but the more I see the more I believe that we might also need to pair with that concept the idea of "rhetorical responding." How do we listen well and respond respectfully, directly, and insightfully, demonstrating that we have listened, engaged our critical abilities, and are responding with sense and sensibility?

In my view, developing critical expertise in listening and responding is a vital and vibrant part of one additional notion that remains a constant for me: the need for all of us, not just the professionals in the field of rhetoric and composition, to do exponentially better than we've done in the past in cross-boundary relationships. The fact that the United States of America is once again at war with another country is inescapable evidence of our ongoing failure to engage genuinely in rhetorical listening and rhetorical responding. Our nation has come up quite short of demonstrating an ability to engage with both sense and sensibility, rather than just power, authority, and arrogance. Since the terrorist attacks of September 11, 2001, I have re-directed much of my attention to the need for our field to use our knowledge and expertise to help the nation to operate more knowledgeably and more responsibly, with better sense and greater sensibility in global relationships. As we are seeing daily, the consequences of our not doing more come with a very high price for us all.

So, as I reflect on "When the First Voice You Hear Is Not Your Own," I am pleased to say that I spoke/wrote in that essay what for me was a truth, and it is comforting to know that, at the remains of the day, I continue to stand by this artifact and to live by it. What is more disturbing and disheartening, both in the profession and outside of it, is that these ideas continue to remain so salient. I've seen one decade pass. How many more will it take before I can review these words and say, "Oh, this piece is really outdated."

–JACQUELINE JONES ROYSTER
The Ohio State University

WORKS CITED

Ratcliffe, Krista. "Rhetorical Listening: A Trope for Interpretive Invention and a 'Code of Cross-Cultural Conduct.'" *College Composition and Communication* 51 (1999): 195–224.

Royster, Jacqueline Jones, ed. *Southern Horrors: The Anti-Lynching Campaign of Ida B. Wells, 1892–1900*. Boston: Bedford/St. Martin's, 1997.

———. *Traces of a Stream: Literacy and Social Change among African American Women*. Pittsburgh: U of Pittsburgh P, 2000.

———, and Ann Marie Simpkins, eds. *Calling Cards: Theory and Practice in the Study of Race, Gender, and Culture*. Albany: State U of New York P, 2005.

1996

Literacy after the Revolution

LESTER FAIGLEY

O ne of the traditions of the CCCC Chair's address is to narrate an anxiety dream. Andrea Lunsford still has the best one, when she dreamed about beginning her address, turning the first page, and finding only the word *linguine* on the next page, and on the page after that, and on the page after that, and on all the rest of the pages. My dream was somewhat less fantastic. I dreamed that I met many of my friends walking out of the auditorium as I was walking in to speak. I wanted desperately to ask them why they were leaving, but then I thought that I probably didn't want to know.

When faced last August with a deadline for supplying a title for this talk, I began reading the addresses of past chairs printed in *CCC*. They comprise a distinguished collection of essays on the values placed on literacy and on what it means to be a college teacher of writing. The tradition of the chair delivering an address at the opening general session began with Richard Lloyd-Jones in 1977, the first year I attended the convention. Reading the addresses I had heard over my years at the annual convention was like reading a personal history of the field, a history I had witnessed.

Together the Chairs' addresses also caused me to reflect on how I came to be before you today. The condition of living in a highly urbanized, mobile, and transient society allows remarkable sets of circumstances to direct the paths of particular lives, and my life is no exception. When I graduated from high school, I never planned to be an English major, never planned to get a PhD, never planned to be a college teacher, and certainly never planned to be Chair of CCCC. In each case I could narrate a series of minor events that were pivotal in shaping years of my life. I'm sure each of you can think of at least one small event where if

This article is a revised version of the Chair's address Lester Faigley delivered at the CCCC Convention in Milwaukee, Wisconsin, on March 28, 1996. It was first published in *CCC*, volume 48, number 1, February 1997.

a particular person were absent or if your presence at a particular location had been just few minutes earlier or later, the subsequent course of your life would have been very different.

But if the particular paths that our lives take are very influenced by seemingly chance events, the broader tracks show a great deal more regularity. After all, there are over 3,000 of us at this convention. Evidently some common forces brought us here. I only gradually became aware of these forces. Like most other college writing teachers of my generation, I was not trained specifically in rhetoric and composition. I taught writing in graduate school as a teaching assistant, but at the universities where I did my graduate work, there was no specialization in rhetoric and composition at that time. Teaching writing was something you did for a living but not something you thought about very much. For those of us who found our way into rhetoric and composition, somewhere along the way we began thinking about teaching writing other than as a drudgery from which we wished deliverance. We realized that likely we would be teaching writing in some form if we were to have a professional career, but more immediate were the positive experiences that we were teaching something quite valuable for our students' lives.

It is not coincidental that early experiences of teaching basic writers figure so prominently among the past Chairs of my generation—Jacqueline Jones Royster, Lillian Bridwell-Bowles, Anne Ruggles Gere, Bill Cook, Don McQuade, Jane Peterson, Andrea Lunsford, David Bartholomae, Miriam Chaplin, Lee Odell, Rosentene Purnell, Jim Hill, and Lynn Quitman Troyka—and among many other of my contemporaries. We came of age when the great social issues of the Civil Rights movement and the Vietnam War were being debated publicly and when education was widely believed to be the chief means of ending social inequality. Early experiences of teaching basic writers exposed for these teachers the role and power of institutions in maintaining social divisions. But these teachers also found spaces where institutional power could be challenged and where students who had been labeled as deficient could succeed.

That the good classroom could help produce the good society seemed self-evident when I began teaching college writing courses. The students I taught were becoming more diverse, and I believed composition teachers were better situated than anyone to adapt to their needs. We were the faculty who were exploring anti-authoritarian ways of teaching and who were encouraging our students to use literacy to participate in democratic community life, to engage civic issues, and to promote social justice. Even though, like nearly everyone else teaching composition, I experienced the second-class status of a writing teacher in an English department, I felt that composition was going to do fine in the long run. We were in step with the new mission of colleges and universities to provide education for all who wanted it. History seemed to be on our side.

Now that we are more than halfway through the 1990s and closing quickly on both the end of the millennium and the fiftieth anniversary of CCCC, it no longer seems like we are riding the wave of history but instead are caught in a rip tide carrying us away from where we want to go. Part of this frustration is linked to the growth of rhetoric and composition as a discipline. Had not the members of CCCC been so successful in creating an expansive discipline, in fostering important research and scholarship, and in broadening the ways in which writing is taught, perhaps visions of restoring rhetoric to the central place in the American college curriculum might have remained nostalgic images of the past. At the same time, however, writing teachers who have been at the forefront of initiating change have run up against a multitude of institutional barriers and attitudes that would limit writing instruction to teaching students to replicate the traditional forms of academic and professional discourses. Most disappointing, the discipline's success has not influenced institutions to improve the working conditions for many teachers of writing. A huge percentage of college writing courses are taught by part-time faculty who endure uncertain employment, heavy workloads, poor pay, nonexistent benefits, and often the lack of the most meager support services such as a desk and a mailbox.

A decade ago, Maxine Hairston in her Chair's address blamed the literature faculty for the problems writing teachers face. Now the situation for writing teachers might seem rosy if the problems could be resolved within English departments, no matter how petty and vicious the politics. I'm going to talk today about how larger forces of change affect how we see ourselves and what we do. These changes are of such magnitude that they have been labeled revolutions—one a technological transformation called the *digital revolution* and the other an economic, social and political transformation called the *revolution of the rich*. These revolutions have been described as having very different impacts—the digital revolution as expanding access and the revolution of the rich as contracting it—but we may eventually come to see them as different aspects of an even larger scale change.

I want to begin with the revolution of the rich. What no one, including writing teachers, foresaw 20 years ago was the extent to which the creation of wealth would be divorced from labor and redistributed, leaving the United States the most economically polarized among industrialized nations, with the divide between rich and poor continuing to widen. The most recent Federal Reserve figures available, from 1989, indicate that the wealthiest 1% of the population, living in households with a net worth of at least $2.3 million each, own almost 40% of America's wealth. The top 20% of U.S. households, worth $180,000 or more, own nearly all of its wealth—more than 80% (Bradsher).

Those in the middle have increasingly struggled to maintain their position. The workweek in America has increased and leisure time has decreased since 1970. Juliet Schor found that the average working American in 1989 put in 163 more hours a year than he or she did 20 years earlier—the equivalent of an extra month of work. Those who work harder for lower real wages and reduced benefits have found life precarious. Business executives take great credit for increasing corporate profits through downsizing, but these profits have come out of the pockets of the workers. During the 1970s and 1980s, corporations succeeded in busting unions and in rolling back government social programs.

But the most important strategy to increase profits has been to seek greater flexibility in hiring workers. Between 1979 and 1995, the *New York Times* estimates from Department of Labor statistics that 43 million jobs were eliminated in the United States (Uchitelle and Kleinfield). The layoffs in the 1990s read like casualty totals from World War I battles: 123,000 gone from AT&T, 50,000 fired by Sears, 18,800 pink slips at Delta Airlines, 16,800 cut from Eastman Kodak. Four companies out of five in America laid off workers in 1995. These reductions came not at a time of economic depression but when the economy was booming and the stock market was setting record highs. While unemployment is currently low in the United States and millions of new jobs have been created, there has not been such job instability since the Great Depression and never before have highly paid, highly educated workers been so vulnerable. Only 35% of currently laid-off full-time workers find jobs comparable to the ones they held.

Workers have not shared in the prosperity of the last 15 years. The median wage in 1994 adjusted for inflation is nearly 3% below what it was in 1979. Household income climbed 10% during the same period, but the richest 20% received 97% of that gain (Uchitelle and Kleinfield). The accumulation of wealth at the top is staggering even when compared to the robber barons of the nineteenth century. On November 29, 1995, Steven Jobs, the co-founder of Apple Computers, made $1.2 billion on paper on the first day of the public issue of his company Pixar Animation Studios, when the stock price jumped from 22 to 39. In August, 1995, Jim Clark, the co-founder of Netscape, made $1.3 billion when it went public. To give some perspective, these sums are over double the annual gross domestic product of a small nation like Belize (CIA). That's what I call empowerment.

What is different today from the era of monopoly capitalism in the 19th and early 20th centuries is that people in the last century looked to government to regulate the monopolies of industries, railroads, and banks. For example, San Francisco newspaper editor Henry George attacked speculators who reaped huge profits from the rising price of land that they did not improve. He proposed a tax on this "unearned increment" that the government would use to address the misery caused by industrialization. Today no one is calling for taxes to ameliorate poverty on money earned by speculation. Instead government is identified with bureaucracy, inefficiency, and waste. Current defenders of the free market go even further than Andrew Carnegie, who justified laissez-faire economics by appealing to Social Darwinism, but nonetheless saw the need for public schools and libraries.

Today the invisible hand of the unregulated market is trusted to do nearly everything, and publicly supported higher education is becoming an institution of the past. Tax-dollar support for higher education is being reduced so rapidly that huge tuition and fee increases cannot keep pace. From 1991 to 1995, the California State Legislature slashed the budget of the University of California at Berkeley by $70 million, or about 19%, and over the same period the City University of New York has been cut $200 million, or 20% (Honan).

More and more, colleges and universities are being ordered to make sweeping changes by politicians who are unfamiliar with higher education. They see colleges and universities as bloated and want to "re-engineer" higher education on the market-driven principles of "downsizing" by imposing heavier workloads, getting rid of tenure, and converting full-time jobs into "permanent temp" positions. In the corporate world, these changes are called "planned staffing." Arizona Regent John Munger, an opponent of tenure, puts it bluntly: "There's plenty of faculty out there who want to teach and are willing to teach without tenure, and frankly who we might be able to obtain at a cheaper price and with more hiring flexibility" (Mayes). Munger and his allies are already far along in these "reforms." According to the Education Department's National Center for Education Statistics, the percentage of part-time faculty in institutions of higher education rose between 1970 to 1991 from 22% to 35%. These jobs are also disproportionally held by women.[1] In this respect writing programs have been pioneers in the new employment structure of higher education.

Given the magnitude of these forces, continuing to argue for a vision of literacy for participation in democratic community life, civic engagement, and social justice feels like swimming against the current. But as in the case of rip tides where there are often complex cross currents, so too are the social and economic forces influencing higher education. The revolution of the rich has been facilitated by another related revolution—the digital revolution of electronic communications technologies. These technologies have grown up along with CCCC. It is very difficult to imagine from the perspective of 1949, the year of the first meeting of CCCC, the development of computer and information technologies and the impacts they would have on the industrialized world. Computers in 1949 were comparable to automobiles in 1899. Computers, like early cars, were bulky, slow, expensive, and difficult to use. Their utility was confined largely to replicating certain functions of mechanical calculators. Even though the transistor had been invented in 1947, the big advances that allowed the rapid increase in computing power and decrease in cost were yet to come, especially the development of the integrated circuit in 1957 and the microprocessor in 1971 (Braun and MacDonald). We can now describe the history of computers in terms of household objects. A throw-away greeting card that sings "Happy Birthday" has more computing processing power than existed in 1951; a home video camera has more than a 1976 IBM 360, the standard mainframe machine that I used as an assistant professor (Huey 37).

Personal computers invaded the academy in large numbers beginning in the early 1980s, and where they were available in composition classrooms, they enhanced process pedagogy by making it easier for students to revise their papers. But as personal computers became enormously more powerful in memory and speed, they began to challenge the unproblematic relationship between familiar pedagogy and new technology. When personal computers became linked to other computers in local-area networks, writing teachers were forced to devise new pedagogies because the traditional lines of authority had to be renegotiated. With the coming of the Internet and the World Wide Web, another major renegotiation of pedagogy and authority is now in progress.

I direct a large college writing program that aims to give every student opportunities to practice the new electronic literacies unless they prefer to be in a traditional classroom. We are committed to teaching the great majority of our writing courses in networked classrooms by 1998. The Division of Rhetoric and Composition and the University of Texas administration believe that college students should be able to use the media of literacy that they will likely use in their later lives. The Division of Rhetoric and Composition also has as one of its central goals to encourage students to read and write about significant public issues.

Discourse on significant public issues abounds on the Internet, and giving students access to participate in these discussions at first seemed like a wish come true. Our instructors quickly explored the potential of connecting students with ongoing world-wide discussions of political and social issues. For example, at the time of the elections in South Africa that brought Nelson Mandela to power, a graduate instructor, Noel Stahle, directed his students to the on-line newsgroup, soc.culture.southafrica, where they were able to obtain first-hand accounts of the elections and to contact people in South Africa. Other instructors have involved students in on-line discussion groups concerning domestic and international issues.

But as talk radio so vividly demonstrates, providing venues for the discussion of public issues does not necessarily lead to a more informed public, increased civic engagement, or enhanced democracy. The problems our instructors have encountered in introducing students to newsgroups reflect larger debates over the impacts of the Internet. In the wake of the exponential growth of the Internet—from 213 host computers in 1981 to over 9,000,000 in early 1996—and sweeping pronouncements on the scale of

John Perry Barlow's that (forget Gutenberg!) the coming of the Internet is the most transformative event in human history since the capture of fire, others have begun asking into what changed state are people being transformed.[2] One of the most strident critics of the Internet, Mark Slouka, sees the appeal of life in virtual worlds motivated by the degradation of our physical environment. Slouka blames technology for our present lack of civic engagement, arguing that when our own communities have become unsafe, uncertain, unpleasant, and ugly, we seek artificial ones.

The stampede to get on-line has prompted much hype and horror about the Internet, but before we pronounce it good or bad for our discipline, we should pause to examine how the Internet developed over several decades and what actually is new about its widespread use. The Internet has its origins in a Cold War project in the 1960s that addressed how the military would maintain communications in the aftermath of a nuclear war, when presumably many if not most lines of communication and most major communications centers would be destroyed. The ingenious solution was to flatten the communications hierarchy, making every node equivalent so that the loss of any one node would not collapse the system. Each node would have the capability to originate, pass, and receive individually addressed messages bundled in packets. The routing of messages became relatively unimportant. Messages would bounce from host to host like a beach ball batted around in the crowd at a free concert until it finally reached its destination.

In 1969 the Pentagon began connecting researchers at military and university sites on the ARPANET, enabling them to transmit data at high speeds and access each other's computers. The ARPANET grew rapidly in the 1970s because its utility was obvious and its structure accommodated different kinds of machines, overcoming the problem of incompatibility. Because the demand for high-speed communications was so great at the time the National Science Foundation took on the expansion of the Internet in 1986, the NSF decided to build a network capable of connecting most of the nation's researchers. By 1990 the Internet had outgrown the community of scientists as corporations and individuals began to take advantage of the Internet's speed and low cost, and by 1993 the growth of the Internet became explosive.

It is not surprising that the Internet would become so widely used so quickly. The Internet became available at a time when other new low-cost, high-speed communications technologies—FAX machines, cellular telephones, and cable television—were also growing in popularity. But what is surprising is how the Internet came to be used. Soon after the introduction of the original ARPANET in 1969, researchers began to do more than access and transfer data at remote sites. Those researchers who had personal accounts soon exploited the net for person-to-person communication that ranged from project collaboration to schmoozing to the first hobby bulletin boards. Just as was the case for older technologies, researchers on the ARPANET quickly discovered new uses that hadn't been imagined by the designers.

A decade later, between 1979 and 1983, programmers wrote the software that led eventually to thousands of newsgroups created on USENET and on other networks.[3] The number of words posted each day on these newsgroups may now exceed the number of words printed each day—a fact that enthusiasts like Barlow celebrate as the overcoming of barriers to communication and that skeptics like Slouka decry as a morass of babel in which reflective thought disappears. Overlooked in these pronouncements is that a significant new medium of literacy has come into existence with the Internet.

In 1982, Thomas Miller and I conducted a survey of 200 college-educated people writing on the job, stratified according to type of employer and type of occupation. We found that everyone in an occupation that requires a college education wrote on the job and wrote frequently. Nearly three-fourths of the people sampled claimed to devote 10% or more of their work time to writing, but very few reported writing much off the job. For many people who have access to the Internet, that situation has changed. They may be using work time for personal writing, but they are nonetheless writing for purposes other than work. For many people on-line newsgroups and chat rooms have become something close to an addiction.

The Internet will soon be as ubiquitous as cable television as the costs of computers and connections continue to drop. At least ten million people today in the United States are connected either directly to the Internet or to commercial on-line services. Even more phenomenal has been the growth of the World Wide Web, which in months became a major medium of publishing. By August 1994, just two years after its introduction by the European Nuclear Research Center, Internet traffic on the World Wide Web was greater than the volume of electronic mail. If this growth pattern continues, traffic on the Web will surpass the total world voice communication traffic by 1998 (Rutkowski).

When the NSF backbone was turned off on April 30, 1995, the Internet became privatized, and with the signing into law of the Telecommunications Reform Act in February 1996, the land rush is on for the control of Cyberspace. Initially, the part of the telecommunications bill that has been most controversial is the Communications Decency Act, which is a truly benighted piece of legislation but which also is likely to be struck down in numerous court challenges.[4] The major long-term impacts, however, will come from removing regulations from corporations involved in computing, communications, publishing, and entertainment. The new media megaliths created by the mergers of Time Warner/CNN, Westinghouse/CBS, and Disney/ABC are only the beginnings of consolidation of power as the giants buy up the technology to control how we work, how we get information, how we shop, how we relax, and how we communicate with other people.

AT&T, which we used to think of as a telephone company, has been fast out of the starting blocks following the Telecommunications Act to reach out and crush someone—notably Prodigy, CompuServe, and America Online along with MCI—by offering five hours of free Internet service monthly to all of its 80 million long-distance customers beginning on March 14, 1996. This move points the way of the future because it not only gives AT&T an advantage in its telephone business but greatly expands its share of telecommunication and financial services. Soon AT&T is going to launch its WorldNet Internet service that will insure credit card transactions for users of its Universal Card, creating a world-wide Home Shopping Network with massive possibilities for cross-marketing with other partners.

As much as I resist AT&T's "you will" advertisements that offer scenes of technological determinism, I do not foresee colleges and universities remaining unaffected by these developments for long. AT&T and the other telecommunication giants are committed to put every household with a computer and disposable income on-line in the very near future, and soon the majority of students we teach are going to come from these households. Many colleges are already responding by giving students easy high-speed access to the Internet. By December 1996, my university will have installed ethernet connections in every dormitory room, boasting "a port for every pillow." Student traffic on the Internet at the University of Texas doubled from spring to fall semester in 1995.

When students enter one of our networked classrooms, they quickly dispel any assumptions of their teachers that they do little writing on their own. Most use email, and many already have personal home pages on the World Wide Web. While many of these personal home pages are little more than self-advertisements, the students who made them have experience producing and publishing multimedia forms of literacy.

Some have made quite remarkable use of this new literacy. Even though Generation X often gets bashed for its political apathy, many students have used their digital literacy to engage social and political issues. For example, the Web site of an undergraduate student at Swarthmore, Justin Paulson, became an important distribution point for the publications of the Zapatista rebels in the Mexican state of Chiapas. Many thousands of people have connected to Paulson's Web site and have read essays, communiqués, and articles about the Zapatistas. The Web site itself has become much publicized through articles in many magazines and newspapers including *The Guardian* (UK) and *Reforma* (Mexico). In April 1995, the Mexican Foreign Minister, José Angel Gurría, declared that the uprising in Chiapas is a "Guerra de Tinta y de Internet" ("a war of ink and of the Internet"). The role of the Internet in the Zapatista uprising becomes evident when Chiapas is contrasted to the Shining Path rebellion in Peru. The Zapatistas have been able to historicize the context of their rebellion and convey the complexity of a peasant society without resorting to ongoing violence.

While I am much encouraged by the creativity and commitment of students like Justin Paulson, their Web sites need to be placed in a larger perspective. Pointing to their work as proof that digital literacy necessarily leads to democratic participation and civic engagement is another version of the good classroom leading to the good society. We as teachers have little control over who gains access to higher education and even less control of access to the Internet. Very simply, the Internet is not the world. Use of the Internet is even more skewed than consumption of the world's energy resources, where less than 5% of the world's population who live in the United States annually consumes nearly 25% of its energy resources (*Economist Book*). In January 1995, nearly 98% of Internet hosts were located in the United States, Western Europe, Canada, Australia, and Japan. The presence on the Internet of much of Africa, Asia, and Latin America is nonexistent (in Africa, there were only 90 hosts outside of South Africa).

Even within the United States, Internet users are far from being equally distributed across the population. A major Internet publisher, O'Reilly and Associates, conducted a survey of United States residents over 18 years of age, which used random telephone dialing to obtain interviews with a statistically representative sample of nearly 30,000 people. This survey, released in October 1995, confirmed findings of other surveys that younger people are the most frequent users of the Internet.[5] Over half the users are between the ages of 18 and 34 (57%) and only 4% are 55 or older. They are also well-off financially. Median annual income in 1994 is reported as between $50,000 and $75,000. And they are mostly white. There is no doubt that African-Americans are severely underrepresented because their percentage of ownership of computers is far lower than that of white Americans. A 1989 U.S. Census Bureau report estimated that nearly 27 million whites but only 1.5 million African-Americans used computers at home (Stuart).

The O'Reilly survey found that a third of Internet users are women, a higher percentage than earlier surveys that gave estimates that 80–90% of Internet users are men. Nonetheless, even the O'Reilly figures have the gender skew at 2 to 1. The disparity of men and women on the Internet indicates that factors beyond merely owning a computer with a connection to the Internet and being literate in English determine access. People must have time to keep up with the abundant discourse if they are to be active participants, and the people who have this time are most likely to be young, affluent, white men.

Up to now the debate over the Internet within the humanities has been conducted in terms of the printed book. In *The Gutenberg Elegies*, Sven Birkerts asks, "What is the place of reading . . . in our culture?" (15), and he answers that it is increasingly shrinking, with the attendant effects of the loss of deep thinking, the erosion of language, and the flattening of historical perspective. Birkerts calls on us to resist the tide of electronic media; his last words in the book are "refuse it." It's disappointing for someone as thoughtful as Birkerts to allow his book to derail by collapsing all electronic media into a single form and then offering an either/or vision of the future. Anyone who has used email knows that it bears little similarity to television beyond light appearing on a screen, and we haven't thrown away pencils, legal pads, or the good books that Birkerts loves to curl up with.

The more misleading either/or that Birkerts posits, however, is that reflective thinking can occur only in acts of reading. I would like to let him in on a little secret that writing teachers know: college students often become more careful, critical, and appreciative readers after a semester in a writing course. I'm learning that little secret again. This semester for the first time I am devoting a significant part of a writing course to graphic design, and I am discovering that after years of attempting to teach students to analyze images, they learn much more quickly when they create images on their own. Active learners can think reflectively about any human symbolic activity whatever the medium.

If we come back to our annual convention a decade from now and find that the essay is no longer on center stage, it will not mean the end of our discipline. I expect that we will be teaching an increasingly fluid, multimedia literacy, and that we will be quite happy that attempts in the past failed to drop our fourth "C," "Communication,"—a term David Bartholomae noted in his 1988 Chair's address that "keeps us from ever completely knowing our subject" (45).

What concerns me much more is whether we as a professional organization can sustain a shared sense of values when in many respects history is not on our side. Benjamin Barber summarizes our condition when he writes that the more hollow values of the Enlightenment: "materialism, solipsism, and radical individualism [have triumphed] over certain of its nobler aspirations: civic virtue, just community, social equality, and the lifting of the economic yoke from what were once known as the laboring classes" (222). These nobler aspirations were developed and spread primarily through the practices of literacy. We know that literacy education has often not lived up to these ideals and has functioned instead to label individuals and groups as deficient, inferior, and unworthy. Nevertheless, these ideals have provided the means of critique for educational practices that uphold illegitimate hierarchies of power.

When I first came to the annual convention in 1977, I needed CCCC for the intellectual community it provided. Over the years I have come to appreciate more the values we share in common. In a culture that is increasingly cynical about the belief that schools should offer equal opportunity to education, we have remained steadfast to the goal of literacy for equality. Even if many of us occupy less powerful positions in less powerful departments, we still have many strengths. We are not tied to narrow disciplinary turf. We can cut across traditional disciplinary boundaries. We can be confident that the need for what we teach will only increase. And as part of a much larger professional organization, we have many possibilities for working with teachers in the schools and with colleagues in the other college organizations of NCTE.

But we also have some hard questions before us. Can we do anything to stop the decline in publicly supported education? Can we promote a literacy that challenges monopolies of knowledge and information? Can we use technology to lessen rather than widen social divisions? The overriding question facing us as a professional organization is: What do you do when the tide seems to be running against you? I don't think there is any big answer but there are some little ones. You have to look outward. You have to be smarter and more aware. You have to look for opportunities to inform people about what you do. You have to practice what you preach and engage in public discourse. You have to form alliances. You have to be more tolerant of your friends and look for common ground. You have to organize.

Our charge is in the last two sentences from *Rhetorics, Poetics, and Cultures*, the recently published final book from Jim Berlin, who sustained me through his work and his friendship. He writes: "It is time all reading and writing teachers situate their activities within the contexts of the larger profession as well as the contexts of economic and political concerns. We have much to gain working together and much to lose working alone" (180). May Jim Berlin remain present among us.

NOTES

1. These numbers come from the National Center for Education Statistics (230, 234). The statistics on full-time higher education faculty count full-time adjuncts; thus the percentage of non-tenure-track faculty is actually much higher than 35%. In 1991, the percentages of full-time women and men faculty were nearly equal, but the percentage of women in part-time positions was over two-thirds (66.8%).
2. This debate is enacted in "What Are We Doing On-Line?"
3. See Salus, chapters 15 and 18.
4. A panel of federal judges ruled the Communications Decency Act unconstitutional in June 1996.
5. A January 1994 survey found that 62% of respondents were under age 35; 73% under age 45 (Quarterman).

WORKS CITED

Barber, Benjamin R. *Jihad vs. McWorld*. New York: Times Books, 1995.
Bartholomae, David. "Freshman English, Composition, and CCCC." *CCC* 40 (1989): 38–50.
Berlin, James A. *Rhetorics, Poetics, and Cultures*. Urbana: NCTE, 1996.

Birkerts, Sven. *The Gutenberg Elegies: The Fate of Reading in an Electronic Age.* Boston: Faber and Faber, 1994.

Bradsher, Keith. "Gap in Wealth in U.S. Called Widest in West." *New York Times* 17 Apr. 1995: A1+.

Braun, Ernest, and Stuart MacDonald. *Revolution in Miniature: The History and Impact of Semiconductor Electronics Re-explored.* 2nd ed. Cambridge: Cambridge UP, 1982.

Central Intelligence Agency. *The World Factbook, 1995.* Washington, DC: CIA, 1995.

The Economist Book of Vital World Statistics, 1990. New York: Times Books, 1990.

Faigley, Lester, and Thomas P. Miller. "What We Learn from Writing on the Job." *College English* 44 (1982): 557–69.

George, Henry. *Progress and Poverty: An Inquiry into the Cause of Industrial Depressions and of Increase of Want with Increase of Wealth.* San Francisco: Hilton, 1879.

Hairston, Maxine C. "Breaking Our Bonds and Reaffirming Our Connections." *CCC* 36 (1985): 272–82.

Honan, William H. "New Pressures on the University." *New York Times* 9 Jan. 1994, sec.4A: 16.

Huey, John. "Waking Up to the New Economy." *Fortune* 17 June 1994: 36–46.

Mayes, Kris. "Tenure Debate Worries Faculty." *Phoenix Gazette* 28 Sept. 1995, B1.

National Center for Education Statistics. *Digest of Education Statistics 1995.* Washington, DC: US Department of Education, 1995.

O'Reilly and Associates. "Defining the Internet Opportunity." http://www.ora.com/survey (31 Oct. 1995).

Paulson, Justin. "Ya Basta!" http://www.peak.org/~justin/ezln/ezln.html (31 Oct. 1995).

Quarterman, John S. "The Internet Demographic Survey." *Matrix News* 4 (January 1994): 2–6.

Rutkowski, Anthony-Michael. "Bottom-Up Information Infrastructure and the Internet." http://info.isoc.org:80/speeches/upitt-foundersday.html (31 Oct. 1995).

Salus, Peter H. *Casting the Net: From ARPANET to Internet and Beyond.* Reading, MA: Addison, 1995.

Schor, Juliet B. *The Overworked American: The Unexpected Decline of Leisure.* New York: Basic, 1992.

Slouka, Mark. *War of the Worlds: Cyberspace and the High-Tech Assault on Reality.* New York: Basic, 1995.

Stuart, Reginald. "High-Tech Redlining." *Utne Reader* 68 (March-April 1995): 73.

Uchitelle, Louis, and N. R. Kleinfield. "On the Battlefields of Business, Millions of Casualties." *New York Times* 3 March 1996, sec.1: 1.

"What Are We Doing On-Line?" *Harper's* August 1995: 35–46.

AFTERWORD: PURSUING SOCIAL JUSTICE

My 1996 Chair's address examined the trajectory of composition studies and CCCC against the backdrop of enormous changes then underway in American society that continue to the present. I contrasted the growth of composition studies as a discipline with the vast redistribution of wealth in America, which I called the "revolution of the rich," and with the digital revolution of electronic communications technologies. At a time when the economy was thriving, millions of Americans were losing their jobs, and a large percentage of the jobs being created resembled those occupied by many college writing teachers — "flexible" positions, often part-time, with little job security and few or no benefits. I ended by posing these questions to the audience.

- Can we do anything to stop the decline in publicly supported education?
- Can we promote a literacy that challenges monopolies of knowledge and information?
- Can we use technology to lessen instead of widen social divisions?

We now have more perspective on the magnitude of the redistribution of wealth that occurred during the last decades of the twentieth century. Data from the 2000 census show that the wealthiest 10 percent of the population continued to do well. Analysis of census data by the Congressional Budget Office found that the richest 1 percent of American households received $515,600 in after-tax income adjusted for inflation in 1999, compared to $234,700 in 1977. The after-tax incomes of the bottom 20 percent of households fell from $10,000 in 1977 to $8,800 in 1999 when adjusted for inflation. The higher on the economic ladder, the more extreme were the gains. Those on the very highest rung in the 99.9 percentile—13,400 households out of 134 million taxpaying households—received 5 percent of the total income of the country, almost $24 million per household. In 1970, this top group received 1 percent of the total national income with $3.6 million per household.

In 1996, support for public higher education was rapidly dwindling, a trend that accelerated in the early 2000s as tax revenues fell. Private colleges and universities have long served the children of the wealthy, and increasingly, selective public universities have joined this mission of conferring status to the haves and denying opportunity to the poor and the lower reaches of the middle class. But many public colleges and universities have been unable to make up for the shortfalls in state support with large tuition increases.

Dwindling support for public higher education has especially affected community colleges. The percentage of part-time faculty has risen steadily to 65 percent in 1999, the latest figure available from the National Center for Education Statistics. Writing programs at all types of institutions have been caught in the squeeze. For 1997, an Association of Departments of English survey reports that at Ph.D.-granting universities, tenure-track faculty teach only 5 percent of the writing courses, and in four-year colleges, fewer than half of writing courses are taught by tenure-track faculty.

I pointed out in my Chair's address that many colleagues of my generation came to rhetoric and composition from early career experiences of teaching basic writing. They were motivated by the belief that quality public education could promote social justice. Public higher education expanded access in the 1960s and early 1970s by admitting far more students and charging low or even no tuition. Today, access to public education is contracting. Low-income students struggle to pay the costs of public education at a time when programs designed to broaden access are being cut or eliminated. (For example, the basic studies program at the local community college that my older son attended after ten years as a rock 'n' roll musician has been eliminated.) The social and economic costs of effectively denying higher education to lower-income students will be enormous in the long run.

Any writing teacher who has taught for long in public colleges knows the wealth of talent that will be lost. Yet it is often hard to see how the impoverishment of working people affects our teaching and our research, and that tells us a lot about how our discipline defines our work. We have become more cognizant of how dependent we are on state funding, but we still need to challenge ourselves to think about how our work with literacy, with technology, and with institutions is related to broader trends in the prevailing political economy. We cannot allow public higher education to either fall into shambles or else become prohibitively expensive for many of those it has traditionally served.

–LESTER FAIGLEY
University of Texas, Austin

1997

The Two-Year College as Democracy in Action

NELL ANN PICKETT

I am a graduate of a two-year college, and I am proud of it. It is an honor to stand here today as your colleague—and as a two-year college teacher. The two-year college is the bringer of dreams to hundreds of thousands of persons across this country, and that I can take part in that dream remains for me the highest honor.

A student wrote on the first day of class:

> My grandpa used to say, "Only in America does a poor man have a chance." Well, I'm here to tell you that if my Grandpa was here today, I'd tell him that only at a college like this does a poor guy who messed up his life get another chance.

This student, in his mid-twenties, was enrolled at Hinds Community College the month after his release from the county penal farm for dealing drugs. (Propitiously, the penal farm is just across the highway from the college.)

He was afraid. He was ashamed. And he had grave doubts about his future. But he came to a college that would take him in, and he was embraced by a faculty who did not care where he came from, just that he had. He had come to better his opportunities and as he said, "to get a clean start." And so the work began. And so did a dream. At the end of almost two years at Hinds, no longer afraid for his future, James is to graduate this summer with an Associate in Applied Science degree in drafting and design technology; he plans to transfer in the fall to a state university. His story is a common one, for the community college is in the business of serving the community. And the best way to serve is to put back into the community.

This article is a revised version of the Chair's address Nell Ann Pickett delivered at the CCCC Convention in Phoenix, Arizona, on March 13, 1997. It was first published in *CCC*, volume 49, number 1, February 1998.

"Only at a college like this," James wrote.

It is because of the Jameses and the Pecks, the Barbaras, the Mary Jeans, the Eileens—and yes, the Nell Anns—that I entitle this address, "The Two-Year College as Democracy in Action."

In the fall of 1966, I was hired at what was then Hinds Junior College on a one-year appointment replacing a teacher on leave. The one-year appointment suited me. I had been teaching at the university level for four years, preceded by three years in high school. Before settling into a career of teaching and before completing a PhD, I wanted to be sure that the level of institution and its expectations complemented my interest in classroom teaching.

At Hinds, I was returning to the two-year college from which I had graduated ten years earlier with an Associate in Arts degree and a major in English. To this day, I have the 3 × 5 cards on which I had written the valedictory address I gave at graduation. As support on that occasion, my mentor English teacher Jim El. Byrd Harris held a copy of those cards so that if I got so nervous I couldn't talk, the speech would be delivered. This morning, a friend and predecessor in this office—Lynn Troyka—holds a copy of the text I'm reading from. So no matter how my knees shake or my voice quivers, this address—now that it's written—will be given.

What I would like to center my remarks around is how an assignment to teach technical writing at a community college has shaped much of my professional life—and continues to shape it. Like many two-year college English teachers who have been around for a while, I've taught everything in the curriculum—including developmental courses, honors courses, writing courses, literature courses. The courses I most often teach, however, form a two-semester sequence of technical writing.

These technical writing courses are service courses for students majoring in such areas as child development, commercial art, criminal justice, dental assisting, drafting and design, electronics, hospitality and tourism management, landscape management, nursing, paralegal studies, veterinary technology. Most of the students are working toward an Associate in Applied Science degree and plan to enter the workforce full-time upon completion of the program at Hinds. Most of them work at one or more jobs, and most will be in school two and a half to five or more years off and on to meet the requirements for the so-called two-year program.

While most are full-time students (12 or more hours per semester), an increasing number are part-time—particularly those in the 30-to-50 age bracket, the baby-boomer generation. The community college often serves these persons through courses at nontraditional times and locations. Taking education to the people—democratizing education— enables individuals to realize the dream of bettering their lives.

Two years ago, Peck Sullivan, 32, a full-time supervisor at a container corporation, decided to do something to get his life out of a rut and to make life better, reports Andy Kanengiser. He has a high school equivalency certificate. He wants to become a nurse. "It would be great to help people," he explains. "I want to make more money and better the lifestyle for our family" (1). Sullivan enrolled at a convenient community college site and is taking two classes a semester. He's making As and Bs. His wife, Brenda, 31, an insurance company employee, is proud of his decision to enter college. She states, "I've been begging him to do it. This is a man who has the brain to do more with his life. I just wish he had done it sooner." Peck Sullivan comments about his leap to college: "I was nervous and didn't know what to expect. The kids are so much younger, but they made me feel pretty welcome" (1).

Mentioning that 27.2 is the average age for Hinds students in associate degree programs gets a "So what?" response from traditional students—those 17, 18, or 19 years of age. Nontraditional students, such as Peck Sullivan, listen with a different ear, a comforting ear, when they begin to understand what that means: of the 13,000 students at Hinds, more than half are 27 or older. At 32 years of age, wanting something better in life, Sullivan is thus in the mainstream of students in two-year colleges across the nation.

Currently, approximately ten million people across the nation are enrolled in both credit and noncredit courses in two-year colleges, according to a telephone interview with the American Association of Community Colleges. This estimate is not surprising. Consider the implications of this statement from AACC: "There are approximately 1300 community colleges strategically located within 25 miles of 95 percent of the nation's population base." Further, AACC reports that "the majority of the nation's first-time in college freshmen, minority students, and women are enrolled" in two-year colleges (*Responding to the Challenge* 5).

But let's narrow the spectrum for the moment and consider the numbers of persons enrolled in credit courses in one state, the state of Mississippi. According to the Mississippi State Board of Community and Junior Colleges, in the 1995–96 academic year:

- 69% of first-year college students were enrolled in community colleges;
- 54% of all college students were enrolled in community colleges.

Let me interject a bit of background. Two-year colleges have been a part of Mississippi higher education since the 1920s. In fact, the state of Mississippi has the oldest state-wide system of two-year colleges in the nation. Further, community colleges in Mississippi emerged from agricultural high schools that provided education and training, work assignments, and dormitories. My institution, founded in 1917, first offered college courses in 1924.

In Mississippi, as in other states, a community college is the most cost-effective choice in higher education. For FY 1996, the Mississippi

State Board of Community and Junior Colleges lists the average yearly tuition and required fees in Mississippi:

- Private colleges and universities $6,190
- Public universities $2,446
- Public community colleges $936

Stated another way, for the same amount of money a student can attend a private college or university for one semester, or attend a community college for four semesters and still have $1200 left over. Or for the same amount of money, a student can attend a public university for one semester, or a community college for three semesters.

Additional statistics concerning Mississippi are particularly significant because of concerted efforts to enroll underrepresented population groups. Last year

- 28% of all community college students were minority (Mississippi State Board); 36% of the state's population was minority (*Mississippi Almanac* 68).

- 67% of all associate degrees were awarded to women (Mississippi State Board); 52% of the state's population was female (*Mississippi Almanac* 68).

Historically, these two groups—minorities and women—have been underrepresented in higher education not only in Mississippi but across the nation.

Mary Jean Evans is in my Technical Writing II class this semester. In two months, Mary Jean, 38 years of age, will realize a dream come true. She will graduate in May with an Associate in Applied Science degree and a major in paralegal technology. Married at 16, she is the mother of three children. A full-time student since she began college two years ago, she is also the accountant for her husband's business. She serves as president of the Paralegal Club, and she works 20 hours a week in a legal firm as a paralegal intern. She writes, "My goal is to excel to my fullest potential; I value my family first but I expect a lot from myself. I think a real important accomplishment for me is to attend school, maintain good grades, and still be the mother and wife I want to be."

For Mary Jean, the only good grade is an A. One year ago at midsemester, she had a B in civil litigation; she talked with the teacher about dropping the course. Astounded to learn that hers was the highest average in the class, Mary Jean responded, "I want to learn everything that a course has to offer."

Peck Sullivan and Mary Jean Evans continue to juggle the realities of the demands of school, work, and family. And the realities of our students are the realities that we as teachers in two-year colleges deal with each day. Syllabi, assignment sheets, paper-due dates, student conferences, portfolio reviews—these are always fluid. Or we lose the student. And the student loses contact with formal education and training—at least for the time being. Encouraging students, making every class meeting relevant to students' goals, using teaching/learning materials that students can identify with: these realities are the continuous challenge for us as teachers. And the challenges can be very frustrating.

Let me share one such frustration. When I was hired in the fall of 1967 as "permanent" faculty at Hinds, I was asked to teach the two sections of technical writing. I said "Sure," and was handed the textbook used since the college first offered technical writing in 1962. This textbook was a revision and extension of *The Engineer's Manual of English*, first published in 1933. The first weeks of class, students and I both realized that this textbook did not meet our needs. It was written for engineering majors in their junior or senior year of college who had completed their general education requirements and many of their engineering requirements.

In desperation, I began producing multipage handouts to get us through the term. Then for the next term, my colleague Ann Laster was also assigned to teach technical writing. All the while, my department chair and I were contacting publishers and publishing representatives pleading for them to send us examination copies of their technical writing books suitable for first- and second-year students. There was no such book.

We visited businesses and industries, we talked with technicians in the workplace, we gathered examples of writing they did on the job. And we read and read and read. We worked closely with technical instructors, audited technical classes, attended craft committee meetings, and made lots of assignments that required students to research what would be expected of them in the workplace. The college supported us and encouraged us.

The following summer, the college gave us a stipend to refine and expand the units on explaining procedures, describing mechanisms, giving various kinds of reports, and writing business letters. The vocational offset printing department at the college printed our materials as a spiral-bound book. That fall, several publishing representatives asked for a copy of our "homemade" book. Shortly, we had offers of contracts from four major publishing houses. We signed a contract, and soon the book was in production.

What happened next was to be the biggest shock of my life. We began to get urgent phone calls from the editor in New York:

First call: We have arranged for a published professor at a well-known Eastern university to write an introduction and to be listed as the senior author.

Our response: We don't know this man. He has had no part in writing this book. Forget it.

Second call: Our editorial staff has decided that using your initials plus last names is sufficient on the title page.

Our response: We like our full names—Nell Ann Pickett, Ann A. Laster. Use those full names or just tear up the contract.

Third call: Identification of your institution is not necessary on the title page.

Our response: We are from Hinds Junior College, in Raymond, Mississippi, and that's the way we want to be known.

Naive as we were, those phone calls within a week just didn't set right with us; there was something innately unfair. Our gut reply was: "Forget this book publishing notion." After all, we had not sought a publisher. Our sole reason for writing and assembling *Effective Communication for the Technical Student* in the summer of 1968 was to offer appropriate classroom materials for our students.

Those telephone calls from the senior editor were our first experience in being treated as inferior because (1) we were women and (2) we taught in a two-year college. As we mulled over those phone calls, we realized that the publisher had made certain judgements:

- A technical writing textbook aimed at the two-year college market was indeed needed and would sell.
- This publishing house wanted to go on record as producing the first technical writing textbook designed specifically for freshman and sophomore level courses.

Further,

- A technical writing textbook authored by two women would not be creditable. (Sada A. Harbarger in her 1923 technical writing textbook was referred to only as S. A. Harbarger, Robert J. Connors points out, "perhaps because the publisher felt that many readers might resent a woman claiming to be able to teach technical writing" [335].)
- A technical writing textbook by two-year college teachers, particularly teachers from a rural, deep South state, would not sell.
- The only voice to be trusted in making publishing decisions is the voice of the publisher.

Well, the book came out several months later than scheduled. Through the grapevine, we learned that two cantankerous Mississippi women were blamed for costing the publisher a bundle of money because they would not listen to reason about something as inconsequential as names and college identification on a title page and an introduction written by a guest author. We also learned that when the publisher telephoned us with those urgent messages, the front matter—the last folio to be printed—was already in press.

Those bits of information were being fed to us with the expectation that two neophyte authors, who happened to be female and who taught in a two-year college, at press time would not question the judgement of an editor at a 175-year-old publishing company. But we felt great pride in being female and in choosing to teach in a two-year college. In that first publishing venture, our focus was sharing with others the classroom materials that we had developed for our students. Although at that point in our lives we did not have the vocabulary to articulate the unfairness we felt in the senior editor's insistences, there was never any doubt about our stance. Accept our work and us for what we are.

Now working on the eighth edition of this textbook (for release in fall 1998), we continue to experience the full support of our college and of our colleagues—and, yes, of senior editors.

I'd like to share another major influence early in my Hinds teaching career that bonded me with the two-year college. The English department chair, Jim El. Byrd Harris, said to me, "Nell Ann, there's a new professional organization for two-year college faculty, and I want you to go to the next meeting. I think you and it can grow together." That meeting was the February 1968 annual convention of the Southeastern Conference on English in the Two-Year College, now known as TYCA-Southeast. The site of that third annual meeting of the new organization was Biloxi, Mississippi. Several hundred people were expected—the lure of the beautiful Mississippi Gulf Coast in winter—who could resist? History was made that weekend, but not in the way we had anticipated. In Biloxi, there was a four-inch snowfall, part of a band of sleet and snow that paralyzed the deep South. Rather than the three hundred we had expected, the three dozen of us who had arrived a day early were the only ones at the conference.

One of the early arrivers was Elisabeth McPherson, featured speaker. Liz, harbinger and champion, whom we specifically honor and commemorate on this day, was chair of CCCC in 1972—the first two-year college person elected to the office. Throughout her life, Liz was a leading voice in the democracy of the two-year college, of the development of the two-year regional organizations, of students' rights to their own language, and of students' rights to educational opportunity.

Since my first attendance at the Regional in Biloxi, I have returned each year. The two-year Regionals have come to mean informative sessions, learning, sharing, belonging, a professional home. It is no wonder that there is such excitement about the inauguration of the Two-Year College English Association-National this week at this conference in Phoenix, for it was CCCC that 32 years ago, in 1965, inaugurated the seven two-year college Regionals.

In closing, I want to comment on an expanding emphasis in the two-year college—workforce improvement—and how it is undergirded by the openness, the acceptance, the flexibility in programming in the two-year college. Let me share one example of how workforce initiatives are making a difference in persons' lives, as reported by Marcy Lamm.

Eileen Rubin, an insurance executive, lost her job, her livelihood, and her self-esteem. Through the local community college, she established an even more rewarding career.

Rubin, through new management of the company where she had worked for years, found herself in a no-win situation. She says, "All of a sudden everything I did was wrong. I could see it [a pink slip] coming, and there wasn't a darn thing I could do about it" (Lamm 11). She quit before she was squeezed out.

At 43 years of age, her world began to crumble. In spite of her strong qualifications and job leads, she could not find employment. Her husband's income was supporting her and their 10-year-old son. But her executive salary had supplied the major income for the family. "I was depressed. I was scared for my family that I was letting them down. I thought nobody's going to want to hire me. I thought I was too old" (11).

Then she attended a career seminar at the community college sponsored by its Women in Trades and Technology program. The series of aptitude tests that she took highlighted her interest in health care and nursing, manifested years earlier as a premed major at Rutgers University. Rubin enrolled in the community college nursing program and graduated with an associate degree in nursing in May 1995. Within a week, she was employed in her new profession, and she continues to receive promotions. Rubin reports that in her new life as a registered nurse she is happier and spends more time with her family, and "my priorities are very different" (12).

Eileen Rubin, in her early 40s, states to the world: "I will never again put work first." Rubin, through a community college, learned new skills that helped her cope with the challenge of workplace competition. She experienced firsthand the concepts enumerated in the AACC's *Developing the World's Best Workforce*. Community colleges

- are accessible to virtually all Americans;
- provide diverse programs and services; and
- receive high ratings from employers for the quality of programs and for program responsiveness to employer needs.

Community colleges have emerged as vanguard institutions in preparing an efficient, skilled, and adaptable workforce.

I salute all the Eileens and the Jameses, the Pecks, and the Mary Jeans across this country. And I salute the 1300 two-year colleges—colleges that bring hope, opportunity, fulfillment of dreams to a large segment of our population for whom otherwise higher education would be very difficult, if not impossible.

Community colleges are open door, they are accessible, they are affordable, they are cost efficient, they offer a broad array of programs and services, and they open the way for transferring to four-year institutions or entering/reentering the workforce.

Familiar words from the Declaration of Independence remind us of the basis of our democracy: "We hold these truths to be self-evident . . ."—you know the rest of the sentence. The abstractions "created equal," "certain unalienable rights," "life, liberty, and the pursuit of happiness" become realities for many because of their community college experiences.

Community colleges are indeed democracy in action.

WORKS CITED

American Association of Community Colleges, Commission on Workforce and Community Development. *Responding to the Challenge of Workforce and Economic Development: The Role of America's Community Colleges*. Washington, DC: AACC. May 1996.

American Association of Community Colleges. *Developing the World's Best Workforce: An Agenda for America's Community Colleges*, Annapolis Junction, MD: Community College P, 1996.

Connors, Robert J. "Technical Writing Instruction in America." *Journal of Technical Writing and Communication* (1982):329–52.

Kanengiser, Andy. "Lifelong Learning Boom Crowds Campuses." *The Clarion-Ledger* [Jackson, MS.] 8 Jan. 1997:A1, 5.

Lamm, Marcy. "Women's Mid-Life Crises Often Inspire New Careers, Upgraded Self-Esteems." *The Clarion-Ledger* [Jackson, MS.] 3 Nov. 1996:B11–12.

Mississippi Almanac 1997–1998. Yazoo City: Computer Search and Research, 1997.

Mississippi State Board of Community and Junior Colleges. "Mississippi Community and Junior Colleges." Fact Sheet. Jackson, MS: n.d.

AFTERWORD: COLLEGE RESOURCES AND STUDENT NEEDS: FINDING THE FIT

Melody Austin, enrolling in September 2004 as a junior in an online baccalaureate degree program, is realizing educational goals in ways unimaginable to her as a traditional college freshman in 1977. Flash to new millennium. Online courses. Austin—in her mid-forties, a single parent, her son in college (Brown)—is "a first student to receive an associate degree, with 50 percent or more online courses, from Hinds Community College" (Hogan). "Once I was involved in online courses, I saw a way. Afraid that I would lose momentum, I took all the courses I needed, without let up" (Austin).

Labeled as dumb, Jerry Barlow barely finished high school. In community college he was identified as dyslexic ("Dyslexia No Barrier"). His high school grades and ACT scores, indicating basic courses (English, mathematics, reading, study skills) forewarned. Barlow knew that his progress might seem slow, but he was eager to learn and prove to himself, his wife, and two daughters that education could better their lives. He took the prescribed developmental courses, Basic

Studies in English and Fundamentals of English Composition, before enrolling in traditional English Composition I and II and a subsequent literature course (Barlow). His favorite hobby, writing—particularly short stories—yielded second place honors in the Mississippi Community College Creative Writing Association competition in spring 2004 (Fatherree). A winner! A statewide published author!

Melody Austin and Jerry Barlow exemplify what can happen when college resources and student needs fit. Austin longed to complete her associate degree, but work and family responsibilities nixed traditional classes (Austin). Ability to work independently and self-discipline: a good fit for online classes. Although Hinds offered several online courses earlier, the surge began in 2000 when the consortium Mississippi Virtual Community College (MSVCC) provided access to all online courses in the system (Pugh). Thus, in fall 2004, while Hinds offers 136 sections of 77 independent courses ("Distance Learning"), Hinds students have access to several times that many sections and courses. Austin sums up her online experience, "All of this has been a positive experience. Online is harder than traditional classes; you really have to be committed to be successful" (Austin). Indeed, she is committed, has made excellent grades, and is now pursuing an emergency management major online at an Alabama university, thankful for online as a venue.

Jerry Barlow, a good fit for community college resources, exclaims, "This is my last day of work. Now I can become a full-time student!" For two years he took night classes while working full-time. With his wife's associate degree in nursing completed, it is his turn to take a full load of day classes. His goal is to graduate from Hinds by 2006 and transfer to a four-year institution to become a high school counselor or history teacher (Barlow).

These two success stories, still in the making, indicate challenges in two areas of biggest enrollment jumps: distance learning and developmental courses preparing students for regular college work.

Definitely, two-year colleges continue to embody democracy in action.

–NELL ANN PICKETT, EMERITA
Hinds Community College

WORKS CITED

Austin, Melody. Telephone interview. 29 July 2004.
Barlow, Jerry. Telephone interview. 31 July 2004.
Brown, Riva. "Online Classes Offer Older Students a Leg Up." *Clarion-Ledger* [Jackson, MS.] 11 July 2004: B1.
"Distance Learning Fall 2004 Courses." Hinds Community College Class Schedule. Summer/ Fall 2004: 139–41.
"Dyslexia No Barrier to Student's Writing Success." *Hindsight* 29.3 (2004): 5.
Fatherree, Beverly. Interview. 22 July and 27 July 2004.
Hogan, Dan. Interview. 27 July 2004.
Pugh, Jason. Telephone interview. 27 July 2004.

1998

Technology and Literacy:
A Story about the Perils
of Not Paying Attention

CYNTHIA L. SELFE

Technological literacy—meaning computer skills and the ability to use computers and other technology to improve learning, productivity and performance—has become as fundamental to a person's ability to navigate through society as traditional skills like reading, writing and arithmetic. . . . In explicit acknowledgment of the challenges facing the education community, on February 15, 1996, President Clinton and Vice President Gore announced the Technology Literacy Challenge envisioning a 21st century where all students are technologically literate. The challenge was put before the nation as a whole, with responsibility . . . shared by local communities, states, the private sector, educators local communities, parents, the federal government, and others. . . .

—*Getting America's Students*
Ready for the 21st Century (5)

We know, purely and simply, that every single child must have access to a computer. . . .

—BILL CLINTON, qtd. in *Getting America's*
Students Ready for the 21st Century (4)

This article is a revised version of the Chair's address Cynthia L. Selfe delivered at the CCCC Convention in Chicago, Illinois, on April 2, 1998. It was first published in *CCC*, volume 50, number 3, February 1999.

A central irony shaping my experience with the CCCC as a professional organization goes something like this: I consider it a fortunate occurrence and a particular point of pride that many of the best ideas about teaching and learning writing, the most powerfully explanatory theoretical insights about language and discourse and literacy that inform education today, grow directly out of conversations among CCCC members. Given this situation, however, I find it compellingly unfortunate that the one topic serving as a focus for my own professional involvement—that of computer technology and its use in teaching composition—seems to be the single subject best guaranteed to inspire glazed eyes and complete indifference in that portion of the CCCC membership which does not immediately sink into snooze mode.

This irony, I am convinced, has nothing to do with collegial good will. CCCC colleagues have been unerringly polite in the 17 years of discussions we have had about technology. After all this time, however, I can spot the speech acts that follow a turn of the conversation to computers—the slightly averted gaze, the quick glance at the watch, the panicky look in the eyes when someone lapses into talk about microprocessors, or gigabytes, or ethernets. All these small potent gestures, as Michel de Certeau would say, signify pretty clearly—technology is either boring or frightening to most humanists; many teachers of English composition feel it antithetical to their primary concerns and many believe it should not be allowed to take up valuable scholarly time or the attention that could be best put to use in teaching or the study of literacy. I have, believe me, gotten the message—as subtle as it is.

These attitudes toward technology issues, of course, aren't shared by everyone in this organization—there are pockets of technology studies scholars and teachers here and there among us; notable occasions when an individual CCCC leader does speak about technology; and, every now and again, a professional conversation among us about the array of challenges associated with technology. These occasions remain exceptions, however, and anybody familiar with the values of traditional humanism knows that, as a group, we tend to hold in common a general distrust of the machine, that a preference for the non-technological still characterizes our community.

Our tendency to avoid focusing on the technological means that—while we are tolerant of those colleagues interested in the "souls of machines," to use Bruno Latour's term—we assign them to a peculiar kind of professional isolation "in their own separate world" of computer sessions and computer workshops and computers and writing conferences that many CCCC members consider influenced more by the concerns of "engineers, technicians, and technocrats" (vii) than those of humanists. It is this same set of historically and professionally determined beliefs, I think, that informs our actions within our home departments, where we generally continue to allocate the responsibility of technology decisions—and often-times the responsibility of technology studies—to a single faculty or staff member who doesn't mind wrestling with computers or the thorny, and the unpleasant issues that can be associated with their use. In this way, we manage to have the best of both worlds—we have computers available to use for our own studies, in support of our classes and our profession—but we have also relegated these technologies into the background of our pro-fessional lives. As a result, computers are rapidly becoming invisible, which is how we like our technology to be. When we don't have to pay attention to machines, we remain free to focus on the theory and practice of language, the stuff of real intellectual and social concern.

WHY WE ALLOW OURSELVES TO IGNORE TECHNOLOGY

As humanists, we prefer things to be arranged this way because computer technology, when it is too much in our face (as an unfamiliar technology generally is), can suggest a kind of cultural strangeness that is off-putting. We are much more used to dealing with older technologies like print, a technology conventional enough so that we don't have to think so much about it, old enough so that it doesn't call such immediate attention to the social or material conditions associated with its use. Books, for example, are already and always—almost anyway—there. At this point in history, books are relatively cheap, they are generally accessible to students and to us, and they are acknowledged by our peers to be the appropriate tools of teaching and learning to use. As a result, our recognition of the material conditions associated with books have faded into the background of our imagination. Thus, although we understand on a tacit level that the print technology in which we invest so readily (and in which we ask students to invest) contributes to our own tenure and promotion, to our own wallets, and to our own status in the profession and in the public eye—this under-standing is woven into the background of our professional attention, and we seldom pay attention to it on a daily basis. If we did, we'd go mad.

There are other things that don't occur to us, as well. When we use the more familiar technology of books, for instance, it is mostly within a familiar ideological system that allows us to ignore, except for some occa-sional twinges of conscience, the persistence of print and our role in this persistence. It allows us to ignore the understanding that print literacy functions as a cultural system—as Lester Faigley noted two years ago—not only to carry and distribute enlightened ideas, but also as a seamless whole to support a pattern of continuing illiteracy in this country.

I provide this example to suggest that composition studies faculty, educated in the humanist tradition, generally prefer our technologies and the material conditions associated so closely with them to remain in the background for obvious reasons, and the belief systems we construct in connection with various technologies allow us to accomplish this comfortable process of naturalization.

In the case of computers—we have convinced ourselves that we and the students with whom we work are made of much finer stuff than the machine in our midst, and we are determined to maintain this state of affairs. This ideological position, however, has other effects, as well. As a result of the inverse value we generally assign to discussions about computers, our professional organizations continue to deal with technology in what is essentially a piecemeal fashion. We now think of computers, for instance, as a simple tool that individual faculty members can use or ignore in their classrooms as they choose, but also one that the profession, as a collective whole—and with just a few notable exceptions—need not address too systematically. And so we have paid technology issues precious little focused attention over the years.

WHY COMPOSITION SPECIALISTS NEED TO PAY ATTENTION TO TECHNOLOGY ISSUES

Allowing ourselves the luxury of ignoring technology, however, is not only misguided at the end of the 20th century, it is dangerously shortsighted. And I do not mean, simply, that we are all—each of us—now teaching students who must know how to communicate as informed thinkers and citizens in an increasingly technological world—although this is surely so. This recognition has led composition faculty only to the point of *using* computers—or having students do so—but not to the point of *thinking* about what we are doing and understanding at least some of the important implications of our actions.

I believe composition studies faculty have a much larger and more complicated obligation to fulfill—that of trying to understand and make sense of, to *pay attention* to, how technology is now inextricably linked to literacy and literacy education in this country. As a part of this obligation, I suggest that we have some rather unpleasant facts to face about our own professional behavior and involvement. To make these points more persuasively, I offer a real-life story about what has happened in American schools and literacy instruction as a result of our unwillingness to attend to technological issues.

An honest examination of this situation, I believe, will lead composition studies professionals to recognize that these two complex cultural formations—technology and literacy—have become linked in ways that exacerbate current educational and social inequities in the United States rather than addressing them productively. The story will lead us to admit, I believe, that we are, in part, already responsible for a bad—even a shameful—situation, and, I hope, will inspire us to do something more positive in the future.

I'll provide readers the moral of this story up front so that no one misses it. *As composition teachers, deciding whether or not to use technology in our classes is simply not the point—we have to pay attention to technology.* When we fail to do so, we share in the responsibility for sustaining and reproducing an unfair system that, scholars such as Elspeth Stuckey and Mike Rose have noted in other contexts, enacts social violence and ensures continuing illiteracy under the aegis of education.

I know, however, that it is not easy for composition teachers to pay attention to technology. As Anthony Giddens would say, our tendency to ignore technology—to focus on humans rather than on machines—is "deeply sedimented" (22) in our culture, in the history of our humanist profession. And the sedimentation of this belief system is so deep that it has come to comprise a piece of what Pierre Bordieu might call *doxa* (166)—a position everyone takes so much for granted, is so obvious, that people no longer even feel the need to articulate it. But by subscribing to this attitude, we may also be allowing ourselves to ignore the serious social struggles that continue to characterize technology as a cultural formation in this country.

Nowhere are these struggles and debates rendered in more complex terms in the United States—and nowhere are they more influential on our own work—than they are in the link between literacy and computer technology that has been established in increasingly direct ways over the last decade. This potent linkage is sustained and reproduced by a complexly related set of cultural influences: workplaces in which approximately 70% of jobs requiring a bachelors degree or an advanced college degree now require the use of computers (*Digest of Education Statistics* 458); a corporate sector focused on exploiting the 89% of "teachers and the public" who believe that the Internet adds value to teaching and learning specifically because it "reduces the costs teachers spend on classroom activities" ("MCI Nationwide Poll"); schools in which 87% of high school students are now writing on computers by Grade 11 (Coley, Crandler, and Engle 27); and homes in which 86% of parents are convinced that a computer is *the* one "most beneficial and effective product that they can buy to expand their children's opportunities" for education, future success, and economic prosperity (*Getting America's Student's Ready* 10).

The tendential force generated by these complexly related formations—which magnify our country's economic dependence on technology—is considerable. However, because it is always easier to ascribe responsibility for such a situation to others—to blame the greed of the corporate representatives who sell computers, or the blindness of school administrators who mandate the use of computers, or the shortsightedness of parents who consider technology a guarantor of learning for their children, I want to focus primarily on our own professional roles and responsibilities associated with this social dynamic.

It is, after all, partly a result of the involvement of English composition specialists, or lack of involvement, in some cases, that the linkage between literacy and technology has come to inform most of the official instruction that goes on within the United States' educational system, most official definitions and descriptions of literacy featured in the documents we write and read, and many of the criteria used to gauge literacy levels within this country. Few government documents about educational goals; few documents outlining national or state educational standards, including our own NCTE standards document; and few corporate job descriptions now fail to acknowledge a citizen's need to read, write, and communicate in electronic environments.

And certainly, like most Americans, we have not felt a responsibility to involve ourselves directly in some of the more public discussions about technology and educational policy because many of us unconsciously subscribe to a belief—both culturally and historically determined—that technology is a productive outgrowth of Science and Innovation (cf. Winner; Virilio; Feenberg; Johnson-Eilola). As a result, we take comfort when the linkage between literacy and computer technology is portrayed as a socially progressive movement, one that will benefit American citizens generally and without regard for their circumstances or backgrounds. Such a belief releases us from the responsibility to pay attention.

It is this last point, however, that makes the American cultural narrative about technology and literacy a particularly potent force in our lives, and that provides a jumping off point for our real-life story about technology.

AN AMERICAN NARRATIVE ABOUT COMPUTER TECHNOLOGY AND ITS GROWING LINKS TO LITERACY INSTRUCTION

This story about technology and literacy could be dated by any number of historical events, but for the purposes of this paper, we turn to the June of 1996, when the Clinton-Gore administration—with direct reference to the larger cultural narrative of social-progress-through-technology that I have just identified—published a document entitled *Getting America's Children Ready for the Twenty-First Century*, which announced an official national project to expand *technological literacy*, the "ability to use computers and other technology to improve learning, productivity and performance" (5).

The purpose of this large-scale project—as outlined by Secretary of Education Richard Riley—was, and is, to help "all of our children to become technologically literate" so that each "will have the opportunity to make the most of his or her own life," to "grow and thrive" within the "new knowledge-and-information-driven economy" (3–4). By "technologically literate," this document refers to the use of computers not only for the purposes of calculating, programming, and designing, but also for the purposes of reading, writing, and communicating (15–19)—at least for the officially-sponsored academic tasks required in schools across the country.

Estimates indicate that this particular literacy project may cost up to $109 billion dollars—averaging either $11 billion annually for a decade or between $10 and $20 billion annually for five years—from a variety of sources at the national, state, and local levels (*Getting America's Students Ready* 6). Where has this money come from and where has it gone? As Todd Oppenheimer notes:

> New Jersey cut state aid to a number of school districts this past year and then spent $10 million on classroom computers. In Union City, California, a single school district is spending $27 million to buy new gear for a mere eleven schools. . . . [I]n Mansfield, Massachusetts, administrators dropped proposed teaching positions in art, music and physical education, and then spent $333,000 on computers. (46)

Secretary of Education Richard Riley, in *Getting America's Students Ready*, lists other funded projects from various states—here is a sampling:

California

$279 million (one time, State Board) for "instructional materials, deferred maintenance, technology. . . ."

$13.4 million (State Board) for educational technology.

$10 million (State budget) to "refurbish and update used or donated computers."

$100 million (current year, Governor Wilson) for "educational technology."

$35 million (Pacific Telesis) for rate overcharges. (60)

Delaware

$30 million (State, three years) to fund "infrastructure initiative." (61)

District of Columbia

$9 million for "hardware and software purchases." (61)

Idaho

$10.4 million (Idaho Educational Technology Initiative) for "technology in the classroom." (62)

Maine

$15 million (Governor) to "establish a distance learning network." (63)

Montana

$2.56 million (NSF) to support "SummitNet"

$100,000 (State) "for technology" (65)

Texas

$150 million (State, Telecommunications Infrastructure Fund)

$30/student (State) for "purchasing electronic textbooks or technological equipment . . . , training educational personnel directly involved in student learning, . . . access to technological equipment." (67)

Wisconsin

$10 million (State) for "improve[d] access to advanced telecommunications and distance education technologies." (68)

[Telecommunications providers] have provided unidentified funds for Advanced Telecommunications Foundation. (68)

In comparison to the miserly federal funding this country is allocating to other literacy and education projects, these amounts stagger the imagination.

To put these expenditures for technology into perspective, we can look at the 1999 budget for the Department of Education that President Clinton has recently sent to the United States Congress. In this budget, the President has requested $721 million of direct federal funding for educational technology but less than half of that amount, $260 million, for the America Reads Challenge and less than one-tenth of that amount, $67 million, for teacher recruitment and preparation (Community Update, No. 56, p. 3).

And we are already in the midst of this project—the administration's deadline for creating such a technologically literate citizenry, one that will think of official, school-sponsored literacy practices as occurring primarily in technological contexts, is "early in the 21st century" (*Getting America's Children Ready* 3).

This project, and the extensive influence it has had on our national understanding of officially-sponsored literacy practices, is a phenomenon that deserves close study not only because of the considerable attention that individual teachers and school districts around the country have already paid to its goals, but, interestingly and conversely, because of the utter lack of systematic and considered attention that our profession as a whole and our professional organizations have accorded it. And so I will move the story forward a bit more.

Since 1996, although our professional standards documents now reflect the core values of this project in that they assume the necessity of computer *use* by communicators in the 21st century, they do not provide adequate guidance about how to get teachers and students *thinking critically about such use*. Moreover, in a curious way, neither the CCCC, nor the NCTE, nor the MLA, nor the IRA—as far as I can tell—have ever published a single word about our own professional stance on this particular nationwide technology project: not one statement about how we think such literacy monies should be spent in English composition programs; not one statement about what kinds of literacy and technology efforts should be funded in connection with this project or how excellence should be gauged in these efforts; not one statement about the serious need for professional development and support for teachers that must be addressed within the context of this particular national literacy project.

Nor have these organizations articulated any official or direct response to the project's goals or the ways in which schools and teachers are already enacting these goals within classrooms. And this is true despite the fact that so many literacy educators in a range of situations — including all English and Language Arts teachers in primary, secondary, and college/university classrooms — have been broadly affected by the technology-literacy linkage for the past decade and will continue to be so involved well into the next century.

In other words, as members of these professional organizations, we need to do a much better job of paying critical attention to technology issues that affect us. Now why is this particular task is so important? By paying critical attention to lessons about *technology*, we can re-learn important lessons about *literacy*. It is the different perspective on literacy that technology issues provide us that can encourage such insights. In the sections that follow, I point out just a few of these lessons.

REMEMBERING THE TRUTH ABOUT LARGE-SCALE LITERACY PROJECTS AND THE MYTH OF LITERACY

The first lesson that the national project to expand technological literacy can teach us has to do with the efficacy of large-scale literacy projects, in general, and with the myth of literacy. One of the primary arguments for the project to expand technological literacy rests on the claim that such an effort will provide all Americans with an education enriched by technology, and, thus, equal opportunity to access high-paying, technology-rich jobs and economic prosperity after graduation. The truth of this claim, however, has not been borne out and is not likely to be so. This fact is one of the primary reasons why we need to pay attention to technology issues.

Scholars such as Brian Street, Harvey Graff, and James Paul Gee note that such claims are not unusual in connection with large-scale, national literacy projects. Indeed, our willingness to believe these claims contributes to the potency of what Graff has called the "literacy myth," a widely held belief that literacy and literacy education lead autonomously, automatically, and directly to liberation, personal success, or economic prosperity. This myth, however, is delusory in its simplicity, as Street says:

> The reality [of national literacy movements] is more complex, is harder to face politically. . . . [W]hen it comes to job acquisition, the level of literacy is less important than issues of class, gender, and ethnicity; lack of literacy is more likely to be a symptom of poverty and deprivation than a cause. (18)

In the specific case of the project to expand technological literacy, the claim is that a national program will provide all citizens equal access to an improved education and, thus, equal opportunity for upward social mobility and economic prosperity. If we *pay attention* to the facts surrounding the project's instantiation, however, we can remind ourselves of the much harder lesson: in our educational system, and in the culture that this system reflects, computers *continue to be distributed differentially along the related axes of race and socioeconomic status* and this distribution contributes to ongoing patterns of racism and to the continuation of poverty.

It is a fact, for instance, that schools primarily serving students of color and poor students continue to have less access to computers, and access to less sophisticated computer equipment than do schools primarily serving more affluent and white students (Coley et al. 3). And it is a fact that schools primarily serving students of color and poor students continue to have less access to the Internet, less access to multimedia equipment, less access to CD-ROM equipment, less access to local area networks, less access to videodisc technology than do schools primarily serving more affluent and white students (Coley et al. 3).

These data, which are profoundly disturbing, become all the more problematic if we trace the extended effects of the technology-literacy linkage into the country's workplaces and homes. There, too, the latest census figures indicate, the linkage is strongly correlated to both race and socioeconomic status. It is a fact, for instance, that Black employees or Hispanic employees are *much* less likely than white employees to use a range of computer applications in their workplace environments (*Digest* 458). It is also a fact that employees who have not graduated from high school are much less likely to use a range of computer applications than are employees who have a high school degree or have some college experience (*Digest* 458). And it is a fact that poor families in both urban and rural environments and Black and Hispanic Americans are much less likely to own and use computers than individuals with higher family incomes and white families (*Condition* 212; *Digest 1996* 458; *Getting* 36).

In other words, the poorer you are and the less educated you are in this country—both of which conditions are correlated with race—the less likely you are to have access to computers and to high-paying, high-tech jobs in the American workplace.

The challenges associated with the unequal distribution and use of computer technology along the related axes of socioeconomic status, education, and race have proven embarrassingly persistent for a number of related reasons. Secretary of Education Richard Riley, for example, citing a 1995 General Accounting Office Survey, notes that

half of all schools do not have adequate wiring (such as outlets) to handle their technology needs. More than half do not have sufficient telephone lines, and 60 percent consider the number of conduits for network cable unsatisfactory. Schools that have all of these infrastructure elements are clearly the exception to the rule. Strikingly, schools in large central cities are even less equipped to meet the demands of technology than other schools; more than 40 percent do not even have enough electrical power to use computers on a regular basis. . . . Classrooms in older buildings, for example, may require expensive renovations to improve electrical systems before computers and networks can be installed, discouraging the community from making a commitment. (*Getting America's Children Ready* 34–35).

As a result of this overdetermined system, the differential distribution of technology and technological literacy continues—albeit, with some complex new variations. In a recent article published in *Science*, for example, Hoffman and Novak identified the following findings:

- Overall whites were significantly more likely than African Americans to have a home computer in their household. Whites were also slightly more likely to have access to a PC at work. (390)

- Proportionately, more than twice as many whites as African Americans had used the Web in the past week. As of January 1997, we estimate that 5.2 million (±1.2 million) African Americans and 40.8 million whites (±2.1 million) have ever used the Web, and that 1.4 million (±0.5 million) African Americans and 20.3 million (±1.6 million) whites used the Web in the past week. (390)

- As one would expect . . . increasing levels of income corresponded to an increased likelihood of owning a home computer, regardless of race. In contrast, adjusting for income did not eliminate the race differences with respect to computer access at work. . . . Notably . . . , race differences in Web use vanish at household income of $40,000 and higher. (390)

- 73% of white students owned a home computer, only 32% of African American students owned one. "This difference persisted when we statistically adjusted for students' reported household income." (390)

- White students were significantly more likely than African American students to have used the Web, especially in the past week. (391)

- White students lacking a home computer, but not African American students, appear to be accessing the Internet from locations such as home of friends and relatives, libraries, and community centers. (391)

Acknowledging these facts, we might understand better why the rhetoric associated with national literacy projects serves to exacerbate the dangers that they pose. When Secretary of Education Richard Riley states, for example, that "Computers are the 'new basics' of education . . ." or that the project of technological literacy can help us give "all of our young people" an "opportunity to grow . . . and thrive" in the "new knowledge- and information-driven economy" (*Getting* 3), he erroneously suggests, in Brian Street's words, "that the acquisition of literacy" will by itself "lead to 'major' impacts in terms of social and cognitive skills and 'development'" within a population (14). As Street reminds us, these "simple stories" that "both politicians and the press" tell about literacy to justify and sustain the momentum of such major programs, frequently "deflect attention from the complexity and real political difficulties" (17). The ultimate effect, according to Street, is an overly narrow understanding of literacy—usually in terms of a single official literacy—and the development of accompanying "patronizing assumptions about what it means to have difficulties with reading and writing in contemporary society. Such rhetoric also serves to raise false hopes about what the acquisition of literacy means for job prospects, social mobility, and personal achievement" (17).

In the specific case of computers and literacy, these stories serve to deflect our attention from the fact that "every single child" does *not* now have access to technology, and some students, especially those who are poor and of color, have less access than others. And so, *if* access to and use of technology in school-based settings *is* now a fundamental skill of literacy and *if* such skills *do* help prepare graduates for the jobs they will be asked to do, these same students can expect less opportunity to assume high-tech and high-paying jobs, not more. As Richard Ohmann described the underlying dynamic in a prescient 1985 *College English* article about the general relationship between technology, literacy, and economic conditions:

> Of course there will be more jobs in the computer field itself. But . . . the field is layered into specialties, which will be dead ends for most people in them. . . . Graduates of MIT will get the challenging jobs; community college grads will be technicians; those who do no more than acquire basic skills and computer literacy in high school will probably find their way to electronic workstations at McDonald's. I see every reason to expect that the computer revolution, like other revolutions from the top down, will indeed expand the minds and the freedom of an elite, meanwhile facilitating the degradation of labor and the stratification of the workforce that have been hallmarks of monopoly capitalism from its onset. (683)

The frustrating cycle associated with this situation is so dismally clear and sickeningly familiar because it mirrors exactly the dynamics associated with more traditional literacy efforts in our country. As Graff notes, official literacies usually function in a conservative, and reproductive, fashion—in favor of dominant groups and in support of the existing class-based system:

> Hegemonic relationships have historically involved processes of group and class formation, recruitment, indoctrination, and maintenance at

all levels of society. For most of literacy's history, these functions have centered upon elite groups and their cohesion and power. For them, the uses of literacy have been diverse but have included common education, culture, and language . . . shared interests and activities; control of scarce commodities, such as wealth, power, and even literacy; and common symbols and badges, of which literacy could be one. (*Legacies* 12)

Thus, the national project to expand technological literacy has *not* served to reduce illiteracy—or the persistent social problems that exacerbate illiteracy. Rather, it has simply changed the official criteria for both "literate" and "illiterate" individuals, while retaining the basic ratio of both groups.

In sum, we have little evidence that any large-scale project focusing on a narrowly defined set of officially sanctioned literacy skills will result in fundamental changes in the ratio of people labeled as literate or illiterate. These categories are socially constructed identities which our current educational system reproduces rather than addresses. Similarly, we have no specific evidence that the current project to expand technological literacy will change the patterns of literacy and illiteracy in this country. Rather, this project is likely to support persistent patterns of economically-based literacy acquisition because citizens of color and those from low socioeconomic backgrounds continue to have less access to high-tech educational opportunities and occupy fewer positions that make multiple uses of technology than do white citizens or those from higher socioeconomic backgrounds.

LITERACY EDUCATION IS A POLITICAL ACT

Given the effects we have just described, the national project to expand technological literacy can also serve to re-teach us a second lesson—that literacy is always a political act as well as an educational effort. In this context, we can understand that the national project to expand technological literacy is motivated as much by political and economic agenda as it is by educational values and goals. To trace the concrete forms of political agenda, one relatively easy starting place is 1992. At that time in history, the Clinton-Gore team was preparing to enter Washington, and this administration had already identified technology as a key factor in both its domestic and international economic policies. At home, the Clinton-Gore team was facing a long-standing slowdown in manufacturing and productivity, persistent poverty, and an increasing income gap between the rich and the poor. As the 1997 *Economic Report to the President* tells the story:

For more than two decades America has faced serious problems: productivity growth has been slower than in the past, income inequity has increased, and poverty has persisted. In addition, serious challenges loom for the future, such as the aging of the baby boom, which threatens to create severe fiscal strains in the next century. (Council 18)

The administration knew well that its ability to address these problems and to inject new vigor into the domestic economy—or to convince the American public that it had done so—would be a deciding factor in the way the effectiveness of their administration was judged. On the international scene, the Clinton-Gore team faced three important and related changes in the world's economic picture: the end of the Cold War and the fall of Communism in the Soviet Union, the emergence of growing markets among the developing countries of East Asia and Latin America that threatened to capture an increasingly large percentage of the world's consumers, and the threatening increase in competition due to the global scope of the international economy.

To kill these two economic birds with one stone, the Clinton-Gore administration focused on the idea of expanding America's technology efforts—the design, manufacturing, and consumption of both technology and technological expertise. On the international scene, the administration took three steps to expand technology efforts. The first step involved defining America's focused area of specialization in the world marketplace as technology and information services:

> The Administration's economic policy has been an aggressive effort to increase exports through the opening of markets abroad. . . . The United States will certainly gain, both as a major exporter of information technology and as an importer, as American industries take advantage of new foreign technologies that will lower their costs and increase their productivity. (*Economic Report* 27)

The second and third steps involved exerting leadership in the development of a Global Information Infrastructure (GII) built on the back of the country's own National Information Infrastructure (NII). As part of this effort, the United States offered other countries—especially those with emerging markets that were hungry for technological involvement—the opportunity to buy American goods and services exported in connection with the GII. As Gore described the plan to the International Telecommunications Union in Buenos Aires in 1994:

> We can use the Global Information Infrastructure for technical collaboration between industrialized nations and developing countries. All agencies of the U.S. government are potential sources of information and knowledge that can be shared with partners across the globe. . . . The U.S. can help provide the technical know-how needed to deploy and use these new technologies. USAID and U.S. businesses have helped the U.S. Telecommunications Training Institute

train more than 3500 telecommunications professionals from the developing world, including many in this room.

Such a system also set up the possibility of continued reliance on American goods and services. Technicians trained in the deployment and use of American technology and American-designed operating systems, and American software, and American networks, for example, would tend to continue to rely on—and purchase—those products and components with which they were most familiar. Gore articulated the economic reasoning behind this plan:

> For us in the United States, the information infrastructure already is to the U.S. economy of the 1990s what transportation infrastructure was to the economy of the mid-20th century.

> The integration of computing and information networks into the economy makes U.S. manufacturing companies more productive, more competitive, and more adaptive to changing conditions . . .

The benefits associated with the GII expansion had political as well as economic effects. If the GII was constructed according to the Clinton-Gore plan, it would not only re-vitalize the American economy, it would also help promote the spread of democracy and capitalism around the globe within the context of a liberalized global economic system. The GII would accomplish this goal by providing forums for democratic involvement and expanded freedom of speech, by increasing privatization of technology resources, and by decreasing government regulation. As Gore noted:

> The GII will not only be a metaphor for a functioning democracy, it will in fact promote the functioning of democracy by greatly enhancing the participation of citizens in decision-making. And it will greatly promote the ability of nations to cooperate with each other. I see a new Athenian age of democracy forged in the fora the GII will create. . . .

> The integration of computing and information networks into the economy makes U.S. manufacturing companies more productive, more competitive, and more adaptive to changing conditions and it will do the same for the economies of other nations. . . .

> To promote; to protect, to preserve freedom and democracy, we must make telecommunications development an integral part of every nation's development. Each link we create strengthens the bonds of liberty and democracy around the world. By opening markets to stimulate the development of the global information infrastructure, we open lines of communication.

> By opening lines of communication, we open minds.

The international effort to expand technology, however, was only one part of the Clinton-Gore agenda. The other—and, in some ways, the more important—effort occurred in the domestic arena and focused on the revitalization of the American domestic economy through the expansion of the American computer industry. The Clinton-Gore team saw this particular industry as an economic "engine" (*Global Information* 3) that would, by increasing technological efforts at home, in turn, jump-start the international effort: providing the resources—the additional technology and the technological expertise—required to exploit emerging world markets.

To carry out this complex plan, the domestic engine of technology had to be cranked up and, to accomplish this goal, the Clinton-Gore administration knew that it had to accomplish two tasks:

- educate a pool of technologically sophisticated workers and technology specialists who could assist in the effort to reach new global markets and export more American manufactured equipment and specialized technology services to the rest of the world; and

- provide an influx of resources into the domestic computer industry so that it could simultaneously support the international effort and assume an increasingly important role in re-vitalizing the domestic economy.

And it was in response to these complexly related economic and political agenda that the national project to expand technological literacy was born. The dynamics that underlie this project were ideally and specifically suited to the economic and political goals we have just sketched out. Touted as an educational effort designed to improve citizens' literacy levels and, thus, their opportunities for future prosperity, the project was targeted at producing a continuing supply of educated workers who both had the skills necessary to design and manufacture increasingly sophisticated technological goods at home, and could offer sophisticated and specialized technological services in international arenas. Central to the task of achieving these targeted goals, the Clinton-Gore team recognized, was its ability to levy the power of the national educational system to reach large numbers of Americans in relatively short order. It was only within such a national system, they recognized, that an appropriately large proportion of the country's population could quickly acquire the training necessary to boost high-tech industries.

Importantly, such a plan was pretty close to self-fueling—citizens who learned the habits of reading, writing, and communicating on computers early in their lives within high-tech schools would tend to demand and consume such goods later in life when they graduated, thus injecting an increasingly continuous flow of money into the computer industry. And the plan's effects in the public sector promised to resonate effectively with its effects in the private sector: when citizens used, or were exposed to, cutting-edge in technologies in their workplaces, or in school settings, they would desire them, as well, in their homes—and they would purchase updated technologies more frequently. Further, to ensure the continuation of the same high-tech careers and industries that have served them so well, such citizens would also tend to vote in support of political and economic programs that involved the further expansion of technology markets both domestically and internationally. Such citizens, moreover, would recognize the key role that technological literacy plays in their own success, and, so, demand a similar education for their children.

From our perspective today, of course, we can see a darker side of this dynamic. The economic engine of technology must be fueled by—and produce—not only a continuing supply of individuals who are highly *literate* in terms of technological knowledge, but also an ongoing supply of individuals who fail to acquire technological literacy, those who are termed *"illiterate"* according to the official definition. These latter individuals provide the unskilled, low-paid labor necessary to sustain the system I have described—their work generates the surplus labor that must be continually re-invested in capital projects to produce more sophisticated technologies.

The people labeled as "illiterate" in connection with technology—as expected—are those with the least power to effect a change in this system. The come from families who attend the poorest schools in this country and they attend schools with the highest populations of students of color. In part because of such facts, these students have less access to technology, in general, and less access to more sophisticated technology during their educational years. Partially as a result of their educational backgrounds, such individuals are hired into less desirable, lower-paid positions that demand fewer official technological literacy skills.

Moreover, because skills in *technological* communication environments are so closely linked with literacy instruction *in general*, and because students who come from such backgrounds are afforded the poorest efforts of the educational system and the lowest expectations of many teachers, the label of "illiterate" has broader implications for these individuals' ability to acquire other skills through their formal schooling years.

REMEMBERING OUR OWN ROLE IN THE LITERACY/ILLITERACY CYCLE

The danger associated with such an extensive ideological system, as Terry Eagleton points out, is the effective processes of naturalization that it engenders. Successful ideological systems "render their beliefs natural and self evident" by so closely identifying them with "common sense" of a society so that nobody could imagine how they might ever be different (58). More importantly, as Eagleton continues,

> This process, which Pierre Bordieu calls *doxa*, involves the ideology in creating as tight a fit as possible between itself and social reality, thereby closing the gap into which the leverage of critique could be inserted. Social reality is redefined by the ideology to become coextensive with itself, in a way which occludes the truth that the reality in fact generated the ideology. . . . The result, politically speaking, is an apparently vicious circle: the ideology could only become transformed if the reality was such as to allow it to become objectified; but the ideology processes reality in ways which forestall this possibility. The two are thus mutually self-confirming. On this view, a ruling ideology does not so much combat alternative ideas as thrust them beyond the very bounds of the thinkable. (58)

It is within this effectively naturalized matrix of interests, I would argue, that English teachers all over this country have become the unwitting purveyors of technology and technological literacy—even as we try to avoid a technological focus by attending to more traditionally conceived topics within the humanities.

The paradoxical dynamics at the heart of this situation are difficult to wrap our minds around especially because they function at so many different levels. Because we fail to address the project to expand technological literacy in focused, systematic, and critical ways within the professional arenas available to us, English composition teachers have come to understand technology as "just another instructional tool" that they can choose either to use or ignore. And, working from this context, we divide ourselves into two perfectly meaningless camps—those who use computers to teach classes and those who don't. Both groups feel virtuous about their choices, and both manage to lose sight of the real issue. Computer-using teachers instruct students in how to *use* technology—but, all too often, they neglect to teach students how *to pay critical attention* to the issues generated by technology use. Teachers who choose *not* to use technology in their classes content themselves with the mistaken belief that their choice to avoid technology use absolves them and the students in their classes from *paying critical attention* to technology issues. In other words, both groups contribute to the very same end. And when such things happen, when we allow ourselves to ignore technological issues, when we take technology for granted, when it becomes invisible to us, when we forget technology's material bases—regardless of whether or not we use technology—we participate unwittingly in the inequitable literacy system I have just described.

PAYING ATTENTION TO ACTION

So can composition teachers address the complex linkages among technology, literacy, poverty, and race? The primary factors determining any individual's involvement, of course, must necessarily start with the local and specific—with social agents' own deep and penetrating knowledge of the specific colleges and universities in which they work; the particular families, communities, cultures within which we live and form our own understanding of the world; the individual students, teachers, administrators, board members, politicians, and parents whose lives touch ours.

As Donna Haraway reminds us, this kind of "situated knowledges-approach" (175) leads to a kind of "coyote" (189) way of knowing—one different from the traditional perspective of Science, but in that difference, capable of offering a "more adequate, richer, better account of the world" that makes it possible to "live in it well and in critical, reflexive relation to our own as well as others' practices" (178). Such an approach may provide "only partial perspective" (181), Haraway cautions, but it allows us to avoid the trap of claiming a scientific objectivity that invites a false sense of closure and overly simple answers.

This kind of paying attention can serve as a collective effort to construct a "larger vision" of our responsibilities as a profession, one that depends on a strong sense of many *somewheres* (e.g., schools, classrooms, districts, communities) "in particular" (187)—especially when such a project is undertaken with a critical understanding of what we are trying to accomplish with such work and a collective commitment to seeing social problems "faithfully from another's point of view" (181) and even when it is clear that such a vision must remain partial, distorted, and incomplete. In this way, our profession can assemble, from many local understandings "stitched together imperfectly" (183), a picture of technological literacy— as it now functions within our culture—that might allow us to act with more strategic effectiveness and force, both collectively and individually.

A situated knowledges-approach to paying attention also honors a multiplicity of responses to technological literacy. Given the constraints of local and specific contexts, and a commitment to engaging with the lives of individual students, for example, some teachers will find their best avenue of involvement to reside in individual agency, others will find increasing effectiveness when they work with other colleagues. Some educators will find work within their own classroom to be the most immediately pressing and others will find the action in local communities to offer the most immediate and successful venue for their work. Indeed, the appreciation of local situations and variations may help composition studies professionals understand the power of large-scale projects when they are built on the critical understandings and active participation of a diverse group of educators.

Operating from this understanding of the local and particular, suggestions for critical engagement with technological literacy issue must allow for wide variations in social, political, economic, and ideological positionings, and wide variations in teachers, students, administrators, citizens, and communities. In deference to this approach, the suggestions that follow focus on the typical *sites* for critically informed action on technological literacy (and on general areas of attention within such sites) rather than on specific projects that should be undertaken within these sites. Individual teachers and groups of teachers, students, parents, and school administrators must determine within such sites how best to pay increased and critical attention to the linkage between technology and literacy—recognizing as fully as possible the local conditions affecting the work they do.

In Curriculum Committees, Standards Documents, and Assessment Programs

We need to pursue opportunities for resisting projects and systems that serve to establish an overly narrow, official version of literacy practices or skills. Such projects and system simply serve to reward the literacy practices of dominant groups and punish the practices of others. They serve to reproduce a continuing and oppressive cycle of illiteracy, racism, and poverty in this country and in others.

Within these venues, composition specialists can lead the way in insisting on a diverse range of literacy practices and values, rather than one narrow and official form of literacy. We have made a start at this effort in the 1996 NCTE *Standards for the English Language Arts*, but CCCC needs to go much further in helping both future teachers and those already in classrooms understand why this work is so important and what implications their successes and failures may have.

In Our Professional Organizations

We need to recognize that if written language and literacy practices are our professional business, so is technology. This recognition demands a series of carefully considered and very visible professional stands on a variety of technological issues now under debate in this country: for example, on the access issues we have discussed, on the issue of technology funding for schools, on the issue of multiple venues for students' literacy practices, on the national project to expand technological literacy, and so on. We need to engage in much more of this kind of professional activism, and more consistently.

In Scholarship and Research

We also need to recognize that technological literacy is our responsibility. We need not only additional examinations of the ideological systems and cultural formations currently informing the literacy-technology link, but also the historical patterns established by other literacy technologies. And we need research like that Regina Copeland has just completed in West Virginia that takes a hard look at the access that individuals in various population groups—students of color, poor students, women—have to computer-supported literacy instruction, and of the expenditure of government and schools and family funds in support of technology and literacy. We also need additional research on how various technologies influence literacy values and practices and research on how teachers might better use technologies to support a wide range of literacy goals for different populations. We need work like that Nancy Guerra Barron has completed in LA to examine the bilingual online discussions of Latino students in a Chicano studies class and trace the ways in which these students manage to shape and use electronic environments productively to mirror the linguistic richness of their lives outside the classroom. These projects represent only some of the many that we can encourage.

In Language Arts and English Studies Classrooms, and in First-Year and Advanced English Composition Courses

We need to recognize that we can no longer simply educate students to become technology users—and consumers—without also helping them learn how to become critical thinkers about technology and the social issues surrounding its use. When English/language arts faculty require students to use computers in completing a range of assignments—without also providing them the time and opportunity to explore the complex issues that surround technology and technology use in substantive ways—we may, without realizing it, be contributing to the education of citizens who are habituated to technology use but who have little critical awareness about, or understanding of, the complex relationships between humans, machines, and the cultural contexts with which the two interact.

Composition teachers, language arts teachers, and other literacy specialists need to recognize that the relevance of technology in the English studies disciplines is not simply a matter of helping students work effectively with communication software and hardware, but, rather, also a matter of helping them to understand and to be able to assess—to pay attention to—the social, economic, and pedagogical implications of new communication technologies and technological initiatives that affect their lives. Knowledgeable literacy specialists at all levels need to develop age-appropriate and level-appropriate reading and writing activities aimed at this goal. This approach—which recognizes the complex links that now exist between literacy and technology at the end of the twentieth century—constitutes a *critical technological literacy* that will serve students well.

In Computer-Based Communication Facilities

We have to put scholarship and research to work as praxis. These technology-rich facilities can serve not only as teaching environments for students completing literacy assignments—as sites within which both faculty and students can develop their own critical technological literacy—but also as sites within which students and faculty can formulate guidelines and policies for critically informed practices that put these understandings to work in complicated social situations. Feenberg offers the possibility of considering such sites in terms of their *underdetermined* potential, a potential which can be exploited by interested and knowledgeable social agents determined to make a difference in their own and others' lives. Technology-rich communication facilities are already replete with such interested agents—the English/language arts teachers involved in designing and teaching within them, the students involved in using them and learning within them, the staff members (often students) responsible for keeping them operational, and the administrators who help to fund them.

In technology-rich communication facilities, students and teachers can develop a more critically-informed sense of technology by actively confronting and addressing technology issue in contexts that matter—contexts that involve real people (peers, faculty, community members, staff members) engaged in a range of daily practices (making decisions about software and hardware purchases, hiring individuals who can help teachers and students deal more effectively with technology, setting lab fee levels for students, deciding on etiquette and use guidelines, identifying access problems) within their various lived experiences and in light of their own goals. When confronted and addressed in these complicated and often contradictory contexts, technology and technological issues become connected with social issues, human values, and material conditions—rather than naturalized and separated from such experiences.

These sets of issues and others are all part of the process of managing technology-rich environments, and each is a component of the critical technological literacy we believe students must develop as they become effective social agents and citizens. Our culture will need these activists—in school board and PTO meetings, in small businesses, on corporate boards, and in government agencies where decisions about communication technologies will influence the personal and professional lives of citizens.

In Districts and Systems and States That Have Poor Schools, Rural Schools, and Schools with Large Populations of Students of Color

We need to resist the tendential forces that continue to link technological literacy with patterns of racism and poverty. We need to insist on and support more equitable distributions of technology.

In Our Voting for School Board Elections, in Committee Meetings, in Public Hearings, at National Conventions, in the Public Relations Statements of Our Professional Organizations

We have to argue—at every chance that we can get—that poor students and students of color get more access to computers and to more sophisticated computers, that teachers in schools with high populations of such students be given more support.

In Pre-Service and In-Service Educational Programs and Curricula

We need to help all English composition teachers get more education on both technology use and technology criticism. In the curricula comprising our own graduate programs and the educational programs that prepare teachers for careers in our profession, we need to make sure these programs don't simply teach young professionals to *use* computers—but rather, that we teach them how to pay attention to technology and the issues that result from, and contribute to, the technology-literacy linkage. It is no longer enough, for instance, simply to ask graduate students or colleagues to use computers in composition classes. Instead, we need to help them read in the areas of technology criticism, social theories, and computer studies and, then, provide them important opportunities to participate in making hard decisions about how to pay attention to technology issues in departments, colleges, and local communities; how to address the existing links between literacy and technology in undergraduate curricula; how to provide more access to technology for more people and how to help individuals develop their own critical consciousness about technology.

In Libraries, Community Centers, and Other Non-Traditional Public Places

We need to provide free access to computers for citizens at the poverty level and citizens of color—not only so that such individuals have access to computers and, thus, can become proficient in computer use for communication tasks, but also so that these citizens have access to the Internet and to online sites for collective political action (Oppel; Hoffman and Novak).

TOWARD AN END . . .

The lessons I have outlined in the preceding pages, as I am sure readers understand, are as much about literacy as they are about technology. But, as Bruno Latour notes, real-life stories *always* lack richness and accuracy when they are told from a single perspective. We require multiple perspectives if we hope to construct a robust and accurate understanding of the ways in which technology functions in our culture. Our profession's occasional respectful attention to technology and the social issues that surround technology may allow us to see things from a slightly different point of view, even if for only a moment in time. And from such a perspective, as Latour reminds us, our interpretations of issues "take on added density" (viii).

I might add that this occasional merging of the technological and the humanist perspectives—into a vision that is more robustly informed—has as much value for scientists and engineers as it does for humanists. Margaret Boden, an early pioneer in artificial intelligence, notes in the Introduction to her landmark 1977 book that she was drawn to the study of artificial intelligence for its potential in "counteracting the dehumanizing influence of natural science" and for its ability to "clarify the nature of human purpose, freedom, and moral choice," those "hidden complexities of human thinking" (4) that machines cannot replicate, that have always concerned us most within this profession.

One technology writer, Mark Weiser, has said that "The most profound technologies are those that disappear," that "weave themselves into the fabric of everyday life until they are indistinguishable from it" (94). I agree, but with a slightly different interpretation—these technologies may be the most *profound* when they disappear, but—it is exactly when this happens that they also develop the most potential for being *dangerous*. We have, as a culture, watched the twin strands of technology and literacy become woven into the fabric of our lives—they are now inscribed in legislation, in the law—in the warp and woof of our culture. But, recognizing this context, we cannot allow ourselves to lose sight of either formation. We must remind ourselves that laws write the texts of people's lives, that they constantly inscribe their intent and power on individuals—as Michel de Certeau says, "making its book out of them" (140).

It is our responsibility, as educators, to commit ourselves every day that we teach to reading and analyzing these texts, these lives of students—honestly, with respect, and to the very best of our collective and personal abilities. The alternative—of ignoring them, of perceiving students only in terms of their numbers in our schools or as members of undifferentiated groups—is simply unacceptable. As Elspeth Stuckey, Mike Rose, Harvey Graff, Brian Street, James Paul Gee, and many others have told us, when we participate in unthinking ways in political agendas, legislative initiatives, or educational systems that support an overly narrow version of official literacy, we all lose, and we are all implicated in the guilt that accrues to a system of violence through literacy.

It is my hope that by paying some attention to technology, we may learn lessons about becoming better humanists, as well.

WORKS CITED

Barron, Nancy Guerra. "Egalitarian Moments: Computer Mediated Communications in a Chicano Studies (ChS 111) Course." MA Thesis. California State U at Los Angeles, 1998.

Boden, Margaret. *Artificial Intelligence and Natural Man.* New York: Basic, 1977.

Bordieu, Pierre. *Outline of a Theory of Practice.* New York: Cambridge UP, 1977.

Coley, R. J., J. Crandler, and P. Engle. *Computers and Classrooms: The Status of Technology in U.S. Schools.* Princeton: ETS, 1997.

Copeland, Regina. "Identifying Barriers to Computer-Supported Instruction." Diss. West Virginia U, 1997.

Council of Economic Advisors. *Economic Report of the President.* Washington, DC: US Government Printing Office, 1997.

de Certeau, Michel. *The Practice of Everyday Life.* Trans. Steven Randall. Berkeley: U of California P, 1984.

Digest of Education Statistics 1996. Washington, DC: National Center for Education Statistics, Office of Educational Research and Improvement, 1996.

Eagleton, Terry. *Ideology: An Introduction.* London: Verso, 1991.

Faigley, Lester. "Literacy after the Revolution." *CCC* 48 (1987): 30–43.

Feenberg, Andrew. *The Critical Theory of Technology.* New York: Oxford UP, 1991.

Gee, James. *Social Linguistics and Literacies: Ideology in Discourses.* New York: Falmer, 1990.

Getting America's Students Ready for the 21st Century: Meeting the Technology Literacy Challenge: A Report to the Nation on Technology and Education. Washington, DC: US Dept. of Education, 1996.

Giddens, Anthony. *The Constitution of Society: Outline of the Theory of Structuration.* Berkeley: U of California P, 1985.

Gore, Albert Jr. *Global Information Infrastructure: Agency for Cooperation.* Washington, DC: Government Printing Office, 1995.

Gore, Albert Jr. "VP Remarks—International Telecommunications Union." Buenos Aires, Argentina, 21 March 1994. <http://www.whitehouse.gov/WH/EOP/OVP/html/telunion.html>.

Graff, Harvey J. *The Legacies of Literacy: Continuities and Contradictions in Western Culture and Society.* Bloomington: Indiana UP, 1987.

———. *The Literacy Myth: Cultural Integration and Social Structure in the Nineteenth Century.* New Brunswick: Transaction, 1991.

Green, Kenneth C. "The Campus Computing Project: The 1995 National Survey of Desktop Computing in Higher Education." 1996. <http://ericir.syr.edu/Projects/Campus_computing/1995/index.html>.

Haraway, Donna. "Situated Knowledges: The Science Question in Feminism and the Privilege of Partial Perspective." *Technology and the Politics of Knowledge.* Ed. Andrew Feenberg and Alastair Hannay. Bloomington: Indiana UP, 1995. 175–94.

Hoffman, Donna L., and Thomas P. Novak, "Bridging the Racial Divide on the Internet." *Science* 17 April 1998: 390–91.

Johnson-Eilola, Johndan. *Nostalgic Angels: Rearticulating Hypertext Writing.* Norwood: Ablex, 1997.

Latour, Bruno. *Aramis or the Love of Technology.* Trans. C. Porter. Cambridge: Harvard UP, 1996.

"MCI Nationwide Poll on Internet in Education." National Press Club. Washington, DC, 3 March 1998.

Michigan Curriculum Framework: Content Standards and Benchmarks. Lansing: Michigan Dept. of Education, 1995.

Ohmann, Richard. "Literacy, Technology, and Monopoly Capital." *College English* 47 (1985): 675–89.

Oppel, Shelby. "Computer Lab Offers Escape from Poverty." *St. Petersburg Times* 17 Sept. 1997: 3B.

Oppenheimer, Todd. "The Computer Delusion." *Atlantic Monthly*, July 1997: 45–62.

"Public Law 102–73, the National Literacy Act of 1991." House of Representatives Bill 751, 25 July 1991. <http://novel.nifl.gov/public-law.html>.

Rose, Mike. *Lives on the Boundary: The Struggles and Achievements of America's Underprepared.* New York: Free P, 1989.

Smith, Thomas M. *Condition of Education, 1997.* Washington, DC: National Center for Education Statistics, U.S. Government Printing Office, 1997. NCES 97–388.

Standards for the English Language Arts. Urbana: NCTE, 1996.

Street, Brian V. *Social Literacies: Critical Approaches to Literacy Development, Ethnography, and Education.* London: Longman, 1995.

Stuckey, J. Elspeth. *The Violence of Literacy.* Portsmouth: Boynton, 1990.

US Dept. of Education. Community Update, No. 56. "President Clinton Sends 1999 Budget to Congress." Office of Intergovernmental and Interagency Affairs, 1998.

Virilio, Paul. *Speed and Politics: An Essay on Dromology.* Trans. Mark Polizzotti. New York: Semiotext(e), 1986.

Weiser, Mark. "The Computer for the 21st Century." *Scientific American* 265.3 (Sept. 1991): 94–104.

Winner, Langdon. *The Whale and the Reactor: A Search for Limits in an Age of High Technology.* Chicago: U of Chicago P, 1986.

AFTERWORD: PAYING ATTENTION TO LITERACY AND TECHNOLOGY

In the CCCC Chair's address I delivered in Chicago in 1998, I asked composition teachers and scholars to pay attention to the increasingly complex linkages between literacy and technology—especially as these related to the digital divide evident in schools and homes in 1998 and to persistent patterns of intergenerational illiteracy and poverty.

Have these relationships changed? Have we altered the inequitable ways in which computer access and digital literacy have been aligned along the related axes of race and poverty? These questions are not simple ones—nor can they be answered in simple ways.

One answer is "No—the fundamental problems continue to exist." Consider these facts taken from updated reports on access to computer technology in U.S. homes and schools:

- Although there have been large increases in computer ownership among families of color and poor families, children from Caucasian families and high-income families remain more likely to have a computer at home (87 percent and 98 percent respectively) than children from African American families (71 percent), Hispanic families (68 percent), and poor families (65 percent) (*Connected* 3).
- This same pattern informs family Internet access. Although there have been large increases in Internet access among families of color and poor families, children from Caucasian families (49 percent) and high-income families (66 percent) remain more likely to have Internet access at home than children from African American families (29 percent), Hispanic families (33 percent), and poor families (29 percent) (*Connected* 5).
- Although schools in general have enjoyed steadily increasing access to technology and the Internet in instructional rooms (from 3 percent in 1994 to 92 percent in 2002), a significantly smaller percentage of inner city schools (88

percent) and rural schools (93 percent) than suburban schools (96 percent) enjoyed such access (Kleiner and Lewis 13).

- Although schools in general have enjoyed steadily increasing access to technology and the Internet in instructional rooms, schools with a high percentage of minority enrollment were less likely to employ a full time, paid technology coordinator (32–34 percent) than were schools with low minority enrollments (49 percent) (Kleiner and Lewis 15).

- Although the ratio of students to computers has improved—especially in schools enrolling a high proportion of poor students—the ratio of students to computers with Internet access remained persistently aligned along the axes of class. The ratio was highest in schools with high proportions of poor students and lowest in schools with low proportions of poor students (6.8 percent compared to 5.5 percent) (Kleiner and Lewis 16).

- Although schools in general have enjoyed steadily increasing access to technology and the Internet, before-school access to computers connected to the Internet remains aligned along the related axes of race and poverty. Such access is less frequent in schools with high minority enrollments (62 percent) and poor schools (57 percent) than it is in schools with low minority enrollments (78–80 percent) and wealthy schools (75–82 percent) (Kleiner and Lewis 18).

A different answer might start with, "Yes—there has been change, but not necessarily for the better." My original CCCC talk focused on the relationship between literacy and technology in the United States. In recent years, sociologists, economists, and technology scholars as well as nongovernmental organizations such as the United Nations and the World Bank have begun to pay increasingly close attention to the digital divide on a global scale—studying the disparity between people who have access to and use of computer technologies, computer networks, and the specialized technological education needed to maintain a digital infrastructure and those who do not.

The primary impetus for this work is the recognition that computers and other digital technologies are not simply an outcome or "reward of successful development," but, rather, that "they can help make change happen"—especially with regard to improving the environment for the acquisition and development of literacy, increasing people's access to knowledge, and connecting them with others who have similar interests and needs. Technology, in other words, can be a "critical tool" for achieving human development (*Human Development Report* iii).

Problematic patterns of technology diffusion, however, exist on the global stage—just as they do within the United States. Consider, for example, the following perspectives:

- Global patterns of access to technology are aligned along existing economic axes. Indeed, the nations that might benefit the most from technological innovation are in the worst position to exploit it. For instance, 94 percent of all Internet users live in the forty richest countries in the world (*Facts and Figures* 31). The average Bangladeshi, in contrast, needs "more than 8 years' income and the average American just one month's salary to purchase a computer" (*Facts and Figures* 31).

- Global patterns of technology use—and digital literacy practices—are also aligned along the axis of education, a condition related directly to wealth. Internet users are, for the most part, both better educated and wealthier than non-users. Approximately 30 percent of Internet users, for example, have a university degree (*Facts and Figures* 31). In Bulgaria, the poorest 65 percent of the population accounts for only 29 percent of Internet users. In Chile, 89 percent of Internet users have had tertiary education, in Sri Lanka, 65 percent, and in China, 70 percent (*Human Development Report* 40).

- Telecommunications and Internet costs are particularly high in developing countries. As the United Nations *Human Development Report* indicates, "Monthly Internet access charges amount to 1.2 percent of average monthly income for a typical US user compared with 614 percent in Madagascar, 278 percent in Nepal, 191 percent in Bangladesh and 60 percent in Sri Lanka" (80).

Adding to the complexity of this global context, I believe, are our country's recent wars in Afghanistan and Iraq. The billions of dollars allocated to these undertakings—especially when combined with the monies spent on increased homeland security—has had a *direct and negative* economic impact on available levels of education and educational funding in the U.S. Given these new fiscal realities, the cost of access to education and literacy programs is bound to increase. In 2003, for example, public college and universities raised tuition by 14 percent. As the Revitalizing Education Project estimates, this increase means that

> 400,000 qualified high school graduates will not pursue a full-time, four-year degree because of an inability to pay. More than 100,000 students are in danger of dropping out of school due to increased tuition costs. Even worse, college costs stop nearly half of low-income students from attending a public four year school. In 1975–76 a Pell grant covered 84 percent of tuition at a four year public school—now it only covers 39 percent ("College Should Be Affordable").

This realignment of priorities—toward war and away from social programs— diverts important funding from projects that might otherwise increase equitable access to computer technology in schools, address the need for smaller class sizes, provide broader funding for literacy programs, lower tuition to affordable levels, and increase the possibility that poor students will have access to an education rich in all of these areas ("Cost of War"). The U.S. War on Terrorism, of course, has also had a direct and negative impact on education and literacy programs in the countries we have invaded. As Bennis reports,

> UNICEF estimates that more than 200 [Iraqi] schools were destroyed in the conflict and thousands more were looted in the chaos following the fall of Saddam Hussein. Largely because of security concerns, school attendance in April 2004 was well below pre-war levels (7).

In sum—our work is far from done. I believe, more than ever, we need to pay attention to the changing nature of literacy and to work with even greater diligence on improving the resources our nation allocates to literacy and education. Further, we need to *expand our commitment* to exploring the complex relationships among literacy, technology, race, and poverty, and to addressing current and persistent inequities in these areas.

—CYNTHIA SELFE
The Ohio State University

WORKS CITED

Bennis, Phyllis; IPS Task Force. "Paying the Price: The Mounting Costs of the Iraq War: A Study by the Institute for Policy Studies and Foreign Policy in Focus." 24 June 2004. 25 Aug. 2004 <http://www.ips-dc.org/iraq/costsofwar/#key>.

"College Should Be Affordable." *Bush's Budget Fails Education: An Issue by Issue Analysis of How Bush Misses the Mark.* The Revitalizing Education Project. 2004. Campaign for America's Future. 25 Aug. 2004 <http://www.ourfuture.org/issues_and_campaigns/educatioin/20040202_edu_budget.cfm>.

Connected to the Future: A Report on Children's Internet Use from the Corporation for Public Broadcasting. Mar. 2003. 25 Aug. 2004 <www.cpb.org/pdfs/ed/resources/connected>.

"The Cost of War for States and Selected Cities." National Priorities Project. 2004. 25 Aug. 2004 <http://www.nationalpriorities.org/Issues/Military/Iraq/CostOfWar.html>.

Facts and Figures 2000. UNESCO Institute for Statistics. 2000. 25 Aug. 2004 <www.uis.unesco.org/en/pub/ doc/facts&figures_eng.pdf>.

Human Development Report 2001: Making New Technologies Work for Human Development. United Nations Development Programme. New York: Oxford UP, 2001.

Kleiner, Anne, and Lauri Lewis. *Internet Access in U.S. Public Schools and Classrooms: 1994–2002.* A Report from the U.S. Department of Education, National Center for Educational Statistics (NCES 2004–011). October 2003. Washington.

1999

On the Rhetoric and Precedents of Racism

VICTOR VILLANUEVA

U na Historia

The scene is Peru. It's the early 16th century. Father Valverde, a Franciscan, is speaking to the Incan philosopher-rhetorician about the ways of the world. The Franciscan intends to be instructive, to attempt to raise the indigenous from its ignorance. But the Incan doesn't recognize the developmental mindset and enters into dialectical interplay. Having heard of how things work according to Father Valverde, the Incan responds:

> You listed five preeminent men whom I ought to know. The first is God, three and one, which are four, whom you call the creator of the universe. Is he perhaps our Pachacámac and Viracocha? The second claims to be the father of all men, on whom they piled their sins. The third you call Jesus Christ, the only one not to cast sins on that first man, but he was killed. The fourth you call pope. The fifth, Carlos, according to you, is the most powerful monarch of the universe and supreme over all. However, you affirm this without taking account of other monarchs. But if this Carlos is prince and lord of all the world, why does he need the pope to grant him concessions and donations to make war on us and usurp our kingdoms? And if he needs the pope, then is not the pope the greater lord and most powerful prince of all the world, instead of Carlos? Also you say that I am obliged to pay tribute to Carlos and not to others, but since you give no reason for this tribute, I feel no obligation to pay it. If it is right to give tribute and service at all, it ought to be given to God, the man who was Father of all, then to Jesus Christ who never piled on his sins, and finally to the pope. . . . But if I ought not give tribute to this man, even

---

This article is a revised version of the Chair's address Victor Villanueva delivered at the CCCC Convention in Atlanta, Georgia, on March 25, 1999. It was first published by *CCC*, volume 50, number 4, June 1999.

less ought I give it to Carlos, who was never lord of these regions and whom I have never seen.

The record of this meeting with Atahualpa notes that,

> The Spaniards, unable to endure this *prolixity of argumentation,* jumped from their seats and attacked the Indians and grabbed hold of their gold and silver jewels and precious stones. (Dussel 53)

A little earlier, 1524, a little further north, Mexico. Twelve recently arrived Spanish Franciscan missionaries have agreed to a dialogue with the indigenous people of the region. The Aztecan delegation consists of a group of *tlamatinime,* or philosophers. Somewhere between the ages of six and nine, young Aztecs (which might have included women) left their families to join the *Calmécac* community. There, they received a rigorous education based on discussions with teachers, or wise ones (*Huebuetlatoli*). The discussions will allow the young Aztecs to acquire the wisdom already known (*momachtique*), a wisdom which is to be rendered in the adequate word (*in quali tlatolli*). This, then, was the Aztecan trivium, displayed in the rhetoric called the flower-and-song (*in xochitl in cuícatl*) (Dussel 95–97).

The *tlamatinime* address the missionaries in the manner of the flower-and-song, in what could be read as a five-part rhetorical rendition. First, there is a salutation and introduction:

> Our much esteemed lords: What travail have you passed through to arrive here. Here, before you, we ignorant people contemplate you.
>
> What shall we say? What *should we direct to your ears?* Are we anything by chance? We are only a vulgar people.

The *proemium*-like intro done, the *tlamatinime* turn to the matter at hand, an attempt to enter into a dialogue concerning the doctrine that the missionaries had brought. The Aztecan flower-and-song enters into a context-setting that is like the classical Roman *narratio*:

> Through the interpreter we will respond by returning the-nourishment-and-the-word to the lord-of-the-intimate-which-surrounds-us. For his sake, we place ourselves in danger. . . . Perhaps our actions will result in our perdition or destruction, but where are we to go? We are common mortals. *Let us now then die; let us now perish* since *our gods have already died.* But calm your heart-of-flesh, lords, for we will break with the customary for a moment and open for you a little bit the *secret,* the ark of the lord, our God.

Next, *dispositio*:

> You have said the *we do not know* the lord-of-the-intimate-which-surrounds-us, the one from whom the-heavens-and-the-earth come. You have said that our gods were not *true* gods.

We respond that we are perturbed and hurt by what you say, because our progenitors never spoke this way.

Refutatio takes the form of three topics not unlike Aristotle's: authority, ideology as worldview, and antiquity. The first is authority:

Our progenitors passed on the *norm of life* they held as *true* and the doctrine that we should worship and honor the gods.

Such doctrine is consistent with the Aztecan worldview:

They taught . . . that these gods give us life and have gained us for themselves . . . in the beginning. These gods provide us with sustenance, drink and food including corn, beans, goose feet (*bledos*), and *chia*, all of which conserve life. We pray to these gods for the water and rain needed for crops. These gods are happy . . . *where they exist*, in the place of *Tlalocan*, where there is neither hunger, nor sickness, nor poverty.

Then the appeal to antiquity:

And in what form, when, where were these gods first invoked? . . . This occurred a very long time ago in Tula, Huapalcalco, Xuchatlapan, Tlamohuanchan, Yohuallican, and Teotihuacan. These gods have established their dominion over the entire universe (*cemanauac*).

Conclusio

Are we now to destroy the ancient *norm of our life?*—the *norm of life* for the Chichimecas, the Toltexs, the Acolhuas, and the Tecpanecas? We *know* to whom we owe our birth and our lives.

We refuse to be tranquil or to believe as truth what you say, even if this offends you.

We lay out our reasons to you, lords, who govern and sustain the whole world (*cemanáhualt*). Since we have handed over all our power to you, *if we abide here, we will remain only prisoners.* Our final response is do with us as you please. (Dussel 112–14)

No multiculturalism there, no cultural hybrid possible, though some try hard now to reclaim the Incan or Aztecan, try hard to be more than the Eurocentric *criollo* of Latin America.

ALGUNAS IDEAS

As academics and teachers we become accustomed to juggling dozens of constraints at a time. We adjust to the multidimensional nature of our jobs. But just for a little while we'd like to focus on one aspect of our careers, work one thing through. Except for the occasional sabbatical leave some of us are granted in our jobs, however, the best we can usually do is set priorities. It's something of the too-much-to juggle mindset, I would say, that gives rise to multiculturalism. So many inequities, so much rampant bigotry leveled at so many things. None of it should be ignored. But if we're to set priorities, I would ask that we return to the question of racism, the "absent presence" in our discourse (Prendergast). Although gays and lesbians are subject to more acts of hate in this country right now than any other group, the attacks are most often leveled at gays and lesbians of color (Martínez 134). Women of color carry a double yoke, to use Buchi Emecheta's words, being women and being of color. And it's a secret to no one that the greatest number of poor are people of color. This is not to say that the eradication of racism—even if possible—would mean the eradication of bigotry and inequity. It is to say that as priorities go, racism seems to have the greatest depth of trouble, cuts across most other bigotries, is imbricated with most other bigotries, and also stands alone, has the greatest number of layers. According to Mike Davis:

> No matter how important feminist consciousness must be . . . , racism remains the divisive issue within class and gender [and sexual orientation]. . . . The real weak link in the domestic base of American imperialism is a Black and Hispanic working class, fifty million strong. This is the nation within a nation, society within a society, that alone possesses the numerical and positional strength to undermine the American empire from within. (299, 313–14)

The numbers have risen since Davis wrote this in 1984. And he failed to mention the Asian Americans and Pacific Islanders, the amazing percentages that don't succeed and the others who are "model minorities" rather than simply assimilated. Or the American Indians. Racism continues to be among the most compelling problems we face. Part of the reason why this is so is because we're still unclear about what we're dealing with, so we must thereby be unclear about how to deal with it.

Part of that insecurity about what it is we face when we talk or write about racism can be seen in our references to "race and ethnicity." I've used the term myself, to distinguish what we are biologically from how we're treated or regarded, to point to the ways in which racism doesn't always affect those who are visibly different from the majority. But referring to ethnicity is tricky and carries connotations that don't necessarily apply to people of color in the U.S.

Ethnicity grows out of a consciousness of an older, less sustainable racism. The concept of ethnicity first evolved in response to Social Darwinism, traveling through the 1920s to the 1960s, at which time class and colonialist concerns came to the fore (Omi and Winant, Grosfoguel, Negrón-Muntaner, Georas). Since the 1960s, the talk of colonialism has taken a new turn, and the realization that racism remains even when there is class ascension had made for something of a separation between discussions of class and of color. So ethnicity is back, now decidedly associated with race. And with ethnicity comes the concept that was historically a subset of ethnicity, *cultural pluralism* (Omi and Winant 12).

Ethnicity received its most complete treatment in Nathan Glazer and Daniel P. Moynihan's *Beyond the Melting Pot: The Negroes, Puerto Ricans, Jews, Italians, and Irish of New York City,* first published in 1963, with a second edition in 1970. Glazer and Moynihan describe a process that sounds much like hybridity, a postcolonial term enjoying currency. Ethnic groups do not necessarily assimilate, say Glazer and Moynihan:

> Ethnic groups . . . even after distinctive language, customs, and culture are lost . . . are continually recreated by new experiences in America. The mere existence of a name itself is perhaps sufficient to form group character in new situations, for the name associates an individual, who actually can be anything, with a certain past, country, or race.

So something new emerges in the acculturation process—neither fish nor fowl, a new language and culture with ties to something older. And this new thing is an *interest group.* Glazer and Moynihan continue:

> But as a matter of fact, someone who is Irish or Jewish or Italian generally has other traits than the mere existence of the name that associates him with other people attached to the group. A man in connected to his group by ties of family and friendship. But he is also connected by ties of *interests.* The ethnic groups in New York are also *interest groups.* (qtd. in Omi and Winant 18)

From this it wasn't much of a leap to the bootstraps mentality, with Glazer and Moynihan writing in 1975 that "ethnic groups bring different norms to bear on common circumstances with consequent different levels of success—hence *group* differences in status," so that any group that fails does so by virtue of flaws in the group's "norms," as in the stereotypical contention that the dropout rate among Chicanos and Latinos are so high because Latino culture does not prize education like other groups do (qtd. in Omi and Winant 21).

Because this country has always consisted of many groupings (even before the first Europeans), the notion of ethnicity rings true. And because so many ethnicities still feel attachments to their ancestry, even if only as nostalgia, the concept of a cultural plurality sounds right. Ethnicity and the cultural plurality suggested by multiculturalism appeal to common sense in ways that can address racism—and sometimes they do, maybe often—but without tugging at its hegemony with the kind force so many of us would wish.

Racism runs deep. Consider some of the litany of the 1980s with which E. San Juan opens his book on *Racial Formations/Critical Transformations*:

Vigilante gunman Bernard Goetz catapulted into a folk hero for shooting down four black youths in a New York subway. Fear of Willy Horton, a black inmate helped elect a president. . . . Antibusing attacks in the early eighties in most big cities. The 1982 murder of Chinese American Vincent Chin mistaken by unemployed Detroit autoworkers for a Japanese. . . . The election to the Louisiana legislature of Republican David Duke, former head of the Ku Klux Klan. (1)

And also:

- We watched the 1992 beating of Rodney King, watched Alicia Soltero Vásquez being beaten by Border Patrolmen.

- San Francisco, 1997. Two young Latino children are found completely covered in flour. They wanted their skin to be white enough to go to school, they say.

- Oxnard, 1995, Mexican and Chicana women working at a Nabisco plant are denied toilet breaks. They are told to wear diapers during their shift.

- Rohnert Park, 1997. Police kill a Chinese engineer, father of three, who had come home drunk and angry after having put up with racist insults at a bar. He's loud. A neighbor calls the police. Still drunk, he grabs a one-eighth inch thick stick, brandishes it. He's shot. His wife, a nurse, is disallowed to administer care. He's handcuffed. Dies while awaiting an ambulance. The reason for shooting him? The police were afraid he would use martial arts with that one-eighth inch stick (Martínez 10–11).

We know that incidents like these are ubiquitous. And we know they're on our campuses—at the University of Nevada, at Miami University of Ohio, at my own campus. Everywhere.

Multiculturalism hasn't improved things much, not even at the sites where students are exposed to such things. Maybe the relatively low numbers of people of color on our campuses or in our journals—or the high numbers at community colleges with disproportionately few of color among the faculty—reinforce racist conceptions. The disproportionately few people of color in front of the classrooms or in our publications, given the ubiquity of the bootstrap mentality, reifies the conception that people of color don't do better because they don't try harder, that most are content to feed off the State. The only apparent generalized acknowledgement of racism as structural comes by way of the perception of a reverse discrimination.

Yet the numbers underscore that there is no reversal. Latinos have the highest poverty rates from all Americans—24%, with Navajo close behind, followed by African Americans (Martínez 7). And there's no use blaming insufficiency in English, as Latinos and Navajo lose their native tongues, the Navajo struggling to hold on to their Dine' language (Veltman, DeGroat).

Among Latinos, 64% are native to the U.S. Half of all Latinos never complete high school, the highest percentage for all groups (Dept. of

Health). Although segregation by race is no longer legal, there is an economic segregation, a white and middle-class flight from inner cities that relegates African American and Latino students to schools that lack a strong tax base and are thereby poorly funded (Martínez 7). While Latinos make up over 12% of the public school population, less than 4% of faculty or administration are Latina or Latino, and less than 1% of those who sit on school boards as voting members are Latina or Latino.

Of course, some do make it to higher education. Twenty percent of those who receive Associate Degrees are of color. Of that 20%, Latinas and Latinos account for 6%. Those rates are relatively the same through Bachelors and Masters degrees. At the doctoral level, Asian Americans earn about 4.5% of all PhDs, African Americans 3%, Latinos 2%, American Indians about .3%, and white folks who are not Latina or Latino 61% (the remaining 27% going to foreign nationals) (37, 39). In English Language and Literature for 1995, Latinos and Latinas received 26 PhDs — not 26% but 26: 8 for Latinos and 18 for Latinas — African Americans 37, Asian Americans 35, American Indians 7. White folks who were not Latino received 1,268 — of which 743 were awarded to women (US Dept. of Education). That's 1,268 white to 26 Latino or Latina PhDs in English. I have so little patience with reverse discrimination.

These numbers could still be broken down by field within English, but there are no clear numbers that include race breakdowns. If CCCC membership demographics can tell us much, though, the numbers aren't encouraging, with a 92% white membership, 5% African American, 1.4% Chicanos or Latino, 1% Asian American, and 0.5% Native American/American Indian. And there is only the most infinitesimal amount of representation in our journals, with *TETYC* giving the most attention to race issues of the three journals searched (*TETYC, CCC,* and *College English*), with none in a search by article titles looking at issues concerning Latinas or Latinos — not even to address the English-Only movement.

Even though members of CCCC and NCTE have tended to treat its members of color with respect and have advanced our numbers into positions of leadership regularly, and even though both NCTE and CCCC will soon be entering into a membership campaign that should increase the pool of people of color, I believe that our best recruiting tool for those graduate students of color, the undergraduates of color, the students who have vaulted the fault line and are in college at all will not be the pictures of people of color in the *Council Chronicle* or in the convention program books or even at our wonderful conventions — since all of those media mainly reach the already-subscribed; rather, it will be through our journals, the journals on library shelves or online, with people of color writing frankly, sympathetically about matters concerning racism, and all of us writing about what matters to those students of color. That's what will attract people of color in sufficient numbers to begin to affect racism. We can do better than 7% among our teachers and scholars of color, better than a representation that is statistically insignificant in our journals.

CUENTOS

A number of graduate students of color in English at my campus write an article for the school newspaper which gains a full-page spread. Its title, "Black Masks, White Masks," parodies a famous book on colonialism and race by Frantz Fanon. The grad students write that they no longer wish to be reduced to wearing white masks if they are to succeed in the university, that the denial of their being of color affords them nothing but their silencing. Among their examples of the racism they feel, they write of a Halloween party in which one of their fellows appeared in blackface (Dunn et al. 6).

A meeting of grad students and department faculty. Tempers run hot. Blackface says he never meant to offend. He was paying homage to the great jazz and blues musicians of the past, playing Muddy Waters tunes. He would have been born in the 1970s, maybe unaware of a dark history of such homages.

> *Holiday Inn*: Bing Crosby in blackface, singing "Who was it set the darkies free? Abraham. Abraham." Mr. Crosby surely didn't mean to offend. But that was then, you might have said before this little *cuentito*.

Stunned silence. A student of color leaves.

A large-seeming fellow, red hair, small, blue eyes, always earnest, always speaking with broad gestures from large, thick hands, all befreckled, always the one to find contradictions. He stands. Says that as he sees it, this thing about silencing doesn't wash, that those complaining about it are the very ones who are always speaking up in classes, and that (without a breath) he can't think of a one from among the faculty present who doesn't speak of multiculturalism, that the damned text used in the first-year composition program is really an Ethnic Studies book, for gosh sake (or words to that effect). (The book is Ronald Takaki's *A Different Mirror*, "a history of multicultural America," according to the subtitle, its author, "a professor in the Ethnic Studies Department" at his university.) All are effectively silenced for a dramatically long moment.

Then, from behind the semi-circle of chairs, a South Asian woman stands. She self-identifies as a person of color, as one of those colonized by another's empire, British accent to her speech, dark brown skin, large black eyes that seem to well with tears, thick black mane framing her small face. She's clearly agitated. Breaks the silence. She speaks about the difference between speaking and being heard, that if one is constantly speaking but it never heard, never truly heard, there is, in effect, silence, a silencing. She says that speaking of ethnic studies or multiculturalism is less the issue than how racism seems always to be an appendage to a classroom curriculum, something loosely attached to a course but not quite integral, even when race is the issue.

She, two Latinas, and one African American woman had attended, then boycotted a graduate seminar on Feminist Theory a few semesters before. Expecting that the most common and longest form of oppression in human history, gender discrimination, would serve as a bond that would tie them to the other class members and the professor, these four women were surprised, then hurt, then angered, at their silencing by their sisters. One of the Latinas does her presentation in Spanish, says "Nobody listens anyway." No one commented, or even acknowledged not knowing what she had said. The African American woman posted a message on an African American listserv warning others not to apply to the school, that it was too deeply racist.

A poem by Puerto Rican poet Victor Hernández Cruz:

Anonymous

And if I lived in those olden times
With a funny name like Choicer or
Henry Howard, Earl of Surrey, what chimes!
I would spend my time in search of rhymes
Make sure the measurement termination surprise
In the court of kings snapping till woo sunrise
Plus always be using the words *alas* and *hath*
And not even knowing that that was my path
Just think on the Lower East Side of Manhattan
I would have been like living in satin
Alas! The projects hath not covered the river
Thou see-est vision to make thee quiver
Hath I been delivered to that "wildernesse"
So past
I would have been the last one in the
Dance to go
Taking note the minuet so slow
All admire my taste
Within thou *mambo* of much more haste.

One of my daughters had had enough with the teacher who singled her and her girlfriends out, except the Latina girlfriend from Venezuela, who bore European features and a French and German name, never called out even though she did in fact cut up with the others when they were cuttin' up. My daughter had shaken her booty at the teacher after a disciplining of one sort or another. The teacher: "That might be okay in your culture, but not in mine." I don't think multiculturalism took.

A meeting with that teacher and the principal. After explanations, I break into a lecture about racism. I do that. Often. From the Principal: "We had some problems with that at the beginning of the year, but we took care of them." And I want to know how he solved the problem of our nation "at the beginning of the year."

A joke to some and not to others tells about an immigration official who detains the Puerto Rican at the border. "But I'm Puerto Rican," says the detained citizen. "I don't care what kind of Mexican you are," says the official.

A poem by Sandra María Esteves:

From Fanon

We are a multitude of contradictions
reflecting our history
oppressed
controlled
once free folk
remnants of that time interacting in our souls

Our kindred was the earth
polarity with the land
respected it
called it mother
were sustained and strengthened by it

The european thru power and fear became our master
his greed welcomed by our ignorance
tyranny persisting
our screams passing unfulfilled

As slaves we lost identity
assimilating our master's values
overwhelming us to become integrated shadows
unrefined and dependent

We flee escaping, becoming clowns in an alien circus
performing predictably
mimicking strange values
reflecting what was inflicted

Now the oppressor has an international program
and we sit precariously within the monster's mechanism
internalizing anguish from comrades
planning and preparing a course of action.

ON BREAKING PRECEDENTS

I have failed some tests, have had a fellow worker bleed in green and red over a paper I had wished to submit for publication, have gotten the maybe-you-could-consider-submitting-this-essay-somewhere-else letter from journal editors. That's just part of the job. But I have only once felt insulted. Some years have passed, and I have forgotten the editor who had written my rejection letter; I've even forgotten the journal, I realize as I write this. But I still bear a grudge. The essay challenged the idea of a postcolonialism, invoking Frantz Fanon. The Rejecter said he saw no reason to resurrect Fanon. The essay also cited Aristotle and Cicero. Their resurrection went unquestioned. Rejecter also said that he feared that in bringing in Fanon, I risked essentializing. *Essentialism,* as I understand the term, is the "belief in real, true human essence, existing outside of or impervious to social and historical context" (Omi and Winant 187). But I had argued in that piece, as I have always argued, that race in America is a result of colonialism, that "racial discrimination and racial prejudice are phenomena of colonialism," to use John Rex's words (75). This is historical, not merely a matter of physiognomy. How was I essentializing?

In the years that have followed that infuriating letter, I have seen my concern of that essay echoed, seen a rekindled interest in Fanon grow and grow, and have heard how others of color have been insulted by a particular use of the word *essentializing.* Henry Louis Gates in an essay titled "On the Rhetoric of Racism in the Profession," for example, writes that

> Long after white literature has been canonized, and recanonized, our attempts to define a black American canon—foregrounded on its own against a white backdrop—are often decried as racist, separatist, nationalist, or "essentialist" (my favorite term of all). (25)

And so maybe that was the problem, that I had been read as taking on an old, 1960s type of argument for nationalism among people of color in bringing up Fanon's rendering of internal colonialism.

Now as I try to think of how this profession can improve on its multiculturalism, do more than assuring that people of color are represented in our materials, more than assuring that people of color are read and heard in numbers more in keeping with the emerging demographics of the nation and the world, I remain tied to the belief that we must break from the colonial discourse that binds us all. What I mean is that there are attitudes from those we have revered over the centuries which we inherit, that are woven into the discourse that we inherit. I believe this happens. But even if not, consider the legacy.

Among all that is worthwhile in the intellectual discourse we inherit from the colonizers of the United States, there is also a developmental and racist discourse. Here is how Kant, in 1784, answers the question as to "What is Enlightenment?"

> Enlightenment (*Aufklärung*) is the exit of humanity by itself from a state of culpable immaturity (*verschuldeten Unmündigkeit*). . . .

Laziness and cowardliness are the causes which bind the great part of humanity in this frivolous state of immaturity. (qtd. in Dussel 20)

For Hegel,

Universal history goes from East to West. Europe is absolutely the *end of universal history.* Asia is the beginning.

Africa is in general a closed land, and it maintains this fundamental character. It is characteristic of the blacks that their consciousness has not yet even arrived at the intuition of any objectivity. . . . He is a human being in the rough.

This mode of being of the Africans explains the fact that it is extraordinarily easy to make them fanatics. The Reign of the Spirit is among them so poor and the Spirit in itself so intense . . . that a representation that is inculcated in them suffices them not to respect anything and to destroy everything.

And as for Spain, Hegel continues:

Here one meets the lands of Morocco, Fas (not Fez), Algeria, Tunis, Tripoli. One can say that this part does not properly belong to Africa, but more to Spain, with which it forms a common basin. De Pradt says for this reason that when one is in Spain one is already in Africa. This part of the world . . . forms a niche which is limited to sharing the destiny of the great ones, a destiny which is decided in other parts. It is not called upon to acquire its own proper figure. (qtd. in Dussel 21–24)

This is the legacy of racism. And how is it passed on? The Naturalization Act of 1790—1790!—denying rights of full citizenship to nonwhites (Takaki, "Reflections"). The Chinese Exclusion Act of 1882. The 1928 Congressional Hearings on Western Hemisphere Immigration:

Their minds run to nothing higher than animal functions—eat, sleep, and sexual debauchery. In every huddle of Mexican shacks one meets the same idleness, hordes of hungry dogs, and filthy children with faces plastered with flies, disease, lice, human filth, stench, promiscuous fornication, bastardly, lounging, apathetic peons and lazy squaws, beans and dried fruit, liquor, general squalor, and envy and hatred of the gringo. These people sleep by day and prowl by night like coyotes, stealing anything they can get their hands on, no matter how useless to them it may be. Nothing left outside is safe unless padlocked or chained down. Yet there are Americans clamoring for more of these human swine to be brought over from Mexico. (Estrada et al. 116)

And after the slurs run through the mind, there comes the question as to how this is an issue of immigration to the Western Hemisphere as a whole, rather than simply to one country of the Western Hemisphere. To understand that, we would need to recognize the discourse of diplomacy toward our neighbors to the South since the time of John Quincy Adams, summed up in an 1820s lecture to new envoys to Central and South America:

> If the United States has received but little gratitude, this is only to be expected in a world where gratitude is rarely accorded to the teacher, the doctor, or the policeman, and we have been all three. But it may be that in time they will come to see the United States with different eyes, and have for her something of the respect and affections with which a man regards the instructor of his youth and a child looks upon the parent who has molded his character. (Schoultz 386)

Or George Bush referring to Daniel Ortega's presence at a meeting as like an unwelcome dog at a garden party (Schoultz vii, 386). And after the summer hurricanes hit Central America during the summer of '98, we all heard Bush's pleas for aid for Honduras, since if such were not granted, those people might come here.

From Kant to our current politicians, from the exclusion of somehow "essentialized" notions of race to ongoing English-Only laws and the end of Affirmative Action, we are steeped in racism. And we are steeped in a colonial discourse, one which continues to operate from a developmental rather than dialectical model—despite our best efforts.

If Latin America is like a child to the U.S., the U.S. continues to act as the colonial offspring of Europe. Here's an analogy from diplomacy. Historian Lars Schoultz writes:

> When a State Department official begins a meeting with the comment "we have a problem with the government of Peru," in less than a second the other participants instinctively turn to a mental picture of a foreign state that is quite different from the one that would have been evoked if the convening official had said, in contrast "we have a problem with the government of France."
>
> What exactly is the difference? To begin, Peru is in Latin America, the "other" America; France is in northwestern Europe, the cradle of the dominant North American culture. Peru is poor; France is rich. Peru is weak; France has nuclear weapons. Peru has Incan ruins . . . ; France has ancient ruins too, but it also has the Louvre. Peru makes pisco; France makes claret. Peru is not so firmly democratic; France is. Peru is a Rio Treaty ally, which, as alliances go, is something of a charade; France is a NATO ally, which is a very serious alliance. In most of our history, Peru has not mattered much in international relations; France has mattered a lot. . . . U.S. policy toward Peru is *fundamentally* unlike U.S. policy toward France, despite the fact that both policies are driven by self-interest. (xvi–xvii)

Now, imagine the phrase "there is a Mexican philosopher" and compare it to "there is a French philosopher." Which carries the greater weight? The analogy holds.

I began this essay with a reference to the logic of the Incas and the rhetorical training and rhetoric of the Aztecs prior to the European conquest. The source was a series of lectures delivered in Europe by an Argentine philosopher who resides in Mexico City, Enrique Dussel. Apart from a couple of dozen students in one seminar I've taught, I don't believe there are many in this country who know him or his work or the ways he might inform our concern with rhetoric or with liberatory pedagogy. His work mainly concerns the Philosophy of Liberation, and a good deal of it is in translation. We don't look to the South. Freire came to our attention only after he became a member of the faculty at Harvard. We tend to get our Great Thinkers from Europe, and too often only after our literary brothers and sisters, themselves too many and too often still quite literally an English colony, have discovered them. I'm not saying we shouldn't. I am grateful for *habitus* and hegemony as concepts that came from Europe. I have a great affection for the rhetoricians of Greece and Rome. But we must break from the colonial mindset and learn from the thinkers from our own hemisphere as well. There is, for example, a community college with a long record of trying to break through structural racism (now facing bureaucratic problems), Hostos Community College. Do we know who the school is named after? Do we know about his educational philosophy? He was a Puerto Rican philosopher, Eugenio María Hostos. Freire refers to many of the European thinkers, but he also refers to others. Do we know them? Might not knowing them be of some worth?

Break precedent! We are so locked into the colonial mindset that we are now turning to the excolonials of Europe to learn something about our own people of color. There again, I'm grateful for the insights. But what are the ex-colonials of the U.S. saying, the ex-colonials of our hemisphere, now caught in neocolonial dependency? In this essay, for example, I have called on the research of a number of Puerto Ricans, a Filipino, a number of Chicanas and Chicanos, an American Indian, African Americans, as well as an Argentine from Mexico — ex-colonials and contemporary colonials of the United States, writing and researching on their colonial relations to the United States. What we know are the writers. And they have a great deal to say that we should hear. But the Grand Theorists, to our mind, must be of "the continent" (as if the Americas weren't). At Hunter College in New York there is a Center for Puerto Rican Studies. What is being said there, not by postcolonials but by still-colonials? Some Puerto Ricans, for instance, are arguing for *jaiba* politics, a strategy of mimicry and parody that might have application in the classroom, a way to think our ways through the contradiction of a political sensibility in the composition classroom and instruction in academic discourse (Grosfoguel, Negrón-Muntaner, Georas 26–33). I haven't studied the concept of *jaiba* further or its possible application in composition studies yet. But I am hoping more of us will.

We shouldn't ignore the concepts that come of the ex-colonies of Europe, nor should we ignore European attempts to think its ways through bigotries of all sorts, since the problems of racism and hatred are Europe's also—but we also should not ignore the concepts that come of members of the interior colonies like Puerto Rico and the American Indian nations, the internal colonies of the formerly colonized as in America's people of color, the neocolonies of Latin America.

From Sandra María Esteves:

Here

I am two parts/a person
boricua/spic
past and present
alive and oppressed
given a cultural beauty
 . . . and robbed of a cultural identity

I speak the alien tongue
in sweet boriqueño thoughts
know love mixed with pain
have tasted spit on ghetto stairways
 . . . here, it must be changed
we must change it.

WORKS CITED

Cruz, Victor Hernández. "Anonymous." *Pueto Rican Writers at Home in the USA: An Anthology.* Faythe Turner, Ed., Seattle: Open Hand P, 1991. 119.

Davis, Mike. "The Political Economy of Late Imperial America." *New Left Review* 143 (1984): 6–38.

De Groat, Jennie. Personal Communication, 21 Nov. 1998.

Department of Health and Human Services. Hispanic Customer Service Demographics, *http://www./hhs/gov/heo/hisp.html,* 4 October 98.

Dunn, Cataya, Azfar Hussan, Abraham Tarango, and Sumatay Sivamohan. "Black Masks, White Masks." *The Daily Evergreen,* 23 April 1998, 6.

Dussel, Enrique. *The Invention of the Americas: Eclipse of "the Other" and the Myth of Modernity.* Trans. Michael D. Barber. New York: Continuum, 1995.

Emecheta, Buchi. *Double Yoke.* New York: Braziller, 1982.

Esteves, Sandra María. "From Fanon." Turner 186–87.

———. "Here." Turner 181.

Estrada, Leonardo F., F. Chris Garcia, Reynaldo Flores Macias, and Lionel Maldonado. "Chicanos in the United States: A History of Exploitation and Resistance." *Daedalus* 2 (1981): 103–31.

Fanon, Frantz. *Black Skin, White Masks.* Trans. by Charles Lam Markmann. New York: Grove, 1967.

Gates, Henry Louis, Jr. "On the Rhetoric of Racism in the Profession." *Literature, Language, and Politics.* Ed. Betty Jean Craige. Athens: U of Georgia P, 1988. 20–26.

Glazer, Nathaniel, and Daniel P. Moynihan. *Beyond the Melting Pot: The Negroes, Puerto Ricans, Jews, Italians, and Irish of New York City.* Cambridge: MIT P, 1970.

Grosfoguel, Ramón, Frances Negrón-Muntaner, and Chloé S. Georas. "Beyond Nationalist and Colonialist Discourses: The *Jaiba* Politics of the Puerto-Rican Ethno-Nation." *Puerto Rican Jam: Rethinking Colonialism and Nationalism.* Grosfoguel et al., eds. Minneapolis: U of Minnesota P, 1997. 1–36.

Martínez. Elizabeth. *De Colores Means All of Us: Latina Views for a Multi-Colored Century.* Cambridge: South End, 1998.

Omi, Michael, and Howard Winant. *Racial Formation in the United States: From the 1960s to the 1990s.* New York: Routledge, 1994.

Prendergast, Catherine. "Race: The Absent Presence in Composition Studies." *CCC* 50 (1998): 35–53.

President's Advisory Commission on Educational Excellence for Hispanic Americans. *Our Nation on the Fault Line: Hispanic American Education.* Washington, DC: USIA, September 1996.

Rex, John. *Race, Colonialism and the City.* London: Routledge, 1973.

San Juan, E. *Racial Formations/Critical Transformations: Articulations of Power in Ethnic and Racial Studies in the United States.* Atlantic Highlands: Humanities P, 1992.

Schoultz, Lars. *Beneath the United States: A History of U.S. Policy Toward Latin America.* Cambridge: Harvard UP, 1998.

Takaki, Ronald. *A Different Mirror: A History of Multicultural America.* Boston: Little, 1993.

———. "Reflections on Racial Patterns in America." *From Different Shores.* Ed. Ronald Takaki. New York: Oxford UP, 1987.

Turner Faythe, ed. *Puerto Rican Writers at Home in the USA: An Anthology.* Seattle: Open Hand P, 1991.

U.S. Department of Education, National Center for Educational Statistics, Integrated Postsecondary Education Data System. "Completions Survey." Washington: US. Department of Education. April 1997.

Veltman, Calvin. "Anglicization in the United States: Language Environment and Language Practice of American Adolescents." *International Journal of Social Languages* 44 (1983): 99–114.

AFTERWORD: 1999 CHAIR'S ADDRESS: REFLECTIONS

I was wandering about a bookstore in Austin, Texas, looking for books on world systems theory, when I came across a book by Enrique Dussel. The title caught my eye—*Invention of the Americas: Eclipse of "the Other" and the Myth of Modernity.* I was particularly taken by the play on *invention*—meaning "discovery" on the one hand and "to make anew" or "to make up" on the other hand. I bought the book. Read it on the plane ride back home. Adopted it for a class in contemporary rhetorical theory. Later that same year I was elected assistant chair of CCCC. The 1998 conference would be mine to put together. I would face the members of CCCC in 1999 with a keynote. I knew already that Dussel's published lectures would inform that talk.

I knew that Dussel would inform the CCCC Chair's address because he pointed to a number of concerns I also had. Although Dussel's concerns were in some ways different from mine, he nevertheless demonstrated that a rhetoric— purposeful oratory—existed among the indigenous peoples of this hemisphere before the conquest by Europe. He demonstrated what folks like George Fredrickson later describes as the evolution of racism (from other forms of discrimination) in the seventeenth and eighteenth centuries. And in that I could find no one in any journal within rhetoric who ever cited Dussel, he demonstrated the degree to which American academics, at least in rhetoric and composition studies, did not seem to bother with academics from the Americas. Dussel himself doesn't say any of this. It's what I saw; it's what I knew needed telling. It needed telling because I knew CCCC to be deeply committed to addressing inequities of all sorts—age, class, gender, sexuality, racism (though like all U.S. institutions, ours tried to get at racism through phenotypes and exoticized cultures—race and ethnicity—when what matters is the racism, not the race or some blurry race-like distinction called "ethnicity," which rarely seems to apply to white, Western European ethnicities, discounting Spain). But if I knew CCCC to be deeply committed, I also knew it to be overly dependent on one discipline's definitions—literary criticism, European literary criticism. The non-Europeans (like Ernesto Laclau, for instance) wouldn't be recognized until acknowledged by Europe.

The first Latino chair of the organization, I needed to show gratitude and point to the fact that only racism could explain my being the first in a fifty-year-old organization. I spent the summer of 1998 writing the piece to be delivered the spring of 1999. Joe Harris, then editor of *CCC*, wanted the keynote to appear in a special fiftieth anniversary issue of the journal, which would come out the summer of 1999. Kay Tronsen, a graduate student, helped with research. Carol, my wife, listened to delivery of drafts of the essay. Even though I was going to send it to Joe, my concern was with the oral. Almost all of my writing is written with the oral in mind and in ear (because I began my career in the era when orality and cognitive dysfunction were used to explain the lack of advancement among folks of color. I felt obligated to show a relationship between orality and cognitive sophistication).

On 25 March 1999 I delivered the talk to a packed room, maybe a thousand seated in the audience (maybe more; I don't know), breaking from script when the feeling was right, getting a laugh when one was needed, slowing down when sinking-in time was necessary. At the end, the usual standing ovation, but the applause seemed long, wonderfully long. It was a rush. I had dared and hadn't been defiled.

Being defiled wasn't out of the question, after all. Someone said to me that when the audience arose, she thought they were going to hurry out of the room, since I had run over time, not stand for an ovation. Someone else, however, a Latina, thanked me with tears in her eyes. Another said something like, "I didn't know you could do like that" (a person of color, choosing a discourse of color).

Later, within the conference, someone said that my talk would overshadow Pratt's contact zones (very flattering, even if not the case). Later, I would hear that someone I respected (still do, despite the rumor) accused me of not including any women in my speech, the selected hearing of one who slipped into the tired old stereotype of Latinos as outrageously sexist men. She hadn't noticed that the denouement of the speech had been supplied by Sandra María Esteves, with her poem "Here." Oh well. I knew to expect the contra in controversy.

I've now seen the speech referred to several times. It's as if folks use it as sanction to explore the rhetorics of figures from Mexico in particular. And I feel compelled to practice what I preach, so that I have now begun conducting research on Pedro Albizu Campos, a Puerto Rican intellectual (a Harvard professor early in the twentieth century), an intellectual targeted by the FBI, condemned to nearly twenty years in jail because of his ideas, ideas found less in his writings than in his speeches — a rhetorician condemned for his rhetoric, a rhetoric of color, a colonial subject who dared oppose colonial rule. It's as if my clarion call was a call to my Self to discover my own heritage, stories from my father before his death, stories known well in my parents' homeland, but lost to the rest of us who share a destiny with that homeland. And I think of more than folks who identify as Puerto Rican. I think of us all in the United States, insofar as we are all "owners" of Puerto Rico, insofar as its peoples have been colored by racism, insofar as eliminating a problem means understanding the problem historically, culturally, and for us who claim language as our special concern, rhetorically.

—VICTOR VILLANUEVA
Washington State University

WORKS CITED

Dussel, Enrique. *The Invention of the Americas: Eclipse of "the Other" and the Myth of Modernity*. Trans. Michael D. Barber. New York: Continuum, 1995.

Esteves, Sandra María. "Here." *Puerto Rican Writers at Home in the USA: An Anthology*. Faythe Turner, ed. Seattle: Open Hand, 1991. 181.

Fredrickson, George M. *Racism: A Short History*. Princeton: Princeton UP, 2002.

2000

Literacy, Identity, Imagination, Flight

KEITH GILYARD

As I prepared to come to Minneapolis for this convention, I could not help, given the locale and theme of our gathering, to remember to pay homage to a special person of great imagination, Dr. Martin Luther King, Jr. When King was gunned down in Memphis in 1968, the nineteenth annual CCCC convention was being held in this city. Fortunately, his dream of non-racist societies lives on and, in fact, has inspired some of the best work done by members of our organization over the past thirty-two years with respect to creating courses that have gestured toward a more socially just world.

When I thought more of King in relation to this present conference, I realized anew the tremendous sacrifices he made beyond the most obvious one. He chose to subordinate certain other imaginative pursuits, such as leisurely study and contemplation of music and literature, to the taxing demands of the civil rights movement. And I thought of how often that kind of tradeoff has been made, how people have set aside particular and perhaps preferred flights of fancy because they have become absorbed in pressing matters that often have weighed them down and have not seemed very fanciful at all. I also thought, as I geared up to come here, about literal, machine-powered flight. Still musing about King and his unfinished mission, I noted how the airways remain our most segregated channel of mass travel, of how flight—both fanciful and business-like—links to economics that in turn link to the color line that concerned King so much and that W.E.B. Du Bois wrote about on several occasions, most memorably in 1903. Then I recalled that in 1903, the same year Du Bois was suggesting that the color line was

This article examines issues of literacy and identity relative to the development of a critical pedagogy and a critical democracy. A revised version of the Chair's address Keith Gilyard delivered at the CCCC in Minneapolis, Minnesota, on April 13, 2000, it was first published in *CCC*, volume 52, number 2, December 2000.

indeed *the* problem of the twentieth century, Wilbur and Orville Wright construed a fundamental problem of the new century to be that of flight. They solved the conundrum that most consumed them, contributing vitally to the age of aviation that has been one of the most spectacular stories of the last ninety-seven years. It is an age during which the world has shrunk considerably, the color line not as significantly. And I conjured up the image—just started imagining and re-imagining all kinds of things because of this convention—of a childhood friend and schoolmate of Orville Wright who had to pass on one of his own notions of flight because he stood in a disadvantaged position in relation to the color line. He desperately wanted to go to Harvard University to pursue becoming a lawyer, but it was not to be. Fortunately, both for him and for us, this fellow, Paul Laurence Dunbar, did get to soar through his poetry and other writings, partly and ironically because of the Wright brothers' assistance.

Among their many creative ventures, the Wright brothers established a printing company in 1890. Wilbur served as publisher, Orville, as editor. One of their publications was a four-page weekly titled *The Tattler* that was aimed at an African American readership. Dunbar wrote and edited this short-lived vehicle. He also wrote a poem on a wall in the office testifying to Orville Wright's genius. A couple of years later, Dunbar approached Orville Wright to see if he would print his first book of poetry. Wright lacked the mechanism to handle a job of that size but directed Dunbar to a printer with whom arrangements were made. By the time Orville Wright took off at Kitty Hawk in 1903, Dunbar had persevered to publish thirteen professionally produced books, including three in 1903 alone as he, at age thirty, was already succumbing to the tuberculosis that would claim his life. A too brief career, like King's, and, like King's, an ascending career despite intense social pressures, ended in 1906.

Now I do not argue that Dunbar or Du Bois or King would not have chosen in any case to devote almost their entire talents to the progress of African Americans and the resultant healing of the national soul. My point is that they could hardly have ignored that option given an enduring racism. I thank them continually for their choice and their example. Nor will I tie up neatly the large and noble notion of humane interaction along the color line, a conception that I am alluding to in some respects. I'll let all that suggestiveness simmer a bit. I want to press directly forward on some specific ideas about me, you, and the topic (Educating the Imagination, Re-Imagining Education) that brings us together today, and about how I hope this convergence is helpful as we continue to work on ourselves and with our students.

I have let my mind roam over this topic, a novel experience, knowing all along that such endeavor would evoke prior experiences, thus leading to a synthesis of new and old. I was encouraged by the fact that you have agreed to hear me and perhaps be kind. I have made connections that maybe only I would, all that politicized African Americaness rubbing up against historical curiosity about poets and the biographies of poets as well as biographies of prominent people in general, not to mention a sense of CCCC's history. But these connections were initially vague, not in the fairly mature form in which I now present them. I had to put in research time to flesh out ideas, to shore up my memory. With your implied indulgence, I was and am motivated to make some of the cultural and personal suppositions that I hold as clear to you as I can. This learning contract, then, is what I propose as a model. If we agree to aim for a radical, transcultural democracy, as King did, then we need pedagogies to foster the development of the critical and astute citizenry that would pursue the task. In this regard, the best strategies involve maximizing various epistomologies, searching for transcultural understandings, opening up spaces for imaginative wanderings, for scholarly recreation. These are our best chances of obtaining and maintaining the widespread student-citizen involvement we seek.

A former student of mine, Chang Chun Tao, helped me to appreciate the educational value of creative cross-cultural conversation. At the end of a semester of first-year English, in which he studied alongside African American and African Caribbean classmates, my curiosity about his perceptions of the course led to a talk in my office. My colleague and friend Steve Cannon intruded, as he usually did, and we all decided to tape the whole exchange, of which I'll share a couple of excerpts.

> **GILYARD:** So what were some of the works you liked this semester? I know you like Tolstoi. You did your research paper on Tolstoi. Now I know about your father [who taught Russian literature in China]. What else drew you to Tolstoi as a writer?
>
> **TAO:** First, he looked at people of different classes. I was also influenced by the sociological approach, Marxist interpretation. I was born in a communist country, and they always use that way to evaluate a piece of work. It's true. So this is why I like the sociological approach. I think Tolstoi does all his literature basically in this approach.
>
> **GILYARD:** You mean it lends itself to a sociological explanation?
>
> **TAO:** That's why I like it. I also like another piece of work very much, *A Raisin in the Sun.*
>
> **GILYARD:** [Lorraine] Hansberry's play. Why do you like it?
>
> **TAO:** Because it reflects the conflict between two generations. A generation comes from an underdeveloped area to a developed area. When they are in the underdeveloped area, they favor the values they had, moral values. But when they go to developed areas, when they go to Chicago and see all the industry, they like money only.
>
> **GILYARD:** So you don't like Walter Lee Younger?

TAO: I cannot say I don't like him. But I say this is a real figure in society. In my country—

GILYARD: They have Walter Lee Youngers in China?

TAO: Yeah. Something like that. Before they came through the economic reform people really appreciated moral values. But after reform they just like money.

GILYARD: Well, money is a value, isn't it?

TAO: It's a value, but it's not a moral value.

GILYARD: No, it's not a moral value, but then maybe it is. You tell me. You like philosophy, economics. You like Marx.

TAO: No, I don't like Marx. I like money, too. But money cannot do everything, especially in a family relationship. You shouldn't choose money over your family. Walter chose money.

CANNON: He chose money over and above the family.

TAO: He chose money over and above anything else.

GILYARD: What about *Antigone?* I know you had fun with that.

TAO: Yeah. I like it, too. This play criticizes dictatorships.

CANNON: The whole idea of dissent.

TAO: So this play is like what happens in communist countries when they take everything over. They don't want to allow the people—

CANNON: To dissent—

TAO: They don't like to listen to different voices.

CANNON: Other points of view.

TAO: This is why they clamped down on the demonstrations in Tienamen Square. That's the same thing. I can imagine—

CANNON: You can immediately identify with that, huh?

Then we rambled about universality, canon formation, and reader-response theory. Both Steve and I sensed that Chang was not likely to make that quick, right, anti-Black turn that several Asian immigrants we knew made. We figured his introduction to Black students and his willingness to see Black texts to be as worthy as others would help him to remain fairly open-minded. We pushed on to popular culture, where Steve and I often wind up.

CANNON: Do you spend time going to the movies?

TAO: I watch movies on television. I don't go to the movies.

CANNON: You don't go sit in the audience?

TAO: I might borrow some tapes from the video store. I'll tell you what I like, *The Color Purple.*

GILYARD: Why do you like *The Color Purple*? I know people who hate that movie.

TAO: This movie reflects how housewives suffer in the underdeveloped areas and how they become strong and finally how they choose their own way.

GILYARD: Now would that interpretation have something to do with the traditional role women have played in Chinese culture?

TAO: It's very similar because in China a husband always dominates a family. Women have little power.

GILYARD: So Steve, he would be sitting there relating the movie to his experiences in China, and he wouldn't even know what all the Blackfolk were fussing about, positive and negative images and all that. He's not even in that one. He's connecting it to something else.

CANNON: Matriarchy-patriarchy.

GILYARD: Or the effects of patriarchy. That's right. Of course, from there he can eventually get to the so-called *Purple* debate—through the side door in a sense, which is actually the front door for him.

Although Chang Chun Tao asserted and demonstrated the universality that all fine literature possesses, he was never seduced, nor should we be, by the argument that because this is so, it doesn't matter if we try for a culturally diverse mix. It may, in fact, *not* matter in the absolute, but the absolute is not where we live and learn and teach. Our choice of materials and our classroom concerns communicate messages as well, largely about whom we value. Chang knew I was in his corner. He, Steve, and I went on for quite a spell, clashed somewhat, contradicted ourselves, tried to work that out, all three of us widening our critical gazes, casting out from our primary cultural shores. We talked about, among many things, Chinese literature, publishing politics, and radical lesbian feminism.

Looking back, I wonder if Chang, who thought I was pretty sophisticated about literature and literary theory, knew that I acquired a lot of knowledge similar to the way he did. A lot of my initial observations are the old "go for what you know" variety that are important back in the 'hood. For example, what I comprehend about structuralism and post-structuralism is due to James Brown. On his recording "There Was a Time," Brown opens by singing/stating that "There was a dance, hah / There was a time, hah / when I used to dance, hah."

Let's examine this. The dance is the structure, the pattern of rhythmic movements. For Brown to repeat the movements establishes a certain meaning inside a particular system of signification. When we understand this dancer in relation to the codified motions that precede him, that's structuralism. Of course, defining these "-isms" can be slippery, but I'm pretty centrist in my reading here according to the *Penguin Dictionary of*

Literary Terms and Literary Theory. So *there was a dance*. And *there was a time*, Brown's acknowledgment of the social construction of dances, his sense that although the dances precede the dancer, they cannot precede history. In other words, they are not natural; they are situated articulations derived from specific human encounters. So there was a time *when I used to dance*. This is Brown talking about specific occasions on which he makes predictable meaning. Again, that's structuralism. Then Brown takes the listener on a tour of structuralist understandings as he speaks of doing the mashed potatoes, the jerk, the camel walk, and the boogaloo. We may even term these substructuralist understandings insofar as these movements are components of the larger socio-historical dance. The song really is this deep. Quincy Troupe wrote that James Brown was "the philosopher of the Black masses" and that has always rung true to me. Brown knows as well as anyone this side of Roland Barthes and Jacques Derrida how meaning can be shifting, unstable, inside a given dance. He thus announces his poststructuralist stamp on the dance with the words, "But you can bet you haven't seen nothin' yet until you see me do the James Brown." In other words, he can extend beyond the received structure in ways he would wager you could not have anticipated had you been a personal witness at Harlem's Apollo Theater in 1967, the very same year Barthes's *Elements of Semiology* was translated into English and Derrida published *Of Grammatology*.

This same street-level approach makes composition theory accessible to me as well. The theorists I'm feeling most right now are Romy Clark and Roz Ivanič, whom I relish for their explicit discussions of writing as a social practice in their book *The Politics of Writing*. As Clark indicates,

> I have learned that it is important to see writing as a social practice, embedded in social relations within a specific community, each with its own complex ideological and conventional practices within which individual students have to find identities as writers that they feel confident and comfortable with. (5)

Of course, there has been voluminous research produced on this side of the pond about writing as a situated and constructed endeavor, for example, Linda Brodkey's *Academic Writing as a Social Practice* and Pat Bizzell's *Academic Discourse and Critical Consciousness*. And, to be sure, Clark and Ivanič call upon this body of work, as I hope we all have. But they and their colleagues at Lancaster University have also coined the term *Critical Language Awareness*, which marks the teaching mission I am on more and more these days in several courses. If the ascension toward a more perfect democracy depends upon citizens being able to interrogate and resist discourses that impede such instantiation, as I suggest is the case, then students need to comprehend as completely as possible how discourse operates, which means understanding how the dominant or most powerful discourse serves to regulate and reproduce patterns of privilege. Who is deemed worthy of being marketed as an author? Whose stories get to be preserved in published, well-distributed formats? Which genres are privileged? Who is included in that consensual "we" that writers habitually try to impose on readers? Why are many of Noah Webster's 1783 preferences still the bane of so many writers' existences? Why, even, is sloppy handwriting a mark of status if one is a doctor or celebrity, but a negative sign if one is an adult of relatively low status, a trait perhaps excusable in the writing of boys, but never in that of girls? In short, students will need to engage in discussions of culture, ideology, hegemony, and asymmetrical power relations—all that rugged theoretical terrain that sometimes seems far removed from the texts they are generating in seemingly smooth sites. The whole journey sometimes gets confusing for them and me. I see their vexation, the eye queries: "What's this all about, professor?"

"Look a here," I say, "There are things operating in the language on the down-low. You use the language uncritically, you are employing what's in it on the down-low. Malcolm X found that out in a prison library more than fifty years ago when he could find only negative connotations associated with the word *black* and positive ones associated with the word *white*. And check this: in your lifetime, according to Donald MacKay, you likely will read the word *he* used as a generic, so-called neutral pronoun more than ten million times (355). What does that say about the standing of women? Even, as Clark and Ivanič point out, the use of the term Standard English as opposed to Standardized English makes it seem like the standard variety dropped from the clouds (211). Get that *IZE* up in there and you can focus more on the fact that the standardIZED variety was selected by the linguistic elite. And this standardIZED variety is packed with all this down-low elite material. So you see how we can perpetuate ideas without even realizing it. But luckily that's not the end of the story. We can become cognizant of how these conceptions circulate and resist them. We can create nonsexist language, for example. We can look at language on the up-high. That's the move to make, to get used to writing on the up-high as much as possible, right at eye level, with ever-increasing awareness of the dynamics of contestation and replication. The media do it all the time to play you, and you need to do it all the time so you don't get played, player."

Again, this is how theory and I get along. Unfortunately, neither theory nor I have all the answers. Even as the view of language and learning I have been describing prompts us to develop courses that are broadly inviting with respect to linguistic and cultural differences, that encourage students to contribute through their writing to fuller accounts of the world, that establish contexts beyond a narrow student-teacher relationship for the dissemination of students' ideas, that question the implications of rhetorical choice, there still is no getting around the double-bind that, whenever we participate in the dominant discourse, no matter how liberally we may tweak it, we help to maintain it. Therefore, we are complicit in whatever that discourse accomplishes with respect to the unjust distribution of goods and services. Yet, not to engage in the dominant discourse may diminish some very real material possibilities for ordinary people struggling to do better. Obviously, these are possibilities we generally should not oppose even if individual successes help to reify wider inequity. Nonetheless, I think we—and by *we* I mean folks who more or less think about literacy the way I do—can remain optimistic in the face of this dilemma if we view it as part of a productive tension, a heightening of the contradiction, to invoke terminology from my old study groups.

In more recent times, with more contemporary critical precepts in mind, this problem has been addressed remarkably well by Rodrigo Crenshaw, the young alter ego of Richard Delgado's brilliant chronicles. He sees normative discourse as being unable to burst the bubble of social inequality given that such discourse is "circular, reassuring, empty, 'inscribed'" (94), given that such conversations "prefigure the answers one reaches, at least unless one is very, very careful" (100). Rodrigo then suggests the need to "seek out someone unlike us, someone who sees things with new eyes" (103–04). He warns that "if we do not do this, we will pay a price, namely the inability to see system-wide defects that cause our bubble, ever so imperceptibly, to drift downward" (104). Then Rodrigo prepares to dash off to work on a paper for one of his law classes (time to play the game). His interlocutor halts him with a series of questions:

> But won't we just be co-opted, you and I, I mean? We'll take our "outsider perspective," as you call it, in your case to the law faculty committee, in mine to the audience at my conference. Won't we just join the bubble, merge whatever meager insight we can offer into the general cultural mix, reinscribing ourselves in the current dysfunctional, hierarchical, and often racist culture of which we both complain? Won't we just become part of that bubble? (104)

Before departing, Rodrigo beams his answer, "At least it'll be a larger bubble" (104).

I take hope in that vision of an expanded bubble, one more likely to burst into a more open state. I am reaffirmed in the notion that being critically careful does make a difference, and I know that there are the likes of Rodrigo, like Delgado himself, who are not fictional insider-outsiders, but real.

As I consider further these ideas about insiders and outsiders and recall Clark's belief that "individual students have to find identities as writers that they feel confident and comfortable with" (5), I am reminded that no matter how we envision literacy and curriculum, we have to reckon with how students, and teachers as well, describe themselves. For any progressive pedagogy to achieve respectable results, students, among whose ranks are some of the important outsiders we need, have to feel invested in the roles they play in the process. This problematic often translates into debates about race, ethnicity, gender, sexuality, disabilities, multisubjectivities, contact zones, essentialism, social class, social constructionism, and postmodernism. There can be no quick or easy tour through the land of identity politics. Nor is anyone going to sum up and settle the issue once and for all. I'll just offer a case study pulled from the G files; they're like the *X Files* but can be more surreal.

I was in the ticket line in the bus station in Syracuse. A woman was taking an inordinately long time at the window. She was buying a ticket for her son who was in college somewhere in New England, and she was asking the same questions repeatedly. Others in line grew frustrated, as did the ticket agent herself. Me, too. But I figured I'd chill, be polite, patient; I worry about kids also. However, this Indian brother right in front of me became quite agitated. If he wasn't drunk, he had a good down payment on it. He started harassing the purchaser and the agent, articulating some of what I was thinking. The purchaser ignored him, but the agent began chastising him and threatening not to sell him a ticket if he were drunk and couldn't calm down. He warned her not to try that stuff this time because he couldn't be late getting to Buffalo. I started chuckling a bit and the guy spun around and asked me pointedly, with a strong whiskey breath, "You Injun?" I said, "Naw, I ain't Injun."

He repeated the question. "You Injun?"

"Naw, I ain't Injun."

Then he showed me his massive, rough fists and explained that he worked steel and that this woman was always giving him a hard time even though he might marry her someday.

"You Injun?"

"Naw, I ain't Injun."

He pointed to another man, apparently his traveling buddy, who was playing video games. "He's Injun," he announced. "We work steel." Then he went back to harassing other folks.

Eventually I got my ticket and waited around a moment to witness his fate. The agent had explained to me that sometimes he got to go, sometimes he didn't. This time he didn't.

I probably have spent too much of my life trying to read profundity into inebriated ramblings, but I did think about this fellow while I was en route to New York City. I thought about this "Injuness" and of my great-grandfather, Toby Townsend, the 6'6" Cherokee shop owner who refused to labor in the fields for anyone else. Good image. I also thought about the "Trail of Tears," the seizure of Cherokee lands. Poignant image. But I recalled reading that the Cherokees were the most assimilationist of the Indian nations. Not the image I want to romanticize. So then I considered how Indian scouts aided the confederacy, but also how Blacks served in the U.S. Army as agents of genocide against Indians. But that was all mental exercise, perhaps useful in widening and deepening perspectives about family history and the world. However, I knew my primary identity. Not a single bad thing has ever happened to me because someone pegged me for Indian. When I arrived in New York City, I tucked my wallet in my shoulder bag and tried not to appear threatening to the NYPD.

I respect postmodernist projects designed to disrupt injustice. I'm for traversing some boundaries myself, aren't I? But what I'm driving at here is that academic postmodernism, including that which gets valorized in composition classes, often gets stuck in passive relativism, just a classroom full of perceived instability. It's useful at times to complicate notions of identity, but primary identities operate powerfully in the world and have to be productively engaged. I think King had it right, for example, when he dreamed of Black kids and White kids holding hands (219). There are whole realities attached to those Black hands and White hands that have been insufficiently dealt with to date and won't be if we insist on prematurely converting King's dream to one of hybridity kids holding hands with junior border crossers. When we engage in discussions about fluidity, we ought to keep in mind the question of who can afford to be anchored to a focus on the indeterminate. As Natalie Cole sings clearly, "You gotta serve somebody." Who are we serving with the identity politics we push? And how are those politics consistent or inconsistent with what we say about pedagogy overall? Those aren't easy questions, and they don't get any easier from here. But we spend a lot of time in classrooms talking about identity, and we need to continue to strive to make those discussions serve a critical, democratic project.

We have a lot to solve. The nation and the academy are going to become even more complex arenas. Given population projections, the largest and most socially diverse teenage population in U.S. history is on the horizon, which may fuel higher and more intense enrollment pressures, which in turn would intensify debates about policies of access and exclusion. I suggest that we are poised between scenarios suggested by Dr. Dre and Jay-Z. In Dre's line — "full effect of intellect so I could collect respect plus a check" — there are prospects for positive engagement with academe and with English studies. If student intellects are indeed in full effect, then our willingness to accord them certain respect along linguistic and identity dimensions can help set them up for the check, which will include basic, old, not to be ignored loot, but may also mean attainment of insight and energy to be spent on achieving social justice. Allow my optimism. By all means, remember King's dream. Also recall Dunbar's early pessimism, as he wrote, "But the work you've got to do / Dreams won't ever do for you / Even if they did come true" (qtd. in Braxton xii). And recall Dunbar's eventual artistic flight, as important as any flight physical, as the inventors of machine-powered flight understood. But let us not lose sight of Jay-Z's apocalyptic warning that "When my situation ain't improvin, I'm tryin to murder everything movin." I would say that we should work on that situation.

If we are to diminish appreciably the hard knock life, if visions of a better society are to come to fruition, I think that we, as teachers, could play a pivotal role in such a movement. I'm not overestimating what compositionists can do. I made that mistake already when I was watching *Saving Private Ryan*. When Tom Hanks's character revealed that in civilian life he was a composition teacher, I figured he would easily make it to the end of the movie. He didn't, so I understand that we have limited powers in the face of all we confront. But we also have great imagination, splendid playfulness, wonderful resourcefulness, and, I think, serious intellectual and social commitment. Both today and over the course of my career, these are qualities that I have always attempted, however inadequately, to perform.

WORKS CITED

Barthes, Roland. *Elements of Semiology*. 1964. Tr. Annette Lavers and Colin Smith. New York: Hill and Wang, 1973.

Bizzell, Patricia. *Academic Discourse and Critical Consciousness*. Pittsburgh: U of Pittsburgh P, 1992.

Braxton, Joanne M., ed. *The Collected Poetry of Paul Laurence Dunbar*. Charlottesville, VA: UP of Virginia, 1993.

Brodkey, Linda. *Academic Writing as Social Practice*. Philadelphia: Temple UP, 1987.

Brown, James. "There Was a Time." *Foundations of Funk, A Brand New Bag: 1964–1969*. A&M Records, Inc. 31453 1165–2. Compilation released in 1996. Song was originally recorded in 1967.

Clark, Romy, and Roz Ivanič. *The Politics of Writing*. London: Routledge, 1997.

Cole, Natalie. "Gotta Serve Somebody." *Snowfall on the Sahara*. WEA/Electra Entertainment, 1999.

Cuddon, John Anthony. *The Penguin Dictionary of Literary Terms and Literary Theory*. 4th ed. New York: Penguin, 1990.

Delgado, Richard. *The Rodrigo Chronicles: Conversations about America and Race*. New York: New York UP, 1995.

Derrida, Jacques. *Of Grammatology*. 1967. Tr. Gayatri Spivak. Baltimore: Johns Hopkins UP, 1976.

Dr. Dre. *Keep Their Heads Ringin'*. Priority, 1995.

Du Bois, W.E.B. *The Souls of Black Folk*. 1903. New York: Penguin, 1989.

Howard, Fred. *Wilbur and Orville: A Biography of the Wright Brothers*. Mineola, NY: Dover Publications, 1998.

Jay-Z. "Hard Knock Life." *Vol. 2: Hard Knock Life*. Def Jam, 1998.

King, Jr., Martin Luther. "I Have a Dream." *The Negro History Bulletin* 21 (1968): 16–17. Rpt. in *A Testament of Hope: The Essential Writings of Martin Luther King. Jr.* Ed. James Melvin Washington. San Francisco: Harper, 1986. 217–20.

MacKay, Donald. "On the Goals, Principles and Procedures for Prescriptive Grammar: Singular They." *Language in Society* 9 (1980): 349–67.

Troupe, Quincy. "Ode to John Coltrane." *Skulls along the River*. New York: I. Reed, 1984. 37–42.

Any genealogy of an academic event can get complicated, and one can hardly hope to account for all the idea strands that find expression in a leader's address to his or her professional organization. In a sense, one speaks out of all that one knows and cares about. So that's the larger story. And the cop out. A partial and more interesting tale commences with Victor and Victoria, which sounds something like a movie but is the real deal.

I was fortunate to be on the dais next to Victor Villanueva as he delivered, in 1999 in Atlanta, one of the most stirring addresses I have heard—or mostly heard. My mind was already leaping ahead to the following year's convention in Minneapolis, and I was contemplating how I might effectively address the largest audience I probably would ever have at a CCCC convention. I figured I could be sufficiently intellectual; I knew I could speak with conviction. But I also knew that erudition and passion alone would never suffice. The bottom line is that I had to represent. In other words, I had to infuse the intellectual and emotional with a style and line of argument that expressed both how I obtained knowledge and how I acquired sense.

Victoria Cliett, my good colleague who hails from Wayne State University, knew exactly what I was thinking. As folks were milling around after Victor's speech, the atmosphere still electric, she came up to me and said simply, "You know what you have to do, right?" She was all up inside the code, expressing in eight words extreme admiration for the day's speaker and issuing the polite demand, if not quite the expectation, that I manifest a similar excellence. She was also requesting a legitimate effort, the idea being that if I became serious enough about the task of addressing the organization as Chair, then we would be all right, the "we" being Victoria and the group of African Americans inside CCCC who viewed me as their representative. Of course, I could address members of the larger group in whatever ways I saw fit. After all, I belonged to them as well. But I did understand all that Victoria did not expressly say. My verbal reply was simple: "Don't even worry. I got it."

Shortly after that I began sketching a number of ideas relative to connections between education and imagination, the theme suggested by Program Chair Wendy Bishop. I generated a text that quickly became unwieldy. So I tried to think less about what I could say and more about what I should never fail to say about language and learning when given the opportunity. I should never fail to address issues of politics and diversity, never fail to make connections between the theoretical and the practical, never fail to speak as plainly as is reasonable, and never settle for pessimism. My hope might get unhopeful, but never hopeless, as Du Bois would say.

So that's how I settled on my specific framework while keeping in mind the overall theme. I bounced a number of ideas off others, including Vorris (another V, which I took as a sign for victory) Nunley, who was my research assistant back then. We always had great discussions, and he kept me on a pretty steady course.

I wouldn't judge how things turned out. Folks who are interested can read the text for the content. For a sense of that morning in Minneapolis, they can ask somebody who was there. I'll just report this: Victoria said I was right, and Suhail Islam, from up in Rochester, New York, was crying. I could never have predicted Suhail's response for I didn't know him all that well. I had only talked with him briefly at a few conventions. I hugged him and kept asking him why he was crying, but he couldn't really explain it. He could probably do better now, and maybe that's the better story to get. Victor and Victoria were great inspirations, but a lot of what the Chair's address meant to me, what I don't even have a complete handle on yet, is tied up in Suhail Islam.

–KEITH GILYARD
Pennsylvania State University

2001

Against the Odds in Composition and Rhetoric[1]

WENDY BISHOP

T eachers of writing and rhetoric work against personal, pedagogical, and institutional odds. They have felt marginal—rebellious, second selves, outsiders, change agents—by historical accident, but they also inhabit these locations by *choice* because it is good work with large emotional and intellectual rewards.

For some time, I've been thinking intently about how fatiguing certain institutional arguments and battles have been, for so many, and for so long. How swiftly a type of generational fatigue knocks at the doors of our classrooms and offices. What would I feel—I began to wonder—and would I be disappointed—or at least dramatically changed—if our field became dominant, the center of English studies or the valued first-year core for all fields as some of us have suggested it should be?

Your first response to this might be similar to mine: "Ah . . . how good to have lost those pressures and to be fairly accepted and roundly acknowledged" (picture here a small ticker-tape parade in front of your institution's library). Here, I want to explore why your second response might also be similar to mine: "I'm actually not so sure." For to become the center might be to become something completely otherwise.

• • •

As an undergraduate and MA student, I studied poetry writing with the late Karl Shapiro. The first day of a new quarter, Karl had us open our royal blue Norton Anthology to Gerard Manley Hopkins' poem "Pied Beauty." Karl read it aloud, looked up at us through the lenses of his coke-bottle glasses and cloak of pipe smoke, and said, "This is the best poem ever written." Most of us were shocked, bemused, absolutely unconvinced.

This article is a revised version of the Chair's address Wendy Bishop delivered at the CCCC Convention in Denver, Colorado, on March 15, 2001. A previous version was published in *CCC*, volume 53, number 2, December 2001.

After that statement and our active silence, after closing our books and storing them in our bookbags, we moved on to discuss each other's drafts.

Pied Beauty

Glory be to God for dappled things—
   For skies of couple-colour as a brinded cow;
     For rose-moles all in stipple upon trout that swim;
Fresh-firecoal chestnut-falls; finches' wings;
   Landscape plotted and pieced—fold, fallow, and plough;
     And áll trádes, their gear and tackle and trim.

All things, counter, original, spare, strange;
   Whatever is fickle, freckled (who knows how?)
     With swift, slow; sweet, sour; adazzle, dim;
He fathers-forth whose beauty is past change:
                   Praise him.

                       –GERARD MANLEY HOPKINS

Hopkins' poetry, including "Pied Beauty," has haunted me since that 1973 workshop. In the years that followed, I would backpack to Europe and discover myself reciting what I could of "Spring and Fall" to the autumn trees outside the window of my Danish youth hostel. I'd use the last line of "Felix Randall" as a calming tongue twister or workshop example: "Didst fettle for the great grey drayhorse his bright and battering sandal" (47). When I fell in love, the sort of men I liked always seemed variations on *counter, original, spare, strange* (and sometimes *fickle* or *freckled*). Teaching at Navajo Community College in northern Arizona, I'd return often to the landscape-igniting words of "Pied Beauty" as I watched sunset unravel along the Chuska Mountains and backlight the piebald reservation ponies that drifted across the small campus commons like equine tumbleweeds. If you know and value the poem, it's likely that similar moments have come to you.

In addition, over time, I learned to admire Hopkins's craft—his desire to wrestle the sonnet form into a nonce version; the sprung rhythm; the poem's movement from man to God to man (to whom on first reading I patiently added women); the celebration of creation through the celebration of the abundance of the world and a deity's grace. I continue to borrow from Hopkins because, for me, such are the ingredients of a life in composition: unusual, oxymoronic, deeply-rooted, long-lasting.

In the preface of his Yale Younger Poets' Award winning collection *Praise*, poet Robert Hass describes a situation in which someone confronted with "a beast so large, terrifying, and unpredictable" is asked what to do. He replies, "I think I shall praise it" (1).

Like Hopkins, like Hass, I think many in composition are appreciators of the underappreciated, individuals who challenge the odds, take on large and difficult tasks, and make much of what is generally overlooked or undervalued. It is our work and we do well to praise it.

• • •

I find it helpful to explore the value of compositionists understanding themselves as a dedicated minority *by choice*: as agents instead of as those acted upon. After years of experiencing myself at odds with English studies, a wannabe not getting past the guardians at the literary gates, but alive and energized by writing classrooms, my biographical movement into composition felt like coming home.

For me, such movement was quite different than were my motions in the English department. For that, the image in Bede's *Ecclesiastical History of the English People*, which I had read in my undergraduate literature courses, comes to mind. In the chapter on the conversion of King Edwin, Edwin has accepted the new faith but needs the green light from his counselors, who look at their old lives in light of the promise of the new Christian life they are being offered, one with an afterlife. One counselor speaks:

> This is how the present life of man on earth, King, appears to me in comparison with that time which is unknown to us. You are sitting feasting with your ealdormen and thegns in winter time; the fire is burning on the hearth in the middle of the hall and all inside is warm, while outside the wintry storms of rain and snow are raging; and a sparrow flies switfly through the hall. It enters in at one door and quickly flies out through the other. For the few moments it is inside, the storm and wintry tempest cannot touch it, but after the briefest moment of calm, it flits from your sight, out of the wintry storm and into it again. So this life of man appears but for a moment; what follows or indeed what went before, we know not at all. If this new doctrine [Christianity] brings us more certain information, it seems right that we should accept it. (184–85)

I felt like a sparrow (not a Hopkins finch), making her mad dash into and out of promised warmth. Invited into and then out of the English studies' meadhall. I worked as a part-time and adjunct teacher for the next ten years before returning to graduate school. Because I had found no middle ground and apparently no afterlife, I was ripe for conversion into composition and rhetoric. The odds did not appall me; they were what I was used to with the added fillip of the promise of a new community, a place to stand, with others. In graduate school I would be introduced to the intriguing idea of a Burkean parlor. Rereading this passage, I am surprised that what I once found welcoming, I now find more similar to the meadhall than I had once thought. More similar, too similar perhaps, because this field really isn't any longer—if it ever was—well represented as a cozy nineteenth-century parlor?

> Imagine that you enter a parlor. You come late. When you arrive, others have long preceded you, and they are engaged in a heated discussion, a discussion too heated for them to pause and tell you exactly what it is about. In fact, the discussion had already begun long before any of them got there, so that no one present is qualified to retrace for you all the steps that had gone before. You listen for a while, until you decide that you have caught the tenor of the argument; then you put in your oar. Someone answers; you answer him; another comes to your defense; another aligns himself against you, to either the embarrassment or gratification of your opponent, depending upon the quality of your ally's assistance. However, the discussion is interminable. The hour grows late, you must depart. And you do depart, with the discussion still vigorously in progress. (Burke 110–11)

In fact, my life in composition more often resembles moments on a convention elevator. Fumblingly, I press a handful of buttons as I enter and move faster or slower at the mechanical beast's whim. Others get on and off at different floors, I disembark and re-enter, multiple times, over time, and arrive at some point at a new floor, then another, then another: enough to keep me interested throughout a professional lifetime, if I so choose. But also much is seen partially, briefly, at a distance as often as close up. I've learned that after conversion, comes longer reflection.

• • •

In Joe Harris's *A Teaching Subject* I found a newly-significant-to-me critique of the term community: "For like the pronoun *we*," says Harris, "*community* can be used in such a way that it invokes what it seems merely to describe" (99–100, emphasis in original). I revised this text with a view to replacing all invoking *we*'s because I can only provide my momentary snapshot, a view that is situated, partial, and heartfelt. Or, as Harris explains, "Most talk about utopias scares me. What I value instead is a kind of openness, a lack of plan, a chance both to be among others and to choose my own way" (107). I have long been one who preferred to be among others *only* if I can choose my own way. Perhaps this is true for you also if my premise holds that many arrived in composition studies to find a refuge from other, less hospitable spaces.

• • •

In the mid-1980s, Gary Olson published a useful teaching essay investigating the cliché. His research reminds me that what is clichéd and expected to me may be new or functional to my younger students. There are also similarities to teaching innovations. As a young teacher, every new teaching theory and strategy was a delight, offered me insights. Then, I found myself helping new teachers learn to use an activity for the first time. I had to remind myself that what was beginning to sound like old news to me might still be new—not over-worked nor mined out—for them.

Part of maturing within a field is to recognize this cyclical process. I began to notice how activities and theories were being discarded or over-written even as I felt I was just beginning to gain success with them. So too scholarly work; researchers, scholars, writers, writing students delight in coining the new.

Generations become shorter—the thirty year span of family generation dissolves into blended families, and scholarship appears to have a decade's currency, if that long, and graduate program generations last from five to seven years. Pressures to professionalize, to produce better writers, to provide inoculating three-day in-services for new teachers that press teachers to work ever more efficiently under stress-inducing conditions wring shorter and shorter half-lives out of many.

Some days, I am not savoring, glorying in, praising, I'm pursued, running after something, or alongside a heavily breathing someone. In her introduction to *Living Rhetoric and Composition*, Andrea Lunsford summarizes the history of the field by pointing to

> the journey from other fields . . . to a new field of study; the institutional struggles and punishments . . . the role that the GI Bill, 1960s activism, and programs like open admissions played in helping scholars (re) imagine themselves as rhetoricians and compositionists; the shock of recognition that teaching, really teaching, seems to have brought to many, along with a growing realization that the teaching of writing and literacies offers rich and compelling rewards. . . . [T]he battles for tenure and promotion . . . always the battles for tenure and promotion. (Roen, Brown, and Enos xi–xii)

In the same volume Ed Corbett provides his own benchmarks of field-maturity in a list that includes the growth of graduate programs, as well as the increase in field-specific books, new journals, and new research (Roen, Brown, and Enos 5–6). Theresa Enos defines her place in composition and rhetoric's generational progression as that of a "notch baby," one who was born

> right after the Great Depression that interrupted the otherwise increasingly generational growth. . . . I'm a one-point-fiver in rhetoric, too. I came along right between the real pioneers like Ed Corbett and Janice Lauer and the first replication of those who created the second wave, the real crest, of doctoral programs in rhetoric and composition. (Roen, Brown, and Enos 76)

Like Theresa Enos, I often find myself trying to figure out what or who my generation is: two-point-five, three? How long does my knowledge have currency, and how do I stay current with new knowledge?

When rhetoricians and compositionists offer "stories of the discipline," you'll find an overflow of celebration and emotion as well as an undertow of concern and worry. John Trimbur revisits Corbett's claim when he voices his own,

> Looking back on this period of time I spent studying composition (rhetoric came later), there is something remarkable about it that I want to note, and that is the fact that in the late 1970s one could actually stay current with the field. I do not believe this is the case anymore. . . . And this doesn't even take into account what people feel they need to read in other fields. When 'theory' hit in the 1980s, it only multiplied the amount of reading one had to do . . . (Roen, Brown, and Enos 136–37)

And in another collection, *Comp Tales*, readers learn of an exhausted teacher-father at a soccer game who says: "Suddenly I had a vision that made me cringe. I was looking through my son's eyes and seeing his dad sitting in the stands, hunched over, marking student papers" (Haswell and Lu 148). After this vision, the writing teacher reluctantly abandons twelve years of graduate school, part-timing, and tenure-line work in order to become a financial advisor with weekends to spend with his family.

• • •

Like many of you, I have a group of friends I met at this convention. I look forward to re-connecting with them each year. Two of these, Libby Rankin and Lad Tobin, solidified their friendship one evening after a session that had been lively and too short (or perhaps it had been dull and too long?); in any event, they continued their talk about student writing by each taking a stack of the student papers they inevitably brought with them on the plane and sharing them in a downstairs bar, an event that came to be called Nerds Night Out.

Regularly, Lad begins our annual convention breakfast with the observation that he's totally burned out, and then cheers up immeasurably as the bacon and eggs and toast and juice and coffee and talk go down. Before long, he is working on his next convention proposal, his new idea for research, and ways to branch out as a writer.

• • •

I looked up the word *burnout*. It's not in my thesaurus, but I am offered *weariness* and its cognates: *fatigue, boredom, repetition, beat, blasé, spent, played out, sleepy, uninterested, on one's last legs*. I had not thought beyond *fatigue*. But *boredom, repetition, disinterest* will certainly bring anyone to his or her last legs. When I turned to a pocket dictionary I fared better: "Burn-out. (1) cessation of operation of a jet or rocket engine and (2) physical or emotional exhaustion, often a result of stress. Antonyms: energy and amusement."

Since I too regularly feel crisp around the edges, I start to consider whether or not I am maturing into a generational cliché myself, less *counter, original, spare,* and *strange,* more *slow, sour,* or *dim.* Myself, but different. I worry not simply about age, time in the field, time in the saddle, but about good people having chosen good work under difficult conditions. I envisioned these colleagues as rocket ships crashing to desert dunes due to physical *and* emotional exhaustion. Yet I know these individuals continue because they have chosen to, because they are engaged intellectuals and activists, because they are teachers in love with writing and teaching. Every working day these individuals tilt the odds, incrementally, in our field's favor.

• • •

As part of my job, I review statistical reports and survey results with NCTE staff. Certain numbers impress me in my 2001 NCTE/CCCC executive committee report binder. First, that of approximately 60,000 college writing teachers in the country, CCCC members total only about 8,000 and of those 8,000 approximately 3,000 attend our annual convention. Second, that from 15 to 30 percent of our 8,000 members are new—annually. That means 15–30 percent of our members *aren't* renewing: We're not losing membership overall but we're not growing as we should. In addition, and most problematic, of those members we lose, nearly half (43 percent) are our newest members, teacher-scholar-researchers who have been with us from one to four years. Although these figures don't factor for those who have become members, stopped out a year or more, and then joined again, they do suggest that a significant number of attendees of the 2001 convention won't renew membership and/or be back in 2002.

Our conference has grown enormously since the CCCC held its first two-day convention in 1949 in the Stevens Hotel in Chicago with only three sessions each day. Although I still delight in the Burkean parlor metaphor, I wonder if it is not disingenuous. Always, as an organization, we want to know if members bored out, burned out, didn't feel at home, or simply couldn't afford to return for some time. Certainly a number of factors influence such a decision; nevertheless, some members—unfortunately—will not find exactly what they have come looking for. And we want to change that.

Joe Harris' chapter on "Community" in *A Teaching Subject* has been most useful to me here as I've been trying to figure out what sometimes goes wrong in what's so right. At the end of his book, Harris notes:

> But I am growing less inclined to valorize notions of conflict or struggle in and of themselves. I want instead to argue for a more expansive view of intellectual life than I now think theories of the contact zone have to offer—one that admits to the ways in which we are positioned by gender, race, and class, but that also holds out the

hope of a more fluid and open culture in which we can *choose* the positions we want to speak from and for. To work as teachers toward such a culture, we need to move beyond thinking in terms of fixed affinities or positions and the possible conflicts between them. We instead need to imagine a different sort of social space where people have *reason* to come into contact with each other because they have claims and interests that extend beyond the borders of their own safe houses, neighborhoods, disciplines, or communities. (124, emphasis in original)

Many of us have gone beyond the meadhall and the parlor, and I believe there is a need to do so. For instance, I find my friends puzzling out the place of the emotions and sentiments they feel about their work. At its best, our own annual convention, to slightly change Harris, allows teachers to examine claims and interests that extend beyond the borders of their safe houses, neighborhoods, disciplines, or communities. To discover what they can see, give what they can give, take back what they can find.

Tom Newkirk describes an expansive teaching space in this manner:

The ideological space of a composition course, while never unbounded, can be expanded or contracted—and students look to determine these degrees of freedom. Teachers who choose to keep this space relatively open are often perceived as being 'soft,' teaching 'low risk' courses, not academically rigorous. Yet if we are to take culture seriously, we are to learn about culture from our students, it follows that we need a space big enough for a diversity of forms of self-representation. (107)

And I find that definition—space enough for "a diversity of forms of self-representation"—works equally well for a convention, for the intellectual arenas created by our journal, for the talk that takes place on our listservs through professional email exchanges, and within programs lucky enough to have more than a single compositionist on staff.

Through individual participation in these venues, we forge new wholes. The more active our membership is in asking for what it needs, the more interested and invested it will become. This is to say, the Conference on College Composition and Communication can and will start initiatives, report on progress, set up new spaces. But it's like voting in a national election—something someone from the state of Florida has learned a lot about—spaces are filled with conversation if people are willing to converse. Panelists are most effective when audiences feel talked *with*, not *at*. Newcomers feel welcome if they are greeted, listened to, and included in continuing groups. Journals publish what we want and need to read if we all become teacher scholars sharing, listening.

I'm concerned with composing communities or configuring spaces in varied ways, counter, original spare ways, ways that require new metaphors. Here's how I believe it works: If I don't want new conference members to feel that they just flew through the meadhall, a sparrow noted but not nurtured, or left as the hour grew late and unsure if they will return, then I need to attend to my life in the field, each year studying my classrooms and current research; each year attending local, regional and/or national conferences, particularly CCCC; each year listening to presenters, attending a caucus, a workshop, a special interest group, participating in the annual business meeting. I need to celebrate and watch for that quiet moment when a few individuals gather unscripted to celebrate and share their work. In that sense, it's not theory or practice, this or that, it's person to person, feeling safe and unsafe, challenged and rewarded, confused and enthused, fatigued and renewed. This comes with the territory, and what a territory it is. As Jim Corder put it: "Rhetoric is love, and it must speak a commodious language, creating a world full of space and time that will hold our diversities" ("Argument" 428).

• • •

These are the spaces I hope we as a conference will continue to keep open; these are the spaces I hope we as members will fill.

Against the odds, this is the life I have chosen to live in composition, captured momentarily and shared in this poem.

My Convention Poem

My convention poem has elevator eyelids and a concierge's phone ringing without remorse all night.[2]

My convention poem flaunts its badges and free samples in the face of a chafing dish lobby breakfast bar with sad fruit baskets and scorched coffee urns.[3]

My convention poem bursts at the heart-seams when the crowd likes its paper even if they didn't attend, didn't listen, didn't seem to quite understand.[4]

My convention poem goes down on its knees at the exhibit hall trampled by a pod of discount purchasers and last day packaways.[5]

My convention poem is an expectant handshake and wink late night lobby dark where the unsayable is finally said and concerns are translated into conversations of sudden sociability.[6]

My convention poem is the swimming pool seen from the 24th floor going down fast on an outside vertigo elevator, the red eye strange city sunset, the looming awake by the rain-misted non-opening window of a barely inhabited room where the insufficient hairdryer and Mr. Coffee sing hey, diddle diddle to the waning moon together.[7]

My convention poem is a good idea tucked in my pocket like a business card, is that break in city traffic when I rush across without crosswalk, suddenly outside, and see all this simply as part of my life, like the moment faces reflect out of a grand ball-room mirrored wall like memory or a piece of familiar luggage settling into the held luggage area for one last long day until shaken into the maw of a departing taxi.[8]

My convention poem is a bee hive an ant colony a home that has spread its architectural wings to the greatest excess, is a myth is a role a delight a fresh and stale breath, is a heart breaker a home breaker a career maker a sob and a snooze, is a galvaniz-ing detour into another phrase of my life.[9]

My convention poem packs up and never goes home — is always al-ready at home — in the exhibit hall when writing teachers give way to tile setters, tile to computer programming, programming to dentists, parochial to medical, law to athletics, and the tides of the world and the turns of the hotel corridors tell us that our conventions will continue to go in and out and ebb and flow with or without us while we return to the reliable ground floors of our everyday lives.[10]

NOTES

1. This Chair's address draws on the poetry of Gerard Manley Hopkins to explore and cele-brate a life in composition. Acknowledging institutional fatigue, I outline possibilities for individual renewal, particularly through the process of mentoring new members. Ending with a convention poem, I invite readers to compose their own.

2. My most persistent convention memories include elevators. Being stuck in them with strangers, waiting so long I want to run up the staircases, thinking, this hotel will never get us all where we need to be, something a little scary and claustrophobic and "not like home."

3. To escape the crowds I wander to a bench, a foyer, a breakfast cart nearby; I'm out of the way, trying to identify the particular smell, alighting finally on that of scorched coffee, brewed too early for too many late risers. Nothing prepared me for the rigor needed — indulging late in talking and taxi rides to dinners and then getting up early to try to pre-pare to face the world of business-like breakfasts. Some people in the coffee shop looked so at home, but I'd notice others, like me, drifting at the fringe, unable to decide just where to go, who to be, what to say.

4. Who doesn't remember her paper-giving experiences? My first: a last slot on Saturday. Three presenters, four audience members: one friend for each speaker and my major professor.

5. First timers have to be initiated into the practical lore — you can get your books at dis-count on the last day. You can eat "free" at publishers' parties.

6. Even for an introvert, eventually, things pick up. Someone talks to you in the lavatory (especially if you're a woman waiting in longer lines), someone drifts by and reads your name tag at a reception, someone you argue with in a Q and A session keeps the conver-sation going, a SIG proves a first network location and suddenly the forbidding late night hotel lounge looks much much more familiar. A foyer. An annex to whom you might become. You clear your voice.

7. One day, it all turns into too many hotel rooms. A bathroom drawer at home crammed full of soap and shampoo samples. That "where am I?" feeling when awak-ened by late night hall door slamming or the realization that you were given a room near the ice-machine or the elevator or have arrived in a city where fun is defined by false fire alarms.

8. Some conventions never see the light of day. If you start to serve, you start to see that the profession is surprisingly like an enormous English department meeting: rife with issues, personalities, possibilities, and problems. Only you elected to talk to these folks, then they elected you to talk.

9. It is camp, old home week, a club. You now start to feel older. You tell stories (you think). Promulgate myths and advice: Never propose alone, never propose as a panel, always propose alone, always use the convention title in your proposal, never go to X, Y, Z, always go to X, Y, Z, don't miss the keynote address, do miss it because it's published anyway, always go to X's talk, you won't regret it, you will. Did you know Y and Z are or aren't? Have you heard. I used to . . . but now I don't.

10. Once you were timorous and afraid, now you may be jaded, or you may be in the middle—seeing what's useful—seeing others just arriving, thinking of those who have recently left. Your bag is cram-packed—promotional buttons, sewing kit and shower cap, catalog, shopping spree, notes, unused handouts, small sheaves of ideas, more notes. You'll return. Or not. You'll enlist in more, or resist. You've been, unwittingly, part of someone else's convention poem. Now you must write your own.

WORKS CITED

Bede, the Venerable, Saint. *Ecclesiastical History of the English People*. Ed. and trans. Bertram Colgrave and R.A.B. Mynors. New York: Oxford UP, 1969.

Bishop, Wendy. "My Conference Poem" (earlier version of "My Convention Poem") first appeared online in *Academic Writing* 2000. <http://aw.colostate.edu>.

Burke, Kenneth. *The Philosophy of Literary Form*. Berkeley: U of California P, 1974.

"Burn-out." *The New American Webster Handy College Dictionary*, 3rd ed., 1995.

Corder, Jim. "Argument as Emergence, Rhetoric as Love." *Professing the New Rhetorics: A Sourcebook*. Ed. Theresa Enos and Stuart S. Brown. Englewood Cliffs, NJ: Prentice Hall, 1994. 413–28.

———. "Hunting for *Ethos* Where They Say It Can't Be Found." *Rhetoric Review* 7 (1989): 299–316.

Crane, Stephen. *The Complete Poems of Stephen Crane*. Ed. Joseph Katz. Ithaca, NY: Cornell UP, 1972.

Harris, Joseph. *A Teaching Subject: Composition Since 1966*. Upper Saddle River, NJ: Prentice Hall, 1997.

Hass, Robert. *Praise*. New York: Echo, 1974.

Haswell, Richard H., and Min-Zhan Lu. *Comp Tales: An Introduction to College Composition through Its Stories*. White Plains, NY: Longman, 1999.

Hopkins, Gerard Manley. *Poems and Prose*. Ed. W.H. Gardner. New York: Penguin, 1953.

Newkirk, Thomas. *The Performance of Self in Student Writing*. Portsmouth, NH: Heinemann-Boynton/Cook, 1997.

Olson, Gary. "The Generational Cliché: Then You Saw It; Now They Don't." *JAC* 6 (1985–86): 105–15.

Reon, Duane, Stuart Brown, and Theresa Enos, ed. *Living Rhetoric and Composition: Stories of the Discipline*. Mahwah NJ: Erlbaum, 1999.

"Weariness." *The New American Roget's College Thesaurus in Dictionary Form*, rev. ed. 1985.

▬▬▬

AFTERWORD: WRITING TEACHERS: A "DEDICATED MINORITY BY CHOICE"

Wendy Bishop's CCCC Chair's address, "Against the Odds in Composition and Rhetoric," reminded me of a conversation I once had with a friend who was not a writing teacher.* Provoked by a recently proposed departmental reorganization at my university, I was venting my frustrations

———————

*Pavel Zemliansky wrote this reflection on the 2001 Chair's address.

about the power struggles within English studies. Afraid that the proposed change would, again, hand composition the short end of the stick, I told my friend that someone always prospers at writing teachers' expense. I must have projected the image of an injured sufferer that evening because after hearing me out, my friend told me to quit whining and to drop the victim mentality.

In her address, Wendy Bishop makes an important distinction between simply being a minority and being a "minority by choice." She writes that teachers of writing and rhetoric are the "Other" of English studies, the backbenchers who work against the odds to win recognition and reward and to effect change. According to Bishop, remaining in opposition to more powerful forces may be beneficial for us as a profession because it pushes us along the road of change and innovation. In her words, we are "agents instead of those acted upon."

Of course, professional recognition and the ability to influence the environments in which we work are important for writing teachers. We should continue to serve on influential committees, have our scholarship recognized by prestigious publishing houses and journals, and convince our counterparts in other disciplines that composition is an established field and not some weird offshoot of English whose members "fix" students' bad grammar and spelling because they could not cut it in literary studies. In a word, we need to keep our professional status up.

But we must also resist making the fight for institutional recognition a defining feature of our professional identities. In addition to fighting for the institutional prestige of our profession, we must elevate our profession through qualities and activities that often distinguish us from others. It is our meticulous attention to our students' learning and writing, to innovative pedagogies and theories that will win us distinction in the long run. It is also the collegiality, the spirit of support that is so evident at CCCC and our other professional meetings and that is often so absent from gatherings in other academic disciplines.

Intradisciplinary debates and struggles are here to stay. It is up to us, both as a discipline and as individuals, to find ways of maintaining our professional identity and dignity while not allowing this fight for recognition to harm our teaching and scholarship. Working with Wendy closely for several years, I could see that institutional conflicts were taking a toll on her. Yet, when talking to students and colleagues, she was always able to shrug them aside and focus on teaching and writing instead. I am confident that our profession can continue to work in the same spirit.

– PAVEL ZEMLIANSKY
James Madison University

2002   *All Good Writing Develops at the Edge of Risk*[1]

JOHN C. LOVAS

[A free write] Just plunge in. Just start. That's it, keep going, keep writing, word-by-word, bird-by-bird, tur . . . who said that? Annie Dillard, no, Annie Staunton, Ann E. Lovas, Annie Lamott, whatever, you've got your A-list now, so Just Do It—oh, don't get me started, this is stupid, it's silly, you just keep writing. Yeah, trust the process, Luke. I'm John. Well, Matthew, Mark, whatever, trust the process. Keep the cursor moving, and you'll get to something. Like what I want to do is make four or five points but to do so in different forms, some of the common forms of college composition. There, I got it in— college composition—that's what we're all about, right? We compose. We're in colleges (ok, universities, too, and adult schools and community schools), and we're always trying to figure out what we're about. So that's the idea—keep going—to write in personal narrative, in the five-paragraph essay, the polemic, the argument, maybe journals and reflections, oh, and e-mails—gotta get e-mails in if it's 2002—and freewriting, generative writing, this stuff, the Macrorie and Elbow stuff. So you've started, now where do you begin?

THE UNIVERSAL, THE COMMON, THE COLLEGIAL: THE MANY VOICES OF OUR PROFESSIONAL CONVERSATION

A five-paragraph essay in exactly 500 words, beginning with a strong declarative sentence. ["I'm suspicious of calls for coherence"—David Bartholomae] We talk to each other through journals, newsletters, and Web pages. We converse formally through panels and informally in the hallways at our conferences. In our search for understanding how the

This article is a revised version of the Chair's address John C. Lovas delivered at the CCCC Convention in Chicago, Illinois, on March 21, 2002. A previous version was published in *CCC*, volume 54, number 2, December 2002.

written word works, we simplify for our students (the five-paragraph essay) and complexify for each other (a Bakhtinian moment in a Vygotskyan process on the margin of the contact zone). Often, our *unum* gets lost in our *pluribus* [thesis statement].

Discovering the universal has long been the goal of the university [topic sentence]. Research takes the universe as its subject, then explores the nooks and crannies of heavens and earth, formulating laws that apply universally. The microscope and telescope blend as we search for the tiniest elements in the farthest reaches of space. Our impulse to find the broadest generalizations can conflict with the desire to experience a single sunset or to love this one person.

Paradoxically [transition word], focusing on the unknown and the particular can blind us to the common: those patterns that bind us in community, those impulses to connect to others, to feel wanted, needed, and supported. The common may be ordinary, hardly worth noting, but it also binds us. The Diaspora story of the Old Testament emphasizes the idea that languages divided us; we lacked a common tongue. Recently, the work of the late Joseph Greenberg and that of Noam Chomsky argues we share the language ability in common [allusion and reference]—that all languages derive from a common languaging capacity. We are a global community if only we could understand our commonality and our commonness.

When we organize institutions of higher education, we call some universities and others colleges. One name emphasizes the search for ultimate truths; the other name suggests joining together, our common enterprise. In 4Cs, we left nothing to chance. All four nouns in our name have their root in Latin *cum* (with). We are together, with one another, gathered in common, to talk seriously about the exchange of ideas and the putting of things into proper position. Let me gloss from the *OED*.

- **conference:** the act of conversing on serious subjects, formal discourse
- **college:** an organized society of persons . . . a body of colleagues, a guild, fellowship, association
- **composition:** the putting of things into proper position, order, or relation to other things
- **communication:** the imparting, conveying, or exchange of ideas, knowledge, information, etc. (whether by speech, writing, or signs)

Perhaps our founders understood our impulse to individual expression so well that they named this group "Together on Together Together and Together."

Our culture—and our own scholarship—has given significant attention to identity, creation of the self, the myriad ways in which humans express themselves: capturing the unique moment in the right word, the apt image. In the face of the larger collective, we formulate little "togethers": committees, special interest groups, caucuses. The university folk seek their own; the community college people gather separately; the small liberal arts colleges ask for their own space. Let's remember we do all of this as ConColCompComm.

IT'S MORE THAN GOING TO SESSIONS: TWO CONFERENCE NARRATIVES

I am in the latter years of an extremely satisfying career as a college teacher, employed by the same district (though two different colleges) for thirty-six years—and counting. Always active in professional organizations, I was president of an AFT local and played a role in founding our union, the Foothill-De Anza Faculty Association. I've also had leadership roles in ECCTYC/TYCA-Pacific Coast, National TYCA, and now CCCC, so I have been to many conferences.[2]

Serving as an officer for TYCA and now CCCC, I have been privileged to travel throughout the United States, discovering many texts in very different streets. I documented some of that in the preview and program books for our meeting in Denver last year. In the last seven years of professional travel, I've wandered in St. Augustine, Disney World, the Mall of America, Opryland, Broadway at night and Greenwich Village, Palm Springs, the Children's Museum in Indianapolis, the Venetian, Bellagio, and Luxor casino hotels in Las Vegas, Charleston, the Town and Country Mall in Kansas City, and Wrigley Field and GospelFest right here in Chicago. While I cannot recount transformative experiences from any of these monuments of our culture, two others have had a deep impact on me.

Let me begin in Memphis, Tennessee. I was the national TYCA representative to the TYCA-Southeast regional conference, February 1999, at a hotel on the outskirts of the city. The Friday evening social hour and buffet were followed by a reception sponsored by a textbook publisher in the National Civil Rights Museum. Although I have been active in civil rights issues since 1959, I hadn't heard of this museum. Large buses ferried us to the locale, very much a tourist moment. But as I stepped off the bus, there was the Lorraine Motel, just as it looked in all that 1968 television footage. Instinctively, I turned my head and spotted the building from which the fatal shot was fired, martyring the greatest American moral leader of my lifetime. Thirty-one years telescoped instantly.

When I recovered my bearings, I joined my colleagues in the museum, which powerfully documents the civil rights movement, as led by Rev. Martin Luther King, Jr., from 1956 to 1968 and as carried out by black college students and everyday black Americans and a wide range of other Americans from every region, background, and walk of life.

A diorama reenacts the Birmingham bus boycott, including the bus that Rosa Parks sat in, refusing to move to the rear. A display documents the sit-ins of early 1960, begun in Nashville but gaining national attention in Greensboro, North Carolina. As a college senior and editor of the campus newspaper, I had brought this issue to the attention of my fellow

students at John Carroll University, an all male, virtually all white, student body. The notion of supporting black students in the south did not sit well with many campus leaders or many of the faculty. The imagery of the museum triggered a flood of recollections: the burned-out bus from the Freedom Riders, a diorama including an actual Memphis garbage truck, with the sanitation workers and National Guardsmen facing off, and a replica of the Birmingham jail cell where Rev. Martin Luther King, Jr., wrote his epistle to the American people, that brilliant essay that I and so many of you have used in our writing courses. Most powerfully, the museum display ends in the only two rooms remaining from the Lorraine Motel: one is the room that Rev. King shared with Rev. Ralph Abernathy, down to a replica of the remains of the catfish lunch they had shared; the other adjoins it, providing an hour-by-hour accounting of the final twenty-four hours leading to the fateful moment at 6:00 p.m. April 8, 1968.

"Living history" is a marketer's phrase, but it fits the National Civil Rights Museum. I was transported to all those times from the late-50s to 1968, reliving wrenching event after wrenching event. Arriving for evening cocktails, I was not prepared for the depth and intensity of emotions that tour evoked. Important parts of my life passed before my mind's eye.

The next day, Saturday afternoon, the conference offered a trip to Graceland, the national shrine to a different kind of hero of my adolescence, Elvis Presley. I sense a deep ambivalence in my cultural responses to Elvis. The seductive richness of his voice, whether singing pop, rock, blues, or gospel, remains a blessing. He simultaneously introduced the rhythms of black music to the full range of American youth and provoked an ongoing debate about the black roots of pop rock.

To my surprise, Elvis's career, as documented in his Memphis home, evoked many of the same emotions I'd felt the night before. The news clippings, album covers and movie posters, and other memorabilia from Memphis and Nashville had me hearing again the sounds I first heard on WJW in Cleveland as the Moondogger (disc jockey Alan Freed) introduced me to rock 'n' roll, those rhythms that moved north from New Orleans to Memphis to Chicago.

This juxtaposition of Elvis with Rev. King was accidental, not historical. The connection may be idiosyncratic but for me emotionally powerful. The voices of Rev. Martin Luther King, Jr., and Elvis Presley remain the most evocative human sounds of my late adolescence. In very different ways, they were like the older brothers I never had, leading me into racial and cultural understandings I could not find in my all-white northern suburb:

> **MLK, JR.:** I have a dream, that one day down in Alabama with its vicious racists, with its senator having his lips dripping with the words of this particular nullification, one day like that in Alabama, little black boys and black girls will be able to join hands with little white boys and white girls as sisters and brothers, I have a dream today . . . ("I Have a Dream")

> **ELVIS:** I believe for every drop of rain that falls, a flower grows, I believe somewhere in the darkest night, a candle glows . . . ("I Believe")

> **MLK, JR.:** I may not get to the mountaintop. Like anybody I would like to live a long life, longevity has its place. But I'm not concerned about that now. I just want to do God's will. And he's allowed me to go up to the mountain and I've looked over and I've seen the Promised Land. I may not get there with you. ("I've Been to the Mountaintop")

> **ELVIS:** Walk on, walk on, with hope in your heart and you'll never walk alone, you'll never walk alone. ("You'll Never Walk Alone")

Why tell this story? And why tell it this way? It would be safer to forget the Graceland/Elvis part—but not honest. The combination of experiences stirred me up for weeks.

Then, just a month after Memphis, I was at the 50th CCCC, my first time in Atlanta. The first six days, I barely left the hotel. Saturday night, I rented a car and reserved a room in a bed-and-breakfast in a residential neighborhood. Sunday morning, I headed for the King Center, first driving around the Sweet Auburn neighborhood to get a sense of place, then going to the main building with the displays of Rev. Martin Luther King, Jr.'s life. The heart of the exhibit is a series of transparent walls with text and photos, each station including a video monitor with key scenes from Rev. King's life and The Movement. At the third station, seeing again those images of massed law enforcement officers, police dogs, fire hoses, young people being washed down the street, tears welled up. I really was so lost in the images and the memories, I'd lost track of myself. Then I felt someone take my hand and squeeze it gently. I turned to see a young

African American woman who said, simply, "It's OK. This is my first time here too. I'm from Nashville."

What else to say? I finished touring the exhibit, floating, on a natural high. I planned to see the Ebenezer Baptist Church next, when I noticed there's a new church, and Palm Sunday services were just ending. I watched the worshippers file away, then went over to have a look at this new structure. From the corner of my eye, I saw a striking woman in a gold suit. Quick double take—yes, it was Coretta Scott King. And I'm looking like a tourist doofus in my Cleveland Indians All-Star game T-shirt. No matter. I walk over, introduce myself, and she graciously engages in a few minutes of conversation, all under the watchful eye of a burly young man who is both chauffeur and bodyguard. At that moment, I fully expected a complete stranger would walk up to me to say I'd won the Lotto and here was my check for $10,000,000. These are moments lived and savored and really need no explication. I'll just recall these words from Keith Gilyard's Chair's address two years ago: "I think King had it right, for example, when he dreamed of Black kids and White kids holding hands."

Fragments of My Literacy Autobiography

All writing is autobiography.

—Donald Murray

I have a ragbag mind full of bits and pieces of useless material I dare not throw away.

—Student paper (the opening of a student paper my second year of teaching, a line I've never forgotten)

Early in my teaching career, I assigned students to research the week of their birth as a way of getting them engaged with periodical sources. In both my developmental and first-year writing courses now, I assign students a reading or writing autobiography. Here, briefly, are "bits and pieces of useless material" I'd draw on in constructing my own literacy autobiography.

The grandchild of immigrants: Frank Lovas and Julia Horvath were Hungarian speakers who learned English. Peter Noone and Anna Staunton were English speakers who knew Gaelic. None of them graduated high school. None of this reached my childhood. My parents were the occasion of language shift, and I was an English-only boy, a working-class kid who got a good Catholic school education (St. Angela Merici in Fairview Park, Ohio; St. Edward High School in Lakewood, Ohio), followed by a Jesuit college education (John Carroll University). My Irish-American mother and Hungarian-American father raised seven kids on a factory worker's wages.

Born November 4, 1939, in St. John's Hospital in Cleveland, Ohio. A few hours earlier that morning, the *Cleveland Plain Dealer* headlined:

NAZI CREW SEIZED, FLINT IS FREED

The *City of Flint*, an American freighter taken by a German prize crew, had been returned to its American crew by Norwegian officials after the ship anchored in Oslo. The other lead story

reported Congress passing the Neutrality Act, a victory for FDR. We always had newspapers at home. My mother delivered newspapers as a girl to help her widowed mother make ends meet. When I was eight, I got a weekly paper route. I delivered dailies all through high school and got a scholarship to college from the Cleveland Press. I still subscribe to three daily newspapers.

As the first-born child, my mother read to me in the afternoon before naptime and in the evening before bedtime. Little Golden Books, *The Little Engine That Could*, the traditional fairy tales. She also read to me from her high school poetry textbook, *The Loyola Book of Verse*, and wrote to me that our favorites were "Trees" and "The House with Nobody in It" by Joyce Kilmer, T. A. Daly's "Da Grata Basaballa" and John Henry Newman's "Lead Kindly Light." Also, Poe's "The Raven," James Ryder's "Why the Robin's Breast is Red," and Tennyson's "The Brook." In the same note she wrote, "The summer you were 4 (1943) you wanted a library card. I couldn't go with you—Jackie was a baby, so you went yourself." The librarian was Ruth Morris, my mother told me, but I remember Bernice

Happer, a woman who clearly loved children and books. If I wanted a book beyond the children's section, she'd check it out to me. I read all the Andrew Lang fairy-tale books, the Childhood of Famous Americans series, the John R. Tunis baseball books, and, starting about age twelve, every one of the Erle Stanley Gardner Perry Mason mysteries.

Letter writing, especially with relatives in Ireland, was a part of my family culture. My mother also regularly corresponded with her Irish relatives, people she'd never met, so I learned early to write to an unknown audience, sending cousin Briena letters two or three times a year and getting back letters like these from her brothers Joe and Tommy: "Mammy is teaching in Carraholly School and she goes down with the rest of the family at nine o'clock every morning. Daddy works at home on the land." "Mammy" was Aunt Babie, my great aunt, a farmwife and schoolteacher, who, after the family moved to the mainland, rowed out to the island where she taught every morning and rowed back every afternoon, even when pregnant.

Then from "Beach Cove," on October 12, 1944, Aunt Babie wrote, "Isn't it a pity ye are so far away. I am sure the children would enjoy today in our garden. We have 12 men working at the threshing machine, getting our wheat and oats threshed. The day is very fine, and that helps too." She closed, "God bless and guard you all. Kiss the children 100 times for their little cousins."

Like most of us, my early literacy was shaped by women: stories and poems from my mother, letters from Ireland from a teacher aunt, and the kindly Bernice Happer, librarian at our one-room local library, who would always bend the rules for a reader. And also by a very special person, Sister Elizabeth Ann, my second-grade teacher (whose career spanned sixty-four years, from age eighteen to eighty-two).

My mother sent me the original of Sister Elizabeth Ann's letter about ten years ago. She'd saved it from March 2, 1947. It recounts an incident in

which I disrupted class by announcing the date of Sister's birthday, breaking a taboo. She wrote my mother: "John, at least had gotten it out of his system, and I stood the embarrassment, for the pleasure I could see he was enjoying, in knowing some of the deep dark secrets of my personal life. It's well he doesn't know my age or that would have been the news-flash of the day!"

Writing I remember: a report on Jefferson's ideas on education when I was 11, a short story with a great beginning and a poor ending when I was 13, a report on Voltaire when I was 15. Recently reading this paragraph, I thought the style a bit precocious: "In his youth Voltaire shocked his simple old father by his gay idle habits and his way of writing bold, witty, cutting, dangerous verses satirizing many of the powerful men of the day. This was dangerous for these were the days of the tyrant Louis XV." But I found my explanation on the "bibliography" page—citations from three encyclopedias and this author's note: "I did not make any direct quotations in the text because of the large number of them. Any of them could be found in the above bibliography." I was way ahead of Stephen Ambrose in my approach to intellectual property.

My freshman college writing course with Aloysius A. Bungart, a white-haired man with a battered leather briefcase and a corncob pipe, shaped my thinking about college composition. Our text, titled *Writing by Types*, modeled narratives, profiles, character studies, and local color pieces as well as explanatory and argumentative essays. What I internalized then and theorized much later is that a writer develops better by facing and working out a range of rhetorical problems rather than being presented the same rhetorical problem over and over. That's probably why this text has taken the forms it has.

My first published essay, "The Art of Eating French Fries," in my high school literary magazine, *Flight*. Wrote news features in the *Carroll News*. And my editor's column—I concluded one with this sentence: "People who don't try striking out on a new course when they are young could hardly be expected to bring fresh insights to world problems when they reach their middle forties." Later, my first professional article. Still later, a book. And an occasional column in our local weekly newspaper.

Then there are the literacies of feminism, where my wife, Brenda, has been my teacher and mentor. The literacies of multiculturalism—here's the reading list for my basic class this term: Sherman Alexie, Julia Alvarez, Rudolfo Anaya, Frank Chin, Linh Dinh, Chitra Banerjee Divakaruni, Laura Esquivel, Duong Thu Huong, Stephan Jaramillo, Chang-rae Lee, Malcolm Margolin, Toni Morrison, Brian Ascalon Roney.

Literacies of later life: illness, death, grief. When my mother entered the hospice, I tape-recorded several of the poems she had read to me as an infant, and she listened to them almost every day. Because my brothers and sisters are spread across the land, we needed to keep in touch. I put together a kind of listserv so those who were with mom could keep the rest of us informed. Only when she was gone did I realize the seven of us always communicated through her, passing on the news. We've maintained that family list since 1997, adding our children as well. "List mom" still keeps the family in touch.

Anne Gere's sensitive comments in "Revealing Silence: Rethinking Personal Writing" about how one selects the personal to make it public have helped me address this final fragment.

Literacies not yet fully developed: a parent's view of brain-based illnesses, such as bipolar disease and schizo-affective disorder; a piece on the taboo around suicide—having lost a son to a chosen death has been compounded by losing touch with all his friends. Suicide silences most conversations. As a society, we have little understanding of suicide, whether by two teenage boys in Littleton, Colorado, or nineteen terrorists commandeering commercial airliners. We need—I need—greater literacy here.

THREE LISTS

Just consider what associations these three lists create:

Harvard	Ohio State	Flathead Valley
Duke	Penn State	Contra Costa
Stanford	Michigan State	Diablo Valley
Yale	Kansas State	Ketchikan
Princeton	Florida State	Heartland
Brown	Washington State	Del Mar
Wesleyan	Arizona State	Waubonsee
Bryn Mawr		Kapi'olani
		Bunker Hill
		Ohlone

WORKING ON EQUITY IN OUR WORK

CCCC has always addressed issues of professional equity. This morning, we saw the tenth group of Scholars for the Dream acknowledged. Encouraging the full participation of scholars of color has been one of our more significant efforts, one we've institutionalized. The February 2002 issue of *CCC* demonstrates the quality of scholarship generated out of this effort, led initially by Bill Cook and Victor Villanueva. We've gotten this direction right and need to maintain our momentum.

Today, I focus on two other issues of professional equity, a notion I regard as indivisible. In addressing these two issues, I do not claim a hierarchy or pecking order. Sometimes progressives develop "liberal fatigue," a feeling that one is doing as much good as one can handle and so any new cause is overload. Organizational theory offers the concept of "idea integration": when faced with a number of good ideas, you seek out a point of integration, a place that allows you to support each of the worthy ideas.

My first point I have elaborated more fully in an article, entitled "Playrooms, Hodgepodges, Soulless Monsters: Why I Can't Imagine Having a Better Job," in the Fall 2001 *ADE Bulletin*. In a nutshell, my claim is that our profession has an intellectual blind spot regarding knowledge building in and about community colleges. The reasons for this have never been entirely clear to me, but part of it lies in an argument developed in the late 1960s and early 1970s. Jerome Karabel and Steven Zwerling and others made an argument something like this: more minority and low-income students entered two-year colleges than other institutions of higher education, but the rate at which they reach upper division was much lower than the rate at which those who entered universities reached upper division. In this construction, the two-year college was the device of a corporate system intended to dampen the aspirations of minority and poor students. Versions of this idea, first advanced by Burton Clark in 1960 as the "cooling out function" of two-year colleges, became virtually the only idea of two-year colleges adopted by progressive, university-based intellectuals in America. The notion was taken up by Samuel Bowles and Herbert Gintis in 1976 and has been rehearsed as recently as 1994 in Kevin Dougherty's *The Contradictory College*. And in an interview with Howard Tinberg in 1999, Ira Shor repeats this argument, albeit in a context sympathetic to working-class students and two-year colleges.

I will not claim these arguments are without merit. I will say they are inadequate, based on a study done forty-two years ago in one California community college district. As I see it, American higher education has been driven by the efforts of top universities to "select the best and forget the rest." Most high schools buy into this value set. But two-year colleges accept everyone and work hard at helping the whole range of students meet their goals. Two-year colleges have a much larger proportion of students who are both ill prepared and uncertain of their purposes. My personal experience tells me I have students who are as good as any that enter university first. They transfer and they succeed. I could stand here for two hours telling their stories and not repeat myself. One such student (I'll call him Jerome) grew up in Brooklyn, attending what he told me was a high school called the worst in America. A family divorce led him to Florida, where he enrolled in the local community college and, as he put it, "played so much, I flunked out in a year." He returned to New York to live with his father and enrolled in a community college in Brooklyn, where he also was not successful. Finally, his godfather, a San Jose lawyer, had Jerome work in his house, taking care of his children. Jerome enrolled in De Anza and a little over two years later transferred to University of California, Berkeley, where he graduated in 2000. I recently wrote reference letters for Jerome to law schools. Jerome typifies the zigzag pattern through higher education so common among community college students. But I also have many students like Adrian, part Hawaiian and part Filipino, who last week gave his oral report on Brian Ascalon Roney's novel, *The American Son*. Before class, he told me, excitedly, it was the first book he'd ever finished. I don't know how far Adrian will get, though he's clearly distancing himself from his gangbanger brother. His progress will be aided, not impeded, by his work at a two-year college.

Just recently at De Anza College, where I teach, we conducted a sociolinguistic survey among all our developmental and ESL students in November 2001, collecting a total of 1,965 responses from about a hundred sections of students. We asked them their primary reason for attending De Anza. The choices: transfer, vocational, AA/AS degree, personal growth, parents, develop a skill, other. Eighty-eight percent of developmental students said their main reason for attending was "parents." Among ESL students, the figure was 73 percent. I was astonished. Most of my colleagues were astonished. I'm not aware of a comparable survey in a major university, but I suspect the result would differ significantly. More to the point, we don't have the data. I suspect we don't know our students and their purposes as well as we think we do.

Because we have no data center on types of writing courses, I can't document *this* claim: most basic writing students and basic writing courses are found in two-year colleges. But you could read every issue of *CCC* from 1980 to now and have no sense that basic writing students are primarily two-year college students. When Donna Burn Phillips, Ruth Greenberg, and Sharon Gibson chronicled the history of *CCC* from 1950–93, no mention of two-year colleges or their writing programs occurs in the article. No citations of two-year college work appear. Even now that textbooks are increasingly authored by two-year college professors, they are rarely discussed in our journals and meetings.

While it's easy to see this issue as political—junior professors in universities need publications and citations to gain tenure and community college professors do not—I see it as a scholarly and intellectual failing. You cannot represent a field if you ignore half of it. You cannot generalize about composition if you don't know half of the work being done. Besides, there's no reason a junior professor at a university couldn't build a scholarly body of work by including studies of two-year college writers and writing programs. We need new and substantial forms of collaboration on a local and regional basis so that the quality of all writing programs can be improved.

Here's the essence of my argument: much of the theorizing in our profession about basic writing, assessment, grading practices, teaching methods, and text production by students has a thin empirical base. This is not to say that two-year college scholars have done an adequate job of documenting the work in these institutions. We are called the "invisible colleges" both because university researchers rarely study our programs and our students, and because two-year college departments rarely publish program and institutional-based studies of our programs and our students. Then, the small but useful body of scholarship on two-year college writing programs is simply ignored by scholars who do publish in our journals.[3]

Let me turn to my second and final point. Our efforts to address issues related to exploited labor of compositionists founder on the problem that we don't understand well enough the various ways in which the exploitation occurs. In general, writing programs are managed very differently in larger universities from writing programs in community colleges.[4] In general, community colleges hire only faculty who have completed graduate degrees and who have already accumulated some teaching experience. In general, large universities still depend on current graduate students, many of whom are facing their first classroom. Community colleges, enacting the ethic of their mission that they accept all adults who can "profit from instruction," met the onslaught of baby boomers by shifting heavily to underpaid, low benefited, part-time faculty, a situation abetted by universities expanding graduate programs in English, rhetoric, and composition even faster than the colleges could absorb them. Community colleges, from the 1970s to the 1990s, failed to educate taxpayers and legislators about the kind of subsidy involved in meeting half the instructional costs at 40 cents on the dollar. Most community colleges are digging out of a very deep hole in this regard.

We do important work and that makes us each an important member of this society and our communities. Yet the importance of our work is not validated by the most common American standard of worth—pay. This contradiction causes us much stress and pain, occupying a great deal of our professional and personal time. Most of us could tell various stories of how limited pay forced unwanted choices. Here's one of my stories.

In 1960 at the age of twenty, I was accepted into the University of Utah MA program and was offered a teaching assistantship. In exchange for teaching six courses in freshman English over three quarters and ten months, I would be paid $1,420—gross. That worked out to $71 (before deductions) twice a month. When payday fell on a Monday, I might have $2 left on Friday to feed myself over the weekend. Baloney and Wonder® Bread was the entrée, peanut butter and Ritz® Crackers the dessert and snack food. One of my fellow grad students calculated our hourly rate, factoring in classes, prep time, paper grading, and office hours. We were making 13 cents an hour. The preceding summer I had worked in the same factory as my father for $1.40 an hour. No matter what rationalization one wishes to create about apprenticeships and interning and the like, my labor was being exploited by the people of Utah. The university composition requirement was primarily underwritten by my fellow TAs and me.

While we probably have few institutions today that have comparably poor conditions, the fact is that the teaching of composition remains seriously underfunded. As a nation, we are unwilling to graduate students without demonstrating academic literacy, and we are unwilling to pay for it. To the degree any of us are individually or collectively complicit in this contradiction, we should be ashamed.

While many of us have mounted theoretical and moral arguments about this situation, finding the fault in the economic system, in a system used to exploiting the labor of women, in vestiges of medieval hierarchies in universities, we really haven't been very effective in defining the issue clearly for a general audience, the political constituency that could ultimately lead to substantive reform. We adopted the Wyoming resolution in 1987, and virtually every Chair's address since has cited the problem. *CCC* published "One Hundred Ways to Make the Wyoming Resolution a Reality" in 1990 (Wyche-Smith and Rose). But in this new millennium, we have made little headway in public awareness and political effectiveness in addressing the overuse and misuse of part-time, adjunct faculty. While the Coalition on the Academic Workforce report suggests the problem is greatest in two-year colleges, we had the lowest response rate from these colleges, resulting in a muddy picture, at best. And so far, the vested interests of senior faculty in universities have resisted examining the overuse and misuse of teaching assistants with the same level of effort.

A colleague in a large state university told me she left the writing program administrator position when the university insisted on raising the number of TAs from fifty to sixty. A few months ago, she said the number was now 110. Most university English and writing departments seem trapped in the economics of this cycle: the need to maintain large numbers of composition classes to employ large numbers of graduate students to justify the loads of full-time professors in upper-division and graduate courses. Then we can't adequately place those who complete our graduate programs.

While I would agree that comparing first year TA's to community college part-time faculty is unfair to both groups, from a functional standpoint, each group represents the way in which the different institutions meet the societal demand for adult literacy standards through teacher subsidy. We do not demand that our states and our institutions bear the true cost of instruction, even at the paltry level that full-time professionals are compensated. Last year, the *San Jose Mercury News* editorialized against the practice in California of paying two-year college faculty about 40 percent of full-time pay, noting that at a median of $60,000 per year, full-time pay was hardly generous.

The recent exchange between James Sledd and Joseph Harris in *CCC* illustrates our dilemma, our inability to agree on the nature of the problem. Sledd correctly points to long-entrenched practices in higher education in which most tenured faculty are implicated. He rails at corporate mentalities and devotion to hierarchical systems. And he's right, to a point. Harris correctly points to the pragmatic institutional circumstances faced by anyone responsible for a writing program and argues for a kind of "bird by bird" approach. While radical, revolutionary reform will not occur, steady, incremental improvements could ultimately reach a critical mass and result in true reform in the long run. He's right, too, to a better point.

Here's why I think Harris had the better point. A few years ago, Harris left Pittsburgh for Duke and Andrea Lunsford left Ohio State for Stanford. I've heard more than a few 4Cs hallway conversations wondering what that could mean. Well, I interviewed both of them recently, just to find out. Joe was hired to bring improvements to the Duke Writing Program. Those improvements are both in the curriculum and the staffing of the program. With significant support from the Mellon Foundation, Duke now staffs its writing program almost entirely with post-doctoral, full-time teachers in the context of a multidisciplinary curriculum and a substantial, ongoing professional development process. At the same time, Duke participates in a Preparing Future Faculty program with several local colleges, including one two-year college. Here's my read on the program: get the university to approximate the full cost of instruction; improve the teaching of writing to undergraduates; focus more on the professional development of faculty than on traditional structures of tenure and hierarchy.

Similarly at Stanford, Lunsford has built support for significant curricular improvements, including a new requirement in oral and multimedia presentations for second-year students, supported by a new writing center and several high-tech classrooms. Associated with those improvements is an effort to create a core full-time faculty with competitive compensation and benefits and long-term contracts and a substantial professional-development program, emphasizing various forms of expertise in rhetoric and writing. In general, the program Lunsford has initiated will more approximate the full cost of writing instruction, will focus on developing expert knowledge about the teaching of writing and related forms of communication, and will emphasize the material conditions of faculty over traditional titles and status concerns.

At De Anza, as in most community colleges, the approach is necessarily different. We have had a negotiated union contract since 1977 that sets forth conditions for pay, benefits, teaching load, and assignments. Early on, we did a few things right. We ensured that all faculty, full- and part-time, have equal votes as union members—and everyone must contribute to the union, though dues are pro-rata based on a percent of pay. Early on, we negotiated indexing of all part-time pay schedules. That means every pay raise goes to part-time faculty without a separate negotiation. We have modest benefits for part-time faculty and paid office hours. We have a guaranteed staff-development fund to support conference travel, and part-timers are fully eligible. In my department, wherever possible, we replace sabbatical-leave faculty with full-time replacements. In short, we make every effort to move the hiring process toward meeting the full cost of instruction, to create conditions where all faculty work to improve both curriculum and teaching methods, and to enact the community college ideology that resists systems of rank and privilege.

The overuse and misuse of part-time, adjunct, temporary faculty, and teaching assistants in composition programs represent a significant failure in equity, a morally repugnant arrangement that is not made more palatable because it is so widespread and so entrenched in our institutional financing arrangements. I know many of you work in states with so-called "right to work" laws, which means that a negotiated union contract is not an option. Each institution and each state requires its own unique approach. I'd like to establish a new standard, a "write to work" law—one that recognizes how critical writing is in the workplace, how essential adult literacy is to our cultural, economic, and political life. Such a law—or principle—would ensure that where writing is mandated in the curriculum, the full cost of instruction would be provided, whether by legislative action or the actions of boards of trustees. As a national organization, we can give voice to this fundamental principle of professional equity. And we can tell our fellow citizens that the "right to work" can best be guaranteed by those who "write to work."

Our Professional Equity Project and the work of the Committee and SIG on Part-Time, Adjunct, Nontenure-Track faculty express our organizational commitment to this principle. Our new Public Policy Committee initiatives can provide us the techniques for mounting a national educational campaign on these principles of equity. Regardless of class, race, gender, ethnicity, age, sexual orientation, institution, or size, every American needs to write to fully participate in life, culture, and society. Our work as a conference, as a profession, should be to find every available means of heightening the contradiction between high standards and low pay, of persuading—even shaming—the larger society into fully funding this important work, this helping our citizens articulate their ideas, their dreams, their feelings to themselves and to one another.

As we each pursue our individual and special interests at this conference, let each of us reflect on points of solidarity with the whole. As each of us returns home with renewed creativity and commitment, let us remain open to learning from one another. Finally, let each of us work to educate our fellow citizens on the moral and practical necessity of enacting professional equity, in all its forms, in all our college writing programs.

APPENDIX A: SCORING RUBRICS

I use these standards for scoring most of the papers I assign in the first two courses of first-year composition.

Grading Standards: Composition   J. Lovas

0 - Unacceptable	1 - Poor	2 - Weak	3 - Average	4 - Good	5 - Excellent

Rhetoric
A point worth making (thesis); clear, sharp focus; effective opening and closing.
1   2   3   4   5

Shape (appropriate to topic, balanced design); adequate development with summary, details, quotations; transitions.

1   2   3   4   5____ ×5 =____

Style

Honesty, individuality, movement, liveliness.

1   2   3   4   5

Phrasing (effective chunking); diction (effective word choice).

1   2   3   4   5____ ×3 =____

Editing

Grammar/sentence structure			1	2	3	4	5	
Punctuation	1	2	3	4	5			
Spelling	1	2	3	4	5			
Format	1	2	3	4	5____ ×1 =____			

TOTAL_____

COMMENTS

I use these criteria in scoring some assignments in the second and third courses of first-year composition. Indicate whether you are scoring my whole speech___(check) or one part_____(name it).

Grading Standards: Expressive Papers   J. Lovas

1 - POOR	2 - WEAK	3 - AVERAGE	4 - GOOD	5 - EXCELLENT

Quality of insight/idea
__1__2__3__4__5 ×4 =_____

Level of risk as a writer
__1__2__3__4__5 ×4 =_____

Evidence of planning and organizing
__1__2__3__4__5 ×4 =_____

LANGUAGE AND STYLE
Authentic voice
__1__2__3__4__5 ×1 =_____

Sentence variety/emphasis
__1__2__3__4__5 ×1 =_____

Vivid, appropriate details/quotations
__1__2__3__4__5 × 1 = _____

Wit, charm, playfulness
__1__2__3__4__5 × 1 = _____

MATTERS OF FORM

Sentence grammar __1__2__3__4__5 × 1 = _____
Punctuation __1__2__3__4__5 × 1 = _____
Spelling __1__2__3__4__5 × 1 = _____
Format __1__2__3__4__5 × 1 = _____

COMMENTS

APPENDIX B: AN IDIOSYNCRATIC BIBLIOGRAPHY OF TWO-YEAR
COLLEGE SCHOLARSHIP, 1953–2001 [based entirely on material
in my personal library]

Fisher, Beverly. "Problems of Motivation in Junior College Communication Courses." *College Composition and Communication* 4.2 (1953): 43–45. [Santa Monica College]

The Report of Workshop No. 2. "The Terminal Student." *College Composition and Communication* 4.3 (Oct. 1953): 77–78.

The Report of Workshop No. 5. "Sub-Freshman Composition—The Poorly-Equipped Student." *College Composition and Communication* 4.3 (Oct. 1953): 83–85.

Baker, J. Gordon. "Measuring Success in Composition." *College Composition and Communication* 5.2 (May 1954): 81–84. [Jersey City Junior College]

Radner, Sanford. "Organizing a Junior College English Program." *College Composition and Communication* 10.1 (Feb. 1959): 40–43. [Staten Island Community College]

Williamson, Richard. "The Case for Filmmaking As English Composition." *College Composition and Communication* 22.2 (May 1971): 131–36. [College of San Mateo]

Bens, John. "Taboo or Not Taboo." *College Composition and Communication* 22.3 (Oct. 1971): 215–20. [Merritt College]

Mills, Helen. "Fanning the Inner Flame." *College Composition and Communication* 22.3 (Oct. 1971): 262–66. [American River College]

Lambdin, William G. "Sociology Made Easy." *College Composition and Communication* 22.5 (Dec. 1971): 363–64. [Northeastern Junior College]

Miller, William. "New Sentence Tactics through Predication." *College Composition and Communication* 22.5 (Dec. 1971): 365–76. [Diablo Valley College]

Croll, Charles. "Teaching Vocabulary." *College Composition and Communication* 22.5 (Dec. 1971): 378–80. [Broome Community College]

Grimes, Geoffrey A. "A Contract System for Freshman and Sophomore Courses." *College Composition and Communication* 23.2 (May 1972). [Mountain View College (Dallas)]

Elgin, Don D. "Freshman Composition Texts." *College Composition and Communication* 24.1 (Feb. 1973): 45–46. [Cleveland State Community College]

Cooney, James P., Jr. "On the Dangers of Pre-Plotting in English." *College Composition and Communication* 24.2 (May 1973): 206–08. [Mount Wachusett Community College]

Willis, Hulon. "A Brief Comment on the Utility of Scholarly-Traditional Grammar." *College Composition and Communication* 24.2 (May 1973): 213–15. [Bakersfield College]

Metzger, Deena. "Silence As Experience." *College Composition and Communication* 24.3 (Oct. 1973): 247–50. [Los Angeles Valley Junior College]

Teaching English in the Two-Year College. Urbana: NCTE, 1974.

Gibson, Walker, ed. *New Students in Two-Year Colleges.* Urbana: NCTE, 1979.

Cloos, Carol. "Staffing in the Two-Year College." *Profession 79*. New York: MLA, 1979. 29–34. [Monroe Community College]

Mognis, Robert. "What Every Four-Year-College Chairperson Should Know about the Training of Two-Year College English Teachers." *ADE Bulletin* 63 (1980). [Modesto Junior College]

Troyka, Lynn Quitman. "Perspectives on Legacies and Literacies in the 1980s." *College Composition and Communication* 33.3 (Oct. 1982): 252–62. [Queensborough Community College]

Bilram, Barbara. "Unrealistic Teaching Loads and Threatened Literature Courses: Or, Why We Need an MLA Community College Commission." *ADE Bulletin* 83 (1986). [Santa Monica College]

Kievitt, F. David. "Tenure and Promotion Policies in the Two-Year College." *ADE Bulletin* 83 (1986). [Bergen (NJ) Community College]

Sledge, Linda Ching. "The Community College Scholar." *ADE Bulletin* 83 (1986). [Westchester Community College]

Tinberg, Howard. "A Model of Theory-Making for Writing Teachers: Local Knowledge." *TETYC* 17.1 (Feb. 1990): 18–23. [Bristol Community College]

McPherson, Elisabeth. "Where Were We, Where Are We As Community College Teachers?" *TETYC* 17.2 (May 1990): 92–99. [Forest Park Community College]

Reynolds, Mark. "Twenty-Five Years of Two-Year College English." *TETYC* 17.4 (Dec. 1990): 230–35. [Jefferson Davis Community College]

Raines, Helon. "A New Era for Two-Year College English Teachers." *TETYC* 19.3 (Oct. 1992): 163–67. [Casper College (Wyoming)]

Tinberg, Howard. "Seeing Ourselves Differently: Remaking Research and Scholarship at the Community College." *TETYC* 20.1 (Feb. 1993): 12–17. [Bristol Community College]

Raines, Helon Howell. "Reseeing the Past, Recounting the Present, Envisioning the Future: The Teaching of English in the Two-Year College." *TETYC* 20.2 (May 1993): 100–08.

Reynolds, Mark. *Two-Year College English: Essays for a New Century*. Urbana: NCTE, 1994.

Griffith, Marlene, and Ann Connor. *Democracy's Open Door: The Community College in America's Future*. Portsmouth, NH: Boynton/Cook Heineman, 1994.

Kort, Melissa Sue. "Crossing the Great Divide: From the Two-Year College to the University, and Back." *TETYC* 21.3 (Oct. 1994). [Santa Rosa Junior College]

Peterson, Jane. "Through the Looking Glass: A Response." *College English* 57.3 (Mar 1995): 310–18. [Richland College (Texas)]

Madden, Frank. "A Job at a 'Real' College: Or, How I Became a Faculty Member at a Two-Year College." *ADE Bulletin* 111 (1995). [Westchester Community College]

Gere, Anne Ruggles. "Stories Out of School." *TETYC* 23.1 (Feb. 1996): 9–18. [University of Michigan]

Bay, Libby. "Teaching in the Community College: Rerouting a Career." *ADE Bulletin* 114 (1996). [Rockland (NY) Community College]

Griffith, Marlene. "Getting Our Story Out." *TETYC* 23.4 (Dec. 1996): 269–73. [Laney College]

Tinberg, Howard. *Border Talk: Writing and Knowing in the Two-Year College*. Urbana: NCTE, 1997.

Gaskins, Jake, Dennis Holt, and Elizabeth Roeger. "Do Two-Year College Students Write As Well As Four-Year College Students? Classroom and Institutional Perspectives." *TETYC* 25.1 (Feb. 1998): 6–15. [Southeast Missouri State and Shawnee Community College]

Pickett, Nell Ann. "The Two-Year College As Democracy in Action." *College Composition and Communication* 49.1 (Feb. 1998): 90–98. [Hinds Community College]

Reynolds, Mark. "The Intellectual Work of Two-Year College Teaching." *ADE Bulletin* 121 (1998). [Jefferson Davis Community College]

Lewiecki-Wilson, Cynthia, and Jeff Sommers. "Professing at the Fault Lines: Composition at Open-Admissions Institutions." *College Composition and Communication* 50.3 (Feb. 1999). [Miami University, Middletown Campus]

Kort, Melissa Sue. "PhD at the JC? Preparing Teachers for Two-Year Colleges." *ADE Bulletin* 122 (1999). [Santa Rosa Junior College]

Hillocks, George, Jr. *Ways of Thinking, Ways of Teaching*. New York: Teacher College P, 1999.

Grubb, Norton W., and Associates. *Honored but Invisible: An Inside Look at Teaching in Community Colleges*. New York: Routledge, 1999.

Lovas, John C. "Coordinated Teaching." *TETYC* (Mar. 2001): 286–92. [De Anza College]

———. "Playrooms, Hodgepodges, Soulless Monsters: Why I Can't Imagine Having a Better Job." *ADE Bulletin* 129 (2001): 43–48.

Tinberg, Howard. "Writing a Book on the (Two-Year College) Job." *ADE Bulletin* 129 (2001): 49–52.

Surveys

Lawson, Lewis A. "National Trends in Remedial English." *College Composition and Communication* 10.2 (May 1959), 113–15. [Surveys 285 colleges accredited for teacher education by NCATE, thus no two-year colleges would be included.]

Gorrell, Robert. "Uses and Limitations of Entrance Tests: A Proposal." *College Composition and Communication* 11.1 (Feb. 1960). [Mention of fit between high schools and colleges, but no mention or recognition of differing assessment needs in two-year colleges.]

Cox, Martha H., John W. Canario, and James R. Cypher. "Remedial English: A Nationwide Survey." *College Composition and Communication* 11.4 (Dec. 1960): 237–44. [Includes responses from seventy-five institutions in forty-seven states, one university and one state college queried per state. No community colleges.]

Raines, Helon Howell. "Is There a Writing Program in This College? Two Hundred and Thirty-Six Two-Year Colleges Respond." *College Composition and Communication* 41.2 (May 1990): 151–65. [Only two-year college survey I have found, rarely referenced elsewhere.]

NOTES

1. Using a variety of common forms from first-year composition, this paper examines the purposes of CCCC, transformative experiences at professional conferences, and the elements of my literacy autobiography. I then argue for recognition of the knowledge-building role of writing programs in two-year colleges and for a "write to work" principle, calling for full pay for all who teach required writing courses. Originally, this manuscript was a speech integrated with a PowerPoint® presentation using more than 100 slides (text, photographs, and music), which cannot be fully represented here.

2. ECCTYC/TYCA—English Council of California Two-Year Colleges and Two-Year College English Association.

3. See my idiosyncratic bibliography of two-year college scholarship in Appendix B.

4. I present a more detailed argument in a chapter titled "How Did We Get in This Fix? A Personal Account of the Shift to a Part-Time Faculty in a Leading Two-Year College District" in Eileen Schell and Patricia Stock's *Moving a Mountain: Transforming the Role of Contingent Faculty in Composition Studies and Higher Education.*

WORKS CITED

Bakhtin, M. M. *The Dialogic Imagination: Four Essays.* Ed. Michael Holquist; trans. Caryl Emerson and Michael Holquist. Austin: U of Texas P, 1981.

Bartholomae, David. "Freshman English, Composition and CCCC." *College Composition and Communication* 40 (Feb. 1989): 38–50.

Bowles, Samuel, and Herbert Gintis. *Schooling in Capitalist America: Educational Reform and the Contradictions of Economic Life.* New York: Basic Books, 1976.

CCCC Committee on Professional Standards. "A Progress Report from the CCCC Committee on Professional Standards." *College Composition and Communication* 42 (Oct. 1991): 330–44.

CCCC Executive Committee. "Statement of Principles and Standards for the Postsecondary Teaching of Writing." *College Composition and Communication* 40 (Oct. 1989): 329–36.

Chomsky, Noam. *New Horizons in the Study of Language and Mind.* New York: Cambridge UP, 2000.

Clark, Burton. "The 'Cooling Out' Function in Higher Education." *American Journal of Sociology* 65 (May 1960): 569–76.

Dougherty, Kevin. *The Contradictory College: The Conflicting Origins, Impacts, and Futures of the Community College.* New York: State U of New York P, 1994.

Elbow, Peter. *Writing without Teachers.* New York: Oxford UP, 1975.

Gere, Ann Ruggles. "Revealing Silence: Rethinking Personal Writing." *College Composition and Communication* 53 (Dec. 2001): 203–23.

Greenberg, Joseph, ed. *Universals of Human Language.* [Associate editors, Charles A. Ferguson and Edith A. Moravcsik.] Stanford, CA: Stanford UP, 1978.

Harris, Joseph. "Beyond Critique: A Response to James Sledd." *College Composition and Communication* 53 (Sep. 2001): 152–53.

———. "Meet the New Boss, Same as the Old Boss: Class Consciousness in Composition." *College Composition and Communication* 52 (Sep. 2000): 43–68.

Karabel, Jerome. "Community Colleges and Social Stratification." *Harvard Educational Review* 42 (Winter 1972): 521–62.

King, Martin Luther, Jr. "I Have a Dream." Audio recording. The King Center, Atlanta.

———. "I've Been to the Mountaintop." Audio recording. The King Center, Atlanta.

Lovas, John. "How Did We Get in This Fix? A Personal Account of the Shift to a Part-Time Faculty in a Leading Two-Year College District." *Moving a Mountain: Transforming the Role of Contingent Faculty in Composition Studies and Higher Education.* Ed. Eileen Schell and Patricia Lambert Stock. Urbana: NCTE, 2001. 196–217.

———. "Playrooms, Hodgepodges, Soulless Monsters: Why I Can't Imagine Having a Better Job." *ADE Bulletin* 129 (2001): 43–48.

Macrorie, Ken. *Telling Writing.* New York: Hayden Book Co., 1970.

Merrill, Robert, Thomas J. Farrell, Eileen E. Schell, Valerie Balester, Chris M. Anson, and Greta Gaard. "Symposium on the 1991 'Progress Report from the CCCC Committee on Professional Standards.'" *College Composition and Communication* 43 (May 1992): 154–75.

Moghtader, Michael, Alanna Cotch, and Kristen Hague. "The First-Year Composition Requirement Revisited: A Survey." *College Composition and Communication* 52 (Feb. 2001): 455–67.

Murray, Donald M. "All Writing Is Autobiography." *College Composition and Communication* 42 (Feb. 1991): 66–74.

Phillips, Donna Burns, Ruth Greenberg, and Sharon Gibson. *"College Composition and Communication:* Chronicling a Discipline's Genesis." *College Composition and Communication* 44:4 (Dec. 1993): 443–65.

Presley, Elvis. "I Believe" and "You'll Never Walk Alone." Audio recordings on *Amazing Grace: His Greatest Sacred Performances,* RCA, 1994.

Roney, Brian Ascalon. *The American Son: A Novel.* New York: W. W. Norton & Company, 2001.

Sledd, James. "On Buying In and Selling Out: A Note for Bosses Old and New." *College Composition and Communication* 53 (Sep. 2001): 146–49.

Tinberg, Howard. "An Interview with Ira Shor—Part I." *Teaching English in the Two-Year College* 27 (Sep. 1999): 51–60.

Vygotsky, L. S. *Thought and Language.* Ed. and trans. Eugenia Hanfmann and Gertrude Vakar. Cambridge, MA: MIT P, 1965.

Wyche-Smith, Susan, and Shirley Rose. "One Hundred Ways to Make the Wyoming Resolution a Reality." *College Composition and Communication* 41 (Oct. 1990): 318–24.

Zwerling, Steven. *Second Best: The Crisis of the Community College.* New York: McGraw-Hill, 1976.

Giving the Chair's address at CCCC in the Palmer House in Chicago was the chance of a lifetime, and I wanted to make the most of it. In thinking about the address, I understood it as a speech to be delivered, not a paper to be read. That purpose guided me throughout my writing process. I also understood my audience to be the fifteen hundred people in the ballroom, not those who would later read the text in *CCC*.

Chairs usually address themes central to their own scholarship and professional work. Because I believe that practice drives theory, I wanted my speech to emphasize what we do as compositionists. That led to the thought of opening with a freewrite. I wrote that piece first and left it exactly as it came out, resisting strong urges to edit—my homage to the expressivist strand in our profession.

In tension with expressivism lies the formalism embodied in the five-paragraph essay, a format still widely practiced even though widely reviled. I tried to capture the paradox, partly by using meta-comments to parody important elements of the formula (thesis statement, topic sentence) while trying to make a substantive comment on our purposes as an organization of professionals. To use exactly five hundred words (as counted by my word processor) reflected the purposes of parody, and provided me a challenge in editing.

Another tension in our work lies between analytical forms such as the "beginning, middle, end" structure and the use of narrative to make a point. In my roles as TYCA and CCCC leader, I had the privilege of traveling to Memphis and Atlanta where chance and choice led me to a personal epiphany: the two shaping voices of my adolescence were Rev. Martin Luther King Jr. and Elvis Presley. I knew this juxtaposition was risky, but it was deeply felt. The ethos of my address was grounded in these juxtaposed narratives—and the emotional center of the speech lay in alternating the actual voices of King and Presley.

Another important strand of our work in composition lies in identity formation, encouraging students to use personal, autobiographical material. I fully appreciated the emotional appeal of old family photographs and used them shamelessly throughout my address.

Classical rhetoric suggests that speakers must convince their audiences of their worthiness if their arguments are to be given serious consideration. Thus, the first half of my speech attempted that authentication. The latter half presented arguments on two moral issues facing the profession: the intellectual failure to regard community college composition seriously and the unconscionable exploitation of part-time labor in composition.

Early on, I decided to incorporate both audio and visual elements, demonstrating the "communication" element of our organization. Fortunately, my former student Gino Do provided critical expertise in the design and execution of the PowerPoint elements. I had never used PowerPoint before. How's that for risk-taking?

Before the speech, we distributed copies of two of my scoring rubrics, inviting the audience to grade me. I received about thirty back, mostly positive, but one comment helped me believe I'd accomplished my goals: "You made me laugh, you made me cry, you made me think."

—JOHN C. LOVAS
De Anza College

2003

Changing Missions, Shifting Positions, and Breaking Silences[1]

SHIRLEY WILSON LOGAN

A nd where the words of women are crying to be heard, we must each of us recognize our responsibility to seek those words out, to read them and share them and examine them in their pertinence to our lives.

—AUDRE LORDE (43)

During the early stages of invention, my initial impulse was to be broadly inclusive. Preparing a paper to be delivered at the annual meeting of the Conference on College Composition and Communication, a professional organization that takes pride in its commitment to diversity, I set out to cite a wide range of scholars—European scholars, Anglo-American scholars, Native American scholars, Latina scholars, and other scholars of various colors and ethnicities. But I ultimately decided to resist what appears to be the current trend towards feigned—and frequently sincere—attempts at some version of multiculturalism, a trend that erases all difference as insignificant, as if difference does not matter as long as you have a good mix. I returned instead to what I know best—the texts of black women. For centuries these women have had good reasons to speak but not always the opportunity. Still, heeding Audre Lorde's imperative in the epigraph, I invoke their voices, believing that within the specificity of their claims resides general truth and proposing that we "read them and share them and examine them in their pertinence to our lives."

Alice Walker writes, "[O]ur mothers and grandmothers have, more often than not anonymously, handed on the creative spark, the seed of the flower they themselves never hoped to see: or like a sealed letter they could not plainly read" (240). And so, somewhat in call-and-response

---

This article is a revised version of the Chair's address Shirley Wilson Logan delivered at the CCCC Convention in New York, New York, on March 20, 2003. It was first published in *CCC*, volume 55, number 2, December 2003.

fashion, I have intermingled their voices with mine throughout this paper. These are as much their thoughts as mine, and they expressed them so much better.

Here we are, the CCCC, assembled in the largest city in the United States with more than 8 million people, ready to articulate Program Chair Kathleen Yancey's provocative call, "Rewriting Theme for English B: Transforming Possibilities." *"Does anybody know we're here?"* The city with 1,098,832 students in 1,204 public schools, taught by 80,000 classroom teachers. *"Does anybody know we're here?"* The city with some 131,129 English language learners enrolled in its schools, learners whose home languages are Spanish, Chinese, Russian, Haitian Creole, Urdu, Bengali, and Korean, to name the most prominent.[2] *"Does anybody know we're here?"*

> My mouth is effective in its speech; I do not go back on my word. Hear ye!
> —Queen Hatshepsut [1490 BCE] (14)

> Methinks I heard a spiritual interrogation—"Who shall go forward, and take off the reproach that is cast upon the people of color? Shall it be a woman?" And my heart made this reply —"If it is thy will, be it even so, Lord Jesus!"
> —Maria Stewart [1832] (6)

The city with more than forty two-year and four-year colleges and universities.[3] *"Does anybody know we're here?"* One NCTE database membership search indicates that 165 subscriptions of *CCC* are sent to a NYC zip code. *"Does anybody know we're here?"* These statistics remind us, on the one hand, of our enormous constituency as educators and, on the other, of our relative insignificance as a conference. But as a conference, I believe that we can still make a difference.

Unlike past CCCC Chair Keith Gilyard, I won't quote James Brown,[4] but consider these lyrics from Stevie Wonder's "Living for the City," a song narrating the experiences of a young man who migrated from the South to New York City, much like the one in the 1951 Langston Hughes poem "Theme for English B"[5]: "I

> We are all bound up together in one great bundle of humanity, and society cannot trample on the weakest and feeblest of its members without receiving the curse in its own soul.
> —Frances Harper [1866] (217)

hope you hear inside my voice of sorrow / And that it motivates you to make a better tomorrow /This place is cruel no where could be much colder /If we don't change, the world will soon be over /Living just enough, stop giving just enough for the city!!!!"

CHANGING MISSIONS

The Executive Committee, over the past year, has revisited our mission statement, our position statements, and other public documents declaring CCCC's views on a number of discipline-related issues. Our revised mission statement, as approved by the EC, reads as follows:

> CCCC, as a conference of NCTE, supports and promotes the teaching and study of college composition and communication by (1) sponsoring meetings and publishing scholarly materials for the exchange

of knowledge about composition, composition pedagogy, and rhetoric; (2) supporting a wide range of research on composition, communication, and rhetoric; (3) working to enhance conditions for learning and teaching college composition and to promote professional development; and (4) acting as an advocate for language and literacy education nationally and internationally.[6]

We are living up to some aspects of this mission better than others. We do sponsor meetings, and we support and publish the results of a wide range of research in rhetoric and composition. The last two goals, however, are much more difficult to accomplish and sustain. The conditions under which much college writing is taught and learned are still below the standards articulated in our own position statements on these matters.

SHIFTING POSITIONS

We have some clearly articulated — some might even say radical — statements on two of the major issues in college composition and communication today — teachers' professional standards and students' linguistic rights. Look at the list of eleven position statements (CCCC, *Position*):

1. Students' Right to Their Own Language (1974)
2. Statement on the Preparation and Professional Development of Teachers of Writing (1982)
3. Scholarship in Composition: Guidelines for Faculty, Deans, and Department Chairs (1987)
4. Statement of Professional Guidance (1987)
5. Statement of Principles and Standards for the Postsecondary Teaching of Writing (1989)
6. Writing Assessment: A Position Statement (1995)
7. The National Language Policy (1998)
8. Statement on Ebonics (1998)
9. Promotion and Tenure Guidelines for Work with Technology (1998)
10. Guidelines for the Ethical Treatment of Students and Student Writing in Composition Research (2000)
11. Statement on Second Language Writing and Writers (2001)

The full texts of all of these statements are posted on the CCCC section of the NCTE Web site <http://www.ncte.org/cccc/positions/index.shtml>. I listed them chronologically, but if we consider them thematically they tend to fall into two or three categories: Of the eleven, four address some aspect of the relationship between students' home languages and the various "school" languages in which they are required to speak and write *and on* and *in* which they will be tested; five address some aspect of working environments and professional development for teacher-researchers in composition. Of the remaining two, the "Statement on Writing Assessment" sits at the intersection of student-teacher interaction and public accountability and, as a more recent statement, incorporates many of the principles articulated in the earlier documents. The eleventh, "Guidelines for the Ethical Treatment of Students in Research," added in 2000, reflects the growth of composition studies as a field of inquiry.

Now I do not intend in this limited space to discuss each one specifically, but I would like to highlight some of the important principles they uphold and to point to their salience at this moment in history. In spite of the fact that the EC's preliminary reviews of these statements recommend that many be either updated, re-contextualized, or simply reaffirmed, I find them rewarding to read. It may be that what we need is not so much a revising as a rereading of the statements we have already made. One of the many disadvantages of having been around for awhile is that one loses the ability to be excited about other people's good ideas; your life becomes one big déjà vu experience. ("Didn't we try that in '83?") Thus, what I propose we do is revisit and reread portions of these documents, perhaps for the first time.

Let's begin with those I have categorized as concerning students' home languages. Whenever I ask my students how many of them speak a dialect of English, usually only a few, somewhat embarrassed, reluctantly raise their hands. More often than not, they are the students of color. And even as I speak of people of color, we should be reminded of the very significant differences among people of color, the significant differences among people in general. All too often when invoking the slippery term "diversity," we

> Oppressive language does more than represent violence; it is violence; does more than represent the limits of knowledge; it limits knowledge. Whether it is obscuring state language or the faux language of mindless media; whether it is the proud but calcified language of the academy or the commodity-driven language of science; whether it is the malign language of law-without-ethics or language designed for the estrangement of minorities, hiding its racist plunder in its literary cheek—it must be rejected, altered and exposed.
> —Toni Morrison [1993] (16)

allow the lazy force of generalization to erase those differences so that all concerned are further disempowered. In the February 2 *New York Times Magazine* article "Forget Diversity," James Traub calls the "affirmative-action-as-diversity" rationale "an elaborate charade to keep us from knowing what we're [really] doing" (16). What we are doing is substituting some version of "diversity" for the hard work of acting affirmatively to correct the consequences of past discrimination and denial of rights, particularly of African Americans. That said, what attention are we paying to our changing linguistic demographics? An editorial in the publication *Rethinking Schools*, "Bilingual Education Is a Human and Civil Right," notes that in 1864 Congress prohibited Native American children from being taught in their own languages. It took 70 years to overturn that law, and now we seem to be going backwards with the federal and local governments taking steps to ban or weaken bilingual education in virtually every state. CCCC needs to play an active role in overturning such legislation as that passed by the ESEA, requiring English language learners to take standardized tests in English within three years of entering the school system (Editorial 26). Consider this rather lengthy quote from "Students' Right to Their Own Language":

> Many of us have taught as though there existed somewhere a single American "standard English" which could be isolated, identified, and accurately defined . . . We have ignored . . . the distinction between speech and writing and have taught the language as though the talk in any region, even the talk of speakers with prestige and power, were identical to edited written English.
>
> We have also taught . . . as though the "English of educated speakers," the language used by those in power in the community, had an inherent advantage over other dialects as a means of expressing thought or emotion, conveying information, or analyzing concepts. . . . We need to ask ourselves whether our rejection of students who do not adopt the dialect most familiar to us is based on any real merit in our dialect or whether we are actually rejecting the students themselves, rejecting them because of their racial, social, and cultural origins. (CCCC, "Students' Right")

Read it in its entirety—it still inspires, challenges.

We must strengthen the links between language and democracy, text and street. During this present moment when various current national constituencies are "discovering" the importance of writing, let's make sure they understand what it means to teach writing and what learning and teaching environments best facilitate it. We have position statements that articulate those conditions. As language arts educators, we ought to be at the center of all policy decisions that affect the teaching and learning of communication skills. Somebody needs to ask *us* the next time decisions are made about how facility with language will be assessed. Somebody needs to ask *us* before proclaiming a national crisis in the quality of college student writing. And we need to have ready answers when they do. We need to thank John Lovas, our past chair, for taking the lead in developing a CCCC fact sheet "On Writing" for general public dissemination.

> I accept this idea of Democracy. I am all for trying it out. It must be a good thing if everybody praises it like that. If our government has been willing to go to war and to sacrifice billions of dollars and millions of men for the idea, I think that I ought to give the thing a trial. . . . I am crazy about the idea of this Democracy. I want to see how it feels.
> —Zora Neale Hurston [1945] (166–67)

We need to be at the center of free speech controversies. How can we reclaim what one writer calls "our hijacked words," words like *democracy, justice, human rights,* and, yes, *terrorism* (Berger 15–16). How do we respond as a conference to the current language of war, a language that often threatens to silence opposition? In the wake of the USA Patriot Act of 2001, authorizing the interception of wire, oral, and electronic communications, the Executive Committee, at its preconvention meeting, adopted a statement opposing the suppression of the right to speak freely and urging policy makers to "vigorously protect this right, especially in times when national security is perceived to be threatened."[7] Our Ad Hoc Advocacy Committee is looking into ways to increase the volume of our public voice and the visibility of our public presence. We must help policy makers and other publics understand the extent to which composition matters and work against the perception that past change was favorable but current change is not; so that we frown upon hip-hop culture and the word work of Talib Kweli or Def Poetry Jam at the same time that we long for the good old days when everyone wrote grammatically correct English.

BREAKING SILENCES

Robert L. Woodson, president of the National Center for Neighborhood Enterprise, writes about the current poverty in Lowndes County, Alabama, where many of the early civil rights battles were fought but apparently still not won. The old wiring in its ten public schools will not even support computers and Internet access. He observes that "[t]he real test of effective redress is not how well we hold up the wrongs of the past, but how effectively we act today to help" students and teachers who learn and teach in substandard environments (A17). We have created an Ad Hoc Committee on Teaching, Learning, and Assessing Writing Digitally to develop a statement on best conditions for teaching writing in the digital age as we struggle to avoid what past CCCC Chair Cindy Selfe called the "perils of not paying attention."[8] Clearly one main component of this statement will be access.

> I am before the American people today through no inclination of my own, but because of a deep-seated conviction that the country at large does not know the extent to which lynch law prevails in parts of the Republic, nor the conditions which force into exile those who speak the truth.
> —Ida Wells [1893] (80)

> The fact that we are here and that I speak these words is an attempt to break that silence and bridge some of those differences between us, for it is not difference which immobilizes us, but silence. And there are so many silences to be broken.
> —Audre Lorde [1977] (44)

At my own University of Maryland, all preservice English teachers are required to take a course designed to help them understand the challenge of teaching diverse learners in the English classroom, mainly ESL learners but, in fact, all students, since, as I was recently reminded, "Everyone learns a new dialect when learning to write."[9] Starting this fall, the successful completion of the High School Assessment (HSA) will be a general graduation requirement in Maryland. The English portions require writing at least one essay, and the revised SAT in 2005 will include, of course, a writing component.[10] I point to these developments without praise or blame but with cautious enthusiasm. My caution is expressed in this excerpt from our position statement on assessment:

> Any individual's writing "ability" is a sum of a variety of skills employed in a diversity of contexts, and individual ability fluctuates unevenly among these varieties. Consequently, one piece of writing—even if it is generated under the most desirable conditions—can never serve as an indicator of overall literacy, particularly for high stakes decisions. Ideally, such literacy must be assessed by more than one piece of writing, in more than one genre, written on different occasions, for different audience, and evaluated by multiple readers. (CCCC, "Writing Assessment")

What are we doing with our rhetorical skills that makes a difference? *Does anybody know we're here?*

A central component of any discussion of professional issues should be how effectively we recruit graduate students. We need to engage in direct mentoring of graduate students who don't always come to us set on degrees in rhetoric and composition. As Stone Shiflet, former broadcaster and graduate student at the University of South Florida, pointed out, many have never heard of rhetoric and composition as a discipline. Properly guided, students are often attracted by the ways in which our field links to the life experiences they often bring to the academy or that are concurrent with their academic experiences.

There is plenty of work for all who have the proper conception of the teacher's office, who know that all men are brothers.
— Lucy Craft Laney [1899] (173)

If the first woman God ever made was strong enough to turn the world upside down, all alone, these together ought to be able to turn it back and get it right side up again.
— Sojourner Truth [1851] (27)

But even as we invite them into our disciplinary homes, we must work to improve the neighborhood. This has been a particularly challenging goal to achieve. In *Moving a Mountain: Transforming the Role of Contingent Faculty in Composition Studies and Higher Education*, Eileen Schell and Patricia Stock write, "It appears to be ironic, but true, that as higher education has become increasingly democratic . . . , academic hiring practices have become increasingly undemocratic" (5). This collection of essays, narrating the contributions, successes, and failures of writing faculty within a variety of institutional contexts, was published just two years ago in 2001. Yet CCCC's first position statement on ideal learning and teaching environments and professional development for teacher-researchers in composition was issued eleven years earlier in 1989. Consider this excerpt from the standard-bearer "Statement of Principles and Standards for the Postsecondary Teaching of Writing":

> Quality in education is intimately linked to the quality of teachers. Higher education traditionally assures this quality by providing reasonable teaching loads, research support, and eventual tenure for

those who meet rigorous professional standards. Such standards are applied and such support extended to virtually all faculties in higher education—but rarely to those who teach writing.

We don't talk nearly enough about the fact that most writing courses are taught by part-time and adjunct faculty and graduate students, most of whom are not even here at our conference. My now-deceased colleague Susan Oswald comes to mind whenever I address this matter. She carried around in her small body enough anger, energy, and wit to fuel a rebellion of part-time instructors at the University of Maryland. Many will recall the data coming out of the CAW-sponsored Roper Starch survey—data that verified what we already knew. The survey confirmed that ten years after the 1989 "Statement of Principles and Standards for the Postsecondary Teaching of Writing" we were not much closer to improving conditions of those who teach postsecondary writing instruction and may in fact be even farther away from that goal today ("Summary"). *Does anybody know we're here?*

> Professors are expected to publish, but no one really expects or demands of us that we really care about teaching in uniquely passionate and different ways. Teachers who love students and are loved by them are still "suspect" in the academy. Some of the suspicion is that the presence of feelings, or passions, may not allow for objective consideration of each student's merit. But this very notion is based on the false assumption that education is neutral, that there is some "even" emotional ground we stand on that enables us to treat everyone equally, dispassionately.
>
> —BELL HOOKS [1994] (198)

I just wonder how many of the part-time nontenure-track instructors who represent 28% of teaching staff in freestanding composition programs and how many of the 31% who represent English departments including composition are at this convention ("Summary")? Or how many even belong to CCCC? Our Professional Equity Project (PEP) is one partial response to this challenge. This year we have close to 80 PEP participants registered. Still when we do pay attention to the reality or the growing use of part-time faculty to teach writing at the college level, we often get it wrong. We assume that the problem is the quality of the teachers and that the answer is different teachers, i.e., tenure-track professors. But in most cases, the problem is the range of environments in which we are asked to teach writing. The cause-effect relationship here is that conditions (the cause) consequently affect the quality of instruction. I don't need to remind this audience of those standards, but we do need to remind the various publics we serve. Given our status as a 501c3 charitable organization, how do we respond to this state of affairs? I want to recognize the work of our members, especially the Committee on Contingent, Adjunct, and Part-Time Faculty in keeping us focused on these matters.

Yet we also must acknowledge that membership in general is declining. The five-year trend shows an 11.3% drop. The economy certainly is a factor here, but it may also be the case that many writing teachers have had to become more discriminating in selecting those organizations and publications that serve their needs best. We need to think of ways to serve those needs better. Of particular concern is the small percentage of people of color who are members of CCCC: 4.4% African American; 1.4% Asian American/Pacific Islander; 1.5% Hispanic American/Latino; 0.5% Native American or Indian; and 92.2% white.[11] *Does anybody know we're here?*

Initiatives like the still much needed Scholars for the Dream awards represent one response to this reality. In the current climate of increasing entitlements for the rich when affirmative action is under siege, we should recall Supreme Court Justice Thurgood Marshall's 1978 separate, dissenting opinion on the *University of California v. Bakke* decision. He marveled that the same Constitution that "did not prohibit the most . . . pervasive forms of discrimination now stands as a barrier when a State acts to remedy the effects of that legacy of discrimination" (qtd. in Traub 15). We have a newly formed CCCC Committee on Diversity, charged to promote and support ongoing dialogues about diversity and difference in all aspects of teaching, graduate study, hiring and professional development practices, and in research on rhetoric, writing, and communication.

Notice that I have discussed only the CCCC position statements. The NCTE, our parent organization, has a separate set of writing-related position statements. "How to Help Your Child Become a Better Writer" is one of my favorites because it highlights the fact that learning to write begins at home (NCTE). The students in our 101 classes have already been "writing" for at least 12 years of formal schooling and earlier.

I want to close with the claim that our main goal should still be to teach effective writing and communication well. Our meetings, our research, our work to enhance learning environments for teachers and students, and our public advocacy should all support this overarching goal. Often in our justifiable concern about students' and teachers' rights, we neglect the other component of this communication triangle, the subject matter, the content. We need to be intentional about making certain that we give our students linguistic options. I strongly believe that we can respect linguistic differences and teach our students various dialect options, particularly the option of edited American English (EAE)—the dialect of power and privilege—at the same time. After we acknowledge students' rights and improve learning and teaching conditions, we still have the obligation to help them become more effective and versatile communicators. What tactics do and should we employ to open our students to the wonders of language? We don't need to throw up our hands. We need to pay attention to the body of scholarship about effective methods of teaching writing. We have more than 2000 years of rhetorical theory as well as the work of contemporary scholars, published in journals like *CCC*, especially the work focused on style, and we have the knowledge produced at our conventions to help us.

> The time is ripe for action. Self-seeking and ambition must be laid on the altar. The battle is one of sacrifice and hardship, but our duty is plain.
> —Anna Julia Cooper [1886] (46)

These women, who have been speaking to us out of their pasts and ours were indeed "effective in their speech." From Queen Hatshepsut to Toni Morrison, we must listen. Their comments have not all been immediately relevant, but their success as women who used language to effect change is indisputable. We must give our students the same facility with language. I challenge us over the next few days of this convention and beyond to consider how we can respect our students' rights to language and work to improve the learning conditions that will enable them to rewrite their *own* themes for English B.

ACKNOWLEDGMENTS

I dedicate this article to two feisty teachers of writing—Susan Oswald, a part-time instructor at the University of Maryland, and my oldest sister Thelma Wilson Wright, a high school English teacher in the State of South Carolina for forty years. Sue died in 1995 and Thelma, last April 2002. I wish to thank Sharon Floyd, Angela Haggins, Enid and Monica Logan, Joyce Middleton, and Jackie Royster for the use of their voices and Malcolm Logan for technical support in the oral version of this article.

NOTES

1. I review the current mission and position statements of the organization by calling attention to the ways in which our current social and political climate challenges our ability to meet our goals and support our positions. I weave into my text the "voices" of historical black women who called for response in their own time and even in ours.
2. Statistics on New York City Public Schools from New York City Department of Education. 3 December 2002 <http://www.nycenet.edu/stats>.
3. Colleges and Universities in New York City. 29 August 2001. Mediabridge Info Systems, Inc. <http://www.ny.com/academia/colleges.html> 3 December 2002.
4. See Keith Gilyard, "Literacy, Identity, Imagination, Flight." *CCC* 52.2 (2000): 260–72.
5. See Langston Hughes, "Theme for English B." *Cavalcade: Negro American Writing from 1760 to the Present.* Ed. Arthur P. Davis and Saunders Redding. Boston: Houghton Mifflin, 1971. 305–06.
6. Minutes of CCCC Executive Committee Meeting, 19 March 2003.
7. Minutes of CCCC Executive Committee Meeting, 19 March 2003.
8. See Cynthia L. Selfe, "Technology and Literacy: A Story about the Perils of Not Paying Attention." *CCC* 50.3 (1999): 411–36.
9. Jeanne Fahnestock, personal communication, March 2003.
10. I thank Mika Troutman for her comments on the state of writing assessment in Maryland.
11. Statistics provided by Kent Williamson, executive director, NCTE, January 2003.

WORKS CITED

Berger, John. Introduction ["Where Are We?"]. *Between the Eyes: Essays on Photography.* By David Levi Straus. Rpt. in *Harper's Magazine* (March 2003): 13–17.

Conference on College Composition and Communication. *CCCC Position Statements.* November 2002. National Council of Teachers of English. 5 January 2003 <http://www.ncte.org/cccc/positions>.

———."Students' Right to Their Own Language" [1974]. *CCCC Position Statements.* November 2002. National Council of Teachers of English. 5 January 2003 <http://www.ncte.org/cccc/positions>.

———."Writing Assessment: A Position Statement" [1995]. *CCCC Position Statements.* November 2002. National Council of Teachers of English. 5 January 2003 <http://www.ncte.org/cccc/positions>.

Cooper, Anna Julia. *A Voice from the South.* New York: Oxford, 1988.

Editorial, "Bilingual Education is a Human and Civil Right." *Rethinking Schools: An Urban Education Journal* 17.2 (Winter 2003/03): 26.

Harper, Frances. "We Are All Bound up Together." *A Brighter Coming Day: A Frances Ellen Watkins Harper Reader.* Ed. Frances Smith Foster. New York: Feminist P, 1990. 217–19.

hooks, bell. *Teaching to Transgress: Education as the Practice of Freedom.* New York: Routledge, 1994.

Hurston, Zora Neale. "Crazy for This Democracy." *I Love Myself When I Am Laughing . . . And Then Again When I Am Looking Mean and Impressive. A Zora Neale Hurston Reader.* Ed. Alice Walker. New York: Feminist P, 1979. 165–68.

Laney, Lucy C. "The Burden of the Educated Colored Woman." *The Rhetoric of Struggle: Public Address by African American Women.* Ed. Robbie Jean Walker. New York: Garland, 1992. 167–74.

Logan, Shirley Wilson, ed. *With Pen and Voice: A Critical Anthology of Nineteenth-Century African-American Women.* Carbondale: SIU P, 1995.

Lorde, Audre. "The Transformation of Silence into Language and Action." *Sister/Outsider: Essays and Speeches.* Freedom, CA: The Crossing P, 1984. 40–44.

Morrison, Toni. *The Nobel Lecture in Literature, 1993.* New York: Alfred Knopf, 1994.

NCTE. "How to Help Your Child Become a Better Writer." November 2002. National Council of Teachers of English. January 2003 <www.ncte.org/positions/how-to-help.shtml>.

Queen Hatshepsut. "Speech of the Queen." *Daughters of Africa: An International Anthology of Words and Writings by Women of African Descent from the Ancient Egyptian to the Present.* Ed. Margaret Busby. New York: Pantheon Books, 1992. 12–14.

Schell, Eileen, and Patricia Stock, eds. *Moving a Mountain: Transforming the Role of Contingent Faculty in Composition Studies and Higher Education.* Urbana: NCTE, 2001.

Shiflet, Stone. Personal interview. 23 November 2002.

Stewart, Maria W. "Lecture Delivered at the Franklin Hall." Logan 6–10.

"Summary of Data from Surveys by the Coalition on the Academic Workforce." March 2001. American Historical Association <http://www.theaha.org/caw/cawreport.htm>.

Traub, James. "Forget Diversity." *New York Times Magazine* (2 February 2003): 15–16.

Truth, Sojourner. "Speech Delivered to the Woman's Rights Convention." Logan 26–27.

"USA Patriot Act as Passed by Congress." 25 October 2001. Electronic Frontier Foundation. 13 March 2003 <http://www.eff.org/Privacy/Surveillance/Terrorism_militias/20011025_hr3162_usa_patriot_bill.htm>.

Walker, Alice. "In Search of Our Mothers' Gardens." *In Search of Our Mothers' Gardens.* New York: Harcourt Brace Jovanovich, 1983. 231–43.

Wells, Ida B. "Lynch Law in All Its Phases." Logan 80–99.

Wonder, Stevie. "Living for the City." *Innervisions.* Motown Record Corporation. T3261, 1973.

Woodson, Robert L. "Beyond the Edmund Pettus Bridge." Editorial. *Washington Post* 4 Jan. 2003: A17.

AFTERWORD: THE CHALLENGE OF WRITING THE CCCC CHAIR'S ADDRESS

The daunting prospect of addressing one's peers, a pervasive and almost paralyzing sense of audience, presented itself as I prepared to write this talk. As do all Chairs, I read over a number of Chairs' addresses, in search of the chief characteristics of a genre called "CCCC Chair's talk." I concluded that this genre, if it is indeed a genre, has few common traits. The most apparent feature was that all Chairs spoke about the issues in rhetoric and composition studies that they cared and knew most about. They all spoke of their passions, and they all seemed to view the occasion as a singular opportunity to address the membership on the state of the profession at that particular moment. Thus, it was no surprise that Cindy Selfe spoke of equity and access to technology, that Keith Gilyard examined issues of literacy and identity, that Victor Villanueva challenged our assumptions about the origins of racism north and south of the border, that Nell Ann Pickett spoke of democracy in the two-year college, or that Wendy Bishop closed her talk with a convention poem. It was refreshing to recognize that everyone decided to "keep it real."

In preparing to write my own talk, I asked myself three questions: What do I know most about? What do I care most about—where lies my passion? What current professional issues do I want to address? The answer to the first question was easiest. I knew that in some way I would incorporate the words and deeds of nineteenth-century black women. I wanted to call forth their words so that we could, as Audre Lorde said, "examine them in their pertinence to our lives." Further, I am passionate about the need to acknowledge rather than erase differences—differences in learning styles; differences in race, ethnicity, and cultural experiences; differences in linguistic practices; differences in perspectives; differences in local situations. Even if the differences are undesirable, they must first be acknowledged. As for the last question, the CCCC Executive Committee had just revised our mission statement, and various subcommittees of the Executive Committee had begun a review of our position statements. This review focused our attention on the ways in which these documents represented, in far too many instances, unachieved goals. The "Statement on Second-Language Writing and Writers," the "Statement of Principles and Standards for the Postsecondary Teaching of Writing," and "Students' Right to Their Own Language" demonstrated this disconnect between real and ideal more saliently than did the others. And they all had to do with how we respond to difference.

So, I had my answers and went to work. It was still a difficult writing assignment, but at least I knew that I would be grounded in what I knew, what I cared about, and what I felt CCCC members needed to hear about our organization.

–SHIRLEY WILSON LOGAN
University of Maryland

2004

Made Not Only in Words: Composition in a New Key

KATHLEEN BLAKE YANCEY

On March 22, 2004, I delivered the "Chair's Address." This talk was twenty-six pages, more or less, double-spaced, and composed in Garamond 12. While I talked, two synchronized PowerPoint slide shows ran independently, one to my right, another to my left. Together, the two slide shows included eighty-four slides.[1] There was one spotlight on me; otherwise, the theatre was dark, lit only by that spot and the slide shows. Oddly, I found myself "delivering" the Chair's Address to an audience I could not see. As Chris Farris pointed out to me later, given this setting, the talk was more dramatic performance than address.

Or: what genre was I invoking?

Words strain,
Crack and sometimes break, under the burden,
Under the tension, slip, slide, perish,
Decay with imprecision, will not stay in place,
Will not stay still.

Sometimes, you know, you have a moment. For us, this is one such moment. In coming together at CCCC, we leave our institutional sites of work; we gather together—we quite literally convene—at a not-quite-ephemeral site of disciplinary and professional work.

At this opening session in particular, inhabited with the echoes of those who came before and anticipating the voices of those who will follow—we pause and we commence.

We have a moment.

These moments: they aren't all alike, nor are they equal. And how we value them is in part a function of how we understand them, how we connect them to other moments, how we anticipate the moments to come. For compositionists, of this time and of this place, this moment—this moment *right now*—is like none other.

I come to this podium this morning fully conscious of the rather daunting responsibility attached to this occasion—a responsibility heightened by what my distinguished predecessors have said in their Chair's Addresses.

—Anne Ruggles Gere 1994

Never before has the proliferation of writings outside the academy so counterpointed the compositions inside. Never before have the technologies of writing contributed so quickly to the creation of new genres. The consequence of these two factors is the

This article is a revised version of the Chair's address Kathleen Blake Yancey delivered at the CCCC Convention in San Antonio, Texas, on March 25, 2004. A previous version was published in *CCC*, volume 56, number 2, December 2004.

creation of a writing public that, in development and in linkage to technology, parallels the development of a reading public in the 19th century. And these parallels, they raise good questions, suggest ways that literacy is created across spaces, across time.

Literacy today is in the midst of a tectonic change. Even inside of school, never before have writing and composing generated such diversity in definition. What do our references to writing mean? Do they mean print only? That's definitely what writing is if we look at national assessments, assuming that the assessment includes writing at all and is not strictly a test of grammar and usage. According to these assessments—an alphabet soup of assessments, the SAT, the NEAP, the ACT—writing IS "words on paper," composed on the page with a pen or pencil by students who write words on paper, yes—*but* who *also* compose words and images and create audio files on Web logs (blogs), in word processors, with video editors and Web editors and in e-mail and on presentation software and in instant messaging and on listservs and on bulletin boards—and no doubt in whatever genre will emerge in the next ten minutes.[2]

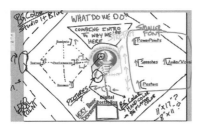

Note that no one is *making* anyone *do* any of this writing. Don't you wish that the energy and motivation that students bring to some of these other genres they would bring to our assignments? How is it that what we teach and what we test can be so different from what our students know as writing?

What *is* writing, really? It includes print: that seems obvious. But: Does it include writing for the screen? How visual is it? Is it the ability to move textual resources among spaces, as suggested by Johndan Johnson-Eilola? Is composing, as James Porter suggests, not only about medium but also specifically about technology? Suppose I said that basically writing is interfacing? What does that add to our definition of writing? What about the circulation of writing, and the relationship of writing to the various modes of delivery?

> But the main insight I have about my own literacy history is that none of the important or meaningful writing I have ever produced happened as a result of a writing assignment given in a classroom.
>
> —Lillian Bridwell Bowles 1995

And what do these questions mean with respect to another kind of delivery, the curricular and pedagogical delivery of college composition, in classroom to seminar room to online chat room to studio?

Collectively, these questions sound a moment for composition in a new key.

To explain what I mean by this more fully, I'll detail what this moment is, and why and how it matters for us, and what

> In planning this address—what some called a script, others a transcript—I designed a multigenred and mediated text that would embody and illustrate the claims of the talk. To accomplish this aim, I developed "stock" of two kinds. I collected verbal material, based on readings, some of my own writings, and some of my students' work. Concurrently, I collected images, again from my own work, photographs from places I knew, and images from the public domain. Collecting these different materials and putting them in dialogue with each other was a key part of *this* composing process.

it is that we might want to do about it in a talk I have subtitled Composition in Four Quartets.

QUARTET ONE

In my beginning is my end.

We have a moment.

In some ways our moment is like that in 19th-century Britain when a new reading public composed of middle- and working-class peoples came into being. Technology played a major role in this creation: with a new steam printing press and cheaper paper, reading material became more accessible. There were political and economic reasons as well. Economic changes of the 19th century came in the context of a globalization connected to travel, adventure, colonialism, and a massive demographic shift from farm to city changing the material conditions of work and life.[4] Economically, what has been called the Industrial Age promoted a "rising" middle class, indeed a bourgeoisie, that had the funds to buy print reading material and the leisure in which to read it and that began to have some political rights—and to press for more. From the perspective of literature, the genre receiving the most attention was the novel, which is said to have encouraged readers and in some ways to have created them. As important

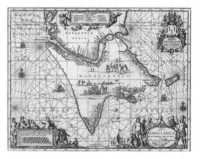

for our purposes, these novels were often *published in another form first,* typically in serial installments that the public read monthly. In other words, the emergence of this reading public co-occurred with the emergence of a multiply genred and distributed novel. All of Dickens's novels, for instance, were so published, "generally in monthly parts." And the readers were more than consumers; they helped shape the development of the text-in-process. Put differently, the "fluctuations of public demand" influenced the ways that Dickens and other novelists developed future episodes. The British novels of the 19th century were from the very beginning developed and distributed in multiple genres made possible by a new technology, the novelist writing in the context of and for very specific readers who, in turn, provided responses influencing the development of the text in question.

People read together, sometimes in "reading circles," sites of domestic engagement, but also in public places. Technological constraints—bad lighting, eyesight overstrained by working

The images, in other words, did not simply punctuate a written text; together words and images were (and are) the materials of composition.[3]

The Chair's Address is, of course, one genre, what Mike Palmquist has called a "call to action" genre. In medium, this address was plural—delivered simultaneously through the human voice and through the PowerPoint slides, both in relation to and also mediated by the twenty-six pages of written text.[5] In response to some requests for the script, I created a version of it in the spirit of an *executive summary.* Another version is being developed for *CCC Online;* its logic is different still. And then there is the text you are reading now, which includes a limited number of slides (reproduced) that are arranged anew. This "Chair's Address" also includes new images and new verbal text—like the meta-text you are reading now.

All of which leads me to ask: how many compositions are in this text?

conditions[6]—encouraged such communal readings, since in this setting no single pair of eyes was overly strained. People also gathered frequently to hear authors read their own works in staged readings. For these 19th-century novels, the patterns of circulation thus included both oral and written forums. Or: new forms of writing—the serials, the newspapers, the triple-decker Victorian novel—encouraged new reading publics who read for new purposes.

And all of this happened outside of school.

Today, we are witnessing a parallel creation, that of a *writing* public made plural, and as in the case of the development of a reading public, it's taking place largely outside of school—and this in an age of universal education. Moreover, unlike what happens in our classes, *no one is forcing this public to write.* There are no As here, no Dean's lists, no writing teacher to keep tabs on you. Whatever the exchange value may be for these writers—and there are millions of them, here and around the world—it's certainly not grades. Rather, the writing seems to operate in an economy driven by use value. The context for this writing public, expanded anew, is cause for concern and optimism. On the one hand, a loss in jobs in this country caused (it is said) by globalization is connected to a rise in corporate profits detailed in one accounting report after another, and we are assured by those in Washington that such job loss is actually *good* for us. As one commentator on NPR put it in early March, we've moved from just-in-time jobs to just-in-time people. Such an approach to labor is not news to those of us in composition: we apparently got there first. On the other hand, those committed to another vision of globalization see in it the chance for a (newfound) cooperation and communication among people, one with potential to transform the world and its peoples positively. At best, it could help foster a world peace never known before. At least, as we have seen over the course of the last year, it is (finally) more difficult to conduct any war in secret.

> Modern physics long since made us learn that the world out there has more space than stuff anyway, and it is in the spaces that we find relationships.
> —Richard Lloyd Jones 1978

Like 19th-century readers creating their own social contexts for reading in reading circles, writers in the 21st century self-organize into what seem to be overlapping technologically driven writing circles, what we might call a series of newly imagined communities, communities that cross borders of all kinds—nation state, class, gender, ethnicity. Composers gather in Internet chat rooms; they participate in listservs dedicated to both the ridiculous and the sublime; they mobilize for health concerns, for political causes, for research, and for travel advice. Indeed, for Howard Dean's candidacy we saw the first blog for a presidential candidate. Many of the Internet texts are multiply genred and purposed: MoveOn.com sends e-mails, collects money, and hosts a Web site simultaneously. Flash mobs gather

It's worth asking what the principles of all these compositions are. Pages have interfaces, although like much that is ubiquitous, we don't attend to such interfaces as we might. The fact that you have one interface governing the entire text, however, does provide a frame. What is the frame for (and thus the theory governing) a composition in multiple parts? For that matter, how does this text—with call outs, palimpsest notes, and images—cohere?

And: How do we create such a text? How do we read it? How do we value it?

Not least, how will we teach it?

The literacies that composers engage in today are multiple. They include print literacy practices (like spelling) that URL's require; they include visual literacy; they include network literacy. As important, these literacies are textured and in relationship to each other. Perhaps most important, these literacies are social in a way that school literacy all too often only pretends to be.

Of course, as Anne Gere demonstrated in her own Chair's Address, writing has always been embedded in an extra-curriculum. Public institutions now design for such a curriculum, bringing together what computer game designer Frank Lantz calls a convergence of digital and physical space. Examples include new public libraries, especially those in Salt Lake City and in Seattle. In their designs, both architectural and curricular, these institutions overlap and interplay "domestic spaces" (like Seattle's "living room" inside the library), "conventional" library spaces, and electronic spaces.[7]

for minutes-long social outings; political flash mobs gather for purposes of political reform. And I repeat: like the members of the newly developed reading public, the members of the writing public have learned—in this case, to write, to think together, to organize, and to act within these forums—largely without instruction and, more to the point here, largely without *our* instruction. They need neither self-assessment nor our assessment: they have a rhetorical situation, a purpose, a potentially worldwide audience, a choice of technology and medium—and they write.

Some of these new Internet genres—e-mail, instant messaging, and so on—divide along lines based in age and in formal schooling. Faculty—the school insiders—use e-mail daily, considering it essential to academic and personal life. In contrast, students use instant messaging at least as often, and unlike most of us, they *like* it. Faculty see blogs—if they see them at all—as (yet) another site for learning, typically in school; students see blogs as a means of organizing social action, a place for geographically far-flung friends to gather, a site for poets and musicians to plan a jam. But our experiences are the same in one key way: most faculty and students alike *all have learned these genres* *on our own, outside of school.* Given *this* extracurricular writing curriculum and its success, I have to wonder out loud if in some pretty important ways and within the relatively short space of not quite ten years, we may already have become anachronistic.

Some disturbing data suggest that traditional English departments already are. According to the list of departmental administrators published in the PMLA, over the last twenty years, we have seen a decline in the number of departments called English of about 30%. Let me state this more dramatically: of the number of English departments whose administrators were included on the list in 1985, about one in three has disappeared. Why? They may have simply stopped being represented for any number of reasons: a shortage of funds, a transfer of the listing elsewhere. Naturally, this statistic doesn't mean that English is disappearing as an institutional unit. Most obviously, it means that fewer units calling themselves English are listed in the PMLA. And when plotted against another trend line—the *increase* of units called something other than English, like departments of communication and divisions of humanities—it

Because we are essentially in partnership with the wider community attempting to share meaningfully in the working out of a community responsibility, we must be in communication with the other parts of the community.

—Vivian Davis 1979

seems more plausible that *something* reductionist in nature is happening to English departments generally. They are being consolidated into other units or disappearing.[8] Another data point tells the same story: according to the Association of Departments of English (ADE), if English departments were graduating English majors at the same rate graduated in 1966, we would congratulate 100,000 students this year. Instead, we will offer English degrees to half that number—50,000.[9] And these data points may well explain why the number of tenure-line jobs in English continues its now altogether-too-familiar decline (which makes the continuing increase in tenure-line jobs in rhetoric and composition all the more remarkable). Of course, for many of us, this may be a moot point. We may not be housed in English departments ourselves, and most of us don't teach courses in the major because the major continues to be defined as *territorias literati*, a point to which I will return. Still, enough of us do reside in English to understand that as English goes, so may we.

These shifts: are they minor tremors signifying routine academic seismic activity that makes the world more stable? Alternatively, are they tremors occurring along the fault lines of tectonic plates that will in the not-too-distant future change the very topography of higher education?

These questions assume greater significance as evidence of other tremors within higher education make themselves felt. In the last two decades, we've seen a shift in the way the country views higher education. According to a 2004 edition of *U.S. News and World Report* (Shea), beginning in the Reagan era, the U.S. began moving away from the view that college is good for the *country*, a view that enfranchises all of us, and began shifting toward the view that higher education is good for the *individual*. Given this shift, perhaps it makes a perverse kind of sense that even though more than half of college students work, they still graduate with debt exceeding $15,000. During this same period, public institutions became state-supported institutions, then state-assisted schools, then state-affiliated schools, and now state-located schools. States

Although interpretations of data around the status of English departments vary, here something in English studies is clearly underway. The data points I report plot one trend line, a line that in its downward direction contrasts with the upward swing of the plot line for rhetoric and composition. In the midst of this moment, a new discourse that repositions English and humanities is emerging. The latest evidence: As I write this, literacy scholar Helen Vendler, in her NEH Jefferson Address, has attempted an English-centric redefinition of the humanities that excludes both history and philosophy.

Composition is a part of a higher education and the persistent problems in composition are tied to larger issues in the world, in our country, in higher education generally and in each academic institution specifically.
—Miriam Chaplin 1988

Additional evidence of our unwillingness, as members of a commons, to support higher education is abundant. Again, as I write this, President Bush's plan to maintain the level of funding for Pell Grants goes almost unchallenged. Given that tuition costs have risen and the number of eligible students has likewise risen, what this means is less support for students.

Part of what's at issue with screen literacy is how it too enables the making of stories, a common question we ask of literary texts, a common question we ask of students and of ourselves. As Daley suggests, the screen is very much part of the thinking around narrative. In reviewing *21 Grams*, for instance, film critic Roger Ebert brings the issue into relief (perhaps ironically?) when he says: "Imagining how heartbreaking the conclusion would have been if we had arrived at it in the ordinary way by starting at the beginning, I felt as if an unnecessary screen of technique had been placed between the story and the audience."

haven't abandoned support of education: rather, they have redirected the revenue streams away from the institutions and toward the consumers, the students. In other words, historically, public funds went to public institutions; today, in many states, including mine, they go directly to the students—chiefly through scholarships titled Hope or Freedom, which one economist has likened to vouchers for K – 12. And the worst-case scenario has already been proposed in Colorado: take all funding for public institutions and distribute it not to them but directly to students.[10] Educationally, in the words of Robert Putnam, we are increasingly bowling alone, and apart from the damage it will do to the individual schools, I worry about the damage it will do to the country as a commons.

Relevant to literacy specifically, we can record other tremors, specifically those associated with the screen, and in that focus, they return us to questions around what it means to write. Further, I'd suggest that they constitute a serious challenge to us. As articulated by Elizabeth Daley, dean of the University of Southern California School of Television & Cinema, this view of literacy makes a clear distinction—both in practice and in institutional home—between print literacy and screen literacy. Linking what happens outside of school to what we might do inside, Daley observes that both in metaphorical analogy and in use, the screen has become ubiquitous. "Metaphors from the screen have become common in our daily conversation," she says ("Expanding" 34). Think about these everyday terms: close up, flash back, frame, cut to the chase, segue. Our daily communicative, social, and intellectual practices are screen-permeated. Further, her argument is that *the screen is the language of the vernacular,* that if we do not include it in the school curriculum, we will become as irrelevant as faculty professing in Latin. "No longer," she declares, "can students be considered truly educated by

mastering reading and writing alone. The ability to negotiate through life by combining words with pictures with audio and video to express thoughts will be the mark of the educated student" ("Speaking"). Specifically, she proposes that the literacy of the screen, which she says *parallels* oral literacy and print literacy, become a *third* literacy required of all undergraduates. Not surprisingly, she believes such literacy should be taught not in composition classrooms but in media studies programs. Not least, Daley argues that education needs to get in step with life practices and should endeavor to assist students to negotiate through life.

What do these conceptions of reading and writing publics, these tremors in the world and in higher education and in English have to do with composition?

QUARTET TWO

A people without history

Is not redeemed from time, for history is a pattern

Of timeless moments.

We have a moment.

What we make of this moment is contextualized by our own history as a discipline. Many have noted the role that first-year composition played in the formation of CCCC: it was our raison d'etre—and a worthy cause. We focused then on the gatekeeping moment, the moment when students enter college and in particular on that transition moment between high school and college. It's worth considering, however, how this gatekeeping situation has changed in the last fifty-five years.

> Someone has estimated that there are at least nine thousand of us teaching in college courses in composition and communication.
>
> —John Gerber 1950

Early in the decade when CCCC was formed, in 1949, only 30% of students graduated from high school; only 20% of high school graduates even began college, typically at four-year liberal arts institutions; and fewer than 6% graduated. Today, depending on your source, about 89% of students graduate from high school, and some 65% begin college ("America's"). In other words, at various times—in high school in AP classes and dual-enrollment classes, just after high school, years after completing high school—many students—indeed most students—do begin college.[11]

But what happens? They don't finish: only 28% of Americans complete four years of college. It looks bleaker as you go to certain categories: 17% of African Americans have college degrees, 10.6% of Latinos, even fewer Native Americans (Wright). Still, too often we define ourselves as that first-year course. Suppose that if instead of focusing on the gatekeeping year, we saw composition education as a *gateway*? Suppose that we enlarged our focus to include *both* moments, gatekeeping and gateway? And further suppose, to paraphrase Elizabeth Daley, that we designed a curriculum in composition that prepared students to become members of the writing public and to negotiate life. How might that alter what we think and what we do?

Such an agenda is consistent with data that account for successful college experiences. Richard Light, for instance, demonstrates that one of the key factors students and alumni cite in studies of how college can work well is writing. The National Survey of Student Engagement—in both two- and four-year school versions—sounds the same note. We know that writing makes a difference—both at the gatekeeping moment and as students progress through the gateway.

> It's almost impossible to know how many students finish high school. Some finish after four years; some finish after another year or two in an alternative setting; some finish through the GED program. And it is so that some don't finish at all. Where they don't finish, typically in urban settings and in impoverished states, life is harder all the way around. Still, if we in college could graduate the same percentage of students as our colleagues in high school do, we'd nearly triple our graduation rate.

In the Portraits of Composition Research Study, respondents spoke in chorus about the move to digital texts. Nearly all respondents expect students to submit texts composed in a word processor; nearly half of the respondents respond to student texts via e-mail. But very few—less than 30%—use a course management system.[12]

Of course, in this moment in composition's history, I'm making certain assumptions about writing that as a disciplinary community, we are still ambivalent about. What should be the future shape of composition? Questioning the role of technology in composition programs—shall we teach print, digital, composition, communication, or all of the above?—continues to confound us. Do we want to confine our efforts to print literacy only —or, alternatively, to print literacy predominately? Given a dearth of resources—from hardware to pro-

fessional development, from student access to what Gail Hawisher calls the bandwidth digital divide—many of us continue to focus on print. Given a concern that postmodernism and infobits could undermine a sustained rational discourse that is fundamental to democracy, many of us vote for the known that is, not coincidentally, what our colleagues expect us to deliver in the composition classroom: the print of CCCC—coherence, clarity, consistency, and (not least) correctness.

At the same time, when reviewed, our own practices suggest that we have already committed to a theory of communication that is both/and: print and digital. Given the way we *produce* print—sooner or later inside a word processor— we are digital already, at least in process. Given the course management systems like Blackboard and WebCT, we have committed to the screen for administrative

purposes at least. Given the oral communication context of peer review, our teaching requires that students participate in mixed communicative modes. Given the digital portfolios coming into their own, even the move by CCCC to provide LCD's and Internet connects to panelists upon request and for free, we teachers and students seem to have moved already— to communication modes assuming digital literacy. And thinking about our own presentations here: when we consider how these presentations will morph into other talks, into articles for print and online journals, into books, indeed into our classrooms, it becomes pretty clear that we *already* inhabit a model of communication practices incorporating multiple genres related to each other, those multiple genres remediated across contexts of time and space, linked one to the next, circulating across and around rhetorical situations both inside and outside school.

This is composition—*and* this is the *content* of composition.

If we cannot go home again to the days when print was the sole medium, what will the new curricular home for composition look like?

> That composition has a content at all—other than process—is a radical claim. The CCCCs was founded with a concern about what the content of first-year composition should be, and it is a concern that continues to energize us even today.

QUARTET THREE

> Words, after speech, reach
> Into the silence. Only by the form, the pattern,
> Can words or music reach
> The stillness, as a Chinese jar still
> Moves perpetually in its stillness.

We have a moment.

At this moment, we need to focus on three changes: Develop a new curriculum; revisit and revise our writing-across-the-curriculum efforts; and develop a major in composition and rhetoric.[13]

Since the limits of time and space preclude my detailing all three, I will focus on the first, developing *a new curriculum for the 21st century*, a curriculum that carries forward the best of what we have created to date, that brings together the writing outside of school and that inside. This composition is located in a new vocabulary, a new set of practices, and a new set of outcomes; it will focus our research in new and provocative ways; it has as its goal the creation of thoughtful, informed, technologically adept writing publics. This goal entails the other two: extending this new composition curriculum horizontally throughout the academy and extending it vertically through our own major. In other words, it is past time that we fill the glaringly empty spot between first-year composition and graduate education with a composition major.

> To accept rhetoric and composition . . . as legitimate parts of the graduate curriculum is not a sign of dissolution, dispersion, and decomposition. It is, rather, a sign that we are regaining our composure, taking composure to mean composition in all of its senses.
> —Frank D'Angelo 1980

And in the time and space that's left, I want to sketch briefly what this new curriculum might look like.

To begin thinking about a revised curriculum for composition, we might note the most significant change that has occurred in composition over the last thirty years: the process movement. Although not everyone agrees that the process movement radically altered the teaching of composition (see Crowley; Matsuda), most do think that process—as we defined it in the research of scholars like Janet Emig and Linda Flower and as brought into the classroom by teachers like us—did revolutionize the teaching of writing. We had a new vocabulary, some of it—like invention—ancient, some of it—writing process and rewriting and freewriting—new. We developed pedagogy anew: peer review, redrafting, portfolio assessment. But nothing stays still, and process approaches have given way

> Erika Lindemann's work on the bibliographic categories that organize and construct composition reveals the role that process both has and has not played in the discipline. Lindemann notes that while in the 1986 CCCC Bibliography *process* was included in three of twelve categories (or 25%), it is completely absent in the 2001 MLA successor to the Cs bibliography.

to other emphases. Recently, we have seen several approaches seeking to update that work, some on the left in the form of cultural studies and post-process; some more interested in psychological approaches like those located in felt sense; others more interested in the connections composition can forge with like-minded educational initiatives such as service learning and first-year experience programs.

What's interesting is that regardless of the changes that are advocated as we attempt to create a post-process compositional curriculum, most (not all but most)  attempt this without questioning or altering the late-20th-century basis of composition. To put the point directly, composition in this school context, and in direct contrast to the *world* context, remains chiefly focused on the writer qua writer, sequestered from the means of production. Our model of teaching composing, as generous, varied, and flexible as it is in terms of aims and as innovative as it is in terms of pedagogy—and it is all of these—(still) embodies the narrow and the singular in its emphasis on a primary and single human relationship: the writer in relation to the teacher. In contrast to the reading public nearly two centuries ago, the "real" reading public of school is solitary, the teacher whose reading consists of print text delivered on the teacher's desk. In contrast to the development of a writing public, the classroom writer is not a member of a collaborative group with a common project linked to the world at large and delivered in multiple genres and media, but a singular person writing over and over again—to the teacher.

What no one, including writing teachers, foresaw twenty years ago was the extent to which the creation of wealth would be divorced from labor and redistributed, leaving the United States the most economically polarized among industrialized nations, with the divide between rich and poor continuing to widen.
— Lester Faigley 1997

I am interested in the terms we use to constitute our subject, the terms we take for granted and the degree to which we take them for granted. Today I'll stick to the three terms of our name, composition, communication, conference. These terms are our legacy; we must not betray those who have given them to us. They are also our problem, our burden, since they resist reflection and change.
— David Bartholomae 1989

John Trimbur calls our school model of writing the in loco parentis model: we are the parents who in our practices continue to infantilize our students as we focus their gaze and their energy and their reflection on the moments of creation, on process. I tend to think of it in another, complementary way, as a remediated tutorial model of writing. In other words, it seems to me that in all our efforts to improve the teaching of composition—to reduce class size, for instance, to conference with students, to respond vociferously to each student paper, and to understand that in our students' eyes we are the respondent who matters—we seek to approximate the one-to-one tutorial model. Quite apart from the fact that such an effort is doomed—about a hundred years ago, Edwin Hopkins asked if we could teach composition under the current conditions,[14] which conditions then are the same conditions we work in today, and immediately answered, "NO"—I have to wonder why we want to work this way, wonder why *this* is the neo-Platonic mode to which we continuously aspire. Not that the process model is bad, I hasten to add: students do engage with each other, often do write to the world, and frequently do develop elaborated processes—all to the good. But if we believe that writing is social, shouldn't the system of circulation—the paths that the writing takes—extend beyond and around the single path from student to teacher?

More to the point, the list of what students aren't asked to do in the current model—and what they might—is long:

- consider the issue of intertextual circulation: how what they are composing relates or compares to "real world" genres;

- consider what the best medium and the best delivery for such a communication might be and then create and share those different communication pieces in those different media, to different audiences;

- think explicitly about what they might "transfer" from one medium to the next: what moves forward, what gets left out, what gets added—and what they have learned about composing in this transfer process;

- consider how to transfer what they have learned in one *site* and how that could or could not transfer to another, be that site on campus or off;[15]

- think about how these practices help prepare them to become members of a writing public.

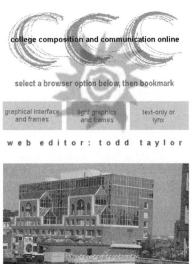

A Boston skyline, the old juxtaposed with the new, old and new interfaced. An architectural intertextuality.

What I'm proposing is that we move to a new model of composing where students are explicitly asked to engage in these considerations, to engage in these activities, to develop as members of a writing public. Such a model of composition is located in three key expressions:

Circulation of composition

Canons of rhetoric

Deicity of technology

Let me begin with circulation: although they are related, I will here outline and exemplify two kinds: (1) the circulation of texts generally, and (2) the circulation of a student's own work

Conceptually, composition itself is in circulation. From music and art, it carries an aesthetic dimension. From chemistry and architecture, it carries an interest in materials. Pedagogically, borrowing from Joe Janangelo and Pablo Picasso, I have talked elsewhere about students as "ongoing compositions." We see such humans-as-compositions in any collected work, summarized minimally in a resume or vita; developed and illustrated more fully and reflectively in a portfolio. Regardless of whether we see such composing or not, it is always in play. In the context of compositionists as professionals, we compose ourselves, both individually, in the words of Elizabeth Flynn, and as participants of a community, in the words of Andrea Lunsford's Chair's Address.

within an educational culture. Texts circulate: they move across contexts, between media, across time. Writers compose in the context of other writers and thinkers and speakers. They imitate them directly and indirectly; they quote them, write in direct reference to them, paraphrase them, and frame their own work in these contexts. This circulation is the one, perhaps, with which we are most familiar: we often talk about it as intertextuality, as a conversation that we invite students to join. The conversation, of course, occurs through genres and is really many conversations, with texts circulating in multiple, interrelated ways.

What I am calling circulation can go by other names: Charles Bazerman and David Russell, for instance, call it activity theory, but basically it's the same point: As they explain,

> Writing is alive when it is being written, read, remembered, contemplated, followed—when it is part of human activity. . . . The signs on the page serve to mediate between people, activate their thoughts, direct their attention, coordinate their actions, provide the means of relationship. It is in the context of their activities that people consider texts and give meaning to texts. And it is in the organization of activities that people find the needs, stances, interactions, tasks that orient their attention toward texts they write and read. So to study text production, text reception, text meaning, text value apart from their animating activities is to miss the core of text's being.

So: circulation.

With the help of David Russell and Arturo Yañez, let me put a classroom face on what this might look like in terms of curriculum. They tell the story of a student caught in an all-too-familiar dilemma. Beth, the student, is an aspiring journalist convinced of the integrity and objectivity of reportorial accounting; moreover, she believes that good writing is good writing is good writing, regardless of the discipline. Which means, of course, that good writing is the writing she understands and practices. The problem: she's enrolled in an Irish literature class that she needs for graduation, a class where good writing— located in interpretation and exercise of judgment—looks very different. To her, this historical writing feels inexact and duplicitous; and it makes history, which she has understood as an exercise in "Just the facts, ma'am"—as completely alien. What activity theory adds to this mix is a means of making sense of these seemingly disparate texts and ways of knowing.

> Professional historians . . . critically examine and interpret (and reinterpret) primary documents according to the methods (rules, norms) of history. They argue and debate to persuade other experts. And when enough experts (or the enough powerful experts) arrive at consensus, that consensus is put into textbooks for high school students and generally perceived as "fact." And, perhaps, that consensus is eventually put into popular

history books, of the kind that journalists review and the rest of us Big Picture People sometimes read—to find the "facts" of history. (Russell and Yañez)

Thinking in terms of circulation, in other words, enables students to understand the epistemology, the conventions, and the integrity of different fields and their genres. Using that as a point of departure allows students to complete the task *and* move closer to the big picture of writing. Trimbur makes an analogous point in outlining a curricular approach where students in health sciences understand how different genres even within the same field function epistemologically: research genres to make scientific knowledge; public health articles deriving from the research genres both diluting and distributing it, each according to its own logic and conventions. His purpose?

> I want students to see that the shift in register and genre between a journal article and a news report amounts to a shift in modality—the relative credibility and authoritativeness invested in written statements—that marks journal articles as 'original' contributions and news reports as secondary and derivative. (213)

Media themselves provide another example of circulation. As Jay Bolter and Richard Grusin explain in *Remediation*, and as McLuhan suggested before that, nearly every medium is re/mediated on another medium. In other words, consciously or otherwise, we create the new in the context of the old and based on the model of the old. Television is commonly understood to be remediated on film, for example, and the Web is commonly understood to be remediated on print. Remediation can be back-ended as well, as we see in the most recent CNN interface on TV, which is quite explicitly remediated on the Web. The new, then, repeats what came before, while at the same time remaking that which it models. This isn't a new phenomenon, however, as we remember from the development of that 19th-century novel, which appeared in multiple genres and media: serials, triple-deckers, performances. Fast forward to the 21st century: imagine that in composition classes students, like Victorian novelists before them, focus on remediating their own texts. Beginning with a handout or one pager, they define a key term of the course and revise that on the basis of class response; in addition, they move the material

We look at the present through a rear-view mirror. We march backwards into the future.
—**Marshall McLuhan 1964**

Who writes the "first draft" of history can change, of course, as can patterns of circulation. Concerns around such issues are not merely academic, as is clear in the following *New York Times* commentary on the relationship between genres and the roles they are currently playing in *this* historical moment: "The sudden outpouring of inside details in books about the Bush administration is all the more remarkable because of the administration's previous success at controlling the flow of information to the press about its workings. It is a phenomenon that is creating an unusual reversal in which books—the musty vessels traditionally used to convey patient reflection into the archives—are superseding newspapers as the first draft of history, leaving the press corps to cover the books themselves as news."

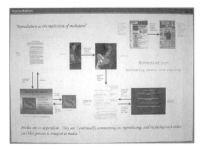

of that handout to a five-slide *PowerPoint* show presented to the class and itself revised. Suppose that they move this material to a poster, then to a presentation, then to a conventional written text. For the conventional written text, they brainstorm in class and on a blog, thinking individually and communally about which of these tasks "counts" as writing—and why. As they move from medium to medium, they consider what they move forward, what they leave out, what they add, and for each of these write a reflection in which they consider how the medium itself shapes what they create. The class culminates with text in which they write a reflective theory about what writing is and how it is influenced or shaped or determined by media and technology. Located in the rhetoric of purpose, audience, genre, this model of circulation is particularly oriented to medium and technology; it permits a student, as Brian Morrison does here, to define composition as "the thoughtful gathering, construction, or reconstruction of a literate act in any given media."

These three related approaches: all oriented to the circulation of texts, to genre, to media, and to ways that writing gets made, both individually and culturally. As important, all three of these approaches, in their analysis of textual relationships and contexts, in their theories and examples of how writing works, and in their situating the student as a maker of knowledge, map the content for new composition. And if you are saying, but I can't do all this in first-year composition, I'm going to reply, "Exactly."

Speaking of Remediation . . .

Have you heard Sheryl Crow's version of Rod Stewart's "The First Cut is the Deepest"?

Or how about *Moulin Rouge*?

First-year composition is a place to begin; carrying this forward is the work of the major in composition and rhetoric.

A second kind of circulation, occurring within the bounds of school and often within the classroom, has to do with the variety of academic texts that students create, with the places in which those texts are created and distributed, and with how *this circulation* contributes to student development in writing. We have some fine research in this sense of circulation that accounts for students moving forward in their writing: research conducted by Lee Ann Carroll, Nancy Sommers and Laura Saltz, Marilyn Sternglass, Richard Haswell, and Elizabeth Chiseri-Strater. Typically, such studies focus on how and what students "transfer" from one site to another; Anne Beaufort's study asks the same question but applied to the site of work. And often we ask students to engage in this activity themselves: in their reflections, students account for the progress (or not) of their texts; of what they have learned in the construction of such texts; in their portfolios—be they digital or print—students comment and demonstrate the circulation of the course.

A vignette composed by Paul Prior and Jody Shipka shows us another way to think about circulation that focused exclusively on a single text.

> A psychology professor reports to us that when she is revising an article for publication she works at home and does the family laundry. She sets the buzzer on the dryer so that approximately every 45 minutes to an hour she is pulled away from the text to tend the laundry downstairs. As she empties the dryer, sorts and folds, reloads, her mind wanders a bit and she begins to recall things she wanted to do with the text, begins to think of new questions or ideas, things that she had not been recalling or thinking of as she focused on the text when she was upstairs minutes before. She perceives this break from the text, this opportunity to reflect, as a very productive part of the process.

What Prior and Shipka point out, of course, is that this text is produced through two activity systems: the domestic and the disciplinary.[16] They raise provocative questions about the role the buzzer plays in the drafting process, about the spaces created here for reflection, about the role reflection plays in composing.

This too is circulation; this too is composition.

As I move into the second expression, the canons of rhetoric—invention, arrangement, style, memory, and delivery—I'm aware that these are hardly new. I wonder about how we understand them, however. Like others before me, I would note that we have separated delivery and memory from invention, arrangement, and style in ways that are counterproductive. Let me further say that too often we treat them as discrete entities when in fact they are interrelated. Let me share with you an image. Don't ask me why, but I have always understood each canon as sitting on a rhetorical shelf, as though a freshly laundered cotton blanket in a laundry closet. I take one canon down—my favorite, if truth be told, is invention—use it, then put neatly back on the shelf. But as my options for delivering texts have widened—from the page to the screen to the networked screen and then back to the page anew—I've begun to see the canons not as discrete entities like those blankets on shelves but, rather, as related to

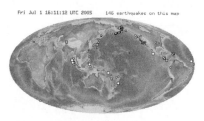

Fri Jul 1 16:11:12 UTC 2005   146 earthquakes on this map

What is the relationship between and among remediating texts, carrying forward materials, finding new sources, and representing and inventing a self?

One thing that is clear to me as I compose this text for the page is that this remediation feels less like a small morphing of a text from one medium to another than it does like creating a new text. And it's not mere perception: this composition is longer by over 2,000 words, most of which comment on, extend, and complicate the earlier voiced text.

Bill Watterson, the creator of Calvin and Hobbes, talks about how circulation of another kind can influence the development of a creator, in this case of a cartoonist. He notes, "The challenge of any cartoonist is not just to duplicate the achievements of the past, but to build on them as well" (9–10). He argues it is thus necessary for the cartoonist to have access to earlier cartoons, through their collection and republication—in book form.[17]

It's instructive to attempt to map the relationship between and among the canons. As I continue to explore delivery—of text, of instruction, of public extracurricula—delivery seems at the heart of the relationship, but I can see how at other times, other canons take that place.

The revolution, if there is one, is the social one of interconnectivity.
—James Porter 2003

We used to have a stable definition of composing and of the author. These have changed. The freedom to invent, to arrange multiply, can be a wonderful thing. It can also evoke anxiety, somewhat akin to discovering that the tectonic plates underlying the continents are not stable but, in fact, are shifting constantly.

The tectonic plate theory of continental drift was "discovered" in 1965. Rohman and Wlecke's stage-model of writing was "discovered" a year earlier; Rohman's *CCC* article detailing prewriting was published the year following, in 1965.

each other in much the same way as the elements of Burke's pentad are related: the canons interact, and through that interaction they contribute to new exigencies for invention, arrangement, representation, and identity. Or: they change what is possible.

Richard Lanham, of course, has argued that with the addition of the digital to the set of media in which we compose, delivery takes on a critical role, and I think that's so. But much more specifically, what a shift in the means of delivery does is bring invention and arrangement into a new relationship with each other. The writer of the page has fundamentally different opportunities than the creator of a hypertext. Anne Wysocki is right about the interface of the page—that is, it has one, and it's worth paying attention to—but even so, as we read the pages of an article, we typically do so line by line, left to right, as you do now: page one before page two. This is the fixed default arrangement. The writer *invented* through such a text is a function of that arrangement. In other words, you can only invent inside what an arrangement permits—and different media permit different arrangements. By contrast, the creator of a hypertext can create a text that, like the page, moves forward. In addition, however, hypertext composers can create other arrangements, almost as in three rather than two dimensions. You can move horizontally, right branching; you can then left branch. The writer invented in a medium permitting these arrangements is quite different—a difference of kind, not degree.

Given my own teaching and research interests, I see such differences, particularly in portfolios. In a print portfolio, remediated on a book, the arrangement is singular. In a digital portfolio, remediated on a gallery, the arrangements are plural. And the students invented in each are quite different. In a print portfolio, the tendency is to tell a single story, one with a single claim and an accumulating body of evidence. In arrangement, a digital portfolio—again, by contrast—is multiple, is defined by links. Because you can link exter-

nally as well as internally and because those links are material, you have more contexts you can link to, more strata you can layer, more "you" to invent, more invention to represent. In sum, the potential of arrangement is a function of delivery, and *what and how you arrange*—which becomes a function of the medium you choose—*is who you invent*.[18] Moreover, I suspect that as multiple means of delivery become more routinized, we will understand *each* of the canons differently, and we will understand and be able to map their interrelationships.

My third and final expression is the deicity of technology. *Deixis*, linguistically, refers to words like *now* and *then*, words whose "meanings change quickly depending on the time or space in which they are uttered" (Leu et al.) or read. The word *Now* when I wrote this text is one time; as I read the word *Now* in San Antonio was a second time; and now, when this talk is published in *CCC* and who knows how many people do (or do not!) read *this* Chair's Address, it will be many, many other times. Literacy is deictic. The speed of technological change has affected literacy, as we know. The particular claim that D. J. Leu, C. K. Kinzer, J. Coiro, and D. Cammack (among others) have made is this: "technological change happens so rapidly that the changes to literacy are limited not by technology but rather by our ability to adapt and acquire of the new literacies that emerge." Deixis, they say, "is a defining quality of the new literacies of the Internet" and other information communication technologies.

According to Leu and his coauthors, there are three sources for this deictic nature of literacy:

1. transformations of literacy because of technological change,

2. the use of increasingly efficient technologies of communication that rapidly spread new literacies, and

3. envisionments of new literacy potentials within new technologies.

Although deixis might be a new term to many of us, the first two claims are familiar. As we saw in the case of the 19th-century reader, technology changes literacy: that's the kind of transformation we are seeing now with regard to writers. Technology, of course, has always been ubiquitous: as Dennis Baron points out, a pencil is a technology. At the same time, however, *this* digital, networked technology continuously promotes itself and new literacies—through the marketing efforts of the corporations that develop these technologies; through open source and shareware and freeware; through our ability to download new programs and formats that are essentially new engines for a literacy no one can quite predict. The dissemination of this potential capacity is built into this model of technology. Given its worldwide distribution and its democratization of authorship, that's new.

The third source—what Leu calls "envisionments of new literacy potentials within new technologies"—is provocative. Here is what he is referring to: the ability or someone to take a given technology and find a use for it that may be at odds with its design. The example he provides is this. Suppose that you

> Leu and his colleagues note how our working in a context of deixis changes the way we teach. No longer, they say, can we speak from the podium with the expertise of old. Instead, faculty and students will consider questions and use various technologies to help address them, with the faculty member guiding the work, and in some cases learning along with the students. In composition, we need to learn how to read and write e-texts—synthesizing, questioning, evaluating, and importing from them—databases and catalogues, hyper-texts and archives, Web essays and portfolios.

> And this means we all need to learn more about how to use images and sources, how to document them appropriately, how to create our own.

> By paying critical attention to lessons about *technology*, we can re-learn important lessons about *literacy*.
> —Cindy Selfe 1999

Envisionment is a practice most of us engage in, typically without thinking about it as such. Teachers use a spreadsheet for grading purposes. A colleague uses a spreadsheet for a digital portfolio template for her class of 120 students. Elementary teachers use PowerPoint for reluctant writers. High school teachers use textboxes for peer review and links for research hypercards. College teachers invite blocked writers to draft in an e-mail program.

A modest proposal: one outcome for all writers is the ability to use many kinds of technologies for their intended purposes and for other purposes, as needed and as imagined.

Or: writers use technology rhetorically.

are writing an e-mail but decide to compose the e-mail inside a word processor, which is a different (if related) technology. In this scenario,

> a word processor can be transformed into a tool for composing e-mail messages, a purpose for which it was not designed, but a function it fills admirably. This potential only comes to life when a person *envisions* a new function for a technology and *enacts this envisionment*. In essence, we can say that she envisioned how to repurpose a technology for a new and different function. Envisionments such as this happen regularly as individuals encounter new problems and seek solutions in new and creative uses of existing technologies. (Leu et al.)

And let me provide another example. For the last several years, I have worked with graduate students in architecture, and one of their practices is meeting monthly to talk about how their projects and theses are developing. Now, given that it's architecture, they do more than talk: they *show* — in pin ups on the walls, in a one-page handout, and in a set of *Power-Point* slides. Something that grabbed my attention almost immediately was how those slides were being used: not for *presentation* of a finished idea, as the design of them would have it — and as the name, pre-

Writing, by its very nature, encourages abstraction, and in the shuttling process from the past to the present, from the particular to the general, from the concrete to the abstract, we seek relationships and find meaning.
–William Irmscher 1979

sentation software, suggests — but, rather, for a different purpose: for exploration, in fact as a new space for drafting ideas. Since then, in several different classes, I've used *PowerPoint* in just this way, as a site for a rough draft, shared with a real audience. Or: envisionment. What other technologies might be re-envisioned and to what effects? What envisionments have students already created that we don't know about? And how do we build this ability — envisioning — into our curriculum?

This new composition includes rhetoric and is about literacy. New composition includes the literacy of print: it adds on to it and brings the notions of practice and activity and circulation and media and screen and networking to our conceptions of process. It will require a new expertise of us as it does of our students. And ultimately, new composition may require a new site for learning for all of us.

QUARTET FOUR

Time present and time past
Are both perhaps present in time future,
And time future contained in time past.

We have a moment.

In her study *Institutionalizing Literacy*, Mary Trachsel makes the argument that when we separate an activity related to curriculum from it, faculty lose control over curriculum to the detriment of students and faculty alike. Trachsel, of course, is speaking of assessment, and how historically it has been cleaved from curriculum, particularly at the gatekeeping moment when students enter college—and she cites the SAT as evidence of the claim. I would make the same observation about technology. If we continue to partition it off as just something technical, or outside the parameters governing composing, or limit it to the screen of the course management system, or think of it in terms of the bells and whistles and templates of the *PowerPoint* screen, students in our classes learn only to *fill up* those templates and *fill in* those electric boxes—which, in their ability to invite intellectual work, are the moral equivalent of the dots on a multiple choice test. Students will not compose and create, making use of all the means of persuasion and all the possible resources thereto; rather, they will complete someone else's software package; they will be the invention of that package.

These spaces—the intertextual, overlapping curricular spaces—between school and the public, including print and screen, are still ours to study, to examine, to work in, and to claim. They are the province of first-year composition but are not limited to it. This curricular change includes renewed attention to WAC. It includes a new major in whatever site: English department, writing studies department, rhetorical studies program. The institutional site is less important than the major itself, which can begin to secure our position in the academy while it makes space for the writing that students do on their own, now, without us.

It is time to speak for ourselves, in our own interests, in the interest of our own work, and in the interest of our students.
—Jacqueline Jones Royster 1996

The metaphors we use to describe also construct. The metaphor of tectonic change, particularly when used in the context of the changes of the 19th century, can help us understand how pervasive our current challenges are, how necessary our efforts to adapt.

So this talk: yes, it's about change. Change, as we saw in the 19th century, and as we see now, can be very difficult, can be unnerving. I used the metaphor of tremors intentionally. A little more than twenty years ago we talked about "winds of change" (Hairston); today the changes are those of tremors. These are *structural* changes—global, educational, technological. Like seismic tremors, these signal a re-formation in process, and because we exist on the borders of our own tectonic plates—rhetoric, composition and communication, process, activity, service and social justice—we are at the very center of those tremors.

Perhaps the most important of the plates on which we stand is advocacy, especially at this moment. As the Dixie Chicks point out, voting is an excellent means of self-expression. In helping create writing publics, we also foster the development of citizens who vote, of citizens whose civic literacy is global in its sensibility and its communicative potential, and whose commitment to humanity is characterized by consistency and generosity as well as the ability to write for purposes that are unconstrained and audiences that are nearly unlimited.

It's an ambitious agenda I laid before you in San Antonio and that I lay before you in these pages today, but yes, this is made not only in words: composition in a new key.

ACKNOWLEDGMENTS

Gracious thanks to the CCCC audience in San Antonio and to those who helped me before I arrived there: Kristi and Shawn Apostel, Michael Crawford, Will Dickert, Teddi Fishman, Morgan Gresham, Doug Hesse, Martin Jacobi, Brian Morrison, Michael Neal, Josh Reynolds, Summer Smith Taylor, and Irwin Weiser. For special help in the selection and placement of images and in the overall design of this text, many thanks to Marilyn Cooper.

NOTES

1. The slides were arranged so that duplicates showed up simultaneously at various points in the presentation: two screens showed the same slide. Also, as the performance progressed, some slides were repeated, in part to provide some contour to the performance, in part to provide some coherence. I attempt to explain the logic of this composition in *Composition in a New Key*, forthcoming.
2. In the 1980s, compositionists were excited about the role that process was playing—in our teaching, in the assessment of student work, in our own research. Given the disparity between the out-of-school, often digitally composed genres that students currently work in and the form that current assessments are taking—even the much ballyhooed new SAT "writing test" includes a component on grammar and usage that is allowed *more* time than the pencil-and-paper draft portion—Marshall McLuhan's point about marching backwards into the future sounds all too true. For a compelling analysis of the disjunction between what we teach and what is being assessed, see Miles McCrimmon, "High School Writing Practices in the Age of Standards: Implications for College Composition."
3. Digital compositions include other materials as well: audio files, for instance. For a discussion of such materials in the context of remediation and composition, see Scott Halbritter.
4. The relationship between and among technology, literacy practices, nation states, and centralized control is considerably more complicated than I can pursue here. For an analysis that focuses on the materiality of literacy practices and technology, see Lester Faigley's *Material Literacy and Visual Design*; for a discussion that emphasizes the centralization of the nation state as related to literacy and technology, see Ronald Deibert's *Parchment, Printing, and Hypermedia: Communication in World Order Transformation* and Deborah Brandt's *Literacy in American Lives*.
5. The talk I delivered was not precisely the same as the written text. For historical purposes, CCCC videotapes the talk, and what seemed obvious to me at the time is so in retrospect: the two "talks" differ.
6. How various technologies—from technology producing light to that associated with various printing presses—interact to influence the development of literacy (and whose needs this literacy serves) is a (another) question worth pursuing.
7. You don't have to be present to see them: online, you can see the home pages for the Seattle Public Library and the Salt Lake City Library. For a fuller discussion of the lessons regarding these spaces that libraries have to teach us, see Yancey, "Episodes in the Spaces of the Plural Commons."
8. The idea that English departments are being consolidated into other units was first drawn to my attention by Tina Good, at Suffolk County Community College, who has conducted a study of the SUNY system, verifying the claim in that context.
9. As David Lawrence, the executive director of the Association of Departments of English (ADE), has pointed out to me, there's no reason to regard the number of majors from 1966 as the ideal or the norm, and it is the case that English majors still rank in the top

ten of all majors (calculated based on a U.S. government database). Point taken. Still, this seems small comfort to me (as a member of an English department) when I remember that more students go to college and graduate today, in 2004, than did in 1966, so the numbers for the English major, it seems to me, ought to grow, not hold steady. In a population that is increasing, maintaining constitutes a decline, as the numbers attest. One reply to such a view, as explained in the *ADE* report "The Undergraduate English Major," is to put the numbers in larger historical perspective. In this case, that entails the observation that the "semicaptive" audience of majors that English used to have—that is, women—are now choosing to major in other fields, especially biology, psychology, and business, which given our interest in gender equity is a good thing. *Of course.* Still, the trend lines—number of majors, number of tenure-line hires, number of English departments—plot a narrative that those of us who are aligned with English should not ignore.

10. On May 10, 2004, the Colorado legislature passed this bill, which provides funding vouchers to all college students in the state to be applied to all kinds of postsecondary institutions, including private schools. The implications of this bill are widespread: for an early analysis, see Chris Kampfe and Kyle Endres.

11. As this list indicates, a number of so-called college classes are actually *delivered* in high school: what does this say about college composition? With several others, I attempt to answer this question: see Yancey, *Delivering College Composition: The Fifth Canon*, Heinemann 2004.

12. The respondents included more than 1,800 faculty members from forty-eight states, split about 40/60 between two-year and four-year faculty. In terms of faculty status, 17% identified as graduate students and 23% as adjunct faculty. For a fuller description and analysis of the results, see Yancey et al., "Portraits of Composition: How Writing Gets Taught in the Early Twenty-First Century."

13. The idea for a major in rhetoric and composition is not new. Keith Miller was kind enough to point me toward the George Tade, Gary Tate, and Jim Corder article in *CCC*, "For Sale, Lease, or Rent: A Curriculum for an Undergraduate Program in Rhetoric." And some 25 years later, Robert Connors makes the philosophical argument in his Afterword to *Coming of Age*.

14. For a full account of the influence of Edwin Hopkins, see the article by John Heyda and Randall Popken.

15. As I look over the list of items here, the key word seems to be transfer: from composing site to composing site, from classroom to classroom, from one experience to the next. As I have suggested elsewhere, Donald Schon's notion of "reflective transfer" is crucial to this development. See Yancey, *Reflection in the Writing Classroom*.

16. The activity systems mapped by Paul Prior and Jody Shipka parallel the spaces architects are designing into various kinds of buildings: both conceive of human activity organized into multiple overlapping spaces. Another way to theorize composition of the 21st century is through the overlapping curricular, activity, and physical spaces where it occurs now and where it might occur. In this construct, the circulation of composition takes yet another definition.

17. Bill Watterson has several books that in their commentary on processes, media, and transfer are models for the observation, analysis, and insight we often find in portfolio reflections.

18. For a fuller account of both kinds of portfolios, see Yancey, "Postmodernism, Palimpsest, and Portfolios: Theoretical Issues in the Representation of Student Work" and *Teaching Literature as Reflective Practice*, especially chapter five.

WORKS CITED

ADE. "Report of the Undergraduate English Major." Report of the 2001–2002 ADE Ad Hoc Committee on the English Major. *ADE* (Fall/Winter 2003): 68–91.

"America's Fortunes." Atlantic Online (January/February 2004) 21 Mar 04 <http:www .theatlantic.com/cgi-bin/send.cgi?pae=http%3A//www.theatlantic.com/issues>.

Baron, Dennis. "From Pencils to Pixels." *Passions, Pedagogies, and 21st Century Technologies.* Ed. Gail Hawisher and Cynthia Selfe. Logan: Utah State UP, 1999. 15–34.

Bartholomae, David. "Freshman English, Composition, and CCCC." *College Communication and Composition* 40.1 (1989): 38–50.

Bazerman, Charles, and David Russell, eds. *Writing Selves, Writing Societies: Research from Activity Perspectives.* Fort Collins, CO: The WAC Clearinghouse and Mind, Culture, and Activity. 1 June 2004 <http://wac.colostate.edu/books/selves_societies/intro.cfm>.

Beaufort, Anne. *Writing in the Real World: Making the Transition from School to Work.* New York: Teachers College P, 1999.

Bolter, Jay David, and Richard Grusin. *Remediation: Understanding New Media.* Cambridge: MIT P, 2000.

Brandt, Deborah. *Literacy in American Lives.* New York: Cambridge UP, 2001.

Bridwell-Bowles, Lillian. "Freedom, Form, Function: Varieties of Academic Discourse." *College Communication and Composition* 46.1 (1995): 46–61.

Carroll, Lee Ann. *Rehearsing New Roles: How College Students Develop as Writers.* Carbondale: Southern Illinois UP, 2002.

Chaplin, Miriam T. "Issues, Perspectives, and Possibilities." *College Composition and Communication* 39.1 (1988): 52–62.

Chiseri-Strater, Elizabeth. *Academic Literacies: The Public and Private Discourse of University Students.* Portsmouth, NH: Boynton/Cook, 1991.

Connors, Robert. Afterword. *Coming of Age: The Advanced Writing Curriculum.* Ed. Linda K. Shamoon, Rebecca Moore Howard, Sandra Jamieson, and Robert A. Schwegler. Portsmouth, NH: Boynton/Cook, 2000. 143–49.

Crowley, Sharon. *Composition in the University: Historical and Polemical Essays.* Pittsburgh: U of Pittsburgh, 1998.

D'Angelo, Frank. "Regaining Our Composure." *College Composition and Communication* 31.4 (1980): 420–26.

Daley, Elizabeth. "Expanding the Concept of Literacy." *Educause Review* 38.2 (2003): 33–40.
———. "Speaking the Languages of Literacy." Speech, University of Michigan, April 2003. 9 Aug. 04 <http://web.si.umich.edu/news/news-detail.cfm?NewsItemID=350>.

Davis, Vivian I. "Our Excellence: Where Do We Grow from Here?" *College Composition and Communication* 30.1 (1979): 26–31.

Deibert, Ronald. *Parchment, Printing, and Hypermedia: Communication in World Order Transformation.* New York: Columbia UP, 1997.

Ebert, Roger. Review of *21 Grams. Chicago Sun Times* (2003) 1 June 2004 <http://www.suntimes.com/ebert/ebert_reviews/2003/11/112606.html>.

Emig, Janet. *The Composing Processes of Twelfth Graders.* Urbana, IL: NCTE, 1971.

Faigley, Lester. "Literacy after the Revolution." *College Composition and Communication* 48.1 (1997): 30–43.
———. "Material Literacy and Visual Design." In *Rhetorical Bodies: Toward a Material Rhetoric.* Ed. Jack Selzer and Sharon Crowley. Madison: U of Wisconsin P, 1999. 171–201.

Flower, Linda, and John Hayes. "A Cognitive Process Theory of Writing." *College Composition and Communication* 32.4 (1981): 365–87.

Flynn, Elizabeth. "Composing as a Woman." *College Composition and Communication* 39.4 (1988): 423–35.

Gerber, John C. "The Conference on College Composition and Communication." *College Composition and Communication* 1.1 (1950): 12.

Gere, Anne Ruggles. "Kitchen Tables and Rented Rooms: The Extracurriculum of Composition." *College Composition and Communication* 45.1 (1994): 75–92.

Good, Tina. Personal discussion, 25 April 2003.

Hairston, Maxine. "The Winds of Change: Thomas Kuhn and the Revolution in the Teaching of Writing." *College Composition and Communication* 33.1: 76–88.

Halbritter, Scott. "Sound Arguments: Aural Rhetoric in Multimedia Composition." PhD diss. University of North Carolina, 2004.

Haswell, Richard. *Gaining Ground in College: Tales of Development and Interpretation.* Dallas, TX: Southern Methodist UP, 1991.

Hawisher, Gail. Personal discussion. Feb. 2004.

Heyda, John. "Industrial-Strength Composition and the Impact of Load on Teaching." *More Than 100 Years of Solitude: WPA Work before 1976.* Ed. Barbara L'Eppateur and Lisa Mastrangelo. Forthcoming.

Hopkins, Edwin. "Can Good English Composition Be Done under the Current Conditions?" *English Journal* 1 (1912): 1–8.

Irmscher, William F. "Writing as a Way of Learning and Developing." *College Composition and Communication* 30.3 (1979): 240–44.

Johnson-Eilola, Johndan. "Writing about Writing." Speech, Computers and Writing Town Hall Meeting, 2002, Illinois State University.

Jones, Richard Lloyd. "A View from the Center." *College Composition and Communication* 29.1 (1978): 24–29.

Kampfe, Chris, and Kyle Endres. "Vouchers to Change the Way Higher Ed is Funded." *The Rocky Mountain Collegian*. 10 May 2004. <http://www.collegian.com/vnews/display.v/ART/2004/05/07/409b21d2bfdee?in_archive=1>.

Lanham, Richard. *The Electronic Word: Democracy, Technology, and the Arts.* Chicago: U of Chicago P, 1993.

Lawrence, David. E-mail to author. April 2004.

Leu, D. J., C. K. Kinzer, J. Coiro, and D. Cammack. "Toward a Theory of New Literacies Emerging from the Internet and Other ICT." *Theoretical Models and Processes of Reading.* 5th ed. Ed. R. Ruddel and Norman Unrau. D.E. International Reading Association, 2004. 4 Aug. 2004 (Preprint version) <http:// www.readingonline.org/ newliteracies/leu>.

Light, Richard J. *Making the Most of College: Students Speak Their Minds.* Cambridge: Harvard UP, 2001.

Lindemann, Erika. "Early Bibliographic Work in Composition Studies." *Profession* (2002): 151–58.

Lunsford, Andrea. "Composing Ourselves: Politics, Commitment, and the Teaching of Writing." *College Composition and Communication* 41.1 (1990): 71–82.

McCrimmon, Miles. "High School Writing Practices in the Age of Standards: Implications for College Composition." Forthcoming.

McLuhan, Marshall. *Understanding Media: The Extensions of Man.* 1964. Cambridge: MIT P, 1994.

Matsuda, Paul. "Process and Post Process: A Discursive History." *Journal of Second Language Writing* 12 (2003): 65–83.

Palmquist, Michael. "Review: Made Not Only in Words: Composition in a New Key." 15 April 2004. *Across the Disciplines* at the WAC Clearinghouse. 1 June 2004 <http://wac.colostate.edu/atd/reviews/cccc2004/viewmessage.cfm?messageid=61>.

Popken, Randall. "Edwin Hopkins and the Costly Labor of Composition Teaching." *College Composition and Communication* 55.4 (2004): 618–42.

Porter, James. "Why Technology Matters to Writing: A Cyberwriter's Tale." *Computers and Composition* 20.3 (2003): 375–94.

Prior, Paul, and Jody Shipka. "Chronotopic Laminations: Tracing the Contours of Literate Activity." *Writing Selves, Writing Societies: Research from Activity Perspectives.* Ed. Charles Bazerman and David Russell. Fort Collins, CO: The WAC Clearinghouse, and Mind, Culture, and Activity, 180–238. 1 June 2004 <http://wac.colostate.edu/books/selves_societies/prior>.

Putnam, Robert. *Bowling Alone.* New York: Simon and Schuster, 2000.

Reynolds, Josh. "Writing Process Map." *My English Portfolio.* 1 June 2004 <http://people.clemson.edu/~jsreyno/Process.htm>.

Rohman, D. Gordon. "Prewriting: The Stage of Discovery in the Writing Process." *College Composition and Communication* 16.2 (1965): 106–12.

Rohman, D. Gordon, and Albert O. Wlecke. "Pre-Writing: The Construction and Applications of Models for Concept Formation in Writing." Cooperative Research Project No. 2174. USOE: Washington, DC.

Royster, Jacqueline Jones. "When the First Voice You Hear Is Not Your Own." *College Composition and Communication* 47.1 (1996): 29–40.

Russell, David, and Arturo Yañez. "Big Picture People Rarely Become Historians: Genre Systems and the Contradictions of General Education." *Writing Selves, Writing Societies: Research from Activity Perspectives.* Ed. Charles Bazerman and David Russell. Fort Collins, CO: The WAC Clearinghouse, and Mind, Culture, and Activity. 1 June 2004 <http://wac.colostate.edu/books/ selves_societies/russell>.

Selfe, Cynthia L. "Technology and Literacy: A Story about the Perils of Not Paying Attention." *College Composition and Communication* 50.3 (1999): 411–36.

Shea, Rachel Hartigan. "How We Got Here." *U.S. News and World Report*, 9 Aug 2004: 70–73.

Sommers, Nancy, and Laura Saltz. "The Novice as Expert: Writing the Freshman Year." *College Composition and Communication* 56.1 (2004): 124–49.

Sternglass, Marilyn. *Time to Know Them: A Longitudinal Study of Writing and Learning at the College Level*. Mahwah, NJ: Lawrence Erlbaum Associates, 1997.

Tade, George, Gary Tate, and Jim Corder. "For Sale, Lease, or Rent: A Curriculum for an Undergraduate Program in Rhetoric." *College Composition and Communication* 26.1 (1975): 20–24.

Trachsel, Mary. *Institutionalizing Literacy: The Historical Role of College Entrance Examinations in English*. Carbondale: Southern Illinois UP, 1992.

Trimbur, John. "Composition and the Circulation of Writing." *College Composition and Communication* 52.2 (2000): 188–219.

Vendler, Helen. "The Ocean, the Bird, and the Scholar." NEH Jefferson Address, 6 May 2004. 9 Aug. 04 <http://www.neh.gov/whoweare/vendler/lecture.html>.

Watterson, Bill. *Sunday Pages 1985–1995: An Exhibition Catalogue*. Kansas City, MO: Andrews McMeel Publishing, 2000.

John Wright, ed. *New York Times 2004 Almanac*. New York: Penguin, 2003.

Wysocki, Anne, and Julia Jasken. "What Should Be an Unforgettable Face." *Computers and Composition* 21.1 (2004): 29–49.

Yancey, Kathleen Blake. "Episodes in the Spaces of the Plural Commons: Curriculum, Administration, and Design of Composition in the 21st Century." Speech, Writing Program Administration, Delaware, 14 July 2004.

———. "Postmodernism, Palimpsest, and Portfolios: Theoretical Issues in the Representation of Student Work." *College Composition and Communication* 55.4 (2004): 738–61.

———. *Reflection in the Writing Classroom*. Logan: Utah State UP, 1998.

———. *Teaching Literature as Reflective Practice*. Urbana, IL: NCTE, 2004.

Yancey, Kathleen Blake, Teddi Fishman, Morgan Gresham, Michael Neal, and Summer Smith Taylor. "Portraits of Composition: How Postsecondary Writing Gets Taught in the Early Twenty-First Century." Unpublished essay, 2004.

AFTERWORD: ONE MORE/LAST TIME: MADE NOT ONLY
IN WORDS: COMP IN A NEW KEY

Sometimes, you know, you have a moment.

In "Composition in a New Key," I echoed a refrain: that (more than we think) *we have a moment* — but/and that *how we value [such moments] is in part a function of how we understand them, how we connect them to other moments, how we anticipate the moments to come.*

In *Reflection in the Writing Classroom*, I spoke to the need to reflect, claiming that in order to reflect, we need psychological space, and that by inhabiting that space, by using it to think capaciously (reviewing, connecting, juxtapositioning), we can know in ways otherwise impossible.

In this, my reflection on my CCCC Chair's address, I want to connect these points.

• • •

I want to begin by noting that creating the space for reflection is never easy. The fabric of our daily lives, pulled by concerns intellectual and personal, doesn't permit much more tension. And yet. Without reflection, the tension is worse, the meaning less. The promise of reflection is that meaning—and action—could be more, could be better.

It is a realistic exercise in hope, social as well as personal.

As I composed the Chair's address, what I hoped was that I could in some helpful way put into dialogue my understanding of the field and of CCCC's role in shaping the field; my sense of higher education; my sense of changing literacies; and my sense of the future. In reading all the former Chairs' addresses that were available and talking to former Chairs, in reviewing issues of *College Composition and Communication* at five-year intervals, and in bringing together my own sense of what our discipline is, I found that I could identify a select number of themes—*the discipline, a set of terms,* and *the major*—that might help give a/nother focus to our work and might assist in charting a path for the future.

> We look at the present through a rearview mirror. We march backwards into the future.
>
> —Marshall McLuhan

Throughout, I (also) attempted to keep a focus on students. And what I said then about our students is still true: we admit (many of) them into college; we do not graduate them. Over the course of the last year, this problem—the failure to graduate students—has grown worse. According to David Leonhardt of the *New York Times,* the myth of increasing social mobility is increasingly mythological: "A nation that believes that everyone should have a fair shake finds itself with a kind of *inherited* meritocracy" (my italics). Why? Because even public institutions find themselves admitting and funding students from the middle and (more often) upper classes. For those in the lower classes, this article claims, and for many reasons, "college just does not feel normal." Students drop out, intending to return. This too is a mythology.

> **A modest proposal: one outcome for all writers is the ability to use all kinds of technologies for their intended purposes and for other purposes, as needed and imagined.**
>
> **Or: writers use technology rhetorically.**

Many of us, perhaps most of us, joined composition because we wanted to open the gateways, to help students enter them and move beyond. Those are still worthy—and unfulfilled—goals. But what was clear to me in 2004 is evermore clear in 2005: we need to help students *complete* the task that first-year composition initiates. And to accomplish this, we need

- to understand (as many of us already do) that first-year composition classes help college *become* normal for students, a dialogic process that changes us as well,
- to develop a composition for the twenty-first century that prepares writers in new ways for composing tasks and technologies old and new,
- to provide students with a vocabulary and set of practices that they theorize through their reflections, and
- to develop a major that provides an/other institutional anchor for much of this activity.

• • •

Sometimes, you know, you have a moment.

Chairs kid each other about the address, about the anxiety it produces, about the chance it presents. I wasn't particularly eager to make the address; my joke was that I'd prefer to chair another conference.

But upon reflection . . .

I was wrong. The Chair's address provides a unique opportunity to speak to one's colleagues, an opportunity (and honor) to be heard.

And one *value* of the Chair's address is that it provides the Chair with a moment, and the opportunity to connect that moment, intentionally, to other moments past, other moments future; to find in that nexus a place to reflect upon who we are, and who we might become.

–KATHLEEN BLAKE YANCEY
Florida State University

WORK CITED

Leonhardt, David. "The College Dropout Boom." *New York Times* 24 May 2005, late ed.: A1+.

2005 *Who Owns Writing?*

DOUGLASS HESSE

[*sung*]
My lord, what a morning.
My lord, what a morning,
Oh, my lord what a morning
When the stars begin to fall.

I've been nervous about singing spirituals since my junior year in a small Iowa high school, in a town fairly German and very white. My chorus teacher, Miss Eggleston, gave me H. T. Burleigh's 1917 *Album of Negro Spirituals*, and she told me to choose a song for the state music contest. Did I have the right to sing from that book? Did

This article is a revised version of the Chair's address Douglass Hesse delivered at the CCCC Convention in San Francisco, California, on March 17, 2005. It was previously unpublished. In this version Hesse includes bracketed material to indicate where Bedford/St. Martin's was unable to secure permission to reprint images he used in his address. Hesse notes: "It turned out, unsurprisingly, that 'who owns writing' has a counterpart question, 'who owns images,' in the case of computer screenshots, even for fair use."

457

I have it here, just now? After all, the title of Marian Anderson's autobiography is *My Lord What a Morning*. Anderson sang that famous 1939 Easter concert on the Mall in Washington D.C. after the Daughters of the American Revolution denied her access to Constitution Hall because she was "colored." What have I done? What claims do I have?

Besides, the song itself perplexes me. It opens with grand affirmation, and then comes that pretty apocalypse: the stars falling. So the cause for jubilation is the end of the world, a dazzling end, yes, but an end

nonetheless. In fact, it's possible to interpret that first lines not as laud but, rather, lament.

The current state of writing might be expressed in similarly conflicted terms. Probably at no recent time has it received so much broad attention. National commissions recommend resources for teachers and students. Higher education groups issue statements and formulate standards. Digital life fertilizes alphabetic literacy along with visual and aural. Writing across the curriculum enjoys rather a new spring. The job listings for rhet/comp remain robust, and new programs, majors, and departments sprout around the country. Our work ought to feel more important than it has in quite some time. And yet, even with all this attention — in fact, perhaps even because of it — the stars threaten to fall on our familiar worlds.

I've chosen such a pushy title that I'm tempted to stalk it through the guise of narrative and metaphor. But let me take it head on. Who owns writing?

I'm not the only one these days to own owning. The president prods us toward an ownership society, albeit one that limits who can own what. On the one hand, individuals should own responsibility for their finances in retirement. On the other, they shouldn't own stem cells or, if they happen to be gay or lesbian, marriage licenses. Teachers shouldn't own how evolution is taught, or not. Teachers may only whisper how well their students read or do math; the shout is left to No Child Left Behind. Other tests tell how well their students write.

To ask who owns writing is to ask most obviously about property rights, the buying, selling, and leasing of textual acreages. But rather I'm asking, Who owns the conditions under which writing is taught? Who owns the content and pedagogy of composition? Who may declare someone proficient or derelict? Who may assign praise or blame? As these questions suggest, ownership has the double sense of controlling use and assuming responsibility. For example, I can paint my kitchen whatever color I choose, but I also have

to shovel my sidewalks in January. I might ask, Who speaks for writing? Who has the right? Who can be heard? These are not the same questions. Does CCCC speak for writing? Am I thus, here, our synecdoche, our avatar? Ah, vanity.

I've posed a largely impossible question, of the form that Wittgenstein declares is best answered by rejecting its very asking. Who owns writing? The possibilities are everyone, no one, someone, and "it depends." Your answer depends on whether you derive it through Wordsworth, Barthes, Althusser, or Rorty. You'll be disappointed or relieved to know that I'm

not going to trace these positions this morning. What I will do is suggest that those who *teach* writing must affirm that we, in fact, *own* it. The question is what we should aspire to own—and how.

• • •

There's a parlor game that many of us have played, with each other and with our students. Call it "beat the digital grader." The rules are simple. Access a computer program that scores writing, and write the worst possible essay that receives the highest possible score. Even undergraduates can get pretty good, as through trial and error they discover assumptions built into the program. These include sentence length and variety, diction, correctness, the presence of semantic chains, and so on.

Last fall several of us on the WPA listserv played an opposite variant. Someone had created a Web site called "the essay generator" which invites you to enter any topic and receive an essay in return. The site isn't very sophisticated, which is part of the fun. Its database stockpiles sentences: several possible first sentences, several second, and so on. Each essay has three headings: Social Factors, Economic Factors, and

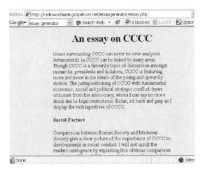

Political Factors. Each essay has a graph. Each essay ends with a fictional quotation. Each essay has three references.

Consider, for example, the essay I "wrote" about CCCC, if by *wrote* you might stretch to mean "typed the topic into a blank." It begins, "Issues surrounding CCCC can never be over analyzed. Advancements in CCCC can be linked to many areas. Though CCCC is a favourite topic of discussion amongst monarchs, presidents and dictators, CCCC is featuring more and more in the ideals of the young and upwardly mobile." The essay continues, "Relax, sit back and gasp as I display the rich tapestries of CCCC."

My essay on CCCC even includes a graph. As you can see, as CCCCs increases, inflation declines. I can only surmise that after Alan Greenspan retires, Jay Wootten should take his place.

Playing the essay generator got me thinking. What if you had a computer generate an essay that was then scored by another computer? So I went to a computer scoring test site. From the choice of three topics, I selected "aphasia," which I then plugged into the essay generator.

An Essay on Aphasia. "Man's greatest achievement? Perhaps not, but can you afford not to read on when I am about to tell you about aphasia?" The essay concludes, "How much responsibility lies with aphasia? We can say that aphasia has a special place in the heart of mankind. It fills a hole, ensures financial stability, and statistically it's great."

I then cut and pasted that essay into the Intelligent Essay Assessor, "a proprietary web-based service developed at Pearson Knowledge Technologies (PKT) that automatically evaluates a student's writing skills and knowledge, and provides scoring and diagnostic feedback to both the instructor and student" (Pearson). I did, however, make one modification: I cut out the graph because I wasn't sure if the site would know what to do. The results are - before you. [*Note:* for my talk in San Francisco, I used a screen shot of Intelligent Essay Assessor scoring of "An Essay on Aphasia." Pearson Knowledge Technologies declined to pro-

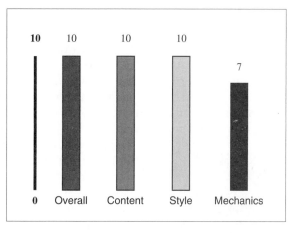

vide permission to use the screen shot in this published version, so I have developed my own visual. Note, further, that since my talk, Knowledge Assessment Technologies has modified its online demonstration site for the Intelligent Essay Assessor. Now (September 2005) instead of individuals being able to write their own essays on aphasia, they may only "select" one of three prewritten sample essays and "submit" it for scoring.]

Now, I want to be precise about why I've told this story. I'm not making a broad claim about the Intelligent Essay Assessor. I tried this just once, and maybe I fluked out. In fact, I'm not even questioning the present or potential sophistication and prowess of machine scoring software. Let's just imagine that programs might well pass a version of the Turing test, producing scores indistinguishable from a trained writing teacher's. In short, for the sake of argument, let's imagine the achievement of a certain machine dream.

This dream would, on the one hand, promise "objectivity" and precision. It would replace the judgments of human readers. After all, teachers are both rotten with imperfection, to twist Kenneth Burke, and also desiring of health insurance. This dream would, on the other hand, "free" teachers of grading, allowing them to teach rather than to judge. But teach what and to what ends?

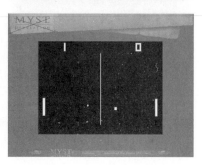

More to the point: how would students understand writing if, when it counted most, writing was something done to be rated by software? Perhaps this would only confirm the view that most students already have, namely that school writing is an exercise to produce required textual features rather than to achieve further rhetorical ends. After all, they know too well five-paragraph themism and its gang. They know pedagogies where the what and why of writing are subordinated to the formalistic how, where writing likens to old school math minus the word problems, the manipulation of symbols to achieve an answer, just don't ask why. In the machine dream, writing would became a sort of dull game, an interaction with software to produce a score. Its consequences would be all regulative, something done to get through a gate. That's the worst-case scenario.

~~forecast~~

Who owns writing?

Ultimately, in terms of students' perceptions, I can predict two others. In a best-case scenario, students would perceive writing for computer programs as a kind of interesting dummy-exercise preparation for "real writing." They would seamlessly translate making for machines into performing for people. In a middle-case scenario, students would experience writing as a forked activity. Down one road would lie writing as a dull activity whose sole function is to generate a score. That's the way of school. Down another road lies writing to accomplish something in a world of writers and readers. School would have almost nothing to say to this world.

[*sung*]
Sometimes I feel like a motherless child.
Sometimes I feel like a motherless child.
Sometimes I feel like a motherless child
A long way from home,
A long way from home.

For decades, the press, both popular and academic, has pundited why Johnny can't write and what Maria, his teacher, should do about it. On the academic side, we have the Association of American Universities' *Standards for Success*, the AAC&U's "Writing in the New Academy," Achieve, Inc.'s *Rising to the Challenge: Are High School Graduates Prepared for College and Work*, and, of course, the studies welling from SAT and ACT as they add writing samples.

Consider the National Commission on Writing for America's Families, Schools, and Colleges. The 2003 report, *The Neglected "R,"* calls for doubling the amount of time students spend writing, for providing "the financial resources necessary for the additional time and personnel required to make writing a centerpiece in the curriculum," for assessments of writing that are "fair and authentic," and so on. Its fall 2004 report, with the foreboding title *Writing: A Ticket to Work . . . or a Ticket Out,* underscores the centrality of writing on the job. It concludes that "individual opportunity in the United States depends critically on the ability to present one's thoughts coherently, cogently, and persuasively on paper" (5). It wants writing for "all segments of the population (19)," reiterates the plea for more time and attention, and while it emphasizes grammar, it also mentions rhetoric and logic, albeit scantly.

As you can see, there's much to celebrate in these reports, even common cause to make. And yet I'm a smidge wary. Probably some of it is plain old male turf-protecting. After all, CCCC didn't get that national press. What are these guys doing on our land? Worse is the guilt of missed opportunity; why didn't CCCC issue national statements on writing? And, worst of all, is the simultaneously salving and smug sentiment that even if CCCC had been there first, it wouldn't have mattered: who pays attention to writing teachers?

So, I confess ignoble motives. But we're justified to be a little cautious, for example, about the commission's fondness for technological fixes. Consider the call that "the nation should invest in research that explores the potential of new and emerging technologies to identify mistakes in grammar, encourage students to share their work, help assess writing samples, and incorporate software into measuring student writing competence" (23). That simply doesn't square, for example, with the "CCCC Position Statement on Teaching, Learning, and Assessing Writing in Digital Environments."

The commission's methodology is narrow, too, relying on business leader reports of satisfaction with workers' writing rather than the messier—and more telling—study of writers themselves. Further, and more subtly, as John Trimbur and Anne Gere have illustrated, writing too

~~we have a moment~~

. . . and we have Yancey

and we have <u>you</u>

often has served as scapegoat for American productivity. I'm no economist, but I doubt that, should everyone achieve marvelous writing skills, everyone will thus have a ticket to salaried work.

Still, I want to see this glass as more than half full. Let's ascribe the best intentions to the National Commission on Writing. Let's imagine its decision to feature the economic dimensions of writing is but a first step. Let's call it a shrewd political and rhetorical strategy. Let's assume that the commission might next turn to other spheres of writing beyond school and work. My question: Can we, here, first articulate those other spheres? Can we complete and speak for the whole of writing? Can we speak to and for the America of writing beyond this room? Can we—and I'm meaning the collective we of CCCC—can we ungate our separate intellectual estates, at least enough to say, together, this is what writing is, all of it, and this how it matters?

I've been thinking about the term *writing* in light of George Lakoff's work on conceptual frames. Famously, after the fall election, Lakoff discussed how the very terms being used to characterize issues frame the

The Circulation of Composition
The Canons of Rhetoric
The Deicity of Technology

Made

not

only

in

Words

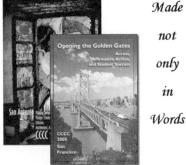

possible ways of thinking about them. If an issue is framed as "tax relief," then the range of desirable actions is constrained; who could oppose "relief"? I'm wondering if the word *writing* may frame our work in ways that aren't always desirable. The term seems neutral enough, but it may well carry the sense of inscribing words on paper; that is, it may focus attention on the physical act of graphemic production, separate from thinking, with all the focus on correctness. I'll note that *writer* functions as a different frame in our culture as a frame than does *writing*. The latter refers to an activity or product, while the former is an identity—and a top-level one at that, on par with electrician or manager or teacher or scientist. But writing is a different frame. By embracing parts of recent reports that make sense to us, we may be perpetuating that frame, perhaps to our detriment. The double bind is that if we critique aspects of these reports, we may seem oddly opposed to writing, shirking the most fundamental aspect of our identity. Now, in response we could reject the term *writing* and reframe our work as *composing*, as several, including Cindy Selfe, have recommended. This oddly retrograde strategy would, on the one hand, open a broader textual territory. On the other, it would carry the heritage of composing as an academic enterprise, a school subject, and one generally gotten out of the way during the freshman year.

Composition is in our name, after all. CCCC was formed in 1949 to address primarily administrative issues in first-year writing. Convention fairly obliges the Chair at this point to retell the founding of the tribe, but I'm simply going to say that we began as a conference on the school subject of composition.

Our originary self-naming signals borders of our terrain: not creative writing (but maybe creative nonfiction) and not journalism (but maybe civic discourse). Yes to "advanced composition," though that idea has been vexed, and "yes" to technical communication, although there have long been tensions between writing as a liberal and as an applied art. And rhetoric? As method? Content? History? Our borders aren't fixed. For example, with writing across the curriculum, we annexed new space or reclaimed old—some of us have chosen to leave English department homelands for that new territory.

What composition owns is marked partially, then, by what parts of the college catalog it controls, whom it hires, and what its budgets say. By these terms, owning the resources of writing has generally been like owning an aging minivan. To provide students the intellectual transportation they deserve and need would really take something safer, more dependable, and more comfortable. But other parts of the institutional budget have needs,

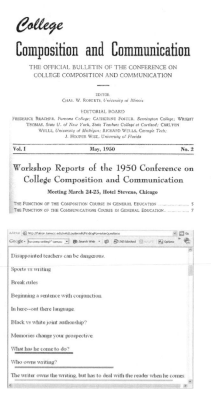

too, and the writing program is asked to get around with whatever parts it can scrounge. Composition turns out to be a cheap way to provide small section experience to lots of students, generating more revenues than it costs. To switch metaphors, composition may be, as Richard Miller says, a resource-rich colony, but its value derives precisely from its colonial status.

The more subtle dimension of ownership relates less directly to material properties than intellectual ones. Here, the question is "Who owns the idea of writing?" In January, I got an e-mail from a liberal arts dean at a state university. Her faculty were embroiled in a debate about the nature of the writing course. As she put it, "we are struggling with the tensions between teaching writing as inquiry and teaching writing as technical skill," and she asked me to suggest an outside arbitrator. I suspect all of us have experienced local versions of this debate, which begins with grousing about undergraduate writing and leads to calls for discipline, rigor, and attention to the basics in English 101. Against colleagues with all-too-common sense, we muster theory and research. We pull George Hillocks off the shelf and worry that 1985 seems ever longer ago. All the while, even as our field matures, we perversely have less respect.

> "We don't give a damn what the teacher thinks, what the teacher feels," Engelmann said. "On the teachers' own time they can hate it. We don't care, as long as they do it."
> —Siegfried Engelmann*

But in many ways lately, we've had less heart for these kinds of fights. Many of us have advocated scrapping required freshman comp for parts and spending the capital on elective courses, freshman seminars, or WAC programs. We've come to shorthand these familiar arguments, grounded in theory and fueled by despair with the conditions for adjuncts, as the abolitionist movement, a very historically charged frame. The term is hyperbolic to the point of being unethical, promising the end of enslavement for both students and teachers, trading the title to the plantation of English 101 for new intellectual acres. These new lands may include a graduate program or a vertical undergraduate, even a major, multiple courses, not one or two. The richest programs of our futures feature writing in a welter of circumstances and genres, creative, journalistic, and professional, as well as civic and academic. They feature work in design—visual and aural as well as verbal. They fully imagine students in complicated worlds of school and work and politics, yes, but also passions, relationships, and

ALBUM of
NEGRO SPIRITUALS
Arranged for Solo Voice by
H· T· BURLEIGH

---

*Quoted by Daniel Radosh in "The Pet Goat Approach." *The New Yorker.* 26 July, 2004: 28.

art. They teach writing to *these* students and not to compliant essay generators producing scripts for Intelligent Essay Assessment.

And yet still remains, for most, English 101, composition, our legacy. For much of its history, English 101 was seen as a sort of giant stem cell whose nurturant medium could be the modes of discourse, current traditional formalism, literary new criticism, process instruction, rhetorical analysis, or whatever. Students could be transplanted from English 101 into whatever circumstance. In a certain longstanding view, process is process, rhetoric is rhetoric, composing is composing, and whether the target discourse is a term paper, a political blog, or a poem, the skill universally develops through the activity itself. In a certain other view, more recent, so profoundly contextualized is all writing that it resists any pedagogy, let alone any generalizability.

So it is today that, we see a national spectrum of first-year writing requirements. At the ultraviolet is the highly focused universal course: this kind of discourse, through these assignments, in this sequence, toward these ends. Its apogee is the standard syllabus—though standard at school X is often sub at school Y. At the infrared is decimalized 101, an array of options, perhaps equivalent in the amount of writing or some other dimension, but otherwise each boldly

differing from each other. Just choose one. Between these two ends—of Calvinist predestination and Unitarian free will—are not only significant theoretical differences about the nature of learning to write, and not only the curricular rights of individual teachers, but also the very nature of our field and the role of CCCC.

Consider just one dimension of contention. Composition has variously concerned itself with five spheres, albeit in different proportions: the academic, the vocational, the civic, the personal, and the belletristic. I'll point out that these spheres can sort into two categories: those concerned with

obliged discourse (to which I'd assign the vocational and the academic), and those concerned with self-sponsored discourse (in which I'd place the personal, the belletristic and, perhaps surprisingly, the civic). By obliged, I mean writing that institutions require and sanction, whether through pay or grades. By self-sponsored, I mean writing that people do for reasons of expression or social affiliation, not for direct material consequence. Note to audience: I know all about invidious binaries, and I could deconstruct the concept "self-sponsored" as totally as anyone in this room. My division is heuristic.

For various reasons, I think that as a profession we must continue to own up to the demands of obliged writing on our students. But we must also attend to self-sponsored writing, not only as target discourses but also as increasingly important forms of action in the world.

I want to say more about one kind of self-sponsored discourse: the civic. The nature of the civic sphere has long been spectral—and not just for writing teachers and students. Paul Starr's masterful history of the rise of "the media" and its relation to governmental and entrepreneurial ownership makes clear that the current issues of access and influence have existed since at least the seventeenth century. Still, for years before the late 1980s gave us discourse communities, compositionists invoked "the general educated reader" in a comfortably assumed public space. Judging from our anthologies, "general reader" really meant subscribers to *Harper's* and *The American Scholar*. But as models for freshman student writing, entering this civic Pleasantville has never been realistic. To expect freshmen to produce texts like those from paid professionals is like expecting freshmen math students to perform as actuaries or freshman psychologists to save marriages. Recognizing this, at least subconsciously, we often have tended to distill civic writing into a school genre. That is, we have students write *about* the civic sphere, not *in* it. In like fashion, our new fine fondness for visual rhetoric manifests itself considerably more in the analysis of, rather than in the production of, images.

New technologies have shifted the possibilities and terms, not by exploding the media as the civic sphere but by fracturing it. Take blogs. People have analyzed, celebrated, and fretted more thoroughly than I can here the relationship of the blogosphere to traditional journalism. I'll simply note the blogger's relative independence from institutional strictures, at least in terms of access to readers. Independence has costs, most substantially a pre-established readership and a source of income. But that seems little to hamper it. Blogs, like e-mails, like letters, like poems, like diaries, are self-sponsored activities. My goodness. That people will write even when not obliged?

Blogs and other sites of civic discourse are not far removed, I suggest, from writing done for personal and belletristic reasons, the welling desire to write oneself into the world by creating textual artifacts. This desire—and I'm perfectly happy to grant it as socially constructed, though I'm also happy to grant it as a quality of being human—is manifested in all sorts of activities. Consider, for example, the rise of journaling and scrapbooking, which have taken on fascinating social dimensions as well as, alas, commercial ones.

Or consider a Web site titled CompanyCommand.com. Two Army majors started it, on a civilian server, as a place for military officers to give and seek practical advice. I quote, "Amazing things happen when committed leaders in a profession connect, share what they are learning, and spur each other on." The quote could be from the 4C's Web site. It proved sometimes faster for field soldiers to learn from Company Command.com than through the chain of command. Now, when soldiers can circumvent a structure as hierarchical as the Army, it's little wonder that traditional media sources, from newspapers to record companies, are trying to figure out how to make a buck. An aside: The Army finally absorbed CompanyCommand.com, loaded it onto military servers, and sent its developers to teach at West Point. [*Note:* My Chair's address in San Francisco included a screen shot of the site, which is at http://company command.army.mil. However, the site's Webmaster declined to allow that shot to be included in this volume.]

One more example. Consider the online open source encyclopedia, *Wikipedia*. As you probably know, anyone can post an article to *Wikipedia*

and, even more tellingly, any can revise what's there. Here's the entry for CCCC, which I put up a few weeks ago. You're all welcome to revise it. If traditional journalism frets blogs, and the Army buys Web sites, you can imagine the challenge that *Wikipedia* poses to *Britannica*. Instead of experts and editors sanctioning knowledge, we have all manner of autotelic encyclopedists, their texts shaped and refined by the digital hive mind.

I haven't even touched on the phenomena of Web casting and pod casting. I haven't explored the ways that composition has yet to embrace sound in the way it has sight, largely ignoring the spoken word, the word set to—and against—music. Instead, I'll just observe that writing in the civic sphere is now manifest as a self-sponsored activity to a greater extent than it ever has been. Yet most of us, and that includes me, teach as if the civic sphere were still institutionally sponsored, as if there were extractable

principles, guidelines, and rules. In fact, our teaching arrangements, from the textbook industry to our plots in the college catalog, fairly depend on it. At stake are structures as fundamental as semesters and thrice-weekly fifty-minute classes.

I started writing the final version of this talk about ten a.m. on Sunday, February 20, 2005, in lane 4 of the swimming pool at the YMCA in Bloomington, Illinois. I've sung in church choirs most of my life, less for the theology than for the aesthetics, and I'm singing in one now. But that Sunday morning, I went to the Y. Turning slow laps I saw the mural at pool's end, announcing the Home of the Waves. I remembered afternoons in this place a long decade past when my son and daughter were on the Waves swim team. Swimming had been different for me as a kid; no teams, no lanes, no times, no ribbons. It had been like baseball, kick the can, Johnny Come over the Ocean, and most every other team sport, all self-organized until high school. All except dodge ball. That one it took PE teachers to invent. Now is the age of clubs and traveling teams. There remain coachless realms, sure, but the

DMZ of the SUV cleaves mere play from serious competition. That last must always be organized by others and always include a fee.

Now, I'm not going to go Rousseau on you and dream some pre-lapsed age of writing now sullied, like, by coaches. I'm simply noting that the nature of an activity changes according to who organizes it and for what ends. We've known that since Werner Heisenberg and Vince Lombardi. Parents organize swimming and soccer and whatever "for the kids," but we do it also for ourselves, for what that experience affords us. Organization isn't a bad thing; whence else come orchestras or choirs?

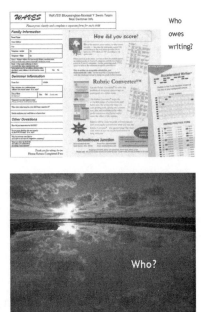

However, it comes down to this. These days all sorts of interests would organize writing. Let's attribute good intentions to them all. But let's remember that my good intentions are likely not yours, that intentions are always cropped and framed by worldviews as basic as what constitutes the good society and what makes the good life. These views bend through the nearly translucent lenses of social and economic interests.

Make no mistake. We in 4Cs refract and frame no less than others. But we have something else—or if we don't have it, we have no particularly right to be in this place, on this March morning. We have the lens of research and reflective practice, polished carefully and long, intentionally scratched at times, even melted. Ours is the knowledge of what writing is and what it can be, the whole of it, in every sphere. Ours is the never done knowledge of how writing develops, within a person or a populace. It is the knowledge of teachers' roles and families', of friends—and foes, of fertile textuality, of fulgent image, word, and sound. And with our knowledge comes responsibility, for writing, yes, but more

our students. ourselves. each. all.

for writers. And so it is that we singly and we together must own and own up to writing, not as colonists or profiteers, but as stewards. Let me, then, remediate that old spiritual:

> [*sung*]
> My lord, what a morning.
> My lord, what a morning,
> Oh, my lord what a morning
> When the stars rise over all,
> When the stars rise over all.

WORKS CITED

Achieve, Inc. *Rising to the Challenge: Are High School Graduates Prepared for College and Work?* Feb. 2005. Achieve, Inc. 20 Feb. 2005 <http://www.achieve.org/dstore.nsf/Lookup/pollreport/$file/pollreport.pdf>.

Anderson, Marian. *My Lord, What a Morning.* 1956. Urbana: U of Illinois P, 2002.

Burke, Kenneth. "Definition of Man." *Language as Symbolic Action.* Berkeley: U of California P, 1966. 16.

Burleigh, H. T. *Album of Negro Spirituals.* Melville: Belwin Mills, 1969.

CCCC. "CCCC Position Statement on Teaching, Learning, and Assessing Writing in Digital Environments." 25 Feb. 2004. 15 Mar. 2005 <http://www.ncte.org/groups/cccc/positions/115775.htm>.

"CCCC." *Wikipedia.* 21 Feb. 2005. 21 Feb. 2005 <http://en.wikipedia.org/wiki/CCCC>.

College Board. The National Commission on Writing. 2005. 28 Feb. 2005 <http://www.writingcommission.org/>.

CompanyCommand: Building Combat-Ready Teams. 2005. 7 Mar. 2005 http://companycommand.army.mil/.

Conley, David T. *Understanding University Success: A Report from Standards for Success: A Project of the Association of American Universities and the Pew Charitable Trusts.* Eugene: Center for Educational Policy Research, 2003.

Gere, Anne Ruggles. "Public Opinion and Teaching Writing." *The Politics of Writing Instruction: Postsecondary.* Ed. Richard Bullock and John Trimbur. Portsmouth: Boynton/Cook, 1991. 263–75.

Hillocks, George. *Research on Written Composition.* Urbana: NCTE, 1986.

Lakoff, George. *Don't Think of an Elephant: Know Your Values and Frame the Debate.* White River Junction: Chelsea Green, 2004.

Lessig, Lawrence. "lessig blog." 2 Mar. 2005 <http://www.lessig.org/blog/>.

Mullen, Dave. "www.EssayGenerator.com." 20 Feb. 2005 <http://radioworldwide.gospelcom.net/essaygenerator/>.

The National Commission on Writing in America's Schools and Colleges. *The Neglected "R": The Need for a Writing Revolution.* Princeton: College Entrance Examination Board, 2003.

———. *Writing: A Ticket to Work . . . Or a Ticket Out: A Survey of Business Leaders.* Princeton: College Entrance Examination Board, 2004.

Pearson Knowledge Technologies. "Intelligent Essay Assessor." 2005. 10 Mar. 2005 <http://www.knowledge-technologies.com/>.

———. "Products." 5 Sept. 2005. http://www.k-a-t.com.

Starr, Paul. *The Creation of the Media: Political Origins of Modern Communication.* New York: Basic, 2004.

Trimbur, John. "Literacy and the Discourse of Crisis." *The Politics of Writing Instruction: Postsecondary.* Ed. Richard Bullock and John Trimbur. Portsmouth: Boynton/Cook, 1991. 277–95.

Yancey, Kathleen Blake. "Made Not Only in Words: Composition in a New Key." *College Composition and Communication* 56 (Dec. 2004): 297–328.

When I chose "Who Owns Writing?" in fall 2004, for a talk to be delivered in spring 2005, I was fretting how "outside" interests were constructing writing and its teaching, often in clear (sometimes, I thought, deliberate) ignorance of the knowledge and research that CCCC had generated over the decades. Student writing—even (or especially) "bad" student writing—had become a surprisingly valuable commodity. There was money to be made testing it and money to be made selling it in glib pedagogical packages. More subtle and powerful than the fiscal capital was the ideological: whoever gets to declare, diagnose, and manage the state of writing in America gets to label—and control—students, teachers, and curricula.

In the few months between my talk and this reflection, I've been struck by how quickly everything has escalated—and how urgent it has become for our profession to turn efforts outward. The spring's catalyzing event was the twenty-five-minute essay added to the SAT. Subject of a session organized by the CCCC Public Policy Committee at the 2005 convention, the new SAT occasioned stories, editorials, and letters across the national media, further fueled by the NCTE statement on testing. People like Dennis Baron and Les Perelman published critiques in *The Chronicle of Higher Education* and the *Los Angeles Times*, but for the most part the profession was defensive. By June 2005, I'd been interviewed by the *Chicago Tribune*, the *New York Times* (which also published my letter), and even the conservative American Family Radio Network, in each instance trying to distill dozens of years of knowledge into a few phrases.

I'm happy that writing generally and CCCC specifically has gotten some press, and I think we've pushed back the darkness a few minutes. But I fear the powerful forces, especially those championing the economy and "objectivity" of computer evaluations of writing, require more than a few of us just saying "no." I fear more that those of us in composition studies can be too easily (even if unjustly) written off as politically motivated obstructionists, concerned less about improving student writing than about advocating self-interests. I fear most that, unless we devise both the means and the motivation to explain our knowledge to others who aren't us, we'll abet our own marginalization. With each new salvo against college composition (this week's, as I write, comes from Stanley Fish), our professional listservs churn splendid analyses and rebuttals, building community, yes, but not extending that community.

One theme my talk sounded was the gap between what I called "obliged writing" (especially school and work genres: the academic essay, the report) and "self-sponsored" writing (civic and personal/relational genres: the literary essay, the blog). I still think we have to attend to both sides of this tricky binary; we best serve individual writers, societal needs, and democratic ideals by insisting on the fullness of writing. But we also need to understand complexities within the obliged and self-sponsored spheres. We need to reconcile our often-idealized (and convenient) classroom views of texts with how writing actually exists beyond our courses. I don't mean this as one-directionally as "follow the market." The challenge for teachers is responding to the discursive world as it is while shaping what it might become, all the while keeping writing interesting, that is consequential, to students.

Giving the Chair's address at once carries great professional responsibility and dangles seductive self-indulgence. Autobiography has been a frequent rhetorical strategy in most of my published work, and yet I worried about abusing it. In the end, I decided that the Chair's address mattered most not for posterity but for its immediate context: this moment in CCCC, this convention, this day, this forty minutes. My choice to sing those spirituals, then, was part self-indulgence, I'll confess, but it was also the best way I could figure to remind everyone there that they *were* there, that morning in San Francisco.

–DOUGLAS HESSE
Illinois State University

Notes on Chairs and Other Contributors

David Bartholomae is Professor and Chair of the English Department at the University of Pittsburgh, where he continues to teach freshman English each fall and where he won the Chancellor's Distinguished Teaching Award (1995). He has served as Chair of CCCC and on the Executive Committees of CCCC, MLA, and ADE. With Jean Ferguson Carr, he edits the University of Pittsburgh series Composition, Literacy and Culture. His books include *Facts, Artifacts, Counterfacts: Reading and Writing in Theory and Practice* (with Anthony Petrosky), *The Teaching of Writing* (with Anthony Petrosky), *Writing on the Margins: Essays on Composition and Teaching, Ways of Reading* (with Anthony Petrosky) (now in its seventh edition), *Reading the Lives of Others* (with Anthony Petrosky), and *Ways of Reading: Words and Images* (with Anthony Petrosky).

Wendy Bishop (1953–2003), Kellogg W. Hunt Distinguished Professor of English at Florida State University, was a teacher, a scholar, a poet, and an essayist. She wrote and edited twenty-two scholarly books, several poetry chapbooks, and numerous journal articles. Her scholarly interests included creative writing pedagogy, genre theory, writing program administration, and many more areas of rhetoric and composition. In all of these areas, she left behind works that will be read, studied, and debated for years to come. Having crossed over from creative writing into rhetoric and composition, Bishop remained true to her original passion, continuing to produce poems and nonfiction alongside scholarly work. She kept showing her students and colleagues that all writing is creative and that all writing teachers should also be writers. In 2001, Bishop's reputation among colleagues earned her the position of CCCC Chair. She also served on various CCCC and NCTE committees. — Pavel Zemlianski

Lillian Bridwell-Bowles received her undergraduate and master's degrees at Florida State University and her doctorate from the University of Georgia. She is currently a Professor of English, Director of Communication across the Curriculum at Louisiana State University, and a member of the Women's and Gender Studies Program. Before coming to LSU, Bridwell-Bowles was a Professor of English, Director of the Center for Interdisciplinary Studies of Writing, and a member of Women's Studies at the University of Minnesota. In addition to serving as Chair of CCCC, she and Hildy Miller cochaired the Second Biennial Feminism(s) and Rhetoric(s) Conference, Minneapolis, in 1999. Her most recent book is *Rhetorical Women*, coedited with Hildy Miller. Other publications include *Identity Matters: Rhetorics of Difference*; *New Directions in Composition Research*; *Word Processors and the Writing*; "Discourse and Diversity: Experimental Writing within the Academy" and "Freedom, Form, Function: Varieties of Academic Discourse," in *College Composition and Communication*; "Experimenting with Diverse Discourse in Writing Classrooms," in *Feminine Principles and Women's Experience in American Composition and Rhetoric*; "Identity Politics," in *Theorizing Composition*; and "Master's Tools," in *Narration as Knowledge*. She also edited an extensive series on writing across the curriculum at the University of Minnesota. More of her work can be found at http://cxc.lsu.edu and at http://writing.umn.edu/isw/publications.htm.

Miriam T. Chaplin is Professor Emerita of Rutgers University, past President of NCTE, and past Chair of CCCC. She is the author of *Reading Comes to College* (1978), coauthor of *Opening the American Mind* (1993), and editor of the Reading Section in *Tapping the Potential of the Black Learner* (1985). She is contributing author to several books in the field of English education. She has also published in the *Journal of Reading, Reading World, English Education, Arizona English Journal*, and many other journals.

Chaplin has served as classroom teacher, reading teacher, and Reading Coordinator in the School District of Philadelphia and Rutgers University. In 1992, she proposed a three-year program to NCTE and served as its Project Manager in Mupumulango, South Africa, for a teacher-development program that involved exchanges between teachers in the United States and South Africa. She also observed early childhood education in the United Soviet Socialist Republic in 1982 and led a staff-development program in Anchorage, Alaska, in 1995.

Chaplin has served as consultant to many school districts and colleges across the United States. For several years, she chaired the Department of Education at Rutgers University in Camden, New Jersey. In addition, she served for two years on the Trustee Board of the Children's Centers in Hilton Head and Bluffton, South Carolina. She lives with her husband in Hilton Head, South Carolina.

William W. Cook: I began as a shoe shine boy on the streets of Trenton, New Jersey, graduated to salaried work in shoe shine parlors, and after that, everything was fortuitous accident and furious silent rages. The accidents in my life were somewhat miracles. The fury at the racism that shaped every day of my life was enough to derange the strongest human being. The miracles sound too much like the old Ragged Dick series, so suffice it to say we were stomp-down poor and there was nothing genteel about our poverty. I began teaching in William Cook Elementary School (I am not lying!); my first students were those with learning disabilities. I went then to Junior High School #1. Both schools were in the poverty zone out of which I came. Because of my own horrible experiences in the same school system, I was going to make damned sure that none of my students were as bored and as angry as I was. I didn't succeed in touching as many as I wanted to touch, but there were some victories. The tool I used was language, oral language, drama, and reader's theater. We dramatized everything imaginable. As the youngest of eleven children, I early learned the value of being always heard. My preacher father loved the sound of my voice, and I memorized everything I could find.

My classes were praised for the neatness of their basal readers each year. We didn't use the damned things but we read a great deal. I went on to Princeton High School, worked in community and regional theater, to Dartmouth College and the founding, with August Wilson and Victor Walker III, African Grove Institute for the Arts (the African Grove Theater was the first professional theater owned by African Americans), a support organization for African American regional and community theaters.

I did many other things, but they don't fit the particular fiction into which I choose to narrate my life today. Like a good Puritan biographer, I use only the parts that fit my present moral message. All biography, given changing notions of what is included and omitted, is simply a duller exercise in fiction. Call it faction.

Kelli Custer completed her BA and MA in English at Idaho State University and is currently a PhD candidate in English Composition at Indiana University of Pennsylvania. In over a decade of teaching at the high school, community college, and four-year college levels in various parts of the country, she has taught composition, literature, basic writing, and first-year seminar courses, as well as directed a writing center and served as an academic advisor. Her current scholarly interests include the formation of teacher identity, teacher preparation, and writing program administration.

Frank J. D'Angelo is Professor Emeritus of English at Arizona State University. He is a former member of the Executive Committee of NCTE, a former Chair of the MLA Writing Division, and a former member of the Board of Directors of the Rhetoric Society of America. He served as an advisory editor for *Rhetoric Review, Journal of Advanced Composition,* and *Focuses*. His publications include *A Conceptual Theory of Rhetoric, Process and Thought in Composition, Composition in the Classical Tradition*, and more than sixty essays in scholarly books and journals. In 1977 he won the Richard Braddock Award, given by CCCC to the author of the outstanding essay on the theory and/or practice of composition. In 1993 he won the Edward P. J. Corbett Award, given by the journal *Focuses* for the best essay that year.

Vivian I. Davis took the bachelor of arts degree from Ball State Teachers College, Muncie, Indiana, with a major in English and minor in Spanish. She taught Spanish at Prairie View A&M College in Prairie View, Texas, before moving to Lubbock, Texas, where she taught high school English and journalism. In 1957, she returned to Indiana, her home state, and unable to find a teaching position, became an Aid to Dependent Children worker in the Department of Public Welfare. After two years as a group social worker in a settlement house, she married, moved to Chicago and took a master's in the art of teaching from the University of Chicago, and ultimately earned the PhD in English Education from Northwestern University in Evanston, Illinois.

Returning to Lubbock, Texas, Davis taught first-year composition and Black Literature at Texas Tech University. In 1978 when she was Chair of CCCC, she was also Chair of the Division of Fine Arts and Humanities at Bishop College. At the end of that school year, she took a job with Warner Amex Cable Television and edited their in-house newsletter. After two years in that position, Davis returned to academe as Chair of the Department of English at Tarrant County Junior College, South Campus. In 1983, she returned full-time to the classroom, teaching developmental writing, first-year composition, and technical writing. In 1992, after retiring, she continued to teach developmental writing and first-year composition part-time. She also taught at Sylvan Learning Center in Dallas, Texas.

In 1999, Emory, her devoted spouse and friend, died. The two had always planned to return to the Midwest to be near family and friends. In 2002, Davis made the move back to Chicago thinking she would finish her career as a day-to-day substitute secondary English teacher. That was not to be. Now Davis teaches GED to adult basic education students and works for the *Chicago Defender*, the last Black daily newspaper in the country. She reads, writes, travels, and enjoys being alive in "difficult times."

Theresa Enos is Professor of English and Director of the Rhetoric, Composition, and the Teaching of English Graduate Program at the University of Arizona. Founder and editor of *Rhetoric Review*, she teaches both graduate and undergraduate courses in writing and rhetoric. Her research interests include the history and theory of rhetoric and the intellectual work and politics of rhetoric and composition studies. She has edited and coedited nine books, including the *Encyclopedia of Rhetoric and Composition* and *The Writing Program Administrator's Resource: A Guide to Reflective Institutional Practice,* and she has published numerous chapters and articles on rhetorical theory and issues in writing. She is the author of *Gender Roles and Faculty Lives in Rhetoric and Composition* (1995) and past President of the National Council of Writing Program Administrators (1997–1999).

Lester Faigley holds the Robert Adger Law and Thos. H. Law Professorship in Humanities at the University of Texas at Austin. He was the founding director of both the Division of Rhetoric and Composition and the Concentration in Technology, Literacy, and Culture at Texas, and he served as the 1996 Chair of CCCC. He currently directs the Undergraduate Writing Center at Texas. Faigley has published ten books, including *Fragments of Rationality* (1992), which received the MLA Mina P. Shaughnessy Prize and the CCCC Outstanding Book Award.

Anne Ruggles Gere is Professor of English and Professor of Education at the University of Michigan, where she directs the Joint PhD Program in English and Education. Her books include *Writing Groups: History, Theory and Implications* (1987), *Into the Field: Sites of Composition Studies* (1993), and *Intimate Practices: Literacy and Cultural Work in U.S. Women's Clubs 1880–1920* (1997). She is currently working on a book about the literacy practices of American Indian women who taught in boarding schools between 1890 and 1930. She has published in, among others, *College Composition and Communication, College English,* the *Michigan Quarterly Review, Signs,* the *History of Education Quarterly,* and the *American Indian Quarterly.* At the University of Michigan, she has received the Distinguished Faculty Achievement Award, the D'Arms Award for Distinguished Graduate Student Mentoring, and a fellowship at the Institute for the Humanities. Nationally, she has served in a variety of capacities for NCTE and MLA. She has received grants from the Spencer Foundation, the U.S. Department of Education, and the National Endowment for the Humanities. Most important, she has helped shape the next generation of composition scholars including Jeffrey Carroll, Shawn Christian, James Inman, Rona Kaufman, Ted Lardner, Margaret Marshall, Alisea McCloud, Deborah Minter, Sarah Robbins, Steve Salchak, Jennifer Sinor, Margaret Willard-Traub, Victor Villanueva, and Morris Young.

Keith Gilyard is Professor of English at the Pennsylvania State University, University Park. He formerly directed the Writing Program at Syracuse University and, before that, taught for fourteen years at the City University of New York. He has served on the Executive Committees of NCTE, CEE, and CCCC. He served as Chair of CCCC in 2000. Author of numerous publications, Gilyard's books include *Voices of the Self: A Study of Language Competence* (1991), for which he received an American Book Award; *Let's Flip the Script: An African American Discourse on Language, Literature, and Learning* (1996); *Liberation Memories: The Rhetoric and Poetics of John Oliver Killens* (2003); and the poetry volumes *American 40* (1993), *Poemographies* (2001), and *How I Figure* (2003). In addition, he edited *Spirit & Flame: An Anthology of Contemporary African American Poetry* (1997); *Race, Rhetoric, and Composition* (1999); *African American Literature* (with Anissa Wardi, 2004); and *Rhetoric and Ethnicity* (with Vorris Nunley, 2004).

Maxine Hairston (1922–2005) came to the academic world late, like many women in composition, starting her work on a PhD at the University of Texas at Austin when she was forty-one. Even as a graduate student, she enjoyed teaching freshman composition and within a year after completing her degree, she became Freshman Director at Texas, a position she held for four years. During those years she was also active in CCCC, serving as Chair in 1985 and publishing articles in *College Composition and Communication* and other professional journals. She authored several composition textbooks, notably *The Scott, Foresman Handbook for Writers* and *The Riverside Reader*. She retired from the University of Texas in 1991 but continued to work on textbooks and to take courses in history and classics at the university, solely for personal enrichment. In 2003 she completed a master's degree in history at the University of Texas.

Amelia R. Herb graduated from Butler University with a major in music and minors in English and psychology in 2000. In 2002, she graduated from the University of Louisville with a master of arts degree in English and American literature. While in Louisville, she studied writing center pedagogy and archival research with Carol Mattingly. Before coming to the University of Illinois at Urbana–Champaign in 2003, Herb taught English as an International Language at the *Institut Universitaire de Formation des Maîtres* (*IUFM*) in Le Puy-en-Velay, France, for the French government's international center of pedagogical studies (*Centre International d'Etudes Pédagogiques-CIEP*). Presently, she is pursuing a PhD in English with a specialization in writing studies at the University of Illinois Urbana–Champaign's English department and Center for Writing Studies. Her current research interests include socio-historicism, social memory, discourse analysis, rhetorical theory, feminist theory and women's studies, composition pedagogy, literacies, early twentieth-century archives, archival theory, classification, and indexing.

Douglas Hesse grew up in the farm town of DeWitt, Iowa, where he worked summers on his father's trash truck, before and while attending the University of Iowa. His mentors included Carl Klaus, Susan Lohafer,

Paul Diehl, David Hamilton, Louise Kelly, and Jix Lloyd-Jones. Beyond stints at Findlay (with Rick Gebhardt) and Miami, he's been at Illinois State, which named him Distinguished Humanities Teacher and Outstanding University Researcher, as Professor of English and Director of Honors and as Director of Writing Programs, Graduate Studies, and the Center for the Advancement of Teaching. Past President of the Council of Writing Program Administrators (WPA) and editor of *WPA: Writing Program Administration*, Hesse has published in *College Composition and Communication*, *Rhetoric Review*, *Composition Studies*, *Computers and Composition*, the *New England Journal of Medicine*; in *Beyond the Postmodern*; *The Private, the Public, and the Published*; *Questioning Authority*; *Sourcebook for Writing Program Administration*; *Passions, Politics, and 21st Century Technologies*; *Kitchen Cooks, Plate Twirlers, and Troubadours*; *Writing Theory and Critical Theory*; *Essays on the Essay*; *Rebirth of Rhetoric, Narrative and Argument*; *Literary Nonfiction*; and elsewhere. Coauthor (with Lynn Troyka) of the *Simon and Schuster Handbook for Writers*, he edited a *College English* issue on creative nonfiction, his main scholarly interest, along with pedagogy, administrative issues, and the public face of composition studies. His wife is a writer, his three children writers and musicians.

James Lee Hill is Professor of English at Albany State University (Georgia), where he also previously served as Chair of the Department of English and Modern Languages, Dean of the College of Arts and Sciences, and Assistant Vice President for Academic Affairs. A member of a number of organizations, including NCTE, CCCC, CLA, CEE and MAWA, Professor Hill has served in professional positions as Chair of CCCC, Chair of the NCTE College Section, Chair of Georgia Humanities Council, board member of the National Federation of State Humanities Councils, and twice as member of the NCTE Executive Committee. He also directed the 1996 NCTE Summer Institute for Teachers of Literature. Currently, he is a member of the Board of Directors of the Georgia Council of Teachers of English and the Board of Governors of the National Conferences on Undergraduate Research. Professor Hill has published in such journals and books as *Black Books Bulletin*, *Arizona English Bulletin*, *American Resources for Literary Study*, and *The Oxford Companion to African American Literature*. He is the founding editor of the Peter Lang series Studies in African and African American Culture, which he edited for ten years (1990–2000); founding editor of *the Albany State University Journal*; and editor of *A Sourcebook for Teachers of Georgia History*. Currently, Dr. Hill is conducting research for a book-length study of Colleen McElroy, an African American writer who lives in Seattle, Washington.

William F. Irmscher graduated from the University of Louisville in 1941 with a bachelor of arts degree in English and history, as Richard Tracey noted in the bibliography he compiled titled "He Takes the Teaching of Writing Seriously."* After graduation, Irmscher taught English at a high school until June 1942, when he was drafted into World War II at the age of twenty-two. He served in the military for three years.

Upon his return from the war, Irmscher earned his master of arts degree in English from the University of Chicago in 1947 and his doctoral degree in Renaissance literature and English language from Indiana University in 1950. For the next decade, Irmscher taught Renaissance literature, drama, and first-year composition at the University of Arizona, directing the first-year composition program beginning in 1954. In 1960, Irmscher left the dry southwest for the rainy northwest, where he directed the freshman composition program at the University of Washington (176–77).

Irmscher began his service to the field of rhetoric and composition in 1965, when he became editor of *College Composition and Communication*. After fourteen years as editor, he served as Chair of CCCC in 1979. Irmscher is perhaps most well-known for *The Holt Guide to English*, published from 1972 to 1983, and for his application of the Burkean pentad, comprised of actor, agent, purpose, scene, act, and means, to composition pedagogy. From 1982 to 1983, Irmscher served as President of NCTE. While Irmscher retired from the University of Washington in 1985, he began editing *College English* the same year, and in 1988 when he officially ended his teaching career, he became the editor for *Writing on the Edge*. Irmscher's extensive bibliography contains contributions to more than twenty-five books and thirty-four journal articles and book reviews. However, Richard Tracey, who wrote his dissertation under the direction of Professor Irmscher, calls to our attention that "Professor Irmscher . . . is more than the sum of his publications. . . . Whether teaching freshman composition or directing dissertations, he is an inclusive mentor, allowing students to forge their own paths, not just follow his own" (177–78).—Amelia R. Herb

Richard Lloyd-Jones is Emeritus Professor of English at the University of Iowa and cofounder of the Iowa Writing Project. He received the first CCCC Exemplar Award, the second ADE Francis Andrew March Award, and the NCTE Distinguished Service Award. These honors reflect his preoccupation with teaching and with the profession itself. He is the coauthor of the benchmark *Research in Written Composition*, he edited the CCCC statement "Students' Right to Their Own Language," and he codesigned the first version of Primary Trait Scoring. In addition to serving as

---

*Tracey, Richard. "He Takes the Teaching of Writing Seriously: A Bibliography of Works by William Irmscher." *Balancing Acts: Essays on the Teaching of Writing in Honor of William F. Irmscher*. Ed. Virginia Chappell, Mary-Louise Buley-Meissner, and Chris Anderson. Carbondale: Southern Illinois UP, 1991. 175–84.

Chair of CCCC and President of NCTE, he served on the boards of ADE, the Midwest Conference on English in the Two-Year College, and SLATE; the NCTE Commissions on Research and Composition; and the Editorial Board of NCTE.

Shirley Wilson Logan, a native of South Carolina, holds degrees from Johnson C. Smith University, the University of North Carolina, and the University of Maryland. Before moving to Washington to teach composition at Howard University, Logan taught in the public schools of Charlotte-Mecklenburg County, and she taught high school English in Prince George's County, Maryland. Logan is Associate Professor of English at the University of Maryland, where she directed the Professional Writing Program. She currently teaches composition, rhetoric, and African American literature within a variety of course designs. Logan served on the CCCC Executive, Nominating, Exemplar Award, and Outstanding Book Award committees before her election as CCCC Assistant Chair. She is past President of the Coalition of Women Scholars in the History of Rhetoric and Composition and served on the Executive Committee of the MLA Division on the History of Rhetoric and Composition. Logan coedits the SIU Press series Studies in Rhetorics and Feminisms with founding editor Cheryl Glenn. Logan is author of *We Are Coming: The Persuasive Discourse of Nineteenth-Century Black Women* and editor of *With Pen and Voice: A Critical Anthology of Nineteenth-Century African-American Women*, and she has essays in several collections. Currently, Logan is completing a study of black sites of rhetorical education, supported in part by a fellowship from the American Association of University Women, and an essay on Ida Wells-Barnett for *A Rhetorical History of the United States: Significant Moments in Public Discourse*.

John Lovas (1940–2005) taught his first section of first-year composition in 1960 at the University of Utah before he was old enough to vote. He taught the equivalent course at De Anza College in Fall 2004, when he was old enough to retire. During that time, he taught all levels of composition, poetry, linguistics, British literature, and children's literature; he cowrote the first ESL curriculum, helped revise the basic skills curriculum, and coauthored an Introduction to Linguistics course at Foothill College. In 1968, he became the first Director of Multicultural Programs at Foothill College. He served as President of the American Federation of Teachers there, then went to De Anza College to serve as Division Dean, Language Arts, from 1977 to 1985. At De Anza, he led efforts to expand the ESL curriculum, to create the College Readiness program, and to revive the student newspaper, and he helped establish the Honors Program. Lovas participated in the English Council of California Two-Year Colleges, serving from 1980 to 1996. Active in CCCC and NCTE, he helped found the Two-Year College English Association, where he served three years in the Chair's rotation, followed by four years in the Chair's rotation of CCCC. He coauthored a book on community college governance and a textbook for developmental writing. His articles have appeared in *College Composition and Communication, Teaching English in the Two-Year College, TESOL Quarterly, ADE Bulletin,* and *Inside English.* In May 2003, he launched "A Writing Teacher's Blog," which documented his teaching and scholarship in a community college.

Andrea Lunsford is Professor of English and Director of the Program in Writing and Rhetoric at Stanford University. She was recently named the Louise and Claude Rosenberg Jr. Fellow in Undergraduate Education. She has designed and taught undergraduate and graduate courses in writing history and theory, rhetoric, literacy studies, and intellectual property. Before joining the Stanford faculty, Lunsford was Distinguished Professor of English and Director of the Center for the Study and Teaching of Writing at the Ohio State University. Currently also a member of the Bread Loaf School of English faculty, Lunsford earned her BA and MA degrees from the University of Florida and completed her PhD in English at Ohio State University.

Andrea Lunsford's interests include rhetorical theory, gender and rhetoric, collaborative writing, cultures of writing, style, and technologies of writing. She has written or coauthored fourteen books, including *Everything's an Argument*; *The Everyday Writer*; *The St. Martin's Handbook, Essays on Classical Rhetoric and Modern Discourse*; *Singular Texts/Plural Authors: Perspectives on Collaborative Writing*; and *Reclaiming Rhetorica: Women in the History of Rhetoric*, as well as numerous chapters and articles. Forthcoming works include *Exploring Borderlands: Composition and Postcolonial Studies*.

Donald McQuade is Professor of English at the University of California, Berkeley, where he has also served as Dean of Undergraduate and Interdisciplinary Studies, Chair of the Department of Dramatic Art, and founding Director of the Center for Theater Arts. He currently serves as Vice Chancellor, University Relations.

McQuade teaches writing, American studies, and American literature at Berkeley and has served as the coordinator of the English Department's writing program. He is also one of three faculty at Berkeley to have been awarded the title "Chancellor's Fellow." He served as the 1991 Chair of the CCCC as well as on the Executive Committee of NCTE and on the Executive Committee of the Teaching of Writing Division of MLA. He has written, edited, and coedited many books on writing, American literature, as well as American culture, and has published numerous articles on the theory and practice of composition. He recently edited volume 9 of *The Correspondence of William James* and is working with his daughter, Christine, on a new edition of *Seeing & Writing*.

Keith D. Miller is Professor of English (and former WPA) at Arizona State University. He is the author of *Voice of Deliverance: The Language of Martin Luther King, Jr., and Its Sources*. He and Theresa Enos recently coedited *Beyond Postprocess and Postmodernism: The Spaciousness of Rhetoric* (2003); he and James Baumlin recently coedited *Selected Essays of Jim W. Corder* (2004).

Lee Odell is Professor of Composition Theory and Research at Rensselaer Polytechnic Institute. His publications include *Evaluating Writing* (first and second editions) and *Research on Composing* (both with Charles Cooper), *Writing in Non-Academic Settings* (with Dixie Goswami), and *Theory and Practice in the Teaching of Writing*. He has published several articles on the relationship between visual and verbal communication and has recently finished a composition textbook (with Susan Katz), *Writing in a Visual Age*, that shows "writers" how to integrate visual and written information. He has served as Chair of CCCC and of the NCTE Assembly for Research. He serves on a number of editorial boards of scholarly journals, including the *Journal of Business and Technical Communication*. His articles have received the CCCC Richard Braddock Award and the NCTE Publication Award for research on technical communication.

Jane Peterson currently teaches first-year composition and world literature at Richland College of the Dallas County Community College District. In her thirty-two years there, she has assumed various administrative duties including English Program Coordinator and Assistant Dean of Communications, but she remains most proud of being honored three times for excellence in teaching.

Considering CCCC her professional home, Peterson served on several committees, including the Executive Committee, before becoming Assistant Chair, which made her the 1989 Program Chair, the 1990 Chair, and the 1992 Winter Workshop Program Chair. Peterson also served on the editorial boards of *Teaching English in the Two-Year College* and the *Journal of Basic Writing*, and was one of sixty participants in the working conference on Future Directions for the Teaching of English, sponsored by the Coalition of English Associations in 1987.

Her publications include articles in *College English* and *College Composition and Communication*; a chapter in *Theory and Practice in the Teaching of Writing*, edited by Lee Odell; a basic writing textbook, *From Course to Course*, coauthored with Judy Lambert; and a ninety-minute Starlink Teleconference, broadcast live and subsequently videostreamed, on Collaboration in the Classroom, copresented with Jennifer Black.

Nell Ann Pickett has long been active in TYCA-SE, CCCC, NCTE, Association of Teachers of Technical Writing, Society for Technical

Communication, and other professional organizations. She is author or coauthor of five books on writing and more than fifty book chapters and journal articles and was an editor of *Teaching English in the Two-Year College*. A former Mississippi Professor of the Year, she is the recipient of numerous awards, several of them named in her honor. "On May 11 [2004], Hinds Community College bestowed a new honor on its one remaining original building, 87-year-old Main Hall, by linking it forever to another of its beloved institutions, retired English Professor Dr. Nell Ann Pickett" (*HCC Hindsight* 29.3 [2004]:4). Now Pickett is a full-time farmer, raising beef cattle and timber on her acreage near Utica, Mississippi. Active in Delta Kappa Gamma, a teachers' honorary society, she serves on the boards of Friends of Utica, Utica Heritage Society, and HCC Development Foundation. She is serving a two-year term as president of the Utica women's service organization and is treasurer of her church and of the community cemetery. She travels extensively.

Rosentene Bennett-Purnell is a native of West Point, Mississippi. She is magna cum laude graduate in English, Tougaloo College, Tougaloo, Mississippi. She has an MA in English (Romantic and Victorian) Literature and American Literature from Northwestern University. She is the first African American to earn the doctorate in English and the second woman to earn the doctorate in John Milton and Renaissance Literature at the University of Okalahoma.

Bennett-Purnell has been an English professor for nearly fifty years. She has taught for Alcorn A&M College, as Assistant Professor; Fisk University, as Professor and Chair; Rutgers University, as Visiting Professor; and is currently English Professor, Pan African Studies, California State University, Northridge. Bennett-Purnell developed and directed the Writing Program in Pan African Studies for nearly twenty years. She also served as University Coordinator of Writing at Northridge for three years. She has been active in NCTE and CCCC since 1968. She is also a life member of College Language Association (CLA), California Association of English, and the California English Council. She is active in the church and other civic organizations, holding national offices in each. She has traveled widely in five continents and did an ambassadorship in South Africa under the auspices of the American Baptist Churches, USA.

Bennett-Purnell has presented numerous papers at NCTE, CCCC, and CLA conventions. She has also served on many committees and commissions in these professional organizations, as well as for the Educational Testing Service. Having done much pioneering in the profession, she has developed and evaluated writing programs throughout much of the country. She is the author of *Bridges: Ways to Understand Written Discourse* (1988); many chapters, including one for Elizabeth Cowan's *Options for Teaching English* (1975); articles including "The Status of Writing

Proficiency" (*College Composition and Communication*, 1982), and "Teaching Them to Curse" (*Phylon*, 1979); and booklets and videotapes on "Teaching Shakespeare" and "Conducting the Writer's Conference" (1984) and "My South African Journey" (1991). She has earned over twenty-five awards for teaching excellence and service to the profession, the university, the church, community, and nation.

Duane Roen, Professor of English, currently serves as Head of Humanities and Arts at Arizona State University at the East campus. Previously, he directed the Center for Learning and Teaching Excellence at Arizona State University at the Tempe campus, where he also had served as writing program administrator. Prior to that, he directed the Writing Program at Syracuse University, and he served as Coordinator of Graduate Studies in English at the University of Arizona, where he also worked as Director of Rhetoric, Composition, and the Teaching of English from 1988 to 1992. In addition to more than 170 articles, chapters, and conference papers, Roen has published the following books: *Composing Our Lives in Rhetoric and Composition: Stories about the Growth of a Discipline* (with Theresa Enos and Stuart Brown); *The Writer's Toolbox* (with Stuart Brown and Bob Mittan); *A Sense of Audience in Written Discourse* (with Gesa Kirsch); *Becoming Expert: Writing and Learning across the Disciplines* (with Stuart Brown and Bob Mittan); and *Richness in Writing: Empowering ESL Students* (with the late Donna Johnson). The royalties from his edited NCTE collection, *Strategies for Teaching First-Year Composition* (with Veronica Pantoja, Lauren Yena, Susan K. Miller, and Eric Waggoner) are being donated to the CCCC Scholars of the Dream Fund. *Writing for College, Writing for Life* (with Greg Glau and Barry Maid), a textbook, is scheduled for release in 2006.

Jacqueline Jones Royster, Professor of English at the Ohio State University, is the author, editor, or coeditor of six books: *Double-Stitch: Black Women Write about Mothers and Daughters* (1991); *Southern Horrors and Other Writings: The Anti-Lynching Campaign of Ida B. Wells, 1892–1900* (1996); *Traces of a Stream: Literacy and Social Change among African American Women* (2000), which was awarded the MLA Mina P. Shaughnessy Prize; *Profiles of Ohio Women: 1803–2003* (2003); *Critical Inquiries: Readings on Culture and Community* (2003); and *Calling Cards: Theory and Practice in Studies of Race, Gender, and Culture* (2005). She is also the consulting author or consulting coeditor of two school textbook series, *Writer's Choice* and *Glencoe Literature: The Reader's Choice*, and the author of numerous articles in rhetorical studies, literacy studies, and women's studies. Royster was the 1995 Chair of CCCC and has served in numerous other leadership roles in professional organizations. She has also been the recipient of numerous awards, including Ohio Pioneer in Education (for higher education) by the State of Ohio Department of

Education (2000); Braddock Award (2000) from CCCC for the best article in their journal, *College Composition and Communication*; Mina P. Shaughnessy Prize (2001) from MLA, as noted above; University Distinguished Diversity Award (2002) from Ohio State; University Distinguished Lecturer (2003) from Ohio State; Exemplar Award (2004) from CCCC; and a YWCA Woman of Achievement Award (2004) from the city of Columbus.

Cynthia L. Selfe is Professor of English at the Ohio State University. Previously, she was Professor of Humanities in the Humanities Department at Michigan Technological University. In 1996, Selfe was recognized as an EDUCOM Medal award winner for innovative computer use in higher education—the first woman and the first English teacher to receive this award. Selfe has served as the Chair of CCCC and the Chair of the College Section of NCTE. Selfe is the author of numerous articles and books on computers including *Literacy and Technology in the 21st Century, the Perils of Not Paying Attention* (1999), *Creating a Computer-Supported Writing Facility* (1989), and *Computer-Assisted Instruction in Composition: Create Your Own* (1986); and she is a coauthor of *Literate Lives in the Information Age: Narratives of Literacy from the United States* (with Gail Hawisher, 2004), *Writing New Media: Theory and Applications for Expanding the Teaching of Composition* (with A. Wysocki, Johndan Johnson Eilola, and Goeff Sirc, 2004), *Computers and the Teaching of Writing in American Higher Education, 1979–1994: A History* (with Gail Hawisher, Paul LeBlanc, and Charles Moran, 1996), and *Technical Writing* (with Mary Lay, Billie Wahlstrom, Stephen Doheny-Farina, Ann Hill Duin, Sherry Burgus Little, Carolyn D. Rude, and Jack Selzer, 1995 and 2000). With Kathleen Kiefer (Colorado State University), Selfe founded the journal *Computers and Composition: An International Journal for Teachers*, which she continues to edit today with Gail Hawisher (University of Illinois).

Donald Stewart (1930–1992) was Professor of English at Kansas State University and the author of *The Authentic Voice* (1972) and *The Versatile Writer* (1986), chapters in books on rhetorical history and theory, and articles in such journals as *College Composition and Communication*, *College English*, *Rhetoric Review*, *the English Journal*, and *The CEA Critic*. Stewart was the 1983 Chair of CCCC, and he held numerous posts in NCTE. He was an avid outdoorsman who spent many summers in Yellowstone National Park as a ranger. His book *The Life and Legacy of Fred Newton Scott* was published posthumously in 1997. — Theresa Enos

Lynn Quitman Troyka, who earned her PhD at New York University, is Professor Emerita of Writing, Queensborough Community College of the City University of New York (CUNY). Also at CUNY, she taught in the graduate Language and Literacy Program at City College and in the Center for Advanced Study in Education at the Graduate School. Former editor of the *Journal of Basic Writing*, her writing appears in journals and scholarly collections. She is author of the *Simon and Schuster Handbook for Writers*, Seventh Edition (2004); the *Simon and Schuster Quick Access Reference for Writers*, Fourth Edition (2003); and various other books. Nationally and internationally, she continues to conduct workshops in the teaching of writing. She served as Chair of CCCC, the Two-Year College Association (TYCA) of NCTE, the College Section of NCTE, and the Writing Division of MLA. She has received the 2001 CCCC Exemplar Award, the highest CCCC award for scholarship, teaching, and service; the Rhetorician of the Year award; and the TYCA Pickett Award for Service.

Victor Villanueva is Edward R. Meyer Distinguished Professor of Liberal Arts and Associate Dean at Washington State University, where he has also been English Department Chair and Director of Composition. He has received the NCTE Russell Award, the CEE Meade Award, been named the 1999 Rhetorician of the Year, and has gotten other kindnesses. He has published and spoken widely on matters of racism, rhetoric, and composition. He was Chair of CCCC in 1998.

Kathleen Blake Yancey is the Kellogg W. Hunt Professor of English at Florida State University, where she is working with colleagues to redesign the PhD program in Rhetoric and Composition Studies. A former eighth-grade teacher in Washington County, Maryland, she has taught at four universities—Virginia Tech; Purdue University; University of North Carolina–Charlotte, where she codirected the UNC–Charlotte site of the National Writing Project; and Clemson University, where she held the Pearce Professorship and directed the Pearce Center for Professional Communication. Her scholarly work includes several books—among them the coedited *Situating Portfolios*; the coedited *Assessing Writing across the Curriculum*; and the single-authored volumes *Reflection in the Writing Classroom* and *Teaching Literature as Reflective Practice*—as well as many articles and book chapters. She has served as Executive Board Member, Vice-President, and President of the Council of Writing Program Administrators; as member and Chair of the College Section of NCTE; and as Chair of the NCTE College Forum. A cofounder and coleader of the National Coalition on Research into Electronic Portfolios, she consults on curriculum, assessment, and portfolio efforts internationally. She is currently beginning the seventh year of partnering with teachers at Virginia Beach City Schools to change the teaching of composition through a continuous faculty development program located in qualitative assessment theory and practice; teacher leadership; and teacher research. She is currently the Vice-President-Elect of NCTE.

Pavel Zemliansky is Assistant Professor in the Writing Program at James Madison University, where he teaches courses in composition, rhetoric, and computers and writing. He coedited (with Wendy Bishop) *The Subject Is Research* (2001) and *Research Writing Revisited: A Sourcebook for Teachers* (2004). His recent book, which he coedited with Kirk St. Amant, is titled *Internet-Based Workplace Communications: Industry and Academic Applications* (2004). His work appeared in the journals *Kairos* and *Composition Forum*, as well as in several edited collections. He also worked as CCCC Assistant Program Chair to Wendy Bishop in 1999. Zemliansky's scholarly interests include research writing pedagogy, computers and writing, and application of new media to teaching and learning of composition.

Photo Credits

John C. Lovas, "All Good Writing Develops at the Edge of Risk": p. 397: Photo of the Lorraine Hotel/Courtesy of the author; **p. 398:** Photos of the National Civil Rights Museum/Courtesy of the author; **p. 400:** *(Top)* Self-portrait/Courtesy of the author; *(Bottom)* Photo of Keith Gilyard/Courtesy of the author; **p. 401:** Photos of author's grandparents/Courtesy of the author; **p. 403:** Photo of Thomas Jefferson's headstone/Courtesy of the author.

Kathleen Blake Yancey, "Made Not Only in Words: Composition in a New Key": p. 431: Sketch for designing a brochure/Courtesy of the author; **p. 432:** Map, Tabula Magellanica qua Tierra del Fuego. Amsterdam: Schenk and Valk (1709?). Hand-colored engraving/Courtesy Geography and Map Division, Title Collection, Chile-Magellan Strait (3), Library of Congress; **p. 434:** Yearbook photograph, l941/Courtesy of Clemson University; **p. 435:** *(Top)* Vasily Kandinsky, *Composition 8*, July 1923. Oil on canvas, 140 x 201 cm (55 1/8 x 79 1/8 inches). Solomon R. Guggenheim Museum, New York, Gift of Solomon R. Guggenheim, l937. 37.262; *(Bottom)* Map of tectonic plates/Courtesy of U.S. Geological Survey; **p. 436:** Photo of multimedia center/Courtesy of the author; **p. 438:** Photo of university gates/Courtesy of the author; **p. 439:** Conference on College Composition and Communication program cover, 2004. Copyright 2004 by the National Council of Teachers of English. Reprinted with permission; **p. 440:** Photo of a classroom/Courtesy of the author; **p. 441:** Cover scan: *College Composition and Communication*, Volume 1, Number 1, March 1950. Reprinted with permission.; **p. 442:** *(Top)* College Composition and Communication sample web design. Copyright by the National Council of Teachers of English. Reprinted with permission; *(Bottom)* Photo of Boston skyline/Courtesy of the author; **p. 444:** PowerPoint presentation/Courtesy of the author; **p. 445:** PowerPoint presentation/Courtesy of the author; **p. 446:** Earthquake map/Courtesy U.S. Geological Survey; **p. 447:** Screen shot of www.punkvoter .com/Courtesy punkvoter.com; **p. 450:** Photo of Boston skyline/Courtesy of the author.

Douglas Hesse, "Who Owns Writing?": p. 459: Photo of sunset/www.iS tockphoto.com; **p. 460:** *(Top)* Cover scan of H. T. Burleigh's *Album of Negro Spirituals*, Melville: Belwin Mills, l969/Used with Permission of Alfred Publishing Co., Inc.; *(Center)* Photo of sunset/www.iStockphoto.com; *(Bottom)* Screenshot of partial page from www.latimes.com, posted February 22, 2005, including headline "Whose Song is it Anyway" by David Pierson/Copyright, 2005, Los Angeles Times. Reprinted with permission, overlapping Screenshot of *The Chronicle of Higher Education*, "Who Owns Islamic Law?"/Copyright 2005 The Chronicle of Higher Education; **p. 461:** *(Top)* Screenshot of Lawrence Lessig's Blog/Lawrence Lessig (www.lessig.org/blog/); *(Bottom)* Photo of a sunset/www.istockphoto.com; **p. 462:** Screenshots of the "Essay Generator"/www .EssayGenerator.com; **p. 463:** Screenshot of generated essay/Courtesy of the author; **p. 464:** *(Top)* Photo of a sunset/www.iStockphoto.com; *(Bottom)* Screenshot of the video game "Pong"/David Winter (www.pont-story.com), overlapping the Web site for the video game "Myst"/© 2004 Ubisoft Entertainment. All Rights Reserved. Ubisoft, ubi.com, and the Ubisoft logo are trademarks of Ubisoft Entertainment in the U.S. and/or other countries. D'ni (TM), Cyan (R), and Myst (R) are trademarks of Cyan, Inc. and Cyan Worlds, Inc. under license of Ubisoft Entertainment. Developed by Cyan Worlds, Inc.; **p. 465:** *(Top)* PowerPoint slide created by Kathleen Blake Yancey/ Courtesy of Kathleen Blake Yancey; *(Bottom)* Photo of sunset/www.iStockphoto.com; **p. 466:** *(Top)* Screenshot of the College Board's National Commission on Writing/ Source: 2003-2004 National Commission on Writing. Copyright © 2005, collegeboard .com. Reproduced with permission. All rights reserved, www.collegeboard.com; *(Center)* Envelope with handwritten recipe/Courtesy of the author, overlapping photo of sunset/www.iStockphoto.com; *(Bottom)* Screenshot of the CCCC Position Statement/ Copyright by the National Council of Teachers of English. Reprinted with permission,

491

overlapping photo of the author's students/Courtesy of the author; **p. 467:** PowerPoint slides created by Kathleen Blake Yancey/Courtesy of Kathleen Blake Yancey; **p. 468:** *(Top)* Overlapping scans of the 2004 and 2005 CCCC programs/Copyright 2004/2005 by the National Council of Teachers of English; *(Bottom) College Composition and Communication*, Volume 1, issue 2, May 1950/© 1950 by the National Council of Teachers of English. Reprinted with permission; **p. 469:** Screenshot of Susan Loudermilk's course Web site/Susan Loudermilk Garza; **p. 470:** *(Top)* Cover scan of H. T. Burleigh's *Album of Negro Spirituals*, Melville: Belwin Mills, 1969/Used with the Permission of Alfred Publishing Co. Inc.; *(Center)* Screenshots of the Valencia, Los Angeles, and New York 826 programs' Web sites/Courtesy of 826 Valencia (www.826valencia.org); *(Bottom)* Photos of the author's students/Courtesy of the author; **p. 471:** *(Top)* Screenshot of course descriptions from Michigan State University/Courtesy Department of Writing, Rhetoric and American Cultures, Michigan State University; *(Bottom)* Screenshot of article from *The Christian Science Monitor*, "Teens Ready to Prove Text-Messaging Skills Can Score SAT Points" by Christina McCarrol/Courtesy of *The Christian Science Monitor*, overlapping photo of Illinois State University/Courtesy of the author; **p. 472:** *(Top)* Collage of graphics: *(Top) Kairos* Web site/*Kairos: A Journal of Rhetoric, Technology, and Pedagogy* (http://english,ttu.edu/kairos). Image originally designed for *Kairos* by Jason Cranford Teague; *(Left)* CCCC logo/Copyright by the National Council of Teachers of English. Reprinted with permission; *(Right)* Book cover *The Creation of the Media* by Paul Starr/Courtesy of Basic Books; *(Bottom)* Screenshot of author's blog/Courtesy of the author; **p. 473:** *(Top)* Envelope with handwritten recipe/Courtesy of the author; *(Bottom) (Left)* Printed by permission of Leisure Arts, Inc. (800-562-5111); *(Right)* Neil F. Neimark, M.D. at www.JournalingSecrets.com; **p. 474:** *(Top)* Wikipedia (http://www.wikipedia.org), text released under the GNU-fdl license; *(Center)* Photo of Illinois State University/Courtesy of the author; *(Bottom)* Photo of Bloomington-Normal YMCA/Courtesy of the author; **p. 475:** *(Top) (Left)* WAVES Bloomington-Normal Y Swim Team; *(Center)* Schoolhouse Junction (www.rubricconverter.com); *(Right)* Accelerated Writer form reproduced with permission from Renaissance Learning, Inc., © 2005. For more information, visit www.renlearn.com; *(Center) (Bottom)* Photos of sunsets/www.iStockphoto.com; **p. 476:** Photo of sunset/www.iStockphoto.com; CCCC logo/Copyright by the National Council of Teachers of English.

Index